PERILOUS PARTNERS

THE BENEFITS AND PITFALLS
OF AMERICA'S ALLIANCES WITH
AUTHORITARIAN REGIMES

PERILOUS PARTNERS

TED GALEN CARPENTER
and MALOU INNOCENT

CATO
INSTITUTE
WASHINGTON, D.C.

Library of Congress Cataloging-in-Publication Data

Carpenter, Ted Galen
    Perilous partners : the benefits and pitfalls of America's alliances with authoritar-
ian regimes / Ted Galen Carpenter and Malou Innocent.
        pages cm
    Includes bibliographical references and index.
    ISBN 978-1-939709-70-7 (hardback : alk. paper) 1. United States—Foreign rela-
tions—1945-1989. 2. United States—Foreign relations—1989- 3. Authoritarianism 4.
Alliances. I. Innocent, Malou. II. Title.

E840.C366 2015
327.73009'04—dc23

                                                                    2015025181

Cover design: Jon Meyers.
Printed in the United States of America.

CATO INSTITUTE
1000 Massachusetts Ave., N.W.
Washington, D.C. 20001
www.cato.org

Contents

Preface

As the United States assumed a global leadership role after World War II, a growing number of cases occurred in which policymakers established close working relationships with allies and security clients. Although such ties varied a great deal in terms of necessity or wisdom, they posed little problem from an ethical or moral standpoint when they involved democratic governments. Outside of Europe and portions of Latin America, East Asia, and Oceania, however, many of Washington's new security partners were anything but democratic. Even worse, some of them had well-deserved reputations not only as corrupt kleptocracies, but also as egregious abusers of basic human rights.

That pattern persisted throughout the long decades of the Cold War. Washington valued its relationships with an assortment of cooperative authoritarian regimes, especially in the Third World. U.S. leaders defended the policy against criticism that such partnerships betrayed fundamental American values and made a mockery of the professed commitment to democracy, the rule of law, and individual liberty.

U.S. officials insisted that cooperation with friendly, but unsavory, regimes was necessary to protect America's own security interests as well as block the expansion of international communism and the nightmare of totalitarianism that system would impose on vulnerable societies. One should not dismiss the extent of the fear that gripped the American foreign policy community and much of the American public during the Cold War. In some cases, the associations made sense from a security standpoint—at least in the short term. In others, the security rationale ranged from questionable to utterly inadequate.

Moreover, American policymakers and opinion leaders frequently went beyond offering a plea of "regrettable necessity." Instead, they lavished praise on Washington's autocratic allies and clients, insisting that such corrupt tyrants were noble members of the Free World. Even in retrospect, it is still sometimes difficult to determine whether U.S. leaders merely engaged in cynical disinformation or succumbed to their own propaganda and actually believed such portrayals.

Whatever the nature or legitimacy of the underlying motives, Washington's support for brutal autocrats disillusioned and alienated populations around the world that groaned under the yoke of U.S.-sponsored dictatorships. When those oppressive regimes finally fell from power, the blowback against the United States varied in intensity. In some cases, such as with South Korea and the Philippines, the lingering resentment was relatively mild. In other cases, most notably Iran, it was virulent, and the animosity poisons bilateral relations to this day. Still other cases, such as Nicaragua, occupy a middle position along the blowback spectrum.

Some of the habits of forging close ties with authoritarian partners during the Cold War did not disappear even when the global rivalry with the Soviet Union ended. Other unhealthy behavioral patterns went into at least partial eclipse during the initial post–Cold War decade, but have reemerged (sometimes in different places) following the September 11, 2001, terrorist attacks and Washington's proclamation of a "war on terror."

In *Perilous Partners*, we examine the official justifications for the U.S. partnerships with corrupt, often brutal, autocrats and assess the credibility and sufficiency of those justifications. We look at both the benefits and costs in blood, treasure, and values to the American republic of more than a dozen specific associations. The various case studies span a wide range in terms of geography, U.S. security interests, and circumstances. Our goal has been to provide a good cross section of examples to illuminate the trends, motives, and consequences of U.S. policies.

As with any book on a large, complex topic, it is not possible to cover in a comprehensive manner all relevant cases. For example, we have chapters on Washington's ties with dictatorships in the East Asian countries of South Korea and South Vietnam during the Cold War, but we do not discuss the equally questionable relationship with Indonesian dictator Suharto. Similarly, we include a chapter on U.S. links to the Somoza family in Nicaragua and the parade of

Guatemalan military strongmen, but we devote only a brief discussion of policy toward the brutal Chilean dictator Augusto Pinochet.

Finally, we endeavor to develop standards to determine when close relationships with friendly autocrats are necessary, when they are gratuitous betrayals of American values, and when they occupy a gray area. We hope that such a treatment will help both policymakers and the American people strike a proper balance in the future.

Introduction: Confronting Ethical Dilemmas in U.S. Foreign Policy

Liberal democracies such as the United States face an acute dilemma in the conduct of foreign relations. Many states around the world are repressive or corrupt to varying degrees. Unfortunately, American national interests require cooperation with such regimes from time to time. To defeat Nazi Germany during World War II, the United States allied with the Soviet Union, despite having to partner with a regime at the height of its barbarity.

But such partnerships have the inherent danger of compromising, or even making a mockery of, America's values of democratic governance, civil liberties, and free markets. Close working relationships with autocratic regimes, therefore, should not be undertaken lightly. U.S. officials have had a less than stellar record of grappling with that ethical dilemma. Especially during the Cold War, Washington was far too casual about sacrificing important values for less-than-compelling strategic rationales. The situation improved somewhat in the decade following the collapse of the Soviet empire, but even during that period, there were some questionable partnerships, including with some rather unsavory regimes in the Balkans and Central Asia. Since the 9/11 attacks, there has been further ethical regression, although U.S. policymakers have remained at least modestly more circumspect and selective than their Cold War–era counterparts.

The ethical rot in U.S. foreign policy began early in the Cold War and grew worse as the rivalry with the Soviet Union deepened. To counter the expansion of Soviet power and the threat of revolutionary communism, the United States acquired several repressive client states, largely for their supposed anti-communist bona fides. U.S. leaders cynically referred to some of the most corrupt and brutal dictatorships as members of the Free World, as long as those regimes cooperated with Washington's geopolitical objectives. Even communist regimes that U.S. officials considered anti-Soviet, such as those in Yugoslavia and Romania, received America's praise and public statements of support and friendship.

George F. Kennan, the principal author of the containment policy during the Cold War, once remarked, "No people can be the judge of another's domestic institutions and requirements." U.S. political leaders and much of the American public, though, tend to regard such realism as unappealing—or at least insufficient—as a basis for the republic's international conduct. Historically, American leaders have seen (or at least portrayed) the nation's mission internationally as something more than the narrow pursuit of national security. Such presidents as Woodrow Wilson and Franklin D. Roosevelt were especially inclined to cloak even mundane geopolitical objectives in the garb of soaring appeals to universal human values.

More recently, President George W. Bush was perhaps the boldest in attempting to eliminate the annoying conflict between interests and values. In his second inaugural address, the president stated: "The survival of liberty in our land increasingly depends on the success of liberty in other lands. The best hope for peace in our world is the expansion of freedom in the entire world. *America's vital interests and our deepest beliefs are now one.*" (Emphasis added.)

It is impossible to separate neatly the realist, sometime cynical, roots of U.S. foreign policy from genuine beliefs in American exceptionalism and other idealistic influences. But the solution to that problem is not Bush's naïve formulation that those elements are congruent. Both visions have characterized the country's foreign policy at various times and in various ways. The tension between them raises many potential dilemmas. Leaders sometimes have to judge tradeoffs between advancing the national interest—especially the nation's security—and advancing America's values.

In doing so, they need to ask hard questions about whether an increase, especially a marginal increase, in U.S. security is worth an often substantial cost in terms of values. Officials also need to determine whether or when it might be appropriate to pressure security clients to reform, both to prevent the potential ouster of the sponsored regime and to reduce the conflict with American ideals. When important U.S. interests conflate with those of a dubious partner, a different, somewhat more lenient, set of standards should apply than when there is only a modest overlap of interests.

2

Finally, the American people need to determine to what extent U.S. aid to oppressive regimes ought to be subject to greater public and congressional scrutiny—and even outright skepticism.

To promote human rights in some countries and simultaneously support the world's most savage and illegitimate autocracies may very well reflect Washington's geopolitical preferences, but such inconsistency also highlights an enormous discrepancy between what the U.S. government claims to do and what it actually does. For U.S. foreign policy to be both effective and reasonably consistent with American values, certain conditions have to be met:

- *The domestic basis of support for U.S. foreign policy must be maintained and strengthened.* Because most Americans believe in the professed values of this country, a foreign policy that ignores or violates those values is likely to lose the public's allegiance sooner or later. That is what happened with such missions as the Vietnam War, the Iraq War, and more recently, the counterinsurgency war in Afghanistan. It is not merely that the ventures failed to achieve quick, decisive results, although that aspect clearly played a role, but that the United States was seen as expending blood and treasure on behalf of sleazy regimes. A disillusioned public turned against those missions, and that development created or intensified bitter domestic divisions. A similar dynamic occurred in response to calls for U.S. intervention to save the Shah of Iran in the late 1970s and block leftist insurgencies in Central America against right-wing governments in the 1980s. For a large number of Americans, it was not worth either the cost or risk to the United States to prop up such political partners. To sustain adequate public support for security partnerships, especially if the policy entails military ventures, the objective must be widely perceived as both worthy and attainable. Without those features, public support for a policy either proves insufficient from the outset or soon erodes, and either development is fatal in a democratic political system.

- *To maintain public support and preserve American values, officials must make an honest assessment of the issues at stake.* Too often, both during the Cold War and the post–Cold War eras, U.S. policymakers have hyped threats to genuine American interests. The alleged dangers posed by such adversaries as North Vietnam, Iraq, Serbia, the Taliban, and Syria border on being caricatures. At times, it appears that U.S. officials have deliberately engaged in distortions to gin-up public support for elective wars and other ventures that could likely be avoided. On other occasions, officials seem to succumb to their own propaganda. In either case, public support dissipates rapidly when evidence mounts that the supposed security threat to America is actually minimal. Although the American public might be willing to hold its collective nose and support a brutal, authoritarian ally—as they did regarding the alliance with Josef Stalin during World War II—to repel a true security menace to the republic, they are not willing to do so for far lesser stakes. It is both inappropriate and unrealistic to expect the public to embrace partnerships with the likes of the Shah of Iran, South Vietnam's Ngo Dinh Diem, or more recently, Afghanistan's Hamid Karzai, unless there is a compelling security justification. In all too many instances, that justification has been lacking, despite Washington's argument to the contrary.

- *To maintain public support and preserve American values, officials must be candid about the nature of Washington's proposed clients.* It is one thing to justify a partnership with an authoritarian ally on the basis of pragmatic considerations. President Franklin Roosevelt epitomized such realpolitik when he once famously observed of a de facto ally in Latin America: "He's an s.o.b., but he's our s.o.b." It is quite another matter to whitewash the behavior of such partners and pretend that they are anything other than corrupt thugs. Yet U.S. administrations have amassed a disturbing track record of doing exactly that. It insulted the intelligence of the American people and publics around the world to portray the likes of the Shah of Iran, Philippine dictator Ferdinand Marcos, South Korean dictator Park Chung Hee, and Egypt's Hosni Mubarak as members of the Free World, but American officials did so. The initial efforts to laud Pakistan's Pervez Musharraf and Iraq's Nouri al-Maliki reflected the same approach during the war on terror. When the actual behavior of corrupt, brutal allies and clients makes a mockery of such portrayals, the American people understandably recoil from embracing them—even when on some occasions there may be a reasonable argument for preserving a particular partnership to protect valid U.S. interests.

- *When partnerships with authoritarian allies are necessary, the association needs to be the minimum required to achieve crucial goals.* The United States has fared best when it has pursued cautious, limited, and pragmatic relationships with autocratic allies. Richard Nixon's rapprochement with China in the 1970s fit that description. That move altered the global balance of political and diplomatic power, forcing the Soviet Union to turn its attention away from applying pressure on the democratic West because it now had to deal with another adversary working in cooperation with Washington. However, most U.S. officials did not delude themselves or try to delude the American people about the nature of China's regime. They recognized that it was an unpleasant, one-party state. Nor did Washington seek to make Beijing a close ally on issues other than countering Soviet power and influence. The two countries were allies of convenience, nothing more. That pragmatic Cold War relationship with Beijing ought to be the model for those other, relatively rare occasions when a security partnership with an authoritarian regime might be necessary.

- *There needs to be a reassessment of America's interests and global security position to minimize the supposed need for entanglements that undermine American values.* As noted above, U.S. leaders have a track record of exaggerating threats to America's security and interests to, among other objectives, justify partnerships with unsavory regimes. Part of the problem is the carryover of a mindset from World War II and the early Cold War period when powerful enemies did pose a significant security threat. But the situation today is substantially different—and it has been for several decades. With an enviable geographic position (weak and friendly neighbors to the north and south and vast oceans on both flanks), the largest economy in the world, a conventional military establishment far superior to any competitor, and a huge, sophisticated nuclear deterrent, the United States is probably the most secure great power in history. The lack of an existential, or even a serious, threat means that U.S. leaders have extraordinary latitude to adopt policies that minimize America's involvement in quarrels in other parts of the world. That factor also means that only on rare occasions should Washington have to face the dilemma of forging close relationships with authoritarian partners. In most instances, an arm's-length relationship with such regimes is all that is either necessary or appropriate. Adopting a more restrained foreign policy would greatly reduce the number of occasions when policymakers have to confront a conflict between America's tangible interests and its fundamental values. Polling data also indicate that the American public would like to see the adoption of a more selective, restrained policy.

The first part of *Perilous Partners* surveys U.S. alliances with authoritarian governments during the Cold War (1945–1991). The second part of the book discusses the contemporary period, recapping the 1990s and going in depth for the period from 9/11 to the Arab Awakening. Those chapters inject historical insight into current dilemmas to create a better understanding of America's past as well as provide possible policy prescriptions for the present and future. Both portions of *Perilous Partners* contain separate chapters for each questionable security relationship.

The concluding chapter, "Closing the Values Gap: Protecting Security, Preserving Values," outlines the standards that should be used to determine when compromising American values is necessary, when it is questionable, and when it is gratuitous and counterproductive. That chapter provides a strategy for resolving, or at least ameliorating, the ethical dilemmas between interests and values faced by U.S. policymakers. It proposes the concept of "an arm's length relationship" with authoritarian regimes and movements, emphasizing that the United States will gain little if it deals with the threat of terrorism—as it too often dealt with the Soviet threat during the Cold War—in ways that routinely pollute American values. The degree of appropriate cooperation with an authoritarian regime should vary depending on how severe the security threat the United States faces in each situation, how valuable a given ally is in meeting that threat, how odious the ally's domestic conduct is, and whether there are reasonable alternatives for achieving U.S. strategic objectives. That is the essence of a strategy based on *ethical pragmatism,* which is the best way to reconcile America's strategic interests and its fundamental values.

PART ONE

WASHINGTON'S QUESTIONABLE COLD WAR ALLIES

1. Uncle Sam's Backyard: Friendly Latin American Strongmen

U.S. policy in the Western Hemisphere since the late 19th century probably deserves an entry in the Hall of Shame. During that period, Washington meddled with increasing frequency in the internal affairs of its southern neighbors. From the 1890s through the mid-1940s, many of the interventions seemed to take place on behalf of powerful business enterprises with important interests in those countries. On other occasions, especially following the onset of the Cold War, ideological and strategic motives appeared to dominate U.S. decisionmaking, although the economic dimension never disappeared. The inclination to meddle was most pronounced regarding the small nations of Central America (often contemptuously labeled as "banana republics") and the equally small and weak island nations of the Caribbean.

Ever since the proclamation of the Monroe Doctrine in 1823, the United States took a special interest in political, economic, and military developments in the Western Hemisphere—especially with respect to the part of the region closest to the U.S. homeland. Monroe's statement (actually written by then Secretary of State John Quincy Adams) emphasized that the United States would not tolerate either the establishment of new European colonies in the Western Hemisphere or European efforts to undermine the independence of the newly sovereign states there.

But Washington's ability or inclination to do much about its concerns was decidedly limited throughout most of the 19th century. U.S. naval capabilities were quite modest and those of U.S. ground forces even more so. Indeed, in an example of irony, America's long-standing rival, Great Britain, ended up being the principal enforcer of the Monroe Doctrine. Washington and London became de facto allies—with the British clearly being the senior partner—in preventing continental European powers from trying to establish colonies or puppet states in the region. American and British interests, while they continued to differ sharply on other issues, overlapped regarding that objective.

The United States shamelessly acted as a security free rider on British exertions in the Western Hemisphere. One of the few occasions that Washington prepared to take strong, unilateral action against a European interloper was in Mexico during the late 1860s. France took advantage of the U.S. Civil War to set up an Austrian client, Archduke Maximilian, as the so-called Emperor of Mexico. Once the Civil War ended, however, the United States openly backed Mexican insurgents and made it clear to France that any attempt to preserve its foothold in Mexico would be met with decisive force. Maximilian fell from power and was captured and executed by Mexican republican forces in 1867, and France did nothing in response.

It was after the Spanish-American War in 1898 and ouster of Spain from Cuba and Puerto Rico, though, that U.S. interventionism became a firmly established policy in the Western Hemisphere. Washington did keep its pledge to grant Cuba independence, with some regret on the part of avid imperialists who believed that William McKinley's administration had made an impetuous, ill-advised promise. Yet even though the United States did not formally annex Cuba as a colony, the new country's independence was severely circumscribed. The Platt Amendment, which Congress passed in 1901, gave the United States great latitude to intervene in Cuba if U.S. officials concluded that stability or good governance in that country was in peril.[1] And Washington exercised that authority on a number of occasions during the succeeding decades.

Roots of Intervention: The Quest for Stability and Order

The key goal with respect to Cuba was order and stability, and that became the mantra with respect to U.S. policy toward other countries in the region as well. The concern was not entirely selfish or hypocritical. One of the recurring problems throughout Central America and the Caribbean was the tendency of corrupt and/or unstable governments to renege on debts owed to foreign creditors. When those creditors were U.S. banks, policymakers in Washington got an earful from angry, well-connected constituents who wanted the federal government to do something about those deadbeat regimes.

Matters were even more delicate when the defaults occurred on debts owed to prominent European governments or financial institutions. U.S. leaders feared that a European country might well use a debt default as a justification—or a pretext—to establish a strong political, and perhaps even a military, presence in the offending country and convert it into a de facto colony.[2] A move to do that would, of course, be a direct challenge to the Monroe Doctrine. Suspicions about Imperial Germany's intentions were especially strong in Washington during the early years of the 20th century. When Germany (along with Britain and Italy) imposed a naval blockade on Venezuela in 1902 to compel the government in Caracas to pay its financial obligations, President Theodore Roosevelt's administration took action. Although London and Rome were also participants in the multilateral campaign of coercion against Venezuela, the bulk of Washington's ire was directed at Berlin because of Imperial Germany's growing assertiveness—often brash behavior—in other regions.

The president issued an implicit warning to Berlin in his 1904 State of the Union Address that the United States would not tolerate coercive moves in America's backyard. At the same time, to sooth the German government and other European governments that were upset about the financial conduct of Venezuela, as well as certain nations in Central America and the Caribbean, Roosevelt pledged that the United States would ensure that its small neighbors would maintain adequate order and fulfill their commitments to foreign creditors—even if Washington had to intervene with its own military forces to do so. That policy became the so-called Roosevelt Corollary to the Monroe Doctrine.

The Corollary quickly became an all-purpose justification for a series of U.S. military interventions in the region. Washington ousted regimes that it considered corrupt, incompetent, or just insufficiently compliant with U.S. wishes. That standard led to multiple missions in such places as Haiti and Nicaragua. Indeed, the U.S. military acted as the de facto government of Haiti continuously from 1915 to 1934.

Uncle Sam's heavy hand was equally evident in Nicaragua. Brookings Institution scholar Robert Kagan succinctly summarizes Washington's conduct: "The United States intervened with troops in 1912 and occupied Nicaragua for most of the next 21 years, assisted in a war against the [populist] rebel Augusto Cesar Sandino from 1927 to 1933, and was involved in the birth of the Somoza dynasty in 1936

13

and its perpetuation for another 43 years." Kagan adds that "most informed Americans were not proud of that history."[3]

Although the official rationale for such missions was the need to preclude major European powers from taking action against offending regimes, some of the episodes clearly were in response to pressure from domestic corporations, especially United Fruit (which became United Brands in 1970), which had massive economic stakes in those often unstable nations.[4] And it soon became clear that leaders in Washington did not especially care whether a Central American or Caribbean regime was democratic or not—despite occasional rhetoric to the contrary. Instead, U.S. officials were concerned about whether a regime could maintain internal order and whether it would cooperate with Washington's goals and those of relevant American business entities. In other words, U.S. administrations had few qualms about backing tyrants—even brutal tyrants—as long as they were sufficiently compliant and effective.

That approach characterized U.S. policy in the hemisphere from the early years of the 20th century to the mid-1930s. Washington's approach shifted somewhat in 1933 when President Franklin D. Roosevelt proclaimed the "Good Neighbor Policy," which included a commitment not to intervene in the internal affairs of hemispheric countries unless there was a threat to the vital interests of the United States. Under both Roosevelt and his successor in the White House, Harry Truman, the parade of military interventions did come to an end. But it was more a shift of tactics than a fundamental policy change. For example, during the mid- and late 1930s, Roosevelt quietly sought to undermine regimes that he thought might be potential allies of the aggressive European fascist powers.[5] Such covert activities might be considered a precursor to the similar, but much more systematic, efforts of the Central Intelligence Agency (CIA) regarding hostile regimes in the post–World War II period.

Moreover, Washington expressed little criticism of friendly authoritarian regimes, of which there were an abundance throughout the Roosevelt and Truman years. In fact, Washington seemed to nurture Latin American military leaders who would later rise to power and impose rigid dictatorships with the blessing, if not outright sponsorship of, the United States. The pattern began even before FDR's administration, and British journalist Grace Livingstone describes that aspect of U.S. policy: "In Central America and the Caribbean, which had borne the brunt of military intervention, the U.S. protected its interests by grooming friendly dictators." Before the U.S. Marines withdrew from Nicaragua in 1933, the U.S. had "created, trained and equipped" a strong National Guard and appointed one Gen. Anastasio Somoza as commander. Somoza seized power from the civilian government in 1936. "The same tactic was used in the Dominican Republic, where Rafael Trujillo was appointed head of the U.S.-trained National Guard. Trujillo led a coup in 1930 and established a tyranny that lasted until 1961." Livingstone notes that "by the mid-1930s, dictatorships had been established across Central America."[6]

And U.S. officials seemed exceedingly tolerant of their authoritarian protégés. Livingstone describes the indulgent U.S. policy toward such leaders:

> State Department officials built up a relationship with the corrupt and sadistic sergeant Fulgencio Batista, helping him to dominate the Cuban political scene. . . . Batista was invited to Washington to meet Roosevelt in 1938; Roosevelt personally met Somoza at the train station when he visited Washington in 1939, and Trujillo was invited for tea with the president and his wife at the White House in 1940. President Roosevelt had become, as Peruvian politician Victor Raúl Haya de la Torre said, "the good neighbor of tyrants."[7]

The Cold War: Interventions Become More Ideological

During the Cold War, Washington's tendency to intervene, either covertly or with military invasions, resurged. But intervention in the internal political affairs of Caribbean and Central American countries took on a more ideological aspect. As U.S. fears that Soviet influence might spread into the Western Hemisphere intensified, American policymakers were determined to prevent the emergence of left-wing regimes and to support virtually any ruler who professed to be anti-communist, regardless of that individual's record of corruption or human rights abuses. Preventing the spread of communist regimes in Washington's neighborhood also was the mantra for sending U.S. troops into the Dominican Republic in 1965 and Grenada in 1983.

The U.S.-led intervention in the Dominican Republic thwarted a rebellion, led by some junior military officers, which sought to restore to office leftist president Juan Bosch, who had won election in 1962 but was deposed in a September 1963 military coup. President Lyndon B. Johnson and his advisers regarded the pro-Bosch insurgents as little more than pawns of Fidel Castro—and, therefore, of Moscow. According to Johnson, Bosch's noncommunist supporters had "almost no control over the rebel movement. For the most part, power rested with the Communists and their armed followers."[8] The United States launched a military intervention, Operation Power Pack, with 42,000 troops to prevent Bosch's return to the presidency. The intervention succeeded, and after complicated maneuvering, Washington placated resentful Dominicans with a promise of free elections the following year. U.S. financial and organizational assistance, both overt and covert, helped pave the way for a more pro-U.S. political figure, Joaquin Balaguer, to defeat Bosch in that election and take office.[9]

Balaguer had served as a loyal aide to Trujillo during the 1940s and 1950s, and his own rule during his first stint as president had more than a few authoritarian features, including the jailing of political opponents. Later in his political career, including several more nonconsecutive terms as president, his policies exhibited greater respect for human rights, and he even acquired a reputation as a genuine democratic reformer.[10]

Ronald Reagan's explanation for the Grenada intervention nearly two decades later was virtually a duplicate of Johnson's justification for the Dominican intervention. Officially, the United States was merely responding to a request from the obscure Organization of Eastern Caribbean States to reverse a coup by hard-line Marxists against a somewhat more moderate Marxist government under Prime Minister Maurice Bishop. According to Reagan, Grenada's island neighbors "told us that under Bishop they had been worried by what appeared to be a large Cuban-sponsored military buildup on Grenada vastly disproportionate to its needs; now, they said, these even more radical Marxists in control of Grenada had launched a murderous reign of terror against their enemies. Unless they were stopped, the Caribbean neighbors said, it was just a matter of time before the Grenadians and Castro moved on *their* countries."[11]

Reagan certainly felt the same way, concluding that there "was only one answer" that he could give to the countries that had asked for Washington's help. U.S. Marines soon went ashore, ousted the new regime, and restored order. Afterwards, Reagan stated that he "probably never felt better" during his entire presidency. "I think our decision to stand up to Castro and the brownshirts on Grenada not only stopped the Communists in their tracks in that part of the world but perhaps helped all Americans stand a little taller."[12]

Countering perceived Soviet influence in the hemisphere was not confined to the Caribbean and Central America, although it was strongest in that region. Washington also forged ties with an assortment of right-wing (often military) regimes in South America—even in those portions of the continent that were geographically more distant than Europe from the U.S. homeland. As noted in chapter 2, the Reagan administration thought it improper to criticize the ruling junta in Argentina, which murdered (or "disappeared') several thousand political opponents and kidnapped their young children for distribution to regime supporters. American Enterprise Institute scholar Mark Falcoff concluded that the Argentine military "liquidated the terrorists and their accomplices. But it also abducted and murdered many who were guilty only of membership in left-wing political movements or intellectual circles, or only of being acquainted with someone who was."[13]

Callousness about the junta's behavior was not confined to the Reagan administration. Following the Argentine military's seizure of power in March 1976, Secretary of State Henry Kissinger seemed to go out of his way to assure junta leaders that Washington was not concerned about allegations of human rights violations. In a June meeting with the new foreign minister, Admiral César Augusto Guzzetti, Kissinger told Guzzetti: "We wish the new government well" and would do "what we can to help it succeed." Kissinger stated that U.S. leaders understood that the Argentine regime was in a "difficult period. It's a curious time, when political, criminal, and terrorist activities tend to merge without any clear separation." He then gave a diplomatic green light to the junta's developing crackdown on dissidents. "We understand you must establish your authority."[14]

At a meeting with Guzzetti in October, Kissinger seemed even more solicitous, despite the mounting evidence of the pervasive abuses that would characterize Argentina's "dirty war." He assured Guzzetti: "I have an old-fashioned view that friends ought to be supported. What is not understood in the United States is that you have a civil war. We read about human rights problems but not the context." Stating again that Washington wanted the junta to succeed, he emphasized: "We want a stable situation. We won't cause you unnecessary difficulties."[15] As in earlier decades, political stability in the hemisphere was a very high U.S. priority, while human rights and democracy occupied a much lower status.

According to Robert Hill, Washington's ambassador in Buenos Aires, Guzzetti was "euphoric" following the October meeting. Even though Hill had originally viewed the coup with some sympathy, believing that it would end the worsening political instability in Argentina, he had become disturbed about the extent of the junta's brutality. Now, he was even more troubled that Guzzetti had come away from his encounter with Kissinger believing that the U.S. government cared little or nothing about human rights abuses. "Guzzetti went to the U.S. expecting to hear some strong, firm, direct warnings on his government's human rights practices; rather than that, he has returned in a state of jubilation, convinced that there is no real problem with the USG [U.S. government] over that issue."[16]

Washington was similarly mute about atrocities that friendly authoritarian regimes committed in such places as Uruguay, Brazil, and Paraguay. In all of those cases, any strategic justification based on geographic proximity was weak, at best.

And then there was Washington's murky involvement in the overthrow and assassination of Chile's leftist president, Salvador Allende, in the early 1970s. At a minimum, Nixon administration officials knew that the Chilean military was engaged in repeated plots against the government and quietly encouraged such maneuvers. At worst, the administration actively plotted with like-minded Chilean generals to remove an unfriendly, populist thorn in Washington's side.[17] Conservative scholar Mark Falcoff contends that "the role of the United States in the events leading to the fall of Allende has been greatly exaggerated," but he concedes that "the Nixon administration and the conservative political community greeted the coup with some relief." Moreover, among many conservatives, "the Pinochet government had definite appeal."[18]

Despite the pervasive propaganda on the left over the decades, Allende was something less than a political saint. Although he had been duly elected, his behavior in office foreshadowed the ugly measures that Venezuelan ruler Hugo Chávez used to stifle independent media outlets, harass opponents, and undermine democracy in that country during the early years of the 21st century. The deepening and accelerating trend of Allende's authoritarian tendencies was worrisome, both to genuine Chilean democrats and U.S. officials. Chilean democracy, much less the health of property rights and civil liberties in that country, was not in great shape during Allende's years in office. Falcoff has a point when he argues that the subsequent coup and military dictatorship led by General Augusto Pinochet was the outcome of actions that "brought Chile perilously close to civil war in 1973."[19]

Nevertheless, the reality is that Washington once again meddled in the internal affairs of another hemispheric nation, even when the justification on security grounds was not especially strong. And whatever Allende's faults, they paled in comparison to the murderous military dictatorship led by Pinochet that replaced him and brutalized Chile for the next 16 years. As in the case of Argentina in the late 1970s and early 1980s, Pinochet's regime imprisoned or executed thousands of ideological opponents.

Washington's relationship with Pinochet, though, remained somewhat aloof, particularly compared to relations with other "friendly tyrants" in the hemisphere. That was especially true during President Jimmy Carter's administration, but it was generally the case during the Gerald R. Ford and Reagan administrations as well. Pinochet was an extremely prominent symbol of odious, right-wing oppression for human rights activists and other liberal, even moderate, groups in the United States and around the world. It became politically and diplomatically toxic for any American president, whatever his personal preferences might have been, to embrace a leader who had achieved that dubious status. Unfortunately, Washington was less squeamish about embracing comparable—or even worse—human rights abusers closer to home.

Guatemala: From Imperfect Democracy to Slaughterhouse

The scope of Washington's determination to thwart the spread of communism in the hemisphere, especially in Central America and the Caribbean, became evident in 1954 when the CIA orchestrated a coup (Operation Success) to oust the left-leaning, democratically elected (by some 65 percent of the vote) president of Guatemala, Jacobo Árbenz Guzmán. It was apparent that Washington had Árbenz in its crosshairs from the moment Dwight D. Eisenhower took the oath of office in January 1953. In his memoirs, Eisenhower asserted flatly that among the dangers the United States faced when he assumed the presidency was that "Communism was striving to establish its first beachhead in the Americas by gaining control of Guatemala."[20] He added that once Árbenz came to power, "his actions soon created the strong suspicion that he was merely a puppet manipulated by Communists."[21]

The first example that Eisenhower cited as evidence, though, pointed to a rather different grievance:

> [O]n February 24, 1953, the government announced its intention, under an agrarian reform law, to seize about 225,000 acres of unused United Fruit Company land. The company lost its appeal to the Guatemalan Supreme Court to prevent this discriminatory and unfair seizure. (Of all lands expropriated, two thirds belonged to United Fruit.) In return the company was to receive the woefully inadequate compensation of $600,000 in long-term non-negotiable agrarian bonds.[22]

Although Eisenhower conceded that "expropriation by itself did not prove Communism," noting that Mexico had expropriated foreign oil companies decades earlier without turning into a communist dictatorship, the president regarded Guatemala's action as a large black mark against Árbenz. His solicitude for United Fruit also was reminiscent of the attitude of many previous U.S. administrations toward Central American governments—and often served as a prelude to a U.S. intervention. The other examples that Eisenhower cited as evidence of Árbenz's alleged communist leanings ranged from ambiguous to trivial.

A key figure in the demonizing of Árbenz was the new U.S. ambassador to Guatemala, John E. Peurifoy. In a report to Secretary of State John Foster Dulles and President Eisenhower, Peurifoy described a six-hour meeting he held with the Guatemalan leader less than a month after taking his diplomatic post: "He listened while I counted off the leading Communists in his regime, but he gave no ground; many notorious Reds he denied to be Communists; if they were, they were not dangerous; if dangerous, he could control them; if not controllable, he would round them up." It was clear that Peurifoy had no tolerance for Árbenz. "It seemed to me that the man thought like a Communist and talked like a Communist, and if not actually one, would do until one came along."[23] The ambassador warned Dulles and Eisenhower that unless communist influences were "counteracted," Guatemala would fall under complete communist control within six months.

In congressional testimony (before the Subcommittee on Latin America of the House Select Committee on Communist Aggression) on October 8, 1954, following the U.S. orchestrated coup, Peurifoy was even more categorical than he had been in his report to the secretary of state:

> The Arbenz government, beyond any question, was controlled and dominated by Communists. Those Communists were directed from Moscow. The Guatemalan government and the Communist leaders of that country did continuously and actively intervene in the internal affairs of neighboring countries in an effort to create disorder and overthrow established governments. And the Communist conspiracy in Guatemala did represent a very real and very serious menace to the security of the United States.[24]

That assessment was a classic case of hyperbole and alarmism. And the last conclusion bordered on preposterous. Even if Guatemala had come under the control of a communist regime, that development by itself would hardly have posed a "very serious menace" to the security of a superpower. Even a lower-grade menace could have emerged only if Guatemala became a Soviet puppet (as Cuba would do at the end of the decade) *and* if it then allowed the USSR to establish military bases on its territory. But Washington had ample means at its disposal to prevent that outcome.

Even the conclusion that the Árbenz government was communist-dominated is questionable in retrospect. Árbenz certainly was a man of the political left, and his wife appears to have been a communist fellow traveler, at the very least. Much of his support came from socialist or communist trade unions, peasant unions, and other far-left organizations.[25] Yet Guatemala continued to vote with the United States and its allies a majority of the time in the United Nations on major issues where Washington and Moscow were at odds.[26] The government's domestic behavior deviated from the communist stereotype as well. For example, Árbenz did not try to create collective farms with the land seized from United Fruit and other large landholders. Instead, the government distributed that land to 100,000 families. The cases for and against land reform in Latin America are complex, since some of that land was originally acquired in less than ethical fashion, while owners of other tracts appeared to have acted in a legitimate manner. Sorting out the merits on the basis of law or morality in that part of the world is not an easy task.[27]

Within the Latin American context, what Árbenz did was not all that radical. Former *Wall Street Journal* reporter Jonathan Kwitny noted: "The land reform of Jacobo Árbenz fell perfectly within the guidelines that would be recommended by the U.S. State Department a mere seven years later as part of President Kennedy's Alliance for Progress program." Indeed, Árbenz's effort "was positively *tame* compared to the land reform program in El Salvador in the 1980s, which the United States not only conceived but enforced."[28]

It is also pertinent to remember that Peurifoy's allegation came at a time when the United States was in the midst of, indeed approaching the culmination of, McCarthyism. To say that the junior senator from Wisconsin and his legion of imitators were rather loose with their accusations of communist leanings would be an understatement.

Whether administration officials genuinely believed that Árbenz was a communist pawn, or whether that was a convenient pretext to conceal the motive of once again having Washington oust a regime that was hostile to United Fruit and other U.S. businesses may never be known. The disturbingly close associations of several policymakers with United Fruit at least warrant some skepticism about the sincerity of their allegations about the Árbenz government's communist leanings.[29] The likelihood is that both factors played a role. What is clear is that the Eisenhower administration moved quickly to remove a neighboring government that it neither liked nor trusted.

The final straw for Washington came when the Guatemalan regime tried to import a shipment of weapons from Czechoslovakia, a move that U.S. officials viewed as an attempt to spread both left-wing revolutions and Soviet power throughout Central America.[30] The weapons purchase was worrisome, but it came only after Árbenz had failed in his efforts to secure weapons from the United States or other Western powers (the latter failure largely because of Washington's pressure on its allies to isolate Guatemala).

Furthermore, even before the attempted arms purchase from the Soviet bloc, CIA officers had approached various Guatemalan political leaders, looking for someone who would be the focal point for a rebellion against Árbenz. In several of those meetings, they were accompanied by executives of United Fruit.[31] The CIA and its Guatemalan allies eventually settled on General Carlos Castillo Armas, living in exile in neighboring Honduras. Castillo Armas was not especially well known in Guatemala and appeared to have almost no political following. Nevertheless, the United States promptly helped him by funding and training an army of exiles. That force crossed the border back into Guatemala in the late spring of 1954, but the advance was sluggish at best. Rebel fortunes changed when a small fleet of old bombers, flown by U.S. pilots, bombed and strafed targets inside Guatemala, especially near the capital.[32] Those attacks had more psychological than military effect, but they served as a catalyst for an uprising by right-wing elements of the Guatemalan army against the country's leftist president. Under increasing pressure, Árbenz resigned and fled to Mexico. The CIA's fingerprints were all over this "domestic rebellion" just as they had been a year earlier in Iran.[33] (See chapter 6.)

John Prados, an expert on intelligence operations, aptly notes the cynical, ultimately myopic, aspect of U.S. policies toward the balky but democratic governments in Iran and Guatemala:

> In the cold war vision of a two-camp world, there was apparently no place for indigenous nationalism. Not only did the United States readily act against countries like Iran and Guatemala, but the actions were initiated regardless of the nations' efforts to maintain friendly

relations with the United States. The operations made a mockery of the oft-reiterated American principle of nonintervention in the internal affairs of other states. The CIA was unleashed in the name of democracy, but democracy as defined by American foreign policy came to mean governments that followed pro-American policies.[34]

Eisenhower's account of the Guatemalan coup was at least as disingenuous as his whitewashed description of the Iranian coup. His version was that Árbenz had not only declared a state of siege, but "launched a reign of terror." Then, "armed forces under Carlos Castillo Armas, an exiled former colonel in the Guatemalan Army, crossed the border from Honduras into Guatemala, initially with a mere handful of men—reportedly about two hundred. As he progressed, he picked up recruits."[35]

The U.S. role, according to Eisenhower, was limited to replacing two old bombers in Castillo's "air force," which had crashed during the early stages of the rebellion. The rest of what happened was purely an indigenous uprising of the Guatemalan military and population. "The major factor in the successful outcome was the disaffection of the Guatemalan armed forces and the population as a whole with the tyrannical regime of Arbenz." And the president had nothing but praise for Castillo Armas, who after some brief jockeying for power was "confirmed first as the head of the military junta, and then, by a thundering majority, as President." According to Eisenhower, Castillo Armas "proved to be far more than a mere rebel; he was a farseeing and able statesman." He also "enjoyed the devotion of his people."[36]

CIA chief Allen Dulles, brother of Eisenhower's secretary of state, was only a shade more candid than his boss about the U.S. role in the Guatemalan "revolution." He acknowledged that once it "became clear" that Árbenz was out to create a communist state, the United States provided aid "to a group of Guatemalan patriots," and thereby "the danger was successfully met."[37]

All was apparently well now that the communist tyrant Jacobo Árbenz was out of the way. In a nationwide television address on June 30, 1954, Secretary of State John Foster Dulles congratulated "the people of Guatemala" for overturning a regime that had been "openly manipulated" by international communism. John Peurifoy gave a more honest assessment of who was responsible for the ouster of Árbenz, when he quipped, tongue in cheek, that his superiors were complaining that he had been "forty-five minutes off schedule."[38] Árbenz was gone, and Washington rejoiced. "Now the future of Guatemala," Dulles proclaimed in his television address, "lies at the disposal of the Guatemalan people."[39]

Not quite. That prediction proved to be no more accurate than the official account of the overthrow of the Árbenz government. Washington's action may have blocked the danger of Soviet influence in Guatemala (if that danger truly existed), but it indisputably subjected the people of that country to brutal military rule for decades, a period in which some 200,000 people perished at the hands of right-wing regimes.

The Castillo Armas government was relatively benign compared to its successors, but it was bad enough, and the legal foundation for the systematic repression that followed was built during his presidency. One of his first actions was to create a new Committee for National Defense against Communism (CDNCC), and in just the first few weeks that bureaucracy imprisoned more than 4,000 suspects. In August 1954, the regime issued Decree 59, which authorized the CDNCC to, among other things, jail anyone on its list of suspects for up to six months without trial. The "temporary" detention power was not a trivial matter, since the suspect list eventually comprised fully 10 percent of Guatemala's population.[40]

The most odious aspect of the provision, though, was that there was no limit to the number of times the CDNCC could arrest and detain a suspect for a six-month period. A member of Castillo Armas's government candidly told a U.S. Embassy official that "with this law, we can now pick up practically anybody we want and hold them for as long as we want."[41] Legally, regime critics (or even unlucky nonpolitical types) could now be imprisoned sequentially for years—and that is precisely what happened.

Such conduct did nothing to discourage the Eisenhower administration from backing Castillo Armas and his successors. Indeed, U.S. officials seemed pleased with the crackdown on leftist elements. Washington gave especially high priority to funding, equipping, and training the Guatemalan military, arguing that it was a crucial bulwark against a revived communist threat. In 1963, that better trained, professional force overthrew a civilian government and ushered in a series of military regimes that engaged in abuses of human rights that made the practices of Castillo Armas's presidency look mild by comparison.

Yet, with the partial exception of the Carter years, U.S. administrations never faltered in their support of the Guatemalan military dictatorships, providing millions of dollars in aid and hardware. Even as military units conducted bloody and largely indiscriminate raids against accused insurgents, U.S. officers worked directly with those units. How bad was the collateral damage? In one especially bloody period in 1971, government forces killed nearly 1,000 people, most of whom seemed to be civilians, in a mere 12 weeks. Army troops raided the National University, where they assassinated three professors and arrested hundreds of students, some of whom subsequently "disappeared." Colonel Carlos Manuel Arana Osorio, selected by the military junta to be the winning candidate in the 1970 presidential election, vowed to eliminate all insurgents "even if it is necessary to turn the country into a cemetery." Arana and his successors worked very hard to achieve that objective in the coming years, utilizing both the military and allied right-wing death squads.

Most of the victims were leftists, and some undoubtedly were hard-core communists, but that label was routinely attached to all people that the government arrested or killed. Moreover, some of the targets were not even arguably communists. In the lead-up to elections in 1974, death squads (which included "off-duty" soldiers) assassinated a dozen officials of the centrist Christian Democratic Party. Cornell University Professor Walter LaFeber correctly concludes that the Guatemalan army "was not content merely to kill those on the Left; it wanted to eliminate everyone between itself and the Left as well."[42]

The army's brutalities reached the point that even its civilian front men sometimes balked. In 1980, the military-backed civilian vice president resigned in protest. "There are no political prisoners in Guatemala," he remarked. "There are only political assassinations."[43] Matters did not improve the following decade. An especially ugly episode occurred in December 1982 in the village of Dos Erres. Twenty Guatemalan *Kabiles* (special forces soldiers) arrived at the village in search of insurgents. They proceeded to run amok. The soldiers ultimately killed some 250 men, women, and children. Gilberto Jordan, one of the perpetrators, later confessed that the first person he killed at Dos Erres was a baby, whom Jordan threw down the shaft of the village well. Investigators eventually found 162 skeletal remains in that well. Evidence also emerged that the soldiers raped and tortured most of the girls and women before killing them.[44]

The Dos Erres massacre may have been marginally more gruesome than the norm, but there were literally dozens of such episodes during the military's decades-long counterinsurgency war. At least 200,000 people perished during that period, mostly among the largely Indian populations in the rural areas of the country. According to Tim Weiner's National Book Award–winning book on the CIA, *Legacy of Ashes*, between 90 and 96 percent of those deaths were at the hands of the Guatemalan military. Moreover, he contends that as late as 1994 "the CIA's officers in Guatemala still went to great lengths to conceal the nature of their close relations to the military and to suppress reports that Guatemalan officers on its payroll were murderers, torturers, and thieves."[45]

As the violence surged during the 1970s and early 1980s, a number of fissures in Guatemalan society developed or intensified. A leftist rebel insurgency gained strength, especially in predominantly Indian rural communities, which had been largely excluded from Guatemala's Mestiso (mixed blood)-dominated political and economic system. The government responded with an ever bloodier crackdown.

But divisions arose within the political and economic elites—and ultimately within the military itself. Mafia-style warfare erupted in the major cities between rival business and political factions. By the early 1980s, the breakdown of unity had reached the top echelons of the military, as generals became little more than warlords presiding over competing gangs determined to maximize their plunder and power. Washington viewed the growing chaos with dismay but seemed largely incapable of crafting a coherent response. LaFeber succinctly summarizes the dilemma that U.S. leaders faced:

> Washington officials were not pleased with their own creation in Guatemala, but—much as one hesitates to stop feeding a pet boa constrictor—they were reluc-

tant to cut off aid and face the consequences. Throughout those bloody, bleak years, they tried to resolve the
irresolvable: extend U.S. military and economic aid
so the army could fight the growing revolution, but
threaten to cut off aid if the 'rival mafias' did not stop
murdering Indians, labor leaders, educators, lawyers,
and each other.[46]

The violence did not truly abate until a peace accord was signed
between the war-weary government and various opposition factions in 1996, and the country began a transition to a genuine
democracy. When one weighs the consequences of Washington's
decision to overthrow Árbenz and later support a series of right-
wing dictatorships in Guatemala, the human costs were horrify-
ingly high.

Washington and the Somoza Family: Nicaragua as an Authoritarian Client

In addition to the parade of Guatemalan military strongmen,
U.S. administrations backed other dubious allies in the hemisphere.
An especially close association existed with the Somoza family of
Nicaragua, which ruled the country with an iron fist from the late
1930s to the late 1970s. Washington bore considerable responsibility
for the rise of the first dictator of that dynasty, Anastasio Somoza García,
since his original power base was as commander of the Nicaraguan
National Guard—the military force that the U.S. occupation
authorities organized and trained.

Right-wing analysts, though, make a valiant attempt to whitewash Washington's record of being the godfather of hemispheric
tyrants. Robert Kagan, for example, asserts that "neither in the Dominican Republic nor in Cuba nor in Nicaragua could the United
States be held responsible for dictatorship. In Nicaragua dictatorship had been the normal state of affairs since its independence;
tyranny and one-party rule had been interrupted only by periods
of revolution and near-anarchy." He concedes that "the United
States had helped create a new army, the National Guard, which
had been used to put its leader into the presidency," but Kagan
seems to consider that action little more than a minor faux pas.

Somoza García had "the skills and wiles to keep himself in power for 20 years. He may, therefore, be considered one of Nicaragua's most successful dictators, but he cannot be considered the creation of the United States."[47]

That interpretation is, at a minimum, a sanitized version of Washington's conduct. The United States may not have been the outright creator of Latin American autocrats, but U.S. policy certainly facilitated the rise of such dictators as Batista in Cuba, Trujillo in the Dominican Republic, Jean-Claude Duvalier in Haiti, and Somoza in Nicaragua. Time and again U.S. officials established and strengthened indigenous military forces, ostensibly to maintain order once U.S. troops would depart, giving would-be dictators an unmatchable power base. American leaders either knew or should have known that building up such institutions would inherently undermine any prospects for democratic rule. But Washington was, at best, indifferent and at worst, supportive of the rise of tyrants—as long as they were friendly to U.S. economic and strategic interests. That is why a succession of U.S. administrations got along splendidly with the Somoza dictatorship for more than four decades.

Yet according to Kagan and other conservative writers, it was the *lack* of sustained U.S. intervention that was the problem. If only the United States had acted in the Western Hemisphere as Britain did around the world at the height of the imperial era, they argue, we could have prevented the rise and perpetuation of autocratic regimes, enabling our neighbors to enjoy good governance and at least quasi-democratic systems under the supervision of Washington's benevolent hegemony. Instead, according to that school of thought, the United States went through cycles of intervention and withdrawal, and once the Good Neighbor Policy was put in place, nonintervention allegedly became the norm.

The best that can be said for that view is that it represents tenacious wishful thinking. The repeated undermining of regimes (even democratic ones) considered insufficiently cooperative, as well as the sustained support for the Guatemalan dictatorships, the Somoza family, and other compliant, autocratic regimes, suggests that Washington's intervention was hardly sporadic. And the alleged policy of nonintervention that the Good Neighbor Policy symbolized was little more than a diplomatic façade. Military intervention may not have been as frequent or as blatant a feature of U.S. policy as it had been during the first three decades of the 20th century, but that tactic never disappeared. And the more subtle tactics of subversion and covert military action were pervasive. Latin America did not suffer from a lack of U.S. geopolitical attention or action. In particular, Washington's partnership with (often brutal) authoritarian rulers remained a key feature of U.S. policy in the hemisphere.

There were always prominent Americans willing to act as apologists for the Somozas and other autocratic U.S. clients. One of the worst was Jeane Kirkpatrick, who served as U.S. ambassador to the United Nations under President Reagan. Kirkpatrick described Anastasio Somoza Debayle (son and eventual successor of Somoza Garcia) as merely a "moderate" autocrat. Lauding Somoza Debayle and the Shah of Iran, she offered the following assessment: "Both did tolerate limited opposition, including opposition newspapers and political parties, but both were also confronted by radical, violent opponents bent on social and political revolution. Both rulers, *therefore*, sometimes invoked martial law to arrest, imprison, exile, and occasionally, *it was alleged*, torture their opponents."[48]

The notion that such dictators used martial law and other repressive policies solely as defensive responses—and solely against violent totalitarian adversaries—is a grotesque distortion of reality. And, contrary to Kirkpatrick, they didn't just "allegedly" torture their opponents—democratic types as well as radicals—it is well documented that they did so. But Kirkpatrick and other neoconservatives remained exceedingly fond of friendly dictators. She expressed an apologia that unintentionally provides a damning indictment of U.S. policy:

> The Shah and Somoza were not only anti-Communist, they were positively friendly to the United States, sending their sons and others to be educated in our universities, voting with us in the United Nations and regularly supporting American interests and positions even when those entailed personal and political cost. The embassies of both governments were active in Washington social life, and were frequented by powerful Americans who occupied major roles in this nation's diplomatic, military, and political life.[49]

That attitude was not far removed from the cynical Leninist view that one cannot make an omelet without breaking some eggs. Apparently, as long as the likes of Somoza were gracious guests at embassy receptions, sent their offspring to study in the United States, voted correctly in the United Nations, and supported Washington's overall foreign policy objectives, Americans shouldn't have been concerned that those allies also looted and brutalized their own people.

Nor was that an isolated, ill-considered comment on Kirkpatrick's part. On another occasion, she gave a similarly favorable portrayal of the Nicaraguan dictator, noting that he "was a West Point graduate with an American wife," and that "he had accommodated successive administrations." Indeed, Somoza and his government were "doggedly friendly to U.S. interests and desires."[50]

Her assessment of Somoza's relationship with Washington and the nature of his rule was extraordinarily sympathetic. Somoza, she said, "had every reason to suppose that his regime would continue to enjoy U.S. favor and no reason to suppose that his power would be brought down by a small group of Cuban-backed terrorists who periodically disturbed the peace with their violence."[51] She was referring to the Sandinista National Liberation Front, the group that would lead the revolution that ousted Somoza in 1979.

Other than that "small group of Cuban-backed terrorists," most Nicaraguans were supposedly content with their ruler. And why shouldn't they be? According to Kirkpatrick, "Nicaraguan politics during the Somoza period featured limited repression and limited opposition. Criticism was permitted and, in fact carried on day after day in the pages of *La Prensa* (whose editor was an opposition leader.)"[52] At least, he was an opposition leader until he was murdered—in all likelihood by Somoza's henchmen. The conduct that Kirkpatrick minimized as "limited oppression" caused the Carter administration to condemn the Nicaraguan government for human rights violations, but she saw Somoza's conduct as merely a reaction to atrocities that the small group of communist terrorists committed.[53] Kirkpatrick's viewpoint was shockingly insensitive, but her attitude seemed to be the norm in Washington regarding U.S. policy in Central America and the Caribbean over the decades.

What was the nature of the "limited oppression" that Kirkpatrick and other defenders of the Somoza dictatorship casually dismissed? Even Robert Kagan, a staunch conservative, concedes that it was not trivial, stating that during the 1970s, "members of the National Guard imprisoned, brutalized, and killed not only Sandinista fighters, but also hundreds of peasants suspected of helping them."[54] Actually, it was more like thousands of peasants, but his overall description of the Guard's brutality was accurate.

Amnesty International was harsh in its assessment of the Somoza government's human rights record. An August 15, 1977, Amnesty report covering the period from late 1974 to January 1977 charged that "torture, arbitrary detention and disappearances" were "increasingly characteristic of the human rights situation in Nicaragua." The report further criticized the extensive "political imprisonment, denial of due process of law, use of torture and summary executions" of peasants by the National Guard. One charge cited the disappearance and apparent deaths of some 300 peasants.[55]

The Catholic Church was even more scathing in an early 1977 statement by Nicaragua's bishops, accusing the Guard of "widespread torture, rape, and summary executions of civilians" in its counterinsurgency campaign against the Sandinistas.[56] A year earlier, several priests from Nicaragua testified before Congress about Guard atrocities. There were the usual accounts of rape and torture, but some of the testimony suggested impressive, sadistic creativity on the part of Guard personnel. One technique apparently was to force a prisoner to swallow a button, which a torturer would then proceed to repeatedly tug upward.[57]

The conventional wisdom among American conservatives is that the weak-kneed Carter administration sold out Washington's loyal ally in Managua because of exaggerated concerns about human rights abuses. But Somoza's conduct had become an increasing embarrassment to Washington even before Carter took office.[58] A December 1976 State Department report strongly criticized the behavior of the Nicaraguan regime. Weeks earlier, Assistant Secretary of State William Rogers had told Somoza that the United States would "be neutral both publicly and privately in all its actions" with respect to the regime and its opponents.[59] Kagan notes that "American policy had been indifferent to Somoza's activities" throughout the 1960s and early 1970s.[60] (Indeed, that was true throughout the decades of the Somoza family dynasty.) But the latest occupant of the presidential palace in Managua was testing the limits of Washington's tolerance for brutality.

The mounting evidence of the extent of corruption accompanying Somoza's rule also began to embarrass U.S. leaders. A series by syndicated columnists Jack Anderson and Les Whitten in the mid-1970s portrayed Somoza as the greediest, most corrupt dictator in the hemisphere—if not the world.[61] And there was enough evidence to give that allegation credibility. The dictator, his relatives, and his cronies in the Guard monopolized all profitable businesses, both legal enterprises and illegal ones. They dominated everything from construction to auto imports to prostitution and gambling. U.S. administrations during the 1950s, 1960s, and early 1970s did not seem to care, even when U.S. aid dollars went into the pockets of the Somoza family. Not only did bilateral aid continue to flow, but Washington pressed the international lending agencies to make large "loans" to Nicaragua.

But the Somoza regime's greed seemed to know no bounds, and matters began to spiral out of control following a devastating earthquake in 1972 that damaged much of the capital city and leveled a good many outlying towns and villages.[62] The National Guard failed to maintain order in the aftermath, with soldiers often joining the looting. Even worse, the government confiscated and sold on the black market medical and relief supplies meant for hardhit communities. The regime also skimmed the $32 million in aid money that the Nixon administration had sent for earthquake relief. When U.S. officials demanded an explanation, the Nicaraguan government managed to provide, at best, sketchy accounting for only $16 million.[63] The rest had simply disappeared. At that point, even some of Somoza's supporters in Congress and the American media began to get restless.

That restlessness coincided with the election of Jimmy Carter as president and the emergence of a new administration that was less inclined to support autocrats in the hemisphere merely because they were anti-communist. In a May 1977 commencement address at the University of Notre Dame, Carter indicated how his foreign policy would differ from those of recent presidents with respect to backing authoritarian clients. He decried the "inordinate fear of communism" that had "led us to embrace any dictator who joined us in that fear."[64]

Early on, though, the administration's actions with respect to Nicaragua seemed more conventional than the president's rhetoric.

The administration even sought congressional approval for $3.1 million in military aid for Somoza's army. But as the year wore on, Washington's policy hardened, despite Somoza's belated attempts to soothe his increasingly angry public and appease the United States. Among other steps, he lifted the state of siege, which had become the principal legal pretext for the National Guard's crackdown and the accompanying human rights abuses.

Such measures proved insufficient on both the domestic and international fronts. Those officials within the Carter administration, including Deputy Secretary of State Warren Christopher, who lobbied for giving human rights issues a higher priority in U.S. foreign policy, soon prevailed regarding Nicaragua. Not only did the State Department withhold the military aid that Congress had passed, but it moved successfully to block distribution of $10 million in developmental aid loans that Congress had approved. As the fighting in Nicaragua accelerated in 1978 and early 1979, the Carter administration became more impatient with, and critical of, the Somoza government. By the spring of 1979, Washington pushed for a resolution by the Organization of American States that called for Somoza's resignation, and U.S. officials prodded Israel—Nicaragua's last remaining arms supplier—to end its sales.

Conservatives later charged that the cutoff of military and economic assistance to Managua was directly responsible for Somoza's subsequent fall from power at the hands of a revolution led by the Sandinistas. Kirkpatrick was especially upset about the elimination of arms sales and the imposition of an oil embargo in 1979. Referring to the fall of South Vietnam in 1975, she fumed that "for the second time in a decade, an American ally ran out of gas and ammunition while confronting an opponent well armed by the Soviet bloc."[65]

Even some liberal hawks adopted the view that U.S. pressure was the decisive factor in the overthrow of Somoza. Writing in the pages of *Foreign Affairs*, William P. Bundy, assistant secretary of state during the Johnson administration, stated flatly that without the pressure that the Carter administration exerted, "it seems a safe bet that Tacho Somoza would still be in charge in Nicaragua, and his amiable brother-in-law still extending abrazzos to all and sundry in Washington as dean of the diplomatic corps."[66]

At most, though, the elimination of U.S. aid played a secondary role. The Somoza regime's own brutality and corruption—especially the mismanagement and mass pilfering of badly needed earthquake aid—alienated ever larger portions of the country's population. Without such a track record of governmental venality and incompetence, the Sandinistas probably would have remained a weak, fringe group, and the severance of U.S. financial assistance, if it had occurred at all, would have had little impact.

The aftermath of the ouster of Anastasio Somoza Debayle in 1979 proved to be another example of blowback, as the United States then faced the anti-U.S. Sandinista government of Daniel Ortega. Fortunately, the blowback was not nearly as severe as it was in Iran after the fall of the Shah, but it was not trivial, either. The Ortega government did cause some legitimate security concerns for Washington, since it quickly became cozy with Moscow. It was not merely that Managua increasingly voted with the USSR in the United Nations and other international organizations, or even that the rhetoric coming from Ortega and other officials often had a shrill anti-U.S. quality. Those were, or at least should have been, nothing more than irritants.

What was more worrisome was the influx of Soviet bloc armaments into Nicaragua. That development rekindled memories of Moscow's moves during the early years of Fidel Castro's rule in Cuba. Equally unsettling was the Sandinista regime's flagrant support for Marxist rebels in neighboring El Salvador—support that included both arms and money.[67] The Reagan administration's fears that a Soviet client state was moving to destabilize all of Central America and turn the region into a communist bastion beholden to Moscow may have been excessive, but they were not entirely unfounded.

Such blowback, though, was at least partially a product of Washington's uncaring, and often unthinking, support for Somoza; the Guatemalan juntas; and other repressive, corrupt regimes in Central America throughout the decades. Their misrule and U.S. sponsorship of their dictatorships created fertile ground for left-wing, anti-U.S. movements. The Sandinistas were the first of those movements to come to power, and similar revolutions were brewing in El Salvador and other Central American nations during the final stages of the Cold War. Washington was lucky that with the collapse of the USSR, the external support for radical leftist causes in Central America dried up. Castro's Cuba undoubtedly sympathized with kindred Marxist movements, but after the ebbing of Moscow's sponsorship, the communist regime in Havana had its hands full preventing bankruptcy and preserving control of its own country.

Washington also was fortunate that the Sandinistas turned out to be relatively mild autocrats rather than the hard-core Leninists the Reagan administration made them out to be. That point became apparent when Ortega and his followers not only held a reasonably free and fair election but accepted the adverse results. Democratic governments that emerged in Guatemala after the 1990s also focused more on preserving and expanding the country's crucial bilateral economic ties with the United States instead of trying to score political and diplomatic points for past grievances. Consequently, the blowback from the decades of supporting friendly, corrupt, and often brutal tyrants proved to be less severe than it might have been. As in the case of the Philippines and South Korea, the United States dodged a bullet in Central America. Sometimes it's better to be lucky than good.

A Troubling History of Intervention

The desire of U.S. leaders to thwart the establishment of Soviet client states in America's strategic backyard was understandable. And the emergence of Fidel Castro's regime in Cuba in 1959 demonstrated that such concerns were not just hypothetical. Moreover, the Cuban Missile Crisis illustrated the serious security problems that could result from the presence of such client states. Nevertheless, there is the question of whether Washington overreacted to the threat of Soviet penetration of the Western Hemisphere. There is also the issue of how badly the United States damaged its reputation for a commitment to democracy and liberty by supporting odious rulers in Central America merely because they were anti-communist. U.S. policymakers never seemed to examine very seriously whether there were other ways that might have been used to block Soviet influence in the hemisphere without embracing such odious allies.

Moreover, the instances of intervention during the Cold War era cannot be divorced from the long history of Washington's interference in the internal affairs of its hemispheric neighbors throughout earlier decades. That policy did not begin with the emergence of the global rivalry with the USSR. Washington's heavy hand was evident in Central America and the Caribbean long before, and the motives for those earlier initiatives ranged from questionable to sleazy. All too often, U.S. policymakers were willing, if not eager, to displace governments that were deemed insufficiently cooperative with Washington's foreign policy objectives or just insufficiently syco-phantic toward powerful American businesses in the region. There was little respect for either the sovereignty of those small neighbors or for the welfare of their populations. It was not a track record that brought honor to the United States.

The Cold War interventions were more ideological but not nec-essarily more honorable. At best, the Guatemala coup was a ques-tionable response motivated by an exaggerated fear of communist influence in general and Soviet power in particular. Washington's sponsorship of, and financial support for, bloody-handed dictator-ships in the aftermath of that coup—support that lasted for the next four decades—compounded the shame.

The intervention in the Dominican Republic was somewhat less repellent, since the successor government was not on the same level as the Guatemalan butchers. Indeed, it was at least quasi-demo-cratic. And in Grenada, the Reagan administration allowed—even facilitated—the emergence of a democratic successor government, instead of installing a cooperative autocrat in power.[68] One might debate the ethics of intervening in the internal affairs of those na-tions, but the outcomes were decidedly superior to previous U.S. interventions.

Washington's record with respect to the Somoza family dictator-ship deserves a spot somewhere between the performance in Guate-mala and the actions in the Dominican Republic and Grenada. The United States was not directly responsible for Somoza García's rise to power or the perpetuation of the dynasty he established. But it is also likely that without Washington's extensive financial infusions and willingness to equip the National Guard, it would have been difficult for the Somozas to squat on, and impoverish, their unhappy country for better than four decades. Washington deserves more than a little blame for that situation, although the hands of U.S. poli-cymakers are not as bloody as they were with respect to Guatemala.

Washington's inclination to meddle in the internal affairs of its hemispheric neighbors has not abated much with the end of the Cold War. The administration of George H. W. Bush sent in troops to oust Washington's one-time client, Panamanian dictator Manuel Noriega (who had been on the CIA's payroll), in December 1989, more than six weeks after the Berlin Wall fell. And in 1994, years after the Cold War was receding into history, the Clinton administration imposed draconian economic sanctions against Haiti. When those measures did not induce the government to relinquish power, Washington prepared to invade. U.S. officials gave regime leaders an ultimatum: leave quietly and enjoy a comfortable exile or dare to resist the invasion and suffer the consequences. They chose the former, and U.S. troops came ashore unopposed.

Only the rationale for such interventions had shifted with the end of the Cold War. In the post–Cold War period, the United States professed to be the guardian of democracy. And in truth, Washington did orchestrate the emergence of a democratic system in Panama following the ouster of Noriega's authoritarian regime. The Haitian intervention was also defended as a democracy-promotion enterprise. The official justification for both the sanctions and the subsequent military deployment was to restore the duly elected president, Jean Bertrand Aristide, to office. The reality was that Aristide was more of an authoritarian than a democratic leader. Mobs loyal to his political machine routinely harassed, tortured, and murdered political opponents.

In marked contrast to previous clients the United States helped place or sustain in power, though, Aristide was not especially friendly to U.S. interests. Indeed, the junta that the Clinton administration removed from power was arguably far more amenable to Washington's interests. Perhaps a new phase of U.S. interventionism in the hemisphere has emerged in which there is a genuine commitment to democracy—or at least democratic forms. That shift might or might not make America's neighbors more comfortable with the ministrations of the colossus of the north. But at least for the time being, U.S. leaders no longer embrace authoritarian clients in the hemisphere merely because they are willing to do Washington's bidding. That is progress of a sort. But it would be better still if the United States learned to avoid meddling in their neighbors' affairs for any reason, unless its own security interests are directly at stake.

Washington does seem less determined to intervene either overtly or covertly to get rid of annoying leftist regimes. A succession of U.S. administrations tolerated Venezuela's Hugo Chávez even as he engaged in shrill, often crude, denunciations of the United States and its leaders and adopted increasingly repressive practices. The same restraint has been evident toward Chávez's "Bolivarian" emulators, such as Bolivia's Evo Morales and Ecuador's Rafael Correa. Washington has reacted mildly even when those governments have pursued populist economic policies, as well as harassed and intimidated democratic, pro-U.S. political factions. The restraint has held even when those rulers established cooperative ties with such nations as Russia, China, and Iran. Similar policies on the part of left-wing Latin American regimes in earlier decades would likely have led to U.S. subversion campaigns, blatant CIA coups, or even direct military invasion.

The new pattern suggests that U.S. leaders may have internalized some appropriate lessons from the shameful policies of the 20th century toward Latin America. It is encouraging that over the past decade or so, administrations have not overreacted to the emergence of authoritarian, often extremely unfriendly, populist governments in the hemisphere. It would have been easy, especially after 9/11, to portray such regimes as posing dire security threats to the United States—especially when some of them developed friendly ties with Iran. There have been efforts to portray Chávez and his disciples as terrorist allies.[69] But those efforts are relatively infrequent, and unlike similar campaigns against allegedly pro-communist regimes during the Cold War, they have achieved little traction. Instead of succumbing to panicky impulses, this time U.S. policymakers appear to regard such regimes accurately as mere annoyances to a superpower, warranting nothing more than diplomatic responses. If that sensible pattern continues, it may produce a new, much better era in Washington's relations with its southern neighbors.

2. Chiang Kai-shek: America's Troublesome "Free World" Client

For nearly four decades, Washington maintained a close relationship with Generalissimo Chiang Kai-shek, first as the leader of China and then after his defeat on the mainland, as the leader of a rump government on the island of Taiwan (Formosa).[1] Throughout that period, Chiang had an image in the United States at sharp variance with reality. The dominant perception—although there were always some outspoken dissenters—was that he was a heroic figure, who, from the late 1930s until the end of World War II, prevented Japan from conquering his country. Historian Barbara Tuchman concluded in retrospect that China's battle against the Japanese occupation made a deep, favorable impression in America:

> Out of sympathy with her resistance or investment in her affairs, correspondents, missionaries, and other observers concentrated on the admirable aspects and left unmentioned the flaws and failures. An idealized image came through. Generalissimo and Mme. Chiang Kai-shek as "Man and Wife of the Year" for 1937 gazed at Americans in sad nobility from the cover of *Time* sober, steady, brave and true.[2]

It was not coincidental that *Time*'s publisher, Henry Luce, had been born in China of religious missionary parents. Missionaries seemed to be the most enthusiastic practitioners of hagiography regarding Chiang. They had spent decades in that country bringing the Christian gospel to the Chinese people, and they were deeply committed to the narrative that the war against Japanese forces was a Manichean struggle between good (China) and evil (Japan). Moreover, Tuchman notes: "They rallied to the Chiangs in self-interested loyalty because the Chiangs' Christianity at the helm of China provided such gratifying proof of the validity of the missionary effort.

41

They overpraised Chiang Kai-shek and once committed to his perfection regarded any suggestion of blemish as inadmissible."[3]

The missionary community became a crucial component of the vocal pro-Chiang faction in the United States that became known as the China Lobby.[4] It was a somewhat nebulous and informal pressure group, but an extremely capable one. In addition to the missionaries and their religious supporters, the China Lobby consisted of Kuomintang (KMT) diplomats, wealthy Chinese and Chinese-American businessmen, and their political allies in the United States. Those allies included powerful business leaders such as textile magnate Alfred A. Kohlberg, who would become a major supporter of Senator Joseph McCarthy; conservative (primarily Republican) members in both houses of Congress; retired generals; and prominent journalists and publishers. Chiang's government also employed 10 (!) lobbying and public-relations firms to make certain that his government's message was vigorously promoted to U.S. policymakers.[5] The China Lobby was a sophisticated, well-oiled operation that was extremely successful in shaping American public opinion on China. Indeed, it was so successful that until the 1970s, anyone who dared question the orthodox policy of strong support for Chiang risked serious, and possibly fatal, damage to their careers and reputations.

But religious enthusiasts and their allies in the China Lobby were not the only people to convey a picture of Chiang that bore little resemblance to reality. Tuchman points out that "as America's ally, China could not be admitted to be other than a democratic power. It was impossible to acknowledge that Chiang Kai-shek's government was what the historian Whitney Griswold, future president of Yale, named in 1938, 'a fascist dictatorship,' though a slovenly and ineffectual one."[6] Griswold's take may have been a bit extreme, but Chiang certainly did not embrace democratic norms, and according to one biographer, he saw himself as nothing less than "the embodiment of the nation."[7] At least until the late 1930s, he also appeared to admire Hitler's Germany, even congratulating Hitler on the Anschluss with Austria in March 1938.[8]

But the American news media's idealized treatment of Chiang and his policies during World War II rarely wavered. Journalists covering the Chinese component of the war, "even when outside the country and free of censorship," refrained from reporting atrocities and other disagreeable actions.[9] That willingness to whitewash the record of an authoritarian U.S. ally would become a common occurrence in many regions of the world throughout the following decades.

The highly favorable view of Chiang and his government continued after the Japanese defeat ended the occupation of China, for the alleged patriotic stalwart faced another ruthless threat. According to his admirers, Chiang led a valiant resistance to Soviet-backed communist insurgents who sought to drag China into the darkness of totalitarianism. That conflict had begun in the 1920s, but it grew more intense following World War II. When the noble fight against Mao Zedong's legions tragically failed, the conventional wisdom argued, Chiang and his supporters created a Free World redoubt on Taiwan and helped preserve America's own strategic position in East Asia.

Some U.S. officials, especially during the presidencies of Franklin D. Roosevelt and Harry S. Truman, privately adopted a more restrained, skeptical view of Chiang and his government. General Joseph "Vinegar Joe" Stilwell, the U.S. military commander in the China-Burma-India theater in World War II, once described Chiang as "a vacillating, tricky, undependable old scoundrel who never keeps his word."[10] In their public statements, though, even Roosevelt and Truman praised Chiang in glowing terms. In one fireside chat, FDR lauded the Chinese leader as "an unconquerable man . . . of great vision [and] great courage."[11] Other policymakers seemed to be true believers regarding both his nobility of purpose and his leadership ability. Warmly describing Chiang as "my old comrade in arms," General Douglas MacArthur, commander of U.S. forces in East Asia during the late 1940s, stated that the generalissimo's "indomitable determination to resist Communist domination aroused my sincere admiration."[12]

The Real Chiang Kai-shek

There was a troubling gap between the pervasive image in the United States of the generalissimo's behavior and competence and the underlying reality. As the leader of China's Nationalist government since the late 1920s, Chiang Kai-shek was not even remotely a democratic model. Indeed, after a brief flirtation with secular democratic values following the revolution led by Sun Yat-sen that overthrew the last Qing dynasty emperor in 1911, the new Republic of China (ROC) and the governing Kuomintang Party gradually adopted a radical leftist orientation. The KMT was reorganized along Leninist lines in the early 1920s with the assistance of Comintern agents dispatched by the Kremlin.[13]

Generalissimo Chiang took over the leadership of the KMT upon Sun's death in 1925, and by 1927, he had emerged as the party's dominant military and political figure. From the earliest days of his preeminence, his governance was unmistakably authoritarian. Conservative analyst Martin L. Lasater concedes that over the next two decades, Chiang "ruled as a military dictator in constant warfare against [competing] warlords, communists, and Japanese."[14] The generalissimo was not shy about imprisoning or executing anyone who got in his way.

From the late 1920s through World War II, various martial law proclamations served as the ostensible legal basis for his repressive policies. U.S. criticism did help prod a reluctant Chiang to hold more-or-less democratic elections in 1947 and promulgate a new, democratic constitution. But he promptly vitiated provisions of that document. Just weeks after the election, Chiang again declared martial law (in response to the growing communist insurgency) and an obedient legislature enacted the Temporary Provisions Effective during the Period of Communist Rebellion. That measure gave the ROC president extraordinary powers to prosecute the civil war against Mao's forces, and, in the process, deny ROC citizens the civil liberties that the 1947 constitution supposedly guaranteed. The Temporary Provisions would serve as the basis for Chiang's autocratic rule in China until he and the KMT fled the mainland in late 1949. Thereafter, it served the same function for his dictatorship on Taiwan and the surrounding islands, the last portion of China under KMT control.

Even before his flight in 1949, the brutality of Chiang's regime was evident on Taiwan. That territory, which had come under Tokyo's control in 1895 with the Treaty of Shimonoseki after Tokyo's victory in the Sino-Japanese war, reverted to Chinese control after World War II. The new rulers were not gentle with the country's newly returned citizens. Nationalist soldiers often treated native Taiwanese as Japanese collaborators, and many of those residents regarded the arrival of mainland overlords with more than a little hostility. Numerous atrocities took place, culminating in a series of anti-regime riots in the spring of 1947. Details of those clashes remain sketchy even decades later, but it is fairly certain that several thousand Taiwanese perished as Chiang's soldiers crushed the riots—and even the relatively peaceful demonstrations.

Chiang's Failure on the Mainland and the Aftermath

Systematic repression enabled the KMT to retain power on Taiwan, but it was not sufficient to preserve Chiang's authority on the mainland. Corruption as well as authoritarianism riddled the Nationalist government and bred growing resentment. Indeed, debilitating corruption,[15] combined with the often legendary incompetence of Nationalist civilian and military officials, would play a major role in the ability of Mao's forces to sweep the Nationalists off the mainland and proclaim the People's Republic of China (PRC) in 1949. Just two weeks before his death in April 1947, General Zhang Lingfu, one of Chiang's more competent military commanders, sent a letter to the generalissimo lamenting that KMT generals and the entire military culture were "corrupt and hopeless."[16]

Chiang displayed a remarkable ability to alienate even moderate, noncommunist elements. Historian Jay Taylor notes that by the middle of 1947, war weariness was prevalent among urban youth, both university students and those in the work force. As a result, a majority of that contingent wanted an end to the civil war and favored the creation of a coalition government. Polls, though, showed that only a small fraction favored a communist regime. For instance, some 90 percent of urban respondents opposed the Communist Party. The problem for Chiang and his followers, though, was that 95 percent disliked the KMT. Student-led anti-government demonstrations beginning in May 1947 "escalated into a 'tide' of demonstrations and strikes that swept through universities, colleges, and middle schools throughout the country."[17]

Chiang's security forces dealt with these demonstrations and the political opposition they represented in a heavy-handed fashion. "Chiang was determined to crack down," Taylor concludes. One of the first actions was to ban dissident newspapers in Shanghai and other metropolitan areas and arrest student leaders. Extensive detentions of suspected "ringleaders" followed in Chungking and other cities. There was an ominous aspect to that move. "Some suspects were abducted by police; other simply disappeared."[18] Chiang soon backed off from such harsh measures. And as bad as they were, they "contrasted with the absolute nontoleration of public dissent in the Communist areas." Nevertheless, the damage had been done. Taylor's conclusion was devastatingly accurate. "Chiang's new crackdown was a fiasco."[19] An already skeptical public found little reason to back continued KMT rule, and Mao's forces moved to exploit the opportunity.

The communist victory came as a bitter surprise to the American public and a substantial segment of the political elite, especially in Congress. It was far less of a surprise to the Truman administration. Indeed, the administration had repeatedly pressed Chiang to end his civil war with Mao and his followers, in part because they felt that a coalition government might be the best, sustainable deal that the KMT was likely to get. A key episode in that policy was the unsuccessful mission by General George Marshall from late December 1945 to February 1947 to try to end the fighting and mediate a settlement.[20] When KMT troops launched an offensive in the midst of Marshall's mission, the administration slapped an embargo on further military aid. Truman also warned Chiang that if he didn't become more serious about peace efforts, "it must be expected that American opinion will not continue in its generous attitude toward your nation."[21]

That comment did not accurately reflect the state of either public or congressional opinion. In early July 1947, Marshall (who was now secretary of state) candidly told a longtime confidant, General Albert Wedemeyer, about the actual situation. "Increasingly fierce accusations from Congress and the 'China lobby' that the administration was pursuing a pro-Communist policy in China were compelling 'a reappraisal of U.S. policy.'"[22] The recent decision to lift the arms embargo, Marshall admitted, was just one manifestation of the administration's response to the growing pressure.

The trend of opinion in China was another matter. There, the position of the Nationalist government slowly but steadily deteriorated between 1946 and 1949. John Leighton Stuart, the new U.S. ambassador to China, already warned Chiang in late 1946 that he was quickly losing public support in China as well as in the United States. Stuart added that, if that situation was to be reversed, there must be no more assassination of political opponents, no more suppression of newspapers, and a serious effort needed to take place to open up the political process.[23] Truman himself had sent Chiang a letter expressing the hope that "a strong and democratic China can yet be achieved under your leadership." But, the president added, there were growing doubts in the United States about the feasibility of that goal. Recent incidents, especially the "increased tendency to oppress freedom of the press as well as expressions of liberal views among intellectuals," had shaken American confidence in the KMT. The worst episode was the "assassinations of distinguished Chinese liberals at Kunming." All of those developments had produced "a growing conviction that an attempt is being made to settle major social issues by resort to force, military or secret police, rather than by democratic processes."[24]

Truman, Marshall, Dean Acheson (Marshall's successor as secretary of state), and other officials could justifiably be criticized for being naïve about the sweeping goals of the Chinese communists, believing that they would be content to share power. Truman, for example, blamed "extremist elements" in both the Kuomintang and the Communist Party for the carnage taking place in China. That comment assumed that there were moderates in the latter, but the Chinese Communist Party in the late 1940s was thoroughly controlled by hard-line Leninists; it was not merely a case of trouble being caused by an extremist, minority faction within the party.

Such gullibility on the part of U.S. officials was most unfortunate, but the administration was at least more realistic than its critics about the authoritarian nature, as well as the widespread inefficiency and mounting unpopularity, of Chiang's rule. Acheson later cited "the bungling incompetence of Chiang Kai-shek's Kuomintang" as a significant factor limiting U.S. policy options in China during the late 1940s.[25] In his memoirs, Truman states bluntly that Chiang "did not command the respect and support of the Chinese people. The generalissimo's attitude and actions were that of an old-fashioned warlord, and as with the warlords, there was no love for him among the people."[26]

That was a reasonably accurate assessment. But such realism was not much in evidence among Congress, the news media, and the general public in the United States. Thanks in large part to the excessively favorable portrayal of the generalissimo in the press throughout the previous decade-and-a-half, many Americans had come to regard Chiang and his government with great admiration and affection. The well-funded China Lobby portrayed Chiang and his followers as heroic figures. That version became embedded in the broader narrative of Chinese resistance to Japanese aggression even before the U.S. entry into World War II following the attack on Pearl Harbor. A well-crafted media image emerged of Chiang as the beleaguered leader of a Chinese population fighting to save their country from conquest by bloodthirsty Japanese militarists. The regime's propaganda apparatus, led by Chiang's wife, Soong Mei-ling (Madame Chiang), came to dominate discussions about China policy.

An inflated image of both Chiang and China intensified following the U.S. entry into the war. Chiang was even allowed to take part in the Cairo summit meeting with Franklin Roosevelt and British Prime Minister Winston Churchill in 1943. Chiang's involvement created the impression that Nationalist China was a great power like those other states and that Chiang was a major world leader. That image of equality was enshrined at San Francisco when China was made one of the five permanent members (with veto power) on the Security Council of the newly created United Nations.

The reality was quite different. Despite having a large population, China under Chiang Kai-shek was a weak, impoverished country. But the perception that it was actually a great power made the communist victory in 1949 all the more shocking and horrifying to Americans. It seemed as though the global communist juggernaut, controlled by the Kremlin, had scored a huge victory in its effort to weaken U.S. power and put the democratic world at greater risk. What had actually occurred was a largely indigenous revolution against a corrupt, sometimes inept, regime in a third-tier power.

The Poisonous "Who Lost China?" Obsession

The American reaction to Chiang's defeat and his retreat to the last remaining Nationalist bastion, the island of Taiwan, bordered on hysteria. And it was not confined to the usual supporters of the China Lobby. Predictably, conservative GOP members of Congress, such as Senator William Knowland of California and Senator Styles Bridges of New Hampshire, denounced the administration's January 5, 1950, statement that the United States would not send military aid to prop up KMT forces on Taiwan. But the panic about the expulsion of Chiang's government from the mainland was not confined to such circles. Even a moderate such as Senator H. Alexander Smith (R-NJ) argued for immediate action to help Chiang Kai-shek and prevent a communist conquest of Taiwan. Smith even proposed sending U.S. troops to occupy Taiwan to stabilize the situation.[27]

Chiang's ouster from the mainland also led to an immediate search for scapegoats. The question "Who lost China?" became a prominent refrain in U.S. politics from 1949 until well into Dwight D. Eisenhower's administration—and to some extent, even beyond that period. Dean Rusk, who served as deputy undersecretary of state for Far Eastern affairs during the late 1940s, cited the fallacy underlying that query. China was not ours to lose, he stated. "If anything, Chiang Kai-shek's inability to govern," combined with the lingering, damaging effects of the Japanese invasion, "not American inaction 'lost' China."[28] Rusk aptly described the intensity of the emotional recriminations in the United States. The reaction to the fall of China, he recalled, was akin to "that of a jilted lover."[29]

Even the usually sensible Senator Robert A. Taft (R-OH) succumbed to the temptation to seek scapegoats to explain the communist victory in China. Taft spoke on the Senate floor in January 1950, charging that the State Department was "guided by a left-wing group who obviously have wanted to get rid of Chiang and were willing at least to turn China over to the Communists for that purpose."[30] His views did not soften with the passage of time. In an August 1951 interview, the Ohio senator insisted that "we abandoned Chiang Kai-shek" because "the State Department absolutely wanted the Communists to win in China." When an astonished reporter asked him if he really believed that, Taft replied, "I think Secretary Acheson and the Far Eastern Division of the State Department did."[31] And Taft's criticism was mild compared to the comments of some other critics of the Truman administration's China policy. The leader of the more strident faction was Joseph R. McCarthy, the junior Republican senator from Wisconsin. It was no coincidence that McCarthy made his famous speech in Wheeling, West Virginia, charging that there was extensive communist infiltration in the State Department, barely two months after Chiang's forces fled to Taiwan. China policy became the centerpiece of McCarthy's case (and the case of conservative Republicans generally) that traitors had heavily influenced U.S. foreign policy. In subsequent forays, the senator charged that China had been lost because of the machinations of communist sympathizers and agents, and he specifically named prominent East Asian policy specialists in the State Department including John Service, John Carter Vincent, and Philip Jessup. He also cited Johns Hopkins University Professor Owen Lattimore, a prominent China scholar and occasional adviser to the State Department, who McCarthy charged was the "architect of our Far Eastern policy." Taft followed up, denouncing the "pro-Communist group in the State Department" who "promoted at every opportunity the Communist cause in China."[32]

Administration officials tried to shield their policy from mounting congressional and public anger. The most feasible way to do that was to quietly discard some of the officials who had urged Washington to distance itself from Chiang and attempt to develop a working relationship with Mao and his followers. Acheson later insisted that, despite speculation about the "attack of the primitives, before and during McCarthy's reign," on China policy, it had little effect on the Truman administration's stance.[33] That view was self-serving, wishful thinking. The ossification of U.S. policy in support of Chiang Kai-shek may have deepened under Truman's successors, but it began during his administration.

The political climate in the United States made it increasingly difficult even to contemplate abandoning Chiang's moribund remnant of a government on Taiwan. Great Britain and other U.S. allies were already moving to normalize relations with the new authorities in Beijing just weeks after the last Nationalist forces departed the mainland. But opposition to such a shift was much stronger in the United States than other Western countries, even before the onset of the Korean War. Once that conflict began, rising bilateral tensions between the United States and China made the idea of abandoning Chiang and recognizing the new regime even more unlikely.

U.S. opinion leaders interpreted North Korea's invasion of South Korea as the worrisome next stage of a general communist offensive in East Asia. Preventing Taiwan from falling under communist control now became part of the larger Cold War struggle. While President Truman was adamant that he would not permit Chiang to use the Korean conflict as a pretext to launch offensive operations and renew the fighting with communist forces on the mainland, the United States was prepared to be more proactive to help defend the Nationalist redoubt on Taiwan.

Truman approved a proposal from his advisers to give military aid to improve the quality of Nationalist forces. More important, he directed the U.S. Seventh Fleet to take up positions in the Taiwan Strait, effectively shielding Taiwan from any contemplated offensive by Chinese Communist forces on the mainland.[34] Yet some of Chiang's American admirers suspected that the new move was directed against Taipei's possible ambitions at least as much as Beijing's. General MacArthur concluded that the order was largely designed to "neutralize Formosa," thereby protecting "the Red China mainland from attack by Chiang Kai-shek's force of half a million men."[35] Among other effects, MacArthur believed, the elimination of that worry made it possible for China to redeploy its forces and intervene in Korea later that year.

China's communist leaders did not seem worried about a Nationalist offensive, however, and they clearly regarded the deployment of the Seventh Fleet as a hostile act. Beijing's hostility toward the United States spiked, as Washington was now seen as an adversary preventing Mao and his colleagues from definitively defeating Chiang and completing their victory in China's civil war. Historian and China expert Michael Schaller emphasizes the decisive importance of the outbreak of the Korean War on U.S. policy toward Nationalist China. "The most significant and ultimately disastrous aspect of the American response to the North Korea attack was the decision to draw a barrier around Communist China and become involved in the civil war . . . . Not only would South Korea be defended, but now Taiwan would be shielded from invasion."[36]

Truman and his main advisers (especially Secretary of State Acheson), however, did not yet regard that new commitment to Chiang as a permanent fixture in U.S. policy. They still considered the possibility that once the fighting in Korea ended, Washington might review and modify its approach to the China issue. And they embraced only a cautious, limited military commitment to Taipei. According to longtime China expert John W. Garver, the administration's policy meant that "while protecting Nationalist Formosa from Communist attack, the United States would keep it at arm's length."[37]

Other influential figures, including General MacArthur, took a different, far more favorable view of Chiang and sought to push U.S. policy in that direction. Garver concludes that, rather than interpreting the increased commitment to defend Chiang's government as a temporary expedient, MacArthur and other staunch supporters of Nationalist China believed that deploying the Seventh Fleet to protect Taiwan required "a fundamental shift in the estimated strategic importance" of the island. "From MacArthur's perspective, Formosa would now play an important role in maintaining American supremacy over the Pacific Ocean." [38]

The general certainly had a far more favorable view than did his boss about both Chiang Kai-shek and the nature of the military relationship with the Republic of China. According to Garver, MacArthur believed that "in its effort to rally Asia's anti-Communist forces, the United States should encourage and support staunch anti-Communists as Chiang."[39] The general was quite troubled following his meeting with Truman's special envoy, W. Averell Harriman, in August 1950. Harriman's comments left MacArthur with the distinct impression "that President Truman had conceived a violent animosity toward Chiang Kai-shek, and that anyone who favored the Generalissimo might well arouse the President's disfavor."[40] Harriman, on the other hand, was concerned about the extent of MacArthur's affection for Chiang, noting that "MacArthur feels that we have not improved our position by kicking Chiang around."[41]

The disagreement regarding policy toward Nationalist China played a role comparable in importance to the disagreement about Korea policy in the eventual rupture of the relationship between Truman and MacArthur and the president's April 1951 decision to relieve MacArthur of his command. Indeed, the two issues increasingly overlapped throughout 1950 and early 1951. Whatever slim hope remained that Washington might adopt a more sober, sustainable China policy and seek at least a limited relationship with Mao's government disappeared in November 1950 when Chinese troops entered the fighting in Korea and began killing American soldiers. MacArthur wanted to "unleash" Chiang—having him launch an offensive against the mainland to give the Communist regime a second front and force Chinese forces to end their advance southward down the Korean Peninsula. Other critics of the Truman administration chimed in as well. Robert Taft stated that Washington should take the "shackles" off Chiang and help him make a "full-scale diversion action" in South China.[42]

Truman stoutly resisted such calls for escalation. But as a result of those developments, U.S. policy enshrined the absurd situation in which an exile regime on a small island of fewer than 20 million people retained China's seat on the United Nations (UN) Security Council and purported to be the legitimate government of a nation of nearly a billion people. Worse, a succession of U.S. administrations perpetuated that diplomatic fantasy.

Those officials, in the State Department and elsewhere, who had pointed out Chiang's incompetence, brutality, and corruption, and urged Washington to establish a working relationship with Mao's new government, were pilloried as naïve dupes at best, and communist sympathizers at worst. The former allegations may have had some validity, especially with respect to those officials who viewed Mao and his followers as vaguely leftist agrarian reformers rather than hard-core Leninists. The imputation of disloyalty, though, was in the vast majority of cases unwarranted, yet it sent a chill through the Foreign Service that led to rote conformity regarding China policy—and East Asia policy in general—helping produce, among other problems, the Vietnam debacle.[43]

The denigration of dissenting views regarding China policy reached a crescendo in the early and mid-1950s, when Senator McCarthy's influence was at its zenith, but the stifling conformity still blocked any innovation in Washington's approach to East Asian issues until the early 1970s. Even those unorthodox China experts who managed to avoid being purged from their posts found their influence on policy at an end. U.S. policy toward Taiwan became even more entrenched during the Eisenhower years than it had been with Truman in the White House.

The influence of the China Lobby made any suggestion of reducing or qualifying U.S. support for Chiang politically hazardous. John Newhouse, a senior fellow at the World Security Institute, who analyzed the influence of lobbies on U.S. foreign policy, concluded that the China Lobby "was the superpower of lobbies representing foreign causes in the United States." That was an accurate depiction. As he notes, "from the 1940s, when [Chiang] addressed a joint session of Congress, to the 1970s, no U.S. president challenged the so-called China lobby, which opposed all contacts with mainland China."[44]

Key GOP leaders, especially in the Senate, were rabid partisans of Chiang, hailing him as a brave Free World champion. Senator Knowland, who became the new Senate Republican leader following Taft's death in the summer of 1953, Styles Bridges, William Jenner (R-IN), and John Bricker (R-OH), were especially vocal in their support of Chiang. Cynics even referred to Knowland privately as "the senator from Formosa." But support for the China Lobby and its uncompromising stance was not confined to the right wing of the GOP. During the 1950s and 1960s, such liberal Democrats as Senators Paul Douglas of Illinois, William Proxmire of Wisconsin, and Hubert Humphrey of Minnesota also endorsed its agenda, even signing petitions circulated by one of the lobby's front groups, the Committee of One Million.[45]

Eisenhower and his principal advisers were somewhat more circumspect regarding Chiang Kai-shek, understanding some of the Nationalist leader's troubling quirks and limitations. Yet, even their comments often reflected the widespread assumption in the United States that Chiang was a heroic figure. In his memoirs, Eisenhower referred to Chiang, along with South Korean strongman Syngman Rhee, in surprisingly glowing terms. "In President Rhee and Chiang Kai-shek the world had to recognize the sturdy qualities of fearless leaders, always ready to incur any risk in support of what they believed right."[46]

Eisenhower also routinely referred to Nationalist China as "Free China," despite the absence of meaningful freedoms under the KMT regime.[47] Not only was censorship of the press pervasive on Taiwan, the KMT suppressed any political opposition by vigorously enforcing vaguely worded sedition laws. Courts imposed heavy, sometimes draconian, sentences on those who ran afoul of such statutes. Sometimes, those outcomes even included the threat of a death sentence, if the accused failed to modify the offending behavior. In addition, defendants who were found guilty often had their property confiscated and their civil rights (such as they were) suspended for lengthy periods after serving their prison sentences.

Scholars have dubbed the systematic repression in Taiwan from the late 1940s to the 1970s the "White Terror."[48] One of the slogans that Chiang's government encouraged as part of its propaganda and indoctrination campaign was that "it is better to capture one hundred innocent people than to let one guilty person go free." That attitude was the antithesis of America's judicial philosophy that it is better to let a hundred guilty people go free than to convict and punish one innocent person. Chiang's government applied the "law and order" standard with a vengeance, and most of the prosecutions were conducted before military tribunals, not civilian courts. More than 10,000 cases involving civilians were adjudicated before such tribunals between 1950 and the beginning of Taiwan's democratic transformation in the mid-1980s.[49]

Even John W. Garver, a conservative scholar generally supportive of U.S. Cold War–era policy toward Taipei, concedes that in the 1950s, "'Free China' was not free, but a highly repressive authoritarian state."[50] Documents from the U.S. intelligence community reached a similar conclusion. A September 1954 National Intelligence Estimate described Nationalist China as "in essence a one-party state; authority is centralized in the hands of a few, and ultimate political power resides in the hands of Chiang Kai-shek.[51]

Risks to America of Protecting Chiang Increase

Two drawbacks of Washington's relationship with Nationalist China were increasingly evident during the Eisenhower years, however. One was that Chiang's domestic political practices did not comport well with American values. The other was that his agenda regarding mainland China differed in important ways from the policy that the United States favored.

The domestic repression in Taiwan was scarcely less than the KMT practiced when it held power on the mainland. Eisenhower noted that in 1960 Chiang was increasingly disturbed by the recent massive student demonstrations in Korea, Turkey, and Japan. "The Generalissimo was determined that such occurrences would not happen in his own domain. He was convinced that these upheavals were Communist-inspired, staged at much expense by the Communist leaders of both Red China and the Soviet Union."[52] Chiang's intolerant reaction in 1960 regarding anti-regime demonstrations seemed not materially different from his attitude in 1947 to the student-led demonstrations in China's major cities.

U.S. officials also had to deal with their often volatile client concerning his external policies. Chiang's New Year's message for 1954 included a pledge to attack the mainland "in the not distant future," and his Easter message that spring called for a "holy war" against the communists.[53] That wasn't exactly consistent with Washington's far more cautious containment policy, which focused on preventing further communist advances in Europe and East Asia. During a summit meeting with Eisenhower in 1960, Chiang asserted that unrest "was growing steadily among the people and even in the Army on the Chinese mainland." The generalissimo also "thought it might be possible to exploit this unrest, if he were to conduct small guerrilla operations, particularly in the outlying districts." Eisenhower indicated that the idea had some appeal, but his skepticism was not far below the surface. "I thought in this instance great caution would be required."[54]

The main risk in Washington's relationship with Chiang Kai-shek, though, resulted from the U.S. determination to prevent Chinese forces from invading and conquering Taiwan. The arena for a dangerous confrontation was the Taiwan Strait. Two major crises in the Strait took place during Eisenhower's presidency.[55] The first one erupted in early September 1954, when artillery batteries on the mainland commenced a barrage against the islands of Quemoy and Matsu, small Nationalist-held islands a little more than a mile off the Chinese coast that blocked access to two key mainland ports. The second crisis began in August 1958, and again involved the Chinese military initiating a campaign of shelling the offshore islands.

Eisenhower and his advisers were uneasy from the beginning about making a U.S. commitment to defend such vulnerable and nonessential territories, but they feared that the Peoples' Liberation Army (PLA) would not stop at conquering those tiny islands, but would use such victories as a steppingstone to move on Taiwan itself. Even so, they were annoyed that Chiang's actions were helping trigger confrontations with Communist China—especially the second crisis in the strait. "Chiang Kai-shek had helped complicate the problem," Eisenhower wrote. "Ignoring our military advice, he had for many months been adding personnel to the Quemoy and Matsu garrisons, moving them forward, nearer the mainland. By the summer of 1958, a hundred thousand men, a third of his total ground forces, were stationed on those two island groups."[56] It was hardly surprising that Mao's government reacted negatively to those deployments.

U.S. officials understood the risks entailed in taking a stand to defend not only Taiwan, but Quemoy and the other offshore islands. In a March 26, 1955, diary entry, the president wrote that "lately there has been a very definite feeling among the members of the Cabinet, often openly expressed, that within a month we will actually be fighting in the Formosa Strait." He conceded that it was "entirely possible that this is true," although he believed war was not so imminent as many of his associates believed.[57] His cautious optimism proved correct; the following month the crisis subsided.

Although they were committed to preventing the conquest of Taiwan, U.S. officials fretted that Chiang was deliberately goading the communist regime and wanted to dragoon the United States into backing a bid to establish a beachhead on the mainland. Chiang's bellicose rhetoric fed those concerns. Lasater and other conservative analysts are off the mark when they contend, as Lasater does, that although "the goal was to return to the mainland and unite China, including Taiwan, under KMT rule, the strategy was an indirect one: instead of using military means to defeat the Communists, the KMT determined that it would use political and economic means to undermine Beijing and regain the support of the Chinese people."[58] Chiang's statements and conduct belied that notion. His New Year's and Easter messages in 1954 certainly indicated a desire to use military force to retake the mainland—and entangle the United States in that attempt. Although Chiang was prone to make grandiose threats that he could not fulfill, that pattern of belligerent impotence was more apparent in retrospect than it was at the time.

The administration had to contend as well with zealous members of the China Lobby, who eagerly backed Chiang's ambitions to return to the mainland. In the midst of the first Taiwan Strait crisis, numerous senators called for a blockade of China, and Senator McCarthy demanded that the United States free Chiang's forces to attack China's "soft underbelly."[59]

U.S. officials repeatedly worried about the United States becoming overcommitted in its security commitments to Taiwan. Eisenhower aptly captured the nature of Washington's dilemma and the resulting delicate balancing act in terms of policy:

> We could not say that we would defend every protruding rock that was claimed by the Nationalists as an 'offshore island.' On the other hand, if we specified exactly what islands we would defend, we simply invited the Reds to occupy all the others of those groups.
>
> Also, the effect on Chiang Kai-shek of a definitive

statement might be undesirable. He was a proud, sometimes stubborn, sovereign ruler, and our ally. . . . [H]e had a right to expect our ready assistance under appropriate conditions. But to restrain him from his cherished ambition of aggressive action against the mainland was not always easy. One way of inducing some caution on his part was to keep some doubt in his mind as to the conditions under which the United States would support him.[60]

Washington Gives Chiang an Official Security Guarantee

The Eisenhower administration consistently pursued the twin objectives of deterring more serious PLA military moves against Taiwan and preventing Chiang from doing something rash that could entangle the United States. Two related measures in response to the first Taiwan Strait crisis were designed to achieve those goals. One was a congressional resolution giving the president extraordinarily broad powers to meet any threat to Taiwan. It certainly did do that, and although its primary purpose was to send a clear warning message to Beijing, it also constituted a major building block in the creation of the imperial presidency:

> The President of the United States . . . is hereby authorized to employ the Armed Forces of the United States as he deems necessary for the specific purpose of securing and protecting Formosa and the Pescedores against armed attack, this authority to include the securing and protection of such related positions and territories of that area now in friendly hands and the taking of such measures as he judges to be required or appropriate in assuring the defense of Formosa and the Pescedores.[61]

The second measure was the negotiation of a mutual defense treaty with the Nationalist Chinese government, signed in December 1954. Although the administration wrung a crucial, secret concession from Chiang that he would not launch any attacks on the mainland without the explicit consent of the United States, that treaty drew America much deeper into the Chinese civil war.[62] The Republic of

China on Taiwan was now an official ally (or more accurately, a protectorate) of the United States. Washington had a treaty obligation to defend Taiwan's security from Mao's increasingly irate government.

Eisenhower administration officials remained nervous about Chiang's behavior, and their exasperation with him was never far below the surface. After the generalissimo's move to strengthen the military garrisons on Quemoy and Matsu in 1958, a furious Eisenhower told Undersecretary of State Christian Herter that he was "just about ready to tell Chiang Kai-shek where to get off."[63] That attitude was mild, though, compared to the sentiments of Secretary of Defense Neil McElroy, who proposed sponsoring a coup against Chiang to bring to power a new leader who would be willing to evacuate the offshore islands. Garver notes that "U.S. leaders were extremely bitter about what they perceived as Nationalist efforts to embroil the United States in war with the PRC."[64]

Despite such expressions of anger and frustration, the United States did not back away from its commitment to Taiwan's defense. Indeed, Taiwan had become a significant component of Washington's overall military containment strategy. Policy regarding Chiang was now more than just about Chiang; it was subsumed in America's general Cold War strategy.

U.S. Policy Remains on Autopilot During the 1960s

U.S. support for Chiang rarely wavered during the Kennedy and Johnson years, although Kennedy and his advisers toyed briefly with changing Washington's China policy. At a private meeting in May 1961, the president asked Secretary of State Dean Rusk about possible options and the likely ramifications. Rusk outlined three options: recognize both Nationalist China and Communist China (the so-called two-Chinas formula), revive an updated version of the approach attempted more than a decade earlier with the Marshall mission and work behind the scenes to promote a reconciliation between the KMT and the communists, or sit tight and await future developments. Although Rusk personally favored the two-Chinas approach, both he and the president recognized that it was not acceptable to either Beijing or Taipei.

Equally important, they understood that even hinting at U.S. interest in that option would arouse vehement opposition from Chiang's political allies in the United States. Rusk stated later that he believed "American China policy in the year we took office, indeed for many years, did not reflect Asian realities."[65] But given the domestic controversy that would inevitably erupt from any weakening of U.S. support for Taiwan, combined with Kennedy's belief that his razor-thin victory in the 1960 presidential election gave him a weak political mandate, the two men decided not to stir up trouble regarding China policy.

Throughout his political career, Kennedy's views on China policy seldom deviated much from the public's favorable view of Chiang. In his memoirs, Undersecretary of State George Ball praised a young congressman Kennedy for his support of the Truman Doctrine, the Marshall Plan, and other important features of U.S. foreign policy in the initial post–World War II decade. But, Ball stated caustically, Kennedy also "had joined the cacophonous caterwauling of the China lobby that Truman had 'lost' China."[66] As president, Kennedy no longer slavishly echoed the lobby's sentiments, but neither was he willing to challenge its dominance regarding U.S. policy.

Rusk's own views about Chiang Kai-shek were an interesting mixture. Although he believed that the generalissimo had performed an important service to his country in staunchly resisting Japanese aggression and tying down Japanese forces, he was far less positive about Chiang's performance since World War II:

> Unfortunately, he [Chiang] had illusory ideas about his own position in world affairs, Taiwan's role, and developments on the mainland. He genuinely believed a second revolution on the mainland would restore him to power. Because he lived in the past, it wasn't easy to do business with him. In the sixties we worked primarily with his cabinet. Chiang was out of touch, a remote, almost ghostly figure.[67]

The secretary of state recalled his final meeting with Chiang in 1968. "He remained true to form and retold his long story about representing the government of all China and how he would one day return to the mainland and resume his rightful place—with massive American support, of course."[68]

The Kennedy administration's flirtation with altering policy toward China was brief and not really serious. During the Johnson years, there wasn't even a hint of changing the stance regarding Taiwan. As Washington's military intervention in Vietnam deepened and Beijing's backing of Hanoi and the communist Vietcong also intensified, support for Chiang Kai-shek's government and the increasingly hoary fiction that it was the lawful government of China, not just Taiwan, went largely undebated and unexamined. U.S. policy was essentially on autopilot.

Matters grew considerably more complex when Richard Nixon became president. Yet, even as he orchestrated the dramatic policy shift of pursuing a rapprochement with Beijing (see chapter 11), the pull of the longtime partnership with Chiang was evident. "It had not been easy for me to take a position that I knew would be so disappointing to our old friend and loyal ally, Chiang," Nixon recalled in his memoirs.[69]

The administration also did its best to preserve at least some aspects of Taipei's membership in the United Nations, despite the broader goal of establishing a solid working relationship with Beijing. Washington initially proposed a compromise solution based on the two-Chinas formula. Both Taipei and Beijing would be members of the UN, with the General Assembly deciding which government would have China's seat as a permanent member of the UN Security Council. When it became evident that international support for such a formula was inadequate, the Nixon administration reluctantly decided to back Beijing for the Security Council role. Henry Kissinger noted that the main problem with any iteration of the two-Chinas strategy regarding UN membership, which the State Department bureaucracy was pushing vigorously, was that both Beijing and Taipei summarily rejected it.[70]

Ultimately Washington had to accept an even less favorable outcome than the two-Chinas formula. In October 1971, the General Assembly voted over Washington's objections to expel Taipei's delegation and to seat Communist China's delegation as the sole government representing China. Although Nixon and Kissinger were not pleased with that vote, it was testimony to how much importance the Nixon administration attached to its developing rapprochement with the PRC that U.S. leaders accepted the result without provoking a crisis at the UN. The public and congressional response was decidedly less passive. "Reaction in Congress was bitter and surprisingly widespread," Kissinger recalled. "There was strong sentiment to retaliate against the UN and against countries that had voted to expel Taiwan."[71] Both conservative and liberal factions introduced measures to cut back U.S. financial contributions to the UN, and it was only with great effort that the administration was able to prevent such penalties from becoming law.

The extent of the change in U.S. policy regarding the Taiwan issue was further underscored by Nixon's state visit to China in early 1972 and the announcement of the Shanghai Communiqué at the end of that visit. The language of the communiqué regarding the Taiwan issue became a classic example of nuanced diplomacy. The Chinese side forcefully stated China's claim to Taiwan, but Nixon got his wish that the passage avoid any bombast and invective. And the statement of the U.S. position was a masterful stroke of diplomatic obfuscation. It stated simply: "The United States acknowledges that all Chinese on either side of the Taiwan Strait maintain there is but one China and that Taiwan is part of China. The United States government does not challenge that position." Contrary to the PRC's wishes—and to allegations from pro-Taiwan elements in the United States—the U.S. side never *endorsed* the position that there was only one China and Taiwan was part of that country.

Nevertheless, the China Lobby (and, indeed, many other prominent conservatives) were stunned and outraged by the Shanghai Communiqué, especially the language regarding Taiwan, and the entire policy of a rapprochement with Communist China. White House speech writer Patrick Buchanan was so irritated that he threatened to quit, and other conservatives grumbled that the president had cynically betrayed America's staunch ally, Chiang.[72]

Chiang's Death and the China Lobby's Last Hurrah: The Taiwan Relations Act

The political turmoil surrounding the Watergate scandal and its aftermath inhibited both Nixon and his successor, Gerald Ford, from pursuing normalized relations with Beijing. Instead, the United States continued the fiction that the Taipei regime was the legitimate government of all China, even as an assortment of informal economic, strategic, and diplomatic ties with Beijing blossomed. A weakened presidency was unwilling to openly defy the China Lobby and sever diplomatic relations with the Nationalist government. But

Chiang Kai-shek's death in 1975 represented the end of an era, especially given the stirrings of political changes on Taiwan under the rule of his son, Chiang Ching-kuo. The Ford administration basically marked time regarding China policy.

Jimmy Carter took a somewhat bolder stance than did Ford about changing Washington's policy toward Taipei and Beijing, but even he proceeded cautiously. Carter had a healthy appreciation—and wariness—of the China (Taiwan) Lobby's still-potent capabilities. Upon taking office, he concluded that "the Taiwan influence was very strong in the United States, particularly in Congress."[73] Indeed, "in the absence of strong presidential leadership, Taiwanese lobbyists seemed able to prevail in shaping United States policy."[74] His understanding of the China Lobby's clout developed even before he entered the White House:

> I began to see how effective they could be after I won a few primaries in 1976. A flood of invitations came to my relatives and neighbors around Plains for expense-paid vacation trips to Taipei . . . . Those who succumbed to these blandishments were wined and dined by the Taiwan leaders, offered attractive gifts, and urged to influence me to forget about fulfilling American commitments to China.[75]

Such techniques were nothing new. They had been the China Lobby's standard operating procedure for decades, and it had been quite successful.

But when Carter finally took action on China policy, he did so decisively. The so-called Second Communiqué in December 1978, transferring U.S. diplomatic recognition from Taipei to Beijing, provoked pro-Taiwanese Americans even more than had the earlier Shanghai Communiqué. The Second Communiqué, which also included the required one-year notice to abrogate the mutual defense treaty with Taiwan, infuriated both Taipei and its supporters in the United States. Part of that reaction was because the Carter administration had conducted the negotiations with Beijing under a veil of secrecy—although rumors swirled in Washington that negotiations were underway, and angry members of Congress demanded (unsuccessfully) to be consulted.[76] But that was hardly the only reason for the denunciations that followed. There were strong objections to a measure that supposedly betrayed a longtime, loyal U.S. ally.

Carter's recollection in his memoirs that "the serious opposition we expected throughout the country and within Congress simply did not materialize," is simply inaccurate.[77] While the bulk of the public may have remained relatively sanguine about the policy change, anger in Congress and among activist political elements—especially dedicated "movement conservatives"—erupted. Ronald Reagan, in a speech at Pepperdine University, epitomized the reaction among many conservatives. He asked rhetorically, but pointedly: "Have we become so unreliable and capricious? Are we so lacking in common decency and morality, so motivated by the dictates of the moment that we can—by the stroke of a pen—put 17 million people over the side and escape the consequences?"[78]

The surging, conservative-led opposition to the termination of the defense treaty with Taiwan led to passage of the Taiwan Relations Act in April 1979. The Act pledged that the United States would "maintain the capacity" to resist any "resort to force or other forms of coercion" that jeopardized Taiwan's security or social or economic system. It also committed the United States to make available to Taiwan defensive weapons and other systems that might be necessary to maintain the island's "self-defense capability." Finally, it established the American Institute in Taiwan, which would function as a de facto U.S. embassy.[79] President Carter concluded that pro-Taiwan forces in Congress had enough votes to override a veto, so he reluctantly signed the legislation.[80]

Passage of the Taiwan Relations Act was the last significant salvo of the old China Lobby, but it has had lasting effects on Washington's policy toward both Beijing and Taipei. It placed Taiwan in a type of diplomatic limbo, with the United States having somewhat vague but potentially entangling security obligations. And it has led to periodic tensions in Washington's relations with the PRC throughout the succeeding decades.

No Restoration of the Status Quo Ante under Reagan and Bush

Those who assumed that Ronald Reagan's defeat of Carter in the 1980 presidential election would fully restore the strategic relationship with Taiwan were ultimately disappointed, however. There was an interesting gap between Reagan's personal views on the matter and the policies his administration pursued. Writing about Secretary of State Alexander Haig in his memoirs, Reagan's continued fondness for Taiwan came through clearly. "He [Haig] and I also differed on Taiwan," Reagan stated:

> I regarded Taiwan as a loyal, democratic [sic!], long-time ally to whom we owed unqualified support. Haig and others at the State Department were so eager to improve relations with the People's Republic of China that they pressed me to back away from this pledge of support. I felt we had an obligation to the people of Taiwan, and no one was going to keep us from meeting it.[81]

The notion that Taiwan under the KMT had ever been a democratic ally was contrary to the historical record. There were few manifestations of democracy under Chiang Kai-shek. Throughout his rule, Taiwan had been a de facto one-party state where would-be political opponents risked imprisonment if they dared challenge the KMT's monopoly on power. Arbitrary arrests and perfunctory trials before military tribunals were the norm for critics of the regime, and there was no semblance of a free press or freedom of assembly. Chiang Kai-shek was a dictator in every meaningful sense of that term. And although his son and successor, Chiang Ching-kuo, had begun to adopt some limited political reforms, the ROC was still a long way from being a democracy when Ronald Reagan was in the White House. John W. Garver admits that "as late as the mid-1980s, Taiwan remained an authoritarian, nondemocratic state."[82] A truly democratic Taiwan would not emerge until the 1990s.

Whatever Reagan's personal wishes, though, China's perceived strategic importance to the United States short-circuited any inclination by Washington's foreign policy elite to terminate the rapprochement with Beijing and return to the status quo ante regarding Taiwan. Instead, a succession of U.S. administrations engaged in a delicate balancing act, continuing to maintain a strategic relationship and strengthen an economic partnership with Beijing while still selling arms to Taipei and acting as Taiwan's ultimate security guarantor. The context of discussions about policy toward Taiwan also changed, as the initial, limited political reforms on the island under Chiang Ching-kuo gave way to full democratization under his successor, Lee Teng-hui. After the 1980s, the United States no longer had to grapple with the dilemma of backing an authoritarian regime under the Kuomintang against a more powerful and even more repressive communist adversary. It didn't make the situation any less dangerous in practical terms, but the issue of morally compromised values had dissipated.

Reflections on Washington's Flawed Policy toward Nationalist China

Chiang Kai-shek was a ruler who embraced ruthless authoritarian practices and led a corrupt, often incompetent, regime in China. At best, he was an authoritarian modernizer with respect to his country's future—and not an especially effective one. But American supporters of Nationalist China had no patience regarding negative views about their hero, and they freely employed the innuendo that such critics wanted a communist victory in China. Douglas MacArthur typified that attitude, largely dismissing the significance of claims that Chiang and the KMT were corrupt. "Somehow, the reasoning ran," MacArthur contended, "that rule by the Kuomintang was even worse than a Communist police state, and, therefore, any change would be for the better."[83] That was a misrepresentation of the views of Chiang's American critics. Although a handful may have secretly supported Mao, most opponents of U.S. backing for Chiang saw insufficient reason to support a corrupt and repressive regime, even against its communist adversaries.

Certainly, the evidence of KMT corruption and repression was quite real during the years of Nationalist rule on the Chinese mainland. Some American conservative scholars contend that Chiang and the KMT learned from their failures on the mainland and governed Taiwan less repressively and with greater competence. Lasater contends that the KMT was "painfully aware that many of its policies had contributed to a loss of popular support on the mainland," and that it "underwent a comprehensive reformation. The party decided to make Taiwan a model province," with the expectation "that the Communist regime on the mainland would eventually falter and the Chinese people would rise up in rebellion as they had done many times in China's history."[84] There is no doubt that Chiang and his associates hoped to return to the mainland as victors, and they continued to indulge in that illusion until the 1970s. But the record does not support the thesis that the party embraced meaningful reform, lessening its stifling authoritarianism. That was certainly not the case while Chiang was alive.

The reality is that Chiang's political behavior improved only marginally during his years as the ruler of Taiwan and the other offshore islands following his ouster from the mainland. His economic policies were another matter, however. Gradually, Chiang adopted more market-friendly policies, and Taiwan's growth rate improved in an impressive manner. Corruption also diminished, although it remained a troubling problem throughout his rule—and, indeed, is still a problem even in today's democratic Taiwan.[85]

The bulk of the economic progress occurred after Chiang's death, but his policies began the process. And by the late 1980s, Taiwan was widely recognized as one of the new "Asian tigers." Per capita gross domestic product in 1951 was a mere $1,016. By the time of Chiang's death in 1975, the figure had nearly quadrupled to $3,991. By 1990, it was $11,284, comparable to that of prosperous Western societies.[86] Chiang's policies helped produce an export-driven economy, with a significant emphasis on market incentives, the recognition of property rights, and other features of capitalism. An intriguing question is whether he would have pursued a similar course as an authoritarian modernizer if he had retained power on the mainland. Some scholars believe that he might well have done so, leading a modern China similar to the current incarnation, but without the suffocating embrace of the Communist Party.[87] Of course, there is no way that we can ever know.

In any case, Chiang deserves some credit for Taiwan's breathtaking economic growth. Yet current citizens of Taiwan have, at best, mixed emotions about Chiang Kai-shek. At a minimum, he is regarded as a symbol of a troubled bygone era. As Jonathon Fenby astutely observes, "though a giant statue of the Generalissimo looks down in the monumental mausoleum erected to his memory in Taipei, his legacy has faded by the year as the island evolves a character distinct from the Nationalist past."[88]

Washington's association with Chiang Kai-shek, beginning in the late 1930s until his death in 1975, followed a difficult and unsatisfying pattern. The substance of his rule, both on the mainland and on Taiwan, never matched the highly favorable image that he enjoyed in many American political and opinion circles. Washington's decision to continue supporting his regime following his ouster from the mainland reflected domestic political considerations and fears at least as much as it did foreign policy calculations. One could make a credible case that, because of its strategic location, Taiwan was a significant military asset for the United States. That was especially true given the context of the Cold War and Washington's determination to maintain its hegemonic position in East Asia. The overall policy may have been flawed, but keeping Taiwan out of the hands of China's communist regime made sense within the Cold War paradigm. A friendly government in Taipei also provided intelligence (albeit of varying reliability) on military dispositions and other developments on the mainland. Chiang's government also made electronic eavesdropping posts available to the United States, so that American operatives could conduct their own surveillance for military intelligence purposes.

But Washington's support for Chiang, even when his ambitions created complications for U.S. foreign policy, went beyond such sober, if debatable, calculations. For a sizable contingent of Americans, especially in Congress and the news media, Chiang Kai-shek was a true free-world stalwart and a hero in the fight against international communism. That perception was largely an illusion. Unfortunately, it is one that has occurred all too often in America's relations with so-called friendly tyrants.

3. A Preference for Authoritarians: Washington Backs South Korean Dictators

The relationship between the United States and South Korea during the Cold War provided a graphic illustration of the tensions that often arise between U.S. values and perceived U.S. security interests. A succession of U.S. administrations from Harry S. Truman's to Ronald Reagan's concluded that it was a crucial geostrategic objective to prevent communist advances in East Asia, especially Northeast Asia. Japan was considered nearly as important an economic and strategic prize as democratic Europe, and to preserve Japan's security, U.S. policymakers considered it necessary to thwart communist offensives elsewhere in the region—especially in nearby Korea.[1]

However, preserving an anti-communist state in the southern half of the Korean Peninsula following Moscow's installation of a communist regime in the northern half entailed more than a few ethical dilemmas for the United States. Regimes in Seoul proved to be chronically undemocratic and during much of the Cold War were outright military dictatorships. Washington's response to that pattern made it clear that in Northeast Asia, at least, U.S. foreign policy goals soundly trumped the promotion of American values. Indeed, when given a choice between backing staunchly anti-communist factions that were authoritarian, even brutally so, or giving the U.S. imprimatur to democratic factions whose anti-communist credentials were less certain—or at least less strident—American administrations consistently opted for the former. Washington's conduct was such that the professed commitment to democratic values and human rights often rang hollow.

The security stakes in Northeast Asia, given the intensity of the global Cold War rivalry, were far from trivial. Nevertheless, Washington's behavior during its four-decade relationship with autocratic South Korean regimes had some very troubling features and implications.

Washington's Search for an Effective, Anti-Communist Korean Leader

Korea was one of the earliest Asian casualties of the Cold War, becoming an artificially divided country. During the waning weeks of World War II, the United States and the Soviet Union both deployed troops on the Korean Peninsula, which had been a Japanese colony. Largely as a matter of administrative convenience, Washington and the Kremlin agreed that the Red Army would be in charge of disarming Japanese troops north of the 38th parallel, while the U.S. military would handle the task south of that line. The two occupying powers, though, also agreed to establish a provisional government under a five-year joint U.S.-Soviet trusteeship. That initiative largely reflected Washington's view that the Koreans were not yet ready for full political independence.

As relations between Washington and Moscow deteriorated in the following years, the temporary administrative division hardened into two competing states backed by their respective superpower patrons.[2] Plans for peninsula-wide elections soon faded from consideration, especially after Soviet-sponsored factions in the north refused to participate in United Nations (UN)–supervised balloting. As communist control of the northern portion of the peninsula hardened, the Truman administration increased its support for noncommunist political factions in the south, eventually backing the establishment of a separate South Korean state, the Republic of Korea (ROK), in August 1948. Moscow then orchestrated the creation of a communist one-party state, the Democratic People's Republic of Korea (DPRK), led by former guerrilla leader Kim Il Sung, in the territory north of the 38th parallel. North Korean leaders officially proclaimed that new state in December 1948. Even without Soviet assistance, Kim would have been a formidable political player, since he was an acknowledged hero of the armed resistance against the Japanese. But neither Kim nor his Soviet sponsors were willing to tolerate the emergence of a multiparty political system.

Washington Finds an Acceptable Autocrat: Syngman Rhee

Finding an acceptable and effective leader for the ROK, however, proved to be a challenge for Washington. The decades of Japanese colonial rule had irrevocably compromised any Korean political figure that had cooperated with Tokyo, and there were not that many individuals of prominence who had both strong nationalist credentials and were deemed by the Truman administration to be reliably anti-communist.

In the months leading up to the formal creation of the ROK, Washington ultimately opted for Syngman Rhee, a businessman who had a respectable amount of domestic support because of his long track record as a vocal opponent of Japanese colonial rule on the Korean Peninsula. Rhee also had close ties to a number of religious organizations in the United States, ties he had cultivated when he had lived in exile in America, and those groups lobbied quietly but effectively on his behalf. Indeed, there were some interesting parallels between Rhee's politically productive exile, and the backing that American church groups subsequently gave him, and the career trajectory of another authoritarian U.S. client, Vietnamese leader Ngo Dinh Diem. (See chapter 7.)

U.S. leaders decided to back Rhee, according to historian Callum MacDonald, because "they considered his regime to be an instrument of containment" and the "only reliable barrier against communism."[3] In choosing Rhee, U.S. policymakers bypassed and tried to marginalize other, generally more moderate, political factions and leaders. George Washington University Professor Gregg Brazinsky contends that Washington "reluctantly" backed Rhee "because it doubted that more moderate leaders would combat leftist influence with sufficient intensity."[4] However, some influential figures exhibited no reluctance about supporting the South Korean leader. General Douglas MacArthur, commander of U.S. forces in East Asia, later expressed gratification that South Korea was being led "by that fine old patriot, Syngman Rhee."[5]

Truman administration officials said little even when Rhee jailed political opponents, shut down hostile media outlets, and generally stifled dissent. The worst incident occurred when dissidents on Cheju, a small island off the South Korean coast, resisted the authority of the Seoul government. Rhee's national police and soldiers conducted a merciless assault against the population, killing between 30,000 and 60,000 people in 1948 and early 1949 and causing another 40,000 to flee to Japan.[6] Some 70 percent of the island's villages were burned to the ground, destroying more than 39,000 homes. The refugee flow may be even more telling than the deaths. That 40,000 Koreans would choose refuge in Japan, the former and widely hated colonial master, suggests just how brutal the military offensive must have been.

Rhee proved to be a cantankerous and unpredictable client for the United States. Not only did he display a brazen disregard for democratic values, he was repeatedly at odds with Washington regarding policy. Time and again he pressed the United States to boost the military capabilities of South Korean forces, even as he threatened to invade the north to achieve the reunification of the peninsula. Once North Korean forces invaded the South and it became apparent how easily and rapidly communist forces overran South Korean defenders, critics in the United States excoriated the Truman administration for not doing a better job of arming ROK units during the years leading up to the war. It was true that Washington was cautious with its military assistance, refusing to give the Seoul government aircraft, tanks, and other heavy weaponry. The Pentagon was so cautious that it provided the ROK with very limited quantities of ammunition for the light weapons the United States did provide.

That restraint wasn't merely a case of underestimating the tense strategic environment and miscalculating the military balance of power. Some U.S. officials worried that Rhee might use U.S.-supplied weapons to crush political opponents and further repress his own population. But the main reason for the Truman administration's parsimonious policy was Rhee's repeated desire (and intention) to launch offensive operations against North Korea. U.S. officials were fearful of giving him the wherewithal to carry out his threats. The upshot, though, was that when North Korea launched its own offensive on June 25, 1950, ROK forces were insufficiently equipped to repel the invasion. Ultimately, U.S. policy regarding South Korea embodied the worst possible combination of features. The Truman administration created and sustained a foolishly aggressive client but left it too weak to do anything but free ride on U.S. protection— while threatening to start a war at America's expense.

Rhee as Washington's Perpetual Headache

The working relationship between Washington and its South Korean client did not improve all that much once the war broke out. Tensions resurged in 1951 when the Truman administration retreated from its initial ambition to oust Kim Il Sung's regime and create a united, noncommunist Korea. The intervention of Chinese troops in the autumn of 1950 had made that an impractical objective in any case, since the Chinese offensive had repelled U.S. and allied troops back from their farthest advance—almost to the Yalu River border between North Korea and China—and had driven them all the way back to positions south of the 38th parallel. Because Truman was not willing to fight a full-scale war against China, expelling communist forces from North Korea became impossible. Dwight D. Eisenhower's new administration was even more adamant on that point, deciding to press for an armistice that would accept the continuing political division of the peninsula.

Rhee repeatedly balked at U.S. policy and remained an extremely difficult wartime partner. Writes historian Clay Blair: "He never relented in his efforts to sabotage the armistice. Throughout the talks, he had demanded that no concessions whatsoever be granted the Communists, that the [Chinese forces] be expelled from North Korea, that the [North Korean army] be disarmed, and that all Korea be united under the ROK government."[7] Such demands were detached from reality, given the military facts on the ground. Eisenhower biographer Jean Edward Smith concludes the principal obstacle to peace "was no longer China and North Korea, but South Korean president Syngman Rhee, who continued to insist on marching to the Yalu."[8]

At one point, he also threatened to detach ROK forces from the U.S. (technically UN) command and continue the war alone. In an April 1953 letter to President Eisenhower, Rhee wrote that if the proposed peace agreement allowed the Chinese to remain on the peninsula, South Korea would feel justified in asking all of its allies to get out of the country, except for those willing to join in a new drive north to the Yalu River. He did suggest that if U.S. forces wished to remain, they might follow the South Korean military offensive, providing them with support and coverage with planes, long-range artillery, and naval guns along both sides of the peninsula. In his memoirs, Eisenhower stated that he found Rhee's letter "drastic in tone and extreme in its terms."[9] A more accurate assessment was that the author of the letter was delusional.

Although Eisenhower contended that he needed to reassure, as well as restrain, the ROK's disgruntled ruler, his reply seemed to emphasize the latter much more than the former. Although he praised South Korea as a "valiant country" that had bravely resisted an unjustified, brutal assault, Eisenhower stressed that the goal had always been to repel the aggression, not overthrow the North Korean regime and liberate the entire peninsula. The goal of repelling Pyongyang's aggression, the president stated, has "successfully been accomplished." Consequently, "it would not be defensible to refuse to stop the fighting on an honorable basis," which was Washington's goal in the armistice negotiations. While the United States and the United Nations had always supported the unification of Korea under conditions of "freedom and independence," Eisenhower wrote, there were "limits to that commitment." Neither the United States nor the United Nations "has ever committed itself to resort to war to achieve this objective."[10] The message could hardly have been clearer. Washington was going to accept a peace accord that left the Korean Peninsula politically divided, even if Seoul hated that outcome.

In a bid to disrupt the negotiating process at one point, Rhee ordered the release of 25,000 North Korean prisoners of war and allowed them to disappear within South Korea, an action that infuriated both Pyongyang and Beijing and complicated the talks, since one provision of the proposed armistice involved the repatriation of prisoners from both sides.[11] Eisenhower wrote later that the communist negotiators "asked at this juncture—and, I must confess, with some right, whether the United States was able to live up to any agreement to which the South Koreans might be a party."[12] Eisenhower sent a blistering letter to Rhee on June 18, 1953, accusing him of violating his verbal and written pledges to cooperate with the UN military command. That letter also contained language that any repetition of such conduct would result in the "needless sacrifice of all that has been won for Korea." In particular, "your present course of action will make it impractical for the UN Command to continue operating jointly with you . . . ." Accordingly, "the UN Commander-in-Chief has now been authorized to take such steps as may become necessary in the light of your determination to defy UN and U.S. policy objectives."[13]

That message was not merely a sharp rebuke to a client regime, it was menacing, albeit in a rather vague fashion. And Eisenhower backed up his chastising missive with a number of pointed actions. Most notably, he ordered General Mark Clark, the new commander of UN forces, to cut off all fuel and ammunition shipments for the ROK army. Smith notes that "as his supplies dwindled, Rhee recognized that he was holding a losing hand."[14]

The language in Eisenhower's June 18 letter could even be interpreted as a threat to terminate the defense of South Korea and bring U.S. forces home—and Eisenhower may have hoped that Rhee would read it that way. But as subsequent White House discussions made clear, a withdrawal was definitely not part of the administration's strategy. As Eisenhower recalled, "it was vital that we not give the Communists the impression that the United States contemplated a withdrawal from Korea itself. Such a result would be a surrender to the Chinese, handing them on a silver platter everything for which they had been fighting for three years."[15]

Yet Washington was increasingly frustrated with what it regarded as Rhee's obstructionist behavior. Privately, Eisenhower was even more disgusted with Rhee than the June 18 letter indicated. In a July 24 diary entry, the president stated that "it is impossible to attempt here to recite the long list of items in which Rhee has been uncooperative, even recalcitrant." Rhee, Eisenhower concluded, "has been such an unsatisfactory ally that it is difficult indeed to avoid excoriating him in the strongest of terms." There is no question that the South Korean leader had an impressive ability to annoy his American patrons, but there were some quite logical policy disagreements between patron and client. Eisenhower highlighted a key difference in the perceptions of Washington and Seoul about the goal of the U.S.-led intervention. "It is sufficient to say," the president wrote in his diary, "that the United Nations went into Korea only to repel aggression, not to reunite Korea by force." But Rhee and most South Koreans obviously wanted nothing less than reunification.[16]

From the perspective of U.S. leaders, a client ruler was taking measures that could torpedo chances for peace and keep U.S. troops in a war that the administration—and more important, the American people—no longer wished to wage. Indeed, Eisenhower recalled that the Seoul government's erratic behavior had "created some confusion in the minds of many people as to the identity of the real enemy."[17] Given that context, it is more likely that the language in Eisenhower's June 18 letter indicated either that U.S. military commanders would bypass both the Seoul government and the ROK military regarding strategy in the future or that those commanders would take steps to remove Rhee from power. The historical evidence suggests that Washington at least flirted with the latter option.[18]

When it became apparent that the United States was determined to reach an agreement ending the war, regardless of Rhee's objections and actions, he stated that he would not sign any armistice that included de facto recognition of the peninsula's division. And ultimately Rhee did withhold his signature.

Rhee's threat to go it alone was always hollow. Although he might bluster, and was obviously unhappy about the conduct of his patron, Rhee was not insane. He realized that ROK troops stood no chance whatsoever of winning a fight against the arrayed forces of North Korea and China. In the end, the instinct of political survival won out over his more grandiose impulses.

Once the war ended, the tensions between Washington and Seoul subsided modestly, and the United States backed Rhee's regime with more enthusiasm—as well as generous quantities of economic and military aid. The relationship became formalized with the establishment of the Mutual Defense Treaty, signed in 1953 and ratified by both governments the following year. One reason the Eisenhower administration agreed to negotiate such a pact was to mollify Rhee, who was still miffed about the armistice and continued to demand more tangible security reassurance from the United States. Indeed, even while the war was going on, Rhee incessantly reminded Washington that North Korea had a security pact with China, and that the latter had one with Russia, but South Korea had no written guarantee of protection from the United States. In a reply to one such complaint on May 30, 1953, Eisenhower assured Rhee that "at the completion of an acceptable armistice," the United States was prepared to negotiate such a treaty with the ROK.[19] That was a major carrot Washington used to dampen the South Korean leader's continuing objections to, and obstruction of, the armistice process.

But while the goal of placating Rhee was a factor leading to the eventual signing of the mutual defense agreement, it was not the most important one. Indeed, given the prevailing assumption in Washington that Korea was an essential theater in the Cold War struggle, U.S. officials probably would have proposed a formal pact, even if there had been no perceived need to mollify Rhee.

Washington's Strategic Rationale for Supporting an Authoritarian Seoul

The mutual aspect of the defense treaty was—and remains—largely a fiction. The military pact merely institutionalized the ROK's status as a U.S. defense protectorate and put North Korea and China (as well as the USSR) on notice that there would be extremely grave consequences if communist forces broke the armistice and again threatened South Korea. The continuing presence of U.S. troops in the ROK, a deployment that still totaled some 60,000 as late as 1969, acted as tripwire to guarantee U.S. involvement—and a devastating retaliatory strike—in the event of a renewed conflict.

There was both a moral and strategic rationale for strong U.S. support of the ROK. As bad as Rhee's government was, the hideous regime of Kim Il Sung in the North was far worse. Perhaps even more important, Washington saw the Korean Peninsula as a crucial strategic prize in the broader Cold War struggle against international communism. Since Pyongyang was backed by both the Soviet Union and China, South Korea became a significant ally, or more accurately, a significant security client. Brazinsky argues that Washington "was only willing to make massive investments to sustain a highly questionable regime because it believed that the security of the United States and of its Asian allies would be jeopardized if southern Korea did not become a bulwark against Communist expansion."[20]

The defense pact was intended to send a message to Pyongyang, Beijing, and Moscow to abandon any intention of forcing the ROK into the communist camp. The treaty with Seoul was also part of the "pactomania" period of the 1950s, when Washington forged bilateral and multilateral alliances with a host of countries around the perimeter of the USSR and China. Most of those pacts, including the one with Seoul, were with weak parties that added very little to the military capabilities of the United States. The purpose was primarily symbolic—to provide reassurance to vulnerable anti-communist states that the United States would not stand by and allow them to be swallowed up by communist adversaries.

During the 1950s—and indeed well into the 1970s—South Korea's main value to the United States was its strategic location. The ROK was simply too poor to be much value as a military partner. Seoul did provide some troops to America's war in Vietnam in the 1960s, and, by and large, those troops performed well. The most the ROK could have done if a full-scale war had broken out in East Asia, however, would have been to help the United States prevent the entire Korean Peninsula from being overrun.

And to U.S. policymakers, keeping South Korea out of the communist camp was a crucial goal. According to the conventional wisdom, a united, communist Korea would be a dagger pointed at the heart of Japan. At a minimum, U.S. officials believed, such a development would intimidate Tokyo and foster the growth of neutralist sentiment throughout the country. At worst, it would give communist forces a forward staging area for attacks on Japan, greatly complicating the defense of America's keystone ally in East Asia. Skeptics could have justifiably noted that merely possessing South Korea would not be all that valuable militarily to communist forces unless they could also deploy extensive air and naval forces in the southern part of the peninsula. And neither the DPRK nor China had much in the way of credible offensive air and naval assets during the Cold War. The Soviet Union did have more forces of that type, but the post-Stalin leadership in Moscow would have displayed an uncharacteristic tendency to gamble by deciding to deploy a significant number of planes and warships in Korea, since Washington would regard such a step as extremely provocative and react accordingly. Subsequent research has shown that the USSR had no such intention.[21] Indeed, even Stalin's aims on the Korean Peninsula and elsewhere in East Asia appeared to be more limited than U.S. officials believed. But such subtleties tended to be lost on U.S. policymakers during the years that marked the deepest chill in the Cold War. Throughout the 1950s and 1960s, both the U.S. government and the American public believed that the Soviet-led communist bloc posed an existential threat to the United States. While Europe was the primary theater for the armed stalemate that characterized the Cold War, East Asia—especially Japan and the rest of Northeast Asia— was deemed a close second in importance. U.S. leaders were convinced that anything that gave communist forces another foothold in East Asia must be adamantly resisted. That meant providing strong military, economic, and political support for South Korea—even if American officials might sometimes wince at the behavior of Syngman Rhee (and his successors).

Rhee Wears Out His Welcome in South Korea and Washington

As he did prior to and during the Korean War, Rhee again began to exasperate Washington. Among other annoyances, he continued to press his American patron to adopt reckless policies. In a speech to a joint session of Congress in the summer of 1954, Rhee proposed that the United States join South Korea and Chiang Kai-shek's Nationalist China in a war against Communist China. He specifically called for U.S. air and naval support for that military offensive. U.S. officials deemed such comments most unhelpful, coming as they did in the midst of a serious crisis with Beijing regarding the Taiwan Strait.

Equally troubling, Rhee's always evident authoritarian tendencies became more obvious as the 1950s progressed, including imprisoning and torturing those South Koreans who dared to criticize his policies. In addition, the corruption that afflicted his regime became more and more of an embarrassment to his American patrons, while South Korea's anemic economic growth made it apparent that the country would never become a capable U.S. security partner under his rule.[22]

By 1960, both the South Korean people and the Eisenhower administration had had enough of Rhee's clumsy, authoritarian rule. When demonstrations broke out against the regime in Seoul and other cities, Washington let it be known to the ROK military and other political players that the United States would do nothing to perpetuate Rhee's hold on power. That deterioration in both his domestic and foreign support left him little choice but to step aside. Rhee's departure, though, did not mean that U.S. leaders were now fond of the prospect of a raucous, and perhaps left-leaning, democracy in Seoul. To the contrary, administration officials fretted that the post-Rhee era risked a dangerous instability in the ROK at a time when both countries needed to present a strong united front against North Korea and its backers in Beijing and Moscow.

The training that the U.S. military provided to its South Korean counterpart also encouraged, whether deliberately or inadvertently, an attitude that was antithetical to democracy in the ROK. Korea National Defense University Professor Yong-Sup Han notes that "the training programs in the United States helped [ROK] officers to define their role comprehensively to include not only military defense but also nation building." From there, "it was only a short step for the armed forces to entertain the idea of military intervention in the country's political and economic affairs as a legitimate and necessary part of its mission." Apparently, the U.S. tradition of civilian authority over the military was not part of the curriculum, or American instructors at least did not give sufficient emphasis to that principle.[23]

The weak and fractious civilian government that took office following Rhee's fall from power did not inspire confidence in Washington. Consequently, when the ROK military stepped in and ousted that government barely a year after Rhee's overthrow, John F. Kennedy's new administration was ambivalent about the development. The coup leader, General Park Chung Hee, had carefully gauged Washington's probable response before taking action. Park asked one of his advisers, Yi Tong won, an Oxford-educated political scientist, how the United States would react to the overthrow of a democratic government. Yi replied confidently that the United States must support the coup "so long as you proclaim anti-communism as your goal."[24] That comment illustrated just how much officials in Asia, Africa, and Latin America understood that Washington would not blink at authoritarian moves—even snuffing out a sister democratic government—as long as autocratic leaders pushed the proper anti-communist emotional buttons.

Although Washington did issue statements lamenting the demise of a democratic government, U.S. officials were quick to accept General Park's assurances that free elections would be held as soon as conditions permitted. Park gained additional support from administration officials and key congressional leaders when he visited Washington shortly after taking power and reiterated those assurances.[25]

The importance of the U.S. political blessing to Park and his junta partners cannot be overstated. Chung-Ang University Professor Taehyun Kim and Seoul National University Professor Chang Jae Baik describe the extent of U.S. power and influence in South Korea during the 1960s:

> Most of the South Korean budget was made up of the counterpart fund originating from U.S. aid, in addition to the large sum spent directly on the South Korean military through the Military Assistance Program. American advisors were present throughout the South Korean military, and over five hundred officials of the United States Operations Mission (USOM) man-

aged aid money and hence the budgetary allocation of counterpart funds, thus overseeing and shaping South Korea's major social and economic policies for all practical purposes.[26]

A New Strongman: Park Chung Hee

Unlike a majority of coup leaders in countries around the world, Park actually kept his word about holding elections. He was narrowly elected president in 1963 in what appeared to be reasonably free and honest balloting. But that would be the last vigorous exercise of democracy that the ROK would see for nearly a quarter century. Almost as soon as he had an electoral mandate (shaky as it was), Park began to consolidate his political power and harass or suppress his opponents. By the late 1960s, South Korea was becoming as much of a personal dictatorship as it had been under Syngman Rhee. Yet the United States remained virtually mute about the mounting authoritarianism in the ROK. As Kim and Baik note: "Even in the economic realm, where the United States appeared to have the resources to make or break Park, the client more often outmaneuvered the patron than was checked and balanced by it."[27]

Any hope that Park might loosen restrictions and orchestrate a transition to democracy vanished in late 1972 when he declared a state of emergency and suspended virtually all political freedoms. That tightening came in the aftermath of a presidential election the previous year. Despite thoroughly rigging the electoral process, including the imposition of rigorous censorship measures to stifle opposition media outlets, Park had barely defeated liberal political activist Kim Dae Jung. Park was apparently determined that there would be no repetition of such an electoral scare. Korean historian Dae-Sook Suh summarizes the measures that he used to consolidate and retain power:

> [Park] instituted a powerful domestic surveillance organization to suppress popular dissent. Contrary to his original pledge and in contravention of constitutional limitations as well, President Park amended the constitution to prolong his tenure in office. He declared martial law to institute the so-called October

Revitalization Reform of October 1972 that virtually assured him the presidency for life. The powerful government intelligence agency made frequent arrests of dissidents, suppressed newspapers, jailed students and writers, and allegedly kidnapped political opponents.[28]

The role of the undercover security forces, operating as the South Korean Central Intelligence Agency, was especially stifling. Under Park's rule, there were an estimated 350,000 agents operating inside the ROK. Given that South Korea had a population of just over 30 million during that period, the ratio of security agents to the population was substantially greater than that of the secret police in the Soviet Union during the Stalin era.[29]

Policymakers in Washington throughout the Kennedy, Johnson, Nixon, and Ford administrations were content to work with Park's increasingly authoritarian regime. Park satisfied two major conditions that U.S. leaders wanted in South Korea. The first was political stability and policy reliability. Washington could count on the Seoul government taking an uncompromising, hard-line stance against the communist world in general and North Korea in particular. That eased worries that an ROK government might someday undercut the U.S. security perimeter in Northeast Asia by trying to appease or at least reach an accommodation with Pyongyang.

Second, unlike Syngman Rhee, Park seemed to understand that major economic policy reforms were needed to begin to make the ROK a modern, prosperous country.[30] That policy change held out the promise that South Korea might eventually become a more valuable partner—perhaps even a true ally, rather than a client—in both the security and economic realms. Given those benefits to America's policy objectives, U.S. leaders were willing to overlook Park's abuse of the political process and even his regime's serious human rights violations.

U.S. leaders were often rather generous in their praise of Park, both publicly and privately. On one occasion President Ford stated that he was eager to "establish a personal relationship with the leader of a great country whom I have greatly admired."[31] Nor was the praise for Park confined to executive branch policymakers. During a state visit in May 1965, Park stopped in New York City, where Mayor Robert F. Wagner Jr. greeted him effusively. The mayor presented Park with a scroll praising his "sterling leadership in the cause of freedom." The scroll went on to describe the South Korean leader and his country as "examples of resistance to absolutism" and "symbols of high destiny in a troubled world."[32]

It was not always easy for U.S. officials to excuse the Park regime's conduct, though. That was especially true in 1973 when South Korean intelligence agents kidnapped prominent democracy advocate and opposition political leader Kim Dae Jung and threw him in prison. To make matters worse, the agents had taken him while he was in exile in Japan—an incident that enraged the Japanese government. This time, Park had gone too far even for the normally supportive U.S. government. Human rights and pro-democracy organizations in the United States and around the world immediately began to pressure the U.S. government to come to Kim's defense. Washington faced the headache of having to placate both domestic opinion and its chief ally in East Asia, whose leaders were mightily upset about such an affront to Japan's sovereignty and laws.

As far as the administrations of Richard Nixon and Gerald Ford were concerned, Park's human rights abuses—even the Kim Dae Jung incident—were little more than a bump in the road in the overall cooperative relationship between Washington and Seoul. Congressional critics of U.S. policy began to express pointed dissents, however. Representative Donald Fraser (D-MN) argued that the "greatest threat to the stability and security of South Korea rises not from external aggression but from the oppressive nature of the South Korean government itself." He added that "the practice of torture has reached alarming proportions" and that Park's government "has created a police state which does not allow for any divergence from the official views of the government."[33]

President Jimmy Carter's administration took a somewhat more critical stance than its predecessors toward Park, which was not surprising given the new president's emphasis on the importance of human rights. Yet even the Carter administration's public criticism was relatively muted, in contrast to the much more robust posture taken toward other authoritarian regimes around the world. And as Sungshin University Professor Yong-Jick Kim states, "Park adopted the strategy of categorically denying the existence of any human rights problems in South Korea."[34]

Key civilian advisers, as well as Pentagon leaders, repeatedly cautioned the White House to be careful about the amount of pressure that it put on Seoul, since the ROK was a critical ally in East Asia, and America's position in that region had already been weakened by the debacle in Vietnam and the subsequent communist takeovers in Laos and Cambodia. National security adviser Zbigniew Brzezinski admitted in his memoirs that, although he was content with proposals to cut off economic and military aid to some other countries because of their human rights records, "for strategic reasons I favored continued U.S. aid to South Korea."[35]

While diplomatic ties between Washington and Seoul were sometimes tense during the Carter years, there was very little change in the substance of the relationship. Naval Postgraduate School Professor Edward Olsen aptly describes the approach as a balance between righteous indignation and geopolitical prudence.[36] The vaunted Carter human rights policy was quite limp when it came to South Korea. Brzezinski noted that on his 1979 trip to Seoul, President Carter expressed strong support for South Korea's "continued independence and freedom" [sic]. At the same time, though, "Secretary of State Cyrus Vance gave Park a list of 100 political prisoners that we were concerned about."[37] One suspects that such a missive did not cause the South Korean military autocrat to lose sleep about the possibility that the United States might end its backing of his regime.

During his summit meeting with Park, Carter had warned that South Korea's disregard for civil liberties was undercutting U.S. public support for a close security link. But subsequent U.S. actions once again vitiated that warning by sending, at best, mixed signals. In early October 1979, Secretary of Defense Harold Brown visited Seoul to consult on defense issues and delivered a letter from Carter to President Park. That letter stated: "*While human rights abuses would not affect the security ties between the United States and the Republic of Korea,* as a practical matter, it would be difficult for us if there was not a return to a more liberal trend."[38] It is difficult to imagine why Seoul would take the administration's moral nagging seriously when Washington stated up front that the ROK's conduct would not alter the security relationship—specifically, the flow of military aid, the U.S. military presence (at least air and naval units), and the defense treaty.

Brzezinski noted with some chagrin: "Our leverage [with the ROK] was clearly limited," although he adds that "we succeeded in preventing some political executions and encouraging some moderation." "Still," he concedes, "in practical terms, our influence was greater with weak and isolated countries than with those with whom we shared vital security interests."[39]

But it was not merely the assumption that South Korea's independence and safety were critical to the stability of East Asia and America's strategic position in that region. There was also a belief that the human rights issue had to be placed in a wider moral context. Secretary of State Vance emphasized that:

> While the situation in the South fell far short of what most of us felt was desirable, we constantly had to weigh the fact that only thirty-five miles to the north of Seoul was a nation in which control of the population was absolute and freedom nonexistent. The contrast could not be ignored, and although some critics felt that we were not vigorous enough in advocacy of human rights in South Korea, I felt that a careful balance was essential, and made sure that it was maintained.[40]

How the increasingly wary relationship between the Carter and Park governments might have evolved became a moot point in October 1979 when the head of the Korean Central Intelligence Agency assassinated Park Chung Hee. That event came as a great shock to Washington, not so much because there had been an assassination (there had been other attempts on Park's life, including one in 1974 that resulted in his wife's death), but that the assassin was a trusted member of South Korea's security apparatus. There was a flurry of initial speculation that the incident might be part of a North Korean plot, and perhaps even the first stage of a new communist offensive against the ROK. It soon became apparent, though, that the shooting was little more than a mundane personal and political rivalry.

Yet Another Dictator: Chun Doo-Hwan

Park's assassination ushered in another brief period of political turbulence and democratic ferment in South Korea, much like the period that followed the ouster of Syngman Rhee in 1960. Once again, though, a weak civilian caretaker government found it impossible to retain power. Within weeks after Park's death, another general, Chun Doo-Hwan, staged a coup and reinstituted military rule (although for a time he allowed the acting civilian president, Choi Kyu-hah, to remain as a figurehead).

Public opinion in South Korea, which already had been gradually turning more anti-American largely because of Washington's habitual tendency to support military strongmen, now became noticeably more hostile. Younger Koreans were especially inclined to place much of the blame for the latest coup on the United States. General John Wickham, the commander of U.S. forces in the ROK, fanned such suspicions when he stated that Koreans were "lemming-like" and needed a "strong leader."[41] Wickham may have been telling the truth when he said later that he had no opportunity or ability to block South Korean troop movements that made Chun's coup possible. It is unlikely that ROK troops would have refused to obey orders from their own commanders and instead followed the dictates of an American general. But Wickham's statements also indicated that U.S. military leaders were not displeased by Chun's action and were distrustful of the possibility of democracy in Seoul. That attitude infuriated many South Koreans.[42]

Matters became worse in May 1980 when Chun's regime brutally suppressed student demonstrations in the city of Kwangju. The official death toll put out by the Korean government was 191, but that figure had about the same credibility as the official figures that the Chinese government put out in 1989 following the eerily similar Tiananmen Square massacre. Private estimates by organizations in the ROK and elsewhere put the toll between 1,100 and 2,000. And, as in the case of the coup, America received much of the blame.[43]

In this case, Washington seemed less complicit than in the earlier episode. General Wickham did not have operational control over the Korean Special Forces units that Chun used to crush the demonstrations. And it is unlikely that U.S. expressions of disapproval would have dissuaded the new dictator from taking measures that he believed were necessary to preserve his, as yet, precarious hold on political power. He had earlier taken the precaution of telling Washington that Pyongyang was the hidden hand in the proliferating anti-regime demonstrations—a ploy that was well-calculated to mute any opposition to his crackdown that U.S. leaders might contemplate.[44] And sure enough, as the Kwangju demonstrations mounted, Ambassador William Gleysteen cabled back to Washington that they constituted "a massive insurrection" that was "out of control and poses an alarming situation."[45] The bulk of the evidence, though, indicates that while the United States may have been gullible in dealing with Chun, and hardly displayed moral courage when it chose to stand on the sidelines, it was not responsible for the resulting bloodshed.

Nevertheless, it is troubling that at his 1998 trial for various crimes, Chun insisted that all of his actions, in both the December 1979 coup and the Kwangju crackdown, were explicitly approved by the United States.[46] That may have been nothing more than a shrewd attempt by his attorneys to obfuscate the situation and minimize their client's culpability, but many South Koreans believed Chun was telling the truth, and it confirmed their worst suspicions about U.S. policy during that era.

In any case, General Wickham's indiscreet—if not outright racist—comments about the readiness of Koreans for democracy, combined with the extremely cordial reception that Chun received from the new Reagan administration in February 1981 during a visit to Washington, intensified the perception among the South Korean public that U.S. leaders would blindly support any pro-American government in Seoul regardless of its brutality.

Secretary of State Alexander Haig summarized the Reagan administration's attitude. Chun's visit was crucial, Haig said, "to mend the rupture in our relations with Korea caused, under Carter, by the threat of withdrawal of U.S. troops from Korea and by the human rights policies of Carter's administration."[47] Haig's contempt for any willingness to take into consideration the human rights records of America's authoritarian "friends" when formulating U.S. policy could scarcely have been more blatant. He boasted that the Reagan administration had assured another autocratic ally (Argentina's murderous military junta) that "it had heard its last public lecture from the United States on human rights." Haig asserted that the practice "of publicly denouncing friends on questions of human rights was at an end."[48] Chun and other dictatorial clients were likely pleased.

In some respects, Chun proved to be a more difficult—and even more embarrassing—client for the United States than Rhee and Park had been. The Kwangju massacre certainly did not enhance America's reputation as a champion of human rights and democracy. And

87

yet that episode was not the limit of the Chun regime's brazenness and brutality. Among other offenses, the military had once again imprisoned dissident leader Kim Dae Jung. To make matters worse, a regime tribunal sentenced Kim to be executed for treason. That prospect horrified even staunch American friends of the Chun government. This time, Washington made its position quite clear to its South Korean client: If Kim were killed, it would threaten the entire U.S.-ROK relationship. Chun apparently realized that he needed to retreat, and instead of being executed, Kim was allowed to go into genteel exile in the United States.

Such mild and belated support for human rights in the ROK did little to appease the growing public anger at the United States. By the late 1980s, anti-American sentiment had reached troubling levels throughout South Korea. The explanation that one demonstrator gave in July 1987 was an apt summary of the consequences of U.S. policy. "It's not that we don't like Americans," he said, "but for 37 years, you've been supporting the wrong guy."[49] That critic had a point. From the rise of Syngman Rhee in the late 1940s to the end of Chun Doo-Hwan's rule in 1987, the United States backed authoritarian client after authoritarian client in Seoul. While Washington's policy may have made some sense in the years during and immediately following the Korean War, U.S. leaders came to prefer reliable, predictable military autocrats in Seoul to South Korea's fractious and sometimes anti-American democrats.

Most U.S. officials were mild in their criticism of those rulers, even in retrospect or in private. In his memoirs, Lyndon Johnson's national security adviser, Walt W. Rostow, described Park Chung Hee as "a rare postwar statesman."[50] Other American policymakers were less effusive and more realistic, but they were nevertheless reluctant to press their autocratic South Korean clients about political repression or even major human rights abuses. For example, when President Ford cautiously expressed concern about Park's increasingly iron-fisted rule during a visit to Seoul in November 1974, warning that congressional and public support for the U.S.-ROK alliance might erode, the South Korean dictator essentially brushed off the criticism. He responded that "domestic unrest" would undermine his ability to defend the country from a North Korean attack, and prevent the ROK economy from "growing at its programmed pace." Park added bluntly that South Korea had made remarkable economic progress, and that he "was not going to let those accomplishments go down the drain merely to satisfy his political opponents."[51]

Ford's tepid response was quite revealing and typified the walking-on-eggshells approach that previous and subsequent U.S. administrations adopted concerning the behavior of South Korean military dictators. "I told him I understood his problems, but urged him once again to be more lenient. Although he didn't commit himself to any specifics, I was led to believe that he would modify some of his more repressive policies."[52] The latter expectation was nothing more than wishful thinking on Ford's part.

Washington Pivots and Finally Supports Democracy

It was not until the mid-to-late 1980s, under growing pressure from pro-democracy forces in South Korea and human rights advocates in the United States, that Washington seemed to become more favorable and more assertive regarding the emergence of democracy in the ROK.[53] An indication of some change in the U.S. posture was already evident when Chun Doo-Hwan again visited the White House in April 1985. In contrast to the uncritical support he received in 1981, both President Reagan and Secretary of State George Shultz (who had succeeded Alexander Haig in late 1982) stressed the importance of Chun's firm commitment to a democratic succession.[54] Chun had previously indicated he would relinquish power in 1988, but U.S. officials suspected that he would merely arrange to have power transferred to another military strongman without much of a nod to democratic norms. Shultz and some other administration leaders were concerned about the building tensions in South Korea and feared that a failure to make timely concessions to democratic aspirations could lead to a dangerous destabilization of America's East Asian ally.

Those fears seemed to be confirmed when another round of demonstrations erupted against the Chun dictatorship in March 1986 in the city of Pusan, long an opposition stronghold. Further demonstrations followed, and on May 3 some of those demonstrations turned violent, with many people injured and hundreds arrested. Secretary Shultz arrived in Seoul just four days later, and the Reagan administration found itself in an increasingly awkward position. U.S. ambassador to South Korea James Lilley epitomized the traditional reflexive support among many American conservatives for autocratic rule in the ROK. Lilley urged Shultz to avoid any mention of democracy in his remarks, lest it cause trouble both for the South Korean government and the United States. Shultz largely ignored Lilley's advice. As he did regarding the demonstrations that had ousted Philippine dictator Ferdinand Marcos earlier that year, Shultz took a more balanced view. At a press conference, he stressed both that the United States wanted to see a continuation of movement toward democracy in South Korea, and that Koreans deal with that process "in a stable and orderly way."[55] Neither the South Korean dictatorship nor pro-democracy advocates were entirely happy with that formulation, but it suggested that the Reagan administration's policy was evolving in a direction that was not just blindly supportive of autocratic allies like Chun.

That trend became even more evident in early 1987, when a new round of demonstrations began, and this time soon spread far beyond university students and other typical anti-regime, pro-democracy demonstrators. Instead, a growing number of business people and other middle-class types joined the demonstrations, creating a crisis for Chun and his associates. At this point, the Reagan administration, fearing that the growing turbulence could destabilize South Korea and tempt Pyongyang to do something rash, began to pressure Chun and the rest of the military elite to adopt reforms and move the country toward democracy. After meeting with Chun in early March, Shultz issued the following statement:

> The United States, as a friend and ally, supports the aspirations of all Koreans for continuing political development, respect for basic human rights, and free and fair elections. President Chun's commitment to leave office in 1988 will set a historic precedent for the peaceful transition of power. We will support all those who are urging moderation and nonviolent political change.[56]

Opposition to Washington's support for Chun also was building in the U.S. Congress. Congressional Democrats introduced legislation in June that would impose economic sanctions against South Korea unless Chun promptly initiated democratic reforms. "It's time we recognize that the best defense against North Korean totalitarianism is the end of dictatorial rule in South Korea," said Senator Tom Harkin (D-IA). Chun's corrupt, autocratic regime "is not why Americans fought at Pork Chop Hill," fumed Senator Barbara Mikulski (D-MD). "What we fought for has been turned into a mockery." Senator Edward Kennedy (D-MA) justified the congressional move as "designed to fill the vacuum created by the administration's default and to place America squarely on the side of human rights and democracy in South Korea."[57]

After further demonstrations throughout South Korea, and some resulting political turmoil, the ROK strongman, knowing that U.S. support was slipping, finally relented. He agreed to hold free, direct elections for president later that year, instead of having the president chosen by the National Assembly that he had stacked with his political allies. (The president appointed one-third of the members of the assembly.) The direct presidential election might have led to a victory by either long-time civilian democracy proponent Kim Young Sam or the slightly more radical Kim Dae Jung. But neither candidate would withdraw from the race, thereby dividing the pro-democracy, anti-regime vote and leading to a victory (with less than 40 percent of the votes cast) by recently retired general and close Chun associate Roh Tae Woo.

Although the more ardent campaigners for democracy were chagrined at the election results, Roh seemed to grasp that the political environment in the ROK had changed fundamentally and that Washington's preference for authoritarian partners had ebbed as well. Consequently, Roh did a credible job of implementing political reforms and governing according to democratic norms during his presidency.

Washington deserved only modest credit for that development. At least this time, no one in the U.S. military or in the civilian policymaking hierarchy tried to undermine the transition to democracy or even express indifference if the ROK military wanted to crush the democracy movement. In fact, U.S. officials let it be known that they favored the emerging political change. Yet many South Koreans remained irritated at Washington's previous behavior. That attitude was unsurprising. After all, observed Olsen, although South Korea was now joining the ranks of democratic nations, that achievement occurred more in spite of rather than because of, the United States.[58]

Tolerating Autocrats—and South Korea's Security Free Riding

In addition to the problems associated with supporting undemocratic rulers in South Korea throughout most of the Cold War, U.S. officials also encountered frustration in getting the ROK to play a stronger role with regard to its own defense and the overall security of East Asia. Washington was tolerant of Seoul's military limitations when South Korea was a very poor country. And the ROK was extremely poor throughout the 1950s and much of the 1960s. In the early 1960s, per capita gross domestic product was estimated to be no more than $100 and perhaps as low as $90. As late as 1968, U.S. military aid accounted for more than 50 percent of South Korea's defense expenditures.

But as the country's level of prosperity rose in the 1960s, and the ROK emerged as a significant regional economic player a decade later, U.S. officials hoped for more military burden-sharing. Despite being a repressive autocrat, Park Chung Hee wisely instituted an export-oriented, market-friendly economic policy. South Korea then rapidly turned into one of East Asia's—and the world's—great economic success stories. From the mid-1960s to the beginning of the 1990s, economic growth averaged a staggering 8.5 percent annually—only a shade less than China's better known growth rate—and during the late 1980s it sometimes reached double digits.

Yet greater prosperity did not translate into a greater willingness to be a more active security partner for the United States. Indeed, when Washington pressed Seoul for greater burden-sharing, U.S. officials encountered repeated promises that went unfulfilled, complaints about even modest retrenchments in the U.S. force presence on the peninsula, and generalized, persistent free riding on the U.S. security guarantee.

Those problems began to emerge with considerable clarity during Richard Nixon's administration when the United States proposed to reduce the number of troops stationed in the ROK from the approximately 60,000 that had been the norm since the mid-1950s. The move was part of the so-called Nixon Doctrine that expected America's allies, especially in East Asia, to bear more of the security load when it came to military personnel, particularly ground forces. Nixon himself described the doctrine in succinct terms. With regard to future defense efforts, the president said, the United States "would furnish only the materiel and the military and economic assistance to those nations willing to accept the responsibility of supplying the man-power to defend themselves."[59]

Park Chung Hee's government was not happy about Nixon's ini-tial plan to reduce U.S. troop levels to about 40,000. South Korean officials not only cited the North's own military superiority, but also claimed that only a robust U.S. presence could deter Chinese and Soviet support for a new DPRK invasion. To placate Seoul, the Nixon administration offered a $1.5 billion, five-year military moderniza-tion program for ROK forces. That package purchased Park's acqui-escence to the departure of U.S. troops, although he remained very unhappy about the move.

Additional troop withdrawals were scheduled to begin in 1973, but that phase never took place. As the Watergate scandal began to consume his presidency, Nixon did not have the fortitude or political capital for a fight over troop levels in South Korea with factions in Congress and the Pentagon who strongly opposed that move. Once Gerald Ford became president, and concerns about America's global credibility increased following North Vietnam's conquest of South Vietnam in 1975, talk of a more modest U.S. military in the ROK faded for a time. Ford initially proposed to withdraw another 15,000 troops in 1975, but an adverse vote in the House of Representatives on the issue following the fall of Saigon caused him to reverse course. Al-though the Ford administration admitted that Chinese involvement in any new Korean fighting was highly improbable, it contended that the existing U.S. commitment to the ROK remained crucial to serve "as a symbol of America's continued interest in the overall stability of that part of the world during a period of some tension."[60]

Washington's willingness to consider additional troop reductions rose again during the Carter administration. The president's new as-sistant secretary of state for East Asian and Pacific Affairs, Richard Holbrooke, had been on record for several years as believing a com-plete withdrawal of U.S. forces from South Korea over the next cou-ple of decades would be a good development.[61] Indeed, Carter him-self indicated his intention to withdraw all U.S. ground forces from the peninsula, leaving just 14,000 Air Force personnel and logistics specialists. In 1978 he pulled 3,000 soldiers out of the ROK as the first installment in that plan. One reason why Carter embraced the strat-egy of ending the ground-force presence in South Korea was a de-sire to show tangible dissatisfaction with the unsatisfactory human rights record of Park Chung Hee's regime and to let Seoul know that there was a price to be paid for such behavior. But Carter and some of his advisers also believed that continuing to station large numbers of U.S. troops in South Korea was an expensive anachronism. In their view, the security situation had changed substantially since the 1950s and 1960s. Neither the Soviet Union nor China seemed likely any longer to back a new expansionist bid by North Korea. And South Korea was rapidly developing the economic strength to build robust defense forces of its own instead of relying so heavily on the United States.

Although the Carter administration may have recognized that times had changed and that South Korea could (and should) take more responsibility for its own defense, the Park government reacted with even more vehement opposition than it had to Nixon's move. In addition to expressing complaints to Carter administration officials, Seoul lobbied its political allies in the Pentagon, U.S. defense contractors, and Congress to try to torpedo the proposed troop withdrawal. For its part, the Carter administration attempted to replicate Nixon's strategy of buying the Park government's sufferance, this time with a $2.2 billion, five-year package of credit and weapons transfers. Unlike in 1970 and 1971, though, such largesse barely budged Seoul's opposition.

And the ROK's lobbying effort within the United States paid off. Carter not only faced intransigence from Seoul, he confronted growing opposition to the move at home, including from the U.S. military commander in South Korea, General John Singlaub, and senior foreign policy figures, both current and retired, within the Democratic Party. A key defection was Richard Holbrooke, who now collaborated with administration officials who wanted the president to abandon the troop withdrawal idea. Former *Time* magazine and *New York Times* correspondent Richard Bernstein notes that Holbrooke "changed his mind and joined what became almost a conspiracy among the leading members of the administration's foreign policy team to get the president to back off the idea. Holbrooke, according to the *Washington Post* reporter Don Oberdorfer, termed this 'a full scale rebellion against the president.'"[62] Indeed, Holbrooke and Ambassador William Gleysteen practically beamed during a session between Park and Carter when the South Korean leader lectured the American president about how even a partial U.S. troop withdrawal would "play into the hands of the North Koreans, would weaken the United States in Asia, and would strengthen the Chinese—all arguments that the rest of the American delegation supported."[63]

Carter backed down and placed his plan "in abeyance." With the emergence of a new military dictatorship in South Korea following General Chun Doo-Hwan's 1980 coup, though, there was some sentiment in the Carter administration, including by Patricia Derian, the assistant secretary of state for human rights and humanitarian affairs, to revive the proposal. Had he been reelected in 1980, Carter might have made another attempt to at least reduce the number of American troops on the Korean Peninsula.

With Ronald Reagan's election, though, that possibility evaporated. Not only was Reagan far less critical of Seoul's behavior in the area of human rights, he scorned any moves in Korea or any other part of the world that he believed might show weakness to communist forces. Although the South's security free riding on the United States did not abate despite the ROK's rapidly growing economy, the Reagan administration seemed even more indulgent than its predecessors. In 1986 Secretary of Defense Caspar Weinberger pledged that American troops would remain in South Korea "as long as the people of Korea want and need that presence."[64] On the issue of troop levels, U.S. policy seemed to be on autopilot throughout the Reagan administration.

Yet the evidence mounted that South Korea could do far more for its own defense. The great economic growth of the 1970s and 1980s had a clear impact on the ROK's defense industries as well as its civilian counterparts. A nation that at the beginning of the 1970s did not even make its own rifles for the military was producing, by the end of the 1980s, virtually all of its conventional arms, including F-5 fighter jets, helicopters, rocket launchers, self-propelled howitzers, M48 and T88 tanks, armored personnel carriers, naval vessels, ground-to-air missiles, and many other weapon systems.

But even gentle prodding from the United States for a more robust defense budget and greater burden-sharing produced either stubborn resistance or promises that never seemed to be fulfilled. A somewhat irritated Jimmy Carter pointedly asked President Park in 1979 why South Korea, which already had a much larger economy than North Korea, did not match the latter's military spending.[65] Park had no good answer to that question; and more important, confident of the continuing U.S. security commitment, he didn't even bother trying to provide much of an answer. The attitude of South Korea's friendly tyrant indicated that the United States had an increasingly cynical, ungrateful client.

When South Korean leaders were not flatly brushing off U.S. requests for greater burden-sharing regarding the country's defense, they offered specious promises. For example, after President Nixon announced his plan to withdraw one U.S. division, Park stated that ROK forces would be superior to those of North Korea by 1975.[66] When 1975 arrived and that goal clearly had not been achieved, he assured Washington that in just a few more years the ROK would be so strong militarily that it would no longer require even air, naval, or logistical support. "We want the capability to defend ourselves, and that will take four or five years," Park told his American patron.[67]

Similar claims were made during the final decade of the Cold War—and beyond.[68] But such promises were never backed up by substantive steps, such as significant increases in defense spending. Even today, Seoul spends a paltry 2.5 percent of its gross domestic product on defense, despite the overt hostility that North Korea continues to display. Moreover, the ROK continues to depend on the United States for key portions of its defense, remaining especially deficient in air and naval force capabilities.

A Mixed and Largely Frustrating Outcome for U.S. Policy

Washington's policy of supporting friendly tyrants in South Korea did not turn out nearly as badly as similar policies toward such countries as Nicaragua, Iran, South Vietnam, or Zaire. Today, the ROK is a prosperous country with a functioning and seemingly stable democratic system. While there is still a significant undercurrent of anti-American sentiment, and abrasive incidents between U.S. military personnel and Korean civilians can sometimes cause that hostility to flare, Washington's support for a series of autocrats did not produce the vehement public hatred of America that emerged in Iran and some other countries.[69] Indeed, the post-authoritarian era in the ROK has turned out even somewhat better than it has in the Philippines, a country where Washington pursued a similar approach, abandoning a dictatorial client and supporting democracy only at the eleventh hour.

And yet, the decades of political, economic, and military support for South Korea have not produced a reliable, self-reliant security partner for the United States. As much as U.S. policymakers continue to praise the U.S.-ROK alliance and emphasize its continuing importance, the South Korean government continues to free ride on the U.S. security guarantee and underinvest in its own defense. At the same time, Seoul acts ever more independently of the United States on both diplomatic and economic issues. Indeed, the ROK's positions on an assortment of matters, from policy toward the Taiwan issue to how to deal with North Korea, mean that Seoul's policies often align more with Beijing's preferences than Washington's. While that growing estrangement was more blatant under the left-leaning presidencies of Kim Dae Jung and Roh Moo Hyun than under relatively conservative presidents Lee Myung-bak and Park Geun-hye, it remains quite obvious to outside observers.

On balance, Washington's policy of supporting friendly tyrants in South Korea from the late 1940s to the late 1980s achieved mixed results. Given the Cold War strategic context, it is understandable that U.S. leaders regarded the existence of a stable, pro-U.S. government in Seoul as a high priority. Northeast Asia was considered second only to democratic Europe as the key arena in the Cold War struggle, and policymakers saw South Korea as a key factor in keeping that region out of the communist orbit. An unwillingness to trust an unpredictable democratic process in a poor and vulnerable ROK following the Korean War—and, indeed, into the early 1970s—was not surprising. U.S. leaders preferred the predictability and reliability of military rule in South Korea.

Even when they were uneasy about some of the ruthless practices of their partners in Seoul, U.S. leaders were reluctant to use significant diplomatic and economic leverage to promote change, lest it destabilize the ROK and endanger America's strategic architecture in Northeast Asia. William Gleysteen, U.S. ambassador to Seoul at the time of General Chun's coup and the subsequent Kwangju massacre, epitomized that caution. He noted that critics in both the United States and South Korea looked to Washington to exert a constructive influence on events. But, he said, they do not realize "that our influence is limited *in large part by the fact that we could not pull our powerful security and economic levers without risk of destroying the ROK's stability.*"[70] As long as U.S. leaders believed that scenario, which they did well into the 1980s, the South Korean authoritarian tail was able to wag the American dog—and did so on a regular basis.

That policy became both less understandable and less justifiable during the 1970s and especially during the 1980s. By that time, the ROK had become a prosperous, technologically sophisticated country that was vastly outstripping its North Korean rival in every meaningful economic category. Equally important, the security context in the region had changed dramatically. The rapprochement between the United States and China in the early 1970s virtually eliminated any danger that Beijing would back another North Korean attempt to unify the peninsula by force. That possibility vanished entirely later that decade as China began to pursue its own economic reforms and explored new commercial ties with South Korea.

Yet Washington acted as though little had changed. The Ford administration's policy toward South Korea backed away from even the modest changes, most notably the initial troop withdrawals, the Nixon administration had made. President Carter did distance the United States somewhat from Seoul's more repressive domestic policies and initially sought to implement greater troop withdrawals, but even his administration ultimately backed an authoritarian client as though America had no alternative. The Reagan administration's initial enthusiastic embrace of the last South Korean dictator, Chun Doo-Hwan, was a step backward and was even less justifiable than Washington's backing of autocratic clients in Seoul during earlier eras. Moreover, none of those administrations did anything in a serious vein to reduce the ROK's penchant for security free riding on the United States.

At a minimum, Washington's policy regarding South Korea was too slow to change. The best that can be said about America's belated shift from a preference for authoritarian rule to an endorsement of democratic reforms is that it is better late than never. That shift in policy probably enabled U.S.-ROK relations in the post–Cold War period to be at least reasonably cordial and cooperative.

4. From Jinnah to Jihad: Washington's Cold War Relations with Pakistan

The Islamic Republic of Pakistan was once America's closest ally in Asia. In Karachi, Pakistan's first capital and its financial hub, military and civilian leaders joined their fractured, multiethnic country with America's international campaign against Soviet communism. Pakistani leaders remained largely obedient and reliable clients, serving a function similar to Washington's other corrupt, non communist allies, such as the Somoza dynasty in Nicaragua, the Marcos family in the Philippines, and the military regime behind Anwar Sadat and Hosni Mubarak in Egypt. Moreover, as with other Third World allies, Pakistan's tiny minority of kleptocratic military and civilian ruling elites stifled the growth of an authentic and working democracy, while staggering levels of U.S. financial and military assistance compounded the burdens on Pakistan's fragile economy.

Appreciating how those relations evolved is the indispensable first step to understanding the alliance's subsequent complications, and Washington's post–Cold War difficulties across the region. First, Pakistan, instead of defending the broader Middle East or containing the Soviet Union, used American weapons, tanks, and planes to launch wars against neighboring Hindu India and slaughter its Bengali Muslim citizens. Second, the methods of U.S. aid distribution cultivated anti-American sentiment across Pakistan and pushed its elites to identify more closely with Communist China—a far cry from the stated U.S. goal of increasing Pakistan's identification with the "free world community." Finally, a common narrative of the U.S.-Pakistan Cold War alliance is that its turbulence sowed the seeds of the two countries' post-9/11 distrust. But a reality far less understood or appreciated is how Washington's Cold War objectives justified policies that indulged Karachi's worst tendencies—policies that repeatedly pushed Pakistan, and the entire region, to the edge of disaster.

"America's Most Allied Ally in Asia"

Admittedly, Pakistan was formed with little money or know-how with which to develop. Inexperienced leaders and religious warfare proved equally inauspicious. But, as discussed below, the military and economic policies Karachi adopted with Washington's encouragement exacerbated many of its weaknesses.

Before the dissolution of the British Indian Empire, religious and communal cleavages cultivated in the subcontinent over the centuries nurtured a rivalry that would shape India-Pakistan relations long after their independence. In August 1947, the bloody birth of a Hindu-dominated India and a Muslim-dominated Pakistan produced the cross-border movement of an estimated 14.5 million people. The partition's emphasis on Hindus and Muslims constituting "two nations" made issues surrounding identity, religion, and nationhood paramount in relations between the countries. With the British-drawn partition line, competition over the northern state of Jammu and Kashmir, known as Kashmir, sucked the two countries into war. Split among Pakistan, India, and China, the administration of Kashmir became a constant source of instability and one of the world's most intractable problems.[1]

Initially, early U.S. Cold War planners considered South Asia— categorized as Afghanistan, Pakistan, India, Nepal, and Ceylon (later Sri Lanka)—of major, but not vital, importance to U.S. national security.[2] They strove for cordial diplomatic relations with both India and Pakistan and took an impartial stance on Kashmir. But India eventually annoyed Washington, both strategically and personally. India's founding fathers, Mahatma Gandhi, Sardar Patel, and Jawaharlal Nehru, charted a largely independent path that rejected both the Soviet and American camps, despite adopting certain policies imbued with pro-Soviet leanings. Not only was neutralism popular domestically, but Indian leadership believed their country had not emerged from colonialism merely to have a distant superpower dictate its policies.[3] Anti-Soviet American officials found New Delhi's nonalignment intolerable.[4] Its prominent status among developing countries threatened to draw the entire postcolonial world into the neutralist bloc. U.S. officials also complained bitterly about Prime Minister Nehru's intransigence on Kashmir. Dean Acheson, Truman's secretary of state, described the Indian leader as "one of the most difficult men I have ever had to deal with." John Foster Dulles, Dwight D. Eisenhower's secretary of state, characterized Nehru as an "utterly unpractical statesman."[5]

Conversely, Pakistan's founder, Mohammed Ali Jinnah, proclaimed that "communism [does] not flourish in the soil of Islam."[6] Pakistan's secular leaders declared their commitment to the Western bloc and offered Pakistan's armed forces to America's Cold War cause.[7] Their reasons for partnering with a superpower were obvious. Economic chaos, communal unrest, and political uncertainty plagued the new country.

Foreign observers, according to Keith Callard, an expert on Pakistan's early years, had "the gravest doubts about the viability of the new state, especially about its capacity for self-government."[8] Pakistan's major cities and five provinces were poverty-stricken, dissimilar, and averse to cooperation: the provinces of Punjab and Sindh were predominately feudal, Balochistan and the North-West Frontier Province (NWFP) were predominately tribal, and East Pakistan was ethnic Bengali and located hundreds of miles away, beyond India's eastern border. Neither fidelity to Islam nor collective hatred of Hindus suppressed bouts of ethnic nationalism. The untimely death of 71-year-old Jinnah barely a year after partition also dealt a massive blow to the fragile new country. Its military, alongside feudal, land-owning, civilian elites, would heavily influence policymaking.

For leaders in Washington, the infant country's struggle for survival would come to justify U.S. assistance. The Korean War propelled President Truman to send troops to the Korean Peninsula. It also motivated the administration to help France suppress a nationalist uprising in Indochina and to deepen America's ties with anti-Communist countries across the greater Middle East, including Pakistan. Meanwhile, in the 1951 book *Wells of Power*, which became the prevailing wisdom in Washington at the time, the final foreign secretary of the British Raj, Sir Olaf Caroe, argued that the security of the Middle East's oil resources—"the wells of power"—resided with the subcontinent's military.[9] India's neutrality left Pakistan as the only credible candidate. Top U.S. defense and intelligence officials prized Pakistan's territory, geographically contiguous with the Soviet Union's, as valuable for U.S. surveillance missions and operations against the USSR.[10] On February 2, 1952, Truman approved the sale of a small amount of military equipment to Pakistan. His successor would greatly expand security relations with the fledging state.

The Northern Tier

In the spring of 1953, after visiting the Middle East, Secretary of State John Foster Dulles suggested a North Atlantic Treaty Organization (NATO)–like security arrangement for states spanning the broader Middle East from North Africa to South Asia—the "northern tier."[11] Pakistan, and NATO ally Turkey in the eastern Mediterranean, would anchor America's containment strategy against the USSR in the broader Middle East. Both lay on the outer ring of the Middle East's expansive oil reserves, the lifeblood of postwar Western Europe and Japan's economic recovery. That autumn, Pakistan's first army commander-in-chief, General Mohammad Ayub Khan, came to Washington and portrayed his country as a vital component in a Western-led alliance.[12] Unfortunately, U.S. strategists had removed Pakistan conceptually from the subcontinent by placing it in the Middle East, implicitly ignoring its perpetual competition for territory and resources with India.

Prime Minister Nehru suspected that America sought to check Indian power and regional influence. He believed that the Cold War's intrusion into South Asia would cause mounting tensions and, potentially, another conflict. Even news of mere discussions between Washington and Karachi over defense-related issues triggered pandemonium in New Delhi. Despite the uproar, on February 25, 1954, President Eisenhower announced a major military assistance package to Pakistan. As the *New York Times* reported, administration planners had concluded that "the importance of bringing in Pakistan on the defense of the Middle East is greater than the importance of preserving pleasant relations with Mr. Nehru."[13]

A key problem with placing Pakistan in a collective security alliance was the country's veneer of unity amid diverging priorities and incompatible goals. Pakistan accepted U.S. military equipment to strengthen itself against India, not to deter the Soviet Union or contribute to the security of the Middle East.[14] Additionally, Pakistan was not Middle Eastern; excepting religion, it shared none of the language, history, or culture of that region. In March 1954, Senator J. William Fulbright (D-AR), who warned against alienating either India or Pakistan, called the sale of U.S. arms to Pakistan an "unwise and improvident decision." America's ambassador to India, Chester A. Bowles, also thought an arms pact would be catastrophic for the region, and he dismissed *Wells of Power* as a "strained bit of geopolitical reasoning."[15]

Trepidation, U.S. officials soon learned, existed on both sides of the Indo-Pakistani border, arousing fear of real or perceived threats from the other party. Even U.S. aid packages to India, many under the Public Law 480 program for agricultural commodities, antagonized Pakistan.[16] Washington's simultaneous assistance to New Delhi and Karachi provoked passionate resentment from both. As Dulles described in a telling cable to Eisenhower years later:

> The one distinct impression that I gained is their [India's] almost pathological fear of Pakistan. I, of course, knew they did not like our alliance with, and armament program for, Pakistan, but I never appreciated before the full depth of their feeling. I had assumed that India with its greater population and economic strength would feel relatively immune from any serious threat. However, they feel that Pakistan, or at least West Pakistan, is essentially a military state, largely run by the Army, that they are a martial people, that they are fanatically dedicated to Islam and may develop the urge to attack India or at least to try to take Kashmir or parts of it by force.[17]

Despite its inherent flaws and many detractors, the U.S.-Pakistan alliance quickly deepened. On April 2, 1954, Pakistan and Turkey concluded a mutual cooperation agreement to advance U.S. regional defense. In May, Washington and Karachi signed a Mutual Defense Assistance Agreement, in which Washington would supply military equipment and technical personnel for training. That September, Pakistan joined the Southeast Asia Treaty Organization (SEATO) alongside the United States, Britain, France, Thailand, the Philippines, Australia, and New Zealand. Pakistan also joined the American-sponsored Baghdad Pact the following February, with Britain, Iraq, Iran, and Turkey.[18]

As the only Asian country in both SEATO and the Baghdad Pact (later renamed CENTO, the Central Treaty Organization), Pakistan became known, as General Ayub Khan later described it in *Foreign Affairs*, as "America's most allied ally in Asia."[19] But Washington's fixation on deterring Soviet expansion led officials to overlook exactly how the Muslim state would or could contribute to collective security. Its regular army of roughly 150,000 at partition was responsible for "performing essential patrol and internal security functions" along its expansive frontiers with India, East Pakistan, and Afghanistan with limited resources, according to U.S. Brigadier General William T. Sexton, the head of the U.S. mission set up to advise and guide the modernization of Pakistan's armed forces.[20]

Few tools to gauge U.S. aid's effectiveness, and a lack of guidance from policymakers, further hampered Washington's ability to realize its objectives with Karachi. For instance, another one of America's top aims for Pakistan was developing its economy to a level capable of functioning without U.S. assistance.[21] U.S. Embassy Counselor to Pakistan John K. Emmerson reported in October 1954 that the embassy was "unable to evaluate [the] proposed program in relation [to] this objective," as it lacked available data and analyses to permit a long-range forecast of Pakistan's investment, economic development, and potential rate of growth. Worse, in February 1955, Assistant Secretary of Defense H. Struve Hensel reported after returning from a trip to Pakistan that not a single member of the U.S. diplomatic, military, intelligence, or foreign-assistance missions could articulate precisely how Pakistan effectively factored into the defense of the Middle East.[22]

Perhaps the biggest blow to the Northern Tier concept came from the Joint Chiefs of Staff, who reported there was no realistic prospect that concepts of regional defense would "result in any significant reduction of the area's military vulnerability." The report also concluded that the tier's indigenous forces "will have little defensive capability against an attack by a major power." The effect of multilateral pacts was "primarily political and psychological rather than military."[23] In Washington, however, incoherence reigned, with the State Department noting, "US support for Northern Tier concept remains strong and we hope to see its steady and even rapid fulfillment."[24]

To some officials, it became clear that Pakistan's military—and U.S. assistance to it—was stifling the growth of a strong, stable, and economically viable country. As early as November 1953, the six-year-old nation spent more than 70 percent of its revenues on defense. Four years later, the National Security Council (NSC) observed not only that Pakistan's "military build-up [was] based upon a commitment by the United States to provide equipment," but also that "without substantial external assistance, Pakistan's limited resources" would be inadequate to sustain either the burdens of that build-up or the military maintenance costs *and* the needs of economic growth.[25] Senior U.S. policy planners and defense and intelligence specialists reported that Pakistan spent U.S. aid faster than it could absorb it.[26]

The military was the backbone of political power and the only well-organized institution. But, although erected to protect the state, it actually harmed the country's internal development. The military's insatiable appetite for, and unfettered access to, lucrative state resources pulled capital and human talent away from sectors of civil society essential for such development. Over the decades, with major economic stakes in everything from sugar mills and universities to fertilizer companies and cable television stations, the military came to enjoy a wealth of perks and personal benefits not shared with the rest of Pakistan's poor population.[27] In a country already lacking the ingredients of internal stability, the military siphoned the massive infusions of Western capital to consolidate its political control. Correspondingly, aid constrained the country's integrity and independence, crippling economic freedom and depriving its entry into the free-market world. The Central Intelligence Agency (CIA) and the intelligence arms of the U.S. Army, Navy, Air Force, and the Joint Staff estimated that Pakistan's military expenditures would require continued U.S. support "probably for an indeterminate period." The poor country's "beggar's bowl" seemed bottomless.[28]

Pakistan's increasing dependence on Washington rose in tandem with the desire of its people for an independent foreign policy. As a U.S. National Intelligence Estimate concluded in November 1956, "the Pakistan government will be under increasing popular pressure to de-emphasize its ties with the West and demonstrate its independence of 'Western domination.'" The NSC had also found that the vast majority of Pakistani citizens sought their country's shift away from the West.[29] At the time, many newly independent states adopted an anti-Western orientation because they looked to the Soviets, who shrewdly exploited the history of European colonial oppression.

That July, Egypt's charismatic leader, Colonel Gamal Abdel Nasser, nationalized a remnant of European colonialism, the British and French operated Suez Canal Company. In response, and amid rising anger over their county's pro-Western policies, over 300,000 protesters in Lahore, West Pakistan's provincial capital, demanded their country withdraw from SEATO and the Baghdad Pact.[30] Such collective security arrangements put Pakistan in league with Britain at a time when many Pakistanis sought to strengthen the bonds of unity among Muslim countries. Yet another U.S. objective for Pakistan—the allegiance of its people and their identification with the free world—was in crisis. Even President Eisenhower lamented America's costly objective to make Pakistan a military ally. In a summary of the discussion at the January 1957 NSC meeting, he observed that "we were doing practically nothing for Pakistan except in the form of military aid." The president said that "this was perhaps the worst kind of a plan and decision we could have made. It was a terrible error, but we now seem hopelessly involved in it."[31]

Eventually, growing divisions among the general populace, vocal educated elements, and corrupt officials would take Pakistan down a pan-Islamist, pro-socialist, anti-American path. The alliance with the United States pitted the prerogatives of Pakistani elites against the wishes and interests of the general public. Washington's assumption that substantial offers of aid and credits to elites would alleviate popular pressures for change was mistaken. The belief that Pakistan's national interests would best be served through nonalignment inspired that doctrine's popular appeal. The only people in Pakistan claiming their country was pro-U.S. and pro-Western, according to America's ambassador to Pakistan, James M. Langley, was "the very small upper crust"—senior army officers, top groups of politicians, leading businessmen, and a few other direct beneficiaries of American assistance.[32] In 1957, Prime Minister Huseyn Suhrawardy, who resisted the notion that Pakistan's security arrangements impinged upon its independence and territorial integrity, helped lead the National Assembly to approve a motion cementing Pakistan's Western-aligned foreign policy. Yet he and other parliamentarians depended financially on their country's military commander-in-chief, General Ayub Khan, who benefited from the largesse of defense contracts with the United States.

Steadily deteriorating popular support exacerbated Pakistan's dysfunctional political system. On October 7, 1958, President Iskander Mirza imposed martial law, suspended the constitution, dissolved national and provincial assemblies, abolished political parties, and canceled scheduled elections. On October 27, chief martial-law administrator Ayub Khan forced Mirza out and assumed the presidency. The coup d'état manifested the disjuncture between the pro-Western direction of the political system and the preferred path envisioned by a cabal in the military-civilian bureaucratic axis. The coup, inspired by and executed to coincide with the anniversary of Russia's October revolution, empowered a minority of civilian and military leaders, artists, professors, and literati who admired the Soviet Union's rapid economic development programs. Unfazed by communism's atheistic ideology, these leaders embraced ideals of egalitarianism, full employment, and public ownership of the means of production.

Despite Pakistan's jarring transition from civilian control to military rule, and its transparently socialist orientation, some in Washington were unfazed. Rather than take the side of democracy and justice, they saw the new military president as a stabilizing force, subduing internal unrest and renewing ties with the West. Secretary Dulles even thought the country's backslide into dictatorship could improve the situation. His brother, CIA Director Allen Dulles, thought the coup provided "further indications of how difficult it was to make democracy work effectively in such underdeveloped countries." In the minority was State Department Intelligence Bureau Director R. Gordon Arneson, who presciently warned that the military dictatorship was unlikely to master Pakistan's problems, and the general Pakistani public was not prepared "for the arbitrary abrogation of constitutional government."[33]

Ultimately, the United States embraced Pakistan, despite the undemocratic overhaul of its constitution and ensuing period of martial law. "The Government of the United States of America regards as vital to its national interest and to world peace the preservation of the independence and integrity of Pakistan," declared the March 1959 Bilateral Agreement of Cooperation.[34] Through sales, grants, and loans, Washington supplied the country's military with armaments and ammunition, artillery, transports, warships, and an assortment of aircraft. From 1953 to 1961, the United States provided nearly $2 billion in assistance and invited many Pakistani military officers to receive training in the United States.[35] Meanwhile, Pakistan agreed to host a secret intelligence facility for American U-2 spy planes in Badaber, 10 miles from Peshawar, the frontier capital of NWFP adjacent to the Soviet Union. (U.S. pilot Francis Gary Powers, whom the Soviets shot down over their territory and captured in 1960, took off from that facility. Adhering to protocol—like the allegedly crafty deception of post-9/11 U.S. drone strikes in Pakistan—Washington claimed it used Badaber without Karachi's permission, and Karachi protested that Washington's use of the facility was unauthorized.)[36]

An Ally, If You Can Keep It

As the United States and Pakistan grew closer together on paper, their perceived threats, interests, and policies drove them further apart. One prominent wedge was America's goal to build India as a powerhouse in Asia as a counterweight to Communist China.[37] Unlike their predecessors, senior policy planners in the John F. Kennedy and Lyndon B. Johnson administrations prioritized India over Pakistan. The results, however, proved even more disastrous. Pakistan cozied up to Red China, while India warmed to the USSR. Moreover, by pumping aid and weapons to avowedly hostile arch-adversaries, Washington fomented an escalating arms race that erupted into full-scale war in 1965.

It all started innocently enough and reflected more logical priorities for U.S. policy in South Asia. President Kennedy appreciated India's democratic aspirations, its sizeable population, and its symbolic importance in the developing world. He even praised Prime Minister Nehru's "soaring idealism" in his first State of the Union address. Recalls presidential special assistant Arthur M. Schlesinger Jr., Kennedy believed the competition between China and India "for the economic and political leadership of the East" would determine Asia's future. Kennedy wanted India to win that race with China, saying "If China succeeds and India fails, the economic-development balance of power will shift against us."[38]

Pro-India sentiments in Congress and among many American journalists and business elites encouraged Washington's engagement with the world's largest democracy and advocated expanded U.S. aid programs for its economic development. Accordingly, Kennedy appointed pro-India diplomats to high-ranking positions: Dean Rusk as secretary of state, Chester Bowles as number two at the State Department, Philips Talbot as assistant secretary of state for Near Eastern and South Asian Affairs, and John Kenneth Galbraith as America's ambassador to New Delhi.[39]

The Pakistanis were not pleased. "Whatever might be your world-wide commitments, do not take such steps that would aggravate our problems and jeopardise our security," General Ayub implored a joint session of Congress on July 12, 1961.[40] During his official state visit to America, he repeatedly warned against U.S. military aid to India. In April, Kennedy had taken the lead in organizing international support for a two-year, $1 billion economic package to India. Beyond that consortium, he requested from Congress $500 million in assistance for India and $400 million for the rest of the world.[41] Still, even as Washington took heat from Karachi, New Delhi remained unswervingly neutral. In response to the August 1961 delivery of 12 American F-104 jet fighters to Pakistan per an agreement signed in 1960, in May 1962—just months after Kennedy offered to help negotiate a settlement on Kashmir—India announced its decision to purchase fighter aircraft from the Soviets.

Washington finally gained some pull with New Delhi when Moscow declared a position of strict neutrality in a war between India and China. Vying for power and influence, New Delhi and Peking were prickly neighbors. In 1959, India dared to challenge China's claim to sovereignty by granting asylum to the spiritual head of Tibetan Buddhism, the Dalai Lama. On October 20, 1962, amid tensions over outstanding territorial claims, the Chinese People's Liberation Army attacked India along their disputed border and overwhelmed the Indian troops within a week. Although busy defusing the Cuban Missile Crisis, Kennedy agreed to provide Nehru with military assistance, exploiting a clear opportunity for closer relations with India and hoping to prevent Communist China from turning a tactical upper hand into a decisive strategic victory.[42] By late November, China declared a unilateral ceasefire, pulled its forces back from all newly captured territory, and retained the border it had originally claimed.

Unexpectedly, dynamics surrounding the Sino-Indian War marked a major shift in Pakistan's assertion of independence from America. As he promised to do if hostilities between India and China erupted, Kennedy told Ayub about America's delivery of weapons to India. Ayub felt betrayed. He had expressed privately to U.S. diplomats that Pakistan had "no intention [of] taking advantage of India's trouble." But some in Pakistan's military viewed Ayub as weak for failing to exploit India's war with China by seizing Kashmir. The moment left a bitter impression about Washington's conduct.[43] The United States was strengthening Pakistan's primary enemy. Foreign Minister Mohammed Ali Bogra condemned Washington's assistance as "an act of gross unfriendliness to Pakistan."[44] Seeing India rewarded once again for its nonaligned stance, Pakistani streets and newspaper editorials raged with anti-American sentiment.

Ingratiation and "Forthcomingness"

Undeterred by the region's perpetual turbulence, U.S. officials continued aid to Pakistan and accelerated assistance to India. Only now, they also sought to negotiate a settlement on Kashmir, using the lure of U.S. largesse to help achieve a compromise. Secretary Rusk recommended that America's "usable leverage," primarily military assistance, serve as inducements to make the parties willing to compromise in exchange for possibly more U.S. aid. He wrote on January 15, 1963, that the parties have a "vested interest in demonstrating disposition to compromise in talks," and that, with the prospect of receiving more U.S. aid, they would "out-vie each other in forthcomingness."[45]

For many reasons, this hoped-for ingratiation contest failed. First, the Kashmir conflict was about far more than competition over land. There was a historical-psychological dimension as well that the United States could not alter. Since partition, Pakistan believed India's goal was to crush its rival; ceding Muslim-majority Kashmir to secular India would underscore Pakistan's congenital weakness and compromise the religious solidarity that birthed it. Second, America's evenhandedness neither realigned India toward the West nor convinced it to budge on Kashmir. As the dominant regional power, India preferred bilateral consultation on Kashmir and strenuously objected to third-party mediation. Third, Pakistan tried to offset its dependence on America by forging deeper ties with Communist China, the very country American strategists hoped to counter by shifting their attention toward India.

But as superficial as America's relations with India were, they stoked Pakistan's latent insecurities about India's relative power advantage and America's sincerity. Feeling vulnerable by relying on assurances from its principal ally, Karachi pursued "philandering"—as the State Department put it in January 1963—with Peking.[46] As CIA Director John McCone wrote in a matter-of-fact assessment of U.S. policy in the region:

> Our interest is to make a strong sub-continent. . . . While doing this we have moved away from the Pakistanis and they are moving closer to the Chinese and against the Indians. We have not been able to persuade the Pakistanis . . . to change their policy on India. These forces were there long before we came on the scene and we cannot do much about it.[47]

That forthright assessment accurately captured Washington's dilemma amid the region's shifting alliances. After President Kennedy approved a $120 million Anglo-American aid package to India in early December 1963, Pakistan and China announced a boundary demarcation accord on December 26. In early March, Pakistan's Foreign Minister, Zulfikar Ali Bhutto, a hawkish politician from Sindh and a strong proponent of a China-centric foreign policy, flew to Peking to sign the Sino-Pakistan border agreement. That month, Kennedy committed equipment to improve India's air defense capability against potential Chinese attack. By May, Chinese Premier Zhou Enlai declared that China "would defend Pakistan throughout the world" since "Pakistan defended China in SEATO and CENTO."[48] In July, amid several Sino-Pakistan agreements on commercial, aviation, and cultural exchanges, General Ayub Khan unsubtly warned Washington that continued reinforcement of India's military would force smaller countries in Asia to seek Chinese protection.[49]

Any notion that Pakistan was a reliable member of the democratic free world, much less a reliable security partner of the United States, was fading fast. Washington found itself in the unpleasant position of maintaining important military ties to a military dictatorship that was clearly becoming a client of Communist China, a power that U.S. officials regarded as a threat to crucial U.S. interests and the overall peace of both East Asia and South Asia. To put it mildly, U.S. policy toward Pakistan was not working out as planned.

According to Undersecretary of State George Ball, even though Washington had "given Pakistan straightforward assurances on coming to its aid if it should be attacked from any source . . . we shall over a period of time see a gradual erosion of our influence with Paks, with mounting pressures for Pak [to] move in general direction of neutralism."[50] Both Washington and Karachi viewed the other as the disloyal partner, and each had compelling justifications for his position. To Washington, Karachi compromised the bilateral alliance by accepting Chinese assistance. To Karachi, Washington upset Pakistan's precarious military balance with India. As a State Department telegram detailed to the embassy in Pakistan, President Kennedy captured the tension with some sharp words:

> Paks display little appreciation of this primary concern of ours and instead apparently feel impelled to move towards Chicoms [Chinese Communists] and away from us because Pak concern about India. In last few months Pak press has exceeded all but Chicom in its attacks on us. One would gather from Pak press, which is closer to GOP [Government of Pakistan] than ours to USG [U.S. Government], that US was enemy number one.[51]

Despite the worrisome developments in Pakistan acrimony, there was no fundamental reassessment of U.S. policy. Yet the changes that had occurred drastically undercut Washington's original assumptions about cultivating ties with Karachi. The ostensible goal in the late 1940s and throughout most of the 1950s had been to strengthen a democratic ally that would be a bulwark against communist expansion and thereby advance important American economic and security interests in that part of the world. But Pakistan was no longer even arguably democratic, and its foreign policy increasingly ran counter to U.S. objectives. Nevertheless, the awkward embrace of an increasingly dubious partner continued.

For narrow strategic reasons, U.S. officials were unwilling to let Pakistan spin out of America's orbit completely. In addition to the U.S. spy facility outside Peshawar, leaders in Karachi allowed Washington to install wind-sampling equipment on the surface of specific planes bound for China—wind sampling checked for fallout from nuclear tests.[52] In early June, President Kennedy explained America's complicated position to Indian President Dr. Sarvepalli Radhakrishnan by saying America wanted to "give India more security" without incurring "heavy costs in terms of our relations with Pakistan."[53] But the United States couldn't have it both ways. Washington's relations with both South Asian countries increasingly suffered.

The 1965 Indo-Pakistani War's Impact on Relations with the United States

During her visit to Washington in April 1964, Indira Gandhi, Nehru's daughter, told the *New York Times* that America was losing goodwill in India because of its "favoritism toward Pakistan."[54] Kennedy's successor, Lyndon Johnson, continued aid to India, but did little to assuage its anxieties. Meeting with President Johnson, Mrs. Gandhi claimed that Indians felt America always took Pakistan's side, in spite of official U.S. policy during the past few years. On June 6, 1964, Washington announced a renewed defense package for New Delhi: $50 million in military assistance and several million in credit offers as part of a five-year, bilateral defense plan.[55]

With India receiving both Soviet and American assistance, Pakistan countered by accepting more Chinese aid. Rather than depend on Washington indefinitely, Pakistan sought to enter relationships as circumstances dictated. China helped build infrastructure, such as the Karokoram Highway, Gwadar port, Ormara Harbor, and dams. Pakistani leaders, seeing the benefits of neutrality, advocated reduced ties with the West and increased links with Afro-Asian nonaligned states. They also matched their convictions with rhetoric.

"Americans do not hesitate to let down their friends," General Ayub charged at an April SEATO summit in Manila. "Today their policy is based on opportunism and is devoid of moral quality." In June, Foreign Minister Bhutto declared before his country's National Assembly, "The time has come for Pakistan to undertake a reappraisal of its foreign policy and to review her political and military commitments."[56] Even the CIA acknowledged the domestic popularity of the new foreign policy in Pakistan.[57]

In January 1965, to discuss the alarming chill in bilateral relations and the yawning gap in their assessment of Chinese actions and intentions, President Johnson invited General Ayub to Washington that April. The meeting never happened. Nine days before Ayub's visit, Johnson abruptly withdrew his invitation. He also delayed the first scheduled trip to Washington of India's Prime Minister, Lal Bahadur Shastri, but the Pakistanis were Johnson's primary target. In his letter to Ayub, Johnson emphasized Pakistan's dual failures: lack of support for Washington's position in Vietnam and Karachi's warming relations with Communist China. A visit to Washington, Johnson ostensibly feared, would focus public attention on the parties' differences, potentially jeopardizing congressional support for the administration's foreign-aid proposal for Pakistan—a strange stance, considering the tension.

Despite Johnson's annoyance with the Pakistanis, U.S. aid continued to flow. By the mid-1960s, military and economic assistance to the subcontinent accounted for nearly one-third of the U.S. foreign-aid budget and inadvertently contributed to a spiraling regional arms race. In a fundamental reassessment of U.S. policy in 1964, Johnson forced a two-month postponement of a World Bank consortium to approve surplus food to Pakistan under P.L. 480. The NSC later stated that the postponement "was designed to show Ayub that American aid was far from automatic." But U.S. Ambassador to Pakistan Walter P. McConaughy told Secretary Rusk he considered the postponement provocative and discriminatory.[58]

On July 3, when McConaughy broke the news to General Ayub, the Pakistani suspended standard diplomatic niceties, stating that America only wanted "satellites, non-thinking followers who blindly acquiesce to US policy." He warned that Pakistan would look elsewhere, especially China, for development aid. Ayub vented his frustrations publicly, calling the United States "power drunk" in an inflammatory speech before a meeting of the Muslim League. He and other prominent leaders also incited massive anti-American rallies across the country.[59]

On August 5–6, officials in the Pakistani Foreign Office and army high command launched Operation Gibraltar, a plan to sneak armed guerillas across the ceasefire line with India in Kashmir. But the effort to ignite a popular revolt suffered numerous setbacks and devolved into a debacle.[60] Ayub resorted to using regular army forces and their U.S. military equipment in his country's latest confrontation with India. On September 1, Pakistan launched Operation Grand Slam as 70 U.S.-supplied Patton tanks roared into southern Kashmir to cut off Indian supply lines. "The situation as it stands today has made us look ridiculous in the eyes of the entire world," exclaimed Congressman James Haley (D-FL). "The blunt truth is that the hundreds of millions of dollars we have given these countries has equipped them to mount war against each other."[61]

Pakistan seemed undeterred by its breach of previous agreements; it was again misusing U.S. military equipment provided to counter Soviet aggression. On September 6, when the Indian army crossed into West Pakistan, President Ayub and Foreign Minister Bhutto called on Washington to fulfill the bilateral defense agreement of 1959 and to "suppress and vacate" Indian forces.[62] Instead, on September 8, Johnson suspended shipments of military arms, spare parts, ammunition, and other assistance to both countries. India, on top of its own armaments industry, had access to both American and Soviet weapons, whereas Pakistan's principal arms supplier was the United States. Bhutto implied to Ambassador McConaughy that Washington acted as an enemy and said relations would never be the same.[63] Given Pakistan's slide into authoritarianism and its open flirtation with China, it was not apparent why that would necessarily be a bad thing from the standpoint of American interests and values.

Rather than acknowledge their ineptitude in trying to infiltrate Kashmir, Pakistani leaders blamed America, and anti-American demonstrations spread across Pakistan. Mobs attacked the embassy in Karachi, the U.S. consulate in Lahore, and burned a U.S. government library. Ayub's 1967 book, *Friends Not Masters*, hit at America not to behave vindictively and make aid recipients subservient. The conflict ended by United Nations (UN) ceasefire on September 22 but, across the subcontinent, America's prestige fell to an all-time low.[64]

The 1965 Indo-Pakistani War reflected more than just regional rivalry. It testified to the failure of America's Cold War policies. Despite decades of American efforts to advance peace and counter communism in the subcontinent, the world's top two recipients of U.S. foreign aid clashed militarily. After the conflict, India replaced thinly veiled neutralism with even friendlier ties with the Soviet Union, while Pakistan's disdain for America moved it further toward China and the non-Western bloc. Moreover, Pakistan would be increasingly dominated by its military sector, even during brief periods when civilian leaders were officially in charge of the government. Any attempt by the United States to portray Pakistan as anything other than an authoritarian partner was either disingenuous or a case of wishful thinking. Washington's ally was neither democratic nor trustworthy.

Pakistan's Second Partition and Nixon's "Tilt" toward Islamabad

Despite such ominous trends, President Richard Nixon diverged from his predecessors by being more accommodating to Pakistan. Islamabad, which became Pakistan's new capital in 1966, was a key player helping the United States establish diplomatic contact with Communist China in July 1971, a bold initiative that forever changed the Cold War order (discussed in chapter 11). But Pakistan proved incapable of translating its international efforts at forging peace into domestic ones. After a third Indo-Pakistani war, Islamabad's government began preaching a strident mixture of pro-Communist, pan-Islamist, and anti-American worldviews.

Amid a tremendous global shift in the Cold War balance of power, multiple upheavals overwhelmed Pakistan. West Pakistan was the country's core political wing. Home to the country's Punjabi-dominated ruling military generals and civilian political class, it ruled over the culturally, linguistically, and geographically isolated East Pakistan, which was ethnically Bengali and contained more than half of Pakistan's population. Sheikh Mujibir Rahman, known as Mujib, headed the east's ethnic Bengali political party, the Awami League. He insisted that the League was merely demanding that Islamabad accord "his people" their political rights and not relegate them to a "colonial status."[65] But Islamabad viewed the Awami League's six-point plan for East Pakistan's political and economic autonomy as tantamount to secession. Political accommodation was something neither side could countenance. After a devastating cyclone struck East Pakistan on November 12, 1970, national elections the following month became a referendum on the central government's handling of the crisis.

On election day, Zulfikar Ali Bhutto's Pakistan People's Party (PPP) won a majority in West Pakistan, but Mujib's Awami League won a landslide victory in East Pakistan—enough to secure a majority of seats in the National Assembly. Although Bhutto claimed he wanted to meet with Mujib and hash out disagreements over the country's constitution, Bhutto was angered by the election outcome and refused to convene the National Assembly scheduled to meet in

Dhaka, East Pakistan's capital, on March 3, 1971. He told his under-ling, hawkish civil servant Roedad Khan: "A law and order situation could be easily created in Dhaka resulting in tear-gassing and firing, etc., a few dead bodies and that would more than justify postpone-ment of the National Assembly session."[66]

Either by accident or by design, Bhutto's Machiavellian dream came to fruition.

Leaders in West Pakistan precipitated a brutal crackdown on the East. The repression and subsequent refugee crisis led to East Paki-stan's secession and the creation of Bangladesh. Those developments also produced another war between Pakistan and India.

The Bhutto-Mujib impasse infuriated East Pakistan. By March, with the Bengali flag flying over much of the province and the West Pakistan–dominated military imposing martial law, Bengali resi-dents began to attack West Pakistani army officers. When officials ordered Mujib's arrest, a wave of civil disobedience engulfed the province. To quell the massive uprisings, on March 25–26, President Yahya Khan and his military junta launched Operation Searchlight. Under Lieutenant General Tikka Khan, later known as the "Butcher of Bengal," 40,000 West Pakistani forces spread out into major cities, towns, and parts of the countryside, eventually swelling to 90,000. A bloodbath ensued.

"Here in Dacca (*sic*)," reported Archer Kent Blood, the U.S. consul general in East Pakistan, "we are mute and horrified witnesses to a reign of terror by the Pak military."[67] Security forces rounded up civil servants, writers, professors, doctors, and others "marked for extinction" and executed them en masse. Blood's dispatches became known as the "Blood Telegrams" and were featured in news stories throughout the West. The accounts described the chaotic atmosphere in horrifying detail: a family with no Awami League connections "wiped out by army"; a home belonging to civil servants "entered by army and inhabitants killed"; and soldiers setting fire to homes and shooting dwellers trying to escape.[68] America's ambassador in New Delhi, Kenneth Keating, reported his concern about the massa-cre and Washington's "damaging association with a reign of military terror."[69] Blood advised Washington to express "our shock, at least privately." He warned ominously, before Nixon removed him from Dhaka, that the "full horror of Pak military atrocities will come to light sooner or later."[70]

They did. On July 12, 1971, the *New York Times* published excerpts of a World Bank report following the organization's visit to East Pakistan in June. That report described the Kushtia district bordering India as looking "like the morning after a nuclear attack." The description of the Jessore district was equally horrifying. "From the air, totally destroyed villages were clearly visible."[71] West Pakistan's extensive use of U.S. arms supplied before 1965, including Chafee M-24 tanks and F-86 aircraft fighters, to slaughter civilians stunned Congress and the American public.[72] More than 8 to 10 million East Pakistani refugees fled to India, while estimates of the numbers killed vary wildly. West Pakistan's Hamood-ur-Rahman Commission Report low-balled the casualty figure at 26,000 civilians. Journalists who covered the crisis estimated that Pakistani troops murdered more than one million Bengalis, whereas other estimates of the final death toll range to upward of three million.[73] U.S. officials in Dhaka and India described West Pakistan's actions as a selective genocide, but the U.S. and Pakistani governments pressured the United Nations not to appoint a tribunal to investigate the crisis.

Nixon's National Security Advisor, Henry Kissinger, characterized the Bangladesh crisis as perhaps "the most complex issue in Nixon's first term."[74] That alleged complexity may explain the conspicuous silence that emanated from the Oval Office. Conflicting imperatives caused the White House not to take a stance, at least publicly. Nixon pressed Yahya privately to make political accommodations, and he vehemently refused to be the "scapegoat" for Pakistan's disintegration; an independent Bangladesh was a threshold Pakistan had to cross on its own.[75] But another consideration, as mentioned briefly above and discussed in chapter 11, was the diplomatic overture to China, to which Pakistan was "the sole opening." Islamabad not only played interlocutor, but also was Kissinger's place of departure for Beijing during the summer of 1971. Nixon and Kissinger estimated that because Chinese leaders placed importance on an ally's reliability, to disassociate from Pakistan in its moment of peril would have jeopardized rapprochement with China. Not all officials agreed, however. Assistant Secretary of State Christopher Van Hollen, for example, argued that publicly denouncing Pakistan's brutal massacre would not have jeopardized the China initiative.

As millions of refugees fled to neighboring India for safety, Nixon and Kissinger came to believe India would use the crisis to exploit

Pakistan's weakness.[76] That caused concerns over a possible Soviet intervention on India's behalf. In late June, U.S. officials learned the Soviets had promised the Indians protection against Chinese reprisals. By assuaging India's fear of a potential Chinese attack, Moscow had increased India's incentive to intervene in Bangladesh. Moreover, Pakistan's dismemberment by India, a Soviet ally with Soviet weapons, would, Nixon administration leaders feared, harm America's system of alliances and encourage similar Soviet tactics elsewhere.[77] On August 1, weeks after the United States announced the unfreezing of its relations with Communist China, India and the USSR signed a 20-year treaty of peace, friendship, and cooperation.

Additionally, it is difficult to dismiss the extent to which Nixon and Kissinger's strong preference for Pakistan and considerable distrust of India shaped policy.[78] Even President Khan, Foreign Secretary Sultan Khan, and their colleagues did not believe India was planning war. Yet Nixon took a moderate and conciliatory tone toward General Yahya, which differed markedly from his visceral contempt for Mrs. Gandhi, epitomized by his usual epithet for her—"that bitch." As Kissinger expressed to Ambassador Keating, "the President has a special feeling for President Yahya. One cannot make policy on that basis, but it is a fact of life."[79] Mrs. Gandhi's visit to Washington on November 4 and 5 reinforced Nixon and Kissinger's belief that she was attempting to fulfill India's grand design to establish regional preeminence. She repeatedly called Pakistan an artificial state, charging that those in East Pakistan who were demanding autonomy from Islamabad—as well as those in Balochistan and NWFP making similar demands—showed they never should have been part of the partition settlement.

By most accounts, the third war between India and Pakistan began on December 3, 1971, when West Pakistani forces attacked eight airfields in northern and western India. Others argue the war started on November 22, when Indian army units crossed into East Pakistan in support of Bengali separatist operations.[80] Either way, West Pakistan's December attack provided India an official justification to retaliate. The near unanimous conclusion of senior representatives from Defense, CIA, and U.S. Agency for International Development, was that India merited greater priority in terms of U.S. interests and would win the war with Pakistan. Instead, Nixon decided to, in Kissinger's words, "tilt in favor of Pakistan." The White House took the view that India was not only interfering in Pakistan's internal affairs with subversive action, but was also a Soviet stooge. As Kissinger bluntly put it, "here we have Indian-Soviet collusion, raping a friend of ours"[81] U.S. officials condemned India as the instigator of the war, and Washington's UN ambassador, George H. W. Bush, branded India "the major aggressor."[82]

The White House also tried to help Pakistan obtain U.S. fighter planes directly and through third-party transfers *after* the State Department and Congress cut off aid to Pakistan and forbade further assistance in April.[83] Partly because of the six-year U.S. arms embargo after the 1965 war, the military imbalance between India and Pakistan had deepened. The Soviet Union had become India's biggest military supplier, meeting Indian requests for accelerated aid and adding deliveries of aircraft, submarines, radars, medium tanks, guns, and large amounts of ammunition. By contrast, Pakistan's military was woefully ill-prepared. It could not simultaneously challenge hostile secessionists and the numerically superior Indian military. On December 18, 1971, barely two weeks after the war began, West Pakistan's army surrendered unconditionally to India, and Bangladesh was born from the wreckage of a united Pakistan.

The details surrounding the war are instructive regarding U.S.-Pakistan relations. "America's most allied ally in Asia" denied democratic rights to its politically excluded and economically neglected Bengali majority and used excessive force to suppress a popularly elected movement and facilitate search-and-destroy operations against it. The White House could have made explicit appeals for restraint early in the crisis, or bluntly criticized the actions of the regime along with suspending economic assistance programs. Such disassociation would have mitigated the ridicule directed at the Nixon administration for seemingly condoning an ally's denial of democratic rights and subsequent slaughter of its citizens. But a rigid—and ultimately myopic—view of geopolitics, not morality, guided Nixon's response. His administration treated the crisis as a legitimate suppression of civil insurrection rather than a ruthless crackdown. By viewing the crisis as an internal affair—yet also oddly an external, Indo-Soviet one—Nixon did little to stop or even publicly oppose Islamabad's brutal repression and even tried to provide yet more weapons to West Pakistan. As Kissinger later acknowledged about the Bangladesh crisis, "there was some merit to the charge of moral insensitivity."[84]

120

Indeed, the Nixon administration's behavior throughout the episode was a textbook example of faulty foreign policy. Nixon and Kissinger got both the geopolitics and the moral considerations wrong. By any rational measure, India was more important than Pakistan to the future of South Asia and to long-term American interests in the region. Yet instead of cultivating New Delhi, the president and his national security adviser allowed personal animus (especially their attitude toward Indira Gandhi) and curiously shortsighted calculations to produce a strategically unwise and morally obtuse tilt in favor of Pakistan. It was not the finest hour in the history of U.S. foreign policy.

Despite Nixon's desired tilt, U.S. government policy was frequently less pro-Pakistan than he wished. Some State Department bureaucrats, either out of personal outrage or fear of external criticism, ignored presidential directives, refused to carry out the spirit of the executive's decisions, and precipitated actions without clearance from the White House. Unaware of Pakistan's role in the opening to China, the bureaucracy held in abeyance Nixon's one-time exception package to Pakistan, cutting off some $35 million in arms and suspending the issuance of new licenses for the sale of munitions and other items in April. Nixon authorized the transfer of spare parts and nonlethal equipment to Pakistan, as well as economic aid to persuade Yahya to arrange a transition "to East Pakistani autonomy." Journalists revealed the effort, which then became a public-relations fiasco.[85]

Whereas Pakistan viewed its partnership with Washington as the cornerstone of its security, the United States had the luxury to take the partnership for granted. During the crisis, this point of difference was one of fundamental importance. Early in the war, Yahya and Bhutto invoked Article I of the 1959 U.S.-Pakistan Bilateral Agreement of Cooperation and Pakistan's membership in the Baghdad Pact. The State Department rejected their request. Washington issued a "clarification" that Article I only spoke of "appropriate action to thwart such aggression," without clarifying what "appropriate action" should be taken.

That stance was more than a little disingenuous. True, Washington and Islamabad had never concluded a mutual defense treaty, but U.S. leaders had repeatedly created the misleading impression of U.S. support for Pakistan's worries about the threat India posed to its security. Citing a November 1962 U.S. assurance to President

Ayub Khan to assist in the event of Indian aggression, Kissinger later conceded that the victim of the Bangladesh crisis was an ally "to which we had made several explicit promises concerning precisely this contingency."[86]

Pakistani leaders badly miscalculated on two levels. First, they believed India would not intervene in response to the bloody crackdown in East Pakistan and the resulting flood of refugees. Even worse, those leaders failed to understand that neither the United States nor China would ride to their rescue.

But defending Pakistan from India would have posed grave risks to America's security. It was foolish to promise or even imply that there would be U.S. military action to support Pakistan in the event of an Indian attack. Extending unrealistic pledges of support and then reneging on them when threats materialized was harmful for Washington's relations with Islamabad, as with any other country. Nixon told Yahya when he visited Washington in October 1970, "nobody occupied the White House who is friendlier to Pakistan."[87] Unluckily for Pakistan, nobody ever had or likely ever will.

Postwar Pakistan: A Wolf in Sheep's Clothing

On May 3, 1973, President Nixon remarked that despite the "crisis and defeat in 1971," which tore Pakistan's political structure and halved its population, the events had "also brought to power the first civilian administration Pakistan has had since 1958 and produced a new and determined effort to develop institutions of representative government."[88] On December 20, 1971, PPP Chairman Zulfikar Ali Bhutto assumed the office of the presidency and chief martial law administrator as the head of Pakistan's newly elected government. Even though Bhutto's actions and decisions in the Ayub and Yahya eras contributed to and accelerated his country's disunity, he promoted himself as the only leader capable of piecing his fractured country back together.

On August 14, 1973, with the signing of the country's new constitution, Bhutto's Pakistan emerged. Bhutto proved remarkably decisive in shaping his country's policies, and in the drafting and passage of the 1973 constitution. Implementing land, labor, and education reforms in the name of "Islamic Socialism," the 1973 constitution brought the country down the path of religious conservatism, communist economic and social policies, and institutionalized discrimination against religious and ethnic minorities: a lethal cocktail of bad policies. The country's political and social transformation was having a profound influence on Washington's interests. Among Pakistani intellectuals and practitioners, negative impressions of U.S. policies colored perceptions of America and its principles. Socialism, Bhutto preached, was "nothing but Islamic equality," and equality was the "cardinal principle in Islam." Bhutto, who adopted Chairman Mao's attire, denounced his critics as "agents of capitalism" and "lackeys of imperialism." His PPP was the self-proclaimed "party of the masses, the peasants, and the workers." It promised food, clothing, and shelter ("Roti, Kapra, aur Makan") for all.

Parts of the 1973 constitution even echoed Marxist rhetoric. Article 3, for example, read: "The State shall ensure the elimination of all forms of exploitation and the gradual fulfillment of the fundamental principle, from each according to his ability to each according to his work." Communism's atheistic philosophy did not faze Bhutto and others apparently. Nor were Communist ideals of egalitarianism, full employment, common ownership of the means of production, and opposition to colonialism called into question in response to the Soviet Union's domestic repression and brutal imperialism in Eastern Europe.

Bhutto's Pakistan also began to shun its alliance with Washington. Islamabad withdrew from SEATO and the Baghdad Pact, and forged stronger ties with Iran, Saudi Arabia, and other Muslim states. It also became a major purchaser of Chinese military equipment. The 1973 constitution codified the country's turn toward the non-Western world. Its foreign and defense policy, as promulgated in Article 40, read:

> The State shall endeavour to preserve and strengthen fraternal relations among Muslim countries based on Islamic unity, support the common interests of the people of Asia, Africa, and Latin America, promote international peace and security, foster goodwill and friendly relations among all nations and encourage the settlement of international disputes by peaceful means.[89]

North America and continental Europe are excluded from mention. Despite the billions of dollars in U.S. assistance following partition, Washington's efforts at building goodwill and gaining benefits had come up empty.

Although some senior U.S. officials had dismissed Bhutto as an anti-American extremist, they accepted Pakistan's new civilian government.[90] But Bhutto's populist message to end exploitation and social injustice cloaked very anti-Western, anti-U.S., and pro-Communist influences—the very ones the alliance was supposed to vanquish. Bhutto had been a major proponent of independence from the West and had served as foreign minister during Pakistan's 1965 war with India. He learned first-hand the costs of the alliance with America. Bhutto and his colleagues believed that U.S. officials repeatedly reneged on defense commitments that Pakistan had been promised. In governing a deeply troubled and demoralized country after another conflict with India, Bhutto pursued the path of foreign-policy independence. The centerpiece of Bhutto's drive was acquiring the ultimate equalizer against India and the highest level of strategic independence from Washington: an atomic bomb.

Nukes of Hazard: Unstable Pakistan Becomes a Nuclear Power

Islamabad's pursuit of an "Islamic bomb," a nuclear weapon for the Muslim world, directly clashed with Washington's nonproliferation agenda.[91] But the Carter administration's efforts to halt Pakistan's nuclear activities took a backseat after the USSR invaded Afghanistan in 1979. In order to facilitate the infusion of money, propaganda, and other assistance through Pakistan to guerillas fighting the Soviets next door, U.S. presidents of both political parties ignored intelligence that Pakistan was actively pursuing a nuclear weapons program. After the Soviets withdrew from Afghanistan in 1989, Washington declared that it was unable to certify whether Pakistan had a nuclear bomb and cut off economic and military assistance.

Pakistan's flirtation with nuclear weapons had intensified after India conducted its "Smiling Buddha" nuclear tests in May 1974. In response, Bhutto declared famously:

> If India builds the bomb, we will eat grass and leaves
> for a thousand years, even go hungry, but we will get

one of our own. The Christians have the bomb, the Jews have the bomb and now the Hindus have the bomb. Why not the Muslims too have the bomb?[92]

Pakistan's nuclear program arguably began in the mid-1950s under Eisenhower's "Atoms for Peace" program. Officially, however, Bhutto embarked on a nuclear weapons program on January 24, 1972. He summoned hundreds of the Pakistani diaspora's top nuclear physicists and engineers to a secret meeting in Multan to develop an atomic bomb. The project gained momentum in 1975 when European-educated metallurgist Dr. Abdul Qadir (A. Q.) Khan arrived with blueprints for a gas centrifuge uranium enrichment plant he had smuggled from the Netherlands.[93]

It was not long before U.S. officials detected various nuclear efforts. Elected on a plank of nonproliferation, President Jimmy Carter's administration tightened export controls on sensitive items and placed restrictions on arms transfers. These efforts came on top of the Symington Amendment, which Congress passed in June 1976. Named after its chief sponsor, Senator Stuart Symington (D-MO), the amendment to the Foreign Assistance Act of 1961 permitted the cutoff of U.S. economic and military aid to any country importing or exporting unsafeguarded nuclear materials, equipment, or technology.[94] In 1978, Congress added the Glenn Amendment to the 1961 Foreign Assistance Act. Sponsored by Ohio Democratic Senator John Glenn, the amendment prohibited U.S. assistance to any nonnuclear weapon state that detonates a nuclear device.[95] But U.S. officials went beyond legislation regarding restrictions and the cutoff of aid. Carter even mulled forcibly shutting down Islamabad's nuclear program through either sabotage or a commando raid. In May 1978, Bhutto told Saudi Arabia's King Khalid he had "ample proof" Washington was plotting to sabotage Pakistan's nuclear program.[96]

Widespread communal unrest compounded Bhutto's troubles. In Sindh, his PPP endorsed a bill to make Sindhi the province's official language, a move that marginalized ethnic minorities and sparked killings and lootings across the region. In Balochistan, Bhutto tried to destroy traditional tribal practices that challenged central government power, leading him to order the military into the province and fire on citizens. Bhutto's secret paramilitary unit, the Federal Security Force, intimidated political opponents, bugging their telephones and seizing their property. Allegations of massive rigging in the March 1977 national elections further magnified the public's outrage. Moreover, uncontrolled inflation, massive unemployment, and government mismanagement exposed the failures of his Bhutto's intensified, and opposition to him grew inside the military, where many blamed him for undermining Generals Ayub and Yahya and feared he would again sacrifice the country for his pursuit of personal power.

On July 5, 1977, field and junior army officers overthrew Bhutto in a bloodless coup. The coup's main instrument, although not its strategist, was General Zia-ul-Haq, Pakistan's chief of army staff. In the name of restoring domestic tranquility, Pakistan's third military ruler declared martial law (which remained in effect until December 31, 1985), suspended the constitution, and promised elections in three months. General Zia subsequently ordered Bhutto hanged for allegations of murder. While awaiting execution in prison, Bhutto portrayed the legacy he hoped for after his death:

> We know that Israel and South Africa have full nuclear capability. The Christian, Jewish and Hindu civilizations have this capability. The Communist powers also possess it. Only the Islamic civilization was without it, but that position was about to change.[97]

Meanwhile, Washington continued erecting barriers to Pakistan's atomic ambitions. In 1978, Congress passed the Nuclear Nonproliferation Act, forbidding the sale of U.S. uranium fuel to countries that refuse "full-scope," the International Atomic Energy Agency's safeguards, and inspections. On April 6, 1979, upon learning of the uranium enrichment facility in Kahuta, President Carter imposed military and economic sanctions on Pakistan.[98] There would soon be a rapprochement between the estranged allies, however.

Jihad in Afghanistan: Pakistan's Role

In April 1978, a Marxist regime backed by Moscow seized power in Afghanistan. By the spring of 1979, anti-Soviet hard-liners in the Carter administration, along with leaders in Islamabad and Riyadh, called on Carter to back the anti-communist insurgents. There was one important caveat. After Vietnam, the United States was unwilling to commit ground troops. At a March 30 meeting of the Special Coordinating Committee, an interagency body with decisionmaking power across several departments, Walt Slocombe, representing Defense, asked about keeping Afghanistan's insurgency going by "sucking the Soviets into a Vietnamese quagmire." The following month, the committee directed the CIA to develop a plan for giving "small-scale propaganda," "nonlethal material assistance," and "indirect financial assistance to the insurgents."[99] On July 3, almost six months before the Soviet Union's invasion of Afghanistan, the United States began funding the mujahideen through Operation Cyclone, setting the stage for more extensive covert actions once the Red Army moved into the country on Christmas Eve.

Pakistan made the ideal corridor for funneling cash and small arms to anti-Soviet guerillas because of its long, porous border with Afghanistan. Through the Khyber Pass linking the two countries, Pakistan became the rear base for the Afghan rebel resistance. But the large sums of cash necessary for a substantial covert campaign required congressional approval and risked running afoul of congressional restrictions on aid to Pakistan. Carter's National Security Advisor, Zbigniew Brzezinski, advised that Pakistan's support required making the goal of countering Soviet interference a higher priority than nuclear nonproliferation.[100] Despite the considerable information on Pakistan's nuclear program already available, the United States and Pakistan shelved their differences after the Soviets invaded Afghanistan.

The assistance was initially portrayed primarily as help for Pakistan, not a bid to oust the Soviets from Afghanistan. In his address to the nation on January 4, 1980, President Carter declared, "Along with other countries, we will provide military equipment, food, and other assistance to help Pakistan defend its independence and its national security against the seriously increased threat it now faces from the north."[101] The Carter administration allowed military and economic assistance to Pakistan by waiving the Symington sanctions and publicly affirmed U.S. security assurances to Pakistan contained in the 1959 bilateral arrangement against communist military aggression.[102] But on January 9, when Carter offered Pakistan a two-year, $400 million military and economic assistance package, General Zia dismissed the proposal as "peanuts," possibly alluding to Carter's previous vocation as a peanut farmer.[103]

Pakistanis played up concerns that the Soviets would strike them next. The loss of East Bengal made Pakistan fearful of irredentist Afghan leaders stirring up trouble on its western frontier, leaving their country even more vulnerable to Indian attack.[104] Zia desired American F-16s to counter Soviet MiGs. At an emergency session of the Conference of Islamic States on January 29, Pakistan helped crystallize Muslim opposition to the Soviets, demanding all troops immediately withdraw from Afghanistan. Years later, Brzezinski remarked that, despite Zia's dismissal of Washington's initial aid proposal, it was still essential for the United States to aid Pakistan to prevent "the damaging effect of what appeared to be a U.S. unwillingness to treat its commitments seriously."[105] The context of that worry was important. The Soviet Union's invasion of Afghanistan came a month after America's humiliating embassy-hostage crisis in Tehran and just weeks after protesters in Pakistan stormed the U.S. embassy in Islamabad.

Foreign policy became a contentious issue during the 1980 U.S. presidential campaign. In November, Carter's staunchly anti-communist Republican challenger, Ronald Reagan, won the White House. By then, hawkish members of Congress were working to re-start U.S. aid to Pakistan. At a stroke, a marginal U.S. partner barred from military and economic assistance became a pivotal U.S. ally receiving hundreds of millions of dollars in aid. On May 13, 1981, the Senate Foreign Relations Committee passed a six-year waiver to aid restrictions imposed by the Symington and Glenn amendments, authorizing the Reagan administration to proceed in offering Pakistan a five-year, $3.2 billion aid package and the cash sale of 40 F-16 fighters.[106]

The CIA shipped light arms and ammunition to the Inter-Services Intelligence (ISI), Pakistan's main spy agency. Saudi Arabia, a long-time enemy of the godless Soviets and an ally of Islamabad and Washington, matched U.S. aid dollar for dollar. The ISI channeled the aid to the various factions of the Afghan resistance. Under ISI direction, the mujahideen received training in explosives, and the ISI provided fighters with explosives disguised as pens, watches, cigarette lighters, and tape recorders.[107] Because many documents from the era remain classified, it is difficult to determine exactly how much U.S. assistance flowed into the hands of the mujahideen, but according to some estimates, by 1982 Washington was providing Islamabad with $600 million a year in military and economic assistance. During the course of the war, Washington and Riyadh flooded Afghanistan with upwards of $4 billion.[108]

As with Carter's senior planners, top Reagan officials believed the Soviet threat overrode the norms, laws, and institutions against nuclear proliferation. They lifted sanctions, loosened supplier controls on sensitive items, and knowingly aided the export of technology useful for Pakistan's nuclear program. A June 1983 State Department briefing paper reported "unambiguous evidence" that Pakistan was "actively pursuing a nuclear weapons development program."[109] Although the Reagan administration was inclined to look the other way, many in Congress were not. In August 1985, the so-called Pressler Amendment modified the Symington and Glenn amendments by requiring the president to certify annually to Congress that Pakistan did not possess a nuclear device in order to keep the assistance flowing.

Those measures failed to stem the Reagan administration's rapprochement with Islamabad. In late 1985, Pakistan was able to buy U.S.- and European-manufactured military hardware and software that assisted its nuclear program. The CIA had also obtained photos of floor plans and bomb designs from a facility near Islamabad.[110] The CIA and the president were aware that Pakistan had twice successfully cold-tested a nuclear device (a test or computer modeling of a nuclear explosive device with nonnuclear components, i.e., without a fissile core) and that China had likely hot-tested a nuclear device (an actual nuclear explosion) on Pakistan's behalf.[111] According to senior State Department officials who spoke to investigative journalists Adrian Levy and Catherine Scott-Clark, the State Department instructed its embassies in Europe to write "only the mildest diplomatic reproaches" when they discovered a European company assisting Pakistan. So tepid were these démarches—requests for action by a diplomat to a host country—that then assistant secretary of defense Richard Perle called them "démarche-mallows."[112] In October 1986, President Reagan certified that Pakistan had no nuclear bomb.

European and Saudi intelligence notified Washington they suspected Pakistan was siphoning U.S. aid intended for Afghan rebels to fund its nuclear program.[113] ISI Director Lieutenant General Akhtar Abdur Rahman received bags of cash, holding the money at the

Pakistan-controlled Bank of Credit and Commerce International (BCCI), the National Bank of Pakistan, and the Bank of Oman, which was one-third owned by BCCI. Founded by Agha Hasan Abdi, a close confidant of General Zia, the "Bank of Crooks and Criminals International," as one U.S. official quipped, was a "black network" financial supermarket for money laundering, international bribery, terrorism, drug trafficking, and assassination of government officials. [114]

The CIA used BCCI to facilitate funding of the Contras, illegal arms to Iran and Iraq, and the Afghan resistance. Saudi financial support for Pakistan's nuclear program had begun as early as the 1970s and possibly used BCCI as a conduit. The details of BCCI's involvement remain murky, but a 1992 Senate Foreign Relations report found that arms trafficking involving BCCI included the financing of Pakistan's procurement of nuclear weapons. BCCI officials assisted the purchase of nuclear technologies paid for by Pakistani front-companies, and a Pakistani tried to procure BCCI-financed nuclear material through the United States. [115]

Alongside Pakistan's budding nuclear weapons program, changes in Pakistan's internal religious character marked another ominous development. Although Bhutto had started the Pakistani education system down a path of Islamization, General Zia intensified the campaign. He overhauled school textbooks to ensure their ideological purity, while removing books deemed un-Islamic from university libraries. He enacted Islamist ordinances within the court system, encouraged prayer in the barracks, posted an imam in every military unit, and made the five daily prayers compulsory for civil servants. [116]

Pakistan's Islamization both shaped and reflected Afghanistan's. Along the Afghan border, Zia oversaw the proliferation of religious schools madrasahs financed by the Saudi government. They aimed at indoctrinating young war refugees with radical Deobandi and Salafist interpretations of Islam that propagated a militant, anti-Western worldview. [117] General Hamid Gul, head of ISI from 1987 to 1989, argued for religious schools being turned into militarized training camps, creating an Army of God. [118] Zia geared his policies toward combating infidel Soviets and assisting the rise of an Islamic government in Kabul friendly to Islamabad's interests. The ISI directed the bulk of U.S. and Saudi money and weapons to the most radical and intolerant factions of the mujahideen, and the bulk of U.S. supplied arms and aid went to seven Peshawar-based Islamist resistance movements that the ISI favored.

But as U.S. economic and military aid to Pakistan continued, the nuclear issues gained increased prominence. In November 1986, the *Washington Post* reported that U.S. intelligence had found Pakistan was producing weapons-grade uranium.[119] In 1987, after A. Q. Khan inadvertently admitted in an interview that Pakistan had tested a bomb, the CIA uncovered a smuggling ring involving one of Khan's key procurement agents.[120] The State Department had inadvertently facilitated the transfer—granting approvals for high-tech equipment to Pakistan that the Commerce Department had refused to license.[121] Nevertheless, Reagan made his annual Pressler Amendment certification to Congress in December 1986, affirming that Pakistan did not possess a nuclear explosive device.

By October 1989, following the Soviet withdrawal from Afghanistan in February, reports started circulating that President George H. W. Bush could not guarantee another certification in accordance with the Pressler Amendment. In October 1990, U.S. Ambassador to Pakistan Robert Oakley told Islamabad that Washington would institute sanctions. President Bush, according to Brent Scowcroft, then national security adviser, was "genuinely sad" about imposing the Pressler Amendment but felt his hands were tied.[122] To some experts, the termination of covert aid on October 1, 1990, coincided too conveniently with the withdrawal of Soviet forces on February 15, 1989. Some argue that time lags in clandestine intelligence-gathering prevented the Reagan administration from certifying in 1987 that Pakistan had already assembled a nuclear device.[123] Others allege willful blindness on the part of the United States. They say the Pressler Amendment was a tool in waiting, as it contained provisions carefully worded to permit unimpeded funding of the mujahideen but ready for activation when the need no longer existed.[124] Much of the available evidence disputes the more charitable assessments.

Immediately after the Soviets invaded Afghanistan, Pakistan became the linchpin of America's proxy war against the Soviets. Its rugged northwest served as a rear base for the resistance. But the country had assumed grave risks to its security, both by being in a position to provoke a major Soviet reaction against it and by absorbing a disproportionate share of the costs of the culture of drugs, guns, and jihad. The U.S. sanctions shocked and enraged the Pakistani public. Explains Hassan Abbas, who served under

Bhutto's daughter, Benazir Bhutto, and Army General-cum-President Pervez Musharraf:

> What really cut deep and wounded Pakistan was that India, which had introduced nuclear weapons in South Asia, instead of being punished, seemed to be having its efforts rewarded by the United States. To the Pakistanis this was an American betrayal, coming as it did coated with insult.[125]

Pakistan never imagined that the formal end of hostilities in Afghanistan would trigger a total split with Washington. It seemed as though Pakistan had fulfilled its role, and the United States had no further need of it.

The End of an Era, the Beginning of Another

Many in Congress, the media, and the American public vocally supported aiding the Afghan rebels against the Soviets. Often touted as America's most successful covert operation, the anti-Soviet jihad was also the longest, the most expensive, and, given its many negative consequences, arguably the most pyrrhic victory.

Though some have claimed the jihad precipitated the USSR's collapse, weaknesses were embedded within the Soviet system. Russian analyst Pyotr Romanov observed, "The U.S. did not win a Cold War against the USSR. The USSR lost it to the U.S. Decay and inefficiency were genetically programmed into the Communist system. For this reason, its disintegration started at birth."[126] It is debatable whether supporting religious militancy on a grand scale against a decaying regime paid sufficient dividends, especially in light of the many negative unintended outcomes that arose from the conflict. The anti-Soviet jihad facilitated a resurging Islamic fundamentalism in Afghanistan and around the world. Some of the conflict's Arab fighters who helped America defeat the Soviets in Afghanistan later committed the horrendous atrocities of 9/11.

Meanwhile, Pakistan would become one of the world's most dangerous proliferators, both of terrorism and nuclear technology. With the help of elements within the military, A. Q. Khan's "Import-Export" nuclear black-market enterprise exported knowledge and technology on warhead components, bomb-making blueprints, and centrifuge technology to North Korea, Iran, Iraq, and Libya.[127] Former International Atomic Energy Agency head Mohamed ElBaradei described it as equivalent to a nuclear "Wal-Mart." Khan, the father of the country's nuclear bomb, became a national hero. His illicit sale and provision of Pakistan's gas-centrifuge-enrichment technology to an assortment of foreign countries years later led to him being placed under house arrest—making him a scapegoat for a network that many believe involved Pakistan's senior generals.

Billions in aid also subsidized Pakistan's Islamization. General Zia propagated militancy, constructed jihadist training camps, and housed thousands of religious schools. As conduits to the Afghan resistance, Pakistan's security establishment turned into what Benazir Bhutto described as "Frankenstein's monster": the military and ISI came to identify with the extremists with whom they were dealing.[128] After the jihad, liberal and religious officers alike believed only jihadists could bog down India and achieve Pakistan's ambitions in the region and around the world.[129] Over the phone to President Reagan, General Zia conveyed that Pakistan had no intention of ceasing assistance to the mujahideen even after the April 1988 Geneva Accords ratified the official terms of Soviet withdrawal. On August 17, 1988, General Zia, former ISI head Rahman, U.S. Ambassador Arnold Raphael, and 27 others died when their C-130 transport plane nose-dived shortly after takeoff from the airport in Bahawalpur and exploded on impact. The crash was widely alleged as sabotage, with fingers pointed at every conceivable capital, including Islamabad.

The end of the jihadi era helped to complete the Islamic Republic's turn away from the West, which was exactly what Pakistani sympathizers with Soviet and Chinese communism had wanted. They sought to generate anti-U.S. sentiment and hate for those who spoke for America. After the Cold War, the United States encountered a radical and militantly nationalistic regime.

A Perpetually Flawed U.S. Policy

Inadvertently, the pursuit of America's Cold War objectives in South Asia pandered to Pakistan's worst military, political, economic, and ideological tendencies. Time and again, these policies pushed Pakistan and South Asia to the edge of disaster. From president to president, the U.S.-Pakistan alliance swung between periods of mutual accommodation (under Eisenhower, Nixon, and Reagan), to times of strain and mutual hostility (under Kennedy, Johnson, Carter, and Bush I). Relations were not solely tied to the leaders themselves but were a reflection of the two countries' sharply divergent interests and expectations.

Washington's early Cold War objectives for Pakistan included its increased identification with the free world community, its ability to help defend the free world, and a sound and developed economy. U.S. policies would achieve none of those objectives. U.S. analysts and officials initiated a vast program of arms packages and regional security projects, but the concepts on which they based their policies were fundamentally flawed. Elites benefited while the newly born state grew an excessive military desperate for yet more external assistance. By the early 1960s, when armaments became part of diplomacy and not strictly a military issue, they became accelerants to war. Too few in Washington rigorously appraised the long-term impact of simultaneous U.S. aid to India and Pakistan or asked whether partnering with one would contradict stated policies with the other.

Pakistan moved toward China's orbit and used American weapons to attack India in 1965 and crush its own citizens in 1971. Finally, after the anti-Soviet jihad achieved victory in Afghanistan, Washington slapped Islamabad with sanctions. Animosities festered within the now nuclear-armed, internationally ostracized country, which then used its nuclear know-how, as well as the legions of Islamic militants America helped spawn, to expand its influence across the region.

The volatile Cold War partnership certainly helped shape Pakistan's reluctance to cooperate fully with the United States under Presidents Clinton, Bush II, and Barack Obama, but, over the decades, Pakistan's self-image as a victim state has become a popular and powerful narrative at home. Pakistani civilians came to view American aid as enlarging the role of its military, while the military came to see America as unreliable for its on-again, off-again aid. While partly correct, this narrative ignores how senior Pakistani military officers and prominent civilian politicians used the Washington connection to strengthen Pakistan's position against India and advance their own self-interests. Policies that America and Pakistan pursued jointly amplified weaknesses built into the Islamic Republic's structure. Their alliance proved an unhealthy symbiosis and produced one of the post-9/11 world's most dreadful outcomes: a nuclear-armed, highly militarized country that is increasingly radical, prone to take dangerous risks, and distrustful of the United States.

5. Cold War to Holy War: The U.S.-Saudi Alliance

The Kingdom of Saudi Arabia's possession of the largest oil reserves in the world made it a highly valued U.S. Cold War ally. Senior policy planners, diplomatic officials, and defense and intelligence specialists deemed the industrial world's access to Saudi crude a vital national interest. That determination led to calls for establishing U.S. military predominance in the Persian Gulf. The means to secure U.S. ascendance involved acts of aggression, intervention, and subversion against prospective regional foes. Additionally, above the Arab kingdom's oil-rich sands lay the Islamic holy sites of Mecca and Medina. That powerful spiritual position in the Muslim world inspired top U.S. officials to forge a Christian-Islamic moral alliance with the Saudi royal family against pan-Arab socialists, secular nationalists, and godless Soviet communists.

For pragmatic reasons, Washington reluctantly accepted Riyadh's austere social dictates, many at odds with America's core foundational principles and basic standards of human rights. Saudi Arabia's absolute monarchy banned free speech, competitive elections, and political parties. It propagated a ferocious intolerance of Jews, prohibited the public mixing of unmarried women and men, and in a disturbing throwback to the Middle Ages, beheaded apostates, adulterers, drug traffickers, and homosexuals in public. The Saudi government enforced the public's observance not just to Islam, but to an ultra-conservative derivation called Wahhabism (Salafism by its adherents). Throughout the Islamic world, the kingdom exported its literalist interpretation of Islam, pouring its oil wealth into a network of religious schools, Islamic missionaries, and charitable organizations of global reach. Successive American administrations proved enthusiastic backers of Riyadh's influence, even as a viciously intolerant religious ideology rivaled oil as Saudi Arabia's chief export.

The U.S.-Saudi alliance's anti-nationalist, anti-communist crusade produced a decidedly mixed record. Reasonably encouraging short-term gains gave way to disastrously terrifying results in the long run. Few officials could have predicted the partnership's most grim and far-reaching consequences: the birth of al Qaeda, the spread of the radical Muslim Brotherhood, and the growth of a fanatical ideology that justified indiscriminate killing and mass murder. The U.S.-Saudi alliance, one of the world's most enduring, complex, and less publicized partnerships, not only extended U.S. security and political cover to an oppressive, reactionary theocracy, but also nurtured that theocracy's diffusion of malignant ideas and movements that continue to infect the world today.

Oil Diplomacy, Corporate Diplomacy

Before the Kingdom of Saudi Arabia evolved into the commercially sophisticated and oil-rich monarchy of today, its rickety fiefdom soared, collapsed, and reemerged through religious proselytizing and military conquest. That struggle for survival, rather than the desert kingdom's seeming intolerance for modernity, drove its alliance with the West. In mid-18th-century Najd, the Arabian Peninsula's central region, Islamic theologian Muhammad Ibn Abd al-Wahhab spearheaded a movement to expunge his religion of practices and innovations arising after Allah's revelations to the Prophet Mohammed in the 7th century.[1]

Abd al-Wahhab made defiance to authority punishable by death, while preaching the virtues of social harmony. He denounced usury, saint worship, and inattention to prayer, while instructing how to properly shake hands, embrace, and laugh, among other social and personal behaviors. After a local village chieftain expelled Abd al-Wahhab for his radical teachings, he fled to al-Diriya, a town on the outskirts of modern Riyadh, where he came under the protection of local emir Muhammad Ibn Al-Saud, the forefather of the Saudi royal family, the House of Saud.[2] In 1744, with Abd al-Wahhab's desire to spread his puritanical teachings and Al-Saud's need to subdue Bedouin tribes, they formed a religious-political alliance and expanded their geographic dominion by the sword of *jihad* (struggle for the faith of Islam). Their spiritual-warrior followers called themselves Unitarians (*muwahiddun*), but outsiders called them Wahhabists.

Over the centuries, that alliance seized, lost, and recaptured vast stretches of the Arabian Peninsula under the Turkicized Islam of

Ottoman rule. By the early 1920s, in a conquest that totaled 40,000 executions and 350,000 amputations, King Ibn Saud[3] and his estimated 50,000-strong religious army (*Ikhwan*) took al-Hejaz, the Red Sea emirate holding Islam's holiest cities of Mecca, toward which pious Muslims turn to pray, and Medina, burial site of the Prophet Muhammad. On September 23, 1932, after putting down revolts from his elite but unruly *Ikhwan* and consulting the region's tribal sheikhs and theologians, King Ibn Saud unified the state, with Wahhabism as its legal and constitutional basis.

The newly formed kingdom's messianic zeal failed to preclude its orientation toward the West. A key reason was that the West provided the capital-intensive tools and open markets necessary for Saudi Arabia to tap its oil wealth effectively. In May 1933, King Ibn Saud granted Standard Oil Company of California (Socal, later Chevron) an exclusive, 60-year concession to explore and extract his country's petroleum in return for a percentage of profits.[4] By 1938, the oil consortium later known as the Arabian-American Oil Company (Aramco)—comprised of Socal, Standard Oil Company of New Jersey (Standard Oil, later Exxon), Mobil, and Texaco—discovered vast petroleum deposits.

After 1941, when Saudi oil fields began pumping commercial quantities for export, the revenue eventually allowed Al Saud kings and crown princes, serving as top officials, provincial governors, and heads of ministerial agencies, to build their country into a centralized, administrative-bureaucratic state. The Saudis were zealous about protecting their national culture, even as they accepted foreign technology. For instance, the contract with Socal contained an "anti-imperial" clause, which prohibited company influence on Saudi policies.[5] Former U.S. Ambassador to Saudi Arabia Chas W. Freeman Jr. clarifies how the Saudis barred Euro-American intrusions:

> When Westerners finally gained access to the Kingdom of Saudi Arabia, it was under contract as 'hired help,' not as conquerors. Americans and Europeans were able to enter the Kingdom only so long as they evinced respect for Saudi religious and social tradition and accepted that any attempt to propagate Western religious, ideological, or secular values would result in summary punishment and/or deportation.[6]

To appease those in society who resisted an oil industry run by infidel expatriates, and modern innovations like planes, automobiles, telegraphs, and radios, the king consulted a body of religious scholars (*ulema*), who adjudicated disputes, issued official religious-legal rulings (*fatwas*), and ensured the observance of Wahhabism.[7]

To contest rival sheikhs and emirs in the Gulf, King Ibn Saud needed foreign assistance. The British Empire, which had colonies in Kuwait, Qatar, Bahrain, Oman, and the Indian subcontinent and protectorates over Iran, Iraq, and Anglo-Egyptian Sudan, helped Saudi Arabia seize al-Hejaz from the Hashemites, the future rulers of Iraq and Transjordan. But British imperial planners encroached on Ibn Saud's sphere of influence in the southern Arabian Peninsula and catapulted the Hashemites to the forefront of Arab leadership. The king began to consider America as the foreign power with which to align for his country's security.[8] Recalls former U.S. Ambassador to Saudi Arabia Parker T. Hart, one reason Ibn Saud gave for turning to America, "you are very far away!"[9]

By World War II, when Saudi territory provided the allies an air route for sending troops and supplies to the India-Burma Theater, oil company representatives and top U.S. officials urged President Franklin D. Roosevelt to expand that nascent cooperation to safeguard U.S. petroleum interests. James A. Moffett, a friend of Roosevelt's, a petroleum adviser to the White House, and acting in the interest of California-Arabian Standard Oil Company, advocated U.S. aid to Ibn Saud by stressing the king's dwindling resources and the specter of Britain monopolizing postwar oil concessions. W. S. S. Rodgers, the chairman of Texaco, circulated a memorandum to the U.S. Secretaries of War, Navy, and Interior, emphasizing Washington's long-term need for an abundant supply of petroleum.[10] Harold Ickes, petroleum administrator for war and secretary of the interior, insisted that oil was too vital a commodity to leave in private hands.[11]

In 1943, Roosevelt instructed Lend-Lease administrator and U.S. steel mogul Edward R. Stettinius Jr. to make the Saudi government eligible for wartime aid. Under Executive Order No. 8926, which laid the groundwork for a broader alliance and decades of U.S.-Middle East policy, Roosevelt's directive read succinctly: "I hereby find that the defense of Saudi Arabia is vital to the defense of the United States."[12]

On February 14, 1945, in one of history's most iconic moments, President Roosevelt met King Ibn Saud aboard the USS *Quincy* on the Great Bitter Lake in the Suez Canal. The countries date their "special relationship" to this personal meeting, but aside from discussing the question of Palestine, nobody knows if they talked about oil.[13] Afterward, the U.S. and Saudi foreign policy establishments entered a formal military alliance, and Washington pledged to protect Riyadh from prospective enemies in order to secure the industrial world's uninterrupted access to Saudi crude. State Department Near Eastern Affairs Division Chief Gordon Merriam called Saudi oil "a stupendous source of strategic power, and one of the greatest material prizes in world history."[14] That tacit oil-for-security partnership underpinned over half a century of sustained global economic growth. It also made U.S. energy and national security policies inextricably entwined.

More expansive policies with the kingdom began under Roosevelt's successor, President Harry S. Truman. His newly formed Central Intelligence Agency (CIA) determined in October 1947 that denying "a major, hostile, expansionist power" control of the Persian Gulf was as essential as maintaining, "access to the oil of the Persian Gulf area."[15] Equating access to oil with control of it, officials rationalized sheltering Saudi Arabia under the U.S. security umbrella. At U.S.-taxpayer expense the previous year, officials had helped the Saudis complete an enormous military and commercial airfield in Dhahran on the kingdom's eastern coast. The undersecretary of the navy believed that "the mere existence of an American military airfield at Dhahran would contribute to the preservation of the political integrity of Saudi Arabia and to the maintenance of our interest in the oil fields."[16]

Dhahran airbase not only placed Saudi Arabia's oil "in American hands," but also enabled the United States to deploy, base, and operate on Saudi soil for other international projects. Dhahran shortened America's route to the Pacific, as the only base under U.S. Army control between Libya and Pakistan. It also allowed refueling on long-haul air operations for the nuclear-armed, long-range bomber force, the Strategic Air Command. Saudi territory became a springboard for the projection of U.S. military power in and beyond the Persian Gulf. The Saudi connection improved America's "world-wide strategic position," wrote Secretary of Defense James Forrestal.[17]

With Saudi Arabia incorporated into America's globe-girdling series of military outposts, top U.S. decisionmakers and leading thinkers steered America's Middle East policy in a direction favorable to oil interests. Many political leaders, academics, and federal and state judges believed America's largest corporations could not act independent of social considerations. Corporations acted as "arms of the state" and constituted forms of "private government."[18]

The Petroleum Reserves Corporation, a U.S.-government entity tasked with acquiring petroleum outside the continental United States, provided the California-based engineering company Bechtel nearly $135 million to construct an oil pipeline for oil consortium Aramco known as the Trans-Arabian Pipeline (Tapline). From the Persian Gulf to the Eastern Mediterranean, Tapline would send oil to markets in Western Europe for its postwar economic recovery. Alas, President Shukri Quwatly of Syria refused Aramco the right of way through his territory. Oil company executives began giving Damascus ultimatums, upsetting King Ibn Saud's anti-imperialist sensibilities.[19]

U.S. officials saw the refusal of Arab leaders to see things America's way "as ample reason and justification for us to overthrow them—or rather, to enable their own people to overthrow them," wrote Miles Copeland, the CIA station chief in Damascus.[20] With the CIA's discreet backing, Syrian Army Chief Husni al-Zaim—"the Americans' boy," as Copeland put it—overthrew President Quwatly in March 1949.[21] Al-Zaim promptly completed several oil deals with U.S. and British companies. By December, after Syrian army officers ousted and executed al-Zaim, pro-American Army Colonel Adib Shishakli restored Western influence. The State Department explained that nothing would interfere with relations between Saudi Arabia and Aramco because, "this relationship was the basis for the harmony between this government and the Arabian government."[22] By December 1950, Tapline was complete.

Along with bringing the kingdom's massive energy resources to Western markets, President Truman opened another facet of the partnership in autumn 1950. In a letter to King Ibn Saud, Truman called their countries "comrades in arms" opposing "the godless forces of Communism . . . endeavoring to destroy freedom throughout the world." The following year, from the CIA's vantage point, threats to Saudi royalists and other pro-Western regimes emerged from both "Communist pressure" and "the anti-Western national-ism of Iran and the Arab world."[23] Officials hoped the Saudi king, as the guardian of the holy places of Islam, could rally Muslims be-hind America's anti-Communist cause and strengthen Washington's standing across the Islamic World. In a meeting with representatives from the CIA, State, and Defense, one official raised the idea of pro-moting King Ibn Saud as a "Moslem Billy Graham."[24] As the "head of the puritanical Wahhabi movement to restore the pure faith and practices of Islam"—wrote William A. Eddy, the U.S. consul general in Dhahran, in a June 1951 letter—the monarch was "the most repre-sentative and influential Muslim in the world today."[25]

That year, in addition to a mutual-defense-assistance pact supply-ing the kingdom with American weapons, permitting "show-the-flag" military visits, and stationing U.S. technical personnel on Saudi soil, Washington showed a genuine interest in forging a moral alli-ance with the kingdom. Eddy described the strategy as "the Chris-tian democratic West joining with the Muslim world in a common moral front against Communism." Although presidents Roosevelt and Truman laid the economic and security foundations of the part-nership, their successors would progressively expand the alliance's moral and ideological dimension.

Into the Vortex: The "Arab Cold War"

Amid its competition with Moscow, the White House worked with the House of Saud to influence Muslim public opinion. The Psychological Strategy Board, a Truman-era creation later renamed the Operations Coordinating Board, headed most of Washington's propaganda activities in the Islamic world. One of its programs, ad-opted by President Dwight D. Eisenhower but planned under his predecessor, stressed the pervading influence of faith on Arab think-ing. The board's psychological operations expert, Edward P. Lilly, wrote "The Religious Factor," a memorandum in early 1953 that called on Washington to use the power of religion more explicitly.[26] Beyond extending the short-term lease on Dhahran that June and pledging a U.S. Military and Training Mission to advise and assist the kingdom's military, U.S. officials devised a variety of ways to work with the Saudis and mold Muslim minds in support of anti-Soviet policies.[27]

Geopolitics makes for strange bedfellows, with Washington's psychological activities putting it in league with one of the 20th century's most influential pan-Islamist movements—the Muslim Brotherhood. Hassan al-Banna (1905–1949), the Egyptian schoolteacher and imam who founded the transnational religious society in 1928, studied under Muhammad Rashid Rida (1865–1935), a religious reformer influenced by Saudi-Wahhabist doctrine.[28] Al-Banna's anti-secular movement believed in defending Islam through political activism and advocated a system of Islamic republics spanning the global Muslim community (*ummah*). By the late 1940s, al-Banna had regular meetings with diplomat Hermann Eilts, who would later become the U.S. ambassador to Saudi Arabia.[29] Officials continued that ardent courting at the White House.

In the Oval Office on September 23, 1953, President Eisenhower met Said Ramadan, the Muslim Brotherhood's chief international organizer and the son-in-law of its founder.[30] Ramadan had established Muslim Brotherhood branches in Jerusalem, Damascus, and Amman, spreading the movement's dogmatic interpretation of Islam through schools, student groups, professional associations, and propaganda. For *El Musliman,* a monthly magazine of Islamic law and culture where Ramadan was editor-in-chief, subscribers ranged "from Tunisia to Indonesia," gushed U.S. Ambassador to Egypt Jefferson Caffery. Ramadan later offered to distribute *Arabic Review,* run by a CIA front organization in Munich, throughout the Arabic speaking world.[31]

The U.S. Library of Congress, Princeton University, and the International Information Administration at the State Department hosted a 10-day colloquium that brought Ramadan and over 50 other leading Islamic intellectuals to Washington. As U.S. officials stated, the colloquium aimed at giving "impetus and direction . . . to the Renaissance movement within Islam itself" and furthering "good will and mutual understanding between Islamic peoples and the United States."[32] Oil consortium Aramco defrayed some of the travel costs for Muslim Brotherhood members to attend.[33]

Although officials hoped to rally the Muslim Brotherhood against communism, another fear that America's North Atlantic Treaty Organization (NATO) allies expressed emanated from "rising Arab nationalism, fanned by extremists in the Arab states." As in Asia, Latin America, and elsewhere around the world, the Middle East's "anti-imperialist" movements unnerved U.S. officials, who viewed such up-risings as fertile ground for Soviet-inspired communism. [34] Indeed, a nationalist uprising in Egypt, the Arab world's most populous state, birthed a secular, nationalist regime headed by Colonel Gamal Abdel Nasser, who eventually became Saudi Arabia's most pressing security threat and Washington's biggest headache in the Near East.

The charismatic Nasser rode a wave of populist sentiment to expel Britain's colonial presence. After King Ibn Saud's death in November 1953, his profligate heir, King Saud,[35] aligned with Nasser. The Saudi monarch, guided primarily by Arab geopolitics, chan-neled money from U.S. oil companies to sponsor Nasser's propa-ganda campaigns against Bahrain and rival Hashemites in Iraq and Jordan.[36] As for Washington, the CIA initially helped propel Nasser to power in the hope of harnessing his sway over the Arab masses. That strategy backfired quickly when he publicly ridiculed U.S.-sponsored regional security arrangements like the 1955 Baghdad Pact, which comprised Britain, Turkey, Iraq, Iran, and Pakistan. U.S. officials would not only come to shun Arab secularists like Nasser, but also to embrace the Saudis, the Muslim Brotherhood, and other conservative monarchs and extreme religious movements.

No Jews Allowed

Straining otherwise solid U.S.-Saudi relations were controversies over Israel, or more specifically, Saudi Arabia's extreme hostility not only to Israel but to Jews generally. That hostility split U.S.–Middle East policy into separate pro-Israel and pro-Arab camps. After World War II and the tragedy of the Holocaust, many Americans deeply sympathized with the plight of European Jewry. Pro-Israel Ameri-can gentiles admired the Jewish people's quest for statehood and Evangelical Christians supported Jewish migration to Palestine as a fulfillment of Biblical prophecy.[37] As early as 1944, the Republican and Democratic Parties adopted pro-Zionist planks. Accordingly, the American people and their elected officials supported the United Na-tions (UN) partition of Palestine into separate Jewish and Arab states.

In sharp contrast, America's diplomatic, intelligence, and defense communities did not. They strongly advised against U.S. support for Palestine's partition.[38] Senior policy planners concluded that the suffering of Palestinian refugees, and the impression that America protected Zionists, would encourage Arab states to retaliate by either limiting Western access to the region or cultivating ties with the Soviets. The Joint Chiefs of Staff urged no action occur that would orient Arabs away from the West.[39] But as a result of Washington's sponsorship of the UN partition plan of November 1947, a report by the State Department's policy planning staff remarked, "U.S. prestige in the Moslem world has suffered a severe blow and U.S. strategic interests in the Mediterranean and the Near East have been seriously prejudiced."[40]

The divergence between American public sympathies and elite strategic consensus created a duality in the shaping of U.S. statecraft in the Middle East broadly, and toward Saudi Arabia specifically. Riyadh's anti-Israel policies punctuated the partnership with a pattern of highly public controversies. For instance, provisions in the Dhahran airbase lease agreement allowed the Arab kingdom to deny transit to Israelis, people of Jewish descent, and visitors with an Israeli-stamped passport. Those provisions affected diplomats, service members, reporters, lawmakers, business leaders, and tourists. Although U.S. officials never formally approved such discriminatory practices, they submitted detailed lists of names, identities, and religious affiliations of U.S. personnel assigned to the kingdom—enabling Riyadh to exclude whomever it wished. President Eisenhower reflected on the matter years later:

> It cannot be denied that many of the Arab actions, irritating to the Israelis, seemed to be inspired by nothing more than hatred of every Jew, merely because he was a Jew. In our government's negotiations for landing rights in Saudi Arabia for American military personnel, one of the conditions imposed by the Saudi government was that no Jew would be allowed on the field.[41]

In early February 1956, during negotiations for America's renewal of Dhahran's lease, Secretary of State John Foster Dulles told the Senate Foreign Relations Committee, "We don't like to acquiesce, but we have to recognize that Saudi Arabia is an ally."[42] Acquiesce administration leaders did, leading to an anemic Senate resolution in July implicitly criticizing Riyadh's practices. That resolution stated that any attempt by foreign nations to discriminate against American citizens based on their individual religious affiliations was generally "inconsistent with our principles."[43]

That feeble condemnation tempered neither the American public's lingering animosities toward the Saudi regime, nor the Saudi regime's hatred of Israel. When UN Secretary General Dag Hammarskjöld invited King Saud to address the General Assembly the following year, New York City Mayor Robert Wagner announced he would not turn on a single traffic light to help "this monkey."[44] Additionally, King Saud derided as a provocation against Muslims when an Israeli company, chartering a U.S. tanker, proceeded through the international waterway Gulf of Aqaba, which he considered an Arab possession.[45]

To some extent, Saudi intolerance regarding Israel (and Jewish people in any locale) reflected its generally illiberal internal disposition. The regime enforced its rigid Wahhabi religious precepts and social behaviors through government-subsided morality police, the *mutawwa'in*, known by their Orwellian title, Committee for the Propagation of Virtue and the Prevention of Vice. These semiautonomous, ultra-conservative zealots inflicted daily human suffering and misery.[46] They harassed, intimidated, abused, and detained citizens and foreigners alike. Yet, for the White House, the oil-for-security partnership trumped American pluralism and basic human rights. Even as the United States professed to stand by the highest of principles, it applied a very different standard to suit its instrumental objectives in countering Arab nationalists. When it came to the Saudi totalitarian theocracy's systemic repression, both U.S. rhetoric and practices regarding human rights took a back seat.

Masters vs. Subjects

Eisenhower administration officials, like Truman's, also suggested grooming the Saudi king as an Arab leader and a religious rival to Nasser. A CIA survey of Radio Cairo's reception discovered that all parts of the Arab world, from Iraq to Morocco, heard Nasser's propaganda promoting the mythology of pan-Arab nationalism through his popular broadcast "Voice of the Arabs."[47] By March 1956, President Eisenhower grew concerned over what he called "the growing ambition of Nasser" and "his belief that he can emerge as the true leader of the entire Arab World."[48] Regardless of Nasser's motives, U.S. officials believed he abetted Soviet penetration of the Near East. In covert plan Project Omega, senior CIA officials and representatives from State and Defense sought to reduce Nasser's influence, counter Soviet arms deals to Arab states, and strengthen pro-Western regimes in Jordan, Lebanon, and Saudi Arabia. Meanwhile, Washington and London worked to subvert nationalists who largely resisted cooperation, coercion, and control by the West.[49] From Iran and Egypt to Syria and Jordan, Washington and London utilized political assassinations, violent covert action, and other cloak-and-dagger operations to bend to Western interests the region's organic process of political emancipation.

The Anglo-American allies differed, however, over how to counter Nasser and the Arab secular nationalists. Those diverging views came to a head with the Suez Canal Crisis, a flashpoint that cemented Washington's long-standing commitment to the region's conservative, oil-rich monarchies. The crisis also brought into sharper focus the so-called "Arab Cold War," the intraregional divide that pitted Saudi Arabia and other Western-backed guardians of the status quo against Egypt and other Soviet-backed secular-nationalist regimes.[50]

In late October 1956, Israel invaded Egypt, and that move was followed in early November with bombings from Britain and France. President Eisenhower—shocked by allied hostilities he thought reeked of 19th-century imperialism—promptly pulled support for the British pound, refused oil deliveries to France, and threatened to back UN sanctions against Israel. The Suez crisis devolved into a political catastrophe and irrevocably damaged the image of Britain and France as world powers. In response to the willingness to confront Israel and Washington's own NATO allies, America's status across the region skyrocketed.[51]

For merely withstanding the Israeli-British-French-"Zionist-Crusader" invasion, Nasser ascended to regional and global prominence. In the decade after Suez, pro-Nasserite parties sprouted in Lebanon, Syria, Jordan, Iraq, and Arab states in the Gulf, as his pan-Arab nationalism and Arab socialism emerged as the mainstream of Arab geopolitics for nearly a generation.[52] Nasser preached defiance to the forces that attacked him in Suez and denounced as subservient puppets, reactionary rulers, and tools of "imperialist interests" neighboring states that remained tied to them. Most importantly, the fiery-tongued ruler poured out his scorn on Saudi Arabia. He castigated the kingdom as "occupied" by foreign troops, called Dhahran airbase a concession to American imperialism, and admonished the royal family for hoarding oil wealth from its destitute Arab neighbors.[53]

With Nasser's blend of anti-Western and anti-royalist attitudes appealing to Arabs living under pro-Western monarchs, the Eisenhower administration decided to fill the void left by its defeated NATO allies. On January 5, 1957, in the annual State of the Union Address, President Eisenhower requested the authority to send America's military forces to repel "overt armed aggression from any country controlled by International Communism" in the Middle East. As he explained, that region "contains about two thirds of the presently known oil deposits of the world." Many nations depended on that petroleum.[54]

King Saud, during his first visit to Washington that month, threw his full support behind Eisenhower. They signed a five-year renewal of America's lease at Dhahran airbase, and King Saud pursued rapprochement with Iraq and Jordan. He signed a communiqué on the need to stand against all "communist activities" and launched a propaganda campaign against "world communism." Washington agreed to pay, train, and expand Saudi Arabia's army, provide the kingdom with $25 million in loans, and supply its military with ground vehicles, aircraft, and naval equipment.[55] On March 9, Congress passed a joint resolution that became known as the Eisenhower Doctrine. It gave the executive branch the authority to wage war in defense of America's Middle East allies. Meanwhile, as America emerged as the primary source of the kingdom's security, U.S. officials worked more aggressively with Islamic leaders to oppose what President Eisenhower described as "the implacable enmity of godless communism."[56]

Amid the Red scare that gripped Washington, Hollywood, and much of America during this time, high-ranking officials regarded such measures as appropriate, particularly given the few Muslim communities Washington could tap into compared to the estimated 30 million Muslim citizens living under the Bolsheviks. As the head of a Western, predominantly Christian nation, Eisenhower authorized half a million dollars to refurbish Mecca.[57] An Ad Hoc Working Group on Islam, under the propaganda activities of the Operations

Coordinating Board, developed an "Outline Plan of Operations" calling for Washington to side with "reform" groups like the Muslim Brotherhood. "The President said he thought we should do everything possible to stress the 'holy war' aspect," detailed the memorandum of a meeting with Eisenhower, the Joint Chiefs of Staff, and CIA covert operations czar Frank Wisner. According to a later estimate by CIA Director William Colby, up to half of the CIA's budget at the time went to propaganda, political action, and paramilitary operations.[58] Additionally, of the more than $100 million the spy agency spent on anti-Nasser operations, some ended up in the hands of the Muslim Brotherhood, according to defense intelligence officer, CIA adviser, and military attaché Wilbur Crane Eveland.[59]

In its quest to counter Arab states allegedly "manipulated by International Communism," Washington embraced the misbegotten inheritance of European imperialism, placing a bulls-eye on the kingdom's enemies and eventually exacerbating the nationalist sentiments it sought to contest. After numerous botched U.S. and British coups against Arab nationalists in Cairo and Damascus, the Egyptian and Syrian governments merged into the United Arab Republic (UAR) in February 1958. In response, second cousins King Faisal II of Iraq and King Hussein of Jordan formed the Arab Federation, alternatively known as the Arab Union. That alliance proved short-lived.

In what would prove to be a prescient statement of the post-9/11 world, U.S. officials at the time, including State Department Near Eastern Affairs Director Stuart W. Rockwell, supported Faisal, but conceded, "there are disadvantages to a close identification of the United States with the regional and internal political policies of the Arab Union and its component governments."[60] That appraisal, albeit accurate, still amounted to a serious underestimation of the complex environment in which America operated. U.S. foreign policy planners were not chiefly responsible for the Middle East's severe political and socioeconomic dysfunction; however, Washington's generous support to the region's repressive tyrants constituted an artificial prop that kept unrepresentative leaders in power. Arab subjects who opposed Western-backed autocrats thus came to view the West as a major impediment to their economic development and political self-determination. For decades, that prominent feature of America's engagement with the Middle East would feed ever-growing, increasingly rabid anti-American sentiment.

Concerns over petroleum supplies and communist machinations, however, precluded a change of course. The intractability of policy resigned even the most cognizant officials to callous indifference. Backing treacherous tyrants naturally muted calls for reform and standing for America's higher purpose. "Popularity," wrote Rockwell, "in itself in this part of the world is not necessarily an essential element for the survival of a government." That attitude, intuitively appealing to some experts, implied that people of the region willingly submitted to undisputed rulers—that somehow, capitulation to despotism was part of Arab self-identity. That monolithic view rationalized abusive practices and rigid social and political structures. It also allowed U.S. officials to blame dynamics beyond their control, exempting their official support for dictators who deprived their subjects of Western-style freedoms.

On July 14, 1958, after years of the CIA blanketing Iraq with pro-Western propaganda and bribing its "mildly pinkish" leaders to accept anti-Soviet alliances, a band of pro-Nasserite army officers seized control in Baghdad. They acquired documents confirming the previous leadership's schemes for U.S. subversion against Syria, the Baghdad Pact's secret military plans, and at least $45 million worth of U.S. military assistance. President Eisenhower relayed the next day that many of the deposed monarchy's leading personalities "were beaten to death or hanged and their bodies dragged through the streets."[61] Iraq's brutal revolution and the collapse of the Baghdad Pact's key regional power sent shockwaves across the region and alarmed the Saudi royal family.

"What is the use of all these pacts?" exclaimed King Saud's personal emissary on America's failure to intervene.[62] CIA Director Allen Dulles stopped short of saying the Soviets would get directly involved, but nevertheless cast Iraq's military coup in terms of the prevailing domino theory, warning that the events in Baghdad threatened to doom pro-West governments in Lebanon, Jordan, and Saudi Arabia. British soldiers deployed to Jordan to save that country's monarch. Eisenhower dispatched 6,000 marines and 2,500 army personnel to secure the territorial integrity and political independence of Lebanon in Operation Blue Bat within 72 hours of Baghdad's fall.[63]

Whatever the cause of Lebanon's unrest, the injection of Western forces provoked anger in much of the Arab world. "The United States seems to have become anathema to the region," President

Eisenhower observed on July 23. Though he wanted to get "to the point where the Arabs will not be hostile to us," Western actions, especially the military interventions, vindicated that hostility.[64] U.S. officials pledged to protect repressive regimes, like Saudi Arabia, and absorb the military and political risks of doing so. Additionally, waning European colonialism and the growth of nationalist uprisings against it put American leaders in an anomalous position. Indeed, Eisenhower remained sensitive to the impression that America stood as a beacon of hope even to anti-colonial, Third World Elements:

> Among all the powerful nations of the world the United States is the only one with a tradition of anti-colonialism. . . . The standing of the United States as the most powerful of the anti-colonial powers is an asset of incalculable value to the Free World.[65]

U.S. officials may have supported self-determination in principle, but global strategy and tactics pushed against such abstractions. While America's values accorded with the postcolonial struggle for freedom, tough questions surrounded how best to achieve that goal. After all, despite Eisenhower's firm stance during Suez—or perhaps even because of it—Nasser's sway over the Arab masses made him increasingly resistant to Western appeals for moderation.

Weeks after America's intervention in Lebanon, the National Security Council Planning Board advised that "We must adjust to the tide of Arab nationalism, and must do so before the hotheads get control in every country."[66] Eisenhower's successor adopted that approach, but unnecessarily ensnared his administration in another intra-Arab conflict.

The Arab Cold War Heats Up

As with India's Jawaharlal Nehru, Ghana's Kwame Nkrumah, and other Third World neutrals, President John F. Kennedy wanted "a reasonably balanced policy" with Nasser to counterbalance communism.[67] His olive branch cast a noticeable chill over Washington's relations with Riyadh, especially as Kennedy championed in his May 1961 message to Congress the importance of social progress and "economic reform and development," chiding foreign

governments unwilling to change with the times.[68] He argued that
U.S. arms and aid alone could not stabilize reactionary regimes, an
oblique reference to Saudi Arabia, which still had a thriving slave
trade and remained far from social progress. That month, Riyadh
informed Washington that it would terminate the lease on Dhahran
upon its expiration the following June.[69] Relations between President Kennedy and King Saud also grew chilly after they exchanged
personal slights in written correspondence. But as Washington's ties
with Cairo improved, including the distribution of U.S. agricultural
commodities to Egypt, the toppling of another conservative Arab
monarch derailed Kennedy's fragile détente with Nasser and swung
U.S. support back to Saudi Arabia.

On September 19, 1962, in Sana'a, Yemen's capital, pro-Nasserite
military officers overthrew the newly installed imam and established the Yemen Arab Republic. The fourth military coup d'état
in the Arab world—Egypt, Syria, Iraq, and now Yemen—horrified
the Saudis. Yemen's closed society bordered Saudi Arabia's to the
south, and its religious, yet corrupted, feudal royal family also ruled
a scattered population susceptible to Arab nationalist propaganda.
Riyadh pumped money and weapons to Yemen's deposed royalists
and tribal sheikhs, and by October, Cairo dispatched a contingent of
18,000 troops to back the country's new revolutionary regime.[70]

"I don't even know where it is," Kennedy reportedly blurted out
upon hearing of Yemen's tumult.[71] Regardless, the proxy conflict
spurred intense debate in Washington over whether to recognize the
military regime. The CIA and the Arabian Peninsula affairs chief reported that Yemen's power struggle was neither conducive to communist influence nor worthy of U.S. involvement.[72] But after Yemen-
based UAR air units attacked the kingdom in November, Kennedy
authorized brief military aircraft demonstrations over Riyadh and
Jeddah. By then, White House National Security Council aide Robert Komer and Secretary of State Dean Rusk argued that delaying
recognition risked extending social revolution into Saudi Arabia.[73]
Some specialists in the Near East Bureau believed recognition would
encourage Nasser to extract his forces and show that America sided
with the nationalist "wave of the future."[74] When the Saudi-backed
royalists looked destined for defeat, the United States formally recognized Yemen's pro-Nasserite government on December 19, 1962.
Rather than abstain from political interference until the dust settled,

Washington recognized a wobbly military regime backed by a nationalist Arab state that had attacked a U.S. ally and publicly called for its overthrow. In the end, the gesture flopped.

President Kennedy, quite rightly, had separated Arab nationalism from external communist control, a volte-face from his predecessors. Communism never was monolithic, nor were its imagined subsidiaries in the Third World. Nevertheless, the administration's recognition of Yemen revealed an attractive temptation that regularly entraps U.S. policymakers: the urge to address complex problems without a constructive way to resolve them. Despite Nasser's promises to withdraw his expeditionary forces, Washington had limited means of stopping further escalation in the absence of securing a formal disengagement agreement from the parties.[75] Officials also left unanswered precisely how Yemen's recognition would give the "Arab Cold War's" two main belligerents a face-saving exit from their proxy conflict, as domestic power struggles guided their response to the crisis.

Wooing Nasser assumed he would readily jettison his pan-Arab revolution to deepen relations with Washington. That assumption proved unfounded. Meanwhile, there was substantial turmoil within the Saudi royal family. A month before Yemen's coup, Prince Talal[76] openly sided with Nasser and defected to Cairo. His brother, half-brother, cousin, and others joined him, advocating a "Free Princes" reformist movement, a constitutional monarchy, and expanded civil rights. The embarrassment compromised the kingdom's legitimacy. When King Faisal[77] took the reins of power in November 1964, his fight against secular nationalists won him support among Saudi religious elites.[78]

Kennedy went from playing peacemaker to throwing fuel on the inferno by tacitly approving Saudi Arabia's funding of Yemen's Muslim Brotherhood against UAR forces. The CIA also arranged for the approval of a passport for the Muslim Brotherhood's globe-trotting ambassador, Said Ramadan, who a year before Yemen's coup founded the Islamic Center of Geneva.[79] The think tank, funded largely by the Saudis, spread the brethren's puritanical brand of Islam across Western Europe. Whether Ramadan received CIA funding is difficult to determine, but nonetheless probable: Swiss authorities later described Ramadan as an "information agent" of Britain and America, and German intelligence documents claimed America financed Ramadan's expenditures.[80]

In addition to international Muslim Brotherhood branches and a mosque in Munich he helped raise money to build, Ramadan helped found the Muslim World League in May 1962. The Mecca-based, nongovernmental organization, in the words of one scholar, aimed to "'Wahhabize' Islam world wide."[81] It sponsored conferences and symposia, published books and papers, and funded an international network of religious charities. With 99 percent of its funding coming from the Saudi state, along with its secretary-generals becoming ministers in the Saudi government and senior religious figures comprising its Constituent Council, the organization acted as a veritable extension of Saudi national policy.[82] Even as the royal family busily spread its puritanical religious doctrine, President Kennedy intended to display another show of military force in defense of the kingdom. But his effort to soothe Saudi anxieties triggered controversy in Washington.

"Personnel of Jewish faith or Jewish extraction will not be selected," began an April 1963 U.S. Air Force operations manual's planned personnel section.[83] The Pentagon later removed the sentence, but Rep. Emanuel Celler (D-NY) disclosed in a June 10th radio interview that Jewish-American personnel might deploy to the kingdom.[84] The Saudi government demanded that Kennedy rebuke the congressman. Assistant Secretary of State Phillips Talbot told U.S. Ambassador Peter Hart that with Martin Luther King Jr. sitting in a Birmingham jail cell and black children being blasted with water cannon, the prospect of Washington defending Saudi discrimination was "totally out of the question."[85] Instead, Washington provided Riyadh political cover, claiming Saudi anti-Semitism had never arisen.

U.S. officials refused to challenge its ally's rampant anti-Semitism, both out of respect for Saudi sovereignty and to satisfy perceived U.S. national interests. But Riyadh's internal disposition precluded reciprocity—it insisted foreigners not interfere in the kingdom's social biases, while demanding that the policies of allied countries bend to Saudi norms. Saudi practices and Riyadh's diplomatic double standard did not merely raise uncomfortable questions, they obstructed a course of action intended to protect the country. At the same time, Washington's defense of the anti-Semitic kingdom risked aerial combat with the Egyptian air force.[86]

Two days after Celler's interview, Kennedy authorized Operation Hard Surface, which provided a squadron of eight tactical fighter aircraft, one transport aircraft, 560 support personnel, and over 800 tons of equipment to the kingdom.[87] General Maxwell Taylor, chairman of the Joint Chiefs of Staff, warned that Hard Surface put U.S. pilots in the difficult position of either responding militarily if engaged or risking America's military credibility. Air Force Chief of Staff Curtis Lemay warned that U.S. aircraft would be sitting ducks. Some at the Pentagon joked that Saudi pilots were too busy defecting to Egypt and called the operation a token defense. By October, Kennedy reduced his military bluff in the Eastern Mediterranean and the Red Sea to two tactical fighter wings, a second Sixth Fleet carrier task force, and a squadron of aging B-47 bombers.[88]

Overall, the conflicts and nationalist uprisings in Yemen, Lebanon, and elsewhere emerged from localized tensions, not broader U.S.-Soviet antagonisms. Kennedy said as much just weeks before his assassination in Dallas. In a speech before the Protestant Council of New York City, he described the dozen or more Third World proxy conflicts, including between "two Arab states over Yemen," as follows:

> The parties to these disputes have more in common ethnically and ideologically than do the Soviet Union and the United States. . . . In almost every case, their continuing conflict invites outside intervention and threatens worldwide escalation—yet the major powers are hard put to limit events in these areas.[89]

Nasser eventually took to calling Yemen's civil war, "my Vietnam,"[90] and, by the end of the decade, Riyadh and Cairo would put aside their many differences.

The Middle East Remade

Top officials often referred to King Faisal as a moderate—a seductive yet myopic judgment. He may have maintained a pro-American stance and reformed his kingdom's administrative bodies, but the modernizer also intensified missionary preaching and Islamic call (*da'wa*), most profoundly in the Saudi higher-education system.

Despite the kingdom's prohibitions on political parties, it granted thousands of Muslim Brotherhood members sanctuary after Cairo banned the movement in 1948, and Nasser drove it underground and into exile following its attempt on his life in 1954. Brotherhood members fled to Jordan, Lebanon, Syria, and especially Saudi Arabia. Indeed, Saudi Arabia emerged as the brethren's chief operating base and principal financial backer.[91]

By the early 1960s, Nasser altered curriculum at al-Azhar, Cairo's thousand-year-old center of Islamic learning, to compete with Saudi Arabia's centrality in Islam. In response, King Faisal founded and lavishly funded the Islamic University of Medina in 1961 and King Abdulaziz University in 1967 and threw open their doors to Egyptian Islamic scholars. Descendants of Wahhabism's founder, the Al ash-Shaikh, controlled the Ministry of Education and its network of Islamic universities. But as they intermarried with members of the Al Saud, some adopted the Muslim Brotherhood's teachings, melding Wahhabism's austere theology with the Brotherhood's political activism. From that cross-fertilization sprung the precursor of Salafi pan-Islamism (*Salafiyya*), the radical, revivalist movement that germinated al Qaeda.[92]

Many university students studied curriculum tied closely to Islamic laws and teachings, including the work of the prolific anti-American writer and influential Egyptian Muslim Brotherhood member, Sayyid Qutb.[93] Rather than jihad understood as one's internal struggle, Qutb endorsed militant jihad, proclaiming that only from the Quran could true Muslims derive principles of government, politics, and economics. He claimed those professing otherwise were afflicted with a barbarous ignorance more insidious than humanity's state before Islam. Sheikh Abdel Aziz bin Baz, one of the kingdom's leading religious authorities, served as vice president and later president of the Islamic University of Medina. Despite medieval Islam's early contributions to celestial astronomy, Aziz bin Baz proclaimed the world was flat, and the Sun orbited the Earth.

Like Qutb, bin Baz condemned those who did not share his worldview as guilty of "falsehood toward God, the Koran, and the Prophet."[94] The kingdom later appointed the blind sheikh to be president of the Directorate of Religious Research, Missionary Activities, and Guidance, a permanent committee that oversaw the contents of religious sermons and was relied upon by many Muslims around the world for clerical legal rulings. These teachings spread in and beyond the Middle East; for instance, at the Islamic University of Medina, non-Saudis comprised 85 percent of the student body.[95] For some in society, travel abroad and exposure to foreign entertainment increased their desire for modern social transformation. For others, however, religious indoctrination bolstered their conservative Wahhabi predilections. Worldly and insular types alike began questioning concepts of life and the royal family's legitimacy (see chapter 13).[96] The significance of such trends failed to register in Washington.

Many top U.S. decisionmakers, diplomats, and defense and intelligence officials endorsed King Faisal's pan-Islamic efforts. The CIA encouraged Faisal's brother-in-law and intelligence chief, Kamal Adham—who had built a network of Islamist agents across the Arab world—to spend millions on the Muslim Brotherhood.[97] "We thought of Islam as a counterweight to communism," said Arabian Peninsula Affairs Chief Talcott Seelye, adding "we saw it as a moderate force, and a positive one."[98]

One CIA officer described the Mecca-based Muslim World League religious charity as "kind of a 'Vatican'-type organism."[99] That assertion was troubling. The Vatican had stopped denouncing pluralism and democracy as early as the 19th century. More important, in the absence of anti-clerical reaction in Islamic society, insofar as an ordered clergy existed, U.S. officials were making poor analogies and drawing erroneous conclusions. One Saudi-based British diplomat reported on the views of Washington and London:

> I take the relaxed view of Faisal's activities. . . . The American Embassy here, with whom we have discussed the subject at several levels, share this view. That is to say that the concept of Islam as an aggressive force has completely disappeared except among some older Saudis.[100]

That Anglo-American attitude grievously underestimated the political and ideological contagion they were helping disseminate.

Impact of the Six Day War of 1967 on U.S.-Saudi Ties

"Our relations with Saudi Arabia have been long, close, and cordial," affirmed President Lyndon Johnson during a meeting with King Faisal at the White House in June 1966. "As the venerable Arabic saying has it, 'Our house is your house.'"[101] Johnson continued his predecessors' commitment to the conservative, oil-rich monarchy. The British and U.S. governments signed an air defense program to fortify Saudi armed forces, including a $400 million initiative to build Saudi bases and $100 million for trucks and military transport vehicles.[102] But Johnson's generous accolades accompanied another public diplomacy embarrassment.

"Unfortunately," King Faisal replied when asked about U.S. companies doing business with Israel, "Jews support Israel and we consider those who provide assistance to our enemies as our own enemies."[103] New York Governor Nelson Rockefeller and New York City Mayor John V. Lindsay promptly canceled their scheduled engagements with the monarch. Faisal's vulgar recriminations were nothing new, but that bigotry was not frivolous. Although Johnson and other presidents believed the Soviets carried influence in the Middle East by exploiting regional tensions, former National Security Council member William B. Quandt explains that, in Faisal's view, U.S. support for Israel played into nationalist and communist hands, making the region more dangerous for the Saudis and other status quo forces.[104]

Raised by his maternal grandfather, a leading religious scholar and grandson of the founder of the puritanical Wahhabist movement, King Faisal expressed his frustration with Israel and Jews openly. He labeled communists and Jews as Islam's main enemies and charged that they were secretly allied to conquer the world. He even distributed copies of *The Protocols of the Elders of Zion,* a notorious, bogus, conspiratorial tract about a Jewish plot for global domination. Faisal called Marxism "a subversive creed originated by a vile Jew," and blamed Zionists for fomenting Palestinian terrorism.[105] Years later, Saudi Arabia strongly, and successfully, pushed for a UN General Assembly vote that equated Zionism with racism and the South African apartheid system. Faisal even described U.S.-Israel relations as a Zionist scheme to weaken Arab-American ties and undermine their Islamic-Christian struggle against communism.[106]

The kingdom's fervent opposition to Israel opened the U.S.-Saudi alliance's first significant breach. Shortly after the Arab League created the Palestine Liberation Organization (PLO) in 1964, the group splintered. Palestinian guerillas (*fedayeen*) launched raids against Israel from positions in Jordan, Lebanon, and the Gaza Strip (under Egyptian administration since 1949), and in retaliation, Israel inflicted heavy military punishment on Jordan in November 1966 and Syria in April 1967.[107] In a provocative attempt to burnish his nationalist image tarnished in Yemen and elsewhere, in May 1967, Nasser evicted UN military forces stationed on the Sinai since the Suez Crisis, moved his troops to Israel's southern border, and closed the Straits of Tiran to Israeli shipping. President Johnson condemned the blockade as illegal and urged Nasser to rescind it.[108]

Nevertheless, the conflict in Vietnam consumed the Johnson administration's attention and sorely shorthanded its foreign policy team. The Middle East post at the Policy Planning Council remained vacant between late 1966 and early 1967. The office of assistant secretary of state at the Near East Bureau stayed empty from November 1966 until April 1967. And Johnson's National Security Council rotated through three different Middle East directors between April 1966 and June 1967.

What Washington may have failed to fully appreciate was the extent to which the question of Palestine transcended intraregional differences and cemented Arab unity. On May 20, when asked by Aramco's vice president why the Saudi kingdom would object to Washington standing up to Nasser, Saudi Minister of Petroleum and Mineral Resources Ahmed Zaki Yamani replied, "We are all Arabs. Your government would be foolish if it does not keep out."[109] Shortly thereafter, Jordan and Iraq entered a military alliance with the UAR, and Syria, and Lebanon, Kuwait, and Saudi Arabia activated their armed forces.

On June 5, 1967, with the Egyptian, Syrian, and Jordanian armies poised on its borders, Israel launched a preemptive attack on all three. Within hours, it devastated Egypt's entire air force, along with Jordan's and half of Syria's. Iraq, Syria, Yemen, Algeria, Mauritania, and Sudan severed diplomatic relations with Washington and London after Nasser claimed falsely over Radio Cairo that they had provided Israel air support. In Dhahran, rioters stoned the U.S. Consulate, assaulted American citizens, and attacked Western vehicles, homes, and offices.[110] Following Kuwait, Iraq, Libya, and Algeria, on June 7, Saudi Arabia banned petroleum shipments to America and Britain. For the Saudis, solidarity came at a high price. The flow of Arab petroleum plummeted 60 percent within days. America, Venezuela, Iran, and Indonesia, though, increased their oil production and replaced the missing imports. Mecca Radio described the lost revenue as, "no less serious than Arab territorial and human losses in the war with Israel."[111]

After six days, Israel vanquished its Arab adversaries and thereby radically reshaped the modern Middle East. Israeli forces captured the Golan Heights from Syria, the West Bank and East Jerusalem from Jordan, and the Sinai Peninsula and Gaza Strip from Egypt. And—although rarely mentioned—Saudi Arabia's Tiran and Sanafir Islands fell to Israel.[112] Israel had dealt a psychological deathblow to the myth of pan-Arab strength. At the Arab League's August 1967 summit in Khartoum, Sudan, member states pledged no recognition of Israel, no peace, and no direct negotiations.[113] The Six Day War would also become the catalyst for Washington's expansive diplomatic involvement in the Arab-Israeli dispute. After the Jewish state defeated the Soviet Union's Arab clients, the U.S.-Israel patron-client partnership fully bloomed. Accordingly, America's image across the region plummeted, while Soviet prestige soared.[114]

Following Egypt's humiliating defeat, Saudi Arabia, albeit by default, emerged from the "Arab Cold War" victorious. As the strongest and most populous Arab state, Egypt had borne the brunt of the human, economic, and political costs of collective Arab wars against Israel. Cairo sought to restrain its ambitious foreign policy, and Riyadh eagerly filled the void. At Khartoum, Faisal and Nasser signed a peace settlement on Yemen, and the kingdom provided financial assistance to Cairo's economically ailing regime. Meanwhile, the region's religious conservatives and hard-line Islamists both blamed secular nationalism and the influence of Western ideologies for the Arab loss.

Perhaps most significant, Saudi Arabia, as the chief defender of Islam, broadened the pan-Arab struggle against Israel into a pan-Islamic one. He called for reclaiming East Jerusalem, and hence, al-Aqsa Mosque, Islam's third-holiest site, back from the Jewish state. On September 25, 1969, in Rabat, Morocco's capital, he convened delegations from 25 countries to establish the Organization of the

Islamic Conference, which advocated for the "struggle" in Palestine. After Nasser succumbed to a fatal heart attack in September 1970, Faisal increased his pan-Islamist efforts and used aid and loans to amplify the kingdom's influence. At the March 1972 Islamic summit in Jeddah, 31 countries agreed to a fund "for the holy war" against Israel and to support Palestinian guerillas.

The Saudi role regarding Palestine became increasingly prominent—and cynical. Weeks after the Six Day War, King Faisal explained to U.S. Ambassador Hermann Eilts during a meeting in Jeddah, "You are dealing with irrational people." Faisal said that Washington seemed unable to grasp what he called the Arab "mob psychology" prevalent among the region's "crazy people." Faisal and other pro-Western monarchs, he insisted, found themselves in a "bad spot," lacking anything they could identify "to show genuine [U.S. government] concern for Arab interests."[115] Those candid remarks manifested the contempt Arab leaders harbored toward Palestinians and their own subjects. It also underscored the prominence that pan-Islamic sympathies for Palestine would play in Saudi foreign policy decisions.

The Yom Kippur War of 1973

Egyptian President Anwar al-Sadat proposed several arrangements to peacefully reclaim the Sinai and its oil fields from Israel.[116] He and Faisal wanted Washington to pressure Israel into evacuating Arab territories seized during the Six Day War, as per UN Security Council Resolution 242, adopted in November 1967. After March 1969, however, an Egyptian-Israeli war of attrition along the Suez Canal derailed their efforts. Prospects worsened the following March when the Soviets supplied Sadat an advanced anti-aircraft missile defense system, accompanied by 1,500 military advisers and technicians. That figure later swelled beyond 10,000. The Soviet presence in Egypt dissuaded President Richard Nixon from pressuring Israel. Yet, even after Sadat expelled the Soviet personnel in July 1972, Washington remained reluctant to push its Israeli client. American foot-dragging infuriated King Faisal.

Self-preservation remained a primary consideration for the Saudi royal family, one in which Palestine and oil figured prominently. After 1969, the Saudis aided the PLO to forestall the danger of PLO attacks against the kingdom. Still, the Palestinian crisis raised Saudi concerns about terror operations on its assets and oil-production facilities. Palestinian refugees ignited the 1970 Black September war in Jordan; pro-Palestinian terrorists touched off the era's wave of airline hijackings; and Palestinian gunmen stormed the Saudi embassy in Khartoum in March 1973.[117]

Another background consideration involved the Organization of the Petroleum Exporting Countries (OPEC). Formed in September 1960, the cartel of oil-producing states collectively bargained to ration exports to oil-importing states. By the early 1970s, OPEC members wanted more influence over the ownership and activities of multinational oil companies operating in their territories. Saudi Arabia, with the world's largest crude reserves, was OPEC's swing producer and had the de facto final say in raising prices by cutting production. Hypothetically, if Arab oil ministers pursued collective action to decrease production and increase costs on targeted states, the Arab kingdom, as OPEC's leading member, felt compelled to wield the "oil weapon."

On the one hand, the world's largest energy producer had to appear supportive of pan-Arab causes against Israel, while on the other, the kingdom remained closely associated with the United States, the leading oil consumer and primary supporter of Israel. Those diverging interests were bound to collide. The pinnacle of hypocrisy occurred as another potential Arab-Israeli crisis loomed. President Sadat began to warn he could no longer accept peace talks' paralyzing stalemate and indicated his willingness to violently shatter the status quo. Meanwhile, in a *Foreign Affairs* article, State Department oil expert James E. Akins observed that in 1972 alone, Arab states threatened to use the oil weapon 15 separate times.[118] King Faisal joined the growing chorus in July 1973, telling American reporters he desired "a reasonable policy to bring a settlement," but "America's complete support for Zionism and against the Arabs makes it extremely difficult for us to continue to supply the United States with oil, or even to remain friends with the United States."[119] By August, Faisal began requesting detailed reports about the consequences of freezing oil production on consuming countries, in particular, the United States. That month, Sadat and Syria's Hafez al-Assad told Faisal that, if necessary, they would use force to reclaim Arab territories. Faisal reciprocated with an offer to defend

Muslim honor symbolically by coordinating an Arab response with the oil weapon.[120]

In Washington, however, skeptical officials refused to take those threats seriously. Secretary of Defense James Schlesinger dismissed Faisal's comments as "hot air."[121] Decisionmakers considered it lunacy that oil producers would sabotage their revenue stream or that Arabs would attack their militarily superior Israeli adversary. U.S. leaders also viewed the pro-West Saudi royal family, and the pro-West Shah of Iran, as the region's twin pillars of stable oil production and the moderate camp within OPEC. Besides, Arab and Saudi oil boycotts in 1956 and 1967 had failed to affect America's economic situation and that of its allies. Washington also relied heavily on Israeli intelligence, which downplayed the imminence of war and the competence of Arab soldiers. Those prevailing assumptions proved powerful.

On October 7, 1973—Yom Kippur, the Jewish calendar's holiest day—Egypt and Syria launched a surprise joint attack against Israel. An hour later, the Defense Intelligence Agency was *still* disputing reports of an Arab military buildup. The Soviets resupplied their Egyptian and Syrian clients, while Iraq, Libya, Algeria, Tunisia, Sudan, Morocco, Jordan, and Saudi Arabia joined the Arab effort with troops, tanks, and planes.[122] After two days, the Jewish state had suffered more casualties than during the Six Day War.

Various factors pulled U.S. officials in opposing directions in the course of aiding Israel. Save for Portugal and the Netherlands, America's European allies refused U.S. requests to use their bases or to over-fly their territories to send assistance. Because the Middle East accounted for 85 percent of oil consumed in Europe and 90 percent of oil consumed in Japan, they sought to avoid inflaming Arab indignity. Additionally, U.S. congressional probes over Watergate consumed the Nixon administration—the day President Nixon announced the airlift to Israel, October 10, Vice President Spiro Agnew tendered his resignation.

Another demand emanated from America's oil companies, which sponsored newspaper advertisements warning of too much support for Israel and emphasizing closer ties with Saudi Arabia. The chairmen of Exxon, Mobil, Texaco, and Socal urged President Nixon in a joint letter against aiding Israel, highlighting a "snowballing effect" in terms of Arab retaliation.[123] A back-channel U.S. envoy to Arab leaders, Jack McCloy, a partner to a firm whose clients included 22 chief executive officers of U.S. oil companies, had written years earlier in a letter to Secretary of State Dean Rusk: "The simple fact is our Israel policy is not operating in favor of our national interest in the Middle East."[124] His letter expressed the view of his petro-clients and reflected the conflicting impulses that animated America's Middle East policy.

Nixon and Kissinger tried mightily to respond to these competing pressures and interests. They concluded that an overwhelming Israeli victory would deepen Arab humiliation, increase Israel's bargaining leverage after the war, and make peace harder to reach. Such unvarnished realpolitik demonstrated another tendency in U.S.-Middle East statecraft: Washington weighed its interest to ensure Israel's survival against preventing, as Nixon later put it, "a hundred million Arabs hating us and providing a fishing ground not only for radicals but, of course, for the Soviets."[125]

As expected, U.S. aid to Israel provoked a swift Arab reaction. At more than 22,000 tons of equipment, the U.S. resupply to Israel (Operation Nickel Grass) exceeded the Berlin airlift. On October 16, after news of the resupply leaked, OPEC announced a 70 percent hike in oil prices. The following day, Arab oil ministers cut production by 5 percent and pledged to keep doing so each succeeding month.[126]

Despite the backlash, President Nixon agreed to give Israel an immediate military aid package of $2.2 billion on October 19. Saudi Arabia and other Arab states ceased exports to America and other supporters of Israel in retaliation.[127] The war finally ended following a UN-brokered ceasefire on October 22, although Nixon put U.S. military forces worldwide on high alert (Defcon III) on October 25 to deter the Soviets from stopping Israel's overwhelming counterattack against Egypt's Third Army. Eventually, through his step-by-step shuttle diplomacy, Secretary Kissinger mediated the Egyptian-Israeli Disengagement Agreement of January 1974 and the Syria-Israel Golan Heights Disengagement Agreement of May 1974. By March of that year, at Saudi Arabia's insistence, OPEC lifted its embargo.

Recycling Petrodollars

Known as the October War to the Arabs and the Yom Kippur War to the Israelis, the 1973 conflict challenged a number of prevailing assumptions and prompted a major rethink of the U.S.-Saudi partnership. For many U.S. officials, the war diminished the credibility of Israeli intelligence and the belief that its vaunted military superiority would deter an Arab assault.

For the Saudis, though they failed to impose their will on America's Israel policy, they managed to convince many in Washington to weigh Arab interests with sufficient seriousness, including U.S. weapons manufacturers desiring new markets, Pentagon officials seeking to reduce the per unit cost of arms and equipment, and diplomats urging stronger Arab-American relations. Eventually, the Saudis began to take over Aramco, and by 1980, owned 100 percent of the company. Finally, Riyadh became a secret conduit for Washington to restore diplomatic relations with Cairo, helping place the most populous Arab state and the richest Arab state firmly in America's camp.[128]

For many Americans, the war and subsequent oil embargo reinforced the impression that oil-rich Arab despots held America hostage. In stark contrast to the picture that U.S. officials and pundits painted, the energy crisis and lines of cars at gas stations stemmed mainly from price controls and import quotas that limited the domestic energy market.[129] Nevertheless, Americans continued to overestimate the influence of Arab oil-production decisions, as the 1973 war and OPEC's embargo generated public interest in energy conservation, growing calls for energy independence, and substituting away from Middle East oil. But for some U.S. officials and commentators, who during the war made veiled threats to seize Persian Gulf oil militarily, the embargo inspired precisely the opposite reaction.[130] They pushed to enhance U.S.-Saudi interdependence.

After the kingdom emerged from the oil embargo with more money than it could spend, U.S. leaders sought to increase the Saudi stake in the U.S. economy in order to prevent future dislocations of the global economy. Toward that end, Secretary Kissinger and Treasury Secretary William E. Simon encouraged the royal family to lend, give, and invest—"recycle"—revenue from oil sales—"petrodollars"—into multinational companies. In the areas of science, infrastructure, education, agriculture, and others, foreign companies would help modernize the kingdom with Western goods and technology.[131] On June 8, 1974, the United States-Saudi Arabian Joint Commission on Economic Cooperation was born. A week later, after concluding discussions with King Faisal in Washington, President Nixon articulated the benefits of heavy Saudi investment in the U.S. economy:

> If Saudi Arabia is strong and secure, as it will be, we will enhance the prospects for peace and stability throughout the Middle East and, in turn, throughout the world. . . . I would say that today American ties with Saudi Arabia have never been stronger and have never more solidly been based than they are now.[132]

Under joint cooperation, American civil servants advised their Saudi counterparts on governing the bureaucracies of a modern state, including planning development, improving financial data collection, and implementing proper banking standards. Those efforts proved less successful than inducing the Saudis to award contracts to American banks, construction and real estate firms, entrepreneurs, and other firms that channeled billions of petrodollars back into the U.S. economy. Joint security cooperation also recycled petrodollars with the sale of U.S.-manufactured military equipment. By the end of the decade, Saudi Arabia became one of the largest foreign investors in the U.S. economy, especially American banks, treasury bonds, and real estate.[133] Those lucrative business deals also increased Saudi Arabia's influence among American lobbyists, senior policymakers, business leaders, and retired diplomats.

Meanwhile, through its Islamic financial system, the kingdom poured petrodollars into the coffers of fellow Arab and Muslim states, Afro-Asian countries, and anti-communist rebel movements stretching from the Horn of Africa to the Philippines. Saudi-backed Islamic banks sprouted in Egypt, Sudan, Kuwait, Turkey, and elsewhere, helping to radicalize the region's politics by internationalizing the Muslim Brotherhood, Pakistan's Jama'at-e-Islami, and other Islamist movements, their writings, and audiotapes. Yusuf al-Qaradani, a cofounder of the Saudi-backed Faisal Islamic Bank of Egypt, condoned Palestinian attacks against Israel—even calling suicide bombings a legitimate act of self-defense. Wittingly or otherwise, Western financial institutions such as Citibank, Chase Manhattan, Goldman Sachs, Fannie Mae, Freddie Mac, and the U.S. Federal Reserve assisted Saudi Arabia's advancements in Islamic banking.[134]

Domestically, Saudi Arabia's immense wealth and rapid development failed to stem—even arguably helped to unleash—outbursts of religious extremism. A young Saudi prince shot and killed King Faisal on March 25, 1975. Some believe the assassin, Faisal's nephew, sought to avenge the death of his brother, whom Saudi government forces had killed a decade earlier as he tried to destroy Riyadh's television transmitter. The introduction of television had rattled rigid Wahhabi conservatives. Whatever the assassin's motive, the authorities beheaded him publicly. Crown Prince Khalid[135] became prime minister, and Crown Prince Fahd[136] oversaw domestic and foreign policy.[137] Notwithstanding that smooth succession, the royal family would face foreign and domestic disorder from even more extremists, and the final period of U.S.-Saudi Cold War relations is best understood in that context.

The Global Spread of Saudi Conservatism

In 1979, three major shocks convulsed the Saudi royal family and carried substantial political consequences for American national interests. The first occurred on January 16, 1979, when Iran's Anglo-American-installed Shah Mohammad Reza Pahlavi fled for Egypt after facing massive demonstrations, and even riots, against his tyrannical reign. For Washington, Iran's tumult justified the creation of combat-ready, rapidly deployable military units known as the Rapid Deployment Force, which by 1983, expanded into the theater-level U.S. Central Command, covering America's military responsibility in a vast region from Egypt to Kyrgyzstan. Despite Washington's "fly-in" of a dozen F-15 fighters to Saudi Arabia—which came three months after Riyadh's request—President Jimmy Carter announced the planes were unarmed. Washington's inability to reinstall the Shah, combined with sending unarmed jets, disturbed the royal family and prompted questions about the sincerity of Washington's security guarantee. Moreover, the threats befalling the kingdom would grow even more staggering.[138]

Arriving in Tehran on February 1, after years of exile in Paris, radical Shiite clerical leader Grand Ayatollah Ruhollah Khomeini rose to power and ignited a dangerous religious fervor across the region. His ascendance also kindled simmering resentments between Arabs and Persians, Sunnis and Shiites. As in this broadcast, Radio Tehran's shortwave Arabic channel beamed virulent anti-Saudi propaganda into Shiite towns in northeastern Saudi Arabia:

> The ruling regime in Saudi Arabia wears Muslim clothing, but inwardly represents the U.S. body, mind, and terrorism (*sic*). Funds are robbed from the people and squandered . . . for the luxurious, frivolous, and shameless way of life of the Saudi royal family and its entourage.[139]

Khomeini's propaganda directly challenged the royal family's spiritual authority, declaring Islam and hereditary kingship inherently incompatible. He emboldened disaffected Shiite minorities in Sunni-ruled Bahrain, Kuwait, and Saudi Arabia to rebel against their Sunni oppressors. On October 22, with turmoil gripping the region, President Carter allowed the Shah to enter America for cancer treatment. Two weeks later, revolutionary Islamist students stormed the American Embassy in Tehran and held 52 diplomats captive.

Radicals in Saudi Arabia tried to replicate the crisis in 1979's second major convulsion. During dawn prayers on November 20, a procession of approximately 500 mourners carrying coffins entered Mecca's Grand Mosque, a common sight as many pilgrims travel to the holy city to bless their dead. These mourners, though, set down the coffins, opened the lids, and took out a stockpile of grenades and assault rifles. They chained shut the doors of the stadium-sized, seven-acre mosque and locked the nearly 100,000 worshippers inside. Hostage ringleader and former Saudi National Guardsman Juhayman al-Utaybi had convinced several hundred Islamic University of Medina students—many of them Egyptian and Yemeni and more extreme than Saudi government-backed puritans—that his brother-in-law, Mohammed Abdullah al-Qahtani, was the messiah (*Mahdi*) returned to Earth to save Muslims from Western impurities. The Sunni zealots showed that Saudi Arabia was susceptible to revolutionary upheaval. They also represented the blend of Saudi Wahhabi extremism and Muslim Brotherhood jihadism. Matters got worse. The Saudi government evacuated the city and imposed a press blackout, which the State Department inadvertently undermined by releasing a press briefing. Over Mecca's loudspeakers, al-Utaybi called for bans on radio, television, and soccer and upbraided

Saudi rulers as "drunkards" who led "a dissolute life in luxurious palaces" and "squandered the state's money."[140]

His criticism struck a chord, as many ordinary Saudis and Wahhabi guardians of the religious establishment did view many royal family members and emirs as corrupt and decadent. After Saudi Army and National Guard units failed repeatedly to break the militants' defenses, with snipers in minarets picking off security forces, the kingdom turned to French counterterrorism commandos. After an instant conversion to Islam, as non-Muslims are strictly forbidden from Mecca, they fought the militants room-by-room in the mosque's underground vaults and chambers. Meanwhile, Saudi units callously exposed the hostages to indiscriminate lethal force, dropping grenades and canisters of disabling gas into rooms and rolling in M-113 armored personnel carriers into the shrine. The two-week bloodbath killed over 200 pilgrims, troops, and radicals and wounded 500 more. In a fitting spectacle of Saudi conservatism at its finest, the regime publicly decapitated al-Qahtani and his 63 surviving coconspirators in the largest mass execution in Saudi history.[141]

The gory standoff in Mecca marked an ominous turning point for the kingdom. The Wahhabi ulema, in its fatwa allowing the use of force inside the Grand Mosque, demanded that more of the kingdom's oil wealth go to spreading Wahhabism globally. The royal family obliged. Threatened by prospective domestic upheaval, it poured billions into the ulema and ambitious mosque-building campaigns. According to former U.S. Ambassador Richard Murphy, "The royal family decided then and there that no one would outflank them on the right."[142]

Already the Arab world's most traditional society, Saudi Arabia embraced an even more strident agenda at home. It fully unleashed its *mutawwa'in*, the ultra-conservative morality police. They flogged women in shopping malls for being improperly cloaked, charged them with prostitution for socializing with men who were not their relatives, and herded men into mosques to comply with the five daily prayers. They broke into private homes and businesses to destroy satellite dishes. And in their quest to stamp out sinfulness, heresy, and carnal sins, *mutawwa'in* even blacked out faces in advertisements and forbade the sale of children's dolls for their human representations.[143] Notwithstanding President Carter's professed commitment to humanitarian values elsewhere in the world, he (like his predecessors) generally acquiesced to the kingdom's subjugation of its citizens and illiberal worldview that inflicted social repression, political intimidation, and daily misery.

The royal family stepped up its efforts to outstrip religious opponents after 1979's third major convulsion: the Soviet Union's invasion of Afghanistan. Decades earlier, in a study commissioned by President Eisenhower, U.S. officials had deemed a Soviet takeover of the landlocked, Central Asian state as practically irrelevant to Washington.[144] That assessment apparently vanished in the mid 1970s. By then, the United States, Saudi Arabia, Pakistan, and Iran (pre-1979) tried to mobilize Afghan Islamists against the political and social modernization efforts of Afghan monarch Zahir Shah and left-leaning Prime Minister Mohammad Daoud.[145]

When Afghan Marxists seized power in Kabul in April 1978, Saudi leaders expressed concern to U.S. diplomats over a communist "pincer movement" encompassing Central Asia, the Horn of Africa, and the southern Arabian Peninsula.[146] National Security Advisor Zbigniew Brzezinski warned President Carter that the Soviets might use Afghanistan as a launching pad for territorial aggression elsewhere in the region.[147] Against nationalist enemies, the Saudi kingdom served more or less the same purpose for Washington. But by December, the Saudis faced their most definitive Soviet danger. The communist superpower sent 80,000 troops to prop up its faltering client regime in Kabul, which put Moscow in striking range of Iranian and Saudi oil fields. President Carter's January 1980 State of the Union Address presented Washington's most declarative public commitment to protect Persian Gulf oil for the industrial world:

> The Soviet effort to dominate Afghanistan has brought Soviet military forces to within 300 miles of the Indian Ocean and close to the Straits of Hormuz, a waterway through which most of the world's oil must flow. The Soviet Union is now attempting to consolidate a strategic position, therefore, that poses a grave threat to the free movement of Middle East oil.

He continued:

> Let our position be absolutely clear: An attempt by any

outside force to gain control of the Persian Gulf region will be regarded as an assault on the vital interests of the United States of America, and such an assault will be repelled by any means necessary, including military force.[148]

Carter's stern declaration relieved the Saudis, who moved to galvanize opposition to Afghanistan's communist occupiers that month at the Islamic conference in Islamabad. But Carter's speech did little to satisfy the American people. Many lost faith in the White House incumbent, who besides presiding over an ailing economy, appeared to horrendously mishandle foreign threats that persistently challenged American power. To rescue their country from its malaise, voters that November elected a staunch, anti-communist president.

Battles over Weapons

Carter's successor, Ronald Reagan, recommitted America's protection to Saudi Arabia at an October 1981 press conference. He stated the following when asked how he would prevent a repeat of the Iranian revolution in the Saudi kingdom:

> There is no way, as long as Saudi Arabia and the OPEC nations there in the East—and Saudi Arabia's the most important—provide the bulk of the energy that is needed to turn the wheels of industry in the Western World, there's no way that we could stand by and see that taken over by anyone that would shut off that oil.[149]

The president's response, though seemingly forthright, avoided the thrust of the question. Reagan sought to prevent the Saudi regime's demise. As did Crown Prince Fahd, who the following June ascended to the Saudi throne and wanted to limit the secularism accompanying the kingdom's modernization. He believed the Shah's modernizing "White Revolution" in the 1960s and early 1970s precipitated his downfall.[150] But by limiting secularism, combined with ongoing Saudi efforts to outshine religious radicals, the kingdom merely constituted a Sunni fundamentalist mirror image of the Shiite theocracy in Iran—a puritanism wildly volatile and ultimately uncontrollable.

Just weeks after Reagan's press conference, extremists led by a member of Egypt's Islamist group al-Jihad (Sacred Combat) assassinated pro-American President Anwar Sadat. His domestic economic reforms, brutal crackdowns on critics, and controversial peace negotiations with Israel alienated Egyptians, but he had also ushered in his country's religiously conservative shift. Sadat welcomed the Saudi-backed Faisal Islamic Bank of Egypt and the Muslim Brotherhood's Saudi-backed Al Taqwa Bank. He assumed the title of "Believer-President," began and ended his speeches with Quarnic verses, and fought the 1973 Arab-Israeli war under an Islamic banner of the "War of Ramadan." Cairo's al-Azhar University forged arrangements with Saudi Islamists, and many Egyptians working in Saudi Arabia returned home "Wahhabi-cized." The way of life in Egypt gradually changed, and long-time visitors noticed its Islamist shift.[151] It signaled the rising dominance of Saudi-Wahhabist ideology and how extremists focused on one target could quickly turn back on their patron.

Regional turmoil, including the September 1980 outbreak of war between Iran and Iraq, forced Saudi Arabia to rectify its military deficiencies. The results were the trade-and-security focused Gulf Cooperation Council with neighboring conservative and Sunni-ruled regimes, along with spending billions of dollars on U.S. construction services to expand Saudi air bases and port facilities.[152] Pro-Israel members of Congress, however, tried to block the sales of advanced American armaments to Riyadh that Saudi officials deemed critical for their security. Reagan thought selling some weapons would not materially affect the Arab-Israeli balance of power, whereas many on Capitol Hill argued that the weapons would either enhance Riyadh's capacity to wage war against Israel or migrate to other Islamist states.

"It is not the business of other nations to make American foreign policy," admonished President Reagan in response to Israeli efforts to pressure Congress.[153] These political battles regarding weapons to Saudi Arabia had erupted before: in 1976 over the transfer of Maverick air-to-ground missiles and in 1978 concerning the sale of F-15 fighter-bombers. By autumn 1981, controversy flared again about a proposed $8.5 billion arms sale that included five all-weather surveillance and command-and-control reconnaissance planes. Reagan expended considerable effort to ensure congressional authorization, meeting individually with 75 senators to close the deal. Although lawmakers narrowly approved the sale, the weapons battles continued and eroded the trust underpinning the U.S.-Saudi partnership.[154] Such sharp policy disagreements between the White House and Congress stemmed at least in part from the legal basis of the U.S.-Saudi alliance itself. The U.S. Constitution requires the advice and consent of the Senate regarding treaties; however, consecutive administrations evaded that requirement through tacit security arrangements with Riyadh that arose not from a formal defense treaty but rather through executive order.

Few leaders asked whether the cumulative result of U.S. assistance packages and repeated military deployments diminished rather than enhanced the kingdom's incentive to expand its defensive capabilities. Saudi Arabia depended upon non-Muslim foreigners to defend it from Colonel Nasser's Arab nationalists in the 1950s and 1960s, from Ayatollah Khomeini's Shiite radicals in the 1970s and 1980s, and from Saddam Hussein's Iraqi soldiers in the early 1990s. America's heavy military profile arguably compromised, to a high degree, the House of Saud's religious legitimacy (see chapter 13). Some Saudi princes saw weaknesses in the kingdom's reliance on the United States for its security. Indeed, the Saudi government ruled out soliciting the CIA's help during the siege in Mecca; Riyadh's lack of confidence in that agency was apparent when Saudi head of intelligence Prince Turki[155] said that strict congressional restrictions under President Carter had "emasculated" the CIA's operational capacity.[156] The kingdom saw congressional impediments to arms purchases as further eroding the credibility of the White House's pledge of protection.

As lawmakers reduced, stalled, and canceled proposed weapons sales, senior decisionmakers began circumventing Congress altogether. That evasion escalated from weapons sales to large-scale covert operations.[157] In the mid-1970s, when congressional and White House scandals blocked CIA activities, then secretary of state Henry Kissinger approved Saudi Arabia's participation in the Safari Club. The organization, comprised of leading officials from the external spy agencies of Britain, France, Saudi Arabia, Egypt, Turkey, Morocco, and Iran (pre-1979), led efforts to counter Soviet-backed Marxist movements in the Near East and North Africa. The Saudis pumped their oil riches into movements and causes in Angola, Chad, Sudan, Eritrea, Somalia, Jordan, North Yemen, Djibouti, Uganda, Mali, Nigeria, Guinea, Pakistan, Bangladesh, and other countries.[158]

Even Latin America emerged as a prominent front for high-level, U.S.-Saudi covert activities. Congress forbade the Pentagon and the CIA in December 1982 from providing military equipment, training, or advice "for the purpose of overthrowing" Nicaragua's leftist Sandinista regime.[159] The House Intelligence Committee voted the following May to cut all U.S. aid to the rebel Contras. Reagan's National Security Advisor Bud McFarlane, at the behest of CIA Director William Casey, contacted the kingdom for assistance. Saudi ambassador to the United States, Prince Bandar, agreed to put $1 million dollars a month into a Miami bank account for the Contras, a figure that eventually swelled to $32 million.[160] Such anti-leftist, U.S.-targeted, and Saudi-financed operations turned to mass violence in Afghanistan.

Headlong into Holy War

The USSR's invasion of Afghanistan in late 1979 shocked the Islamic world. After the revolution that roiled neighboring Iran and the insurrection that challenged its spiritual authority in Mecca, a Saudi royal family already dedicated to out-radicalizing religious radicals decided to reclaim its position as Islam's chief defender and back Afghanistan's rebels in their war of liberation. Saudi Arabia's General Intelligence Directorate (GID), alongside the CIA, flooded Afghanistan with billions in assistance—an estimated $4 billion alone from the Americans between 1982 and 1990, with the Saudis matching dollar for dollar. From 1979 to 1989, Saudi Arabia and the Gulf Arab sheikhdoms of Oman, Kuwait, Bahrain, Qatar, and the United Arab Emirates gave $600 million to Arab volunteer Osama bin Laden. The United States kept its funds in Pakistan's Bank of Credit and Commerce International (BCCI), a global network for money laundering, drug smuggling, and other skullduggery. Former Saudi intelligence chief Kamal Adham recalls then CIA director George H. W. Bush giving BCCI's activities "the official blessing."[161]

Through the Khyber Pass connecting Afghanistan and Pakistan, the CIA and GID, together with Pakistan's Directorate for Inter-

Services Intelligence (ISI), directed money and military hardware to the most radical and intolerant Afghan rebel factions (discussed in chapter 4). Most Afghan volunteers turned away from suicide bombings because of their extensive familial ties and patronage networks within the country. Non-Afghan volunteers had few such qualms. Foreign fighters from Saudi Arabia, Egypt, and elsewhere were willing martyrs, and hit soft targets like Kabul cinemas and cultural shows. According to Milton Bearden, a CIA field officer in Afghanistan from 1985 to 1989, many Muslim governments emptied their prisons and sent their criminals off to jihad hoping they would become martyrs. The Saudi kingdom disseminated flyers and pamphlets urging its youths to join the jihad; an estimated 12,000 complied. Saudi national airlines even gave a 75 percent discount to Afghan-bound volunteers.[162]

The kingdom soon became a haven for extremists. Blind Sheik Omar Abdul Rahman, a spiritual adviser to Egypt's Islamic Jihad and cofounder of the Saudi-backed Faisal Islamic Bank of Egypt, resided in the kingdom from 1977 through 1980 and was later convicted for his role in the February 1993 World Trade Center attack. Ayman al-Zawahiri, the future second-in-command and leader of al Qaeda, dwelled in the kingdom in the 1980s. Palestinian activist Abdullah Azzam, founder of al Qaeda's predecessor, Mekhtab al Khidemat (the Office of Services), was on the faculty of King Abdulaziz University. In the early and mid-1980s, Azzam toured across the United States—26 states total—recruiting for holy war. In Afghanistan, he received funding from Saudi intelligence, the Mecca-based Muslim World League, and Saudi princes. But he also called for jihad beyond Afghanistan—in Palestine, Burma, Somalia, Lebanon, Chad, the Philippines, and elsewhere.[163]

On the ground in Afghanistan and Pakistan, the Saudis also remained active. Sheikh Abdul bin Baz, the heliocentric-skeptic leader of the Wahhabi religious establishment, sent millions of dollars in cash and hundreds of volunteers to create an emirate in the isolated Kunar province abutting Pakistan's lawless tribal region. He managed the activities of Saudi charities, the International Islamic Relief Organization and the Muslim World League. In the Pakistani frontier city of Peshawar, which functioned as the Afghan rebellion's rear base, Saudi charities set up shop and built schools, hospitals, and battlefield medic services.[164] But even as private and public Saudi funds advanced Washington's anti-Soviet policies, the kingdom prioritized its own interests. When an Iraqi Mirage fighter attacked the American frigate USS *Stark* in 1987, the Saudis refused U.S. requests to intercept the Iraqi aircraft. The Saudis supported Iraq in its war with Iran, and 37 Americans lost their lives.[165]

U.S. deference to Saudi wishes appeared to pay off when Soviet troops withdrew from Afghanistan in defeat on February 15, 1989. But after the anti-Soviet holy war emerged a miasma of stateless renegades. International guerillas long-supplied with U.S. and Saudi money, weapons, and training sought new ventures in Chechnya, Sudan, Bosnia, and—ultimately—America. Other fighters returned to their home countries to topple their apostate regimes.

Well after the withdrawal of Soviet forces from Afghanistan, and the subsequent collapse of the Soviet Union itself, Saudi Arabia continued to export its Wahhabi religious doctrines and social traditions throughout the Islamic world. In mid-1995, a classified Federal Bureau of Investigation intelligence report listed the semiofficial Saudi government charity, the International Islamic Relief Organization, and the largest Saudi-government sponsored religious charity, the Muslim World League, as important sources of a new generation of Sunni Islamic extremists.[166] By the 2011 Arab Spring, when radical uprisings and calls for self-determination bloomed across the Middle East and North Africa, the long-time Saudi-backed Muslim Brotherhood movement emerged as the most highly organized political force in Egypt, Tunisia, Jordan, and Syria—a reflection of the Cold War past became a harbinger of the region's future.

In Afghanistan, the war continued to reverberate. The medieval-style Taliban regime, a Sunni-Pashtun dominated movement backed by Riyadh and Islamabad, assumed power in September 1996. Its harboring of al Qaeda, despite the group's responsibility for the 9/11 attacks, prompted the 2001 U.S.-led invasion. The Taliban regime echoed the Saudi kingdom's overzealous condemnation of the human spirit, destroying depictions of human images in photos and statues, outlawing singing and dancing, and amputating limbs for thievery. Taliban jurists also sentenced homosexuals and apostates to public executions. The ruthless regime even repurposed anti-Soviet, jihadist-era schoolbooks developed by the University of Nebraska at Omaha and federally funded by the U.S. Agency for International Development, scratching out human figures and keeping violent images and pictures of Kalashnikovs.[167] Tellingly, Saudi-financed religious schools also flourished. In the Pakistan-based Islamic seminary Dar-ul-Uloom Haqqania, from which eight Taliban ministers arose, a sign in one classroom read: "A Gift of the Kingdom of Saudi Arabia."[168]

Conclusion

From Roosevelt to Reagan, the United States protected the Kingdom of Saudi Arabia, while Riyadh provided Washington and its industrialized allies preferred access to its crude. That tacit oil-for-security partnership set in motion more expansive policies. U.S. foreign policy planners crafted bilateral relations around the importance of military bases, lucrative business ties, and mutual hostility toward leftists, communists, and otherwise uncooperative leaders. As top American leaders expressed their avowed commitment to democracy, human rights, and the rule of law, they deliberately ignored the realities of Saudi culture and its repressive, socially reactionary, anti-Semitic regime.

Although that arrangement neither alone nor primarily led to the rise of Islamist fanaticism, their Islamic-Christian alliance played a major role in the region's radicalization and destabilizing disintegration. The U.S.-Saudi Cold War alliance sacrificed America's commitment to liberalism for the sake of security and undermined both. The virulent strain of Wahhabi Islam, not shared by a majority of Muslims, particularly beyond the Arabian Peninsula, became an assertive ideological force across the Muslim world. It transcended ethnic and linguistic cleavages to become a malignant force defining the beginning of the 21st century.

6. Subverting Democracy: Supporting the Shah of Iran

One of Washington's favorite "friendly autocrats" during the Cold War was the Shah of Iran. Indeed, had it not been for U.S. support, the Shah might well have been enjoying a posh exile on the French Riviera after 1953 instead of perpetuating his controversial rule for the next quarter century. In the early 1950s, democracy seemed to be taking root in Iran, symbolized by the election of Prime Minister Mohammed Mossadegh, a long-standing fixture in Iranian politics, who had first been elected to the *Majlis* (parliament) in 1906. Mossadegh's goal was to reduce the power of the Shah and make him a Western-style monarch—someone who would "reign but not rule." The prime minister's popularity enabled him to gradually erode the Shah's constitutional powers and bring that goal tantalizingly within reach.

U.S. officials worried, though, that Mossadegh was getting too cozy with the Soviet Union, as well as being hostile to Western economic interests. His move to nationalize British and American oil assets significantly increased the degree of uneasiness in both London and Washington about his economic views. The new U.S. president, Dwight D. Eisenhower, epitomized an all-too-common American attitude during the Cold War when he linked those two developments. In his memoirs, Eisenhower stated succinctly: "Premier Mossadegh had nationalized Iran's oil resources, and the country was drifting dangerously toward Communism."[1]

The British were still smarting over the takeover of the Anglo-Iranian Oil Company two years earlier.[2] According to recently declassified Central Intelligence Agency (CIA) documents, Foreign Secretary Anthony Eden was especially adamant in his belief that the Iranian prime minister posed a serious threat to Britain's economic and strategic interests.[3] Although that belief existed before the nationalization of the oil company, it spiked dramatically thereafter. British officials were shrewd enough, though, not to emphasize their economic quarrels with Mossadegh, since Washington might have had mixed emotions about that problem. After all, the British oil companies were global competitors of U.S. firms. London instead highlighted the alleged growth of Soviet influence, knowing that the Eisenhower administration was especially worried about that danger. As senior British intelligence official Christopher Montague Woodhouse would later admit: "I decided to emphasize the Communist threat to Iran rather than the need to recover control of the oil industry."[4] It was a cynical tactic that anti-communist governments around the world had used to gain American assistance and would continue to use in the coming decades.

In his memoirs, Eisenhower repeatedly refers vaguely to "reports" coming in that Mossadegh was forging closer and closer ties with domestic communist factions.[5] It is likely that many (perhaps even most) of those reports came from British intelligence sources, furthering London's agenda to get rid of the Iranian prime minister. Although Washington fretted that Mossadegh was a Soviet stooge, in retrospect those fears seem largely unfounded. His political vehicle, the National Front, an alliance of centrist and left-of-center factions, did receive support from Tudeh, the Iranian Communist Party, but that support was less than enthusiastic. Indeed, Tudeh frequently scorned Mossadegh and other members of the National Front as "Iranian bourgeoise."[6] And Mossadegh's police forces were not shy about cracking down on Tudeh street demonstrations whenever those demonstrations threatened to get out of hand.

Mossadegh's government was in negotiations for a bilateral trade agreement with the Soviet Union, and talks were also underway to receive economic aid from Moscow, developments that agitated both U.S. and British leaders. But the proposed aid package would have been very modest—a mere $20 million a year—and several other countries (including India) received far more aid from the USSR without becoming Soviet puppets. Indeed, without the continuing British-led embargo against nationalized Iranian oil, which greatly reduced the amount of revenue coming into Tehran's treasury, it's not at all certain that the prime minister would have been even that cooperative with Moscow. Moreover, less than a month following the overthrow of the Mossadegh government, the United States agreed to give Tehran $68.4 million in "technical assistance" and "emergency" economic aid—more than three times the amount that the Kremlin had offered, which Eisenhower had cited as evidence of Moscow's undue influence in Iran.

While the prime minister was hardly a Soviet puppet, he was a staunch, abrasive nationalist, and that orientation got him into trouble with the United States. Author and veteran *New York Times* correspondent Stephen Kinzer describes Mossadegh's intense commitment to Iranian sovereignty: "Two central beliefs shaped Mossadegh's political consciousness. The first was a passionate faith in the rule of law, which made him an enemy of autocracy and, particular, Reza Shah. The second was a conviction that Iranians must rule themselves and not submit to the will of foreigners."[7]

Kinzer is absolutely correct on the second point, but only partially so on the first. As noted below, Mossadegh's commitment to the rule of law was somewhat fragile and inconsistent. He was inclined to view ideological opponents as outright enemies, and he was not above cutting constitutional corners to further his own agenda. Nevertheless, Mossadegh's government offered at least the hope that Iran might progress—however lurching the process might be at times—toward a mature, stable democracy. Conversely, the Shah and his inner circle were unabashed autocrats. Yet Washington and London chose to back the latter faction over the former.

Washington Helps Snuff Out Democracy and Restore the Shah

To forestall the growth of Soviet influence and to reverse the nationalization of British and American oil companies, Washington and London orchestrated a coup in the summer of 1953 to oust the prime minister and help reinstall the Shah as an absolute monarch. Crucial documents, finally declassified in 2013, released under the Freedom of Information Act, and published by the National Security Archive at George Washington University, confirm the nature and extent of the U.S. and British involvement in the effort to undermine Mossadegh and put the Shah back in power.

Those documents are especially important. As the National Security Archive noted upon their publication in August 2013, "the public release of these materials is noteworthy because CIA documents about 1953 are rare. First of all, agency officials have stated that most of the records on the coup were either lost or destroyed in the early 1960s, allegedly because the record-holders' safes were too full."[8]

One can certainly speculate about the veracity of the agency's explanation for the demise of such important documents.

There is no longer any credible doubt that the CIA was a major participant in the Iranian coup, codenamed TPAJAX and informally referred to as "Operation AJAX." (The British called their venture Operation Boot—probably with the meaning of "giving Mossadegh the boot.") Kermit Roosevelt, chief of the CIA's Near East Operations Division, was the on-the-ground manager of the coup. In his own account of the episode, published in 1979, Roosevelt discussed the U.S. role but presented it more as one of encouraging and supporting an indigenous uprising by the military, together with anti-communist Iranian civilians, against an increasingly undemocratic, left-leaning prime minister, rather than as a U.S.-British directed effort with (at most) modest Iranian input.[9] A few right-wing Iranian exiles, most notably former Ambassador Ardeshir Zahedi, still insist that the domestic uprising was genuine and that "clumsy" efforts by the CIA and Britain's MI6 merely worked in parallel with the campaign by Zahedi's father, General Fazollah Zahedi, to weaken Mossadegh.[10]

But the bulk of the evidence does not support that thesis, especially in light of the information in the recently declassified CIA documents, although some American scholars have produced new analyses roughly similar to Ardeshir Zahedi's account.[11] To be sure, Mossadegh was a controversial figure with the Iranian public, and it would be wrong to assert that the Shah had no domestic support beyond elements of the military. But it is equally inaccurate to argue that the United States and Britain were little more than bit players in a largely Iranian political drama.

Indeed, it would be difficult to exaggerate the extent of Washington's involvement in the operation. A previously excised portion of an internal CIA history, "The Battle for Iran," states candidly: "The military coup that overthrew Mossadegh and his National Front cabinet was carried out under CIA direction as an act of U.S. foreign policy, conceived and approved at the highest level of government."[12]

Not only did U.S. officials encourage the Iranian military to take action against the elected leader of the Iranian government, but the CIA spent lavishly to encourage high-ranking military officers who were prepared to turn against Mossadegh, as well as to recruit pro-Shah demonstrators to fill the streets. Even the correspondent for the *New York Times*, Kennett Love, seemed to be working for the CIA.

In a report to CIA chief Allen Dulles, Love described his role in the coup:

> A half-dozen tanks swarming with cheering soldiers were parked in front of the radio station. I told the tank commanders that a lot of people were getting killed trying to storm Dr. Mossadegh's house and that they, the tank commanders, ought to go down there where they would be of some use instead of sitting idle at the radio station. They declared my suggestion to be a splendid idea. They took their machines in a body to Kokh Avenue and put the three tanks at Dr. Mossadegh's house out of action after a lively duel with armor-piercing 75-millimeter shells.[13]

The U.S.-British strategy worked, and the untidy democracy in Iran was snuffed out. The Shah's new prime minister, Fazollah Zahedi, crushed National Front and Tudeh demonstrations. He also moved rapidly to consolidate power by marginalizing more moderate elements in the transitional government, choosing instead to do the monarch's bidding and establish unabashedly authoritarian rule. By the end of 1953, more than 2,100 people were imprisoned—a small down payment on the thousands who would enter the Shah's prison system in the coming years.

Mossadegh was hardly the perfect model of a democratic leader. He had troubling personality traits, including apparent egomania, and was not above playing the populist demagogue from time to time. One CIA assessment described him as one of the "most mercurial, maddening, adroit and provocative leaders" with whom U.S. officials had ever dealt.[14] On the eve of the 1953 crisis, Mossadegh asked parliament to make him commander-in-chief of the armed forces, in place of the Shah, and when the legislators refused, he dissolved the parliament and scheduled a snap plebiscite to ratify his decision. Even before that episode, he had asked—and received—parliamentary authorization both the previous year and in early 1953 to rule by decree, which he did at times.

Those are not healthy developments in any democratic system, especially an embryonic one that did not have a strong tradition of free elections, constitutional restraints on executive power, and respect for the rule of law. Yet, such deviations from democratic norms hardly warranted blatant U.S. and British interference in Iran's internal affairs to remove that government from office. Moreover, the new regime that the restored Shah appointed did not even make a pretense about being democratic. And whatever political and civil liberties abuses might have occurred under Mossadegh, they soon paled compared to those that the Shah and his appointees committed.

At least some of the motives for the coup were downright unsavory. Security concerns, albeit exaggerated, did play a role, but so did the desire to preserve narrow British and American economic interests—specifically to overturn Mossadegh's measures against the Anglo-Iranian Oil Company. Iranian-Armenian historian Ervand Abrahamian is at least partly right when he concludes that the coup was designed "to get rid of a nationalist figure who insisted that oil should be nationalized."[15]

Yet Abrahamian and other analysts who express similar views overstate matters when they conclude that the security justifications were nothing more than a cynical pretext for destroying a democratic regime that dared to pursue leftist economic policies. Contending that "there was never a realistic threat of communism," Abrahamian concludes that the way to justify the coup or any other act "was to talk about the communist danger, so it was something used for the public, especially the American and British public."[16] There is some truth to that observation, but the fear of communism and its seemingly inexorable advance around the world was very real in the 1950s. It was not just political or ideological posturing. The genuine nature of that fear, however, did not change the fact that it produced highly questionable policies toward Iran and other countries.

Whatever the mixture of motives, the coup continues to scar relations between the United States and Iran. Abbas Milani, director of the Iranian Studies Program at Stanford University, notes that in the immediate aftermath of the 1979 revolution overthrowing the Shah, the Iranian people seized the first opportunity available to commemorate Mossadegh. "More than a million of them converged on his estate a few kilometers outside Tehran and paid their tributes to an icon of their anti-colonial and democratic longings."[17]

Current Iranian politicians portray the country's pursuit of nuclear capability as a matter of national pride, and they specifically compare that goal to Mossadegh's oil-nationalization efforts. Whether sincerely believed or not, the comparison intentionally taps into a long-standing reservoir of resentment on the part of the Iranian people about the coup and its aftermath. But for the Islamic politicians, citing Mossadegh is somewhat risky, since he symbolized the goal of a secular, democratic republic, not a theocratic state.[18]

The Shah as America's "Friend"

During the quarter century following the coup, the Shah was Washington's designated gendarme in the Persian Gulf. The monarch's role became especially prominent after Britain essentially liquidated its military presence in that part of the world—largely for reasons of cost. President Jimmy Carter's national security adviser, Zbigniew Brzezinski, emphasized the adverse impact of the British decision and Iran's resulting importance: "During the sixties Iran became our major strategic asset in the wake of the British disengagement from 'east of Suez.' That pull-out created a power vacuum in the Persian Gulf region, and American policy was to fill it by building up the military capability first of Iran, then of Saudi Arabia, and by enhancing their political status as the two American-backed pillars of regional stability."[19] Of the two allies, Iran was considered the more important and reliable.

A succession of U.S. administrations showered Iran's growing military with the most modern hardware, and Tehran and Washington were military allies in every way despite the absence of a formal bilateral treaty. (Iran was a member of the Baghdad Pact, later renamed CENTO, but that arrangement provided few security obligations and was soon moribund.) U.S. leaders saw the Shah as a key barrier to the expansion of Soviet influence into the oil-rich Middle East. From a security standpoint, there was a plausible rationale to Washington's policies, but the United States did far more than form a limited relationship with an unsavory autocrat; it treated the Shah like a valued friend.

That friendship included U.S. equipment and training for SAVAK, the Shah's infamous secret police. Such action caused many Iranians to see the United States as a direct accomplice in the government's abuses against its own people. And there were abuses aplenty. The regime routinely imprisoned anyone suspected of being a critic, and by the 1970s, political prisoners numbered in the thousands. Such prisoners were not treated gently. Torture methods included electric shock, whipping, beating, insertion of broken glass into the rectum, the pouring of boiling water into the rectum, tying weights to the testicles, extraction of teeth, extraction of fingernails, rape, the mutilation of women's breasts, and the use of an apparatus called the *heK met*, which when worn over the head of the victim, magnifies his own screams.[20]

Human rights organizations repeatedly denounced the Shah's regime for torture and other outrages, and those complaints, already becoming noticeable in the late 1960s, mounted steadily during the 1970s. A 1969 report by Amnesty International noted that the organization "has been concerned for some time over the treatment of political offenders in Iran, both in court and at the hands of the police. Available information has suggested that changes in penal practice have lagged far behind the impressive reforms undertaken by the Government in other fields during the last few years. In particular, we have observed the continuing, and unconstitutional practice of trial by court martial in political cases, and the apparent license afforded to SAVAK in their pre-trial interrogation of prisoners."[21]

The report focused on the arrest and trial of 14 intellectuals accused of holding communist beliefs and of subversive activities. Amnesty sent an investigative team to Tehran, which found the trial procedures extremely troubling. The investigators noted that the trial took place before a military court, with meager due-process protections, and resulted in the conviction of all the accused, who received sentences ranging from 3 to 15 years. Upon the report and recommendation of the investigative team leader, Betty Assheton, an American-trained journalist, Amnesty International adopted several of the defendants as "prisoners of conscience," despite the serious nature of the formal charges brought against them.

The Shah's government did not react well to Amnesty's increasingly intrusive probes of the regime's human rights conduct. In a 1971 assessment, the group mentioned that consistent reports were reaching the international press over the previous year of continuing arrests, lengthy detention, and police brutality in Iran. In response to those reports, the Austrian Amnesty Section, which had recently been formed, decided to send its own mission of inquiry. Dr. Hans Heinz Heldmann, a German lawyer, traveled to Tehran in early October, accompanied by an interpreter, Hossein Rezai, an Iranian national and student at Mainz University in West Germany. They carried accreditations as delegates of the Austrian Section of Amnesty, but in October Iranian authorities expelled Heldmann and arrested Rezai.

Amnesty made "urgent and continuing approaches" to the Iranian government that Rezai's status as a delegate be recognized and that he be released and allowed to return to his university in Germany. The Amnesty report sharply criticized the official reply "that Rezai must stand trial, and that any visa application for an Amnesty delegate to attend his trial will be refused—a direct reversal of the Government's announcement in January that henceforth political trials would be open to observers from recognized international organizations."[22] The Iranian government spurned all appeals for Rezai's release. Instead, he was put on trial and sentenced to 10 years in prison.

An Amnesty report the following year was noticeably critical of the government in Tehran. "The celebrations of the 2,500 anniversary of the Persian Empire not only successfully avoided mention of Iran's political prisoners and inadequate judicial system, but also resulted in many more people being imprisoned for their opposition, or suspected opposition, to the present government." Noting that "detailed and accurate information on those arrested is hard to obtain," the organization nevertheless concluded that "it is certain that many have been sentenced to death, and executed after trials before a military tribunal without independent evidence or witnesses being heard and without effective defense."[23]

In September 1971 Amnesty International issued a press statement appealing to the Iranian government to release all prisoners of conscience as part of an amnesty to mark the 2,500th anniversary of the founding of the Persian Empire. The statement also recalled specific proposals that Amnesty had made to the government in 1970 and 1971, which aimed to provide some protection for political prisoners during the phase of pretrial investigation. Those proposals included visits by civilian magistrates; the use of civilian, rather than military, courts to try civilian defendants; the right of appeal in political cases to a civilian higher court; and an amendment to legislation relating to SAVAK establishing penalties for officials responsible for physical mistreatment of prisoners under investigation.

The Shah's regime refused to announce any amnesty. Instead, more than 2,000 people were arrested, and early in October, probably during the 2,500th anniversary celebrations, Hossein Rezai was tried before a secret military court in Teheran. At its November 1971 meeting, Amnesty International's executive committee issued a statement commenting on Rezai's trial, as well as other recent arrests and sentences. It recalled official assurances that there would be a reform of the legal system for political cases, and that future political trials would be held in open court in the presence of foreign observers. The statement concluded that "these new events cast fundamental doubt on such assurances and suggest that the Iranian government has now set aside its stated intention of treating political prisoners in accordance with the rule of law and the practice of responsible nations."[24]

In January 1972 a series of political trials was announced, at which 120 people who had been arrested during 1971 would be tried before the Tehran Military Tribunal. All were charged with violent offenses against the government. Although observers from international organizations attended some early sessions of the tribunal, the court was closed after a report had appeared in the French newspaper *Le Monde* commenting adversely on the conduct of the trial. A large number of those on trial were sentenced to death, and 23 were executed. In December 1971, and again in February 1972, Amnesty joined with other international nongovernmental organizations in statements expressing concern at torture allegations and at the manner of trial.

On March 1, 1972, Amnesty's secretary general signed a letter to the Iranian prime minister asking for death sentences to be commuted. That letter also criticized the lack of fairness in the trials of regime opponents. "We do not question your government's right to bring to trial individuals charged with violent or criminal offences, but the reports suggest that the defendants have been denied certain defense rights which are normally regarded as fundamental to the rule of law . . . . As civilians, the accused are being tried in military courts; this means that they are defended by military lawyers who would not necessarily have been their first choice as legal representatives. Perhaps most important of all, the Tribunal is reported to have accepted as evidence confessions of guilt which the defendants themselves had already repudiated in court on the ground that they were made after torture."[25]

Amnesty International published a report in August 1972 on trial procedures for political prisoners in Iran. The report, which was based on Iranian legal documentation as well as accounts from lawyers who had attended trials in Iran over a period of several years, concluded that "the denial of individual rights to political prisoners between arrest and imprisonment or execution is obvious. Also apparent is the breach of various international undertakings, many of which may be binding in international law on Iran. The repudiation by its domestic practice of the principles of human rights publicly espoused by Iran is unfortunately manifest." In a press statement that accompanied the report, Amnesty expressed "grave concern at the high number of executions of political offenders which have taken place in Iran this year."[26]

Concerns about reports that political prisoners were being beaten and ill-treated in other ways at Adel Abbad prison in Shiraz and at Qasar prison in Tehran were raised in a letter from Amnesty's secretary general to Prime Minister Amir Abbas Hoveida in September 1973. The letter also asked about the health of particular prisoners. There was no response to that letter or to a subsequent one sent to the Iranian ambassador in London, in which the secretary general requested that an Amnesty observer be admitted to the trial of 12 people in January 1974. Although Amnesty leaders conceded that it was impossible to estimate with any degree of accuracy the number of political prisoners being detained in Iran, the organization concluded that there were "many thousands" and that the number appeared to be expanding rapidly.[27]

In November 1976, Amnesty International published a Briefing Paper on Iran, in which it stated that the issues the organization was particularly concerned about in Iran were arbitrary arrest of suspected political opponents, the use of torture, lack of legal safeguards, unsatisfactory trial procedures, executions, and unofficial executions. This publication and the accompanying campaign designed to publicize it provoked an official reaction from the Iranian authorities for the first time in several years. The following January two government-controlled newspapers in Iran accused Amnesty of conducting an "anti-Iranian" campaign. That was followed immediately by an open letter from the Iranian foreign ministry to the British parliament, the Western news media, and Western commercial firms doing business in Iran. The letter charged that "Iran has been made the target of a concerted worldwide campaign of denigration launched by Amnesty International." It concluded with a related allegation that the human rights body had a "proven record of political bias against Iran."[28] That is a standard charge that authoritarian regimes have directed against Amnesty and other human rights watchdogs, and it is one without validity.

In April 1977 a trial of 11 political prisoners took place in Tehran. Those prisoners, who were charged with supporting communist groups, received sentences of between 3 years and life imprisonment, later reduced on appeal to between 2 and 10 years imprisonment. The trial was significant, though, because it was the first judicial proceeding since February 1972 that foreign observers and journalists were allowed to attend.

There were ominous signs both of greater resistance to the regime and of a skittish reaction by an Iranian government feeling the mounting pressure. In addition to the four official executions of political prisoners the government reported during the year, the number of political activists reportedly killed during battles with the police noticeably increased. At the same time, the Shah made some cautious moves to try to placate his critics. Several amnesties of prisoners, including political prisoners, were announced between June 1976 and March 1977. Most of those announcements were gestures to mark the 50th anniversary of the Pahlavi dynasty; others were in honor of the Shah's birthday and the Iranian New Year. Reports of the numbers released in each amnesty varied, but according to an announcement published by the official Pars news agency on February 27, 1977, nearly 5,000 prisoners had been freed since the jubilee year began in March 1976.

Iranian officials also sought to downplay the overall number of political prisoners being held. Parviz Sabeti, deputy director of SAVAK, stated in a September 3, 1976, *Washington Post* interview that "in all Iran there are only 3,200 political prisoners."[29] Independent sources, though, insisted that the total was much higher.

And negative press comment in the United States about Tehran's human rights record continued to grow. A typical example was a May 1976 piece by syndicated columnists Jack Anderson and Les Whitten in the pages of the *Washington Post* and other newspapers around the country. The authors cited the Shah's decision to mark the celebration of the U.S. bicentennial by flying 150 American celebrities to Iran for a week of partying. "They were wined, dined, and entertained in a splendor that rivaled the excesses of [ancient Persian emperor] Xerxes." But "behind all the glitter," Anderson and Witten emphasized, "the Shah rules by torture."[30]

An especially sickening case they cited came from "a courageous Iranian poet, Reza Baraheni," who spent time "in a SAVAK dungeon." They described some of his account in detail. "He was beaten, whipped, and exposed to the sound of screaming prisoners. From his experiences and those of other inmates, Baraheni described how prisoners were lashed to the top of an iron, double-deck bed, which was transformed into a human toaster. 'With the heat coming from a torch or small heater, they burn your back in order to extract information,'" Baraheni confided. "'Sometimes the burning is extended to the spine, as a result of which paralysis is certain.'"

As horror stories like that began to circulate on a regular basis in the U.S. news media, criticism of Washington's association with the Shah's government mounted, causing greater public and congressional uneasiness. That trend coincided with the rising discontent inside Iran with the occupant of the Peacock Throne. But while the American public gradually turned against the Shah because of his regime's human rights abuses, at least until the administration of Jimmy Carter, the executive branch remained deaf to such protests. And even the Carter administration's response seemed ambivalent.

To make matters worse, a majority of SAVAK's victims were secular types. Although some were Leninists or communist sympathizers, others appeared to be genuine democrats. Many of the Islamic radicals who would come to dominate the 1979 revolution either fled into exile or wisely held their tongues. Ironically, America's assistance to the Shah may have weakened democratic forces in Iran at the expense of religious factions, helping to pave the way for a radical Islamic takeover and the establishment of a rabidly anti-Western theocracy.

Perhaps the moral low point in the relationship with the Shah came on New Year's Eve 1977, when President Jimmy Carter made a lavish toast to the Iranian tyrant during a state visit to Tehran. "Iran, because of the great leadership of the Shah, is an island of stability in one of the more troubled regions of the world. This is a great tribute to you, Your Majesty, and to your leadership, and to the respect and admiration and love which your people give to you," Carter gushed. Apparently concluding that America's vocal enthusiasm for the Shah and his policies during the previous quarter century did not link the United States sufficiently to his conduct, the president emphasized: "We have no other nation on earth who [*sic*] is closer to us in planning for our mutual security." But according to Carter, the United States and Iran shared more than security interests. "The cause of human rights is one that is also shared deeply by our people and by the leaders of our two nations."[31] Given the Iranian regime's record of human rights abuses, which were well documented by the late 1970s, that praise was astonishingly inaccurate and insensitive.

Such an effusive toast was ironic on two levels. First, it came not from a president like Richard Nixon who was an unabashed practitioner of realpolitik, but from the lips of a president who stressed the importance of democracy and respect for human rights as a high priority in his administration's foreign policy. Second, the toast came at a time when the Shah's power was not at its zenith, as it was from the mid-1950s to the early 1970s, but at a time when his authority was already beginning to wane.

Missing the Signals: Both Washington and the Shah Miscalculate

Barely a year later, the Shah's regime lay in ruins, soon to be replaced by a virulently anti-American government. Carter's assumption that the Shah was loved by the Iranian people was a classic case of wishful thinking. Some CIA operatives in the field were already warning their superiors that the administration's perception was a delusion and that the regime in Tehran was increasingly fragile, but those reports were ignored by senior CIA officials in Washington because they did not reflect established policy.[32] Instead, the intelligence reports passed on to administration policymakers painted a picture of continued stability in Iran. Blind to reality, the Carter administration identified itself and American security interests with a regime that was already careening toward oblivion. Washington's relationship with Tehran was, therefore, not only morally questionable, it was strategically unsound.

The Carter administration reacted to the growing turmoil in Iran in 1978 and early 1979 with noticeable indecision. Partly, that reflected deep divisions within the administration about how to deal with the problem. The State Department, led by Secretary Cyrus Vance, wanted the Shah to loosen his authoritarian grip and make common cause with democratic reformers. Even during the early months of Carter's presidency, before the turmoil in Iran became acute, Vance had stressed the need for a "balanced" policy. He recalled that, although the administration "recognized the importance of Iran in Persian Gulf security matters," he and his colleagues were "also determined to hew to our position on human rights and to our goal of restraining the sale of American weapons."[33]

The latter was a particular sore point with the new administration. Vance and other officials believed that during the Nixon and Ford years, the U.S. relationship with Iran had focused far too much on the military dimension. Among other unfortunate consequences of that approach, they concluded, was that it led the Shah to deviate from the original trajectory of his White Revolution of the 1960s and its broad-based effort to create a diversified, modern economy to a policy in the 1970s that overemphasized an enormous (and expensive) military buildup and a greater focus on establishing a robust indigenous defense industry. It had also become awkward for the United States to be showering Iran with military sales, even as the Shah's human rights record remained dreadful. Indeed, that juxtaposition of lavish arms sales and rights abuses had become a major grievance for American human rights groups and their allies in Congress.

Carter State Department officials believed that Washington should exert subtle, but significant, pressure on the Shah to move toward both democratic reforms and better human rights practices. Part of that strategy reflected a genuine commitment to those values that was noticeably stronger than in previous U.S. administrations. But there were also more pragmatic motives. Brzezinski recalled that "we knew that our ties with Iran would suffer if our principal regional ally was seen by the American public as flagrantly violating human rights."[34] He had ample reason to be concerned on that score. Anti-Shah demonstrations were becoming larger and more vocal in the United States during the 1970s, and reports of the Iranian regime's human rights abuses were growing.

During 1977, Carter administration officials felt that the new, more balanced, U.S. approach was having a beneficial impact on Tehran's behavior. According to Vance:

> We applauded and supported the measures that the shah was beginning to take to improve human rights; he already had begun to curb SAVAK . . . in its use of extralegal measures to control subversion, and he was working to strengthen judicial and police procedures for dealing with political opponents. He also appeared to be contemplating modest political liberalization in an attempt to reach the more moderate elements of the secular opposition, thus bringing them into association with the imperial regime. These measures, while overdue, were important, and they received our support.[35]

Although there was some truth to Vance's assessment, the changes in regime behavior were actually quite modest. And like so many autocratic allies of the United States, the Shah was adept at playing the communist-threat card to ensure Washington's continued backing and dilute any pressure for political liberalization. That strategy was on full display when the secretary of state met with the monarch during a May 1977 visit to Tehran. The Shah listened patiently to Vance's comments that human rights were a high-priority objective in U.S. foreign policy around the globe. The secretary of state could hardly have been pleased by the Shah's response to that presentation, however. Vance recalled: "He said that his regime was under attack from within by Communists and assorted fellow travelers and that there were limits on how far he could go in restraining his security forces. He warned that if Iran were to slip into civil strife, only the Soviet Union would benefit. He had no objection to our human rights policy, he said, as long as it was a question of general principle and not directed at him or did not threaten his country's security."[36]

In other words, U.S. officials could pontificate all they wished about respect for human rights in the abstract, provided that they didn't seek to pressure Tehran to change the substance of its behavior.

President Carter received a similar response during a private summit meeting with the Shah during the monarch's November

1977 visit to Washington. Carter expressed relatively mild criticism of the regime's human rights practices, even putting that criticism in the larger context of praising the "great improvements which have been made in your country." The president tried to be the consummate diplomat, merely stating that "a growing number of your own citizens are claiming that [human] rights are not always honored in Iran." That comment had to rank as a rather remarkable understatement. Carter closed his comments by asking: "Is there anything that can be done to alleviate this problem by closer consultation with the dissident groups and by easing off on some of the strict police policies?"[37]

To his credit, the Shah managed to conceal any contempt he might have felt for Carter's naiveté. The president recalled that the monarch paused for a few moments before he replied "somewhat sadly": "No, there is nothing I can do. I must enforce the Iranian laws, which are designed to combat communism." Having invoked the bugaboo most likely to agitate an American political leader, the Shah then added that communism "is a very real and dangerous problem for Iran—and, indeed, for the other countries in my area and in the Western world. It may be that when this serious menace is removed, the laws can be changed, but that will not be soon." He also sought to puncture any enthusiasm that the American president might have had for critics of the regime. "In any case, the complaints and recent disturbances originate among the very troublemakers against whom the laws have been designed to protect our country." But the Shah was not worried. "They are really just a tiny minority, and have no support among the vast majority of the Iranian people."[38]

It is uncertain whether the Shah sincerely believed that internal communist forces posed a serious threat to his rule, or whether he invoked that specter because he knew that it was the argument most likely to frighten Washington and deflect the growing pressure he was receiving about the need for reform. Whatever the case, a domestic communist threat proved to be the least of the Shah's—or America's—worries when political turmoil erupted the following year and soon spun out of control. The real threat to the Shah's power came from reactionary religious elements, not the radical, secular left. Indeed, in retrospect it is striking how irrelevant communist factions were in the Iranian revolution. Yet even as that revolution deepened and it appeared likely that the Ayatollah Khomeini would proclaim an Islamic republic, Washington's chief worry was that Iran would drift toward communism.[39] Tehran and Washington were focused on a communist threat that was, at the least, highly exaggerated, while they woefully underestimated the strength of the religious factions.

The trouble in Iran began slowly, with sporadic street demonstrations. Dissatisfaction about corruption, continued repression, and most of all, declining job prospects accompanied by mounting inflation, appeared to be the primary grievances. The economic problems were especially prominent and had an importance that American officials tended to underestimate. The "stagflation" that characterized much of the global economy during the mid- and late 1970s was an annoyance in the United States and other prosperous, developed countries. In a relatively poor, developing country like Iran it was potential social and political dynamite. Most worrisome, but largely missed by U.S. officials at the time, was that religion had become the principal factor uniting the various factions in the demonstrations.

National Security Advisor Zbigniew Brzezinski, to an even greater extent than Vance and his State Department subordinates, believed that the Shah was an indispensable U.S. strategic ally. Consequently, he urged the United States to convey to the Iranian monarch that Washington backed him "without reservation."[40] As the situation worsened, Brzezinski urged Carter to prod the Iranian leader to crack down harder on anti-regime demonstrations, and, if necessary, to impose military rule. Brzezinski also wanted Washington to convey to the Shah in explicit terms that he would have full U.S. backing if he decided to take that drastic step.[41] The national security adviser fretted that pressuring the Iranian autocrat to embrace democratic reforms might merely whet the appetite of his domestic adversaries. On that last point, he was probably correct. The Shah had so alienated key portions of the population that there was little willingness on their part to compromise.

President Carter found it difficult to decide which course to take, given the increasingly sharp divisions between his top security advisers. Brzezinski conceded that "disagreement within the U.S. government widened as the situation in Iran deteriorated."[42] The divisions within the administration were so pronounced that even the Shah and his inner circle were aware of them, and they expressed loathing for the Vance State Department faction, especially Henri Precht, who headed the Iran desk that kept prodding Tehran to take steps toward political liberalization. At one point the Iranian monarch reportedly referred to Precht as "that son of a bitch McGovernite" who caused "confusion" in Washington's policy regarding Iran.[43]

Carter's own instincts were fairly close to those of Vance; both men wanted to support the Shah but also to press him to accelerate political reforms and seek alliances with the more moderate, democratic elements to fend off the religious extremists. If there was a difference in their approach, Vance tended to place more emphasis on the need for reform, while his boss placed a little more emphasis on the need to reassure the Shah and give him consistent backing.

More than Carter, and far more than Vance, Brzezinski reflected the more traditional U.S. Cold War policy of jaundiced skepticism regarding democracy in developing countries. He admits in his memoirs, "I did not think that Iran as a country was ready for democracy." That assessment was only a little less patronizing and ethnically insensitive than General Wickham's infamous comment at the beginning of the 1980s about the South Koreans' supposed lack of suitability for democracy (see chapter 3). Indeed, Brzezinski appeared to prefer authoritarian rule in Iran. At one point in early November, when the Shah seemed intent on proclaiming martial law, Brzezinski stated that such a decision "greatly relieved me." On another occasion, during the final stages of the crisis when the Shah designated a new reformist prime minister, Shahpur Bakhtiar, and prepared to go into exile, President Carter asked his national security adviser point-blank what he recommended, since he was apparently unhappy with the current policy. "I told him we should have encouraged the military to stage a coup," Brzezinski recalled.[44]

Even though Carter seemed a bit miffed at Brzezinski's militancy, Carter never fully signed on to the competing approach, either. As the crisis deepened, he even complained that some of Vance's State Department subordinates seemed determined to dilute White House policy when it came to backing the Shah. He was especially irritated at the U.S. ambassador in Tehran, William Sullivan, who by late 1978 had concluded that the Iranian ruler had no chance at political survival and urged a course of reaching out to opposition forces—even to the Ayatollah Khomeini and his followers. Sullivan apparently did not agree with White House (or Vance's) directives that embraced a different course, and his response, Carter believed, was one "bordering on insolence."[45]

What shows through clearly regarding the Iranian crisis is that U.S. officials overestimated the Shah's ability to retain power (at least until the final weeks), overestimated the willingness of the Shah and democratic forces to forge an alliance against the religious factions, and grossly underestimated the strength of Khomeini and his supporters. It was as though Carter administration policymakers could not fully comprehend that a seemingly strong ruler, and a long-standing useful ally of the United States, was poised to fall from power. The CIA's analyses fed that complacency. An August 1978 CIA assessment concluded that Iran "is not in a revolutionary or even a pre-Revolutionary situation." Carter related later that the report emphasized that the military was loyal to the monarchy and that opposition forces, both violent and nonviolent factions, did not "have the capacity to be more than troublesome."[46] As late as October—barely three months before the Shah would be forced to go into exile—Carter and his principal advisers still believed "that the Shah was our best hope for maintaining stability in Iran."[47]

By the time the Shah and Carter administration officials did grasp the extent of the political tsunami that was building in Iran, it was probably too late to stop it—short of a massive U.S. military intervention. And that was never considered a feasible option.

In the end, both the Shah and his American patrons acted like deer caught in headlights. The Shah at least had the excuse of a serious illness for his lack of an effective response. His cancer, which had first surfaced in 1973, had become advanced and aggressive by 1978, and it took both a physical and emotional toll on the monarch. How much the need to deal with his illness may have affected his decisionmaking is impossible to tell, but it certainly did not help matters.

U.S. officials had no such excuse for their policy paralysis. They could not seem to decide whether to endorse a military coup and a brutal crackdown on demonstrators or, conversely, to embrace a comprehensive agenda of democratic reforms, with the Shah fully ceding power to democratic political figures. Consequently, they temporized, trying to craft an arrangement that would make concessions to the opposition while still enabling the Shah to exercise some power and influence. They never came up with the right formula, and in the end, events simply overtook all of their plans.

Most telling, U.S. leaders continued to underestimate the skill of Khomeini and his religious followers and the overall strength of that faction. Brzezinski explicitly concedes that point, noting that Islamic fundamentalism was "a phenomenon largely ignored in our intelligence reports."[48] Even worse, American policymakers never comprehended the depth of the anger that had built up among the Iranian people toward the United States for its long-time support of the Shah—an anger that would make revolutionary Iran a mortal enemy of the United States for decades to come.

America's Rationale for Backing the Shah: Reasonable or Short-Sighted?

Washington's support for the Shah was a curious mixture of realist foreign policy calculations and a genuine (even slightly sentimental) admiration for the man and his agenda for Iran. That mixture was evident in the assessments of two very different officials, Henry Kissinger and Jimmy Carter. Kissinger is considered to be almost a caricature of a realpolitik practitioner. Carter, on the other hand, stressed the importance of moral values in American foreign policy—too much so, in the opinion of his conservative critics. Yet both men reached surprisingly similar conclusions about the Shah and the U.S.-Iranian relationship during his reign.

Kissinger's version of realpolitik is certainly in evidence. "Whatever the failings of the Shah," Kissinger wrote in his memoirs, "he was for us that rarest of leaders, an unconditional ally, and one whose understanding of the world situation enhanced our own."[49] The former secretary of state elaborated on the geostrategic importance to America of Iran during the Shah's rule.

> Under the Shah's leadership, the land bridge between Asia and Europe, so often the hinge of world history, was pro-American and pro-West beyond any challenge. Alone among the countries of the region—Israel aside—Iran made friendship with the United States the starting point of its foreign policy. That it was based on a cold-eyed assessment that a threat to Iran would come from the Soviet Union, in combination with radical Arab states, is only another way of saying that the Shah's view of the realities of world politics paralleled our own. Iran's influence was always on our side; its resources reinforced ours even in some distant enterprises.[50]

There was a long list of useful actions that Kissinger could cite: "The Shah absorbed the energies of radical Arab neighbors to prevent them from threatening the moderate regimes in Saudi Arabia, Jordan, and the Persian Gulf. He refueled our fleets without question. He never used his control of oil to bring political pressure; he never joined any oil embargo against the West or Israel."[51] Such support for U.S. policy aims was far more than merely useful, according to Kissinger. "It was imperative for our interests and those of the Western world that the regional balance of power be maintained so that moderate forces would not be engulfed nor Europe's and Japan's (and as it later turned out, our) economic lifeline fall into hostile hands."[52]

Given Kissinger's twin assumptions that hostile (implicitly, Soviet) control of the oil flow from the Middle East would threaten Western economic health and that a victory by Arab radicalism would threaten the geostrategic balance—not just of the Middle East, but of Europe—it was not surprising that he saw the Shah as a crucial, indeed indispensable, U.S. ally. America, in Kissinger's view, did not have the option of a laissez faire attitude about developments in that part of the world. That left only two options. "We could either provide the balancing force ourselves or enable a regional power to do so." America's domestic political realities, even in the 1950s and 1960s, but especially once the public turned against the Vietnam War, he contended, made the first option impossible. "Fortunately, Iran was willing to play this role."[53]

Kissinger's views largely reflected the conventional wisdom in Washington—then and now—regarding the alleged imperative value of the Middle East/Persian Gulf region. A decent case could be made for the strategic calculations during the intense Cold War rivalry with the Soviet Union. Various scholars, including David R. Henderson, the senior energy economist on President Ronald Reagan's Council of Economic Advisers, have debunked the notion of the "oil weapon" being wielded by local regimes, however.[54] The reality is that Middle East governments would have little choice but to put their oil into the global market, since for most of them it is overwhelmingly their most important source of revenue. Indeed, for some of them, it is the only meaningful source of income to keep the incumbent regimes in power. And once in the global market, oil will flow to the highest bidders, regardless of politics. Only if the

Soviet Union could have gained secure control over the oil supply and—for Moscow's own political and strategic motives—prevented indigenous countries from maintaining the supply, would it arguably have posed an economic threat to the democratic West.

So, one of Kissinger's assumptions about the value and importance of the Shah was based on an unfortunate, albeit all too common, myth. And if keeping the oil flow in "friendly hands" is not a vital American interest, then the need to maintain a pro-Western tilt in the politics of the Middle East (his other assumption) becomes less compelling as well. But given his assumptions, it is understandable that he felt that the only choices were a direct U.S. military presence or outsourcing the stabilization role to a friendly, major regional player. And it is not coincidental that once the Shah fell from power, the United States did adopt a much larger military footprint in the region—after a brief, and only partially successful, flirtation with Iraq's Saddam Hussein as a possible substitute U.S. client in the 1980s. Since the 1990–91 Persian Gulf crisis, Washington has implemented Kissinger's first option—the one that he described as not possible in the 1970s.

It would be a mistake, though, to assume that Kissinger's support for the Shah was based solely on realist strategic calculations. Arguments about friendship, honor, and even morality to justify the relationship between Washington and Tehran abound in his memoirs. He repeatedly describes the Iranian monarch as a "friend," not just a useful ally, of the United States. "Iran under the Shah," he asserted, "was one of America's best, most important, and most loyal friends in the world." Kissinger railed at those who criticized the Shah following his overthrow in 1979. "It hardly enhances our reputation for steadfastness to hear the chorus today against a leader whom eight presidents proclaimed—rightly—a friend of our country and a pillar of stability in a turbulent world."[55]

Such sentimentality seems a bit odd coming from a policymaker who regards himself as a calculating realist. As the 19th-century British statesman Lord Palmerston rightly observed, nations do not have permanent friends or allies, they only have permanent interests. Indeed, it is even more accurate to say that while individuals may have friends, nations don't have friends—permanent or otherwise. And the Shah certainly did not view the United States in terms of friendship. Especially as he grew older, he appeared to have barely concealed disdain for American (indeed, Western) cultural and political values. Although the Persian monarch considered the West a model for his economic modernization plans, that is about as far as the admiration went. By the late 1960s and early 1970s, he saw the United States and the other Western powers as decadent societies that were headed for decline, if not outright collapse.[56]

Kissinger's apparent fondness for the Shah not only caused him to overestimate the Iranian leader's regard for the United States, it led him to distort the historical record. The secretary whitewashed both the unsavory U.S. role in overthrowing the Mossadegh government and the Iranian monarch's authoritarian, even brutal, practices once back in power. Kissinger's version of the 1953 coup was that the Shah "had been restored to the throne" by "American influence" when "a leftist government had come close to toppling him."[57] That description is a grotesque distortion. In particular, referring to the U.S. role as merely one of "influence" is an affront to historical truth.

Unfortunately, such dissembling is typical of the accounts that U.S. leaders have given. Kissinger's boss, Richard Nixon, described the 1953 events as follows: "A violent coup had taken place and pro-communist government of Prime Minister Mohammed Mossadegh was overthrown by the military. A government supporting the Shah . . . was installed under Prime Minister Fazollah Zahedi." Leaving aside Nixon's drive-by smear of Mossadegh's government, there was not a hint of the extensive role that U.S. and British intelligence agencies played in that episode. Writing in 1978, shortly before the Shah's downfall, Nixon also blithely argued that without the leadership of the Shah and Zahedi, "I am convinced Iran would not be an independent nation today."[58]

Kissinger's assessment of the Shah's domestic policies is only marginally more accurate than his deceptive account of the 1953 coup. "Without a doubt, the Shah was an authoritarian ruler," he concedes. But an apologia quickly follows in every case. Such authoritarianism, "was in keeping with the traditions, perhaps even the necessities, of his society." Indeed, the Shah was, Kissinger insisted, "despite the travesties of retroactive myth—a dedicated reformer."[59]

More than two generations of U.S. political leaders presented highly sanitized versions of the Shah's rule to the American people. For example, President Eisenhower contended that the monarch was "far from being a dictator," although Eisenhower did concede that he possessed more authority "than any constitutional monarch in Europe."[60] Such an assessment was absurd on its face. Twentieth-century European monarchs exercised little or no authority, whereas the Shah's power was unchallenged and almost unlimited. If the Shah was not a dictator, then that concept has no meaning.

Gerald Ford offered a similarly sanitized historical interpretation. According to Ford, the Shah's regime "had made remarkable progress in its efforts to transform a backward land into a modern industrial state." But "not everyone agreed with the Shah's plans for development; resistance emerged, and Savak, the Shah's secret police, sometimes resorted to brutality to put it down." Despite making that grudging (and mild) concession, Ford went on to argue that "the hard geopolitical reality was that Iran served as an indispensable buffer between the Soviet Union and the oil-producing states of Saudi Arabia and the United Arab Emirates." In addition, "the Shah let us use facilities close to his northern border from which we could monitor Soviet strategic arms research and development."[61]

The presumably "moralistic" Jimmy Carter provides an assessment of Washington's three-decade relationship with the Shah that does not differ all that much from the assessment that supposed realist policymakers such as Eisenhower, Nixon, Kissinger, and Ford, presented. "I continued, as other Presidents before me, to consider the Shah a strong ally," Carter explained in his memoirs. "I appreciated his ability to maintain good relations with Egypt and Saudi Arabia, and his willingness to provide Israel with oil in spite of the Arab boycott."[62]

Even when the crisis deepened in late 1978, Carter recalled that "there was no question in my mind" that the Shah "deserved our unequivocal support." In part, that support was warranted because he "had been a staunch and dependable ally of the United States for many years."[63]

Like Kissinger, Ford, and Carter, Cyrus Vance made a valiant effort to make the case for why America's de facto alliance with Tehran made sense. The Shah, he argued, "had been helpful in reducing tensions in Southwest Asia. Iranian forces had aided the pro-Western ruler of Oman to defeat an insurgency backed by the leftist regime in Aden." But it wasn't just his regional security role that Washington valued. "Iran was a reliable supplier of oil to the West, and its exports were critical to our NATO allies and Japan. The shah had refused to join the 1973 Arab oil embargo or to use oil as a political weapon." Vance also had to concede, though, that the Shah "was a strong advocate of higher OPEC prices."[64]

Yet, even his apostasy on oil prices was not entirely hostile to U.S. interests. His support for high prices occurred—in part, at least—because of his need to finance Iran's purchase of military equipment. And most of those purchases were from the United States. It was debatable whether Washington's alliance with Tehran benefited the overall best interests of the American people, but it indisputably benefited the interests of America's defense and aerospace industries. Moreover, despite the Shah's support for profit-maximizing OPEC pricing, Vance (and other U.S. policymakers) regarded that position as a minor flaw in an otherwise beneficial association. In virtually every other respect, the secretary of state believed, "there was considerable harmony between the shah's policies and our regional interests."[65]

When viewed from a narrow and short-term perspective, that assessment was undoubtedly true. But it ignored the debasement of important American values. It also ignored the longer-term, extremely adverse implications for America's interests of alienating the Iranian people and giving Islamic radicalism throughout the region an emotional grievance against the United States. America was lucky in places like South Korea and the Philippines that Washington's support for unpopular tyrants did not lead to a bitter and violent backlash when those rulers fell from power. We did not have the same good fortune in Iran.

Conservative Nostalgia and the Making of a Myth

The Shah's fall from power fostered a myth among American conservatives that began almost immediately and persists to this day. A core belief was that the feckless Carter administration failed to support a vital ally in his hour of need and thereby badly damaged America's position in the Middle East and the republic's overall security. Even Zbigniew Brzezinski, while not conceding the first part of that assessment, did implicitly concede the second. "The Iranian disaster shattered the strategic pivot of a protected tier shielding the crucial oil-rich region of the Persian Gulf from possible Soviet intrusion. The northeast frontier of Turkey, the northern frontiers of Iran and Pakistan, and the neutral buffer of Afghanistan created a formidable barrier, which was pierced once Iran ceased to be America's outpost."[66]

According to Ronald Reagan's first secretary of state, Alexander Haig, the United States, thanks to the Carter foreign policy team, "had not merely countenanced the fall of its steadfast ally, the Shah, it had accepted that his overthrow was not just inevitable but, in some inexplicable sense, moral and desirable."[67] President Reagan himself sneered that the Carter administration made a decision to "stand by piously" while a man "who had been our friend and solid ally for more than thirty-five years" was forced from office.[68]

Fox News talk-show host Sean Hannity refers to Carter's "betrayal of Iran," and accuses him of having "broke faith with the Shah," whom Hannity describes as a "moderate." According to Hannity, "with the Shah's government under assault, Carter offered no assistance—indeed he actually urged the Iranian *not* to defend himself." That statement is an extraordinary distortion of U.S. policy during the final year of the Shah's reign. But Hannity typifies the conservative view of the Shah's fall from power when he contends that Carter "could not see past his own inclination to moralize over the Shah's transgressions."[69]

At least Hannity concedes that the Iranian monarch was guilty of (undefined) transgressions. That's more than Council on Foreign Relations senior fellow Max Boot seems willing to do, referring to "America's great friend, the Shah," and accusing the Carter administration of doing very little to help the monarch in his hour of need because of a misplaced U.S. desire to "woo support among the revolutionaries."[70] Author Steven F. Hayward goes even further, contending that although the Shah was "easily stereotyped in the West as an unappealing and unimaginative autocrat," he was in reality "a relatively progressive ruler." Hayward does concede that SAVAK's activities fell short of "Western standards of due process." Nevertheless, "on balance, Pahlavi was not a great oppressor. He wanted to be loved rather than feared. For all the notorious excesses of SAVAK, Pahlavi did not permit the full force of the security organization to be brought to bear on his enemies."[71]

According to Hayward, there was only one serious option for the Shah to shore up his position once the crisis erupted, "and that was a firm crackdown on the opposition—probably through a declaration of martial law." He contends that "many leaders of the Iranian military expected this, and were certain that the U.S. would make sure such a plan succeeded."[72] How the United States could have made sure that martial law would have quelled the growing opposition, Hayward does not say.

His vagueness about alternatives is consistent with the indictments that other conservative critics make of the Carter administration's handling of the crisis that led to the Shah's exile and the emergence of a vehemently anti-U.S. Islamist regime. They rarely give specifics about what they think Washington should have done differently—much less provide evidence that a more hard-line approach had a reasonable prospect of success. Prominent neoconservative scholar Michael Ledeen's vague policy prescription is typical, contending on the one hand that it was "imperative for us to act," but insisting that "the actions required were political not military."[73] Whatever that might mean.

Almost no credible figure has argued that the United States should have intervened with its own forces to prop up the tottering monarch. Alexander Haig did come fairly close to such a stance at the time, advocating in an emotional phone call to General Robert Huyser, Carter's special envoy to Iran in late 1978 and early 1979, that the United States should send an aircraft carrier task force into the Indian Ocean and deploy military aircraft in Saudi Arabia.[74] Yet even the hawkish Haig did not suggest going beyond such posturing to actually introduce American combat forces into Iran. And short of such a drastic step, it is not clear that either the Shah or the successor government that he designated at the last minute could have survived.

America's Support for the Shah: A Balance Sheet

A more reasonable assessment of the factors that led to the implosion of the Shah's regime would conclude that Washington's image of the Iranian monarch was always at variance with reality. Washington saw a steadfast ally (and even a friend)—an enlightened reformer who was taking his country into the modern era. There was some truth to that image, but only some. The Shah was assuredly a modernist, and his educational and economic reforms (the so-called White Revolution), especially during the 1960s, helped build the foundation for a modern economy.[75] And he did embrace reforms that improved the lives of women and softened some of the harsher features of Islamic traditions. Those policies were what made him anathema to the religious reactionaries that Khomeini and other mullahs eventually mobilized.

But the Shah as reformer was only one part of the picture. The other part was an autocratic rule that was both brutal and corrupt. The suppression of political critics, and especially their arbitrary imprisonment and torture, is ample testimony to the first negative characteristic. Such conduct helped explain why secular democratic activists, who might otherwise have been supporters of the Shah's agenda aimed at reducing the power of the mullahs and bringing Iran's economy into the 20th century, were so thoroughly alienated.

If the regime's repressive measures had not been sufficient to antagonize reasonable political factions, the pervasive corruption added to the anger and created an overwhelming tide of dissatisfaction. Even Ardeshir Zahedi, Tehran's ambassador to the United States and a staunch Shah loyalist from a family of long-standing Shah loyalists, conceded the extent of the corruption problem in his country during a conversation with Zbigniew Brzezinski. Zahedi "acknowledged that there was a great deal of corruption in Tehran, even involving some members of the royal family. He volunteered that he felt that the Shah needed to change course dramatically, to clean house."[76] Years earlier, during the early and mid-1970s, the Shah had received warnings, including from SAVAK, about the extensive corruption and the mounting public anger about it, but he repeatedly dismissed such reports.[77]

U.S. officials, throughout the nearly three-decades-long relationship with the Shah, seemed unable or unwilling to see—and certainly not confront—the manifest flaws in their ally. That is likely why Washington was blindsided when the crisis erupted in the late 1970s. And having invested so much visible diplomatic capital in supporting the Shah, the United States had very little credibility with any successor government in Iran. Indeed, having looked the other way while the Shah suppressed and brutalized democratic opponents, Washington inadvertently made it easier for the religious zealots to fill the power vacuum that occurred when the monarchy finally lost its grip on power. Khomeini and his followers were able to outmaneuver the weakened and divided democratic forces.

From the standpoint of tangible U.S. interests, the investment in the Shah over the quarter century that he held power produced a mixed result, at best. It seemed a reasonably successful strategy over the short and medium term. Ousting a left-leaning, nationalistic prime minister and cementing the power of a more compliant young monarch, who obligingly appointed pro-Western officials to head his government, appeared to pay solid dividends.

Critics, however, excoriate that move and contend that the 1953 coup was the origin of Washington's current headaches in Iran and the surrounding region. Stephen Kinzer epitomizes that interpretation. "The 1953 intervention in Iran may be seen as a decisive turning point in twentieth-century history. By placing Mohammad Reza Shah back on his Peacock Throne, the United States brought Iran's long, slow progress toward democracy to a screeching halt. The Shah ruled with increasing repression for twenty-five years. His repression produced the explosion of the late 1970s." Kinzer adds: "In 1953, the United States deposed a popular Iranian nationalist who embraced fundamental American principles and replaced him with a tyrant who despised much of what the United States stands for. Today, the West finds itself facing a regime in Tehran that embodies threats far more profound than those that it sought to crush in 1953."[78]

Kinzer overstates matters somewhat. One cannot rerun history and state definitively what would have happened if the United States and Britain had refrained from meddling and allowed Mossadegh to remain in power. Iran's embryonic democracy might have matured and thrived, but there was also a possibility that Mossadegh would have either faltered as an effective leader or succumbed to his periodic authoritarian instincts. It is also possible that the communist Tudeh, with Moscow's support, might have displaced Mossadegh and installed a Leninist regime. That is what occurred next door in Afghanistan in the 1970s. Still, even if Kinzer and similar analysts might be too sanguine in their speculation about developments if the 1953 coup had never occurred, it is hard to imagine an outcome in Iran much worse than the one we've had to confront over the past three-and-a-half decades.

Backing the Shah and equipping his military with modern weaponry undoubtedly gave Moscow—and some of Moscow's more radical Arab allies—a geopolitical problem they would not otherwise have faced. To the extent that the Soviet Union had expansionist ambitions in that part of the world, Iran stood athwart those ambitions. It is even arguable that a strong Iran, backed by the United States, prevented greater instability in the Middle East and Southwest Asia.

But Kinzer and other critics are correct that in the long term Washington's ties to the Shah backfired. U.S. policy alienated the Iranian people and led to the emergence of a stridently anti-American regime. A policy that produced such a result cannot be considered either wise or effective. By overthrowing Iran's indigenous democracy in 1953 and then ostentatiously backing a corrupt, repressive autocratic regime for the next quarter century, Washington sowed the wind in Iran—and reaped the whirlwind.

7. Navigating a Quagmire: Sustaining South Vietnamese Dictators

Although Washington's containment policy against the Soviet Union initially focused on Europe, the fall of China to a communist insurgency in 1949 and the onset of the Korean War in 1950 elevated U.S. worries about East Asia as well. Given Japan's inherent strategic and economic importance, it was hardly surprising that Washington would pay considerable attention to Northeast Asia. That would likely have been true even without the additional Cold War incentives. The strong belief that the Kremlin instigated North Korea's attempt to unify the Korean Peninsula under communist auspices reinforced worries about Japan's security and (as noted in chapter 3) made Northeast Asia into a high U.S. policy priority.

Absent the larger, extremely tense, Cold War context, it seems unlikely that the United States would have become terribly concerned about developments in Southeast Asia, a sleepier and less relevant assortment of countries. But given the pervasive view in U.S. policy circles that Mao Zedong's regime was an obedient junior partner, if not an outright puppet, of Moscow's, that attitude changed. Washington feared that Beijing would be willing to do Moscow's bidding along China's entire perimeter. Consequently, Southeast Asia soon became a theater in the Cold War.

American policymakers fretted about evidence of communist penetration of the region. That worry grew as it became increasingly evident that France might not be able to hold on to its colonial empire in Indochina (present-day Vietnam, Laos, and Cambodia). Soviet enthusiasm for, and financial backing of, the communist-led Viet Minh insurgency intensified that worry, especially as Viet Minh forces gained control of more and more territory. As early as February 1950, President Harry S. Truman's secretary of state, Dean Acheson, bluntly described Viet Minh leader Ho Chi Minh as "the mortal enemy of native independence in Indochina."[1] The implication was that Ho was not a Vietnamese nationalist but instead served communist masters in Moscow and Beijing.

In March 1953, barely two months into the new Dwight D. Eisenhower administration, Secretary of State John Foster Dulles likewise expressed his alarm about developments in Southeast Asia. The struggle between the French and the Viet Minh was relevant not just to that region, he told the president, but to Washington's overall strategic position. Dulles argued that Indochina ought to have a high priority in U.S. foreign policy. Indeed, it was "in some ways more important than Korea." Why? Because "a loss there could not be localized, but would spread through Asia and Europe."[2]

Dulles's reasoning was both revealing and troubling. His notion that a communist victory in Indochina would ripple far beyond the region anticipated Eisenhower's famous (or notorious) domino theory that the president expressed at a news conference in April 1954. Eisenhower warned that the communization of Vietnam would have far-reaching implications. "You have a row of dominoes set up, you knock over the first one, and what will happen to the last one is a certainty that it will go over very quickly. So you could have the beginning of a disintegration that would have the most profound influences." The president warned that the abandonment of Vietnam would lead to the loss of all Indochina, then Burma, then Thailand, then Malaya, then Indonesia. Nor was that all. The toppling dominoes would move on to threaten the Philippines, Australia, New Zealand, and the principal geopolitical prize in East Asia: Japan. He concluded that "the possible consequences of the loss [of Vietnam] are just incalculable to the free world."[3]

But Dulles's version of the domino theory was even more expansive than Eisenhower's. The president asserted that a communist takeover of Indochina would menace all of East Asia from the border of India to Japan. But Dulles was arguing that a Viet Minh triumph would even have a detrimental impact on *Europe*—many thousands of miles away. The advice that he was giving, and the president's receptivity to it, underscored just how U.S. officials viewed every foreign policy challenge exclusively through the lens of the titanic Cold War rivalry with the Soviet Union.

Even before the end of 1953, the Eisenhower administration was providing France with $385 million in foreign aid to support its war effort in Indochina. The president justified that expenditure as "the cheapest way" to combat "a most terrible threat."[4] In addition to the financial assistance, some of the military funding that France received as a NATO ally through the Military Assistance Program, first launched in 1949, indirectly aided Paris's counterinsurgency campaign against the Viet Minh. But such assistance would not stave off defeat. During 1953 the casualties that the French officer corps suffered in Indochina exceeded the number of newly commissioned officers that year. Then, in November 1953, the French military command made the fatal error of attempting to lure Viet Minh forces into attacking what was thought to be an impregnable French position at Dien Bien Phu, near Vietnam's border with Laos. Instead, the siege and subsequent battle became a decisive, humiliating defeat for the French military in May 1954 and marked the beginning of the end for Paris's empire in Indochina.

Although Eisenhower rejected the advice of some of his key advisers, including Vice President Richard Nixon and Chairman of the Joint Chiefs of Staff Admiral Arthur Radford, to intervene militarily to lift the siege of Dien Bien Phu and save the French forces,[5] the president was not resigned to accepting communist domination of Southeast Asia. Instead, the administration tried to salvage what it could from the fall of France's colonial empire in Indochina. The danger to the Laotian and Cambodian portions did not appear to be acute, since the newly independent successor regimes were noncommunist and ostensibly nonaligned in the great struggle between the United States and the Soviet Union. The situation in the Vietnamese portion of Indochina was a different matter, though. The Viet Minh was indisputably the strongest political force in Vietnam and already controlled most of the northern part of the country.

The 1954 Geneva Accords that ended the conflict in Indochina provided for a withdrawal of French forces and the establishment of a "provisional military demarcation line." Viet Minh troops were to withdraw to the north of that line (the 17th parallel), while Vietnamese troops loyal to the French cause (and French troops prior to their promised complete departure from Indochina) were to withdraw to positions south of the line. That disengagement process was to be a prelude to supervised free elections that were to be held in July 1956 for a new, independent Vietnamese government. Not only France, but Britain, the Soviet Union, and China signed the accords reached at Geneva, but the United States declined to do so. Washington did, however, agree not to use force to disturb the settlement.

Viet Minh leader Ho Chi Minh had already established a provisional authority in the north, with Hanoi as the capital. In the south, Emperor Bao Dai, who had served as a colonial client (in Richard Nixon's candid admission, a "figurehead") of the French since 1949, appointed Ngo Dinh Diem as prime minister for a government based in Saigon.[6] It was an ominous development that Diem refused to sign the Geneva Accords. What was meant to be a temporary division of Vietnam for the purposes of military disengagement and provisional administration soon hardened into two competing states.

Washington Makes Ngo Dinh Diem a Client

U.S. leaders seemed to have no intention of respecting the provision of the Geneva Accords calling for countrywide elections for a national government in July 1956. That was not too surprising. Eisenhower admitted in his memoirs that if an election had been held before the collapse at Dien Bien Phu, "possibly 80 percent of the population would have voted for the Communist Ho Chi Minh as their leader rather than Chief of State Bao Dai."[7] The reality was that, although Diem might have fared better than the notoriously ineffectual Bao Dai in an electoral showdown with Ho Chi Minh, it was unlikely that he would have fared much better. One reason was because the communist forces that controlled the north would have used their power to rig the balloting. Senator John F. Kennedy expressed the consensus in the United States on that point in a June 1956 speech, asserting that the election was "obviously stacked and subverted in advance."[8]

But even in a free and fair election, a majority of Vietnamese might well have endorsed Ho. Although it galled U.S. policymakers to admit it, the Viet Minh in general, and Ho in particular, had reaped considerable nationalist political capital by waging the war of independence against the French. Again, Eisenhower conceded as much, lamenting that the French and their Vietnamese clients faced an insuperable obstacle of trying to convince "the average Vietnamese peasant" that they represented the cause of freedom, whereas the Viet Minh "were fighting on the side of slavery."[9] Moreover, Bao Dai had very little indigenous support. Even in the south, many Vietnamese regarded him as a colonial stooge or at least an agent of Western influence. Diem had a somewhat better reputation, but being a Catholic in a predominantly Buddhist country, plus having spent much of his life in the United States, did not enhance his credentials as a Vietnamese nationalist.

Eisenhower was sensitive, however, to the prospect that intervention by white Western governments would exacerbate hostile emotions among Asians. In a passage originally written for his memoirs but not included in the published version, Eisenhower explained why he had been so wary about suggestions within his own administration to intervene militarily to save the French at Dien Bien Phu. "The presence of ever more numbers of white men in uniform would have aggravated rather than assuaged Asiatic resentments." He added: "Among all the powerful nations of the world the United States is the only one with a tradition of anti-colonialism." That legacy, he contended, was an asset of great value. "It means our counsel is trusted where that of others may not be." In Eisenhower's view, "the moral position of the United States was more to be guarded than the Tonkin Delta, indeed than all of Indochina."[10] One only wishes that his policies toward the Saigon regime and the larger Vietnam question had better reflected that cautious realism and sensitivity to the impact of nationalism in the region.

While Diem did not share Bao Dai's widespread reputation as a French colonial stooge, neither did he have Ho's cachet as a revolutionary hero. Diem had respectable Vietnamese nationalist credentials, having spoken out against French rule on a number of occasions, but he had also spent much of the prior decade in comfortable exile in the United States. Ho and his Viet Minh colleagues, by contrast, had waged an armed struggle against French forces, often under difficult and dangerous conditions. Neither Diem nor U.S. leaders felt they could accept the risk of waging an election fight that would produce a united Vietnam as envisioned in the Geneva Accords.

Washington's policy goals were clearly set out in NSC 5429/5. According to that document, the United States intended to "make every effort, not openly inconsistent with the U.S. position as to the armistice agreement, to defeat communist influence . . . to maintain a friendly, non-communist government in South Vietnam, and to prevent a communist victory through all-Vietnam elections."[11] The president's approval of a National Security Council (NSC) recommendation in June 1955 made the implicit U.S. position official, although not confirmed in public: Washington would support Diem's refusal to hold the 1956 elections.[12] As early as October 1954, Eisenhower wrote a letter to Diem stressing Washington's support for the Saigon government and outlining the goal of "developing and maintaining a strong, viable state, capable of resisting attempted subversion or aggression through military means."[13] However, the president also indicated that America's support was neither unlimited nor unconditional. The letter stated that Washington intended to provide only monetary, not military, assistance, and even the financial aid would be offered only if Diem met a set of democratic standards, including the establishment of a stable civil government.

Although that may have been the original intention, America's support for the Diem government soon began to escalate and gradually become less and less conditional. The June 1955 NSC recommendation committed the United States to train South Vietnam's embryonic National Army—a step that clearly went beyond mere "monetary aid." Powerful lobbies in the United States pressured the Eisenhower administration to step up support for the Saigon government. In a May 1955 *Life* magazine editorial, publisher Henry Luce asserted that Diem was "a Roman Catholic and a Simon-pure Vietnamese nationalist, thus doubly proof against communist force." Luce went on: "Diem's growing strength immensely simplifies the task of U.S. diplomacy in Saigon. The task is, or should be, simply to back Diem to the hilt."[14] Luce published story after story in the *Time-Life* media empire about Diem's stature as a heroic defender of democracy against the communist onslaught. Other prominent opinion outlets were equally laudatory. Max Lerner of the *New York Post* hailed him as nothing less than a "calendar saint."[15] Later in the 1950s, *Newsweek* correspondent Ernest K. Lindley described Diem as "one of the ablest free Asian leaders."[16]

As he prepared his run for the presidency, Senator John F. Kennedy was nearly as effusive as Luce and other pro-Diem cheerleaders. "In what everyone thought was an hour of total communist triumph [in Indochina], we saw a near miracle take place," Kennedy wrote. "Despite the chaos, despite the universal doubts, a determined band of patriotic Vietnamese around one man of faith, president Diem, began to release and to harness the latent power of nationalism to create an independent, anti-communist Viet Nam."[17]

Eisenhower administration officials, though, were more aware than Luce, Kennedy, and other admirers of Diem of the man's flaws. Even John Foster Dulles, in spite of his pro-Diem public rhetoric, conceded to the U.S. ambassador to France that Diem was "by no means a perfect head of government."[18] The Joint Chiefs were reluctant to have the United States support Diem until a strong civil government was established in Saigon. Despite his own uneasiness, Dulles countered such caution by arguing that helping to fund, reorganize, and strengthen the South Vietnamese army was "one of the most efficient means of enabling the Vietnamese government to become strong."[19] Army Chief of Staff Lawton Collins, though, fretted about evidence of Diem's autocratic and erratic political style, as well as the blatant cronyism in his government. Even as Diem began to outmaneuver or suppress potential political opponents, Collins argued that such short-term successes "will not change Diem's basic incapacity to manage the affairs of government." Indeed, "his present success may make it harder for us to persuade him to take competent men into his government."[20]

It is apparent that, unlike some of Diem's admirers in Congress and the American news media, Eisenhower administration officials perceived his deficiencies. Diem's tolerance of, if not active involvement in, corruption, combined with his persistent inability to institute constructive changes in governance, signaled to U.S. leaders a crucial and growing problem. Yet the belief in the domino theory and the perception that South Vietnam was a crucial—perhaps *the* crucial—domino continued to drive policy thinking in Washington. Administration policymakers concluded that supporting Diem, despite his flaws, was a preferable option to bowing out of South Vietnam and watching the embryonic state fall to the communists, which seemed a probable outcome.

That was the situation that the new president, John F. Kennedy, inherited in January 1961. Given that Kennedy pledged in his inaugural address that America would "support any friend, oppose any foe" to "assure the survival and success of liberty," it seemed that he would be even less likely than Eisenhower to abandon the U.S. commitment in South Vietnam. The embarrassing fiasco of the Bay of Pigs invasion, the humbling inability of the United States to stop the construction of the Berlin Wall, and the emergence of a less than desirable political settlement in Laos reinforced Kennedy's inclination to take a strong stance in Vietnam. As early as June 1961, shortly before the Berlin Wall went up, he privately worried about the erosion of U.S. global credibility, saying: "Now we have a problem in making our power credible, and Vietnam looks like the place" where Washington would have to take a stand.[21]

The new president seemed to believe in the domino theory at least as firmly as did his predecessor. In June 1956, then senator Kennedy delivered a speech on U.S. policy in Southeast Asia that made Eisenhower's analysis seem relatively sophisticated and nuanced by comparison. In a near record-setting use of mixed metaphors, he insisted that Vietnam was "the cornerstone of the free world in Southeast Asia, the keystone to the arch, the finger in the dike." Burma, Thailand, India, Japan, the Philippines, as well as Laos and Cambodia, were among those countries whose security would be threatened "if the red tide of Communism overflowed into Vietnam." South Vietnam, he asserted, was "not only a proving ground for democracy in Asia," but "a test of American responsibility and determination in Asia." Americans, Kennedy proclaimed, were "if not the parents of little Vietnam, then surely we are the godparents. We presided at its birth, we gave assistance to its life, we helped to shape its future."[22]

That same thinking permeated the intelligence and policymaking bureaucracies in both the Eisenhower and Kennedy administrations. In August 1961 a National Intelligence Estimate went so far as to warn about an extension of communist aggression in *India* if the growing insurgency in South Vietnam were not curtailed.[23] In retrospect, that might seem like a far-fetched notion, but to policymakers in 1961 it did not.

And it was clear to the Kennedy administration that the security situation in South Vietnam was becoming increasingly worrisome, with communist Viet Cong guerrillas now in control of at least 20 percent of the countryside. Diem prodded his American patrons to escalate the U.S. commitment. On October 1, 1961, he asked for a formal, bilateral defense treaty—in reality a written commitment from Washington to use military force to defend South Vietnam. On October 13, he specifically requested a major increase in weaponry for his military and, even more ominous, sought the introduction of U.S. combat forces.[24] President Kennedy responded by sending a fact-finding mission led by General Maxwell Taylor later that month. In early November, the Taylor Mission submitted a report to the president concluding both that the United States needed to stand firm in Vietnam and that the threat posed by communist forces to the Saigon government was becoming severe. The report advocated a more robust military response.

Washington moved to beef up the U.S. commitment, greatly boosting the number of military advisers in the country. In the autumn of 1961, there were only 700 such personnel assigned to South Vietnam. By mid 1962, the total had risen to 3,400, and it would reach more than 16,000 by the end of 1963. A new command—the Military Assistance Command, Vietnam—was formed with General Paul D. Harkins in charge, to direct all aspects of the rapidly expanding U.S. effort. Moreover, many of the "advisers" were doing far more than what one would normally expect from personnel with that title. Some of them were accompanying South Vietnam military units into full-blown combat settings. As a result, U.S. troops began to suffer casualties.

Washington Sours on Diem

As the Kennedy administration's political and military commitment to South Vietnam deepened, however, the evidence of Diem's corrupt and undemocratic practices became so flagrant that U.S. officials were soon exasperated. Under Secretary of State George W. Ball, the strongest skeptic about the Vietnam mission within the administration, noted caustically, "we were rapidly discovering that the tiger we were backing in Vietnam was more of a Tammany tiger than a disciple of Thomas Jefferson."[25] The nepotism, which centered around Diem's brother, Ngo Dinh Nhu, and sister-in-law, Tran Le Xuan (Madame Nhu), was also becoming worse. And the circle of advisers surrounding the South Vietnamese president became ever smaller and more insular. Even worse, support for the Diem government among the South Vietnamese population was declining fast. Frustrated American officials warned Diem to purge his administration of corrupt elements and to broaden the regime by taking in some political critics. If he did not do so, Washington indicated that the United States might have to withdraw its support.

Diem largely ignored both the U.S. requests (which were increasingly outright demands) for reform and the threats of abandonment. That was not surprising. Having stated publicly on so many occasions that South Vietnam was strategically crucial—lest it become the first domino leading to a communist triumph throughout East Asia—U.S. officials could not credibly threaten to cut the country loose. With great frustration, George Ball admitted that Washington's hectoring of Diem was mainly bluster. In retrospect, Ball believed that the United States should probably have given Diem a nonnegotiable demand to purge the Nhus before Ambassador Lodge approached discontented South Vietnamese generals about a possible coup. But, Ball concluded, "such a move would probably accomplish little, since if he called our bluff—as he almost certainly would—I doubted my colleagues would ever carry through with a threat of withdrawal."[26]

And Diem probably knew that as well. He also realized that Washington would be reluctant to cut him adrift as South Vietnam's leader because there was no obvious acceptable replacement waiting in the wings. Secretary of Defense Robert McNamara later conceded as much. "Whatever his faults, and they were many, I and others believed that the prospect of getting anyone better than Diem was chancy at best."[27] Robert Kennedy apparently reached a similar conclusion at the time. "Nobody liked Diem," Kennedy admitted. "But how to get rid of him and get somebody who would continue the war, not split the country in two and, therefore, lose not only the war but the country—that was the great problem."[28]

What Diem did not seem to fully appreciate was how perilous his domestic position was becoming. Matters finally came to a head between May and August 1963, when Buddhist monks began to lead massive anti-government demonstrations in Saigon, Hue, and other major cities. From the beginning, there had been a significant degree of tension between the Catholic president and the predominantly Buddhist population, but that tension spiked in the early 1960s and reached crisis levels in 1963. Some of the Saigon government's responses were extraordinarily clumsy and insensitive. For example, Diem's administration banned the display of the Buddhist flag even on the anniversary of Buddha's birthday, an action that enraged even those Buddhists who had not yet become staunch opponents of the regime. The protests then expanded, first involving university students and ultimately including high school students and even middle-class professionals and businessmen.

In his memoirs, McNamara aptly described the root of Diem's domestic problems, and in so doing, inadvertently underscored why

Washington's reliance on Diem and many other Third World clients during the Cold War ultimately proved so disappointing:

> We thought that Diem aimed to move his people toward freedom and democracy. That he had studied in a Catholic seminary in New Jersey in the early 1950s seemed evidence that he shared Western values. As we got closer and closer to the situation, however, we came to learn otherwise. Diem, those around him, and the political structures that he built lacked a connection to the South Vietnamese people; he never developed a bond with them. We totally misjudged that.[29]

Government police repeatedly suppressed the Buddhist-led demonstrations with brutal force. Troops even invaded pagodas, an action that devout Buddhists found especially offensive. Some of the monks then began immolating themselves in the streets in protest, creating horrifying visuals that were seen on television sets in the United States and around the world.

Criticism of Diem in Congress and the U.S. media, which had been almost absent in the mid and late 1950s, and which had still reached little more than a loud murmur over the previous two years, became loud and insistent. Writing in early September 1963, *New York Times* correspondent Tad Szulc concluded that there was now "a firm conviction" in the United States that "because of its brutal excesses against the Buddhists," Diem's government "is no longer capable of maintaining even a semblance of national unity required for the continuation of the war against the Communist Vietcong guerrillas unless it undergoes major internal reforms." Szulc added that there was a growing awareness among administration officials and the American people that "the United States can no longer afford to be identified with a regime as brutal and repressive as the Saigon rulers."[30] For many Americans, Diem had become a brute and a villain, and opinion leaders began to question why the United States was supporting such a man.

Publicly, and sometimes privately, Kennedy administration officials placed most of the blame for the corruption and brutality of Diem's government on Ngo Dinh Nu, who was in charge of the police forces, and Madame Nhu. McNamara described the latter as "bright, forceful and beautiful, but also diabolical and scheming—a true sorceress."[31] Ball was even more negative about both Nhu and his "vicious and vindictive wife—whose talent for repulsive comments was unparalleled."[32] Ball had a point. In response to the fiery suicides of Buddhist monks, Madame Nhu stated that the government should "ignore the bonzes [monks], so if they burn thirty we shall go ahead and clap our hands." On another occasion, she referred contemptuously to the "bonze barbecue."[33] But Ball realized that the problems with Diem's government were not solely because of the influence of the Nhus. Ball noted that by mid-1963, "I became increasingly convinced that we had tied our nation's fortunes to a weak, third-rate bigot with little support in the countryside and not much even in Saigon."[34]

Washington's objective was to mitigate the growing public backlash in the United States, which was now being directed at the Kennedy administration as well as at its Vietnamese client. Yet, in spite of everything, Diem still had his admirers in Washington. Senate Majority Leader Mike Mansfield, a key administration ally, recalled that "my very strong belief was that Diem was the only one who could do the job in South Vietnam." Mansfield conceded that "there were very serious questions, very serious questions about his brother and sister-in-law." But, asserted the senator, about Diem himself, none."[35]

That charitable interpretation, though, was fast becoming a minority view. Even the administration's supporters in Congress began to waver. And as 1963 wore on, administration officials also were having second thoughts about Washington's continued backing of Diem. Even as they publicly expressed continued confidence in his rule, they privately discussed whether to support, perhaps even encourage, a coup to remove him from power. A key point in that shifting position came in a State Department message sent to the U.S. embassy in Saigon. Vice President Lyndon Johnson later described the thrust of that message:

> In effect, it told Ambassador [Henry Cabot] Lodge to advise Diem that immediate steps had to be taken to correct the situation and to meet the outstanding Buddhist demands. If Diem did not act promptly, the Ambassador was instructed to advise key Vietnamese military leaders that the United States would not con-

tinue to support the Saigon government militarily or economically. This ultimatum meant the removal of Nhu and his politically active wife from any continued influence or responsibility in the government. If Diem refused, the United States would no longer support him. If the military leaders then took over, we would support them.[36]

Johnson believed that "hasty and ill-advised message was a green light to those who wanted Diem's downfall."[37] Yet, the Kennedy administration seemed to have made the decision at the highest levels to encourage a coup. An August 29, 1963, memorandum stated: "The Secretary of State said that we have now had the replies from Lodge and Harkins. Both are agreed that the war cannot be won with a Diem-Nhu regime."[38] Lodge bluntly told his superiors about the larger implications of what U.S. policy now had in mind:

> We are launched on a course from which there is no respectable turning back: the overthrow of the Diem government. There is no turning back in part because U.S. prestige is already publicly committed to this end in large measure and will become more so as the facts leak out. In a more fundamental sense, there is no turning back because there is no possibility, in my view, that the war can be won under a Diem administration.[39]

In the following weeks, the administration began to abandon Diem—barring a last-minute move on his part to purge his brother and other unsavory elements from his government—and quietly support a coup against him. One planning document contained the option of providing "inducement (financial, political or otherwise) for opportunists or recalcitrant types to join in a coup."[40]

George Ball aptly summarized the ambivalence of U.S. policymakers during this period and implicitly underscored the moral dilemmas that were building as Washington acquired more and more questionable client regimes around the world. "Encouraging coups, of course, ran counter to the grain of America's principles," he averred. But in this case, an exception might be warranted. "Diem's legitimacy was dubious at best; we had in effect created him in the first place. Now the Nhus were destroying what little moral justification remained for our position in Vietnam."[41]

On November 1, 1963, with the CIA's acquiescence if not encouragement, the South Vietnamese military deposed Diem. What apparently was not anticipated in Washington was that soldiers involved in the coup did not merely arrest Diem and his brother, they executed them the following day. U.S. officials were not happy about that development, but they did not let the matter deflect them from what they regarded as a much more important objective: stabilizing South Vietnam and repelling the communist insurgency.[42] At an NSC meeting immediately following the coup and assassination, Secretary of State Dean Rusk expressed the dominant view that "the important question is how to get along with the war against the Viet Cong." Secretary of Defense McNamara posed the question of when the U.S. would recognize the new government and resume economic and political aid, although he conceded that perhaps a brief decent interval might be required. It was most telling that no one in the meeting even considered the question of *whether* the United States should continue its support of Saigon.[43] Although President Kennedy publicly expressed shock and grief at the coup and subsequent murders, the administration barely paused before granting even more aid to the new regime in South Vietnam. Indeed, the CIA apparently presented the coup leaders with $42,000 in compensation within weeks of their seizure of power.[44]

Washington's behavior in the months leading up to the coup was revealing, not only with respect to policy in Vietnam, but with respect to the broader Cold War policy of supporting friendly autocratic allies. For all the talk about considering South Vietnam an independent country and regarding Diem as a friend of the United States, the reality suggested a very different calculus. Diem had become a political and strategic liability, and when that happened, U.S. policymakers barely hesitated to create a situation in which his violent removal from power was inevitable.

During the summer and autumn of 1963, American officials gave, as Lyndon Johnson candidly admitted, a "green light" to the South Vietnamese military to overthrow Diem. They may not have wanted him killed, but they certainly wanted him out of power. Such actions belie the notion that Washington considered South Vietnam a sovereign state, much less that U.S. leaders respected the prerogatives of such a state. It was treated as little more than a security protectorate, and the Kennedy administration was determined to have a pliant, competent government in place that was capable of waging an effective fight against communist forces. When Diem no longer seemed able to fulfill those criteria, administration policymakers regarded him not only as dispensable, but an annoying obstacle to U.S. policy objectives. One way or another, that obstacle had to be eliminated. All of the talk about him being a brave and noble free world ally, which had been so prevalent in official U.S. statements and in media coverage just a few years earlier, was quickly forgotten.

Chaos in Saigon

Finding a stronger, more credible political client in Vietnam, however, proved extremely difficult. The initial assessment of the coup by Ambassador Lodge and some other officials was that it was "a remarkably able performance," and that it would shorten the war and speed the time American forces could be withdrawn.[45] McNamara, Taylor, and other policymakers were more skeptical, however, and events soon validated their skepticism.

A period of mounting political instability followed the coup, with various military strongmen maneuvering for dominance. The rather cumbersome coalition of generals that had overthrown Diem did not last even three months. That junta was ousted in late January by a rival group of officers led by General Nguyen Khanh. But Khanh was so obviously a heavy-handed autocrat that Washington was eager to have him pushed to the sidelines. The CIA described him candidly as "ambitious and ruthless."[46] And he didn't last long at the top.

President Johnson described (with some chagrin) the game of political musical chairs that began with Khanh's coup:

> More political turmoil followed. Six months later, religious rivalries, which had been pushed into the background, broke out again. From then until well into 1965 governmental changes seemed to take place every few months. There was military rule, then civilian, then military again. First one man was in charge. Then there was a triumvirate. Then a council. General Khanh was in, and out, and then in again.[47]

225

The South Vietnamese, Johnson concluded, "often seemed to have a strong impulse toward political suicide."[48]

As he took possession of the Oval Office following Kennedy's assassination (barely three weeks after Diem's demise), Lyndon Johnson faced a choice of whether to continue trying to establish political stability in an increasingly chaotic post-Diem South Vietnam and to back a successor regime with a more robust U.S. military presence, or to deescalate and develop an exit strategy for American forces. The latter course, administration policymakers realized, would likely mean a communist victory within a few years (or perhaps even a few months) and the reunification of Vietnam under communist auspices.

Journalist Leon Hadar aptly describes why U.S. leaders recoiled from taking that step. He notes that "the specter of Munich" haunted the Johnson administration's deliberations during the crucial year of 1964. The Munich analogy made it seem to policymakers that they had "no other choice but to hang tough and stay the course in Vietnam lest U.S. policymakers would be perceived as lacking the resolve to stand up to Hitler-like aggressors."[49]

Robert McNamara explicitly acknowledges the suffocating influence of the Munich analogy. He noted that former secretary of state Dean Acheson, one of the senior "wise men" informally advising the Johnson administration, had warned that abandoning Vietnam would cause the communist world to reach conclusions about Washington's lack of resolve and would "lead to our ruin and almost certainly to a catastrophic war."[50] McNamara conceded that younger Americans might find it "incomprehensible" that an intelligent man like Acheson foresaw such dire consequences merely from the fall of South Vietnam. But, McNamara adds, "I cannot overstate the impact our generation's experiences had on him (and, more or less on all of us.)" In particular, members of that generation "had lived through appeasement at Munich," and saw the terrible consequences.[51]

As during the Eisenhower and Kennedy years, Johnson administration officials seemed unable to view the struggle between communist and anti-communist factions in Vietnam as a localized conflict. Indeed, Johnson himself subscribed to a domino theory that dwarfed anything that Eisenhower and Kennedy had expressed. Upon returning from a visit to Vietnam as vice president in 1961, he stated that the choice Washington confronted in Southeast Asia was "whether we are to help these countries to the best of our ability or throw in the towel *and pull back our defenses to San Francisco.*"[52] [Emphasis added.]

The notion that the emergence of communist regimes in three tiny, impoverished nations in Southeast Asia would not only erode America's strategic position throughout East Asia but apparently lead to the forced abandonment of such American territories in the Pacific as Guam and Hawaii (the latter of which had become a state of the Union two years earlier!) set a new standard of absurdity. But that is the kind of "thinking" that shaped Washington's policy decisions regarding Vietnam. As Hadar notes:

> For the American foreign policy establishment as well as for the general public, North Vietnam was perceived to be an integral part of a monolithic Communist bloc led by the Soviet Union, including its Eastern European satellites, China, and Cuba. The only serious debate in Washington was over the mix of diplomacy and military force that the U.S. needed to employ in defending South Vietnam and confronting North Vietnam. And in that context, it wasn't difficult for the "hawks" to suggest that just like Czechoslovakia in 1938, South Vietnam was being threatened by a regional satellite of an antagonistic global adversary and thus required forceful American support.[53]

After a few months of hesitation, the Johnson administration plunged forward in Vietnam, not only dramatically escalating the U.S. military commitment but also trying to prop up a seemingly endless series of South Vietnamese military strongmen who vied for power in the post-Diem political vacuum. In the process, U.S. officials grappled with the reality that none of those individuals was more honest, effective, or popular than Diem had been. Indeed, the political convulsions in Saigon were the main factor that caused Washington initially to hesitate about committing more forces. In a crucial meeting between President Johnson and several key officials, including Maxwell Taylor and Henry Cabot Lodge, in Hawaii in June 1964, Taylor opposed further escalation until, in Ball's words, "we had installed a government in Saigon that we could be sure would not sell us out."[54] That was a revealing way to put it. By mid-1964, almost all pretense that the United States was merely assisting a sovereign ally was disappearing. The Vietnam War was rapidly becoming America's war, and the government in South Vietnam was seen as merely an adjunct to that effort.

Following the Gulf of Tonkin incident in early August (involving alleged North Vietnamese attacks on two U.S. naval vessels) and the subsequent congressional blank check in the form of the Gulf of Tonkin Resolution, the process of escalation accelerated. Washington launched major bombing strikes against targets in North Vietnam and began to consider an increase in the number of ground-force personnel, which would require abandoning the official fiction that U.S. military personnel in South Vietnam were merely combat advisers. Ball noted despairingly, "my colleagues in Washington and our Saigon embassy were standing logic on its head. What we charitably referred to as a government in Saigon was falling apart, yet we had to bomb the North as a form of political therapy." The political leadership in South Vietnam, he concluded, "was rotating among various cliques of military grafters."[55]

That assessment was relatively mild compared to his recollection of the situation in November and December 1964. Noting that General Taylor and the embassy in Saigon continued to press for political reforms, Ball observed that "the placemen momentarily holding power in Saigon did promise reform. They always did, but the half-life of such promises was, as I predicted, numbered in hours." Willfully "flouting our conditions," they did such things as making "night arrests of their political opponents, making sure that Saigon's fetid air would never be diluted by even a single whiff of democracy."[56]

As 1965 progressed, with an especially key decision occurring in July, Washington for the first time began to introduce major ground combat units. In addition to gradually deploying large numbers of its own combat troops to stem the military gains of the communist Viet Cong insurgents—and increasingly, North Vietnamese regular army forces—the United States continued to search for a credible, stable Vietnamese leader. The political chaos in Saigon finally ebbed in early June 1965 when yet another coup, this time led by rather young South Vietnamese officers, ousted the civilian government of Phan Huy Quat. Those "young Turks" installed Army

General Nguyen Van Thieu, a mere 42 years old, as president and the even younger Air Force General Nguyen Cao Ky, age 35, as prime minister.

Walt W. Rostow, a key foreign policy adviser in both the Kennedy and Johnson administrations who ultimately became national security adviser in 1966, provided an apt summary of the characteristics and impact of the chaos during the period between Diem's assassination and the Thieu-Ky coup:

> Efforts were made to bring into political life the fragmented civil political establishment through a "leadership committee" in September 1964 and a National High Council in October; and there were several experiments with civilian Prime Ministers. But the military pressure imposed by the communists, the powers inevitably reserved by the Armed Forces Council (with its own rivalries), and the inexperience with national leadership and administration on the part of civil politicians decreed a succession of failures. In the twenty months before the Thieu-Ky administration emerged, then, there was no stable authority in South Vietnam, and this fact corroded every aspect of the nation's life.[57]

Such was the political nature of Washington's Southeast Asian client. Rostow noted that all the objective data reflected "uniformly the deterioration of South Vietnamese fortunes," during that period, "but they do not adequately catch the sense of crisis that suffused Saigon and Washington in the early months of 1965."[58]

The latest coup offered renewed hope to officials in Washington regarding the Vietnam mission, although uneasiness persisted. Thieu seemed relatively colorless and cooperative, but the same definitely could not be said of Ky. Deputy Ambassador Alex Johnson described him as "an unguided missile," and the outspoken general provoked controversy almost from the outset. When a reporter asked him whom he most admired, Ky replied, "I admired Hitler." He added, "we need four or five Hitlers in Vietnam."[59] Assistant Secretary of State for Far Eastern Affairs William P. Bundy later described Ky as "the bottom of the barrel, absolutely the bottom of the barrel!"[60] Ky's behavior was more than a matter of academic concern to U.S. officials, because initially it appeared he might be the more influential member of the Thieu-Ky partnership—although that assessment proved to be erroneous.

Even though the emergence of the Thieu-Ky regime appeared to dampen the political turbulence, George Ball did not share the cautious optimism of his colleagues. In a July 21 meeting of the administration's national security team at the White House, Ball emphasized: "We must stop propping up that travesty of a government in Saigon."[61] As on so many other occasions with respect to Vietnam policy, though, Ball was once again a minority of one.

And at least on the surface, political developments in Saigon seemed modestly encouraging for a change. In January 1966, Prime Minister Ky delivered a major speech pledging a referendum in October on a new constitution, to be followed in 1967 by "genuine democratic elections." That was precisely what Washington wanted to hear. Johnson and his advisers had earlier invited Thieu and Ky to a meeting in Honolulu (in February) and Johnson came away from that meeting with the judgment that both men were patriots who would fulfill their promises to go forward with a democratic political process.[62]

Washington Finally Finds an Acceptable Client

Washington's often frantic search for a credible political partner in Saigon finally ended when the Johnson administration settled on General Thieu as its favorite. In September 1966, South Vietnam held the first seriously contested national elections (for a Constituent Assembly) in its brief history. The following September, elections were held for president, with Thieu elected on a ticket with his sometimes rival, Ky, as vice president. But his rather anemic vote total (34.8 percent) in a multicandidate field indicated that while he might be the Johnson administration's preferred leader, the majority of the people in South Vietnam remained skeptical. Yet, from the standpoint of Washington's policy objectives, Thieu was a vast improvement on the chaos that had been the norm after Diem's assassination. In a December 1967 meeting, President Johnson effusively congratulated Thieu on "the completion of a constitution, the holding of successful national elections, and the installation of a constitutional government."[63] President Nixon's national security adviser, Henry Kissinger, stated in his memoirs that under Nguyen Van Thieu, "South Vietnam seemed more stable politically than at any time in the previous four years."[64]

Nixon himself praised Thieu as a "very capable man" and an excellent politician who should not be underestimated. Indeed, at a press conference during a state visit to India in the summer of 1969, Nixon called Thieu probably one of the "four or five best political leaders in the world." The U.S. president expressed his view that South Vietnam's governmental institutions were strong, and in a spectacularly wrong prediction, stated that Saigon was never going to become Ho Chi Minh City.[65]

Officials in both the Johnson and Nixon administrations generally gave Thieu high marks for his political leadership. And they tended to minimize his increasingly flagrant undemocratic behavior, including the harassment and jailing of political opponents. Nixon administration officials, for example, notably declined to express criticism of Thieu following the national presidential election in October 1971—even though the rigging of that election was so blatant that Ky and every other significant candidate dropped out of the race under protest. As a result, the election became a strange de facto referendum in which voters had the options of voting for an unopposed candidate (Thieu), defacing their ballots, or boycotting the polls. Under those conditions, Thieu received 94 percent of the ballots cast, a total just slightly lower than candidates typically garnered in the farcical elections in the Soviet bloc and other authoritarian systems that Washington routinely scorned.

Walt Rostow later concluded that "it would appear that Thieu overplayed his hand." A better approach, Rostow said, would have involved "a less vigorous use of his assets," primarily his top-to-bottom control of the machinery of government. A more subtle approach "might have made the presidential race competitive while not endangering his re-election." That comment reflected an all-too-common feature of Washington's attitude toward political affairs in South Vietnam. U.S. officials seemed more concerned about the appearance of democracy than the actual substance. Another indicator of such hypocrisy was Kissinger's frantic messages to Ambassador Ellsworth Bunker in Saigon urging him to "explore the possibility of finding other opposition candidates" once Ky and other major figures dropped out.[66] Not that such minor-league substitutes would have any chance of actually winning, but having their names on the ballot would at least create the illusion of a multicandidate, competitive election.

A point that Rostow and Kissinger never acknowledged was that any honest election automatically involves some danger of the incumbent losing. They didn't object so much to Thieu rigging the electoral process as they did that he was so brazen about it that the resulting election had no credibility whatsoever. In a masterful understatement, Rostow conceded that "in terms of the development of South Vietnamese constitutional life, the October 3, 1971, Presidential election was a disappointment and a setback."[67]

The integrity of the political process in Saigon, however, was always a secondary consideration, at most, from the standpoint of U.S. policymakers. Kissinger stated later that, despite the South Vietnamese leader's sometimes heavy-handed rule, "neither Nixon nor I were prepared to toss Thieu to the wolves; indeed, short of cutting off all military and economic aid and thus doing Hanoi's work for it, there was no practical way to do so."[68]

But it wasn't just cynical realpolitik that caused the Nixon administration to give virtually unconditional backing to Thieu's government. Kissinger, for one, believed that pressure among some opinion leaders in the United States for more democracy in South Vietnam was both unhelpful and naive. He felt that such Americans "were seeking to force the developing of a democratic tradition to its culmination in a matter of months, among a people who had been killing each other in a civil war for two decades, in circumstances where loss of political power meant not only giving up office but risking one's life."[69]

President Nixon was also inclined to be tolerant about the Thieu government's decidedly imperfect commitment to democracy. "I was not personally attached to Thieu, but I looked at the situation in practical terms," Nixon recalled in his memoirs. "As I saw it, the alternative to Thieu was not someone more enlightened or tolerant or democratic, but someone weaker who would not be able to hold together the contentious factions in South Vietnam. The South Vietnamese needed a strong and stable government to carry on the fight" against the Hanoi and the Vietcong, "who sought to impose a Communist dictatorship on the 17 million people of South Vietnam."[70] "Because of the way the U.S. media portrayed Thieu," Nixon complained, "many Americans thought of him as a petty tyrant who suppressed his political opponents." Such a view, the president contended, was unfair. "Political dissent was substantially curtailed in South Vietnam, but Thieu still had to deal with an elected National Assembly and face a formidable range of open domestic political opposition."[71]

What Nixon did not mention was that the elections for the National Assembly also fell substantially short of the standards for being "free and fair." And neither the president nor members of his national security team ever wanted to talk about the Saigon government's disturbing human rights abuses, including arbitrary imprisonment and torture. Perhaps the most notorious example of the latter was the Thieu regime's policy of confining suspected insurgents in "tiger cages"—detention devices so small that occupants could never stand, or even rise above a painful crouch. It was a sad comment on American moral scruples that U.S. firms were involved in the manufacture of such hideous torture mechanisms for the South Vietnamese government, and U.S. officials conveniently looked the other way.[72]

Most independent observers' opinions were decidedly less favorable than those of Johnson and Nixon administration policymakers regarding Nguyen Van Thieu and his performance in office. *New York Times* correspondent Robert Shaplen, an expert on East Asia who spent three decades in the region, concluded that Thieu was "an unpopular, vacillating and conniving leader who could never pull the country together, let alone control the bickering members of his own palace guard."[73]

The strategy of backing Thieu never worked very well. Thieu's political legitimacy, despite his official election victories, always remained suspect in the minds of many Vietnamese, and his brutal treatment of opponents did not help matters. Neither the South Vietnamese government nor the South Vietnamese army was able to parry the communist forces without substantial U.S. combat assistance during Thieu's rule. Moreover, throughout his presidency, almost all of the crucial decisions about the war were made by Washington, not by his government. After Diem, the war had become thoroughly Americanized. What had started in the mid-1950s as limited U.S. aid for a client state became by the mid-1960s a U.S.-dominated and directed effort. Even when the Johnson administration finally realized that a definitive military victory was not achievable—or at least not achievable at any reasonable level of cost—and the Nixon administration continued that policy shift with its "Vietnamization" strategy, the decisionmaking power was never transferred to Saigon. The United States controlled the entire process, including the diplomatic effort that led eventually to the Paris Peace Accords in January 1973.

The reality was that Nguyen Van Thieu was never more than a supporting actor in Washington's Vietnam foreign policy pageant.[74] And if there was any doubt that Washington was calling the shots, with Thieu expected—however reluctantly—to fall into line, a candid comment in Richard Nixon's diary should erase all doubt. Noting that the South Vietnamese president resisted many of the proposed provisions of a peace agreement with Hanoi, Nixon concluded: "We are now in a position where, if he doesn't come along after the [1972 U.S.] election, we are going to have to put him through the wringer. I think then he will come along."[75] One doesn't normally put the leader of a sovereign country, who was supposedly a valued U.S. ally at that, "through the wringer." That kind of treatment is reserved for client regimes, and not especially respected client regimes.

As the Nixon administration tried to extricate the United States from the Vietnam conflict by both drawing down U.S. forces and negotiating with Hanoi, tensions between Washington and Saigon increased. Such tensions emerged early in Nixon's presidency. Already in the summer of 1969, Thieu objected to the plan for a gradual withdrawal of U.S. forces from his country. Nixon recalled, "I privately assured him through Ambassador [Ellsworth] Bunker that our support for him was steadfast."[76] Saigon's reluctance to support Washington's negotiations with Hanoi for a peace settlement heightened the tensions, and the Thieu government's repeated foot-dragging in the months leading up to the January 1973 agreement signed in Paris clearly made U.S. officials uncomfortable.[77] At one point in 1972, Nixon bluntly informed Thieu: "If the evident drift toward disagreement between the two of us continues . . . the essential base for U.S. support for you and your government will be destroyed."[78]

Nixon might have had a sense of déjà vu. As Eisenhower's vice president, he had experienced similar tensions between Washington and South Korea's Syngman Rhee over provisions of the proposed armistice to end the Korean War in 1953. It is an inherent problem in relations between a great power and a client state whenever the client state openly balks at a policy that its patron favors. The great power must then either bring the client to heel, or else have its policy dictated by that client. As in the case of the final stages of the Korean War, the U.S. government opted to end any illusion about equality of status between itself and Saigon. The Nixon administration overrode the objections of its South Vietnamese client and concluded the Paris Peace Accord to finally terminate U.S. involvement in the Vietnam conflict.

George Ball, by then a private citizen, identified the nature of the intractable problem in the relationship with South Vietnam. A key defect in the administration's strategy, he contended, was the "failure to separate our interests from those of the Saigon government." The "incompatibility of America's aims with those of the ruling clique in South Vietnam was obvious. America wanted to get out of the Vietnamese mess with the least harm to its reputation; while the Saigon government could survive only if we drove out the North Vietnamese, exterminated the Viet Cong, and restored its sovereignty over the whole territory of South Vietnam." Yet Washington was not honest with its client. "We continued to pretend schizophrenically that we were determined to achieve the very objectives that we were simultaneously abandoning, hoping to placate Saigon with assurances we knew would not be kept."[79]

A prime example of what Ball was talking about occurred in January 1973, just days before the signing of the Paris peace agreement with Hanoi. Thieu had continued to oppose many of the proposed provisions, but President Nixon bluntly told him that the United States was determined to sign. To soften the blow, Nixon offered the following commitment:

> At the time of the signing of the agreement I will make emphatically clear that the United States recognizes your government as the only legal government of South Vietnam; that we do not recognize the right of any foreign troops to be present on South Vietnamese territory; and that we will react strongly in the event that the agreement is violated. Finally, I want to emphasize my continued commitment to the freedom

and progress of the Republic of Vietnam. It is my firm
intention to continue full economic and military aid.[80]

Given the military realities on the ground in Vietnam, and especially the political realities in the United States, Nixon's assurances
were either an example of uncharacteristic naiveté or cynicism. The
chances of making good on those assurances when—not if—Hanoi
violated the peace agreement were roughly midpoint between slim
and none.

Faulty Assumptions Produced a Tragedy

In all of four relevant administrations, U.S. officials believed that
Vietnam was about much more than Vietnam. In the report following his mission to South Vietnam in late 1961, General Maxwell Taylor epitomized such thinking. "It is my judgment and that of my
colleagues that the United States must decide how it will cope with
Khrushchev's 'wars of liberation,' which are really para-wars of guerrilla aggression. This is a new and dangerous communist technique
which bypasses our traditional political and military responses."[81]
It was rare that U.S. leaders focused on Hanoi as the source of aggression, without also blaming the Soviet Union and/or China. Even
when they did, they acted as though North and South Vietnam were
two distinct nations rather than one nation artificially divided into
two hostile states. Attorney General Robert Kennedy provided a
textbook example of such distorted analysis during a February 1962
visit to Saigon. "In a flagrant violation of its signed pledge at Geneva in 1954," Kennedy stated, "the North Vietnamese regime has
launched on a course to destroy the Republic of Vietnam."[82]

As did so many other officials, Kennedy conveniently failed to
mention that the Geneva Accords never contemplated the permanent existence of two Vietnamese states. The final declaration issued
by the conference could not have been more explicit on that point.
The military demarcation line at the 17th parallel was "provisional
and should not in any way be interpreted as constituting a political or territorial boundary."[83] The conflict in Vietnam was from beginning to end a civil war, not an external "war of aggression." Yet
American policymakers from all four administrations believed, or at
least professed to believe, that it was the latter.

236

When U.S. leaders spoke of the threat to South Vietnam, and, therefore, to American interests, they were highly inconsistent about the primary source of that threat. Sometimes it was Hanoi. Sometimes it was Moscow. On other occasions, it was China. In an interview on CBS in September 1963, President Kennedy affirmed his belief in the domino theory as it applied to South Vietnam and stressed the threat from Beijing. "China is so large, looms so high just beyond the frontiers, that if South Vietnam went, it would not only give them an improved geographic position for the guerrilla assault on Malaya but would also give the impression that the wave of the future in Southeast Asia was China and the Communists."[84]

At a minimum, such comments reflected sloppy thinking. If Hanoi was the principal adversary, then the United States was interfering in a civil war—a parochial conflict that had little relevance to America's security. Even if one accepted the Orwellian interpretation that the Geneva Accords intended that there be two Vietnamese states rather than one, it was difficult to expand that issue into one that menaced the well-being of the United States. If, on the other hand, one regarded Hanoi as merely a cat's paw of a major power, U.S. policymakers were confused or contradictory about which major power that was—the Soviet Union or China. It was impossible to regard both as the puppeteer, unless one accepted the premise that Moscow and Beijing were merely two components of a monolithic threat. But even by the early 1960s, that notion had become implausible. The Sino-Soviet split had already emerged in the late 1950s, and by the early or mid-1960s should have been apparent to all except the most diehard conspiracy theorists.

The thesis that Hanoi was Moscow's willing servant was rather far-fetched and ignored strong signs of Vietnamese nationalism, if not chauvinism, both in the Viet Minh insurgency and later in propaganda put out by the North Vietnamese government. But the notion of North Vietnam as a Soviet puppet was plausible compared to the argument that Hanoi was doing China's bidding. That belief suggested a shocking historical illiteracy within the American policymaking elite. Tensions between China and Vietnam went back centuries. Indeed, worries about an undue dependence on China was likely the underlying reason Ho Chi Minh put out feelers to Washington during Truman's administration about the possibility of cooperation with the United States. Even Vietnamese communists preferred to preserve as many options as possible rather than have no choice but to rely on their allies in Moscow and Beijing.

China was literally the last country in the world that Vietnamese, of any political persuasion, would want to have as a patron, much less as a master. That point was confirmed with a vengeance barely five years after the withdrawal of U.S. forces from South Vietnam and three years after the collapse of the South Vietnamese state, when Chinese and Vietnamese forces fought a short but nasty war. Even McNamara admitted later just how "limited and shallow" was Washington's analysis of the situation in South Vietnam and the overall stakes in Southeast Asia.[85]

Faulty analysis by a series of U.S. administrations led to the conclusion that preventing a communist victory in Vietnam was a critical element of America's entire global security posture. Secretary of State Dean Rusk was especially candid on that point:

> The principal lesson that I learned from World War II was that if aggression is allowed to gather momentum, it can continue to build and lead to general war . . . . If I thought there was no connection between the events in Southeast Asia, the broad structure of world peace, the possibility of a third world war, I might have advised differently on Vietnam. But in Southeast Asia, and in that pattern of aggression practiced by North Vietnam, I saw what I thought were the seeds of conflict for future war.[86]

But such apocalyptic thinking was not confined to Rusk and the rest of the Democratic Party's foreign policy establishment; it was a bipartisan folly—and the GOP's participation lasted far beyond the Eisenhower administration. Like his predecessors, President Nixon insisted that America's credibility was squarely on the line in Vietnam. "For the United States, the first defeat in our nation's history would result in the collapse of confidence in American leadership, not only in Asia but throughout the world."[87]

That overemphasis on the issue of credibility[88] dovetailed with both a sense of guilt and a desperation to "save face," leading to the perpetuation of the U.S. commitment to maintain a noncommunist South Vietnam, even when policymakers tacitly conceded as time went on that the war had become a mess and a burden. Nixon's rationale captured all three of those motivations:

> A precipitate withdrawal would abandon 17 million South Vietnamese, many of whom had worked for us and supported us, to Communist atrocities and domination.... We simply could not sacrifice an ally in such a way. If we suddenly reneged on our earlier pledges of support, because they had become difficult or costly to carry out, or because they had become unpopular at home, we would not be worthy of the trust of other nations and we certainly would not receive it.[89]

Hadar argues that if there had been a recognition that "nationalism and not adherence to communist ideology or solidarity with the Soviet Union or China was the main driving force behind North Vietnamese policy," that recognition "could have changed the strategic calculations of policymakers in Washington."[90] Indeed, the belated realization that the notion of a monolithic communist bloc was an illusion enabled the United States to reach out to China and establish, first, strategic cooperation against the USSR, and later, a wide-ranging political and economic relationship. But that realization (and the opportunities it produced) was still years in the future.

U.S. leaders invested an enormous amount of American blood and treasure in backing a succession of authoritarian, corrupt, and ineffectual regimes in Saigon. In fairness, most American policymakers had at least a vague recognition of the deficiencies of Washington's Vietnamese clients. True, some Eisenhower administration officials overestimated Ngo Dinh Diem's competence, honesty, and popularity—especially early on in his rule. Yet even they did not buy the absurdly heroic portrait that some of Diem's admirers in Congress and portions of the news media painted. And during the Kennedy years, officials realized all too well what a flawed client they were supporting. Washington was even more acutely aware about the incompetent and unsavory nature of Diem's would-be successors during the chaotic, "revolving door" period of government changes in South Vietnam in 1964 and 1965.

Once Nguyen Van Thieu consolidated his power, his patrons in Washington hoped that they had at last found an effective, stable partner for the war effort. Yet, as noted, with the partial exception of President Nixon, they harbored few illusions that Thieu had any serious commitment to democratic values. They were a little less realistic about his support among the Vietnamese people, but they continued to believe that most South Vietnamese preferred his government to the brutality and repression that the communists represented. What U.S. leaders in both the Johnson and Nixon administrations seemed unable to grasp was that the massive U.S. military presence in the country, and the suffocating political sponsorship, doomed any chance that Thieu might have had to win the allegiance of the Vietnamese people. Even more than Diem, Thieu was seen as Washington's puppet.

U.S. leaders cared, but not strongly, about the popular legitimacy of the Saigon government. Increasingly, they displayed tunnel vision, bordering on an obsession, with the military dimension of the war. If a government in Saigon was willing to follow Washington's directives about how to win the armed struggle, and showed a modicum of competence in doing so, U.S. leaders were content to leave it in place. But if such a government faltered, and thereby seemed to jeopardize the war effort, Washington looked for a replacement. That was the underlying reason the Kennedy administration decided to encourage a coup against Diem, why the Johnson administration was dissatisfied with most of the candidates who briefly took power after Diem's assassination, and why Washington preferred the relatively pliable Nguyen Van Thieu to the volatile Nguyen Cao Ky. It is also clear that Washington was not overly concerned about respect for South Vietnam's sovereignty, general democratic norms, or even basic moral considerations in deciding whether to support or discard a particular South Vietnamese political client.

Even within the narrow context of their goal of preventing a communist military victory, though, U.S. officials failed to grasp an important point. A South Vietnamese government that was widely perceived as illegitimate was incapable of galvanizing the population, or even the Army of the Republic of Vietnam (ARVN), to wage a vigorous war against communist forces. The low morale and general incompetence of ARVN units were a chronic problem throughout the period that the United States tried to preserve a noncommunist South Vietnamese state. As with the rest of South Vietnam's political structure, the army was riddled with corruption and cronyism. Veteran *New Yorker* writer Robert Shaplen, the author of several books on Southeast Asia, observed that Americans "should have asked ourselves long ago, how an army can go on functioning when it is simply a business organization in which everything is for sale—from what you eat, to transfers or promotions."[91]

Johnson and Nixon administration officials, as well as the commanding generals in Vietnam (William Westmoreland and his successor, Creighton Abrams) insisted that the ARVN actually performed quite well. Following the 1968 Tet Offensive by communist forces, which was so crucial in turning American public opinion against the war, Abrams asserted that most ARVN units had fought effectively. "We would have had a catastrophe, if they had not fought well," he argued.[92] According to a U.S. military assessment, only 8 of the ARVN's 149 maneuver battalions had performed unsatisfactorily.[93] Yet, even if that were true, and U.S. commanders had every incentive to portray the record of South Vietnamese troops in the most favorable light to justify the ongoing mission, the ARVN could count on the support of the massive U.S. military presence in 1968. How well South Vietnamese troops would perform with a far smaller U.S. backstop was always a troubling question.

U.S. leaders got their answer in 1971. The intractable nature of the ARVN's deficiencies became all too clear that year when the Nixon administration, proud of its Vietnamization strategy as it drew down the number of U.S. combat forces, prodded the ARVN to launch an offensive against North Vietnamese units across the border in Laos. As University of Chicago Professor John J. Mearsheimer succinctly observes, ARVN forces were "badly chewed up by North Vietnamese ground forces."[94] Indeed, there were graphic television images of South Vietnamese soldiers clinging to the landing gear of helicopters in a frantic attempt to escape the fighting.

There is a tenacious historical myth, especially in conservative American political circles, that, despite earlier mistakes, the United States and its South Vietnamese ally were on the brink of victory in the early 1970s—in the sense of keeping South Vietnam out of the communist orbit. That argument, so common during the 1970s and 1980s, received a new lease on life in 2007 with the publication of military historian Lewis Sorley's book *A Better War: The Unexamined Victories and Final Tragedy of America's Last Years in Vietnam*.[95] According to the myth, public and congressional anti-war sentiment pressured the Nixon administration into agreeing to the dubious Paris peace agreement in 1973, and—even worse—prevented the United States from taking action when Hanoi predictably violated the provisions of that agreement and renewed its offensive against South Vietnam.

That allegation became a staple early on for Republican hawks. Presidential candidate Ronald Reagan excoriated Congress as communist forces closed in on Saigon. "This Congress is the most irresponsible and dangerous I have ever known," said Reagan. The failure of Congress to provide the military aid that Nixon promised created a "worldwide belief that the U.S. breaks its promised word and abandons it allies."[96]

Nixon himself made a similar argument. Writing in 1978, he charged: "The war and the peace in Indochina that America had won at such cost over 12 years of sacrifice and fighting were lost within a matter of months once Congress refused to fulfill our obligations. And it is Congress that must bear the responsibility for the tragic results."[97]

Although conservatives were—and are—the most inclined to embrace that argument, some interventionist liberals have done so as well. In his 1990 memoirs, Dean Rusk stated his belief that the United States could have prevailed "if we could have maintained solidarity on the home front." He added that "it wasn't until we pulled our forces out and Congress cut off supplies that North Vietnam overran the South."[98] Walt W. Rostow still made a similar argument in the late 1990s.[99]

Mearsheimer correctly points out the fallacy of that thesis, citing the failure of the 1971 Laos venture as evidence. "To stand any chance of holding off Hanoi's offensives, the South Vietnamese army needed massive amounts of American airpower, which effectively meant that the U.S. military would have to continue fighting in Vietnam indefinitely just to maintain a stalemate. That hardly qualifies as being on 'the brink' of victory."[100]

Indeed, the speed of South Vietnam's final collapse in the spring of 1975 suggests the extent of the military and political rot in Washington's client state. One rarely sees such a precipitous unraveling (quite literally in a matter of weeks) if the military and government truly has the support of a population determined to preserve the independence of their country. While the absence of expected U.S.

military hardware may have made the ARVN's problems worse at the margins, that hardly accounts for the anemic resistance in that final stage. A more likely explanation is that most Vietnamese, including most members of the military, were not willing to make even a serious, much less a Herculean, effort to maintain an independent South Vietnamese state.

The reality is that a series of impotent and corrupt regimes in Saigon, widely scorned by their own population, made a North Vietnamese victory virtually inevitable—unless the United States was prepared to continue propping up its client with a large military presence over the very long term and to bear the costs in blood and treasure of doing so. As he did so often in discussions on Vietnam policy, George Ball offers a concise and devastating analysis of why the U.S. effort to sustain an anti-communist government in Saigon was probably doomed from the beginning:

> We fought, as we said, for South Vietnam, but it was never a country—merely an artificial slice of territory created by an improvised dividing line as a diplomatic convenience to obtain the 1954 settlement. Lacking the cohesion, drive, legitimacy, and common purpose of a nation, South Vietnam had no chance to survive against a cruel, fanatical revolutionary clique in Hanoi that responded to, and was driven by, not merely a lust for power, but an atavistic anticolonialism.[101]

By the late 1960s, to say nothing of the 1970s, there was insufficient domestic will in the United States to pay the horrific price in blood of continuing to prop up South Vietnam.

The tragedy of America's Vietnam debacle is that it was all so unnecessary. Preserving a noncommunist government in South Vietnam rather than seeing Vietnam united under communist control (however brutal that was certain to be) was never a vital security interest of the United States. Indeed, it was never even a reasonably relevant security interest. Two decades of U.S. policymakers whipped themselves into a frenzy over the specter of a communist tide sweeping over all of East Asia, destroying America's strategic and economic position in that region and undermining Washington's credibility globally. That fear was based on the twin fallacies of a monolithic communist threat and the simplistic domino theory. (Unfortunately, the myopic view of the Vietnam conflict as the manifestation of a Soviet global power play, and hence a necessary theater in the Cold War, has not entirely gone away, as evidenced by the publication of Michael Lind's revisionist history.)[102]

As a result of such faulty analysis, the United States waged a needless war that killed more than 58,000 Americans and well over a million Vietnamese. Washington also supported a succession of unsavory, as well as ineffectual, political clients in Saigon. By so doing, U.S. policymakers did not serve the legitimate security interests of the American republic, and, equally tragic, they betrayed core American values.

8. Heart of Darkness: U.S. Policy toward Mobutu's Dictatorship in Zaire

Although Mobutu Sese Seko (Joseph Mobutu) did not fully come to power until 1965, the United States was heavily involved in Congolese affairs from 1960—when the country was still the Belgian Congo, the crown jewel of the decaying Belgian colonial empire. As the decade of the 1960s approached, it was increasingly obvious that the Congo would soon join the ranks of European colonies that would be granted independence. And Dwight D. Eisenhower's administration was extremely worried about that process—especially the potential for Moscow to exploit it and gain footholds in the newly independent states.[1]

Administration officials early on gravitated toward the notion that the militaries in these countries could be bulwarks against communist influence. On June 18, 1959, President Eisenhower met with the National Security Council (NSC) to discuss a State Department report, "Political Implications of Afro-Asian Military Takeovers." In a memorandum that detailed the summaries of the meeting, Eisenhower made intriguing and revealing statements about U.S. policy regarding the rise of military dictatorships in postcolonial states. In response to a comment by National Security Advisor Gordon Gray, the president stated "that it seemed to him likely that the trend toward military takeovers in the underdeveloped nations of Asia and Africa was almost certainly going to continue. Accordingly, we must do our best to orient the potential military leaders of these countries in a pro-Western rather than in a pro-Communist direction."[2] That perception guided the policies of the Eisenhower administration (and later, the John F. Kennedy and Lyndon B. Johnson administrations) with respect to the Congo.

Prospects for a smooth transition and a stable, prosperous future in the Congo were not good. The population was overwhelmingly poor and illiterate, and Belgian officials had done very little over the more than seven decades of colonial rule to prepare that population for self-government. At least as troubling, the future country was little more than an amalgam of mutually hostile tribes. A sense of national identity, much less a sense of national cohesion, was weak to nonexistent. Like so many other African states, the Congo was an artificial entity that European officials in the late 19th century cobbled together to suit their convenience. All too often, such colonies were created without reference to ethnic, linguistic, or historical factors. The Congo was almost a caricature of that process.

If the Congo had been located in a geopolitical backwater and possessed little of value, it might have joined other societies similarly characterized as obscure, chronically dysfunctional states and received little more than an occasional glance from the United States. But the Congo was a huge presence in the heart of Africa, with a population of 15.2 million, and a territory of more than 905,000 square miles—roughly the size of Western Europe. Those factors meant that its political status could have an impact in all directions on several other emerging countries. It was also a repository of vast quantities of important metals and minerals, which were in high demand in the United States and other advanced economies. Perhaps most significant on that front, the Congo was the principal source (accounting for some 70 percent of global supply) of cobalt. Among other purposes, cobalt had become a crucial component in the manufacture of jet aircraft—an industry that was beginning to surge at the end of the 1950s, especially as jets replaced propeller-driven planes in commercial aviation fleets.

Chaos in the Congo and the Rise of Mobutu

All of those factors combined to make the Congo extremely interesting to several key countries, including the United States, the Soviet Union, and the departing colonial master, Belgium. As the May 1960 elections for the Congolese parliament approached, the various outside powers maneuvered for advantage. Those governments began to assess the principal indigenous political players, lining up to promote their favorites and undermine the favorites of rival powers.

The strongest political figure appeared to be Patrice Lumumba, a charismatic, left-leaning politician. Lumumba's ideological inspiration came less from the Soviet Union and other hard-core Leninist governments than it did from the idiosyncratic "African socialism" of Ghana's leader, Kwame Nkrumah. But U.S. officials made little distinction between those ideological wellsprings, and they viewed Lumumba with growing apprehension. Eisenhower later described him as "radical and unstable," and, even more damning, "a Communist sympathizer, if not a member of the Party."[3] That perception promptly put him on the list of Cold War enemies of the United States.

When the ballots were counted, Lumumba's party won a plurality—35 of the 137 seats—in parliament, boosting his prospects for prime minister. It was an impressive, but hardly an overwhelming, showing, and it confirmed that the Congo was a deeply divided society. The numerous riots and skirmishes leading up to the balloting, especially in provinces that were inhabited by multiple tribes, further underscored that point.

After considerable deal-making with other political and tribal leaders, Lumumba was able to form a cabinet with himself as prime minister. A somewhat more conservative figure, Joseph Kasavubu, assumed the less powerful, mostly ceremonial, post of president. But before the new government could mark the official date of independence (June 30), even more violent riots erupted. The Congolese army, freed of Belgian control, began to fragment, and multiple armed struggles broke out. Moise Tshombe, the leader of Katanga province, the principal mining center and wealthiest region of the country, declared the province to be an independent state, and the leaders of other provinces indicated an intention to follow suit. The remaining Belgian troops began to meddle, taking sides (often with a pro-Tshombe tilt) in the growing political disputes as the disorder mounted and the country spiraled toward chaos. After conferring with Nkrumah, Lumumba asked the United Nations (UN) to send in peacekeeping troops to restore order and enable his government to establish its authority. Washington backed that move, believing it was the best chance to forestall Soviet mischief. Indeed, an American official, Ralph Bunche, directed the UN mission.

But Lumumba's dissatisfaction with the situation grew, as evidence mounted that the Belgians were covertly supporting the secessionists in Katanga. At this point, the prime minister made a fatal error. In a joint statement with Kasavubu, he asked the USSR to monitor developments and consider sending help if "certain Western countries" did not halt their meddling in the Congo's internal affairs.

Lumumba repeated that comment a short time later, although pointedly, Kasavubu backed away from his previous stance. Lumumba's request (however conditional) for Soviet aid also upset the majority of legislators in parliament, who wanted only UN peacekeepers, not Belgian or Soviet troops, in their country.

Even more damaging to Lumumba's fortunes, the United States now became intensely hostile to Lumumba, convinced that he was a Soviet client. That suspicion deepened in late August when a Soviet ship arrived in the capital, Leopoldville, loaded with trucks, technicians, and air crews. Eisenhower later termed this action (with more than a dollop of hyperbole) a "Soviet invasion."[4] The Eisenhower administration now became determined to neutralize the troublesome Lumumba. The only question was whether neutralizing meant undermining him politically, staging a coup, or assassinating him.

As in so many other arenas, U.S. officials tended to see the turbulence in the Congo solely in terms of America's Cold War struggle with the Soviet Union for influence in the emerging postcolonial world. The CIA believed that Lumumba would not only open the Congo to Soviet control but pave the way for that process in all of Africa. In testimony in 1975 before the Senate committee chaired by Senator Frank Church (D-ID), assigned to investigate questionable actions of U.S. foreign policy around the world, C. Douglas Dillon, undersecretary of state in 1960, stated that the entire National Security Council, including President Eisenhower, believed that not only was Lumumba "an impossible person to deal with," but that he "was dangerous to the peace and security of the world."[5]

The notion that a novice prime minister in an extraordinarily weak and poor country posed a security threat of global magnitude was a rather large logical stretch, but Washington acted on that over-the-top assumption. On August 17, 1960, U.S. ambassador Clare H. Timberlake recommended to his superiors in Washington that the United States instigate a coup against Lumumba. The next day, the Central Intelligence Agency (CIA) station chief in the Congolese capital cabled CIA Director Allen Dulles that the Congo was experiencing a "classic communist effort [at a] takeover," and there might be "little time left in which to take action to avoid another Cuba." At a National Security Council meeting later that day, Eisenhower reportedly stated that Lumumba needed to be eliminated.[6]

It is also clear that Lumumba's clumsy and inflammatory actions galvanized other domestic political factions against him. In September the prime minister resisted Kasavubu's attempt to dismiss him from office. At that point, the commander of the Congolese army, Lt. General Joseph Mobutu, staged a coup and established a new "interim" civilian government. It was rather clear, though, that Mobutu and his troops were the real power. It was equally apparent that Washington approved of the coup as the best strategy to restore order. In his history of the CIA, *New York Times* correspondent Tim Weiner charges that the agency "had already selected the Congo's next leader: Joseph Mobutu, 'the only man in the Congo able to act with firmness,' as Dulles told the president at the NSC meeting on September 21. The CIA delivered $250,000 to him in early October, followed by shipments of arms and ammunition in November."[7] Mobutu endeared himself to U.S. officials from the outset when he closed the Soviet embassy and ordered all Soviet diplomatic personnel to leave the country.

Ironically, Joseph Mobutu was a member of Lumumba's political party, and the prime minister had been responsible for his meteoric rise to prominence. A failed journalist, Mobutu was only 29 years old at the time of his coup, and just months earlier he had been a mere sergeant in the colonial army. But when that army rebelled against its Belgian officers, the troops made him an instant colonel. The new prime minister then appointed him to be the chief of staff of the embryonic national army following independence. The pervasive absence of even semicompetent personnel in the military and other Congolese institutions made such an extraordinarily rapid rise possible, and it was not clear whether Lumumba thought that he had appointed a loyal political lieutenant to command the troops or whether he merely selected someone he knew was popular with those troops. In any case, it proved to be a grave miscalculation. Whether from personal ambition, the lure of U.S. dollars, or a combination of the two factors, Mobutu quickly turned on his patron.

Following the September coup, Mobutu's troops tracked down Lumumba and placed him under house arrest. On February 13, 1961, barely three weeks after the new Kennedy administration took office, the former prime minister was assassinated while in the custody of his political adversaries, headed by Moise Tshombe.

Immediately after Lumumba's arrest, U.S. officials stated publicly that he deserved both humane treatment and a fair trial. Washington even had Ambassador Timberlake make an appeal to the central government in Leopoldville for Lumumba's safety. However, the Church Committee's report in 1975 revealed not only a U.S. wish to have Lumumba eliminated, but also evidence of Washington's tangible support for nongovernmental groups seeking to assassinate the troublesome political leader. Indeed, the CIA apparently developed and delivered special poisons to the Congo intended to assist that effort.[8] Historian Michael Schatzberg concludes that "there is no longer much doubt that the United States was the major force behind Lumumba's ouster and assassination."[9]

Wall Street Journal correspondent Jonathan Kwitny's analysis, depressing as it is about the coup and its aftermath, has the ring of truth:

> Considering the way the Congo was misrepresented to the U.S. public, it's conceivable that the coup, and perhaps even the attendant murders, might have been popularly approved of even if the government had confessed to planning them. Few government or journalistic opinion makers knew much about the leading characters in the Congo drama, or about the long-simmering tribal disputes that formed the context of Congolese political life. Pundits in the United States provided one main explanation for what went on—Soviet plotting.[10]

Unfortunately, the oversimplified notion that Moscow's scheming was behind every adverse development in Third World countries was not unique to the narrative about the situation in the Congo. It permeated U.S. policy toward many countries in Asia, Africa, and Latin America throughout the Cold War, and that myopic perspective brought a great degree of suffering to the people of central Africa.

Washington's Support for Mobutu Grows

Once Lumumba was no longer a factor, Washington adopted a somewhat lower profile in the Congo.[11] From mid-1961 through early 1965, the United States did not take much direct action, although both the U.S. military and the CIA were involved behind the scenes—primarily in bolstering Mobutu and his military establishment.[12] During this period, the United Nations was the most prominent player, making a concerted effort to end the simmering civil war in that country, with the so-called peacekeeping troops clearly taking sides on behalf of the central government. The twin U.S. priorities throughout that period were, first, to stymie the perceived Soviet campaign of subversion and, second, to support the preservation of the fragile country's territorial integrity.

That second goal caused Washington to oppose Tshombe's effort to secure independence for Katanga, even though he professed to be strongly pro-Western, and he had considerable support in the United States among conservatives, especially in Congress. Secretary of State Dean Rusk explained why Washington deemed the preservation of the Congo's territorial integrity to be so important:

> We opposed Moise Tshombe's efforts to have Katanga secede from the Congo for the same reasons we opposed altering any political boundaries in Africa: First, most African nations opposed any boundary changes, and second, if existing political boundaries were altered to take into account tribal, cultural, and religious background, the whole continent would have split up into hundreds of tiny principalities.[13]

During this relative lull between mid-1961 and early 1965, now-General Joseph Mobutu began to solidify his power, and the United States became one of the biggest supporters of that effort. In May 1963, Mobutu left the Congo and traveled to the United States to discuss acquiring training and other aid for the Congolese military. During those meetings, President Kennedy succinctly expressed the primary rationale for supporting Mobutu: "General, if it hadn't been for you the whole thing would have collapsed and the communists would have taken over."[14]

According to the *New York Times*, the United States had already decided to give supplies and equipment for the retraining of the Congolese army even before Mobutu arrived on American soil; the Kennedy administration was keeping that decision quiet, though, because it was still hoping to acquire official UN support for the retraining effort.[15] That hope proved illusory, because UN officials did not trust Mobutu, and they worried that strengthening the Congolese army would undermine the fragile civilian government. In the end, six nations acted independently of the UN to train Mobutu's troops.[16] Subsequently, in February 1964, the United States decided to unilaterally train Mobutu's police forces as a supplement to the military training.[17] On June 30, 1964, the United Nations officially withdrew the last peacekeeping troops from the Congo, despite a security environment that remained decidedly unsettled. Not coincidentally, the United States made a major shipment of military equipment to Mobutu's forces on that same day.[18]

Yet another secessionist rebellion broke out in 1964 in the eastern provinces of Congo just as the UN troops departed. Pierre Mulele led Congolese insurgents calling themselves "Simba" (Lions) against the government in Leopoldville. The Simba Rebellion gained ground against the central government forces, conquering the city of Stanleyville and setting up a new government. The United States and other Western powers were especially alarmed, because the Simbas routinely targeted American and European citizens residing in Congo, including missionaries, priests, nuns, and school teachers.[19] Washington decided to support the Mobutu-led national forces by providing money, planes, and pilots for the Congolese government's counteroffensive against the rebels. That support would culminate in November 1964, when American planes dropped Belgian paratroopers into Stanleyville.[20]

Mobutu's role in the military campaign against the Simbas further strengthened his already powerful position in the Congolese government hierarchy. And there were increasing signs of the brutal behavior that would characterize his rule as the country's dictator. The United States (particularly the CIA) already had clear evidence of appalling human rights abuses committed by members of the government's intelligence agency, the National Surete, which Mobutu controlled. A CIA report issued in August 1964 documented how a paramilitary team attached to the National Surete systematically targeted members of the National Liberation Committee (CNL) for assassination. However, Washington did not hesitate to continue furnishing Mobutu's forces with aid.[21]

On November 24, 1965, Mobutu staged another coup against the Congolese civilian government, making his political supremacy official. Sheldon Vance, who from his post in the State Department's Central African Bureau had a substantial influence on U.S. policy during the early and mid-1960s and would become U.S. Ambassador to Zaire from 1969 to 1974, defended the aid to Mobutu to put down the Simba rebellion. He also seemed to show little dismay at Mobutu's new coup or its aftermath. In a 1989 interview, Vance stated that "there certainly, since then, has not been a great deal of what we call democracy, but at least the Congo became a country and most of the inhabitants began to think of themselves as Congolese or, today, Zairians."[22] Vance's view both overestimated the degree of national cohesion in the Congo (and similar creations of European colonialism) and was callously dismissive of the horrors Mobutu perpetrated. Unfortunately, it was an attitude that typified much of the U.S. foreign policy bureaucracy during the Cold War.

Although Secretary of State Rusk later insisted that a Mobutu military dictatorship "was not what we had worked for," U.S. officials could hardly have been surprised by that outcome.[23] Mobutu would continue to rule the country with an iron fist for the next three decades. Until the final stages of that period, he could rely on the friendship of the United States—and more important, on U.S. financial and military assistance. He had become Washington's man in Africa.

The U.S.-Mobutu Relationship Becomes Official

After Mobutu took power in 1965, his relationship with the United States became even closer than before. U.S. officials pressed their client to open up the Zairian economy to greater foreign private-sector investment, especially from U.S. corporations. Ambassador Vance was especially enthusiastic about that approach. "Very shortly, less than a year after I arrived, we were able to arrange an official visit by Mobutu to the United States. We urged him and our government to use this occasion to encourage the U.S. private sector to see the opportunities for foreign investment in the Congo. This, indeed happened." Vance contended that the approach was so successful, and the improvement of the Zairian economy so noticeable, "that we moved Zaire from grant assistance to loan assistance."[24] He attributed the subsequent nosedive of the economy in the mid- and late 1970s not to the corruption and ineptitude of the Mobutu government, but to higher oil prices engineered by the Organization of Petroleum Exporting Countries (OPEC).

Although the importance of official U.S. diplomatic, economic, and military channels to the Congolese government increased, the covert CIA connection remained crucial. Tim Weiner summarizes that component of the bilateral relationship. "The Congo was a cockpit of the cold war, and Mobutu and the CIA worked in closest harmony." Indeed, "Mobutu got whatever he wanted from the CIA—money and guns, planes and pilots . . . and the political security of close liaison with the American government—while the CIA built its bases and stations in the heart of Africa."[25] And in the process, the United States became an accomplice in the creation of an extraordinarily corrupt and vicious police state.

For all its aid, both economic and military, Washington's ability to moderate Mobutu's behavior seemed very limited. On May 31, 1966, the new dictator ordered the execution of four politicians who had been caught in a failed plot against him. The order was seen as far too excessive by many in the international community, including the United States. U.S. officials personally appealed to Mobutu, asking him to grant clemency to the four men. But Mobutu rebuffed Washington's pleas and had the men hanged in a gruesome spectacle in front of a crowd of more than 100,000 people.[26]

A CIA report published later that month (June 1966) made several damning statements about the hangings and, in particular, what the hangings revealed about Mobutu and his reign. "The plot never was a serious danger, but politicians are an ever-present potential threat to Mobutu's position, and the treatment of these four was clearly designed to discourage other would-be plotters, military as well as civilian. In this context, there is little doubt that this 'solution,' too, will 'work,' at least for a little while."[27] The report continued: "Actions such as this have important implications for the future. Mobutu is likely to be more and more inclined to summary handling of political problems, and he probably will frequently order actions which do not sit well in some quarters in the Congo and abroad."[28]

A scathing article in the *Chicago Tribune* by correspondent John Latz, a journalist who had lived in the country for almost 20 years, concluded: "The Republic of Congo is today a police state." Latz went on to describe Mobutu's campaign to solidify control, which involved both mass imprisonments and anti-white race baiting.[29]

All of this took place in just his first year of full control, and yet the United States continued to support his regime.

In October 1966, Mobutu surprised many in the international community by ordering the U.S. ambassador to the Congo, McMurtire Godley, to leave the country—and do so within 48 hours or suffer the humiliation of being expelled. Godley, in his telegram to the Department of State asking for an early departure, speculated that Mobutu was trying to create an impression of distance between him and the United States, when he actually had no intention of becoming anti-U.S. In other words, the whole controversy was simply a scheme Mobutu concocted to make himself appear more independent of the United States.[30] U.S. officials apparently interpreted his action the same way. As the *Washington Post* reported, Washington would not allow this incident to affect its relations with Mobutu's regime because it "sees no immediate alternative to his leadership."[31]

Mobutu's reputation did not improve in the late 1960s. He imposed a new constitution, which among other things made the Congo a one-party state—with Mobutu, of course, as the head of the sole legal party. Voters ratified his constitutional "reform" in a farcical referendum. According to the official government tally, Congolese voters approved his handiwork by an astonishing 98 percent. The U.S. government, which routinely vilified and ridiculed such phony elections in communist countries, had little to say about the charade its African ally carried out.

Mobutu was not done consolidating his power. His government arranged the kidnapping and imprisonment of former prime minister Moise Tshombe (probably Mobutu's most prominent remaining rival) in Algiers, Algeria. Mobutu, who had previously sentenced Tshombe to death for opposition to his regime, was working hard to expatriate him to the Congo in order to carry out the death sentence without delay.[32] But the imprisonment of Tshombe led to a new uprising in his home province—mineral-rich Katanga—in July 1967. Even as he tried to eliminate his rival, Mobutu urgently requested that the United States supply him with additional military aid. And he wasn't talking just about financial subsidies or new weapons. He wanted a unit of American paratroopers to help him defeat the rebels.

Incredibly, the Johnson administration seriously considered such a direct military intervention. Robert McBride, Godley's successor as U.S. ambassador to the Congo, typified the attitude of one faction: "Failure of USG to respond appropriately to Mobutu and Congo in this hour of need," McBride cabled to the State Department, "could create the possibility of [an] eventual swing of this key African country towards UAR [Gamal Nasser's United Arab Republic], Algeria, or Soviets, all of whom have demonstrated their willingness to fish in troubled waters of Congo and Southern Africa."[33]

Johnson and his top advisers stopped short of taking the drastic step of introducing U.S. combat personnel, but the administration did provide more limited aid to Mobutu's effort to put down the rebellion. By July 1967, the U.S. government had sent three C-130 transport aircraft to the Congo with the stated goal of providing "noncombat" logistical support.[34]

But both Republican and Democratic leaders in Congress immediately united in opposition to that venture. Chairman of the Senate Foreign Relations Committee J. William Fulbright (D-AR) compared the move to the intervention in Vietnam—which was already faltering and provoking strong anti-war sentiment in the United States. He warned that the Vietnam intervention started with similar "toe in the water" mission of military assistance.[35] On August 5, the administration decided to end the mission of the C-130s because of mounting congressional criticism.[36] The withdrawal of the air support caused an outburst of protest from Mobutu and a surge of anti-American rhetoric on Congolese government radio broadcasts.

Ambassador McBride detailed the outburst in a telegram to the State Department in which he stated his own perception of the crisis. "While Congolese behavior obviously enrages me, I would recommend against any strong action on Dept's part now beyond quiet but firm denial of accusations contained in radio broadcasts."[37] Given the congressional criticism of the July intervention, it is no surprise that when Mobutu inquired about possibly visiting the United States later in the year, the State Department sent a telegram to the U.S. embassy in Leopoldville stating that "we should do everything possible to discourage it."[38]

The 1967 incident produced a notable, but brief, strain in the relationship between Washington and Mobutu's regime. From the beginning, Mobutu regarded the U.S. assistance in suppressing the Katanga rebellion as insufficient, and he was enraged at the withdrawal of even that modest support. The Johnson administration clearly wanted to be more supportive, but vocal opposition in the news media and Congress made it politically risky to continue even a marginal military intervention. There was noticeably more congressional push-back on this issue than there was regarding Washington's embrace of other friendly tyrants, such as those in South Korea, Iran, the Central American states, or (later) the Philippines. In fact, there seemed to be even more distaste about aiding Mobutu than there was in assisting the South Vietnamese regime.

The greater resistance to the emerging partnership with Mobutu appeared to reflect two major factors. One was the sense that the argument for backing a tyrant in central Africa on the basis of American security interests did not seem as strong as that argument with respect to the other regions. As noted, another reason for the reluctance was the growing skepticism among members of Congress about the wisdom of the U.S. intervention/nation-building venture in South Vietnam, as evidence mounted that the mission was not going well. That made at least some in the legislative branch wary of any new interventions that had the potential of turning into a quagmire. In any case, congressional hostility toward Mobutu would become an increasingly important factor in Washington's relations with the Congo.

The executive branch, though, was determined to maintain a strong partnership with the African leader. That was true during Lyndon Johnson's final year in office, but it was even more the case with Johnson's successor, Richard Nixon.

A Deepening, but Turbulent, Partnership: The Nixon-Ford Years

In August 1970, the strong ties between the United States and the Congo were on display to the world through a 12-day visit by Mobutu to the United States, including a meeting and reception at the White House. On August 4, Nixon opened with a welcoming speech to Mobutu, in which he stated: "You come from the heart of Africa and I can assure you that the hearts of all Americans go to your country and to you as you go forward in a program of progress and peace for your people and for all the people of Africa."[39] Later on in the evening, Nixon proposed a toast in which he lauded Mobutu:

An enormous amount of the credit for that development goes to its leaders and particularly to our honored guest tonight. I know that all Americans, as they
think of the Congo, know that the President has often
referred to his country as being the heart of Africa. I
think all of us at this table tonight would speak from
our hearts to the heart of Africa when we raise our
glasses to the health of the President of the Congo and
Mrs. Mobutu.[40]

It was yet another example of an American chief executive making a
glowing tribute to a thuggish tyrant.

But Mobutu was becoming wary of his highly public relationship
with Washington—which was not playing well with African publics
or most other African governments. A new dynamic was introduced
into the relationship as Mobutu began to realize that he was viewed
as an American stooge in Africa and the rest of the Third World. He
responded with efforts to burnish his Third World, specifically African, credentials in a variety of ways—some symbolic and some substantive. A key symbolic move was to ostentatiously "Africanize"
his country's culture and institutions. In 1971, he changed the name
of the country itself from the Republic of the Congo to the Republic
of Zaire. The capital, Leopoldville, became Kinshasa, and the names
of other cities also were altered to eliminate any vestige of colonialism. Mobutu even changed his own name from Joseph Mobutu to
Mobutu Sese Seko.

As he had done in 1966, Mobutu also made a tactical course ad-
justment in terms of his rhetoric and official policy positions. He began to criticize the United States publicly in an effort to appear nonaligned in the Cold War. Michael Schatzberg argues in his book: "As
Mobutu successfully consolidated power in the early 1970s, he tried
to diversify the sources of his dependency while asserting a role for
himself in the councils of the Third World and the nonaligned movement. These new thrusts strained bilateral relations during the administrations of Richard Nixon and Gerald Ford."[41]

While Schatzberg claims that Mobutu's rhetoric strained the relationship, at least in the short term, U.S. officials at the time saw
Mobutu's criticism as a necessary show he put on to convince the
nonaligned nations he was one of their leaders. In a meeting with

the African autocrat, Henry Kissinger laughed off the critical speech Mobutu had recently given about the United States. "You are obviously a master at the art of speaking," Kissinger joked. "You can say one thing and mean another." Kissinger also stated, "We understand you sometimes have to take public positions which define your African relationships, so it is therefore especially appreciated when you act independently." Mobutu replied with laughter and responded (using the "royal we"): "We are condemned to take such positions. . . . At the present time we are trying to divest ourselves of certain ambiguities which have plagued our image until now."[42]

Kissinger took over as secretary of state in September 1973 and remained a staunch ally of Mobutu's until he left that post in January 1977. In speaking of Zaire on one occasion, Kissinger stated that "The United States was present at the birth of this nation and we have been a proud partner ever since."[43]

A number of declassified State Department telegrams to and from the embassy in Kinshasa provide insight into the U.S.-Zairian relationship during the Nixon administration and the subsequent administration of Gerald Ford. In November 1974 President Ford sent a telegram to the Zairian leader expressing "his warmest personal regards."[44] While the president may have thought that the relations between the two countries were rosy, the diplomats on the ground grasped the actual situation and were considerably more cautious. Mobutu's support for the West was based on his own interest and could change on a whim, they warned:

> It should be reiterated . . . that Mobutu perceives of himself as an African leader. As long as Western interests coincide with his in Africa, he can be expected to be cooperative. At the moment that Mobutu senses that Zairian interests in Africa are seriously compromised by alignment with the West, he will hasten to detach himself from his former friends.[45]

Following an official visit to Zaire in early 1976, Secretary Kissinger sent Mobutu a letter emphasizing that "the United States attaches great importance to the continued security and economic prosperity of Zaire and remains committed to assisting your government in achieving those objectives."[46] But the reality was that the United States was buying Mobutu's support primarily through military aid.

During those years, Mobutu engaged in implicit attempts at blackmail. His technique was rather simplistic: either you give me the military aid that I demand or I will turn to the communists. For example, in March 1974 Ambassador Vance sent a telegram to the State Department detailing his conversations concerning Mobutu's request for the importation of M-16 rifles. Vance stated that "From all information available to us here, unless U.S. agrees to this sale, GOZ [Government of Zaire] will acquire AK-47s from Chinese. Both from our point of view and Portugal's it would seem infinitely preferable to have the US furnish [a] limited number of M-16s (with end user safeguards) than to have GOZ turn to Chinese with all that this implies."[47]

Mobutu's attempts at blackmail were apparently not confined to the United States. Toward the end of the year, he began to use his upcoming trip to the USSR as leverage to gain more military aid from Washington's European allies. Deane Hinton, who became ambassador to Zaire in 1974, recalled a conversation he had with the Belgian ambassador in which the Belgian diplomat "suggested Mobutu was using Soviet trip to blackmail US, Belgium, and others."[48] Mobutu's efforts to play off the West against the Soviet bloc continued, although never quite as overtly as in 1974.

He seemed increasingly suspicious about the reliability of his American patron and was especially uneasy about Ambassador Hinton. The relationship between Mobutu and Hinton was always rocky, and telegrams and other indicators suggest that Hinton was more outspoken than previous ambassadors in his disagreements with Mobutu. In February 1975 a Zairian official reported to an embassy employee that "I have the impression that President Mobutu is afraid of the ambassador."[49] Only a day later, the American embassy transmitted a front-page story from a major Zairian newspaper (government controlled, of course) alleging Hinton was a part of a CIA operation that worked to overthrow governments not deemed friendly enough to the United States.[50] In June, the Zairian press broke a dubious story that there had been an attempted coup, centered on assassinating President Mobutu.

Within days the press claimed that Washington was behind the plot, and the Zairian government ordered Ambassador Hinton to leave the country.[51] An editorial appeared in the government-sponsored newspaper railing against the United States and warning that "if any misfortune should come to the President—through attempts to sabotage his work or his person—let the Yankees know that none of them will leave Zaire alive."[52]

The U.S. government flatly denied the allegations in such stories. However, within a few days Washington sent a Mobutu favorite, former ambassador Sheldon Vance, on a conciliatory mission to Zaire. Hinton soon departed his post, and within a few months Nathaniel Davis, the head of the State Department's Bureau of African Affairs (and one of Mobutu's prominent targets), resigned. In addition, the United States offered Zaire $60 million in aid to placate its restless client.[53] Clearly, the Ford administration seemed willing to tolerate Mobutu's annoying posturing in order to maintain his cooperation and supposed friendship.

The timing of Mobutu's anti-U.S. outburst was not coincidental: 1975 was the same year that Washington sought to use Zaire to funnel arms to the pro-Western factions in the emerging civil war in neighboring Angola. Beginning in 1975, as the new Angola nation received its independence from Portugal, it would be torn for over two decades by fighting between pro-West and pro-communist factions. That struggle also had a pronounced tribal aspect that was at least as important, if not more important, than the ideological differences. The two largest armed groups were the People's Movement for the Liberation of Angola (MPLA), dominated by the Mbundu tribe, and the Union for the Total Independence of Angola (UNITA), which the Ovimbundu tribe dominated. The charismatic Jonas Savimbi led UNITA and rapidly acquired an enthusiastic following among staunch conservatives in the United States who saw him as a freedom fighter against the Soviet and Cuban-backed MPLA.

But during the early years of the conflict, there was a third, smaller faction in the struggle, the Front for the National Liberation of Angola (FNLA). The head of the FNLA was Holden Roberto, a leader of the Kongo tribe in northern Angola near the border with Zaire. From the beginning of his struggle against the Portuguese, Roberto had a close ally in Mobutu, and indeed appears to have been a distant relative of the Zairian president. The linkage to Zaire was not especially surprising since more Kongo people lived in Zaire than in Angola itself.

261

Because of congressional restrictions, though, the Ford administration could not openly provide military assistance to supposed pro-Western elements. That problem became especially acute following passage of the Clark Amendment to the U.S. Arms Export Control Act in December 1975. Consequently, the administration focused on providing indirect help, channeling money and weaponry to friendly Angolan forces through Mobutu. That made him a key player, a fact that he knew and exploited to the fullest. While Washington seemed inclined to support any Angolan faction that professed to be anti-communist and anti-Soviet, Mobutu wanted most of the aid to go to his ally, Roberto.

In a meeting with the American ambassador, Mobutu "said the only way to get the necessary arms into Holden's hands in time would be for the US to send Zaire American equipment, thus permitting him to release further arms now in the hands of his own troops."[54] U.S. officials harbored doubts about Roberto's popular appeal and military effectiveness, believing that Savimbi's UNITA forces were a better bet, but they ultimately bowed to Mobutu's preferences. Washington and Kinshasa devised a type of arms-laundering scheme to allow the United States to unofficially support the Angolan militants.[55] That operation would continue throughout the 1980s.[56] During the early portion of the joint effort, a disproportionate amount of the aid went to Roberto, as Mobutu insisted. Indeed, to Washington's acute frustration, evidence surfaced that Mobutu himself pocketed a large portion of the funds.[57]

When evidence of Roberto's meager strength became irrefutable (as MPLA forces routed his fighters and drove them back into Zaire in early 1976), Washington began to shift the focus of its aid, and Savimbi ended up being the principal recipient. The dependence on Mobutu as the intermediary in the Angolan operation did not go away, however. Indeed, with the emergence of the Reagan Doctrine in the 1980s, the Zairian role reached new levels of importance (see below).

Henry Kissinger's comments in his memoirs succinctly illustrate Washington's assumption that the U.S. policy options regarding Angola and Zaire could not be separated and that both countries had become important arenas in the Cold War:

> In 1975, any American involvement in Angola had to
> be based logistically in Zaire. I told my staff meeting

that I preferred other dinner companions to Mobutu, but he was "the only game in town." The alternative was to acquiesce in a Soviet scheme to tilt the African equilibrium. Mobutu would be far easier to deal with than a Moscow-dominated government in Luanda.[58]

A final point that emerges from an analysis of the State Department telegrams is the way in which the United States dealt with Mobutu's human rights violations. Throughout the early and mid-1970s, the United States either denied or minimized the many abuses the Mobutu regime committed. In April 1974, a U.S. diplomat sent a telegram to Washington in which he claimed that Zaire had "no established pattern here of arbitrarily imprisoning or interning citizens for political purposes."[59] However, by September the embassy was reporting censorship of Western press operations by the Zairian government.[60] A report from the embassy in 1976 claimed that Mobutu had "successfully eliminated or neutralized his major political opponents" in order to solidify his regime.[61] Interestingly, in September 1976, the State Department sent a draft report on human rights violations in Zaire to the embassy for its review. The draft report slammed Zaire for many abuses, including a lack of political rights, torture and detention of political prisoners, a lack of judicial rights for citizens, and forced removals of local populations deemed disloyal to the Mobutu regime.[62] However, only a few days later, the U.S. embassy sent back a revised report that substantially watered down many of the allegations.[63] Again, the American government could not bring itself to acknowledge the reality of Mobutu's behavior.

The Carter Presidency: A (Slight) Chill in the Air

In his campaign for the presidency, Jimmy Carter pledged to make human rights a major consideration of his foreign policy. Accordingly, Carter sought to change Washington's perspective on Mobutu. Michael Schatzberg contends that "not only did Carter's people take notice of the less than admirable aspects of Mobutu's rule, they set out to improve matters." [64] However, geopolitical developments led to pressures on the new administration to back away from taking a hard-line stance against the Zairian tyrant. The principal factor was the continuing restlessness and secessionist attempts by Zaire's mineral-rich province of Shaba (formerly Katanga). The secession of such an economically vital region would threaten Zaire's viability—and the continuing territorial integrity of that country had been a key feature of Washington's Africa policy since the beginning of the 1960s.

Carter, to his dismay, had to confront two crises involving Shaba, with the first one erupting less than two months after his inauguration when a force of Katangan exiles, supported by Angola's MPLA government, launched a military offensive in a bid for the province's independence. Angola's aid was, according to U.S. officials, at least partly in retaliation for Mobutu's (and indirectly, Washington's) assistance to Holden Roberto's forces.[65] Secretary of State Cyrus Vance's memoirs offer important insights into the policy assumptions that impelled even the Carter administration into backing Mobutu in the Shaba crises—and more generally. The underlying ambivalence of U.S. attitudes, at least in that administration, also comes through clearly in Vance's writings. "The tangible U.S. interests in Zaire were primarily economic," he contended. "Mobutu was a source of consistent, if sometimes embarrassing, political support to the United States. We had supported the territorial integrity of Zaire since its troubled birth as the Congo in the early 1960s." According to Vance, "we had small economic and military aid programs but sought to avoid linking ourselves too closely with Mobutu's political position."[66]

Both aspects of that interpretation are highly debatable. Assisting the Mobutu regime to the tune of tens of millions of dollars each year seemed a bit more than "small" aid programs. And while the Carter administration might have wanted to avoid being identified closely with Mobutu's rule, preceding administrations—and the succeeding one that was in office when Vance published his memoirs—seemed to have no such compunctions.

And ultimately the Carter administration also backed Mobutu—especially during the two Shaba crises—including by providing ammunition to Zairian troops. That escalation occurred after the administration initially decided to send only "non-lethal aid." The second Shaba crisis, which erupted in mid-December 1977, confirmed the extent of continued U.S. support for Mobutu. When Katangan rebels, who had been driven back into Angola earlier that year by a joint force of Zairian, Belgian, and French troops, launched a new offensive, Washington provided extensive aid to the Kinshasa regime. The United States sent military transport planes to assist Belgian and French paratroopers to repel the latest rebellion—and (a not trivial consideration) to secure the economically lucrative Shaban copper mines.[67]

Again, Vance explains why administration officials believed the United States could not stand by on the sidelines: "None of us wished to face the uncertain consequences that might flow from the collapse of the regime and consequent disintegration of Zaire into unstable segments open to radical penetration."[68]

Unlike his predecessors, and even some of his colleagues in the Carter administration, though, Vance was unwilling to view the situation in Zaire as solely part of the East-West struggle. He recognized that many of the conflicts in that country, and elsewhere in Africa, primarily had indigenous roots. And he worked hard to get Nigeria and other African states to take the lead in dealing with the Shaba conflicts and other problems. He also sought to open a dialogue with the Angolan government to induce it to end support for the Katangan (Shaban) secessionists, instead of merely viewing the MPLA regime as a puppet of the Soviet Union and Cuba.

While the new president felt compelled to support Mobutu during those two crises, his support was always tepid. "Carter was unwilling to be pushed into a position of responding automatically to Mobutu's security needs," author Sean Kelly contends, "but he was obliged to make some supportive move, if only to protect his administration against charges that it had failed to come to the aid of an ally under Communist attack."[69] Later in the year, Andrew Young, the U.S. Ambassador to the United Nations, hailed Carter's "whole change of style" toward Africa, a change that stresses "development and food, not warfare and destruction."[70]

While this strategy seemed good in Washington (at least among liberal elements), the reaction in Zaire was quite different. The *Los Angeles Times* reported that "President Mobutu was shocked when his request for military assistance met resistance in Washington."[71] Indeed, the congressional hostility toward continued U.S. support for Mobutu was growing so strong that it had been a struggle for the White House to win consent for even limited military aid.[72] Carter's new policy, while certainly justified on both moral grounds and practical domestic political calculations, deepened the chill in U.S.-Zairian relations.

Despite his caution about giving extensive military aid to Mobutu, Carter was nearly as willing as his predecessors to express support for him in public. When asked about Zaire in a March 1977 press conference, Carter said: "Over a period of years, President Mobutu has been a friend of ours. We've enjoyed good relationships with Zaire. We have substantial commercial investments in that country."[73] Another visible episode of the administration's support for Mobutu came in 1979, when President Carter welcomed him to the White House and held a private meeting with him regarding prospective assistance from the International Monetary Fund.[74] Despite the mounting evidence of Mobutu's corruption and human rights violations, Carter was not willing to end or even tone down the public relationship between the United States and the central-African dictator.

However, during the Carter years, criticism of Mobutu's conduct—especially his human rights abuses—became more commonplace in the American press and on Capitol Hill. Carter's acknowledgement that human rights should be an important part of America's foreign policy equation gave that issue greater prominence in congressional and public discussions. In particular, it led to numerous negative articles, speeches, and hearings about Mobutu's regime.

The *Los Angeles Times* published an investigative report in June 1978 that concluded that "for ruthlessness, Mobutu rivals Idi Amin in neighboring Uganda." The report detailed how 700 people had been killed by government forces in Zaire for opposing the regime.[75] Later that month, the Foreign Affairs Committee of the House of Representatives held a hearing on human rights in several countries, including Zaire. The report emerging from the hearing concluded that Zaire had serious problems with respect to both individual liberties and basic political rights.[76] That hearing was followed up in 1981 with a hearing of the Committee's Subcommittee on Africa, which included policy experts who argued that Mobutu maintained dictatorial power through a veritable reign of terror carried out by government military forces. The hearing heard multiple witnesses document Mobutu's massive violations of human rights.[77] That Congress was willing to expose Mobutu's brutal rule so publicly was a new phenomenon in U.S. politics, but, once unleashed, that attitude would continue until the end of Mobutu's regime in the 1990s.

In late 1979, the *Washington Post* published the claims of Robert Remole, a former American diplomat to Zaire, about Washington's cozy relationship with the country's repressive rulers. Remole alleged that his attempts to inform the U.S. government of Mobutu's human rights violations were either stifled by the U.S. ambassador in Kinshasa, Walter Cutler, or were ignored by Cutler's superiors in Washington. Remole claimed that he was forced into an early retirement because of his recommendations that the U.S. government begin to distance itself from Mobutu. In the article, Remole asserted that the "Mobutu government, its police and its military are the worst enemies of the Zairian citizens."[78] Despite Remole's whistleblowing efforts, the United States continued to back Mobutu. Indeed, with the departure of the Carter administration, that level of support would increase, not diminish.

1981–1989: The Reagan Administration Embraces the African Autocrat

Just as the Ronald Reagan administration reversed the Carter-era tendency to put some distance between Washington and authoritarian U.S. clients in such places as South Korea, Central America, and the Philippines, it did so as well with respect to Zaire. By the mid-1980s, when the attempt to implement the Reagan Doctrine of assisting anti-Soviet insurgents in the Third World fully took hold, the rapprochement with Mobutu's regime was complete. The desire to apply the Reagan Doctrine by assisting Jonas Savimbi's rebel army in Angola again made Zaire a key player.

CIA Director William Casey conducted negotiations with Kinshasa in late 1985, and in December of that year preliminary arrangements were in place for the intelligence agency and the Defense Department to establish a supply and training base for UNITA on Zairian territory. The centerpiece of that operation was a refurbished air base at Kamina, near the Angolan border. Soon, a contract airline, Santa Lucia, was conducting four or five flights per week into the facility. Those flights carried a variety of weapons, including the lethal Stinger ground-to-air missiles, destined for UNITA.[79] In addition, U.S. military trainers gave UNITA foot soldiers instruction in the use of those missiles and in several phases of guerrilla warfare. All of this was done with the active cooperation of the Mobutu government.

Not only did the Reagan administration restore substantial cooperation with Kinshasa, Reagan himself seemed to be the most vocal public supporter of Mobutu of all the American presidents during the Cold War. In late 1981, he welcomed Mobutu to a warm reception in the Oval Office and offered his support for Mobutu's meetings with congressional and business leaders.[80] Reagan, in a February 1986 letter, went beyond simply praising the relations between the two nations and actually praised Mobutu's personal character. "Your strong leadership, manifest in so many issues which affect your continent's future, is something which I value greatly. My government looks forward to being able to rely on your continued council and support."[81]

However, even while Reagan lauded Mobutu, most of the attention that the Zairian leader received from either Congress or the American news media involved criticism regarding his human rights record. In 1982 the House of Representative began to reduce military funding for Zaire because of the regime's abuses. For fiscal year 1983, the House slashed the Reagan administration's military request from $20 million to a mere $4 million. That chamber also eliminated $15 million in economic aid.[82] An angry Mobutu then renounced all of the proffered U.S. aid.[83] Despite that ostentatious temper tantrum, Zaire still received approximately $33 million in U.S. aid for fiscal year 1983.

The pace of congressional hostility toward Mobutu, though, not only continued, but quickened. The House held another hearing in 1984 on the human rights situation in Zaire, which again included a parade of experts who criticized Mobutu's rule.[84] By 1988 Mobutu was frustrated with this criticism and attempts by Congress to subvert the aid that he received from the United States.[85] However, the mounting congressional scrutiny and funding cuts during the 1980s marked the beginning of the end for the U.S.-relationship with Mobutu.

Last Gasp: The Bush Years and the End of the Relationship

The relationship between President George H. W. Bush and Mobutu stretched back to Bush's years at the CIA, during which he presumably gained an admiration for Washington's most prominent African ally. When he became president, Bush demonstrated that he was determined to continue Reagan's policy of enthusiastic backing for Mobutu. The Zairian president received the signal honor of being the first African head of state to make an official visit to Washington during the Bush presidency.[86] During that June visit, President Bush lavished praise on him:

> We thank President Mobutu for coming to the United States at this critical time, and we thank him for his leadership in central Africa. And we look forward to continued cooperation between our countries. Mr. President, the strong ties of friendship between Zaire and the United States endure and prosper. And we are proud and very, very pleased to have you with us to-day.[87]

Despite Bush's comments, events that would undermine the U.S.-Zairian partnership were moving fast. Administration officials continued to wage a rear-guard struggle to preserve the supportive U.S. policy toward Mobutu. In September 1990, with reports of Mobutu's soldiers massacring over 300 students just days before, the assistant secretary of state for Africa proclaimed that the United States would direct future foreign aid toward "emerging democracies" and included Zaire in that category.[88] Only the most optimistic official—or the most cynical—could describe the Zaire of 1990 as an emerging democracy. In reality, that country groaned under the increasingly repressive and corrupt rule of Mobutu Sese Seko.

Such statements of support from the U.S. government would all but disappear after 1990, however. And on November 4 of that year, Congress finally took decisive action against Mobutu, cutting off all military aid and forcing the Bush administration to funnel the $40 million in economic aid through international organizations.[89] By November 1991, Assistant Secretary of State Jay "Hank" Cohen, at one time a strong supporter of Washington's pro-Mobutu policy, agreed that "the present regime under President Mobutu has lost legitimacy to govern Zaire during the transition to democracy."[90]

The growing opposition to Mobutu within the U.S. foreign policy community would eventually penetrate to the top levels of the executive branch. On January 29, 1993, Richard Boucher, the new State Department spokesman for Bill Clinton's administration, made a point of telling reporters that President Bush had sent Mobutu three letters over the previous 10 months urging him "to turn over all effective power, particularly over economic and financial affairs, to the transition government that was selected by the now concluded national conference."[91]

By the time Clinton entered the Oval Office in 1993, Mobutu was not only encountering surging opposition at home; he no longer had any influential supporters in the executive branch of the U.S. government. It was only a matter of time until his regime unraveled.

In the end, it was clear that without the support of his patron, the United States, he could not maintain his iron-fisted rule.[92] Indeed, he had already been compelled to bring some opposition forces into his government as early as 1991, even though he retained the bulk of political power in his own hands. After 1993, both his powers and his health (as a victim of cancer) steadily waned. Following growing violence throughout much of the country, Mobutu fled into exile in May 1997 and died the following September.

The damage that his dictatorship inflicted on the country lasted long after his departure, however. Mobutu's successors soon altered the name of the country to the Democratic Republic of the Congo, in part to repudiate his legacy, but the bloodshed that often tainted Zaire did not diminish.[93] Indeed, it became even worse under the country's new incarnation. A civil war has flared and ebbed for well over a decade, causing an estimated 1.4 million deaths as well as stomach-churning accounts of torture, mass rape, and other atrocities.

No one can be certain whether the people of that unhappy land could have averted such a fate if Mobutu had not so thoroughly looted, devastated, and demoralized the society, but the outcome could scarcely have been worse in any alternate scenario. Mobutu's rule was a disaster for his people, and a succession of U.S. administrations bear considerable responsibility for what happened to Zaire during his dictatorship and the genocidal aftermath.

Washington's Culpability in Zaire's Misfortune

Jonathan Kwitny, writing in the mid-1980s, offered an appropriate, albeit sarcastic, indictment of Washington's long, warm relationship with Mobutu. "The people of Zaire can be grateful to the people of the United States for one thing: we have kept their country from communism. What is less widely considered, but equally true, is that we have kept it from capitalism—or at least anything that might remotely resemble a free market."[94] Or, he might have added, anything that remotely resembled an honest, much less democratic, political system.

Indeed, the degree of corruption that Washington's ally practiced in Zaire dwarfed even that found in most other Third World countries. A prime example was the currency "reform" that the Mobutu regime carried out just before New Year's Day in 1980. With the encouragement of the International Monetary Fund and the U.S. government, the regime implemented two changes that ravaged Zaire's embryonic middle class. Kwitny describes both the goal and the impact of the first currency measure. "To ensure that all the earnings from mineral sales were kept in the central bank, where they could be seized by the big foreign creditors (or by the crooks who run the Zairian government), Zairians were prohibited from converting their money into solid foreign currency."[95]

That was bad enough. But the government's second decree was even more devastating. Again, with International Monetary Fund and Washington's prodding, Mobutu invalidated all existing currency and forced holders to exchange it for a new (and substantially devalued) currency. Worse, the plan gave people a mere three days to visit a bank and exchange a maximum of $1,000 of old money for new. That incredibly short timetable applied to a country in which banks outside of Kinshasa and a few other metropolitan centers were relatively rare and in which the transportation system to get to the banks that did exist was inadequate and unreliable. Kwitny noted that "communications and transportation are such that most people never got to a bank at all in the three days. Those who did found crushing lines, demands for bribes from banking officials, and sometimes an exhausted supply of new banknotes."[96]

The $1,000 ceiling also was a problem. Anything over $1,000 was worthless according to the decree, which especially punished people who kept their money outside the banking system. Although most Zairians didn't possess anything approaching $1,000, members of the small middle class did—and that was the sector that was so essential to any hope of lifting the country out of its dire poverty. The dollar ceiling hurt—and in some cases devastated—that group. The $1,000 limit should also theoretically have been a disaster for cor-

rupt speculators and the officials they had bribed over the years—
providing at least some measure of cosmic justice. But of course it
didn't work out that way. First of all, most of those people kept their
money in currencies that had real value and deposited their wealth
in banks and investment firms far away from Zaire. For the remaining funds, they merely arranged further bribes to ensure that they
were able to exchange as much old money for new as they wished.

That episode was emblematic of the corruption that permeated
Mobutu's rule for more than three decades. America's man in Africa
earned a prominent presence in the pantheon of Third World kleptocrats. And yet U.S. support for Mobutu persisted with little evidence
of regret. Ambassador Vance typified the myopic indifference. In a
1984 interview on the CBS television news program *60 Minutes*, host
Mike Wallace asked Vance if Mobutu was a brutal dictator. Vance
replied: "I'm sure there are examples of brutality, but, on the whole,
compared to a really brutal dictator, I don't think he fits the description."[97] Regarding the issue of corruption, Vance described allegations that Mobutu had stolen between $4 billion and $6 billion as a
"ridiculous ascertion (*sic*)."[98]

During another interview five years later, the former ambassador
to Zaire opined: "I think, on the whole, as I look back on our policy
toward Zaire with regard to Mobutu, it wasn't all that bad. He certainly is not perfect, but I think Zaire could have, and still could, do
much worse."[99] The first part of that statement was obtuse, given
the extent of the abuses Mobutu committed. The second part was
tragically prophetic—but Vance failed to anticipate that the gross
misgovernment of the Mobutu years was a major factor that would
produce the periodic civil wars and appalling bloodletting of the
subsequent era.

U.S. policy in the Congo/Zaire was an unprincipled mess from
the very beginning of the country's existence. Washington helped
orchestrate a coup against a duly elected prime minister primarily
because American policymakers believed that he was getting too
friendly with the Soviet Union. U.S. officials grossly oversimplified
the situation in that fractious, newly independent country, interpreting virtually any adverse development as an unacceptable setback in
an essential arena of the Cold War. Even CIA Director Allen Dulles
later conceded that Washington's perception of the communist

threat in central Africa may have been exaggerated. In a 1962 interview, Dulles stated:

> Well, I think we overrated the Soviet danger, let's say, in the Congo. They established a Lumumba Institute in Moscow, and it looked as though they were going to make a serious attempt at take-over in the Belgian Congo. Well, it didn't work out that way at all.[100]

Following that bad start, Washington continued to meddle in the country's internal affairs, eventually helping to bring to power an exceptionally autocratic and corrupt ruler. U.S. political support, arms shipments, and financial assistance helped Mobutu hold on to power and loot his country for the next three decades.

That conduct would have been bad enough if the United States had had crucial strategic or economic interests at stake. But that justification was even less valid in the case of Zaire than it was with regard to such countries as South Vietnam, the Philippines, Nicaragua, or South Korea. Zaire was never essential to the security of the United States, even if the Soviet Union had demonstrated a clear intent to establish a strong presence there. And although the Kremlin certainly sought to meddle in central Africa, as it did in many other parts of the world, its efforts with respect to Zaire were not especially intrusive.

Moscow's malign intentions were the principal rationale for Washington's backing of Mobutu, but U.S. officials exaggerated the Soviet offensive in central Africa even more than they tended to do elsewhere. Even Kissinger conceded that by the time he became secretary of state, Mobutu's conduct "was approaching the egregious." Nonetheless, he insisted that U.S. policy was justified:

> It is enough to point out that he was sustained by successive American and European administrations because they feared chaos in Zaire more than they objected to Mobutu's conduct. For nearly forty years, every American administration supported both Zaire's independence and Mobutu's rule. Presidents Kennedy, Ford, Carter and Reagan maneuvered to maintain Zaire's territorial integrity against assaults from radical neighbors.[101]

In his memoirs, Kissinger shows repeated contempt for critics—including those who served in the State Department's Africa bureau when he was secretary of state—who wanted to make moral values and human rights a key consideration in Washington's policy toward Zaire in particular and Africa in general.[102] But neither Kissinger nor officials in other administrations ever made a compelling case why having a friendly government in Zaire was essential to America's own security and well-being. Kissinger argues that the alternative to Mobutu was chaos in central and southern Africa fomented by the Soviet Union and culminating in a proliferation of Soviet satellites. But even if one concedes that argument—and it is possible to visualize any number of possible, less negative, outcomes—Kissinger and other defenders of U.S. intervention never explain why turmoil in that region would have posed a dire problem for the United States. They simply assume that point. Given the remoteness, poverty, and lack of serious military capabilities in central and southern Africa during the Cold War, it is a highly dubious presumption.

How little Zaire truly mattered to the security of the United States is confirmed by the general silence about the country and its ruler in the memoirs of Presidents Johnson, Nixon, Ford, Carter, and Reagan. If that country had really been a crucial battlefield in the Cold War struggle, it is unlikely that so many chief executives would have virtually ignored it when they gave their personal perspectives on the important issues they confronted and their record of achievements while in the Oval Office.[103] It seemed that—the hyperbolic rhetoric of some cold warriors to the contrary—Zaire was never much more to them than a convenient geopolitical pawn.

Even Zaire's economic relevance to the United States was only marginal. The country was never a significant U.S. trading partner or a major investment arena for American firms. True, Zaire was—and remains—a source of important rare metals and minerals, but that source was not irreplaceable. Moreover, whatever regime ruled Zaire would have been compelled by economic necessity to continue selling mineral exports in the global market or risk financial suicide.

Even if the country had been an important economic player, that is not a sufficient reason to overthrow an elected government, much less help install and maintain in power for decades an utterly thuggish and corrupt successor. Yet that is what the United States did, and the policymakers who were responsible deserve to feel more than a little shame.

9. Flying Blind in Manila: Enabling Ferdinand Marcos

For more than two decades, beginning in the mid-1960s, Washington hailed Philippine President Ferdinand Marcos as not only a security partner in East Asia but also a democratic partner. The strategic rationale was relatively straightforward. Washington was extremely worried that communist revolutions might sweep the region, and U.S. officials were determined to prevent its former colony, especially given its location astride important sea lanes in the western Pacific, from succumbing to a red tide. Marcos shrewdly exploited those fears and never missed an opportunity to stress his anti-communist credentials. In addition to Washington's general strategic calculations, the Philippines became important as a platform for the projection of U.S. naval and air power in the Vietnam War. Both Subic Bay Naval Base and Clark Air Force Base were significant assets in that conflict.

The strategic location of the islands and the importance of Clark and Subic remained crucial considerations for U.S. policymakers even after the Vietnam intervention came to a close. In his memoirs, President Ronald Reagan stated the continuing strategic case succinctly: "The future of the Philippines was of great importance to the United States. Our huge military stations there, Clark Air Force Base and the Subic Bay Naval Base, were among our largest in the world and the anchor of our defense in the western Pacific; and we had no stronger ally anywhere than Marcos."[1]

The Early Years: Washington Sees Marcos as a Model Leader

The image of Ferdinand Marcos as a democratic political figure had some validity in the beginning. He first became president in 1965 in an election that was, by nearly all accounts, free and fair. Moreover, he was a young, dynamic politician and a charismatic speaker, in some ways reminiscent of John F. Kennedy—an idealized image that was still fresh in the minds of Americans following the horrifying assassination in November 1963. Marcos held out the promise of being the template for a new generation of East Asian leaders—someone who was bold, progressive, but also strongly anticommunist and committed to the Western values of capitalism and democracy.

Throughout the more than six decades since the end of World War II, the emergence of such leaders has always been the professed goal of U.S. governments. And in the post–Cold War period in East Asia, some major political figures, including Lee Teng-hui and Ma Ying-jeou in Taiwan and Kim Young Sam and Kim Dae Jung in South Korea (among others), generally lived up to those expectations. But in Ferdinand Marcos, as with Ngo Dinh Diem a decade earlier, Washington's hopes were misplaced. The behavior of the chosen client failed to match the image.

U.S. enthusiasm for the Philippine leader was evident from the very beginning. Even before his initial election as president in 1965, both the U.S. government and the American news media portrayed him in the most glowing terms. Typical was a *New York Times* profile published shortly after that election contending that Marcos "was 'No. 1' to his countrymen long before they voted him into the highest office."[2] Other media outlets echoed those simplistic sentiments. During a visit to Manila in October 1966, President Lyndon Johnson seemed deeply impressed with the Philippine government's plans for economic advancement, especially in the areas of agricultural modernization and increased food production. Johnson told Marcos: "You are pointing the way for all of Asia to follow, and I hope they are looking. I hope they are listening. And I hope they are following."[3]

Washington's professed admiration for Marcos was not confined to the economic arena. Johnson had been most grateful to the Philippine leader for organizing a summit of anti-communist East Asian leaders to back U.S. policy in South Vietnam. During a state visit to Washington by President and Mrs. Marcos in September 1966, the two heads of state discussed the possibility of such a summit. Johnson recalled: "I told the Philippines President that we approved of the all-Asia conference and would take part, but that the United States would not organize it. He or other Asian leaders should take the lead."[4] Marcos willingly did so, issuing an invitation in his name and the names of South Korean President Park Chung Hee and Thailand's Prime Minister Thanom Kittikachorn—two of Washington's prominent authoritarian allies in East Asia. Since America's reputation in that region, as in the rest of the world, was already in decline because of the increasingly controversial Vietnam War, having a receptive ally take the lead in promoting an important U.S. policy so that Washington's role was less conspicuous generated considerable gratitude on the part of U.S. officials.

Even early in the relationship, though, a gap existed between the enthusiasm for Marcos that U.S. leaders expressed publicly and some of their private misgivings. In particular, President Johnson and his chief advisers, including Assistant Secretary of State for East Asian affairs William P. Bundy, grew weary of Marcos's incessant pressure for more and more U.S. financial assistance. That annoyance increased as he simultaneously resisted Washington's pressure to make a more substantive contribution to the Vietnam War effort. When Marcos tastelessly used the occasion of Australian Prime Minister Harold Holt's funeral in December 1967 to lobby for yet more aid, Johnson reportedly exploded to Bundy: "If you ever bring that man near me again, I'll have your head."[5] But such private distaste did not translate into public criticism, much less substantive policy changes.

Marcos, Martial Law, and Washington as Enabler

By the early 1970s, especially after he imposed martial law in 1972, any reputation that Marcos might have had as a democratic leader was rapidly fraying. Indeed, there were already signs of trouble in the late 1960s. Sterling Seagrave, a journalist who spent many years in East Asia, noted that between 1965 and the end of the decade, "what Filipinos were witnessing was the consolidation of power in the hands of one man—the creation of a police state and the birth of a dictatorship." A key step was changing the military "into a super-police force" by changing its mission "from external defense to internal population control." According to Seagrave, "the remodeling of the police and army was directed toward one end: suppressing internal dissent." Marcos "intended to suppress any and all resistance to his personal rule, whether it arose from political activity by rivals, criticism by journalists, protests by students, demonstrations by labor, or armed resistance by farmers."[6]

Washington aided and abetted Marcos's campaign to "reform" the police and military. President Johnson secretly authorized a multimillion-dollar program to reorganize and retrain those forces. The U.S. Embassy in Manila and the U.S. Agency for International Development (AID) even helped Marcos develop and refine the reorganization strategy.[7]

In marked contrast to the 1965 election, which most observers concluded had been clean, the 1969 balloting that saw Marcos win by a two-million-vote margin out of nine million votes cast gained the opposite reputation. The election was widely seen as riddled with fraud—if not outright rigged. (Critics noted, for example, that the president even swept districts where virtually everyone seemed opposed to him.) Matters became steadily worse with respect to political corruption, financial corruption, and the treatment of political opponents between the murky 1969 election and Marcos's proclamation of martial law three years later.[8]

The United States did not have entirely clean hands regarding that executive coup d'état. True, U.S. agencies, including the Central Intelligence Agency (CIA), were not as involved as in the 1953 coup in Iran—which Washington and London largely orchestrated—or the "made in Washington" rebellion that overthrew Guatemalan President Jacobo Árbenz Guzmán. But American officials were more than passive observers regarding the Marcos presidential coup. Indeed, there seem to be more explicit U.S. acceptance of the destruction of what remained of Philippine democracy in 1972 than there was in the military ouster of South Korean civilian governments in 1961 and 1980.

Despite later denials from the State Department that it "was not informed in advance of President Marcos' intention to declare martial law," both the CIA and U.S. Ambassador Henry Byroade (who had extremely close ties to Marcos) were aware of what was coming and that hundreds of regime critics would be arrested and imprisoned. Journalist Raymond Bonner, who has written the most comprehensive account of Washington's relationship with the Marcos family, assessed the official U.S. response: "At best, the denial was a half-truth; the 'surprise' feigned." Bonner concludes that "Maybe the United States didn't know the exact hour and minute, but it knew just about everything else."[9]

"If Washington had wanted to defend democracy in the Philippines," Bonner notes, "it could have sent a very strong message to Marcos that martial law would not be tolerated, that there would be a cutoff of aid, or some other step taken, if he usurped democracy. No such message was ever sent."[10] And given the U.S. track record with respect to other countries, the failure to convey such a warning was not out of an abundance of respect for Philippines' sovereignty and an unwillingness to interfere in the internal affairs of an ally. The reasons for such acquiescence had far more to do with the belief that Marcos was a critical pro-U.S. political and strategic partner in East Asia.

Indeed, Washington's posture regarding the Marcos proclamation of martial law was only a little less supportive than its posture toward pliable South Vietnamese generals in the weeks leading up to the coup against Ngo Dinh Diem. In both cases, U.S. leaders were aware of the evolving plans and, at a minimum, did nothing to discourage them. Indeed, just a few months before Marcos perpetuated his rule by declaring martial law, Ambassador Byroade had returned from Washington with a clarification of U.S. policy. The policy was, the ambassador apparently told Marcos, that if martial law was needed to put down the communist insurgency, then Washington would back his decision.[11] That was exceedingly close to an outright green light for a presidential coup.

In short, the United States government bore more than a little responsibility for the demise of democracy in the Philippines in 1972. And, as in the South Vietnamese and South Korean episodes, major segments of the Philippine population held Washington responsible for both the coup and what followed.

The reaction of U.S. officials and much of the American news media certainly did not indicate much dissatisfaction with the martial-law proclamation. Chairman of the Joint Chiefs of Staff Admiral Thomas Moorer reportedly told aides that Marcos's action was "the best thing" for the Philippines. Former Secretary of Defense Robert McNamara, who had moved on to become head of the World Bank, promised a key Marcos aide that the World Bank would double its loans to the Philippines if Marcos truly would use his new powers to accelerate the country's economic development. A meeting between that aide, Alejandro Melchor, and key U.S. senators, including Majority Leader Mike Mansfield (D-MT) and Senate Foreign

Relations Committee Chairman J. William Fulbright (D-AR), was marked by a notable comity. The maelstrom of protest in Congress that Ambassador Byroade had feared when Marcos first began to hint of a coup simply did not materialize. *Newsweek* columnist Tony Clifton concluded that Marcos was "sincere" in his desire to use martial-law powers to benefit the Filipino people and that complacent view epitomized the prevailing attitude within the American political and media elites.[12]

Even after the imposition of martial law and the signs of mounting repression and corruption, U.S. leaders continued to fawn over Marcos as though his manifest flaws did not exist. Economic and military aid from Washington continued to pour into the country, and a succession of American political leaders described Marcos as an important Free World leader. Raymond Bonner observes:

> The Marcoses' spell over American policy continued to hold, long after their popularity at home had begun to erode. In the streets and at the polls, Filipinos registered their disapproval of the Marcos administration. But the Marcoses discovered that they could rely on American leaders to bail them out when it seemed that many Filipinos wanted to throw them out.[13]

U.S. Support Remains Steadfast

Despite the mounting authoritarianism and cronyism of the Marcos regime, U.S. aid continued to flow throughout the Gerald Ford, Jimmy Carter, and Ronald Reagan years. It would be difficult to exaggerate the extent of the cronyism and corruption. Political scientist Mark Thompson notes that by 1975, 32 of the 35 most economically influential people in the Philippines were closely connected to the Philippine president.[14] Even the Carter administration, which touted its commitment to human rights as a crucial component of U.S. foreign policy, was reluctant to put any serious pressure on Marcos. The aid issue illustrated the continuation of the status quo. In addition to the unimpeded flow of bilateral aid, the Carter administration cast votes on some 61 World Bank and other multilateral development bank loans for the Philippines. Administration officials never voted no on any of those loans and decided to abstain a mere 11 times, mostly on small, especially dubious proposals.

Carter himself never expressed meaningful criticism of the Marcos regime, and he dispatched Vice President Walter Mondale to Manila for a high-profile visit that turned into a propaganda festival for Marcos. Mondale's posture toward Marcos during that 1978 visit was only a little less fawning than George H. W. Bush's infamous toast a few years later.

The lack of any distancing of U.S. policy from the Philippine dictator during the Carter years was not surprising, given that the official in charge of that policy was Richard Holbrooke, the assistant secretary of state for East Asian and Pacific Affairs. Holbrooke cared little about human rights issues—especially if he believed they might interfere with what he regarded as far more important matters: retaining the military bases in the Philippines and having a reliable, anti-communist ally in Manila. When bureaucratic battles arose between Holbrooke and other advocates of a generous military and financial aid policy for the Philippines and skeptics such as Assistant Secretary of State for Human Rights and Humanitarian Affairs Patricia Derian, who wanted to use the aid issue to exert at least some leverage to get Marcos to ease his repressive rule, the decision that emerged was invariably in favor of more, rather than less, aid. The implicit message to Marcos was that he could persist in his behavior without fear of any loss of U.S. support. One bitter Foreign Service officer later concluded that the Carter policy "in fact sanctioned Philippine authoritarianism."[15]

Even Derian later admitted that Washington had been extremely cautious about condemning the Philippines and other autocratic U.S. allies in East Asia—much less reducing aid or taking other tangible steps to express displeasure with those governments. The reason was simple: East Asia was seen as a vital region geostrategically. Derian was quite candid about the reason for Washington's reticence regarding Marcos's abuses: "We must maintain our bases at Subic and Clark Airfield."[16]

If an official for whom human rights issues were supposedly a top priority was nevertheless willing to concede that strategic considerations trumped concerns about democracy and civil liberties in the Philippines, it is not surprising that officials and opinion leaders who were far less committed to those values were even more inclined to look the other way. The highlight (or lowlight) of Washington's policy came during a 1981 visit by Vice President George H. W. Bush to

Manila, when he lavishly praised Marcos. Bush emphasized the U.S. government's respect and admiration for Marcos: "We stand with you sir. . . . We love your adherence to democratic principle and to the democratic processes."[17] The reality was that the Philippine strongman had been a full-fledged dictator since his imposition of martial law in 1972, and he had displayed pronounced authoritarian tendencies and practices for several years before that official proclamation.[18]

Evidence of Corruption and Brutality Mounts

Hailing Marcos for his alleged commitment to democracy was a stance that infuriated genuine Philippine democrats. The U.S. embrace seemed even more bitterly ironic to democratic forces two years after Bush's laudatory toast when former Philippine senator Benigno Aquino, a long-time Marcos critic and widely acknowledged leader of the democratic opposition, was assassinated moments after landing at the Manila airport following his return from exile in the United States on August 21, 1983. Most Filipinos greeted the official story put out by the Marcos government (a lone, pro-communist assassin with no ties whatsoever to the government) with a mixture of anger and derision, especially since Aquino had been escorted from the aircraft under military guard.[19] Indeed, there was evidence that the so-called assassin had actually been shot to death hours earlier, with security forces dumping his body on the tarmac next to Aquino's seconds after the assassination.[20] After Aquino's murder, Marcos increasingly became an embarrassment to his American patrons. But that uneasiness did not lead to an immediate change in Washington's policy. The Reagan administration would continue backing the Marcos regime for nearly three more years.

Yet Marcos's corruption undermined the very segments of Philippine society that were most important for building a modern economy and creating political and economic bulwarks against communism—which was Washington's professed policy goal. As former *Wall Street Journal* foreign correspondent Jonathan Kwitny pointed out shortly before the dictator's fall from power, "Marcos took much of his wealth directly from the people who earned it—businessmen large and small, whose assets have been effectively expropriated."[21]

While Marcos's behavior may have been perfectly logical from the standpoint of personal enrichment, his actions hardly seem to advance U.S. goals or interests. Indeed, a radical leftist regime would have been hard pressed to undermine those goals and interests any more than Marcos was doing. Kwitny's summary is an all-too-accurate portrayal of the regime's conduct during the last 15 years or so of the Marcos era:

> City and countryside alike, Marcos has made himself such an implacable enemy of business that the relatively wealthy classes are already aiding a budding guerrilla movement, although they know very well they may lose control of it. The Marcos government itself has fundamentally stifled free enterprise. Using the power of the state, it has in effect nationalized many large and medium-sized businesses that in other countries live in fear of communism. From the richest to the poorest, Filipinos make clear that they believe this couldn't have happened without the full, active support of the United States.[22]

Raymond Bonner's evaluation was more succinct, but in the same vein. "Marcos was not just corrupt; he was anti-capitalist, anti-free market. He created more government monopolies than the most dedicated of socialists."[23] Conservative scholar Theodore Friend's analysis was only a little less scathing. Although Friend argued that during the 1960s and early 1970s—even for the first two years or so after the establishment of martial law—Marcos had adopted land reform, export-oriented policies, and other useful reforms to make the Philippines economy more robust and competitive, that had all changed by 1975:

> The Philippines old oligarchy had given way to a new one—Marcos's cronies. Into their hands went the supposedly reformed land, and into their hands too went capital-intensive projects (in nuclear power, steel, copper, etc.), justified by a rhetoric of "economic independence." . . . The projects were devised to bring in huge foreign loans, from which the cronies siphoned off large portions. Cronies also developed commodity cartels in the coconut and sugar industries.[24]

What Friend does not mention is that most of the "foreign loans" came either directly from the United States or from international lending agencies in which U.S. influence was dominant. The economic corrosion that Marcos's policies caused was bad enough, but the economic corruption also led to an alarming political corrosion. As Friend notes: "Good men left or lost influence as the cronies gathered around Marcos."[25] And the communist New People's Army (NPA), which numbered barely in the hundreds when Marcos took office, numbered at least 20,000 during the final years of his rule.

The growing strength of the NPA caused consternation among pundits and policy experts in the United States. Conservative analyst Ross H. Munro, a former correspondent for *Time* in Southeast Asia, published a lengthy piece in *Commentary* in late 1985 warning of the growing communist threat in the Philippines.[26] According to Munro, the NPA could "credibly boast" that it had "way beyond" 20,000 guerrillas, plus at least 10,000 other members, and the insurgent army was fighting in at least 59 of the nation's 79 provinces.[27] As did many other American experts, especially those who were favorable to Marcos, Munro tended to exaggerate the power of the NPA and the group's prospects for a successful revolution. Unless matters improved, he warned, NPA leader Rodolfo Salas "will be heading the People's Democratic Republic of the Philippines sometime in the 1990s and unveiling 'a Pol Pot future.'"[28]

American Conservatives as Apologists for the Marcos Regime

The conservative Heritage Foundation, which was highly influential in GOP circles (especially once the Reagan administration took office), published a study in 1984 asserting that the Philippine bases were more important than ever in the aftermath of the communist victory in Vietnam. Growing instability in the Philippines, the study argued, "threatens to bring a change in leadership that could very well seek to abrogate the bases agreement that has secured the stability of Southeast Asia since the trauma in Vietnam."[29] Conversely, "it is clear that as long as the Marcos administration remains in office in Manila, the United States will be assured access to the Philippine bases."[30]

The Heritage study was bluntly hostile to the democratic opposition and implied that Washington would be foolish to lessen its support for the Philippine leader. Conjuring the nightmare of the virulently anti-American successor regimes in such places as Nicaragua and Iran, the analysis asserted that the "accession to power of even a 'moderate' anti-Marcos opposition would very well threaten U.S. security, economic, and political interests. The 'moderate' anti-Marcos opposition is sufficiently anti-American to make its advent to power in Manila a cause for alarm."[31] The use of scare quotes around "moderate" was not just careless stylistic excess. Heritage scholars, and most other conservatives during the Reagan years, made little distinction between democratic and radical leftist opponents of America's authoritarian clients. In the case of the Philippines, the Heritage study insisted: "In terms of U.S. security and economic interests, it is difficult to distinguish 'moderates' from an anti-Marcos opposition that is 'radical.'"[32]

That sort of sloppy thinking characterized most conservative writing about U.S. policy options in the Philippines during the 1970s and 1980s. The assumption, implicit or explicit, was that the only alternatives were continued support for Marcos or watch the Philippines descend into the maw of international communism. Some conservatives were at least a bit chagrined at having to advocate support for the lesser of two evils. *National Review* editor William F. Buckley Jr. clearly adopted that approach. "One could say about Marcos today what one could have said about Chiang Kai-shek in China in 1949. He is infinitely better than the organized opposition."[33]

Other American supporters of Marcos, though, went well beyond such resigned pragmatism. Former ambassador to the United Nations Jeane Kirkpatrick asserted that "day after day, American newspapers, news weeklies and network newscasts treat Marcos's real and imagined failures, inefficiencies, and corruption as though they were extraordinary and unique. They are not. Of the 159 member states of the United Nations, at least 100 are probably governed more poorly than the Philippines." But while "many countries in the world are worse governed than the Philippines," Kirkpatrick argued, "None is more important to the stability and security of the United States, Japan and other independent nations in the Pacific."[34]

As the 1980s advanced, though, the ostentatious corruption of the Marcos government made its supporters in Washington increasingly uncomfortable. Indeed, Marcos emerged as the poster child of what was wrong with America's foreign policy—especially its foreign-aid program. Although generous amounts of U.S. financial assistance continued to arrive in Manila, there was a dearth of evidence that it benefited the Filipino people. The Philippine economy remained in the doldrums, even shrinking during the mid-1980s (a whopping decline of 7.1 percent in 1984 and another 4.2 percent drop in 1985). That miserable performance stood in marked contrast to the soaring economic growth rates of so many other countries in East Asia—the emergence of the so-called Asian Tigers during the 1980s.

Nonconservative media accounts in the West now increasingly portrayed Marcos and his wife as symbols of corruption and decadence. *New York Times* columnist Anthony Lewis charged that Marcos had resorted to "thuggery, theft, and intervention" to consolidate his power. The Philippine dictator was "a plunderer who knows that his people understand what he has done to them."[35] Not only had Marcos and his relatives emerged as the richest family in the Philippines—with estimates of their wealth reaching into billions of dollars—but the couple's narcissistic excesses had become blatant. Imelda Marcos's notoriously huge collection of expensive shoes was an especially visible symbol of the problem. That collection caused one Washington wag to observe that the only beneficiary of America's aid program in the Philippines appeared to be the shoe industry.

And even some conservative analysts increasingly worried that Marcos's continued rule might strengthen the power of the NPA. Ross Munro commented that in Western news reports from the Philippines, nearly all the responsibility for the Communist upsurge was being put at the doorstep of Marcos. While that view was an oversimplification, Munro contended, it contained more than a little truth:

> Indeed he has played an essential role. During his twenty years in power, the country has suffered from colossal mismanagement of its economy, corruption akin to looting, and the near destruction of the nation's basic political institutions. Without all this help from Marcos, it seems, the Communists would have remained about as inconsequential as they are today in, say, Indonesia or Thailand.[36]

Munro's view, however, remained a minority perspective among conservatives in the policy community and, more important, within the Reagan administration. But that situation was about to change for the better—just in time to avert disaster.

Catalyst for Change: Secretary of State George Shultz Becomes Uneasy

It was not until the corruption and unpopularity of the Marcos regime had reached epidemic levels that the Reagan administration belatedly switched its support to democratic forces led by Corazon Aquino. The key player in that policy change was Reagan's second secretary of state (replacing Alexander Haig), George Shultz. In contrast to previous U.S. officials, and most of his colleagues in the administration, Shultz seemed wary and cynical about the Marcoses from the very beginning. Recalling his first meeting with the couple in 1974, Shultz described them as "intelligent and energetic," but in a telling comment, also as "cunning." That skepticism did not diminish when he headed the State Department. During a lavish state luncheon marking a brief visit by Shultz to Manila in June 1983, President Marcos made a toast hailing the value of a healthy private-sector economy. Shultz, a long-time, staunch advocate of free markets, recalled his reaction. "I almost laughed, as I well knew that state-sanctioned monopolies were in fact the dominant businesses."[37]

While Shultz did not depart from the conventional wisdom that the Clark and Subic Bay bases, which had always been the main justification for backing Marcos, were crucial to America's position in East Asia, he had a slightly different and insightful take on the issue, even given that assumption:

> From my standpoint, I was concerned about Clark Air Force Base and the Subic Bay Naval Station, two of the most important elements in the U.S. presence and strategic posture in the Pacific. The environment surrounding these historic facilities was turning sour. Marcos's support for us and the erosion of support for him among the people of the Philippines were creating political opposition to our bases.[38]

He was certainly more perceptive about the likely outcome of Washington's continuing embrace of the Philippine dictator than most other U.S. officials. Even during this early stage in his tenure as secretary of state, Shultz recognized the mounting danger to Washington's policy goals, and he wondered whether continued support for Marcos was wise. "Where would Marcos take the Philippines?" he pondered. "As matters stood, we and our bases were linked to him and to a large degree dependent on him. I felt uneasy."[39]

The assassination of Benigno Aquino and the increasingly brazen nature of the corruption and arrogance riddling the Marcos regime made Shultz even more uncomfortable over the following year. When opposition factions made surprisingly large gains in the May 1984 elections for the National Assembly (despite the usual rigging of the process), Marcos reached new heights of arrogance with his response. When questioned about the outcome during a May 15 interview with *CBS News*, he stated: "I would presume our instructions to our people to allow the opposition to win some seats might have been taken too literally."[40] Shultz's reaction was one of astonishment. "It was an incredible statement for Marcos to have made, but there it was."[41] That episode deepened his doubts about whether continued U.S. support for Marcos really benefited America's interests.

The consensus strategy that Shultz, Secretary of Defense Caspar Weinberger, CIA Director William Casey, and National Security Advisor Robert McFarlane developed at a February 1985 meeting was to try to revitalize key institutions in the Philippines, including the military and business and professional associations. The hope was that Marcos would support, or at least acquiesce to, such reforms. Shultz and his colleagues "saw Marcos as a survivor, not a reformer, but also as someone who would respond to pressure." The secretary of state conceded, though, that as the year progressed, "I became increasingly convinced that Marcos was the problem, not the solution."[42]

Although they didn't say so explicitly, U.S. officials also were preparing for a post-Marcos era, with the goal of minimizing instability in the country. It was increasingly evident that Marcos was in ill health, and the belief was that even if he could cling to power and thwart the growing political opposition for a few years more, Washington had to hedge its bets. But Shultz and other proponents of a policy change, most notably Michael Armacost, who had been U.S.

ambassador to the Philippines at the time of Benigno Aquino's assassination and was now undersecretary of state for political affairs, had to proceed cautiously.[43] Following a meeting with President Reagan, in which Shultz presented the consensus view reached at the February session, he concluded: "I could see that Ronald Reagan wanted to support this man who had been a friend of the United States over many years, a staunch anti-Communist, and head of a country that was host to important U.S. military bases."[44]

The End of the Marcos Era: The 1986 Crisis

But U.S. efforts to get Marcos to reform before it was too late were doomed to failure. A diplomatic mission by special presidential envoy Paul Laxalt in October 1985 produced disappointing results. Shortly thereafter, Marcos made the fateful decision to move up the date of the presidential election from 1987 to January 1986 (soon moved to early February). His assumption was that the surprise move would give the opposition virtually no time to organize and wage an effective campaign. That assumption proved wrong, as the normally fragmented opposition coalesced behind Corazon Aquino (Benigno Aquino's widow) as its presidential candidate and Senator Salvador Laurel as the vice presidential nominee.[45] Massive pro-democracy demonstrations occurred in Manila and other cities, and key figures such as church leader Jaime Cardinal Sin ultimately sided with Aquino.

It was clear as the election drew near that Marcos was in deep political trouble. Yet the State Department continued to encounter entrenched White House support for the Philippine autocrat. Even generic expressions of support for free and fair elections, which Ambassador Stephen Bosworth expressed in a late January interview, provoked warnings from White House aides to be more circumspect. Shultz describes the attitude of the president himself:

> I was quite aware that President Reagan wanted Marcos to change, not leave. However bad the Philippine situation might be, Ronald Reagan felt that Marcos had been a friend and ally of the United States, and Reagan stood up for people when the going was tough. That trait was criticized but also admired. Reagan had been

outraged by the way the United States turned its back on the shah of Iran; he did not want to treat Marcos that way, to have it said that the United States abandoned its friends.[46]

The domestic crisis in the Philippines reached a culmination in February 1986, when Marcos made a transparent attempt to steal the election after the balloting clearly had not gone his way and Aquino's supporters poured into the streets of Manila and other cities in protest. Yet the White House astonishingly seemed prepared to act as if the fraud had not occurred. (Reagan himself at one point suggested that both camps may have engaged in electoral chicanery, even though embassy officials and other international observers found no evidence of such activity by Aquino and her followers.) Chief of Staff Donald Regan was obsessively anti-Aquino and to the bitter end urged the president to continue Washington's support for Marcos. Days after the balloting, White House Press Secretary Larry Speakes nonchalantly declared that Marcos had won. Shultz was furious, and the State Department lobbied hard for a "clarifying" statement. The White House press office then issued a more neutral comment, but by that time there was a widespread perception in both the United States and the Philippines that the Reagan administration was brazenly backing Marcos.

To Shultz, the situation was becoming both clear and perilous. The burgeoning street demonstrations throughout the Philippines protesting the fraud confirmed to him the strength of the pro-democracy movement and Marcos's untenable position. What the secretary feared most was that a U.S. failure to back Aquino and insist that the real results of the election be recognized would likely mean seeing the moderates shoved aside by more radical elements, who would then control the opposition to an ever-weaker Marcos. That development would increase the likelihood of massive instability in the Philippines, with the prospect of the United States being drawn in militarily (to protect its bases) and, as Shultz fretted, "quite possibly on the wrong side."[47]

Even as the evidence of the Marcos camp's massive electoral fraud and the rapid evaporation of support for the dictator among members of the Filipino political, economic, and military elites became indisputable, President Reagan stubbornly resisted pressure coming from his own foreign policy team for a change in U.S. policy. Ultimately, the shifting allegiance of those Filipino elites, especially the defection of Defense Minister Juan Ponce Enrile to the Aquino camp, presented both Marcos and Reagan with a fait accompli.[48]

But the experience of a new special presidential envoy, veteran diplomat Philip Habib, during his trip to Manila illustrated just how corrosive Washington's long-time support of Marcos had been to the political culture of the Philippines. After a Marcos aide suggested that he talk to four major power brokers who were supposedly pro-Marcos, Habib discovered that all four had concluded that Marcos was finished. Yet they all assumed that only Washington could push him from power. Habib reported that the prevailing attitude was: "Marcos had got to go, and you Americans have got to get rid of him. You're the Godfather, *You* do it." Similar was the plaintive plea of Cardinal Sin: "Tell the president to pick up the phone and tell Marcos to go."[49]

That another country (and a one-time reasonably functional democracy at that) would exhibit a pathetic dependence on the United States to solve its internal political problems should have been a distressing and sobering realization for U.S. officials. In the end, fortunately, Aquino's "people power" movement was much stronger than Washington had anticipated and played the decisive role in impelling Marcos to relinquish his office and go into exile. A blatant exercise of a U.S. "imperial prerogative," which is essentially what Cardinal Sin and others were requesting, did not become necessary. Nevertheless, it was a sad comment that Washington's policies toward the Philippines over the previous two decades had so drained any sense of self-reliance, even among members of the elite, that the result was a supplicant mentality toward the former colonial master.

Anti-Communist Policy Blinders Regarding the Philippines

When he finally relented and accepted the inevitable, President Reagan was still unenthusiastic about dumping Washington's long-time client. In his memoirs, Reagan states that he and his top advisers all agreed that Marcos no longer had sufficient domestic support to remain in power and that Aquino had far more backing. "Given these facts, the decision I made wasn't difficult," Reagan recalled, "but it wasn't enjoyable either."[50] A major reason for that reluctance, he admitted, was uneasiness about Aquino; he was "skeptical about whether she had enough determination to fight the Filipino insurgents."[51] As in so many other instances and arenas during the Cold War, U.S. policy regarding the Philippines was seen almost entirely through the prism of America's global struggle against Soviet-led communism.

And Marcos had always known how to exploit that U.S. obsession with the specter of communist advances for maximum effect. He used that fear, playing American officials as a virtuoso would play a violin. It was no coincidence that of the 23 "whereas" clauses in his 1972 proclamation justifying the imposition of martial law, 19 of them referred to some aspect of the allegedly dire communist threat to the government and society of the Philippines. He realized that not only was that argument the most likely one to neutralize domestic opposition to his power grab, it was—by far—the argument most likely to inhibit any criticism from the United States.

Reagan's views certainly exemplified a reflexive support for any ally, however autocratic, who professed to be anti-communist. When asked during a televised presidential campaign debate with Walter Mondale in October 1984 what he would do about the mounting evidence of corruption and repression in the Philippines, the president responded that events in that country "do not look good to us from the standpoint right now of human rights." But, he asked, "What is the alternative?" Reagan saw only one possibility: "It is a large Communist movement to take over the Philippines." And that prospect made America's policy rather clear-cut. "I think that we're better off trying to retain our friendship and help them right the wrongs we see rather than throwing them to the wolves and then facing a Communist power in the Pacific."[52]

Reagan's comment illustrates the ideological blinders that constrained U.S. policy toward the Philippines throughout the Marcos years. The reality was that the communist insurgency in that country was never as large or powerful as U.S. officials believed. Marcos simply hyped the threat, and U.S. policymakers in five administrations bought that hype. Moreover, to the extent that communist forces were gaining in strength, that trend was in no small measure because of the abuses of the Marcos government—abuses that were alienating wide segments of the Filipino population. Washington's support for Marcos, in short, was undermining, rather than advancing, U.S. policy goals—even within the context of inflated American fears about a powerful communist menace in that country. Even in terms of internal logic, therefore, Washington's continued backing of Marcos made little sense.

One conservative analyst asserted that "at the climax of the crisis [in 1986] the United States government acted with timely daring to strengthen democratic forces in the Philippines, extract the autocratic Marcos from the situation, and minimize bloodshed."[53] But that analysis both gives too much weight to U.S. actions in 1986 and ignores the long record of U.S. foot-dragging in the years before 1986 that undermined democracy and helped keep Marcos in power.

Fortunately, the Reagan administration's policy change, belated as it was, came in time to contain the damage to America's relations with the Philippines. Although anger at the United States remained high, and played a role in Manila's decision in 1992 not to renew the leases to the Subic Bay and Clark military bases, America did not experience the massive blowback that marked the aftermath of its policies in such places as Iran and Nicaragua.

Raymond Bonner provides an appropriate assessment—or indictment—of U.S. policy toward the Philippines during the Marcos years:

> The Marcoses carried on through five American administrations—three Republican and two Democratic. American governments watched as the Marcoses robbed the Philippine people of between $5 and $10 *billion*, larceny and looting that began even before Marcos had declared martial law. Washington looked on as he emasculated the country's democratic institutions: the courts; the schools; the political parties. He corrupted the superb army that had been created by General Douglas MacArthur, sapping it of the ability and morale to fight the Communist-led insurgency.[54]

A succession of American administrations apparently believed that they had a useful client in Ferdinand Marcos and that they were skillfully using him to advance U.S. policy goals. But Bonner is right that the reverse was probably more accurate:

> [Marcos] was an absolute master of the American po-
> litical system. He knew more about that system, its
> intricacies and nuances, and about the men who ran
> it than they ever did about his country and the man
> who ran it. He deployed his knowledge, ingenuity,
> and cunning to extract far more from Uncle Sam than
> he ever gave. At each turning point, each showdown,
> whether over Vietnam or human rights, Marcos stood
> his ground. It was always the powerful United States
> that blinked.[55]

The evidence supports that conclusion. Ferdinand Marcos was never as useful to the United States or as cooperative as American policymakers seemed to believe. For example, although Washington was able to use the Clark and Subic Bay bases for troop deployments and logistical missions to Indochina during the Vietnam War, it would have been difficult for any Philippine government to block such uses in any case, since the United States had valid leases to both facilities. Beyond not causing static over the use of the bases, Marcos did little of value in connection with the war. Several other Pacific and East Asian allies, most notably South Korea, Thailand, and Australia, sent far more troops to support the U.S. military campaign in South Vietnam than did the Philippines. Australia sent 7,500 troops, while the Philippines—with three times the population—sent a 2,000-man engineering battalion.[56]

For two decades, Washington invested a sizable amount of diplomatic and economic capital in a client who provided, at best, very modest benefits. And even more so than in some other cases, U.S. officials allowed their corrupt and repressive client to manipulate his patron. Marcos was not shy about playing diplomatic hardball when the United States seemed to be wavering in its support or became too pushy about wanting reforms. As U.S. pressure on his regime cautiously but steadily mounted during 1985, he responded with barely veiled threats. As Shultz recalled, "Marcos was already making quiet threats about our tenure at our military bases and had hinted to the Soviets that they might gain access to Philippine naval facilities."[57] Such actions should have disabused U.S. officials of any lingering illusion that Ferdinand Marcos was a committed anti-communist and a reliable friend of the United States. He was out for his own gain and little else.

Washington's conduct with respect to the Marcos dictatorship was even more ethically unsound than U.S. policy toward many other authoritarian allies. In most of those other instances, the choice was between a friendly, albeit undemocratic, ruler or faction versus the prospect of a much less friendly (perhaps overtly hostile) alternative. Even in such cases as Iran and South Korea, where democratic governments were briefly in place, democracy seemed fragile at best, and the communist threat seemed not only real, but dire. In retrospect, U.S. officials may have underestimated the strength and sustainability of democratic trends and overestimated the extent of the communist menace, but the situation was more opaque at the time.

With regard to the Philippines, however, a functioning democratic system had been in place for better than two decades—ever since Washington granted its colony independence after World War II. Only the most compelling national security stakes could have justified U.S. leaders acting as—at the very least—passive accomplices in the destruction of that democratic system and the consolidation of a dictatorship. Extensive evidence that the Marcos dictatorship was not only brutal and repressive to political opponents, but was increasingly corrupt and dysfunctional as well, made U.S. policy indefensible. The assistance that Manila gave to Washington's ill-starred mission in Vietnam could not come even remotely close to providing an adequate justification. The same was true of Marcos's largely symbolic support for general U.S. efforts to thwart communist influence in the international arena.

The Military Bases: An Insufficient Justification for Supporting Marcos

The Philippines' strategic location along key sea lanes in the western Pacific may have provided a stronger argument for backing an odious regime, but even that rationale ultimately proved inadequate. Indeed, the mostly benign outcome that emerged once the post-Marcos democratic government asked the United States to leave Clark Air Base and Subic Bay Naval Base confirmed that U.S. warnings about the catastrophic consequences to American security interests if we ever lost those facilities were either overwrought or disingenuous. But the assumption throughout the Cold War that the bases were irreplaceable features of America's strategic posture in East Asia was pervasive. One of the few prominent foreign policy figures to dispute that view was George F. Kennan. When U.S. negotiators in the 1970s, starting with Secretary of State Henry Kissinger, offered to increase the U.S. lease fees to more than $1 billion to placate Marcos (who wanted even more money), Kennan suggested that Washington bluntly tell Marcos what he could do with his financial demands. "I see no reason at all to pay any tribute of this nature, whether it is a billion dollars or any other sum; nor can I see any reason why the bases should not be removed at once." Writing in 1977, Kennan asserted that a more realistic view of America's air and naval interests in East Asia meant that there was no longer a "serious need" for those bases.[58] That, however, was most decidedly not the majority view within officialdom in Washington.

Some of the assertions about the importance of the bases bordered on hysterical. The 1984 Heritage Foundation study, for example, concluded that an attempt by a post-Marcos government to end the U.S. presence would be "incalculably dangerous" to America's interests and the security of the region.[59] Such a comment was a rather substantial overstatement. But it was all too typical of the attitude in U.S. policy circles. Vice President Bush's fawning toast to Marcos drew a bitter, cynical rebuke from syndicated columnist Carl Rowan. "Bush is no dummy. He knows that Marcos snuffed out democracy in the Philippines years ago. But he made his vomit-inviting comments" for a very basic reason: "The U.S. wants to retain the air and naval bases in the Philippines."[60]

Comments from U.S. officials lent credence to Rowan's charges. Paul Wolfowitz, at the time assistant secretary of state for East Asia and the Pacific, stated that if the U.S. "lost access to the bases . . . it will be a communist victory."[61] Reagan himself stressed the importance of continued access. At a press conference in February 1986, he was asked: "Are the two U.S. bases in the Philippines of paramount importance when you consider U.S. policy for the Philippines? Or would you put the future of those bases at some risk if it meant standing up for democracy?" Reagan's reply certainly did not suggest that democracy in the Philippines was comparable in importance to Clark and Subic Bay. "One cannot minimize the importance of those bases, not only to us but to the Western World," he stressed. The president cited the basing of the blue-ocean navy that the Soviet Union had built, "which is bigger than ours, and how they have placed themselves to be able to intercept the 16 chokepoints in the world." The United States, he argued, had to be prepared to intercept a threat to those chokepoints and reopen those that a Soviet naval offensive may have closed. Reagan concluded that "we have to have bases [from which] we can send forces to reopen those channels. And I don't know of any that's [sic] more important than the bases in the Philippines."[62]

The tendency to exaggerate the importance of Clark Field and Subic Bay persisted into the administration of George H. W. Bush. As the "Soviet threat" became less and less credible at the beginning of the 1990s, the rationale for why the bases were important shifted. A few hawks still trotted out the alleged menace posed by the USSR and its supposed clients (apparently meaning Vietnam and North Korea), but the far more popular mantra was "regional stability" and the importance of the U.S. military presence in the Philippines to that goal.[63]

In an implicit dig at Japan, Assistant Secretary of State for East Asia and the Pacific Richard Solomon asserted in November 1990 that "no power other than the United States" was able "or welcome" to "play the role of regional balancer." Another high-ranking Bush administration official stated that the United States has become "everyone's Linus blanket."[64]

Some of the so-called threats to stability were exaggerated to the point of being ludicrous. Senator Richard Lugar, the senior Republican on the Senate Foreign Relations Committee, worried that without the U.S. military presence at Clark and Subic Bay, Japan would become the dominant military force in the region. That development, in his view, would be highly undesirable. And the revival of imperial Japanese regional hegemony would not be the only tragic result of U.S. withdrawal from the Philippines, Lugar warned. Members of the Association of Southeast Asian Nations (ASEAN) would also probably have to reconsider cooperation with the United States on security matters.[65]

Of course, neither of those specters became reality. ASEAN cooperation with the United States on security issues actually increased over the following two decades, as concerns in the region grew about China's rising power and influence. And Japan's preference to be a reticent regional power—as well as a security free rider on the United States—did not significantly abate. Yet, arguments like those

of Solomon and Lugar continued until the eruption of Mount Pina-
tubo in June 1991 buried Clark Field in volcanic ash, and the Philippine Senate refused to accept U.S. terms for renewal of the lease on
Subic Bay Naval Base.

Granted, when the United States finally lost its leases to the two
bases, the Cold War had already ended and the security environment
in East Asia was more quiescent than it had been when Marcos first
came to power or when he consolidated his dictatorship. Yet even during the early 1970s, shortly after he declared martial law, the strategic
importance of Subic and Clark was already fading. The Vietnam War
was coming to an end and the rapprochement between Washington
and Beijing was underway. By the late 1970s and early 1980s, a de facto
Sino-U.S. alliance existed against the USSR, and the notion of Chinese-
led communist expansionism in Southeast Asia—always an exaggerated fear in any case—was clearly not an issue. The Philippine bases
were then not even arguably imperative to sustain U.S. interests in the
region.[66] They were a convenience, but hardly a necessity—a point that
became apparent when the United States ultimately withdrew and
none of the parade of horrible consequences that military and civilian
hawks had long predicted for the U.S. strategic position in East Asia
came to pass. Even the much-feared communist insurgency in the Philippines itself turned out to be largely an illusion.

Yet even though Clark and Subic were fast becoming dispensable
military assets, Washington's commitment to Marcos remained undiminished and the financial aid to his regime continued to flow. At the
least, that suggested poor judgment on the part of U.S. policymakers.

Philippine Aftermath: America Was Very Lucky

Washington's support of the Marcos government was both morally offensive and strategically myopic. About the only positive thing
that can be said about America's conduct is that Reagan administration policymakers, largely because of the influence of Secretary of
State Shultz, at least had the good sense finally to abandon their corrupt, autocratic client—albeit at the eleventh hour.

U.S. leaders were also luckier than they deserved to be that Marcos's successor, Corazon Aquino, was not a demagogue who sought
to whip up anti-American sentiment.[67] Remarkably, she did not seem
to hold a grudge against the United States, either for what Wash-

ington had done to her country or for the personal heartache she had suffered when America's brutal client likely had her husband murdered. Relations between the United States and the Philippines have sometimes been strained during the post-Marcos era, and public resentment played a role in the decision by the Philippines Senate not to renew Washington's leases to the Clark Field and Subic Bay military bases. But the tensions and animosity have not been nearly as bad as they might have been—and perhaps deserved to be. The United States was very fortunate indeed with the relatively mild aftermath of its support for the Marcos dictatorship.

10. The "Good Communists": Tito and Ceauşescu

Throughout the Cold War, U.S. leaders viewed communism with a mixture of distaste, suspicion, and fear. Their hostility was partly because they regarded the ideology itself as dehumanizing and repulsive, but the primary reason was the belief that communist movements and governments were invariably under the thumb of the Soviet Union. American officials usually clung to the latter belief even when there was little evidence of Soviet control and in some cases (North Vietnam) where there was credible evidence to the contrary.

Yet there were two cases in which Washington adopted a more nuanced approach and established fairly close relationships with "independent" communist regimes. The first case was Yugoslavia under Marshal Josip Broz Tito from the late 1940s until Tito's death in 1980 (and under Tito's successors until the end of the Cold War). The second case was Romania—especially during the rule of Nicolae Ceauşescu, from the mid-1960s to his overthrow and execution on Christmas Day 1989. The U.S. approach regarding Yugoslavia and Romania epitomized what historian John Lewis Gaddis termed the "wedge strategy"—the attempt to promote and exploit fissures within the Soviet empire.[1]

Washington's flexibility regarding those two countries occurred even though both regimes were ruthlessly authoritarian—indeed, in Ceauşescu's case even more brutal than most of the other East European communist states that were indisputably in Moscow's satellite empire. The willingness of American policymakers to deviate from the norm of unrelenting hostility toward communist states with respect to Yugoslavia and Romania begs the question why U.S. administrations were unable or unwilling to try the same approach with respect to such countries as North Vietnam, Cuba, and Nicaragua.

The Rocky Road to Partnership with Yugoslavia

Washington did not start out with the intention of forging a de facto strategic partnership with either Yugoslavia or Romania. In fact, the relationship with Marshal Tito's government during the years immediately following World War II was downright frosty. Harry S. Truman administration officials were wary of Tito, even though he had been an extremely capable military leader against Nazi occupation forces. From Washington's standpoint, it seemed more important that he had also received political training in the USSR and made no secret that he was a committed communist. As early as April 1945, Richard Patterson, the U.S. ambassador to Belgrade, warned Secretary of State Edward Stettinius that Tito had established "almost complete control" over Yugoslavia's territory and was establishing a "complete dictatorship."[2] Tito's ruthless suppression of political competitors included the arrest—and later execution—of the chief noncommunist leader of the resistance to the Nazi occupation, General Draza Mihailovic. There were certainly no manifestations of press freedoms, multiple political parties, free elections, or other features of democracy in post–World War II Yugoslavia.

Even more worrisome to U.S. officials, Tito's regime began to pressure its neighbors, especially Greece, in a variety of ways. Washington soon concluded that these initiatives were not Tito's alone, but that he was doing the bidding of Soviet dictator Josef Stalin. At this point, there was no indication yet of the rivalry and hostility between Tito and Stalin that would emerge in a few years. Instead, the two communist rulers seemed to be on the best of terms.

Thus, when Yugoslavia began to send arms to communist guerrillas in Greece and engage in saber rattling toward Italy regarding Trieste, the disputed border region between the two countries, Truman administration officials viewed those matters as something more than bilateral spats. They interpreted those moves as probes by Stalin's obedient servant to advance Soviet power and influence. In other words, such maneuvers were seen in the same light as Moscow's more blatant actions to establish a satellite empire in Central and Eastern Europe. It was a misinterpretation of the actual situation (see below), but for a time, that jaundiced view heavily influenced U.S. policy.

Washington began to take a hard line toward the Yugoslav dictator almost immediately. In a White House meeting with Patterson on August 30, 1945, President Truman told the envoy that he could "use a two-fisted, tough policy with Tito."[3] Patterson subsequently informed Tito that the United States would provide no reconstruction aid whatsoever as long as he continued his repressive domestic policies and pursued mischief toward neighboring states.[4] That was not a trivial threat, since the United States was providing hundreds of millions of dollars in humanitarian assistance to Yugoslavia, primarily through the United Nations Relief and Rehabilitation Administration.

As the Cold War with the Soviet Union got underway in earnest in 1947, Washington's pressure on Tito also mounted. President Truman's speech to Congress in April of that year, promising U.S. aid to countries that were experiencing or threatened with aggression from outside sources or subversion by armed minorities (the Truman Doctrine speech), was implicitly directed against Tito as much as Stalin. After all, Yugoslavia was the principal source of—and channel for—the weapons flowing to communist forces in Greece. That country, along with Turkey, quickly became a major recipient of economic and military aid under the Truman Doctrine.

The administration also adopted a very confrontational line regarding the Trieste issue. When Belgrade steadfastly refused to withdraw its troops from occupied portions of the disputed region, tensions spiked. And when Tito's government threatened to have those military units advance further into Trieste, the United States warned that it would resist such a move "by force, if necessary."[5]

That episode brought U.S.-Yugoslav relations to their nadir. Tito was fast making an enemy of the United States. In addition to Belgrade's destabilizing conduct toward Italy and Greece, there were direct military tensions involving the United States. During the summer of 1946 there had been a series of incidents between U.S. and Yugoslav military aircraft, and, in one case, an American plane crashed, killing everyone on board. Belgrade contended that the plane had violated Yugoslavia's airspace and, given the growing practice of surveillance (spy plane) missions along the perimeter of the Soviet satellite empire, that allegation may well have been true.

Whatever the actual situation, the Truman administration reacted angrily to the growing number of attacks by Yugoslav fighter planes on U.S. aircraft. And the administration came under mounting pressure from Congress and the media to do something about Belgrade's aggressive behavior. Congress at one point even demanded that Washington sever diplomatic relations with Yugoslavia. Articles in such publications as *Newsweek* and the *New York Times* portrayed Tito as a malignant aggressor toward his neighbors and as an enemy of the United States.[6]

Yet even during this period of markedly deteriorating relations, there were hints of the rapprochement that would soon take place. Dissenters within American diplomatic ranks disagreed about the nature of U.S. policy toward Yugoslavia and advocated a more conciliatory approach. A State Department document in July 1946 expressed concern that, in all of the quarrels between Belgrade and Washington, "the U.S. had employed the most negative instruments of its containment policy; nothing had been done to entice Yugoslavia away from the Soviet orbit or drive a wedge between the two Communist states."[7] The same document urged the administration to avoid getting involved in Yugoslav domestic politics by trying to undermine Tito's rule and back noncommunist factions. Instead, it recommended that U.S. policymakers focus on implementing the wedge strategy.

As mavericks within the bowels of Washington's foreign policy bureaucracy made the case for shifting toward a more nuanced strategy for dealing with Yugoslavia, a distinct chill began to develop between Tito and Stalin. The Soviet dictator tended to view Yugoslavia in the same way that he did the other new communist regimes in Central and Eastern Europe—as a puppet that would do Moscow's bidding with few objections. But Tito always occupied a different status from the USSR's client states. Those governments had all been installed in power by virtue of the Red Army's presence at the end of World War II and the Soviet Union's overall clout. Their indigenous domestic support, even in the immediate postwar period when communist factions received credit for opposing the rule of Nazi Germany and its allies, ranged from modest to minimal. Several of them would never have come to power absent the USSR's imperial domination, and most of the others would probably not have retained power for very long.

The situation in Yugoslavia was dramatically different. Tito was a successful leader of a guerrilla army that had given Nazi occupation forces fits throughout the war and had ultimately ousted those forces with little help from the Soviet Union. Tito certainly had his share of domestic enemies, for both political and ethnic reasons. Noncommunists loathed him, as did ethnic nationalists and even relatively nonnationalistic Serbs, who felt that the ethnic Croat Tito discriminated against them. Nevertheless, he also had a sizable pool of domestic support, and he was never beholden to Moscow for his position of power.

Tito therefore rebuffed Stalin's efforts to bring him into line with the other communist clients in the Soviet empire. An early, and ultimately crucial, area of disagreement involved policy toward Greece. Stalin wanted to proceed cautiously, both because he didn't entirely trust the Greek Communist Party and because he was wary of provoking Great Britain and its now exceedingly powerful ally, the United States, by blatantly intruding into an important, traditional British sphere of influence in the southern Balkans and eastern Mediterranean.[8] But Tito had his own nationalistic reasons for favoring a more active policy of supporting the Greek communist insurgents and causing trouble for the government in Athens. Among other things, he hoped to gain some territorial concessions along Yugoslavia's border with Greece.

Ironically, Washington would end up courting the ruler who advocated the more activist, subversive policy. But the dispute between Stalin and Tito created an opportunity for the United States to use the wedge strategy to split the alleged communist monolith, and that seemed the more important consideration. By early 1948 relations between Belgrade and Moscow became so bad that Stalin directed the COMINFORM (the Communist Information Bureau, the chief organizational vehicle for fomenting communist revolutions) to expel Yugoslavia, a move that took place in June. The Kremlin followed that expulsion with the imposition of an economic blockade against Yugoslavia. There were even dark hints of a possible invasion, which Tito vowed to resist with all of his country's military power.[9]

Truman administration officials recognized in these developments an opportunity to implement the wedge strategy. Washington adopted a policy of "keeping Tito afloat" as a means to perpetuate the impairment that his defection had caused the Kremlin. The U.S. government made it clear to Moscow that any attempt to invade Yugoslavia would be regarded as a grave breach of the peace in Europe that the United States could not tolerate. However much Stalin might have wanted to oust Tito and bring Yugoslavia back into the Soviet-controlled camp, he was not willing to risk war with the United States.

In other respects, though, Washington proceeded cautiously regarding the embryonic rapprochement with Belgrade. Not until it became clear that the Tito-Stalin split was so severe that any reconciliation was improbable did the Truman administration begin to relax its economic restrictions on Yugoslavia. Military aid and active strategic cooperation would come even later.

But officials did sense that the new fissure in the communist bloc could prove beneficial to U.S. policy objectives in several ways. Yugoslavia's break with Moscow significantly changed the military equation. Instead of facing a solid phalanx of Soviet-led forces from the Baltic to the Adriatic, there was now a large gap of independent, neutral territory. That made Washington's task of forging a credible defense of Western Europe, which would be institutionalized in 1949 with the creation of the North Atlantic Treaty Organization (NATO), much easier.

There was also an important political and ideological dimension. Yugoslavia was not a small, East European state with minimal influence; it was a serious, midsize country, and its newly independent course might have a contagious effect on other Slavic populations. Administration policymakers hoped that other nations in the region, already restless about heavy-handed Soviet domination, would try to emulate Tito's break with Moscow. According to historian Robert Garson, administration officials wanted to hold up Yugoslavia as an example to other regimes in Eastern Europe that Washington was willing to tolerate communist states, as long as they were not under Moscow's control.[10] The CIA concluded that Tito's rebuff of the Kremlin would make it far more difficult for Stalin to "discipline other nationalist factions" within the communist bloc and keep satellite states under control.[11]

Although the expectation of "more Yugoslavias" proved overly optimistic in the short term, Poland's pressure to replace a subservient regime with a more acceptable, nationalistic one in 1956, and the violent Hungarian uprising in that same year for full independence, bore some resemblance to the events in Yugoslavia in the late 1940s.

The same was true of Alexander Dubcek's "Prague Spring" bid in 1968 for greater autonomy—and domestic political openness—for Czechoslovakia. And the increasingly independent stance of Romania's communist government during the late 1960s and the following two decades certainly emulated Tito's model. The principal difference between Belgrade's successful break with Moscow and the later unsuccessful bids of some of the other East European countries was that Tito had a strong domestic political base and did not have to deal with a large Soviet occupation force. The other would-be maverick communists (except for Romania) were not so fortunate, although Poland's effort to loosen the Kremlin's yoke was partially successful.

But the crucial differences were not so obvious to U.S. officials during the Truman years. Yugoslavia's defection from the Soviet bloc seemed to validate the patient containment policy that State Department official George F. Kennan had outlined. The developments in Yugoslavia confirmed to Truman administration leaders that the Soviet empire could be pushed back without resorting to force. That was relevant with respect to not just foreign policy but also domestic politics. Hard-liners, especially in the Republican Party, were making noises about using U.S. military power to liberate the East European satellites and "roll back" Soviet power. But the Truman administration regarded such a strategy as unacceptably dangerous—even before the USSR exploded its first atomic bomb in 1949. The emergence of even a small Soviet nuclear arsenal made the grave risks entailed in an aggressive U.S. policy to liberate the Soviet satellites obvious to all except the most obtuse hawks.

Administration officials pondered how best to exploit the Tito-Stalin split. One opportunity surfaced rather quickly. Economic suffering in Yugoslavia rose sharply after Moscow imposed stringent financial and trade sanctions in 1948. U.S. economic aid began to fill the gap left by the abrupt end to the subsidy that the Kremlin had provided. Within weeks of Tito's break with Moscow, the Truman administration dispatched $17 million in new funds to Belgrade.

Military assistance was a more contentious matter. Despite Tito's feud with Stalin, the GOP-controlled 80th Congress remained strongly opposed to providing weapons or other military aid to someone who was, after all, still a communist dictator. Matters changed only marginally once Democrats regained their congressional majority following the 1948 elections. Tito's refusal to formally align with NATO fueled congressional suspicions about his reliability as an adversary of the USSR. Ultimately, though, the executive branch was able to provide the initial contributions of military assistance to Belgrade despite the ongoing congressional opposition.

In return for Washington's economic and military aid, Tito soon made a variety of concessions. The most important was his willingness to abandon support for communist guerrillas in Greece—a move that sealed their fate and ended any credible threat they posed to the government in Athens. Belgrade's decision to close Yugoslavia's border with Greece was especially damaging, since it ended the flow of weaponry and the infiltration of fighters for the communist cause. In addition to such moves on security issues, the Yugoslav strongman also began to crack open his country's economy to U.S. trade and investment, although most American businesspeople remained wary of placing funds at risk in the communist-run state.

The shift in attitude among U.S. officials regarding Yugoslavia also progressed. As early as June 1948, the State Department Policy Planning Staff sent a telegram to all diplomatic posts arguing that, while the United States should not "fawn" on Tito, it was also important not to be "too cold," since the Kremlin would cite that reaction as "proof that foreign communists have no alternative but to stay with Moscow."[12]

The State Department's instructions to all of its diplomatic representatives were straightforward:

> This Government would welcome a genuine reemergence of Yugoslavia as a political personality in its own right. Its attitude toward a Yugoslav Government which had cut loose from Moscow would depend primarily on the behavior of that government with regard to this country, to the other European countries, and to the international community in general. We recognize that Yugoslavia's internal regime continues to be one that is deeply distasteful to our people, and that as long as such a regime exists, Yugoslav-American relations can never take on quite the cordiality and intimacy which we would wish. On the other hand, we also recognize that if Yugoslavia is

not to be subservient to an outside power, its internal
regime is basically its own business. The character of
that regime would not, in these circumstances, stand
in the way of a normal development of economic relations between Yugoslavia and this country.[13]

The cautious, balanced perspective grew stronger over time and
the path was now open for a productive relationship, on both security and economic issues, between Washington and Belgrade. That
milder, more pragmatic view of the breakaway communist state was
hardly universal, though, even within the ranks of the Truman administration, much less in other portions of the U.S. government or
the news media.

But policymakers in that administration and succeeding ones
came to the realization that the choice was between an independent,
nationalist communist regime run by Tito or a COMINFORM (Soviet puppet) regime in Belgrade. Although a third option—an anti-
communist government—would clearly have been Washington's
preference, there was no realistic possibility of that happening.
Given the available alternatives, U.S. leaders opted to back Tito.

And they buttressed their rhetorical and diplomatic support with
more substantive measures. In 1950, following a series of Soviet-
encouraged military probes from neighboring East European satellites, forces that included disgruntled pro-Kremlin Yugoslav defec-
tors, the Central Intelligence Agency (CIA) arranged for a covert shipment of arms to Belgrade to help counter Moscow's pressure. The
following year, President Truman approved $29 million in aid under
the Mutual Defense Assistance Program (MDAP). A little later, the
president provided an even larger aid package—some $75 million.[14]

There was at least a modest amount of irony in those actions. The
MDAP was originally intended to assist democratic Europe to build
up its military forces so that they could contribute more effectively to
NATO's capacity to resist communist aggression and subversion.[15]
In this case, though, the operating principle was to help a communist regime resist *Soviet* aggression. Unlike in other times and places,
when U.S. officials tended to regard communist and Soviet power
as synonymous, with regard to Yugoslavia, they made a distinction.

Economic and military aid to Yugoslavia remained controversial,
however, especially among conservatives in Congress and the me-

dia.[16] An exchange between President Dwight D. Eisenhower and influential GOP Senator Styles Bridges (R-NH) illustrated both the nature of conservative objections and the realpolitik that governed U.S. policy toward Tito under both Republican and Democratic administrations. Eisenhower biographer Stephen Ambrose relates the exchange:

> Bridges managed to put in a protest—he did not like giving money to Yugoslavia. Eisenhower snapped back, "Tito is the only man in Europe who succeeded in breaking away completely from the Soviets." Eisenhower said that he wanted more aid for Yugoslavia because "I do not by any manner or means want Tito to find that he has no place to go except back to the Soviets." Bridges asked about the danger of Tito using the military equipment against the United States. Eisenhower scoffed at the notion.[17]

But congressional pressure on the Eisenhower administration to reduce or terminate military aid to Yugoslavia was always a factor during the 1950s. And following the unpleasant surprise of a friendly visit by Soviet leaders to Belgrade in late May and early June 1955, that pressure compelled the administration to "suspend" further deliveries of aid. The suspension remained in effect until the spring of 1957, when Eisenhower finally lifted it unilaterally. After that episode, it was Tito who asked that the program be terminated because he viewed it as an increasing source of friction with Congress. It was typical of Tito's practical approach, though, that he did not request the end to the military aid program until Washington had sent him a large shipment of modern jet fighters and other sophisticated hardware. And a significant tie remained, because the United States still periodically supplied Belgrade with the spare parts that the Yugoslav military needed to keep those weapon systems in good operating condition.[18]

The desire to keep Yugoslavia out of the Soviet orbit affected U.S. policy beyond the issue of economic and military aid. It also had subtle diplomatic consequences. That point became very apparent regarding the issue of Trieste—the territorial dispute that had festered between Italy and Yugoslavia since the end of World War II. When the feud flared in 1948, Washington strongly backed Italy's claims to the whole territory, warning both Stalin and Tito that the United States was willing and able to defend its democratic ally by force, if necessary. But that policy was adopted before Belgrade's split with the Kremlin. Eisenhower, noting that "the quarrel was still raging" when he became president in January 1953, candidly admitted that the changed circumstances limited Washington's options. "Wanting to keep Tito split from the Soviet Union, the United States could no longer, as in 1948, back Italy to the hilt in its claim to everything."[19]

Writing in his diary on October 8, Eisenhower lamented that the Trieste issue had been a "source of irritation and mutual recrimination for years" between Italy and Yugoslavia. "We need both nations as friends," he wrote, and concluded that his administration had to press for a compromise solution.[20] The solution he pressured Rome and Belgrade to accept, despite considerable grumbling on Italy's part—along with unsubtle attempts at blackmail—was a partition of the territory. Although Tito did not get all that he desired, the U.S. move was a significant concession—and one taken at the expense of a major NATO ally. Eisenhower's willingness to take that step, even at the cost of incurring Rome's resentment, was testimony to how important Washington had come to regard the relationship with Belgrade.

That view continued during the John F. Kennedy and Lyndon B. Johnson administrations. Josip Močnik, a former scholar at the Woodrow Wilson Center, noted that, as a young congressman, Kennedy had visited Tito and that by the late 1950s Senator Kennedy "had become a notable supporter of strong U.S.-Yugoslav relations."[21] That point was underscored when Kennedy appointed George F. Kennan, the intellectual architect of Washington's containment policy toward the Soviet Union and perhaps America's most prominent diplomat, as ambassador to Belgrade. Močnik pointed out that *Time* featured Kennan's appointment in a cover story along with the appointments of Edwin O. Reischauer to Japan and John Kenneth Galbraith to India. "By implication," Močnik concluded, "this 'high profile' appointment and the placement of a small, socialist, nonaligned Balkan country on the same pedestal as Japan and India suggested that Yugoslavia mattered and that the Kennedy administration was committed to building strong relations with Yugoslavia."[22]

Despite those intentions, relations between Belgrade and Washington cooled somewhat during the Kennedy years—although Tito did come to the United States in a well-promoted state visit to meet with Kennedy in October 1963. Močnik correctly concludes that, despite Tito's posturing as a leader of the Non-Aligned Movement, the pragmatic relationship between the United States and his regime worked well during the Eisenhower administration because U.S. officials "showed no disposition to take Belgrade's anti-western ideological and political utterances seriously into account" when formulating Washington's policies.[23] But Ambassador Kennan was not satisfied with that arrangement. Washington's approach, he argued, allowed Belgrade to "eat its cake, in the form of American aid, and yet have it too, in the privilege of taking an anti-western and anti-American stance in regard to many world problems, thus defending its respectability as a 'socialist' and anti-imperialist power." Kennan pressed Kennedy and Secretary of State Dean Rusk to get tougher on Tito. Belgrade's behavior was unsatisfactory, he argued, because the Yugoslavs "were getting the bulk of their economic and financial aid from us, and yet seemed to be supporting the Soviet position on almost every important issue in world affairs ulterior to their own bilateral relations with the Soviet Union."[24]

Washington's efforts to show displeasure with Belgrade for its nonaligned posturing in the United Nations and other international arenas proved to be half-hearted and largely ineffective. The relationship, on both the security and economic fronts, settled into a pattern of a wary balance between cooperation and estrangement. Three historians summarized the nature of the bilateral economic relationship during the Kennedy and Johnson years, noting that, despite that overlay of tension, economic ties "broadened significantly" over that period. But it was not a smooth process, those analysts concluded. "Cooperation and useful relations" were "punctuated by periods of conflict and misunderstanding." The emerging balance in the relationship was increasingly evident, though, since the ebb and flow always stopped short "of either confrontation on the early postwar pattern or the sort of Yugoslav reliance on massive American aid that the emergency conditions of the early 1950s demanded."[25]

If Kennedy's successor, Lyndon Johnson, had been able to implement his preferences, Washington's relations with Belgrade might have become stronger than they did. Increased trade with Yugoslavia was the centerpiece of Johnson's initiative to "build bridges" to Eastern Europe by increasing economic links with those countries. But Congress again weighed in against more cooperative ties. Not only did the repressive nature of the East European governments strengthen congressional hostility to the president's goal, so did the aid that Belgrade and other regimes provided to North Vietnam. John Lewis Gaddis argues that, although Johnson's initiative had a great deal of merit, it ran aground on the shoals of domestic political realities. "The not-so-subtle attempt to weaken Moscow's control over its satellites foundered when Congress, angry over Soviet and East European assistance to North Vietnam, refused to relax discriminatory tariff barriers on trade with communist countries. In retrospect, it can be argued that all of those initiatives . . . [including] the improvement of ties with Eastern Europe reflected interests more vital than those at stake in Vietnam." Hard-liners in Congress, though, "did not see it that way at the time."[26]

Domestic politics and ideology intruded with respect to other issues. Both the Kennedy and Johnson administrations sought to maintain and strengthen cooperation between the U.S. and Yugoslav militaries to discourage any Soviet inclinations toward adventurism in Southeastern Europe. But sales of defense replacement parts to Belgrade had to be suspended in early 1964 because of a provision in the Foreign Assistance Act of 1961. The pertinent clause barred aid to any country that had failed to take "appropriate steps" to prevent ships under its registry from transporting goods of any sort to or from Cuba. Thus, Washington's ongoing feud with Fidel Castro impacted security policy halfway around the world with respect to (at that time) the only communist regime willing to defy Moscow's attempt at domination. It took two years before the White House was able to resume shipments of spare parts to Yugoslavia's military.

Despite the continuing congressional sniping at the notion of a friendly U.S. policy toward Yugoslavia, Johnson remained committed to that course throughout his presidency. In an October 1968 meeting with C. Burke Elbrick, who succeeded Kennan as ambassador to Belgrade in early 1964, "The President cited our long tradition of assistance to Yugoslavia and expressed his admiration for Yugoslavia's people and their dedication to freedom. The President made very clear his continuing interest in that country's independence, sovereignty and economic development." Elbrick, for his part, reported that especially in light of the Soviet-led invasion of Czechoslovakia, Tito "hopes we will give Yugoslavia some economic help and stand up with him against the Russian threat."[27]

Historian John Campbell argued in 1967 that U.S. policy toward Yugoslavia "was based on a cold-blooded calculation of self interest."[28] That was generally true. There was certainly less gushing, publicly or privately, from U.S. officials about Josip Broz Tito than there was about the Shah of Iran, Philippine dictator Ferdinand Marcos, South Vietnam's autocratic president Ngo Dinh Diem, or other right-wing authoritarian allies. Tito remained a staunch communist, albeit an independent one in terms of foreign policy, and a slightly more flexible one regarding nonpolitical domestic freedoms (especially after constitutional reforms in the 1960s and 1970s) to the end of his life.[29] That fact limited his appeal to anti-communist U.S. policymakers.

So, too, did his ostentatious promotion of the Non-Aligned Movement. To most Americans, especially conservatives, neutrality in the struggle between the United States and the Soviet Union was unacceptable, even odious. Tito's decision to join with India's Nehru, Indonesia's Sukarno, and Egypt's Nasser to establish the Non-Aligned Movement at the Bandung Conference in April 1955 did not help his reputation in the United States. Indeed, that move made it more difficult for the Eisenhower administration and its successors to continue providing economic and military aid to Belgrade.

The distinct anti-U.S. tilt (at least on the rhetorical level) flowing from Tito's role as a leader of the Non-Aligned Movement also irritated U.S. policymakers, especially Kennan and other officials in the Kennedy administration. Johnson and Richard Nixon administration officials were somewhat more tolerant of such posturing, since they concluded that it did not alter Belgrade's behavior on the central issue of European security, where U.S. and Yugoslav interests substantially overlapped. Yugoslavia's condemnation of U.S. policies on such issues as Vietnam, the U.S. invasion of the Dominican Republic, and Washington's support for the right-wing Greek junta in the late 1960s and early 1970s may have been annoying, but did not fatally undermine the basis for pragmatic cooperation.

Belgrade's position regarding the Vietnam War was a case in point. Moćnik highlights the gap between the Tito regime's diplomatic stance and its actual behavior. Throughout the Johnson administration, Yugoslavia persisted in expressing strong criticism of American action in Vietnam, reaching an officially orchestrated crescendo at a mass meeting in Belgrade on April 6, 1968. Tito's regime, however, did not carry on trade with North Vietnam, and Yugoslav shipments to that country were limited to gifts of medical supplies, plasma, school supplies, and clothing transmitted by the Yugoslav Red Cross."[30]

Ambassador W. Averell Harriman, a close adviser to Johnson, made that important distinction as well. In an oral history interview for the LBJ Presidential Library, Harriman recalled that he was convinced that Yugoslavia was not giving any substantial military assistance to Hanoi. Consequently, it was both "silly" and counterproductive for Congress to want to put Yugoslavia "on the same list as those who were helping the North Vietnamese." According to Harriman, Belgrade "only sent a few hundred thousand dollars worth of medical supplies."[31]

A March 1965 CIA analysis even concluded that "Yugoslavia does not wish the United States to withdraw from South Vietnam and Southeast Asia." According to a high-level source within the Yugoslav government, the analysis reported, a total North Vietnamese victory, backed by China and the USSR, would set a "dangerous precedent" for similar behavior "all over the world." It could even undermine "independent communist centers" in international affairs. Interestingly, according to the CIA document, Tito primarily wanted reassurance that the United States was not trying to provoke a broad military conflict that might escalate to a global conflagration or at least might force the Soviet Union to "adopt a more hostile, anti-American, anti-imperialist line." That was especially important to Belgrade because such a development would "make life more difficult in Eastern Europe, particularly for Yugoslavia and for 'liberal communist' elements in satellite countries."[32]

In marked contrast to his often most unrealist tendency to portray right-wing autocrats in glowing terms, Henry Kissinger adopted a calculated, sensible view of Tito:

> Tito had broken with Stalin over the issue of national autonomy, not over the validity of Communist theory. Through all the vicissitudes Tito remained a member of the Leninist faith. The requirements of survival forced him to reinsure himself against Soviet aggression; they did not significantly alter his convictions.[33]

Kissinger implicitly chastised U.S. and Western officials whom he believed adopted a less realistic view of the tyrant in Belgrade. "Yugoslavia was an asset to us in the Balkans and to a lesser extent in Eastern Europe," he conceded, since it symbolized the possibility of independence. It also to some extent relieved the military threat to NATO. But "outside of Europe, Tito pursued his convictions, which on the whole were not hospitable to Western interests or ideals." In particular: "His sympathy for revolution in developing countries did not differ significantly from Moscow's. Indeed, Tito was even more aggressive in catering to the radical developing nations."[34]

Kissinger was unsurprised by this posture. "I faced this with equanimity," he wrote, "Yugoslavia had not broke (*sic*) with Stalin to do us a favor." Nevertheless, "Yugoslavia's autonomy improved our global position. Stalin was quite right in worrying about the disruptive example it established for other countries of Eastern Europe. In addition, the security of Europe was enhanced by Tito's refusal to join the Warsaw Pact."[35]

Tito himself understood full well that the USSR, not the United States, was his principal adversary. In a February 7, 1961, report before leaving his post in Belgrade, Ambassador Karl L. Rankin related a conversation he had that day with the Yugoslav strongman. According to Rankin, Tito conceded "that Yugoslavia had been more critical of the US and [the] West in general than of the Soviet Bloc" in recent years, but he saw an opportunity for closer relations because Yugoslav differences with the West "were specific and practical," while those with Moscow were ideological and strategic.[36] In other words, Tito believed that he could take public stands against the United States and its allies to score political points at home and diplomatic points in the Third World, but he was confident that only the Soviet Union might take active steps to undermine his rule.

The Warsaw Pact's intervention against Czechoslovakia's reformist communist regime in 1968 deepened Belgrade's already strong, long-standing suspicions about Moscow's goals. Political scientist William Zimmerman observes: "The Soviet action in Czechoslovakia [further] convinced the Yugoslavs that the main danger to Yugoslav security stemmed from the Soviet Union and reconfirmed the wisdom of being part of the international system rather than a part of Eastern Europe—where the norms of socialist international relations (to wit, proletarian internationalism with its doctrinally legitimated justification for Soviet intervention) obtained."[37]

Kissinger grasped the reality that the United States was in a strong bargaining position toward Belgrade. Although Tito might tweak the United States in international forums and cause problems for U.S. policy in the Third World, "there was a limit beyond which he would not go: He could not afford to antagonize us to a point that made his security depend on the goodwill of the Soviet Union." Therefore, U.S. officials "were under no pressure to curry his favor. We had no reason to be obsequious or reluctant to stand up for our own interests with the same intensity as he pursued his own."[38]

That perspective should have been a template for Washington's relations with friendly autocrats around the world. Unfortunately, the policy toward Yugoslavia was an all-too-rare example of such a detached, sober approach.

The American news media likewise adopted a relatively restrained and balanced view of the Yugoslav tyrant. Upon Tito's death in 1980, *Time*'s cover story was generally favorable, describing him in the title as "The Maverick Who Defied Moscow," but there was little attempt to whitewash his record of repression.[39] That record included the imprisonment (and sometimes torture) of people who were merely suspected of being political opponents, the execution of hundreds who were confirmed to practice such political heresy, and the pervasive censorship of media outlets. The aloof restraint of journalists and other U.S. opinion leaders stood in contrast to much of the media's gushing treatment of other dictators who were friendly to the United States.

A Working Partnership While Holding One's Nose: Washington's Policy toward Nicolae Ceauşescu

Washington's relationship with Romania's Nicolae Ceauşescu was more limited in scope than the connection with Tito. Some aspects of the rapprochement with Bucharest began even before Ceauşescu rose to power in 1965. His predecessor, Gheorghe Gheorghiu-Dej, had gone from being a loyal servant of Stalin in the 1940s to being a political figure who sought greater independence from Moscow. Already in the mid 1950s there were signs of a campaign to distance Romania from the post-Stalin leadership in the Kremlin. A *New York*

Times article in 1956, "Peaceful Shifts in Rumania Seen," analyzed those embryonic changes in Bucharest's policies. The article noted that Gheorghiu-Dej was in contact with Tito and appeared interested in adopting a similar, more nationalistic brand of communism.[40]

That expectation proved too optimistic in the short term, but by the mid-1960s the country was showing increasing maverick tendencies. Among other developments, Gheorghiu-Dej actively cultivated trade ties with the United States and West European countries, even when Moscow was uneasy about the extent of those economic openings.

Both the maverick tendencies and warming relations with the West would intensify under Ceauşescu. A *New York Times* article in 1966 contended that "it may now be appropriate to say that Nicolae Ceausescu is the man who has taken charge of breaking up the Soviet Empire."[41] That was a bit of an overstatement, but a *Times* article two years later more accurately described a concerted campaign aimed at "loosening ties with the Soviet Union" and "protecting Romanian independence."[42] So, too, did a 1967 article in *Time*, noting that Ceauşescu "had gradually moved Rumania away from Moscow's orbit and toward closer ties with the West."[43]

Johnson's administration put out feelers to see how independent Romania was willing to be. In late 1967 Johnson sent special envoy W. Averell Harriman to visit officials in Bucharest and gauge their willingness to act as informal intermediaries between the United States and North Vietnam. Harriman discovered that the willingness, while cautious, was very real. A high-level Romanian official visited Hanoi and talked to leaders there shortly after Harriman's lobbying effort, conveying the U.S. position regarding peace talks and other measures that might dampen the war. Although that diplomatic mission—and a subsequent one seeking "further clarification"—did not produce tangible beneficial results, it was telling that the Ceauşescu government was willing to play that role rather than emulate Moscow's unquestioned support for Hanoi.[44]

President Richard Nixon's high-profile state visit to Romania in 1969—a visit that generated diplomatic shock waves on both sides of the East-West divide—increased the scope of diplomatic cooperation between Washington and Bucharest. Nixon personally asked Ceauşescu to use his ties with North Vietnam to convey a warning to Hanoi to back away from its uncompromising stance or the United

States would be compelled to "re-evaluate" its policy—with the clear implication that the administration was prepared to escalate its military pressure. The Romanian leader readily promised to convey that message and to be as helpful as possible.[45]

Various policies that Bucharest adopted throughout the late 1960s and early 1970s demonstrated the goal of a more independent posture, despite Moscow's wishes. Romania became the first communist country to join the General Agreement on Tariffs and Trade (GATT), the Western-dominated international trading system. And in 1967, the Ceaușescu government established diplomatic relations with West Germany—years before the USSR or other communist countries would do so.

U.S. officials were certainly encouraged by those decisions, and they believed that another major nationalistic communist fissure had opened up in the Soviet empire. Moscow finally seemed to be encountering "another Yugoslavia" led by another Tito.

Washington rewarded that independence both symbolically and substantively. Early in his administration, President Nixon visited two, and only two, East European capitals—Belgrade and Bucharest. Kissinger noted: "The symbolism was inescapable. The United States would pay special attention to those Eastern European countries pursuing an autonomous foreign policy." That aspect irritated Moscow, but it also had implications far beyond Europe. "The Chinese were to notice this," Kissinger observed with satisfaction, and that development helped pave the way for the rapprochement between Washington and Beijing.[46]

The Ceaușescu government did not underestimate for a moment the symbolic importance of a state visit by the U.S. president. Kissinger relates that in 1969 Ceaușescu "had postponed a scheduled visit by [Soviet leader Leonid] Brezhnev on one week's notice to enable Nixon to come instead and had even had the welcoming posters for Brezhnev, already hanging in the airport, painted over."[47] One can only imagine how the Kremlin felt about that snub!

Adding substance to symbolism, the Nixon administration and Congress granted Romania most-favored-nation trade status in 1972. And although conducted quietly, discussions between NATO and Romanian military leaders became a routine aspect of the relationship with Bucharest, just as they had been with Yugoslavia over the previous two decades. Romania might have been only an informal military ally of the West, but that association was nevertheless quite real.

Indeed, Washington carefully kept both Belgrade and Bucharest in the loop on major security matters outside of Europe. In his memoirs, President Jimmy Carter notes that, during the Soviet invasion of Afghanistan in late 1979, he "consulted closely with our European allies, President Tito of Yugoslavia, [and] President Ceauscescu (*sic*) of Romania," as well as "the leaders among the Moslem countries, and particularly President Mohammad Zia of Pakistan, to plan our most effective response to this aggression."[48] Consulting with the NATO allies and with Pakistan and other key Islamic states was certainly expected. But putting Romania and Yugoslavia in that same category indicated just how important Washington regarded the strategic ties with those two countries.

A similar desire for closer security links with the West was also occurring on Romania's side from the late 1960s to the early 1980s. Bucharest's wariness about Moscow deepened in August 1968 when the Kremlin led the rest of its Warsaw Pact allies in launching a military intervention against Alexander Dubcek's unorthodox communist government in Czechoslovakia. Ceaușescu flatly refused to join that invasion, and he promptly put out feelers to see if the United States and the other NATO powers would assist Romania if Moscow tried to use military force to bring that country to heel. Nixon's visit the following year was designed not only to show appreciation for Bucharest's diplomatic assistance with respect to the Vietnam War but also to provide visual support for Romania's defiance of Moscow in Europe.

If the Kremlin's crackdown on Dubcek was designed in part to intimidate Tito and, especially, Ceaușescu, the effort backfired. After the crushing of the Prague Spring, Bucharest seemed even more determined to flaunt its independence on a variety of issues. At the same time, though, it projected an image of confidence and aloofness so that the United States would feel the need to offer generous benefits to keep Romania from drifting back into the Soviet camp.

Ceaușescu repeated that strategy of playing hard to get following the Kremlin-inspired crushing of the Solidarity labor movement in Poland in the early 1980s. But U.S. officials had a fairly good understanding of the facts on the ground. During a visit to Bucharest in early 1982, Secretary of State Alexander Haig noticed large numbers of troops and tanks patrolling the mostly darkened streets of the city. Nervousness about Soviet intentions was palpable. How concerned Ceauşescu was about the potential danger to his regime became apparent when he replaced his foreign minister as the host of meetings with Haig.

But the Romanian president was also determined not to convey an impression of weakness in those sessions. Haig recalled that Ceauşescu did not mention the looming Soviet menace by name, and "in his tone and opinions, he sounded remarkably like the leader of a nonaligned Third World country." He also spoke of the need for $1 billion in U.S. aid, presenting it as a thinly veiled demand. When Haig demurred, reminding his host of the role that Congress had to play in approving foreign-aid measures and hinting that congressional sentiment about providing that sum to Romania was uncertain at best, Ceauşescu responded "in a gruff tone, wagging a finger, 'We have other alternatives.'"[49]

In a refreshing, all-too-rare, example of U.S. realism, the secretary of state would not be stampeded into capitulating to Ceauşescu's attempt to extort foreign aid. "Be realistic, Mr. President," he replied. "Look out that window and you will see the alternative."[50] Haig understood that Romania needed the United States far more than the United States needed Romania. The Reagan administration, therefore, had no inclination to act as a supplicant toward its sometime diplomatic and security partner.

And to their credit, U.S. policymakers from the late 1960s to the end of the 1980s harbored few illusions about the fundamental nature of the Romanian regime with which they were dealing. Kissinger, reflecting on President Gerald Ford's visit to Bucharest, contended that "nowhere else in Eastern Europe was the gap between the professed egalitarianism of Communist ideology and the imperial style of the rulers so pronounced." Nor did Kissinger try to obscure the extent of Ceauşescu's brutal, stifling rule. The Romanian leader, he admitted, "ran the closest approximation to a Stalinist dictatorship in the entire Soviet orbit."[51] Indeed, there were probably more secret police on the streets and more political prisoners in custody per capita in Romania as a percentage of the population than anywhere else in the communist states of Eastern Europe. Moreover, human rights organizations documented the extent of arbitrary imprisonment and torture in Romania. U.S. officials fully understood that reality. The

U.S.-Romanian relationship was based on cold-eyed calculations of mutual security interests, nothing more.

And when the wave of anti-communist, pro-democracy sentiment swept through Eastern Europe in 1989 and 1990, the administration of George H. W. Bush had little problem jettisoning America's association with Nicolae Ceaușescu. The Romanian tyrant's use of nationalist communism, based on a willingness to defy Moscow, did not help him in the end. His regime was swept from power just as were the governments elsewhere in Eastern Europe that were reliably subservient to the Kremlin. Portions of his security forces remained loyal for a time, making the transition to a noncommunist regime the bloodiest in the region, but ultimately that bastion failed and Ceaușescu and his wife were captured and executed. As he fell from power, Washington did little to save him, correctly concluding that his usefulness to America's foreign policy was over.

U.S. Policy toward the Independent Communists: Textbook Realism

U.S. policy toward the independent communist regimes in Yugoslavia and Romania was, on the whole, balanced and realistic. It shrewdly exploited fissures in the Soviet camp to cause further discontent in Moscow's satellite empire, causing Kremlin leaders to have to worry about matters close to home. That was beneficial from a diplomatic and political standpoint, forcing the USSR to make concessions that it might otherwise have been able to avoid. It was no coincidence that Belgrade and Bucharest were among the most enthusiastic proponents of the 1975 Helsinki Accords, which established human rights standards throughout Europe and, even more important, put the Kremlin on record as renouncing the right to intervene in the internal affairs of other countries. Both President Gerald Ford and Secretary Kissinger understood the role that Washington's support for Yugoslavia and Romania played in getting those countries to lobby so intently and effectively for the Helsinki Accords.[52]

Nine years later, the United States achieved a more limited and focused diplomatic victory, but one that had significant symbolic value at the time, when Romania and Yugoslavia both sent teams to the 1984 Olympics in Los Angeles despite a Soviet-led boycott of those games. Romania was the only Warsaw Pact country to defy Moscow on that issue.

But exploiting the ruptures in the Soviet sphere of domination, epitomized by Yugoslavia and Romania, also had important strategic implications. If the Kremlin ever had ambitions to militarily threaten or assault democratic Western Europe, the defection of two key countries in Southeastern Europe made such a venture even riskier than before. Indeed, Soviet leaders had to worry that one or both of the maverick communist states might even go beyond remaining neutral in such a fight and actively collaborate with NATO forces.

Tito and Ceauşescu were prone to making ostentatious proclamations of neutrality and nonalignment regarding the Cold War struggle. But the two governments tilted toward the United States and NATO in their actual conduct. Both Tito and Ceauşescu understood that their survival, both politically and physically, depended on the continuing U.S.-led containment of Soviet power. Whether they relished the idea or not, they were de facto security partners of the United States.

Washington's limited courtship of Yugoslavia and Romania came at relatively little cost, either financially to U.S. taxpayers or in terms of American values. The United States was not an important prop keeping Tito and Ceauşescu in office. Both leaders had their own substantial, indigenous bases of power—although they found those bases weakening as time went on—and in Ceauşescu's case—fatally so. U.S. military and financial aid made little difference on the domestic front in either country; it merely helped them resist Soviet pressure. And U.S. leaders did not make the mistake of gushing about their allies of convenience, as they sometimes did with right-wing allies and clients. The association was never that intimate, and so the populations in Yugoslavia and Romania had little reason to resent the United States in the post-Tito and post-Ceauşescu period.

Kissinger's assessment of the benefits and limits of the relationship with Tito was a model of how U.S. policymakers should view ties to useful, friendly, but nonetheless repressive rulers. It was a policy based on sober calculations of the national interest. American officials, for the most part, understood that Tito and Ceauşescu established ties to the United States solely to balance against Soviet power and to secure their country's independence and their own ability to stay in power despite the Kremlin's hostility. There was no naïve sentimentality involved on their side of the relationship with the United States.

And Washington generally viewed its side of the relationship in much the same way—as a national security "business arrangement" for mutual benefit, nothing more. The United States did not overinvest in that relationship. U.S. leaders understood that they were dealing with brutal, hard-nosed communist tyrants, albeit tyrants decidedly independent of the Soviet Union. Neither Tito nor Ceaușescu hesitated to imprison or kill political opponents, including opponents that may have been significantly closer to American ideals. U.S. policymakers usually refrained from trying to hide or rationalize that unpleasant reality, either to the world or themselves. They portrayed Washington's strategic partners in Eastern Europe as merely allies of convenience.

That pragmatic attitude took root early on. The same State Department policy planning document in 1948 that asserted that Yugoslavia's split with the Kremlin offered an opportunity for a productive bilateral relationship also noted:

> Yugoslavia remains a communist state, dedicated to an ideology of hostility and contempt toward the "bourgeois capitalist world," and committed at home to government by the methods of communist totalitarian dictatorship . . . . It would therefore be a frivolous and undignified error on our part to assume that because Tito had fallen out with Stalin he could now be considered our "friend."[53]

That type of realism was sensible and appropriate. Unfortunately, it was all too infrequent in Washington's dealings with useful, but repressive, security partners during the Cold War, and it is frequently absent as well in the current struggle against radical Islamic terrorism.

CHIANG KAI-SHEK, leader of China's nationalist government and, after the 1949 Communist revolution, leader of the remnant based in Taiwan that Washington continued to recognize as the legitimate government of China until 1979.

ABDUL AZIZ (bottom left), King of Saudi Arabia, with other members of the Saudi royal family.

SYNGMAN RHEE (left), first President of South Korea, meeting with U.S. and South Korean military leaders.

JOSIP TITO (center), dictator of Yugoslavia, at a White House ceremony with President JIMMY CARTER and First Lady ROSALYNN CARTER.

MOHAMMAD REZA PAHLAVI, the Shah of Iran, Washington's major ally in the Persian Gulf region after the U.S. helped overthrow Iran's elected government and restore him to power in 1953. He was overthrown in Iran's 1979 Islamic revolution.

ANASTASIO SOMOZA DEBAYLE (center), dictator of Nicaragua, meeting with President RICHARD NIXON and White House Chief of Staff ALEXANDER M. HAIG.

AYUB KHAN (right), Pakistan's first military ruler, who came to power after leading a coup against the civilian government in 1958.

NGO DINH DIEM (front right), first president of South Vietnam until his assassination in November 1963, at an airport greeting with President DWIGHT D. EISENHOWER and Secretary of State JOHN FOSTER DULLES.

JOSEPH MOBUTU (MOBUTU SESE SEKO), the longtime dictator of Zaire (now Democratic Republic of the Congo). MOBUTU came to power following a military coup in 1965.

FERDINAND MARCOS and IMELDA MARCOS, of the Philippines, at a White House ceremony with President LYNDON B. JOHNSON and First Lady CLAUDIA "LADY BIRD" JOHNSON. At this point, MARCOS was seen as a dynamic, democratic Asian leader.

MAO ZEDONG (right), China's communist ruler, meeting with Secretary of State HENRY KISSINGER.

NICOLAE CEAUŞESCU, dictator of Romania from 1965 until his overthrow and execution in December 1989. He was one of the few communist rulers that had a cooperative relationship with Washington.

PRESIDENT RONALD REAGAN (third from left) meeting with leaders of the Afghan mujahideen, the factions resisting the Soviet occupation army. Many mujahideen turned out to be Islamic radicals and enemies of the United States.

Bob Sullivan/AFP/Getty Images

MANUEL NORIEGA, Panamanian dictator and a U.S. client until ousted in a 1989 U.S. invasion.

SADDAM HUSSEIN, longtime dictator of Iraq and a de facto U.S. ally during Iraq's war with Iran in the 1980s. He was ousted from power following the U.S.-led invasion in 2003.

HOSNI MUBARAK (left), Egypt's strongman and a close U.S. ally for more than three decades, until his ouster in the 2011 Arab Spring uprising, at a White House meeting with Israeli Prime Minister BENJAMIN NETANYAHU and President BARACK OBAMA.

ISLAM KARIMOV (right), longtime dictator of Uzbekistan, with U.S. Secretary of Defense DONALD RUMSFELD.

NURSULTAN NAZARBAYEV (left center), leader of Kazakhstan since the breakup of the Soviet Union in December 1991, at a summit meeting with President BARACK OBAMA.

PERVEZ MUSHARRAF, President-General of Pakistan, who came to power after leading a 1999 military coup against a civilian government.

11. Playing the China Card: Strategic Rapprochement with Beijing[*]

Perhaps the most surprising U.S. strategic partnership with an authoritarian regime during the Cold War was the rapprochement with Communist China. The preparatory trip by National Security Advisor Henry Kissinger to Beijing in 1971 and the subsequent state visit by President Richard Nixon early the following year led to a dramatic reversal of Washington's policy toward that country. Since the communist revolution in 1949, the United States had sought to isolate China, and relations between the two governments were exceptionally hostile. U.S. and Chinese forces waged a bloody armed conflict in Korea during the early 1950s, and hostilities nearly erupted twice more later that decade over Beijing's skirmishes with Taiwan, the last remaining province under the control of the Nationalist Chinese government, which Washington still recognized as the legitimate government of China.

It would be difficult to overstate the degree of American animosity toward China's communist regime throughout the 1950s and 1960s. As noted in chapter 2, the communist revolution in that country came as a bitter development to both U.S. officials and the general public. The American reaction to Chiang Kai-shek's defeat and his retreat to the island of Taiwan led to an immediate search for scapegoats. The hostile question "Who lost China?" became a major refrain in U.S. politics for more than a decade.

Hatred of "Red China" Dominates U.S. Policy during the 1950s and 1960s

Any lingering possibility that Washington would accept reality and recognize that the Beijing government controlled the Chinese mainland and that the establishment of diplomatic relations was prudent disappeared when Chinese forces intervened in the Korean War, attacking U.S. and allied forces that had advanced deep into

North Korea and approached North Korea's border with China. The reaction of Dean Rusk, who served as deputy undersecretary of state for Far Eastern affairs, epitomized the response of his administration colleagues and the vast majority of influential people throughout the political and foreign policy communities. "Many people, myself included," Rusk recalled in his memoirs, "toyed with the idea of recognizing the People's Republic of China in the late 1940s, but that idea died on November 26, 1950, when tens of thousands of Chinese 'volunteers' poured across the Yalu River." He added: "At the end of the Korean War, with the anti-Communist Chinese sentiment the war had built up, the China Lobby backing Taiwan, and congressional opposition, no president could have narrowed the gap with Peking even if he had wanted to. The Korean War hardened American attitudes toward Peking; it certainly hardened mine."[1]

In addition to dealing with GOP hard-liners who delighted in using the China issue to bash the administration, Harry S. Truman even had to contend with the uncompromising views of his own secretary of state, Dean Acheson.[2] The British government argued that the allies should concede a key point and allow Communist China to be seated at the United Nations (UN). Even though Acheson was no fan of Chiang Kai-shek and his Kuomintang government, he "took the position that we should not even consider" giving the UN seat to Mao Zedong's regime, Truman wrote. "If we did, we would in effect be saying to the Communists that they had won the game and could now collect the stakes; it would be like offering a reward for aggression."[3]

That attitude would prevail, not only during the remainder of the Truman years, but through the next three administrations. Dwight Eisenhower openly disagreed with Britain and other close allies on the issue, and his standard for endorsing China's UN membership was so stringent as to make the point moot:

> Though the British had recognized Communist China in early 1950, I explained that I would ignore the claim of Communist China that it should be received into the United Nations or at a conference table, until it had established its right to be treated as a respectable member of the family of nations. Among the requirements were withdrawal from Korea, cessation of sup-

port for the Communist faction in Indochina, adoption of a decent deportment in its contacts with the Western world and a commitment to abandon its military threat against Formosa.[4]

In other words, Communist China would have to capitulate to virtually every one of Washington's foreign policy goals in East Asia before it could be a member of the United Nations.

The anger of U.S. political leaders and the American people toward Communist China went far beyond the issue of UN membership, though. They saw Red China as the reservoir of ugly, anti-American, anti-Western totalitarianism. Mao Zedong vied with Joseph Stalin and, later, Nikita Khrushchev, as the face of the great global communist threat. Communist China was the symbol of ruthless tyranny and godlessness, a menace not only to the security of the United States, but also to the values this country embraced.

That attitude would not begin to wane until the 1970s. Meanwhile, Washington's policy toward Beijing was essentially on autopilot, governed by unrelenting and undifferentiated hostility. The discrediting of China experts who had urged a softer policy toward Mao's government in the late 1940s and early 1950s had sent a chill through the Foreign Service that led to rote conformity on China policy—and East Asia policy in general. The conservative wing of the Republican Party led the charge against anything other than uncompromising hostility toward the communist regime in Beijing, but a considerable faction of conservative Democrats joined in.

The two crises in the Taiwan Strait during the Eisenhower years illustrated how Washington's policy toward China was devoid of flexibility.

How much Eisenhower loathed the Chinese regime and how uncompromising he was on the issue of dealing with it comes through clearly in his comments to British Prime Minister Winston Churchill in connection with the first Taiwan Strait crisis in 1954:

> There comes a point where constantly giving in only encourages further belligerency. I think we must be careful not to pass that point in our dealings with Communist China. In such a case, further retreat becomes worse than Munich because at Munich there

> were at least promises on the part of the aggressor to
> cease expansion and to keep the peace. In this case
> the Chinese Communists have promised nothing and
> have not contributed one iota toward peace in the For-
> mosa area. Indeed, they treat the suggestion of peace
> there as an insult.[5]

U.S.-China relations reached their nadir during the Eisenhower years. So entrenched were the twin views of China as an odious to-talitarian country and a Soviet foreign policy tool that even when the split between Moscow and Beijing began in the late 1950s, U.S. poli-cymakers were agonizingly slow to comprehend that development.[6] Indeed, well into the 1960s some officials and a considerable portion of the media and policy communities remained in denial that the split had taken place. Conspiracy theories abounded that the appar-ent hostility between the two communist powers was nothing more than an elaborate ruse to lure the United States and its East Asian allies into a dangerous sense of complacency.

Even when evidence that the Sino-Soviet split was genuine reached the point that rational people could no longer deny it, there was little change in American attitudes or policy. To the limited ex-tent that a shift in attitude did occur, it typically took the form of regarding China as the more dangerous of the two U.S. adversaries. That view even penetrated popular culture. A best-selling novel and subsequent major movie, *The Manchurian Candidate*, was based on a paranoid premise that Communist China was able to infiltrate and manipulate America's political system by utilizing a brainwashed prisoner of war. In Ian Fleming's book *Goldfinger*, the conspirators behind that arch-nemesis of hero James Bond were Russians. But in the 1964 movie based on the book, the villains were changed to Chi-nese. A similar escalation of using Communist Chinese as the epit-ome of evil occurred in other books, movies, and television episodes.

Even members of the policy community came to regard China as a more dangerous enemy than the Soviet Union. During Lyndon John-son's administration the Kremlin sent out feelers about whether the United States would consider a joint operation to eliminate Beijing's embryonic nuclear weapons program.[7] And the administration gave that option some consideration. Conservative opinion leaders, including *National Review* founder and editor William F. Buckley Jr., openly advocated preemptive strikes on Chinese nuclear facilities.

The State Department, under Dean Rusk's leadership, considered China, even more than Moscow, to be the principal instigator of North Vietnam's war of conquest against South Vietnam. For Rusk and his policy team, the number-one reason for having U.S. troops in Vietnam was to stymie China's alleged broader regional geostrategic ambitions.

Nixon, Kissinger, and Hints of Change

Henry Kissinger, who would become Richard Nixon's national security adviser, noted the Johnson administration's pervasive anti-China obsession and was determined that the incoming administration would be quite different. From the beginning, Kissinger stressed, the Nixon administration "never cited, or even hinted at, an anti-Chinese motive for our Vietnam involvement." We "needed no additional enemies."[8]

During the initial months of the Nixon administration, Moscow again floated a trial balloon about taking joint action to curb "Chinese aggression."[9] There had already been clashes between Soviet and Chinese military forces along their lengthy border. Kissinger was appalled that the State Department seemed receptive to that suggestion, or at least to a more modest policy tilt toward Moscow. In his view, China was clearly the weaker of the two communist powers, and for the United States to ally with a much stronger adversary against a weaker one made no strategic sense. "History suggested that it was usually more advantageous to align oneself with the weaker of two antagonistic partners," Kissinger wrote in his memoirs, "because this acted as a restraint on the stronger."[10] But so potent was the fear of, and hostility toward, China that some U.S. officials—not only in the Johnson administration but even in the Nixon State Department—were pushing the myopic strategy of aligning with the USSR against China.[11]

The lengthy record of animosity toward China (which was fully reciprocated) made the Nixon administration's policy shift all the more unexpected and dramatic. In a brief television message on July 15, 1971, President Nixon announced to the nation and the world that National Security Advisor Henry Kissinger and Chinese premier Chou En-lai had held a series of meetings in Beijing, that Chou had extended an invitation to Nixon to visit China in early 1972, and that the invitation had been accepted "with pleasure." The goal of the president's trip was clear and dramatic. "The meeting between the leaders of China and the United States is to seek the normalization of relations between the two countries and also to exchange views on questions of concern to the two sides."[12] That statement underscored that the presidential visit would be substantive, not cosmetic. And if the Soviets were reading between the lines, they likely understood that one of the chief "questions of concern" to the two sides was the USSR's behavior.

Although the July 1971 announcement stunned observers at home and around the world, there had been signs for several years that the new president was interested in adopting a different course from his predecessors.[13] His article in the fall 1967 issue of *Foreign Affairs* offered intriguing hints of a more flexible and realistic approach to dealing with Communist China. Although Nixon spurned suggestions of conceding a "sphere of influence" in Asia to Beijing, he also rebuffed those who favored continuing the policy of unrelenting hostility, or even worse, adopting a U.S.-led crusade against China. "Others argue that we should seek an anti-Chinese alliance with European powers, even including the Soviet Union. Quite apart from the obvious problems involved in Soviet participation," Nixon stated, "such a course would inevitably carry connotations of Europe vs. Asia, white vs. non-white, which would have catastrophic repercussions throughout the rest of the non-white world in general and Asia in particular."[14]

His policy prescription for the short run was one of "firm restraint" augmented by efforts to build up the power of China's noncommunist Asian neighbors (especially the offshore powers) so that they "no longer furnish tempting targets for Chinese aggression." In the long run, though, a wise strategy meant "pulling China back into the world community—but as a great and progressing nation, not as the epicenter of world revolution."[15]

A further signal of greater U.S. flexibility occurred during Nixon's presidential visit to Romania in 1969, when the president referred to the "People's Republic of China," the first time ever that an American chief executive had used that country's official name. Nixon and his advisers then waited to see what moves Mao's government would make and whether such moves would indicate a willingness to end the deep freeze of relations that had been in place for more than a generation. At first, there seemed to be little encouraging reaction in Beijing, but gradually the Chinese government responded with equally subtle measures that indicated at least a cautious receptivity.

Most of the substantive signs of a desire for a rapprochement, however, came from Washington. The section on China in the president's February 1970 Foreign Policy Report to Congress clearly signaled that goal, contending that "it is certainly in our interest and in the interest of peace and stability in Asia and the world, that we take what steps we can toward improved practical relations with Peking." One month later, the State Department announced the lifting of most official restrictions on travel to China, and in April the administration substantially eased restrictions on trade with that country.[16]

Converging Sino-U.S. Interests

Given the personalities of Richard Nixon and Henry Kissinger, it is not surprising that they approached the task of changing U.S. policy toward China with calculating realpolitik and little sentimentality. Indeed, in his memoirs, Kissinger proudly states that their goal was "to purge our foreign policy of all sentimentality" regarding relations with the two communist powers.[17] In a November 1970 memorandum to Kissinger, the president instructed him to have his staff prepare a study of "where we are to go with regard to the admission of Red China to the UN." Nixon's motive for wanting that study was most revealing. "It seems to me that the time is approaching sooner than we might think when we will not have the votes to block admission."[18] In other words, the president sought to make the best out of a deteriorating diplomatic situation. The administration opted to try for a "two China" solution—having seats in the General Assembly for both the People's Republic of China (PRC) and the Nationalist Government on Taiwan.

Nixon's recollection of that shift in Washington's position illustrated the president's realistic sense of changing global dynamics and the need for a cooperative relationship with mainland China. Although he would have preferred a slower process regarding Beijing's membership in the UN, the president understood that the diplomatic tide was not favorable to that strategy:

> I had learned as early as the spring, however, that the traditional vote bloc opposed to Peking's admission had irreparably broken up, and several of our erstwhile supporters had decided to support Peking at the next vote. Personally, I have never believed in bowing to the inevitable just because it is inevitable. *In this case, however, I felt that the national security interests of the United States lay in developing our relations with the PRC.*[19]

As the back-channel negotiations with Mao's regime progressed slowly, using both the Romanian and Pakistani governments as intermediaries, the scope of the discussions during the proposed visit by President Nixon became the principal stumbling bloc. The Chinese government wanted the talks to focus almost exclusively on the Taiwan issue; Washington insisted on wide-ranging discussions. That was yet another indication that the Nixon administration wanted a rapprochement with China for broad global strategic reasons, not merely to deal with subregional issues such as Taiwan or Vietnam. On this matter, Chinese leaders blinked, indicating that at the proposed summit "each side would be free to raise the principal issues of concern to it."[20] Nixon observed triumphantly that "the Chinese had agreed to virtually everything we proposed" regarding the trip. Indeed, Kissinger's preliminary talks "had covered the whole range of issues and problems that lay between our two countries."[21]

In his meeting with Mao and the several meetings with Chou, Nixon repeatedly, and usually with subtle skill, exploited China's growing worries about its Soviet neighbor. His comments during a face-to-face session with Mao were a classic example of how he exacerbated Chinese security concerns, if not paranoia, regarding Moscow's intentions. "We, for example, must ask ourselves—again in the confines of this room—why the Soviets have more forces on the border facing you than they do on the border facing Western Europe?" Nixon noted that Chou had argued, with respect to the projection of power, that "the United States reaches out its hands, and that the Soviet Union reaches out its hands." The president responded: "The question is, which danger does the People's Republic of China face? Is it the danger of American aggression—or of Soviet aggression?"[22] Given the developments along the border and the rise of other tensions between China and the USSR in recent years, Nixon was reasonably confident what implicit answer Chinese leaders would give to that question.

Kissinger was even more candid than his boss about wanting to benefit from the fears that China and the USSR harbored about each other. "Our relations to possible opponents," Kissinger wrote, "should be such . . . that our options toward both of them were always greater than their options toward each other."[23] Yet although the president and his national security adviser wanted to develop a "triangular relationship" with China and the Soviet Union, Kissinger admitted that initially they both "considered the People's Republic of China the more aggressive of the Communist powers." They even thought that China had probably started the fighting along the Ussuri River in early 1969.[24] (Most evidence subsequently indicated that Soviet forces likely initiated the conflict.)

It was not until Moscow's subsequent heavy-handed diplomacy, which among other things sought to get Washington to accept the proposition that China was "everybody's problem," that Nixon and Kissinger began to change their assumption about which adversary was the more belligerent, which caused them to explore more seriously the potential strategic gain to the United States of repairing relations with China. The outbreak of extensive combat along the Amur River between the Soviet republic of Kazakhstan and the Chinese province of Sinkiang in March and April 1969 reinforced their view that a shrewd U.S. policy meant tilting at least slightly toward China.[25]

The conclusion that the Soviet Union now posed the more troubling challenge worried Kissinger, because a full-scale Soviet invasion of China "might tip not only the geopolitical but also the psychological equilibrium in the world." A U.S. rapprochement with China, he believed, would not only dampen the possible PRC threat to Washington's allies in East Asia, but "by evoking the Soviet Union's concerns along its long Asian perimeter, it could also ease pressures in Europe."[26] But the initiative had to be pursued cautiously. We "considered the Chinese option useful to induce [Moscow's] restraint," Kissinger wrote later, "but we had to take care not to pursue it so impetuously as to provoke a Soviet preemptive attack on China."[27]

Nixon's 1972 Visit and the Shanghai Communiqué

That mutual security interests were the foundation of the new China-U.S. relationship became evident in the drafting of the Shanghai Communiqué, which was made public at the end of Nixon's visit. "Perhaps the most vitally important section of the Shanghai Communiqué," the president stated later, "was the provision that neither nation "should seek hegemony in the Asia Pacific region and each is opposed to efforts by any other country or group of countries to establish such hegemony." By agreeing to that provision, Nixon conceded, "both the P.R.C. and the United States were imposing restraints on themselves." However, "far more important, particularly as far as the Chinese were concerned, was that the provision subtly but unmistakably made it clear that we both would oppose efforts by the U.S.S.R." to dominate Asia.[28]

Always lurking in the background of the embryonic rapprochement, though, was the president's awareness of the pro-Taiwan lobby and the price he might pay politically for any misstep—a point that he stressed to his Chinese hosts. Nixon's recollection of the dilemma perfectly captures the interaction of serious foreign policy considerations and domestic political realities, especially when dealing with an unpopular, authoritarian (indeed, totalitarian) state that most Americans still regarded with great suspicion:

> We knew that if the Chinese made a strongly belligerent claim to Taiwan in the communiqué, I would come under murderous cross fire from any or all of the various pro-Taiwan, anti-Nixon, and anti-P.R.C. lobbies and interest groups at home. If those groups found common ground on the eve of the presidential election, the entire China initiative might be turned into a partisan issue. Then, if I lost the election, whether because of this particular factor or not, my successor might not be able to continue developing the relationship between Washington and Beijing.[29]

The two sides managed to finesse the Taiwan issue in the Shanghai Communiqué issued at the end of Nixon's state visit (see chapter 2). The communiqué and all that it symbolized underscored how much both the United States and the PRC were thinking in broad geopolitical terms. China expert John Garver correctly summarizes the importance of the changing global dynamics. "In 1971–72 the two sides were able to set aside the Taiwan issue because they now agreed on a wide range of major global issues. . . . One striking aspect of the rapprochement of the early 1970s was the rapidity with which robust cooperation on a range of important issues replaced conflict over Taiwan."[30] He adds that "once Chinese and U.S. interests began to converge, the Taiwan issue was easily set aside. The global balance of power was the most important element."[31]

Not even profound differences in their political and economic systems and continuing disputes over such issues as Vietnam, Cambodia, and Beijing's support for revolutionary movements in other portions of the Third World proved sufficient to derail bilateral cooperation. The diplomatic relationship deepened following another trip by Kissinger in February 1973, when the two governments agreed to establish "liaison offices" in Washington and Beijing. Those offices amounted to de facto embassies.

An Emerging De Facto Strategic Partnership between Washington and Beijing

Mutual concerns about the Soviet Union were especially significant in serving as a catalyst for rapprochement. And that factor would become even more important during the following years.[32] Henry Kissinger later stated that, in his conversations with Deng Xiaoping, Deng was "if anything," even "more anti-Soviet than Zhou." During his trips to Beijing in 1974 and 1975, Chinese officials acted as though "containment of the Soviet Union was a joint enterprise—as if, in fact, we were members of the same alliance."[33]

The most tangible manifestation of the growing strategic partnership was Washington's astonishing willingness to share sensitive intelligence information with Beijing. Journalist James Mann describes how extensive the cooperation was even during the early years of the new relationship. "During a trip to Beijing in 1974, [National Security Council aide Robert McFarlane] carried stacks of notebooks with hundreds of pages of U.S. intelligence information, lugging them into the Great Hall of the People to give Chinese officials briefings so thorough that the process took three full days. On a Kissinger trip in 1975, he repeated the performance."[34]

Following the Nixon administration's policy course correction, the United States and China became de facto strategic allies against the Soviet Union. Yet Kissinger and Nixon both insisted that the rapprochement was not directed against Moscow. "We did not consider our opening to China as inherently anti-Soviet," Kissinger contended. "It was not to collude against the Soviet Union, but to give us a balancing position to use for constructive ends—to give each Communist power a stake in better relations with us."[35] Although there was some truth to that justification, it was at best a half-truth. Washington did seek to build a triangular relationship, but the impetus for restoring ties with China was an increased hostility toward and worries about the USSR.

And while Kissinger and Nixon were relatively subtle—and even somewhat ambivalent—about the anti-Soviet motive, other members of the U.S. political and foreign policy community were not. It was increasingly common during the 1970s and 1980s for experts and pundits to boast openly about the shrewd move to "play the China card" against Moscow. James Mann notes that the "novel idea" of a China card in the early and mid-1970s was confined to a few officials in the Pentagon, but later in that decade it became "an important element in mainstream American policy toward Beijing."[36]

The New China Policy Divides American Conservatives

The appeal of the China card split the ranks of American conservatives and muted what might otherwise have been a very potent source of opposition to the new relationship with Beijing. It was apparent that a sizable number of conservatives were less than enthusiastic about the Nixon-Kissinger strategy. *National Review* editor William F. Buckley Jr. was caustic in his assessment following his return from China, where he and a handful of prominent journalists had covered the president's initial trip. "Watching the face of Chou," Buckley wrote, "one could not help but reflect that the smile must have been similar on the face of his hero, Stalin, when the boys got together to toast peace and dignity and self-determination of all peoples at Yalta."[37]

Mann aptly describes the nature of the growing split in American conservative ranks:

The anti-Communist right, represented by Republicans like Reagan, Goldwater, Buckley, and Buchanan, were still determinedly opposed to the normalization of relations with China, particularly if it would require cutting off ties with Taiwan. However, anti-Soviet sentiments had much wider appeal, and a growing number of conservatives were attracted to the idea of forming a stronger relationship with China, or using a "China card" to counteract the Soviets. When Senator Henry M. Jackson, the Democrats' leading opponent of détente with the Soviet Union, called for the normalization of relations with China, Buckley's *National Review* accused Jackson of moral blindness about China.[38]

The criticism of Jackson underscored the bitterness of the division that had emerged between conservatives who loathed the Soviet and Chinese (and all other communist) regimes with roughly equal fervor and those who directed their hostility first and foremost at the USSR. That difference between "anti-communists" and "anti-Soviets" weakened the opposition to Washington's new China policy and enabled the Nixon and Gerald Ford administrations to pursue rapprochement successfully.

The Carter Years Produce a Normalized Relationship

Despite the complaints of some conservatives, the Ford administration, with Kissinger's guidance as secretary of state, largely continued Nixon's policy—although Ford seemed somewhat less trusting of the Chinese than had his predecessor. However, little additional progress in the relationship occurred during this period—primarily because the aftermath of the Watergate scandal and the onset of severe domestic economic woes made it politically impossible to pursue the next step—the full normalization of relations, including official diplomatic recognition, between Washington and Beijing.

That cautious trend, much to the Chinese government's growing annoyance, initially continued into Jimmy Carter's administration. Interestingly, Carter and his advisers did not start out with the intention of simply perpetuating the Nixon-Kissinger approach. Before sending one of his advisers to Beijing, Carter instructed him not to "ass-kiss them [the Chinese] the way Nixon and Kissinger did." Carter's new appointee to the U.S. liaison office in Beijing, United Auto Workers chief Leonard Woodcock, clearly shared his boss's combative attitude, telling the staff there: "Never again shall we embarrass ourselves before a foreign nation the way Henry Kissinger did with the Chinese."[39]

The administration's policies, though, never came close to matching the brash rhetoric. That pattern would occur again and again in U.S. policy regarding China over the next three decades. New administrations typically promised (perhaps even intended) to take a harder line than their predecessors toward China. But such bravado soon gave way to the kind of pragmatic, cooperative diplomacy that Nixon and Kissinger pioneered.

That is clearly what happened during the Carter years. Despite the administration's pledge to make human rights issues a cornerstone of U.S. foreign policy, that issue quickly faded with respect to China—much as it did with respect to South Korea and some of Washington's authoritarian allies. Indeed, the Carter administration moved to reactivate the policy of moving toward full diplomatic relations—a goal that had been on hold throughout the final year of Nixon's presidency and throughout the Ford administration.

The "anti-communist versus anti-Soviet" policy dynamic that split conservatives also impacted the liberal Carter foreign policy team. Secretary of State Cyrus Vance wanted to move slowly on relations with China, including giving some prominence to human rights issues and trying to preserve a consulate in Taipei as a condition for U.S. diplomatic recognition of the Beijing government.[40] National Security Advisor Zbigniew Brzezinski led the opposing faction that viewed China policy predominantly in terms of countering Soviet power. Gradually, but inexorably, Brzezinski's perspective prevailed as President Carter's views increasingly tilted toward those of his national security adviser.

On December 15, 1978, the U.S. and Chinese governments signed the so-called Second Communiqué, in which the United States agreed to shift diplomatic recognition from the Nationalist government on Taiwan to the PRC effective January 1, 1979. As noted in chapter 2, the enraged, conservative-led opposition to the Second Communiqué and the diplomatic recognition of the People's Republic led to passage of the Taiwan Relations Act (TRA) in April 1979. The TRA pledged that the United States would "maintain the capacity" to resist any "resort to force or other forms of coercion" that jeopardized Taiwan's security or social or economic system. It also committed the United States to make available to Taiwan defensive weapons and other systems that might be necessary to maintain the island's "self-defense capability." Finally, it established the American Institute in Taiwan, which would function as a de facto U.S. embassy.[41] That legislation produced more than a little grumbling in Beijing, but it did not derail the new, official Sino-American diplomatic relationship.

The Strategic Partnership's Surprising Continuation under Reagan

Anti-China factions in the United States assumed that Ronald Reagan's election as president would greatly restrict, and perhaps even reverse, the evolving political partnership with China. PRC leaders were simultaneously agitated and puzzled by Reagan's rhetoric in the 1980 presidential campaign. His statement at one point that his administration would seek to restore official relations with Taipei especially alarmed the Chinese government, but Reagan quickly backed away from that pledge.[42] Beijing simply did not know what to expect with the new conservative chief executive.

But those who expected that Reagan would repudiate the new relationship with China and return to the pre-Nixon policy of hostility toward the PRC soon had their hopes crushed. The same split between those conservatives who gave highest priority to countering Moscow's influence and those who maintained the attitude of "a pox on all communists" was reflected in Reagan's foreign policy team. His first secretary of state, Alexander Haig, favored a China policy not much different than that of his one-time boss and mentor, Henry Kissinger. In his memoirs, Haig asserted that China was not only an important geopolitical player but also "strategically, the most important nation on earth." He added that the Chinese "had been promised much by both Democratic and Republican administrations and had been given little."[43]

National Security Advisor Richard Allen and other administration officials attached more modest importance to China's global position and were decidedly less favorable than Haig toward the communist Chinese regime. Haig viewed such individuals with barely disguised scorn:

> I was stubbornly opposed by other men in the Admin-
> istration who could not bring themselves to believe
> that not all Communists are the same, that national in-
> terests are at least as reliable a guide to national behav-
> ior as ideology, and that American interests can some-
> times be served by arrangements with such people as
> the leaders of China. The President himself was slow
> if not unable to see merit in my views.[44]

As noted in chapter 2, Reagan personally leaned toward the anti-Beijing, pro-Taiwan faction.[45] But ultimately, the president signed on to the more pragmatic approach favored by Haig and most of the State Department. That point became clear regarding continued arms sales to Taiwan and the prelude to the Third Communiqué with China.

Beijing's chief concern was the continuing U.S. arms sales to Tai-wan. It was not a new concern, but it flared in June 1980 when the Carter administration approved a $280 million package for Taiwan. Beijing immediately denounced the deal as a violation of the Second Communiqué. Haig attempted to resolve the arms-sale problem on a trip to China in June 1981 by proposing that the United States sell de-fensive arms to the PRC as well as Taiwan. That formulation pleased neither American critics of China nor the Beijing government.[46] The former saw the proposal as appeasement of a dangerous totalitar-ian aggressor, while Chinese officials saw it as an attempt to distract them from their real complaint—Washington's continued military support for Taiwan.

Negotiations proceeded for the next 14 months, leading to the signing of the Third Communiqué in August 1982. That document led to profound disillusionment with Ronald Reagan's foreign pol-icy among Americans who still viewed China with suspicion and distaste. In the Third Communiqué, the United States stated that it had "no intention of infringing on Chinese sovereignty and territo-rial integrity, or interfering in China's internal affairs, or pursuing a policy of 'Two Chinas' or 'one China, one Taiwan.'" And in a passage that angered critics of China the most: "The United States Government states that it does not seek to carry out a long-term policy of arms sales to Taiwan, that its arms sales to Taiwan will not exceed, either in qualitative or quantitative terms, the level of those supplied in recent years since the establishment of diplomatic relations between the United States and China, and that it intends to reduce gradually its sales of arms to Taiwan, leading over a period of time to a final resolution."[47]

Reagan and subsequent U.S. presidents insisted that the reduction of arms sales—much less their elimination—was contingent on China's willingness to pursue only peaceful means to resolve the Taiwan issue. In his memoirs, Reagan's second secretary of state, George Shultz, favorably quoted a *New York Times* editorial on that point. The *Times* emphasized that "Washington's words on arms for Taiwan were formally linked to China's declared policy of 'striving for a peaceful resolution of the Taiwan question.'" Shultz even asserted that in the negotiations for the Second Communiqué, "the Chinese stated their peaceful intent toward Taiwan, acknowledging that should their peaceful intent change, U.S. policy would also change."[48]

But that is not how Beijing or its adversaries in the United States interpreted the language of the communiqué. They saw it as a firm U.S. pledge to gradually disengage from arms sales and, more broadly, from political and diplomatic support for Taiwan. And that difference of interpretation became a growing irritant in the U.S.-China relationship over the succeeding three decades.

The willingness of the staunchly conservative, anti-communist Reagan administration to preserve and even strengthen the de facto alliance with Beijing seemed puzzling to some observers. But the underlying reason was not that hard to discern. The Soviet Union was a growing threat in the eyes of both China and the United States. That factor had been the initial impetus for cooperation during the Nixon years, and Moscow's conduct since the early 1970s had done nothing to diminish that incentive. The USSR's invasion of Afghanistan in late 1979, Moscow's growing presence in Vietnam (and elsewhere in the Third World) after the communist takeover of South Vietnam, and an increasingly belligerent posture in Europe alarmed the United States, still smarting from its defeat in Vietnam. Moscow's moves in the first two arenas also unsettled Beijing. The Chinese had grown particularly alarmed at the USSR's deployment of well over 100 SS-

20 nuclear missiles pointed at the PRC. That new threat augmented the ominous presence of heavily armed Soviet divisions along the border between the two countries.

Despite undiminished ideological differences, fundamental Chinese and American security and diplomatic interests continued to converge. Accordingly, both military and economic linkages between the United States and China grew dramatically during the 1980s. It may have been ironic that this cooperation expanded so greatly under an arch-conservative U.S. president, but no one could deny that it was occurring.

Although pragmatic strategic and diplomatic considerations were the glue that bound the U.S.-China relationship during those years, there was another increasingly important factor. With the onset of economic reform in China in 1978 under the leadership of Deng Xiaoping, the two countries developed ever more substantial trade and investment relations to accompany the strategic links.[49] That element would become the primary source of cooperation as the mutual threat posed by the Soviet Union faded and ultimately disappeared.

Tiananmen Square and Its Aftermath

For a time in the late 1980s, it looked as though the already cordial ties between the United States and China might grow even closer. American attitudes toward China became noticeably more positive. Harry Harding, a prominent scholar on China, states that during the mid- and late 1980s "American euphoria about developments in China reached its zenith."[50] Public opinion surveys confirmed that trend. A Gallup poll showed that 70 percent of Americans had a favorable view of China, compared to just 21 percent shortly before the normalization of relations in 1978. Press coverage and political commentary became noticeably more positive as well. China was no longer seen merely as an ally of convenience, much less as a menacing adversary.

Changes taking place in China fostered that positive impression. A growing number of Chinese economists and other experts were beginning to question the Marxist model, albeit cautiously. Their arguments went beyond just adopting Deng Xiaoping's rather agnostic view that it didn't matter whether a cat was white or black as long as it could catch mice. Maverick economists now dared to assert that at least some aspects of free-market economics were superior in principle to their Marxist counterparts.

There were also hints in their arguments of the need for overall liberalization of the Chinese system, involving both political and social reforms. Some Communist Party leaders seemed to be entertaining similar notions. Indicative of the zeitgeist in China during that period was a conference sponsored by Fudan University and the staunchly free-market American think tank, the Cato Institute. Several hundred Chinese students and prominent academics spent nearly a week listening to American advocates of free-market capitalism, including Nobel laureate Milton Friedman, and generally reacting favorably to what they heard. The highlight occurred when a meeting took place between Friedman and Communist Party chief Zhao Ziyang—a discussion that appeared to be extremely cordial and productive.

The intellectual ferment in China became even more intense in the months following that conference. Matters came to a head in the spring of 1989 with the rapid growth of pro-democracy demonstrations (mostly student-led) in Beijing's massive Tiananmen Square. Demonstrators even erected a large statue, the goddess of democracy, which bore a striking resemblance to America's Statue of Liberty. Most intriguing, there were indications that Zhao Ziyang was seriously considering endorsing at least some of the political reforms the demonstrators were pushing.

Unfortunately, the Tiananmen Square demonstrations ended badly when the hard-liners within the Communist Party leadership ultimately found (after several unsuccessful tries) a Chinese military unit willing to use brutal force against the demonstrators. Even now, no one is certain how many people died when the troops and tanks launched their assault on the night of June 3. Estimates vary from a few hundred to well over 1,000. It was an awful episode in any case, and it produced angry denunciations from important opinion leaders in the American policy community and news media. (A rare exception was former secretary of state Kissinger, who initially observed that no government could tolerate the occupation of a huge square near the seat of government by thousands of people who repudiated the legitimacy of that government.)

Even the communist government's bloody crackdown in Tiananmen Square did not disrupt the economic and strategic partnership between the United States for long, though. Just hours after the tanks rolled in, Richard Nixon called President George H. W. Bush and urged him not to let the episode, which he admitted was "deplorable," derail the bilateral relationship. The United States needed to "take a look at the long haul," the former president stressed.[51] Bush agreed, and he emphasized that while he would have to impose sanctions and put the relationship on hold for a while, he would not recall Ambassador James Lilley home from Beijing, and he intended to keep the lines of communication open.

The nasty backlash in American public opinion was another matter; it lasted much longer—and to some extent, it has never gone away. The Bush administration faced intense pressure from influential figures across the political spectrum. Senator Jesse Helms (R-NC) galvanized fellow conservatives to demand a strong response from the administration to Beijing's atrocities. Representative Stephen Solarz (D-NY) led the charge by the Carteresque human rights constituency in the Democratic Party. And they tapped into a strong current of revulsion throughout the American public. The haunting images of bloodied students, many fatally injured by Chinese tanks and bullets, were difficult to ignore. Congressional pressure gradually caused the administration to impose additional economic sanctions beyond those the president implemented shortly after the massacre—harsher sanctions that Bush and his advisers would have preferred to avoid.[52]

Secretary of State James A. Baker III acknowledged that the administration was placed in an extremely uncomfortable position. "In considering our response to the massacre, there was simply no dispute that we had to strike a delicate balance between the need for decisive steps and the need to safeguard the underlying strategic relationship." Beyond the "political realities at home," Baker noted, "the Chinese also needed to understand that we weren't paper tigers on the matter of human rights."[53] But possible congressional reaction was always at the forefront of concerns among administration officials. "In expressing our outrage and condemnation of the bloody crackdown," Baker stressed, "it was important for us to do so, if possible, in a way to preempt punitive congressional legislation that might be difficult to reverse and could do needless long-term damage to the relationship" with Beijing.[54]

George H. W. Bush Flirts with Appeasement

Despite the surge in negative attitudes in the United States regarding the Chinese government, the administration was determined not to let the Tiananmen Square tragedy lead to a cold war with Beijing. In mid-July, barely a month after the bloodshed in Tiananmen Square, the White House dispatched National Security Advisor Brent Scowcroft, accompanied by Lawrence Eagleburger, on a secret trip to Beijing to mend ties. That trip followed an impassioned personal letter that Bush sent to Deng Xiaoping on June 20, expressing, among other points, a willingness to send a "special emissary" to help repair relations.[55]

Bush's letter captures both the importance that the White House attached to preventing a breach with the PRC and the worry the president felt about how what had happened to the students was perceived in the United States and around the world. His missive seemed to straddle the line between foreign policy realism and kowtowing behavior toward a brutal, autocratic regime. "I write in the spirit of genuine friendship," Bush stated. The letter, he emphasized, came "from one who believes with a passion that good relations between the United States and China are in the fundamental interests of both countries. I have felt that way for many years. I feel more strongly that way today, in spite of the difficult circumstances." He asked Deng for his help in preserving that relationship, adding that "I have tried very hard not to inject myself into China's internal affairs."

Bush seemed almost apologetic about the actions that he took to express public revulsion about the crackdown in Tiananmen. Given fundamental American principles and values, "the actions I took as president could not be avoided." (Bush had suspended all military sales to China and all military contacts between the two countries.) Indeed, the president warned, "the clamor for stronger action remains intense." He assured Deng that "I have resisted that clamor, making clear that I do not want to see destroyed this relationship that you and I have worked so hard to build." In particular, "I explained to the American people that I did not want to unfairly burden the Chinese people with economic sanctions."

Bush noted later that Deng replied to that letter within 24 hours, and the White House sent Scowcroft to Beijing on a secret mission shortly thereafter. That mission was so secret, Bush wrote, "that their plane was nearly shot down when it entered Chinese airspace unannounced." The president was quite pleased at the outcome of the subsequent meetings. "The trip was successful in that it conveyed to the Chinese how serious the divide was between us but also how much we respected our friendship."[56]

Diplomatic efforts to soothe tensions continued in the following weeks and months. On July 21, shortly after Scowcroft's return, the president sent a second letter to Deng, this time with the salutation: "Dear Chairman Deng, Dear Friend:"[57] Once again, the president endeavored to strike a balance between realpolitik and appeasement, but this time the balance seem to shift a bit more toward the latter. Bush noted, for example, that the communiqué of the recently concluded summit of the G7 nations addressed the developments in China. "I can tell you in total confidence," the president rushed to assure Deng, "that the U.S. and the Japanese removed some rather inflammatory language from the Communiqué. It was still a Communiqué which I'm sure you'd rather not have had at all, but in the final form it did not urge any new action affecting China."

Later in the letter, Bush again went out of his way to placate the Chinese regime. "I have great respect for China's long-standing position about nonintervention in its internal affairs," he wrote. "Because of that, I also understand that I risk straining our friendship when I make suggestions as to what might be done now. But the U.S.-China relationship, which we have both worked so hard to strengthen, demands the candor with which only a friend can speak." Bush's principal policy suggestion was that Deng's government show "forgiveness" to the students and other demonstrators—an idea that seemed more than a little naive. Another passage reinforced a disturbing impression that the president's behavior verged on supplication. "Please do not be angry with me," he pleaded, "if I have crossed the invisible threshold lying between constructive suggestion and 'internal interference.'"

In his memoirs, Bush noted that "Deng's reply was respectful, but he held steadfastly to their position that this was their internal affair. Eventually, our relationship and friendship would recover, but it took a while to work through the problems."[58] Deng's response indicated that the Chinese leadership understood the principles of foreign policy realism better than did the Bush White House.

A key feature of the U.S. effort to prevent a breach in the relationship with China was a second secret trip by Scowcroft in December. But whereas the first trip had remained secret, the second one soon became public. And the White House then had to admit that that there had been two secret diplomatic missions, with the first one taking place just weeks after Chinese tanks rolled over students in Tiananmen Square. To say that the Scowcroft trips became extremely controversial would be a bit of an understatement.

Despite the best efforts of the Bush administration, the Tiananmen bloodletting and its aftermath led to the nadir in U.S.-China relations since the Kissinger-Nixon opening in the early 1970s.[59] The tensions came at an especially sensitive time in the relationship. Even those members of the policy and political elites in the United States who viewed the Chinese political system with distaste for the most part grudgingly accepted the proposition that playing the "China card" was useful in the bitter struggle against the Soviet Union. All except the most hard-core conservatives and human rights activists seemed willing to overlook China's domestic repression as long as it didn't reach outrageous levels.

But in late 1989 the Soviet empire began to unravel. By the spring of 1990, it was clear that the Kremlin had lost control of its East European satellite empire and that Soviet leader Mikhail Gorbachev and his advisers seemed intent on adopting a more accommodating foreign policy as well as liberalizing political and economic policies at home. The most dramatic concession on the international stage was the willingness to accept the reunification of Germany under a noncommunist government and allow united Germany's membership in NATO.

As Soviet aggressiveness—and overall power—faded, the appeal of China as a de facto strategic ally of the United States also faded. To at least some influential Americans, there was clearly less need for an association that sullied American values. That questioning of the desirability of maintaining close ties with Beijing would probably have occurred even without the brutality on display in Tiananmen Square, given the threat reduction emerging from the Soviet bloc. The Tiananmen crackdown made the case for a reconsideration of the relationship with China even stronger.

A Changed Strategic Environment, but a Largely Unchanged Policy

In retrospect, it is rather surprising that the United States did not greatly de-emphasize its relationship with China during the early 1990s. The principal reason that change did not happen is that President Bush and his closest foreign policy advisers, especially Scowcroft and Baker, believed that there were compelling medium- and long-term reasons for not allowing such a deterioration to occur. And they were willing to defy the increasingly disgruntled public opinion in the United States to preserve the existing policy.

The Bush administration refused to be intimidated by the domestic criticism, and U.S.-China relations gradually got back on track. The growth of economic ties actually accelerated during the rest of the 1990s. During the 1992 presidential campaign, though, the continuation of that trend seemed anything but certain.

Democratic Party nominee Bill Clinton repeatedly blasted the Bush administration for pursuing an excessively soft policy toward Beijing. He especially focused on Scowcroft's trip, which he considered indecent so soon after the carnage in Tiananmen Square. Clinton accused the administration of kowtowing to the "Butchers of Beijing," and he argued that such needlessly deferential behavior extended to trade ties as well as security issues.[60] The focus on trade had less to do with China's unsatisfactory human rights record, as real as that problem was, than it did with pressure from labor unions and other protectionist constituencies in the Democratic Party.

For much of the campaign, the criticism must have sounded to the incumbent president as though it was occurring in stereo. Independent candidate Ross Perot vied with Clinton to see who could engage in the most biting comments about the administration's trade and human rights policies toward China.

Clinton's victory in the 1992 election led to expectations in both China and the United States that a new, much more hard-line policy was in the offing. But the incoming president's confrontational rhetoric was rarely matched by actual deeds. And even the rhetoric faded noticeably after his first year in office.[61]

That shift underscored the changed nature of the U.S.-China relationship. From the early 1970s to the end of the Cold War, mutual security concerns—especially worries about Soviet intentions—were the principal sources of cohesion. From the early 1990s on, economics took center stage. But as James Mann points out, the effect was similar. It caused U.S. policymakers and opinion leaders to ignore, excuse, or downplay the more odious behaviors of the Beijing regime. During the Cold War, the basic response to critics was that China's political and strategic importance in the struggle against the Soviet Union precluded risking the relationship because of domestic repression and human rights abuses. In the post–Cold War period, the argument became that China's growing economic importance and its long-term geopolitical importance precluded making repression and human rights abuses significant policy concerns.

The 9/11 terrorist attacks revived some aspects of the security partnership rationale. Both Beijing and Washington were worried about the threat from Muslim extremists. But that issue also placed the administration of George W. Bush in an awkward position. Chinese officials interpreted any efforts toward greater autonomy by the Uighur population in Xinjiang province as a manifestation of the terrorist threat—a rather self-serving thesis. As Aaron L. Friedberg, a prominent scholar on China, notes, because of Washington's uneasiness about Beijing's treatment of the Uighurs, and an array of other policy differences, Sino-American cooperation on the issue of terrorism "has turned out to be limited in scope and significance."[62]

The Growing Anti-China Public Backlash

The growth of hostility toward China and criticism of the cooperative policy that Washington has pursued toward Beijing since the early 1970s raise serious questions about whether China and the United States are now rivals more than partners. It clearly has become more awkward to maintain a partnership with a regime whose authoritarianism shows few signs of diminishing. The importance of the trade relationship provides some of the necessary glue for a continuing partnership, but even that factor is ambiguous and complicated. Although China's economic importance to the United States has soared since the 1970s and 1980s, the perception has also grown among Americans that China has become a major economic competitor of the United States and the only serious potential strategic peer competitor on a global basis. Indeed, one prominent public opinion poll taken in 2009 found that respondents regarded China as America's number two adversary—behind only Iran and ahead of such odious regimes as North Korea's. Another survey, by Pew Research, found that 53 percent of the public considered China's emergence as a great power to be "a major threat" to the United States.[63] Some 53 percent of Americans in a February 2014 Gallup poll viewed China unfavorably, while only 43 percent had a favorable view of that country.[64]

Add to that factor the reality that the two countries have no major common adversary to cement their one-time de facto alliance. Cooperating against radical Islamic terrorism provides some basis for a strategic partnership, but it does not even remotely offer the same incentive for mutual action as did the perceived need to contain Soviet power. And on other strategic issues, such as dealing with breakout nuclear powers such as Iran and North Korea or assessing the desirability for humanitarian interventions or regime-change missions, Beijing and Washington are more likely to be on opposite sides than on the same side.

The opening to China and the deepening cooperation was always controversial, especially among conservatives. But as China's economic power increased and spawned serious efforts at a military buildup in the 1990s and the first decade of the 21st century, conservative anger and criticism also rose. That core opposition bloc has gained strength from labor unions and other economic nationalists who fear China's potent competition and from human rights activists who are appalled at Beijing's continuing repression of domestic dissidents. The PRC's periodic belligerence toward Taiwan has also angered Americans outside the traditional anti-communist base, especially once the island emerged as a genuine democracy in the mid-1990s instead of being the corrupt authoritarian system under Chiang Kai-shek and his son and successor, Chiang Ching-kuo.

Beijing's increasingly assertive behavior toward various neighbors regarding conflicting territorial claims in the South China Sea also has caused uneasiness among U.S. political figures and opinion leaders. China's claims are so far reaching (encompassing nearly 90 percent of that body of water and its scattered islets) that Vietnam, Malaysia, the Philippines, and other countries have charged that their large neighbor is engaging in a major power play that impinges on important security and economic interests. U.S. leaders also worry about Beijing's motives and wonder if Chinese leaders are attempting gradually to convert the South China Sea from international waters into Chinese territorial waters.[65] As the world's leading maritime power, the United States is not at all willing to see that change occur regarding a region through which many of East Asia's most essential sea lanes pass.

China's actions in the East China Sea have created even greater tensions in the bilateral relationship with Washington. A source of major friction is the Sino-Japanese dispute over a chain of uninhabited islands called the Senkakus in Japan and the Diaoyus in China. Beijing has become ever more insistent in pressing its claims in the past few years, and Tokyo (which currently controls the islands) shows no willingness to back down. The Obama administration adopts the odd stance that it takes no position on the substance of the territorial controversy but simultaneously insists that the U.S.-Japan mutual defense treaty covers those islands.[66] Beijing views that argument as illogical and disingenuous. In any case, the Senkaku/Diaoyu issue is yet another factor roiling relations between the United States and China.

Public criticism of the bipartisan, status quo policy toward Beijing has been on the rise since the Tiananmen Square incident, and it flares whenever the Chinese regime represses dissidents, engages in questionable trade policies, presses debatable territorial claims, or takes positions counter to Washington's foreign policy preferences on issues in East Asia and other regions. The case is building in influential ideological and political circles to take a stronger stand toward China.[67]

Going forward, the probability is that the United States and China will be increasingly wary geopolitical competitors.[68] The extensive trade ties and financial links may be sufficient to prevent such sharp-edged competition from becoming a bitter rivalry, much less cause the two countries to become outright enemies. But the political and strategic partnership that began in the early 1970s appears to have drawn to a close.

Was Washington's Partnership with Beijing Sensible and Decent?

The strategic rationale for cooperation with China during the Cold War was stronger than the case for such cooperation with almost all of Washington's authoritarian partners. Although the war-fighting

353

capabilities of China's antiquated military were overrated by some opinion leaders in the United States, the de facto alliance between Washington and Beijing did cause a shift in the global balance of power and certainly complicated Moscow's political, diplomatic, and strategic calculations.

James Mann describes the relationship as "a strategic marriage of convenience," and its foundation as "a classic example of Kissinger's obsession with geopolitics." Mann argues that while "in private, some American leaders, particularly Nixon, could be candid about the regime they were dealing with," in public U.S. officials "portrayed the relationship as something different from and greater than their wartime association with Stalin. Washington's Cold War partnership was colored by romance and sentimentalism."[69]

Although that assessment of U.S. attitudes has some validity, overall it is too harsh. Some American officials tended to whitewash China's authoritarian characteristics, but U.S. administrations generally maintained a realistic and pragmatic view of the U.S.-China relationship. They understood that they were dealing with an autocratic, one-party state that had committed egregious human rights abuses during the Maoist era and had improved just modestly on that front under Deng Xiaoping and his successors.

Oddly enough, occasional comments by the supposed arch-realist Henry Kissinger were a partial exception to the pattern of realism. One of his secret messages to Nixon during a trip to China in 1973 made the astonishing comparison of China with Great Britain as a potential friend of the United States. In fairness, though, Kissinger's actions rarely reflected such naiveté.[70]

The biggest exception to the tenets of realism regarding U.S. policy toward China was the behavior of George H. W. Bush's administration (especially the actions of the president himself) during the months immediately following the Tiananmen Square massacre. In their efforts to repair the—admittedly important—bilateral relationship, Bush and his advisers engaged in behavior that verged on kowtowing. Sending Brent Scowcroft to China so soon after the killings was unseemly at best. But worse were the two letters that Bush sent to Deng Xiaoping. The tone in those letters was just short of fawning, and there certainly was no indication that the president realized that the United States was in the stronger position. It was appropriate that Washington made some effort to restore the relationship, but given the growing importance of the U.S. market to the Chinese economy, and Beijing's residual worries about Moscow's geopolitical ambitions in Asia, there was no need to go to such rhetorical extremes to placate the PRC.

During that period, U.S. officials acted toward the Chinese government much as they had done too often throughout the Cold War toward authoritarian partners that committed egregious acts against their own people. The Bush administration's response to Tiananmen was not realism; it was insensitive behavior that came across to public opinion in the United States and around the world as a hypocritical policy based on a greedy desire to preserve a lucrative economic relationship with the PRC—even if that meant betraying professed American values.

In general, though, Washington's policy toward China during the last decade of the Cold War and the early years of the post–Cold War era was more sensible and justified than the policies toward other authoritarian allies. China was substantially more important than almost all of those allies, and Beijing's behavior, although certainly repressive, usually fell short of the atrocities that many other friendly regimes committed. It therefore met the test of being an appropriate—albeit far from perfect—strategic relationship for the United States.

PART TWO

AMERICA'S AUTHORITARIAN PARTNERS AFTER 9/11

12. Pyramid of Cards: Washington's Policy toward Egypt from Mubarak to El-Sisi

On February 11, 2011, after 18 consecutive days of massive nation-wide protests, Egyptians forced the resignation of President Hosni Mubarak after 29 years of authoritarian rule. But underneath the euphoria, courage, and self-determination, Egyptians had not forgotten that the United States had tacitly embraced a harsh dictatorship that perpetuated its power through the denial of free speech, arbitrary imprisonment, torture, and other forms of savage repression. While diplomatic and economic engagement with loathsome foreign powers is unavoidable in statecraft, active endorsement should be avoided.

Washington's devotion to Cairo's tyrant—at a cost of more than $60 billion dollars in military and economic assistance and nearly three decades of political support—contradicted the basic moral principles America purports to want for the world. But even in terms of the alliance's strategic, ideological, and economic justifications, collaboration carried grave risks. On a strategic level, post-9/11 Egypt provided the United States with extensive counterterrorism assistance. However, Mubarak's authoritarianism—and America's patronage—also served as a potent rallying cry for extremists determined to attack the U.S. and Egyptian governments—the latter a holdover from Mubarak's predecessor and staunch American ally, President Anwar al-Sadat.

In terms of ideology, Cairo's secular regime ruthlessly suppressed deeply conservative Islamist forces at odds with U.S. and Egyptian interests. Such activity, however, also marginalized moderate, reform-minded critics and proponents of liberal, secular thought, producing a poisonous dynamic that allowed underground Islamist movements to thrive.

On the economic front, the strongest case given for America's support for Mubarak was the preservation of Egyptian-Israeli peace—the primary rationale for more than 30 years of continued

U.S. military and economic assistance to Egypt. But aid concealed several flaws: first, because U.S. aid bought obedience, not loyalty, Egyptians continued to view Israel as an enemy, an animosity that leaders in Washington failed to take seriously during the explosive Arab Spring; second, U.S. military assistance to Egypt made Cairo's domestic atrocities traceable to Washington; and third, rather than incentivizing political and economic reforms, aid corroded the relationship between the Egyptian people and their state.

America's alliance with Egypt underscored a persistent tension in U.S. grand strategy between cold-blooded strategic objectives and crucial American values. In terms of what U.S. policy planners perceived as America's vital interests, the partnership proved problematic. In this respect, as Washington's alliance with Cairo vividly illustrates, sometimes the case for discarding an alliance is as at least as forceful as the case for pursuing it.

Prelude: The U.S. Relationship with Anwar Sadat

In the 1970s, the nexus of Palestinian terrorism and Soviet-backed Arab actions against Israel would forever deepen U.S. diplomatic and economic involvement in Egypt and throughout the Middle East. Before, and especially after, the Arab-Israeli war of 1973—October War to the Arabs and the Yom Kippur War to the Israelis—President Sadat made appeals to religion, not Arab nationalism, ushering in a religiously conservative shift to Egypt's domestic and foreign policies. Sadat assumed the title of "Believer-President," began and ended his speeches with verses from the Quran, and fought the 1973 war under the banner of Islam, calling it the "War of Ramadan."[1] He also leaned more on Saudi Arabia, Kuwait, and other wealthy Gulf states awash in petrodollars following the 1973–74 oil embargo. During this time, Al-Azhar, the thousand-year old Islamic center of learning based in Cairo, was forging ties with Saudi Islamists.[2] With many Egyptians working in Saudi Arabia and returning home "Wahhabi-cized," the way of life in Egypt gradually changed.

As long-time visitors saw an Islamist shift in Egyptian society, though, Washington and Cairo began to put aside their decades of distrust. In October 1975 Sadat became the first Egyptian leader to visit the United States, and on November 5, he had the rare honor of addressing a full session of Congress—a privilege that had not yet been bestowed even on an Israeli leader.[3] To reward Egypt for its new moderate tone and firm rejection of the USSR, the United States sold Egypt six C-130 Hercules transport jets and gave it $750 million from the U.S. Agency for International Development (USAID). Despite the détente, Egypt's sovereignty over the Sinai Peninsula, seized by the Jewish state during the war, still remained unresolved, while perceptions of Washington going out of its way to appease Israel lingered in Cairo.[4]

On November 9, 1977, fed up with America's apparent inability to exert pressure on Israel for a full-scale withdrawal from the Sinai, President Sadat announced that he would travel to Jerusalem to further the cause of peace. His decision was both courageous and unprecedented. As then secretary of state Henry Kissinger later commented, Sadat's initiative "constituted perhaps the first serious act of policy taken by an Arab ruler in the thirty-year-old conflict."[5] On November 20, before the Israeli Knesset, the Egyptian president declared he had come to Jerusalem to build a durable peace in which "Israel lives within her borders, among her Arab neighbors in safety and security, within the framework of all the guarantees she accepts and that are offered to her."[6]

President Jimmy Carter praised Sadat's "historic breakthrough" and proclaimed that the road to peace that had led through Jerusalem "will now go to Cairo." William B. Quandt, a member on the National Security Council under President Carter, recalls the reaction in Washington was "one of admiration for the personal courage required."[7] The Israeli government, however, was disappointed.[8] The right-of-center Likud Party, which assumed power in June, opposed the previous Labor Party government's approach to territorial compromise. Moreover, Sadat's speech, while historic, was delivered in Arabic and in a lecturing tone.[9] Such diverging worldviews among the Americans, Israelis, and Egyptians presaged the arduous path to peace that lay ahead.

From September 5 to 17, 1978, at the invitation of President Carter, President Sadat and Israeli Prime Minister Menachem Begin convened with their advisers for peace talks at the presidential vacation facility in Camp David, Maryland. Procedurally, the Egyptians would draft an agreement, the Israeli delegation would write a counter-draft, and the American team would negotiate with both parties to elicit reactions to proposals. As the parties revised and polished drafts, disagreements surfaced quickly. One of the biggest obstacles was achieving Carter's main goal of comprehensive peace. As the president wrote on July 19, 1977, comprehensive peace involved normalized Egyptian-Israeli relations, Israel's withdrawal from occupied territories in stages, "a Palestinian entity," and "Palestinian self-determination."[10] But at Camp David, the inclusion of a Palestinian representative proved impossible given staunch Israeli opposition.

The October 1974 Arab League summit in Rabat, Morocco, had recognized the Palestine Liberation Organization (PLO)—a union created by the Arab League in January 1964 to give a voice to Palestinian refugees—as the "sole legitimate representative of the Palestinian people" and the negotiator for the future of the West Bank and Gaza. But the PLO represented a threat to Israel's security and endangered the integrity of another close U.S. ally, Jordan, which endured its own negative spillover from the Palestinian refugee crisis during the Black September conflict in 1970. The PLO's deplorable acts of terrorism had become synonymous with the Palestinians more generally and undermined the Palestinian cause. Some U.S. officials at the time also believed the PLO's inclusion in peace talks might spark a civil war within the PLO between moderates and radicals.[11] Known for his idealism and seeming naiveté, even Carter later compared the PLO to the Klu Klux Klan and the Nazis.[12] The PLO had also rejected the idea of Sadat as its spokesman and refused to deal with Egypt within the Camp David framework—for that matter, so did much of the Arab world. The refusal to negotiate with Israel had long been the glue that bonded Arab unity.

A further obstacle to including the PLO in the Camp David talks was a 1975 Memorandum of Understanding between the United States and Israel. The United States promised that it would neither recognize nor negotiate with the PLO without Israeli consent. Carter's secretary of state, Cyrus Vance, later wrote about that self-imposed restraint on American diplomacy:

> The Israelis interpreted [this] commitment as giving them a veto over the presentation of U.S. ideas for peace to the Arabs. It ... was to make our task of finding a way to deal with the PLO close to impossible at a time when the Palestinian question had become a pivotal issue.[13]

With no Arab leader able to speak on behalf of the Palestinians, Camp David provided no opportunity to gain Israel's acceptance of concessions that might lead to a comprehensive peace.

A persistent challenge to the peace process was the controversy surrounding Israeli-occupied Arab land. After the Suez Crisis, President Dwight D. Eisenhower put sanctions on Israel until it abandoned all Egyptian territory. To do otherwise, he said, would have undermined the United Nations (UN) charter. In his words, "No nation should be allowed to occupy foreign territory and be permitted to impose conditions on its own withdrawal."[14] Two decades later, Prime Minister Begin rejected one significant passage of UN Security Council Resolution 242 of November 22, 1967: "the inadmissibility of the acquisition of territory by war." Begin argued that the defensive nature of the Six Day War granted Israel the right to retain all the land it had conquered. He also opposed the principle of "Palestinian self-determination" and justified his position on the grounds of Palestinian rejection of Israel.[15] Begin instead called for a Greater Israel (Eretz Yisrael) encompassing all of Palestine, including the West Bank, which he called Judea and Sumaria. In this respect, and what would later lead to a critical and recurring problem in the peace process, Begin fought tooth-and-nail over every detail of the Camp David negotiations to ensure that an agreement between Egypt and Israel remained independent of the question of Palestine—the heart of Carter's concept of comprehensive peace.[16]

Yet another obstacle to progress at Camp David, surprisingly enough, was President Sadat. His primary goal was the restoration of the Sinai to Egypt. But unlike Begin, who was consumed with technicalities, Sadat cared little for specifics and spoke in generalities. He thought the Palestine question could wait until a later stage, whereas others in his delegation wanted "linkage" between Egypt's agreement with Israel and a future peace deal for other Arab land. This divergence within the Egyptian delegation was a source of great contention, especially because Sadat was shelving the question of Palestine under the cover of an honorable and comprehensive solution to the Arab-Israeli dispute. He also tended to keep his subordinates out of the loop. Sometimes the Americans knew Cairo's diplomatic instructions before they reached the Egyptian negotiators.[17]

Egypt's third consecutive foreign minister to resign, Mohamed Ibrahim Kamel, did so mainly over an agreement that he foresaw as an instrument for Israel's "expansionist intentions." In his memoirs he lamented, "Sadat's fickle whims and abrupt and indiscriminate changes of behaviour without prior notice and consultation . . . shook my faith in Sadat's leadership and led me to despair of achieving any progress." Kamel elaborated, "Sadat agrees to something in the morning, and an hour later he rejects what he had previously agreed to, and then in the afternoon he agrees to the same thing again!"[18]

Carter's National Security Advisor Zbigniew Brzezinski underscored the limitations of the Camp David process. He observed that socializing at the retreat was "almost entirely" between the Americans and the Egyptians and the Americans and the Israelis—never between the Egyptians and the Israelis.[19] Such poor communication later proved important. Camp David may have removed the underlying sources of conflict between two arch-adversaries, but it fell short of cultivating the respect and mutual tolerance necessary for normalized relations.

Nevertheless, the Camp David Peace Accords, reached on September 17, 1978, rank as one of the more important achievements in modern diplomacy. The agreement comprised two parts. First, "The Framework for Peace in the Middle East" was an agreement for the conduct of negotiations among Egypt, Israel, Jordan, and "the representatives of the Palestinian people" for reaching a comprehensive and durable settlement to the Palestinian problem. Second, a "Framework for the Conclusion of a Peace Treaty between Egypt and Israel" stipulated Egypt's sovereignty over the Sinai Peninsula, and Israel's freedom of navigation, overflight, and agreement to remove its military forces from the Sinai, which it did in April 1982.[20]

"The future is with Egypt," Israeli Foreign Minister Moshe Dayan told President Carter. "If you take one wheel off a car, it won't drive. If Egypt is out of the conflict, there will be no more war."[21] The Camp David Peace Accords successfully removed Egypt from the pan-Arab struggle against Israel and ended the days of Radio Cairo calling for the overthrow of pro-Western Arab governments. Sadat and Begin shared the 1978 Nobel Peace Prize for their efforts to defuse bilateral tensions and signed the Egyptian-Israeli Peace Treaty at the White House on March 26, 1979.

Seemingly, no good deed goes unpunished. American leaders expended considerable time and energy at Camp David, but any movement toward a settlement prompted fierce debates in the United

States, with much of the American news media depicting U.S. officials as anti-Israeli.[22] Meanwhile, any request the Egyptian delegates perceived as against Arab interests they labeled "for Carter's sake." Egypt faced harsh Arab blowback, but its delegates at Camp David assumed that the United States was powerful enough to deliver the support of key regional and world leaders.[23] That did not happen.

Arab resentment toward Sadat had been building for several years. After Sadat's speech at the Knesset in November 1977, Damascus state radio denounced him as "a traitor" and a "betrayer of the Arab cause." At the Baghdad summit in November 1978, two months after Camp David, the Arab League called on Cairo "to go back on these agreements and not sign any reconciliation treaty with the enemy." The League formally suspended Egypt on March 31, 1979. Saudi Arabia and other status quo regimes favored using discrete political and economic measures to reprimand Sadat, whereas Iraq demanded a "total rupture" of relations.[24] In the face of such Arab hostility, Sadat went down swinging. He cut diplomatic ties with nationalist regimes that opposed his peace initiative and derided Arabs not ready for peace as nomads and Bedouins who counted for little. When asked what U.S. leaders could do to placate opposition from Damascus, Sadat replied that they could inform Syria that Egypt was the center of the Arab world.[25] For leaders in Cairo and Washington, the strange mixture of overwhelming accolades and unrelenting vilification became the double-edged sword of peace.

Sadat's "Open Door"

After Camp David, the United States became a crucial source of financial aid to Egypt. Washington gave Israel, on average, $3.2 billion and Egypt $1.8 billion, annually, with more than half of that money going to purchase American-manufactured military equipment.[26] What remains unclear is whether U.S. assistance was necessary from the standpoint of America's interests, as Washington was merely subsidizing national interests that Cairo already had. Over the course of several decades, USAID also provided Egypt with tens of billions of dollars in economic and development assistance earmarked for infrastructure, health, food, and public-sector reforms. Sadat had inherited from his predecessor, Gamal Abdel Nasser, a socialist economy in crisis: a growing population, a bloated public sector, rampant inflation, and widespread unemployment and illiteracy. Arab socialism did more than wreck Egypt's economy; it destroyed human capital.

Accordingly, some American officials justified U.S. aid to Egypt in the belief that it would alleviate Cairo's economic woes. Assistance would supposedly cement Egypt's partnership with America and move Egypt along the path of economic progress. But those large doses of U.S. military and financial assistance failed to put Egypt on the path of self-sustained economic growth. After a quarter century, corrosive corruption and overregulation continued to strangle the Egyptian economy.[27] More important, U.S. aid turned America into a scapegoat for the adverse consequences of Sadat's broader economic and social initiatives. Before Camp David, Sadat had opted for privatization and welcomed foreign investment. These changes, known as the "open-door" (*infitah*) policies, rolled back state planning; removed government subsidies for basic necessities; eliminated price controls; and altered production, trade, and labor laws. Open door policies provoked widespread discontent, with demonstrations at public-sector companies, strikes in a number of major cities, and bread riots in January 1977.[28] In 1974, the Muslim Brotherhood had declared that all members supported the government's austerity policies. By the end of the decade, many in the movement had become openly hostile both to the government's economic policies and to the perceived U.S.-Israeli imposed peace. One policy that connected those two grievances was a Camp David preferential treatment clause that compelled Egypt to sell Sinai crude to Israel at below market rates.[29]

For many Egyptians, these mounting economic challenges, and the broader geopolitical changes that accompanied them, prompted a period of self-reflection, mainly involving issues of justice and identity. Writing of this angst in the context of Egypt's wars with Israel, Sadat wrote in an April 1974 working paper: "The years of defeat afforded us with the opportunity to put our conscience to a severe test, in which we passed through a period of soul-searching and put all the facets of the national work under the microscope of criticism."[30]

Resentment against Sadat and his policies was becoming a potent brew even before Camp David. In the same month that Sadat presented his working paper, bouts of unrest plagued the country, and the Islamic Liberation Organization, an Islamist terrorist movement, attacked the Heliopolis military academy near Cairo, hoping to obtain the academy's munitions and use them to overthrow the government.[31] Several years later (in July 1977), the Islamist group Takfir Wal Hijra kidnapped and assassinated the former government minister of religious endowments and condemned Sadat's regime as infidel. Islamists in Egypt were becoming increasingly radicalized even before Sadat's November 1977 trip to Jerusalem, although that event and the rapprochement with Israel that it triggered greatly intensified the animosity.

To eliminate Islamists, Sadat approved a bill authorizing death or hard labor for anyone convicted of belonging to a secret organization. He cracked down on the Brotherhood, the nationalist Al-Wafd Party, and other opposition groups—save for three government-created "opposition" political parties. By 1981 1,500 prominent political activists were in prison. Years prior, Sadat had ordered the arrest of the speaker of the national assembly; members of the central committee; and the ministers for war, information, and presidential affairs, whose "inane socialist slogans," he claimed, were "at variance . . . with our religious faith."[32] In a perverse premonition of Egypt under Hosni Mubarak, private property was supposedly sacrosanct while the government zealously attacked abuses of what it deemed public property, such as the image of the president, the state, and the military. Such draconian laws circumscribed the Egyptian people's exercise of political rights.

Consternation toward Sadat also flared among elements of the military. In 1978 members of a New Free Officers movement were arrested for plotting against Sadat after Camp David, and 11 air force officers suffered a similar fate in September 1979 for their alleged anti-regime activity. Even the onset of bountiful flows of U.S. military aid did not stem the growing discontent. On October 6, 1981, a truck stopped in front of Sadat's podium during a military parade in Cairo honoring the eight-year anniversary of the October War. The soldiers inside, led by a member of the Islamist group al-Jihad (Sacred Combat), which had opposed both Sadat's domestic crackdown and peace negotiations with Israel, opened fire on the president, killing him.[33] In contrast to the vast outpouring of grief by an estimated five million Egyptians who had turned out for Nasser's funeral, the magnitude and intensity of the mourning for Sadat was noticeably less. But a record number of foreign dignitaries came to Egypt for Sadat's ceremony, including three former U.S. presidents. Such a contrast underscored that the Egyptian leader was far more respected abroad than he had been at home.

The Rise of Hosni Mubarak

As close as U.S.-Egypt relations were under Sadat, they grew much closer under his vice president and handpicked successor, Lieutenant General Hosni Mubarak. The former air force commander, who had led the first air strike against the Jewish state in the 1973 war, now declared Egypt's adherence to the peace treaty with Israel. In February 1982 President Mubarak visited the White House and negotiated a $1.3 billion arms sales agreement. The deal included $200 million as an outright grant, an amount which President Ronald Reagan soon increased to $400 million. Such generosity—with American taxpayers' money—was funded largely through U.S. Foreign Military Sales loans, a method by which the U.S. government sells military equipment to foreign governments and thereby creates a larger market for U.S. arms manufacturers.[34]

Egyptian factories turned out hundreds of millions of dollars worth of military goods for domestic use and for export markets, while the Reagan administration considered Egypt "the best market for the Northrop F-5G Tigershark fighter." One of the main pillars of U.S.-Egyptian political and security ties was the coproduction of the M1A1 Abrams tank. According to *Aviation Week*: "US and Western European aerospace industry officials believe Egypt is the key to doing business in Africa and the Middle East. . . . Egypt, and all of Africa through Egyptian licensed or coproduction, is a market far larger than China was considered several years ago."[35]

U.S. assistance to Egypt continued despite Cairo's internal repression and fading hopes that assistance would lead to a growing Egyptian economy. Instead, with Egypt's military in control of large commercial industries, U.S. aid helped to further entrench the military's role in the economy. That, along with aspects of open door policies, widened the socioeconomic gap between well-connected elites and the Egyptian people, a condition hardly conducive to internal stability.

Although President Mubarak adhered to the Camp David Accords, the full utility of any agreement depends upon whether the parties achieved what was promised. Camp David's "The Framework for Peace in the Middle East" was a broad declaration of principles encompassing Palestine that lacked firm linkage to the Egyptian-Israeli agreement. William Quandt recalls the conventional wisdom at Camp David that the Egyptian-Israeli peace would serve as a model for future negotiations between Israel and its other Arab neighbors. "Egypt's task," wrote Egypt's foreign affairs minister Boutros Boutros-Ghali, "was to convince the Arab sides of the necessity of negotiation and that negotiation could lead to positive results." Zbigniew Brzezinski also argued that Camp David is best described not as an "agreement," but as a "framework" for negotiating another transitional arrangement.[36] Israeli Defense Minister and Camp David delegate Ezer Weizman made a similar observation: "Whereas the Egyptians saw the Sinai agreement as the model for similar understandings with Jordan and Syria over the West Bank and the Golan Heights, Begin saw it as the precise opposite. As far as he was concerned, the withdrawal from the Sinai would be the end of the story."[37]

Some experts, such as Harold H. Saunders, an assistant secretary of state in the Carter administration, and Avner Yaniv, the former vice president and professor of political science at the University of Haifa, conclude that the Camp David Accords had another, very negative impact. They believe that by helping Israel hold onto Gaza and enlarge its program of settlements in the West Bank, Camp David freed Israel to drive out and destroy vestiges of the PLO by invading Lebanon. Those operations led to the horrific massacres at the Sabra and Shatila Palestinian refugee camps in Beirut by Israel's Lebanese Christian militia allies in 1982.[38] Thereafter, Mubarak froze the normalization of relations with Israel, causing considerable uneasiness in Washington.

The perception of Western domination, writes Hisham Sharabi, "gave rise to a feeling of inferiority and frustration which often expressed itself in nihilism and despair."[39] Many in the region blamed Washington for their political and economic misfortune. Although the criticism was in some respects justifiable, given Washington's history of interference in the Middle East, it overlooks the region's own shortcomings. As scholar Barry Rubin put it, states and movements blamed America for blocking their ambitions, even as "those advocating an Islamic society or united Arab state would not attribute failure to the impossibility of these goals or their own people's refusal to rise up in support of them."[40]

This way of thinking also demonstrated the new public-relations minefield that lay ahead for U.S. leaders, as PLO leader Yasir Arafat labeled Washington "the chief engineer of the plot against the Arabs."[41] To many in the region, the United States appeared as more of a divider than a peacemaker. Strikes and demonstrations persisted in the West Bank and Gaza throughout the 1980s, culminating in the first coordinated uprising (*intifada*), which began in December 1987 and would last for nearly four years. The Palestinians wanted the homeland of their ancestors, and over 200 million other Arabs agreed, including most Egyptians, and stood behind them—at least symbolically. Festering questions over Palestine, which U.S. officials lacked the wisdom, energy, and interest to address fully, did little to advance America's interests or even its image in the Muslim world. After spending billions of dollars and decades of effort, America emerged from the Camp David process as one of the most hated influences in the Middle East.

Egypt in the "War on Terror": Operational Necessity or Strategic Liability?

Because Egyptian President Hosni Mubarak was a long-time ally of the United States, Washington intensified its assistance to his regime after 9/11. Ironically, the Islamist radicalism Egypt's authoritarian government spawned may have negated the usefulness of its counterterrorism support. On September 15, 2001, President George W. Bush called for a full-scale covert attack on international terrorism. A major component of Bush's strategy used hundreds of millions of dollars to secure the cooperation of foreign intelligence services in Jordan, Algeria, and Egypt. The Central Intelligence Agency (CIA) provided these foreign operatives with training, new equipment, money for their agent networks, and whatever else they might need to triple or quadruple the CIA's resources.[42]

Another covert program, which began under the Bill Clinton administration and expanded dramatically after 9/11, was "extraordinary rendition." Rendition gave the U.S. government robust authority to track down terrorist suspects worldwide and then "snatch" those persons, either using foreign intelligence services or other paid assets, to render (transfer) them to countries where they were wanted for security or law enforcement proceedings. Egypt's ruthless dictatorship became a popular third-party state to send alleged terrorist suspects. Egypt's prime minister said the United States had transferred some 60 to 70 detainees to his country during just the first four years of the Bush administration.[43] "If you want a serious interrogation, you send a prisoner to Jordan," according to former CIA agent Robert Baer. "If you want them to be tortured, you send them to Syria. If you want someone to disappear—never to see them again—you send them to Egypt."[44]

Torture inside Egyptian detention facilities included, but was not limited to, water-boarding, electric shock, severe beatings, solitary confinement, sleep deprivation, sexual humiliation, and suspension from metal hooks.[45] Egypt's security services used techniques to extract information from suspects that would have been considered monstrously illegal if done on American soil. Much of that brutality predated the U.S.-led war on terror after 9/11, and U.S. officials certainly should have been aware of Cairo's unsavory record. In May 1996, the UN Committee against Torture issued a report summarizing a confidential inquiry carried out since November 1991, which concluded that "torture is systematically practiced by the Security Forces in Egypt, in particular by State Security Intelligence." Ron Suskind, a former *Wall Street Journal* reporter and winner of the Pulitzer Prize, told ABC News, "When we wanted someone to be tortured, we'd send him to Egypt to have them tortured." United Kingdom's director of Amnesty International, Kate Allen, stated in 2007, "We are now uncovering evidence of Egypt being a destination of choice for third-party or contracted out torture in the 'war on terror.'"[46] Yet a 2006 U.S. State Department memorandum called America's collaboration with Egypt on anti-terrorist measures "probably the most successful element of the relationship."[47]

Presumably, the United Nations Convention against Torture and Other Forms of Cruel, Inhuman, or Degrading Treatment, which Congress ratified in 1992, would have deemed the extraordinary rendition program in violation of U.S. criminal law, but it remains unclear whether the convention would have prohibited the rendering of persons seized outside the United States. Whatever one's attitude regarding the appropriate line between security and liberty, fundamental American principles would dictate that the means of achieving anti-terrorism goals should have been a prominent concern.[48] After all, the United States—the most outspoken advocate of accountability and the rule of law—was sending terrorist suspects to a country known for its deprivations of due process and use of torture.

Cooperation with Egypt may have been effective on tactical and operational grounds, but aligning more closely with Mubarak's regime ignored an important symptom of the systemic terrorist problem. In a broader context, the phenomenon of al Qaeda terrorism was a reaction to the region's Muslim tyrannies. Al Qaeda's training manual, "Military Studies in the Jihad against the Tyrants," includes references to the torture endured by Muslims at the hands of "apostate" rulers.[49] The issue was not just the grievance about the use of force by illegitimate rule, but illegitimate rule *and* its use to serve an infidel.

A recurring theme in the radical Islamist discourse was the widespread and systematic practice of torture by police and security services across the Middle East. Experts blame the torture at Egyptian detention facilities for turning run-of-the-mill Islamists into hard-core extremists.[50] That transformation remained true for several members of al Qaeda, including its long-time deputy commander Ayman al-Zawahri, who evolved from a relatively minor player in the Egyptian radical group al-Jihad after prolonged stays in Egyptian prisons into a prominent fanatic.[51] It is no coincidence that senior members of al Qaeda, including Sayf al-Adl, Mohammed Atef, Abu Ubaidah al-Banshiri, and Sheikh Saeed al-Masri, as well as Muhammed Atta, the tactical leader of the 9/11 plot, and four other 9/11 hijackers, were of Egyptian origin. According to Michael Scheuer, the former head of the CIA's Osama bin Laden unit, merely being behind bars makes one into a martyr.[52]

Torture and abuse wove a fabric of conflict between violent Islamic extremists and U.S.-allied Arab dictatorships. "Al Qaeda's beginnings trace back to the prisons of Egypt and Mubarak's persecution of the Muslim Brotherhood," said career Air Force interrogator Matthew Alexander, whose team achieved a series of intelligence breakthroughs in Iraq. He observed that Ibn al-Shaykh al-Libi, one victim of the CIA rendition program to Egypt, where he was then tortured by local interrogators, provided the false information that Saddam

Hussein was working with al Qaeda. And that lie "was cited as one of the primary reasons for going to war in Iraq."[53]

The sexual, cultural, and religious humiliation of torture imbues victims with an insatiable hunger to exact revenge as a legitimate response to Egypt's secular authoritarian dictatorship. That feature of U.S. cooperation carries long-term ramifications, as a report from the DoD's Defense Science Board acknowledged: "If it is one overarching goal they [Muslims] share, it is the overthrow of what Islamists call 'apostate' regimes: the tyrannies of Egypt, Saudi Arabia, Pakistan, Jordan and the Gulf States. . . . *Without the U.S. these regimes could not survive.*"[54]

That craving for vengeance cannot be understood apart from Washington's steadfast support for Cairo and other cooperative Muslim regimes. Americans remain a major target of international terrorism in part because terrorists from specific foreign countries perceive U.S. actions as brutalizing Muslims and, thus, come to deem American citizens as legitimate targets.[55] That anger does not legitimize attacks on innocent civilians, of course, but it does at least partly explain the underlying maniacal hatred. An important caveat is needed, however. The Muslim world is expansive, and, despite the mounting anger at Washington's foreign policies, radicals (especially those willing to resort to terrorism) constitute only a small part of that huge population. Thomas H. Kean, chairman of the 9/11 Commission, elaborated on that point in July 2004 before the House Committee on Government Reform's Subcommittee on National Security:

> The small number of Muslims who are committed to Osama bin Laden's version of Islam, we can't dissuade them. We've got to jail them or we've got to kill them. That's the bottom line. *But the large majority of Arabs and Muslims are opposed to violence, and with those people, we must encourage reform, freedom, democracy and perhaps, above everything else, opportunity.*[56]

While the majority of Muslims oppose violence, that means neither that the United States must encourage reform and democracy nor that it knows how to do so. A pious Muslim could conceivably view the concept of forgoing God's law for man's law as heretical.

Still, many Egyptians, like the majority of Muslims, strive earnestly for a better life. But under the rubric of cooperation and regional stability, Egypt continued its state-directed torture, daily misery, and systematic mistreatment, plaguing alleged terrorists and political dissidents alike.

An Ideological Affinity for Countering Islamists

Egypt's secular government had long suppressed the Muslim Brotherhood, an underground opposition movement formed in 1928 and dedicated to establishing a state run by Sharia or Islamic law.[57] To establish an Islamic state in Egypt, their grassroots strategy has been to Islamicize Egyptian society. Because the group also espouses strong anti-American rhetoric, Mubarak often brandished the Muslim Brotherhood to justify political repression. In this respect, despite Mubarak's secular leanings, he was not a force for moderation. Through a labyrinth of legal tactics and a series of sham elections, Mubarak's authoritarian grip marginalized progressive, secular opponents and moderate, reform-minded critics. Among Islamists, though, persecution built cohesion and organization. Over time, the Muslim Brotherhood and other reactionary elements emerged out of Egypt's broken political landscape as the strongest political movement.

Although the Egyptian constitution protects freedom of speech and of the press, Mubarak restricted those rights through numerous interlocking decrees. The country's long-standing Emergency Law (Law No. 162 of 1958, as amended), invoked after Sadat's assassination in October 1981, gave Cairo the authority to detain anyone for up to 45 days without charge, prohibit public demonstrations of five people or more, and limit the range of legitimate political activity. The Anti-Terrorism Law (Law No. 97 of 1992), which provided the legal basis for trials of civilians before military courts, augmented that earlier statute. Together, those measures greatly curtailed civil rights and expanded authoritarian power.[58]

Mubarak's regime often used the two laws in combination with provisions of the penal code, such as Article 80(D), which criminalized "harming Egypt's image"—a vague standard that let the regime censor newspapers, ban books, imprison journalists, and incarcerate citizens for their online writings. Cairo's official argument for these laws was preservation of the "national interest," and, on occasion, authorities could rightfully claim they were targeting violent Islamist extremists or other subversive elements. But more often than not, the "anti-terrorism" laws were used against peaceful critics of the establishment.

In September 2007, a judge sentenced four newspaper editors to prison on charges of defaming Mubarak and his son, Gamal. That same year, a court sentenced prominent blogger Abdel Kareem Nabil Soliman to four years in prison: three years for insulting Islam and one year for insulting Mubarak. In 2001, a court sentenced Egyptian author Salahuddin Muhsin to three years in prison with hard labor—later reduced to six months—after prosecutors deemed two of his books to be "offensive to Islam." Both books promoted secular thought, not anti-Muslim sentiments—other than the most intolerant versions of that religion.[59] American diplomats observed years later that the regime's political obstructionism included the "suppression of activists and demonstrators," "state-influenced media attacks on reform advocates," and "continuing arrests and harassment of opposition activists."[60]

Another feature of Mubarak's political repression was the thin façade of a multiparty system, a political feature not all that different from Saddam Hussein's Iraq or Bashar al-Assad's Syria. In Mubarak's case, it amounted to extreme authoritarianism without the extreme cult of personality. Egypt's National Democratic Party (NDP), a coalition of business and political elites loyal to Mubarak, used several formal and informal measures to ward off opposition. For instance, the Political Parties Committee, which was responsible for registering political parties and was dominated by the ruling NDP, had the broad authority to close party offices, seize their funds, and refuse to recognize a party altogether. Such sweeping powers made it nearly impossible to run for office as an independent, thereby forcing opposition parties to compete among themselves rather than for power.

A series of sham elections was also the norm. Mubarak officially served five consecutive six-year presidential terms, but he ran virtually unopposed for most of those electoral contests. For example, in a token effort at reform during the lead-up to the 2000 legislative elections, the government announced that the judiciary, rather than representatives of the executive branch, would supervise polling stations in order to prevent rigging. But in many cases, only NDP supporters were permitted to reach the polls.[61] There were numerous reports of state-directed violence, with plainclothes officers picking fights with citizens and throwing pepper sauce into peoples' eyes and security forces using tear gas and live ammunition to disperse frenzied crowds. All told, Egyptian security bore responsibility for approximately 80 percent of the more than five dozen killings and injuries during the 2000 elections.[62]

A further illustration of political repression occurred during the 2005 elections, before which President George W. Bush urged President Mubarak to "show the way toward democracy in the Middle East."[63] Mubarak did as asked, but the results were tailored to convince Washington why Cairo supposedly needed a dictator. He allowed just enough political openness for the Muslim Brotherhood to form the main opposition in parliament.[64] At the same time, the regime detained several high-profile, moderate judges who had spoken openly about election abuses committed by pro-government forces. The regime also imprisoned opposition leader Ayman Nour for having the temerity to run against Mubarak. As one prominent American commentator remarked in the pages of the *Washington Post*, Nour's arrest was intended to "eliminate all moderate opposition." Mubarak's objective was to "present the U.S. with a choice between continuing his rule—and the eventual succession of his son Gamal—and an Islamist fundamentalist movement."[65]

Even American diplomats later conceded that Mubarak was using the "implicit threat of the Muslim Brotherhood's rise" to "temper foreign pressure for more and faster democratic reforms."[66] Mubarak's use of the Brotherhood's rise as a pretext to crush dissent ironically played a significant role in the Brotherhood's eventual ascendance. In 2007 the government enacted a series of constitutional amendments, one of which banned any party with a religious orientation from registering to run for office. The amendment was aimed directly at the Brotherhood, but it had the unintended consequence of shifting the organization's internal balance of power: reformers were discredited and hard-liners gained clout.[67]

Many secular Egyptians blamed the Brotherhood for the subsequent Islamic revivalism that pulsated through mainstream Egyptian society: the promoting of head scarves and later face veils on women, the stifling of public debate, and a crackdown on alcohol consumption.[68] During the Mubarak years, the Brotherhood had some crucial advantages over secular opponents of the regime. For example, if secular dissidents held a meeting in a cafe, the place was shut down; "but the authorities could never go into mosques and shutter those," writes Middle East observer Scott Atran, "so the MB survived."[69] One Cairo-based American diplomat opined, "Mubarak had systematically and 'legally' eliminated virtually all political opposition, leaving only the MB standing."[70]

One of the leading justifications for Washington's tacit endorsement of Mubarak's authoritarianism rested on ideology. But America's unrelenting hostility toward Islamist forces such as the Brotherhood obscured the extent to which Mubarak's illiberal secularism penalized leftist and liberal opposition parties by closing their options for peaceful opposition.[71] Rather than acting as a force for moderation, Mubarak inadvertently strengthened the Islamists, allowing them to become the only well-organized and effective resistance to his rule.

U.S. Economic Assistance and the Limits of Influence

Preservation of Egyptian-Israeli peace stood as the strongest case for Washington's partnership with Mubarak. Indeed, it was the basis for over 30 years of continued U.S. military and economic assistance to Egypt. After Israel, Egypt was the second-largest recipient of U.S. military aid, roughly $1.5 billion annually since 1979. Additionally, USAID provided Egypt with $28.6 billion between 1975 and 2011, ostensibly to promote human rights and democratic institutions.[72]

American money bought mixed results. U.S. aid to Egypt did influence the policy of its government to some degree. Egypt withdrew from the pan-Arab nationalist confrontation against the Jewish state, maintained the blockade of Gaza, and helped U.S. efforts in Sudan, Syria, and elsewhere. However, Mubarak offered either the most minimal cooperation necessary to retain American aid or pursued policies that already aligned with Egypt's geopolitical interests. Within Egypt, despite the noble aims of USAID's heavily subsidized arrangements, foreign assistance enhanced the regime's capacity for political and economic repression.

In the decades following the U.S.-brokered 1978 Camp David Accord between Egypt and Israel, the absence of a major conventional land war in the Levant was a major development in the history of the modern Middle East. But many examples that have passed without comment in Washington undercut the glowing image of Mubarak as a dutiful ally of U.S. policy and a good neighbor to Israel.

That Mubarak and his cadre of military leaders viewed U.S. aid as "untouchable compensation for making peace with Israel," as explained in the U.S. State Department's internal records, is a telling description.[73] The implied threat underlying "untouchable compensation" exposes the artificiality of peace derived through bribes and coercion. In 2008, while the Egyptian army engaged in military exercises simulated against an "enemy" Israel—an event seldom discussed in Western media—U.S. officials in Cairo fretted over the "backward-looking nature of Egypt's military posture" and its focus on "force-on-force warfare with a premium on ground forces and armor."[74] Such comments, even narrowly interpreted, suggest a failure by leaders in Washington to seriously consider that Egypt's military leaders still view the Jewish state as an enemy.

Egypt's preoccupation with conventional warfare despite decades of peace is not the only example of its uncertain posture. One instructive example is Hala Mustapha, editor-in-chief of Egypt's *Democracy* magazine. Three months after President Barack Obama's June 2009 conciliatory speech to the Arab world in Cairo, Mustapha invited Israel's ambassador to Egypt to her office for a discussion about an upcoming Middle East peace conference. Although pursuing people-to-people contact would ostensibly be critical to promoting peace, Mustapha had to break the Egyptian Journalists' Syndicate's ban on contacts with Israeli diplomats with her invite. As punishment, the Mubarak government stationed security officials in Mustapha's office on a permanent basis and demanded she relinquish half the space the magazine occupied in the building. "The regime manages to keep this relationship on the official level," she said. "At the same time, for political reasons, the regime is not willing to defend the concept of peace."[75]

That official/unofficial, two-tiered quality at the heart of regional stability signifies how Cairo apparently cooperated with Washington while also stifling broader elements of lasting peace. The primary victim of Mubarak's betrayal of permanent peace was the full normalization of Egyptian-Israeli relations (e.g., expanded cultural relations, educational exchanges, tourism).[76] There is, after all, a reason why Israeli officials and analysts commonly describe their country's relations with Egypt as a "cold peace." A similar official/

unofficial pattern existed with U.S. aid meant to affect the conduct of Cairo vis-a-vis its support for specific Israeli interests. But dollars do not make ancient antagonisms disappear.

Take Hamas, a violent outgrowth of Egypt's Muslim Brotherhood that calls for the destruction of Israel. After Hamas won Palestinian Authority elections in January 2006, both Egypt and Israel had an interest in diplomatically and economically isolating the group. Yet in late 2007 Israeli authorities complained that goods were still being transferred by sea and above ground by weapons networks bribing Egyptian soldiers, and that Egypt was failing to effectively control the smuggling of arms and explosives in tunnels under its Rafah border crossing with the Gaza Strip. One theory, proffered by Israeli Security Agency Director Yuval Diskin, was that leaders in Cairo refused to crack down because they viewed Israel as a safety valve channeling extremists away from Egypt. Furthermore, according to U.S. officials, Egypt's Defense Ministry strongly resisted, and then finally relented to, a $23 million, U.S.-funded countersmuggling system on the Gaza-Egyptian border.[77] After the Israeli government sent a video to leaders in Washington showing Egyptian security officials helping Hamas smuggle weapons into Gaza, lawmakers on Capitol Hill threatened to withhold $100 million in military aid to Egypt. In response, Egyptian Foreign Minister Ahmed Aboul Gheit fumed about what he derisively called the "Israel lobby" and warned that Egypt would retaliate if Israel ever damaged its interests with Washington.[78]

Another demonstration of Egypt's conflicting behavior, especially since the Arab Spring, was its stance on Iran's Shiite Islamic Republic, which, along with Israel, was also long viewed as a threat to regional stability. However, in December 2009, when Ellen Tauscher, America's under secretary for arms control and international security, visited Israel to set the stage for an upcoming nuclear proliferation conference, her Israeli interlocutors lambasted her. What was the problem? Egypt's insistence on establishing a nuclear weapons free zone (NWFZ) in the Middle East, a posture designed purposely to divert attention away from Iran's nuclear program by linking it with Israel's. Israeli Deputy Director General for Strategic Affairs Alon Bar, when describing Egypt's "obsession" over the NWFZ, argued that Egyptian officials were using Israel's nuclear program as a "wedge issue" to prevent better relations between Israel and its neighbors. According to U.S. diplomats, Deputy Director General of the Israel Atomic Energy Commission David Danieli concurred, arguing that Egypt was trying to put Israel "in a corner."[79]

Interestingly enough, U.S. leaders persistently evaded these realities by continually framing the U.S.-Egypt alliance as essential and, therefore, beyond scrutiny. But a failure to take such obstacles to lasting peace seriously allowed them to fester. At the heart of the matter, many Egyptians resolutely opposed Mubarak and his coterie on important regional questions. Most damaging were feelings of considerable responsibility for the suffering of the Palestinian people and the Egyptian leadership's subordination to American will regarding Gaza. For many Arabs, such a meaningful, value-laden, identity-based policy resonated far more than the receipt of American aid money—which most Egyptians were never beneficiaries of in the first place. As a result, U.S. aid bought Mubarak's cooperation at the expense of placing him in a precarious position. Maintaining peaceful relations with Israel ensured a continued flow of U.S. aid, while perfunctory, pro-Palestinian and other pan-Arab nationalist gestures allegedly mollified popular resentments. But by rebuffing domestic popular sentiment and pursuing unpopular regional policies, Mubarak provoked bouts of vitriolic protests that threatened his regime's survival and damaged relations with America and Israel.[80]

One striking example was Israel's reoccupation of the West Bank in March 2002, which prompted massive anti-Israeli and anti-American demonstrations across Egypt.[81] Conveying the resonance of pro-Palestinian solidarity, protesters circulated postcards that read, "Boycott them" next to logos of American companies. Some included a picture of a martyred Palestinian child with the words, "Their weapon is resistance and ours is boycott. Boycott is our weapon against America that butchers us."[82] To appease his disgruntled public, the following month Mubarak announced that his government would suspend all relations with Israel, excluding political ties, and he subsequently withdrew Egypt's ambassador.[83]

Another acrimonious episode occurred in July 2006 when Lebanese Shiite political party-cum-terrorist group—and Iranian and Syrian proxy—Hezbollah kidnapped two Israeli soldiers. Thousands of demonstrators gathered in Cairo to condemn the Israeli campaign against Lebanon and criticize their own government's lack of response to the crisis. The protesters waved Lebanese and Hezbollah flags, carried portraits of Hezbollah leader Hassan Nasrallah, held photos of wounded Lebanese civilians, and chanted "Down, down, Hosni Mubarak" and "Down with the U.S.-Israeli terrorist alliance." Local U.S. Embassy staff reported that the Muslim Brotherhood was well represented at the demonstrations. Highlighting the gulf between the Arab street and the consensus in Washington, President Bush pressed Mubarak to side with the United States against Hezbollah. Rather than offer tacit obedience or grumbling reluctance, Mubarak waited for the crisis to subside. While other examples of Egyptian agitation included reaction to Mubarak's anti-smuggling efforts and the 2009 Gaza war, which aimed at ending rocket attacks into Israel, such protests were so common that examples can be chosen virtually at random.[84]

U.S. aid not only encouraged the Egyptian government's unfaithfulness to its people but in some cases perversely incentivized failure to further the cause of peace with Israel. Such was the case for Egypt in its constructive, yet also detrimental, role as a primary intermediary in the peace process between Israel and the Palestinian Authority. In a 2010 meeting with then U.S. Foreign Relations Committee chairman John Kerry (D-MA), Egyptian Prime Minster Hamad bin Jassim Al-Thani admitted candidly that Egypt had a vested interest in dragging out talks, given that its sole utility to the United States was brokering peace. He said, equating the situation to a doctor with only one patient to treat, "the physician is going to keep the patient alive but in the hospital for as long as possible." To add insult to injury, he candidly stated that the Egyptian "people blame America" for the lack of progress on Palestinian reconciliation.[85]

By promoting stalemate during arbitration and diplomatic bargaining on such a sensitive issue, Egyptian leaders repeatedly helped contribute to the deteriorating regional situation and helped heighten hostility among Arabs toward the Jewish state. That behavior hardly warranted a U.S. vote of confidence in Egypt's willingness to promote peace.

Up in Arms: The Politicization of Aid

Beyond the policy of providing financial aid and military hardware to Mubarak, American leaders argued for strengthened ties between the two countries' militaries. U.S. planes enjoyed access to

381

Egyptian airspace and U.S. Navy warships received expedited processing through the Suez Canal. According to former secretary of state Hillary Rodham Clinton, during Egypt's Arab Spring uprising cooperation with the Egyptian military also produced more subtle and pervasive benefits. Having "trained a generation of Egyptian officers," she argued, "we saw them refusing to fire on their own people under tremendous pressure."[86]

U.S. military assistance and training certainly bolstered America's negotiating leverage with the regime, but there were still limits to how far that could go. President Obama inadvertently explained the more persistent problem in his June 2009 speech in Cairo: "No system of government can or should be imposed upon one nation by another."[87] It is startling how a country like the United States, whose leaders and citizens demand control of their political destiny, either failed to fully grasp or were all too willing to dismiss how military assistance and training can stifle a foreign population's ability to remove an unjust regime. Aside from whether close military ties to a dictatorship advanced important U.S. interests, such generosity contradicted America's broader commitment to advance democratic self-government abroad.

More than half of the estimated $60 billion in U.S. military and economic assistance to Egypt has been in the form of grants and loans for the purchase of military hardware and services from American defense manufacturers. Excluding economic and development assistance, Washington gave the Mubarak government $1.3 billion a year in military aid since 1987. Most of that aid, namely grants and loans, came through Foreign Military Financing (FMF).[88] Under FMF, U.S. arms manufacturers contracted with the Defense Department to provide Egypt with weapons systems and services, upgrades, and follow-up maintenance. Items included M1A1 Abrams battle tanks, armored personnel carriers and self-propelled guns, Apache helicopters, and F-4 and F-16 fighter jets. Although such weaponry is distinct from the crowd-control devices commonly used against student disturbances and worker demonstrations, according to Ahmad Al-Sayed El-Naggar, editor-in-chief of *The Economic Strategy Trends Report* published by the Al-Ahram Center for Political and Strategic Studies in Egypt, "aid is devoted mainly to strengthening the regime's domestic security and its ability to confront popular movements."[89] The Congressional Research Service estimated that U.S.

military aid during the Mubarak years covered as much as 80 percent of the Egyptian Defense Ministry's weapons procurement costs. One expert adds, "there's never been any civilian oversight in how the Egyptian military was acquiring weaponry from the U.S. or anybody else for that matter."[90]

Training operations, as well as the transfers of military hardware, helped foster interoperability of U.S. and Egyptian forces for U.S. Central Command. U.S. taxpayers also facilitated the coproduction of both the M1A1 and the M1A2 Abrams tank. Some parts were made in Egypt, while others were produced in America and then shipped to Egypt for final assembly. The main contractor, General Dynamics, which had a major facility in Michigan, was among the many defense companies and consulting firms involved in deals related to Egypt. Other firms with plants in key political locales included Lockheed Martin in Texas and Florida, US Motor Works in California and Texas, and Boeing in Arizona and Missouri.[91] That economic and political presence helped entrench U.S. military cooperation with Mubarak's regime. U.S. taxpayers also paid for other forms of assistance, such as a community policing training program and U.S. sponsored anti-terrorism classes for Egypt's Central Security Services. Furthermore, Egypt's State Security Investigative Service (SSIS) maintained strong ties with the FBI and received training at the FBI Academy in Quantico, Virginia.[92]

Unfortunately, Washington's training efforts failed to draw a sharp boundary between accommodation and direct complicity in the ruthless behavior of Egypt's law enforcement and state security forces. According to the State Department, the Egyptian Interior Ministry used SSIS to "monitor and sometimes infiltrate the political opposition and civil society" and to "suppress political opposition through arrests, harassment and intimidation."[93] It also employed "methods such as stripping and blindfolding victims; suspending victims by the wrists and ankles in contorted positions or from a ceiling or door frame with feet just touching the floor; beating victims with fists, whips, metal rods, or other objects; using electric shocks; dousing victims with cold water; sleep deprivation; and sexual abuse, including sodomy." Police brutality was so "routine and pervasive" that local embassy sources estimated there were literally hundreds of torture incidents every day in Cairo police stations alone.[94] As U.S. Ambassador to Egypt Margaret Scobey wrote, the government of

Egypt has yet to make "a serious effort to transform the police from an instrument of regime power into a public service institution."[95]

None of the aforementioned evidence insinuates the U.S. government explicitly trained Egyptian security agents to brutalize Egyptian citizens. Indeed, the official rationale for the training was to transfer American ideals of respect for human rights. But simultaneously extolling a repressive regime as "a steadfast ally in the GWOT" (global war on terrorism) and America's "strong law enforcement cooperation with the State Security Investigative Service (SSIS)" is incriminating, no matter the aims.[96]

U.S. aid also deprived Egyptians of control over their destiny by economically empowering the government and security apparatus over the rest of society. The enrichment of kleptocrats divorces the rulers from the people. Scholar Paul Amar observes how U.S. assistance bought off Egypt's generals, shaping them "into an incredibly organized interest group of nationalist businessmen." Egypt's military, run by retired generals, commands an array of commercial enterprises and industries such as water, olive oil, cement, construction, hospitality, and gasoline.[97] As the late economist Peter T. Bauer once observed about foreign aid and economic development: "since official wealth transfers go to governments and not to the people at large, they promote the disastrous politicization of life in the Third World."[98]

Egypt is a powerful example of that politicization, given how the military has staunchly opposed economic reforms, both under Mubarak and since his removal from office. Indeed, reform efforts would jeopardize the government's lucrative economic position within society. Elites who run the military's vast business and commercial empire neither pay taxes nor have to deal with red tape; many have converted public land into gated communities and a network of exclusive luxury resorts. As U.S. diplomats concede, "We see the military's role in the economy as a force that generally stifles free-market reform by increasing direct government involvement in the markets."[99]

The counternarrative to the Arab Spring, representing the dawn of a new era of secular democracy and human rights, was that it instead underscored the extent of political and economic failure. Decades of retrograde agricultural policies from Nasser's Arab socialism, such as land collectivization, turned the ancient world's breadbasket into the modern world's top importer of wheat. It installed economically retarding subsidies, concentrated capital in the hands of kleptocrats, and led to a genuine collapse in agricultural production. Egypt's malnourished population was fertile ground for rebellion. And amid the Arab world's myriad revolts, U.S. policymakers reacted so haphazardly because they often misinterpreted the causes.

U.S. officials sidestep those uncomfortable truths by pointing to other wealth transfer programs intended to foster Egypt's democratic institutions. Between 1975 and 2010, USAID provided Egypt with nearly $30 billion. But independent civic groups and nongovernmental organizations (NGOs) found themselves left out of the loop because the vast majority of funds went directly to government-to-government projects. As an October 2009 inspector general audit of USAID's efforts concluded:

> The impact of USAID/Egypt's democracy and governance activities has been limited based on the programs reviewed. In published reports, independent nongovernmental organizations ranked Egypt unfavorably in indexes of media freedom, corruption, civil liberties, political rights, and democracy. . . . the impact of USAID/Egypt's democracy and governance programs was unnoticeable in indexes describing the country's democratic environment.[100]

Some experts argued for USAID to decrease its support for the Egyptian government and increase its support for civil society. [101] But as USAID discovered between fiscal years 1999 and 2009, after spending $24 million to promote democracy and good governance by directly funding NGOs, such efforts had limited impact. Cairo showed "reluctance to support many of USAID's democracy and governance programs" and "impeded implementers' activities."[102]

The Mubarak regime's obstructionism seemed clear. First, as with any regime, Mubarak's top priority was to remain in power. Without meaningful pressures to reform, he was unwilling to oblige calls for change from Washington or any other source, despite his regime's manifest inability to deal with the country's innumerable challenges: stark social inequality, endemic corruption, labor unrest, and the realignment of institutional forces within civil society. Ironically, U.S.

aid probably helped keep incompetent and unaccountable leaders at the helm.

The U.S.-Egypt alliance during the Mubarak years underscored two recurring themes: American ungainliness as an empire and the corrupting power of foreign-aid money on recipient countries. Aid bought compliance, not allegiance. The concept of "aid" premised on helping another country develop encourages bribery without the effectiveness. In old-fashioned geopolitics, bribes were the carrot offered to prospective puppet rulers. The stick was the explicit or implicit threat of replacement by force. With Egypt under Mubarak, however, Washington channeled tens of billions of dollars to a semi-compliant puppet it was unwilling to treat as disposable.

Second, far from being cooperative, any regime concerned for its survival—particularly an authoritarian one—would deem talk of reform (or political linkage or conditioning of assistance on reform) as a worrisome, perhaps fatal, intrusion into its domestic affairs. At one point, the Mubarak regime sternly enjoined the United States to stop financing organizations that were "not properly registered" with the Egyptian government, and the interim military regime that replaced Mubarak in 2011 even detained foreign NGO workers.[103] Mubarak and other U.S.-backed Arab allies did not view U.S.-desired reforms in the Middle East as promotions of peace and order, but as incredibly destabilizing.

"We have heard him lament the results of earlier U.S. efforts to encourage reform in the Islamic world," Ambassador Scobey wrote in a May 2009 memorandum about Mubarak to officials in Washington. "Wherever he has seen these U.S. efforts, he can point to the chaos and loss of stability that ensued."[104] Although Mubarak had no love for a regional rival like Saddam Hussein, he nevertheless consistently railed against President Bush's decision to invade Iraq, contending that it facilitated increased Iranian influence across the region. Mubarak's antipathy toward past U.S. initiatives was so profound that Scobey wrote in an earlier memorandum, "The Egyptians have lost confidence in U.S. regional leadership."[105]

Although U.S. officials had been calling for reform in Egypt for decades, a confluence of material interests—from sustaining close ties with the Egyptian military to U.S. congressional districts with a stake in Egypt's continued defense procurement—typically won out. Even U.S. government audits and observations that contradicted the conventional wisdom were deemed irrelevant to changes in policy. Yet it was always a curious belief that aid money channeled to a government that had a vested interest in the status quo would somehow enhance reform. Egyptians who had to live under the cruelty and mistreatment of dictatorship could no longer wait for genuine change from without. It would have to come from within.

The Road to Revolution

When asked in a March 2009 interview with Arabic-language news channel Al-Arabiya if there was any connection between President Mubarak's then upcoming visit to Washington and a U.S. State Department report criticizing his government's human rights record, Secretary of State Clinton replied: "It is not in any way connected. We look forward to President Mubarak coming as soon as his schedule would permit. I had a wonderful time with him this morning. I really consider President and Mrs. Mubarak to be friends of my family."[106] That candid admission reveals why U.S. policymakers struggle to criticize an ostensibly friendly dictatorship. They forget, or choose to ignore, that the "friends" who seem so pleasant at dinner parties in Washington are the same tyrants responsible for inflicting atrocities on their subjects at home. The incentive to retain Mubarak as an ally explained Washington's tendency to tolerate his abuses, a disposition that did not impress political dissidents like Ayman Nour, the secular and liberal-minded opposition figure imprisoned after daring to run for president against Mubarak in 2005.

Languishing in a jail cell in southern Cairo, Nour wrote to then secretary of state Condoleezza Rice. In his letter, he includes a poignant quote from popular Egyptian author Mostafa Amin:

> The American loves speed, and that is the secret behind the alliance between American policy and dictatorships, but what it gains quickly, it loses quicker. . . . Maybe America gains a lot when it exports to us arms and cars or planes, but it loses more when it does not export the best that its civilization has produced, which is "Freedom and Democracy and Human Rights." The value of America is that it should defend this product, not only in its country but throughout the world! It

> may harm some of its interests, but it will make gains
> that will live hundreds of years, for the friendship of
> peoples live forever.[107]

Many U.S. officials, however, regarded Mubarak as an "ally," a "force of stability," and ultimately, a "friend."[108] Quite naturally, when the 2011 Arab Spring eventually blossomed, U.S. officials were torn between fidelity to America's liberal values by supporting the popular uprising for freedom and siding with a loyal despot. The Egyptian Arab Spring's chaotic early months certainly gave its revolution a liberal appearance, but the aftermath soon dashed hopes for a new, liberal political system. The Muslim Brotherhood and other Islamists were the best-organized component of the opposition to Mubarak's rule, and their agenda was anything but liberal. And although Egypt's military hierarchy staunchly opposed the Islamists, it also had little enthusiasm for the emergence of democracy and liberalism.

When Tunisian President Zine El Abidine Ben Ali fled his country on January 14, 2011, after 23 years of one-party rule, it suggested to other Arab publics that their tyrants could fall just as quickly through popular demonstrations. For Egypt in particular, one important stimulus was the Internet-coordinated, Facebook-driven mobilization inspired by the brutal murder of Khaled Said. In June 2010 plainclothes security agents in Alexandria beat Said to death after he refused to show his identity card upon entering an Internet cafe. In his memory, political activists organized a "Day of Rage" on January 25, Egypt's official "Police Day" celebration, to protest the government's appalling violence. Three days later, the "Friday of Rage," Egyptians marched from their mosques after Friday prayers to the central squares. To the surprise of organizers, the protest drew tens of thousands to Tahrir ("Liberation") Square, the symbolic heart of downtown Cairo.

As protests spread to Alexandria, Suez, Mansoura, Luxor, and other cities, the government shut down the Internet, cut off mobile telephone service, and jammed television signals, except for state-run channels. In response to the frenzy directed against a besieged ally, Secretary Clinton urged "all parties [to] exercise restraint and refrain from violence."[109] As protesters hurled bottles and rocks at security forces firing water cannons and teargas bearing the label

"Made in the USA," Vice President Joe Biden explained to PBS *News-Hour's* Jim Lehrer why he could not refer to Mubarak as a dictator. According to Biden, Egypt's cooperation on key U.S. foreign policy issues made Mubarak an "ally."[110]

Washington's response to the country's unfolding political turmoil laid bare the U.S. government's strategic thinking. It feared the loss of one of its most coveted geostrategic assets in the region and a severe blow to American influence with other Arab allies, such as the monarchs of Jordan, Saudi Arabia, and the Gulf Arab sheikhdoms. President Obama urged "an orderly transition to a government that is responsive to the aspirations of the Egyptian people," but the administration showed its cards early in the face of the rapidly deteriorating crisis. Despite calibrated, and occasionally haphazard, diplomatic responses to the course of events, Secretary Clinton publicly announced there was "no discussion as of this time about cutting off any aid."[111] The die of political change in Egypt, however, was already cast.

On February 11, following 18 consecutive days of nationwide protests, President Mubarak resigned, handed power to the Supreme Council of the Egyptian Armed Forces, and appointed as his successor Vice President Omar Suleiman, the chief of the Egyptian intelligence service who had worked closely with the CIA in the rendition and torture program. Mubarak left behind more than a political structure molded in his image. Successor regimes revealed their inability to break free from the repressive features of military rule, nor could they tame decades of deeply entrenched anti-U.S. and anti-Israeli sentiments among the Egyptian public. That August, with the military in charge, protesters in Cairo stormed the Israeli Embassy, forcing Israel's ambassador, his family, and other officials to flee the country. The following month, Egypt's first democratically elected head of state, Mohamed Morsi, a Muslim Brotherhood politician and the movement's point of contact for Hamas prior to coming to power, waited two days before taking action or even saying anything after Egyptian protesters scaled the U.S. embassy walls in central Cairo and tried to rip down the American flag.

In assessing the full extent of Egypt's revolution-in-progress, the United States was reluctant to lose a pillar of its regional alliance system—a fact not lost on average Egyptians. An April 2011 poll released by Pew Global Attitudes Project, the first taken after

Mubarak's downfall, found that 79 percent of Egyptians held an unfavorable opinion of the United States.[112] Such visceral attitudes, though, are not static. They remain sensitive to changes in policies, such as efforts by the United States to promote its stated values. For instance, when President Bush condemned the Egyptian government's use of violence against protesters in late May 2005, every major regional Arab media outlet ran the news as a lead story in celebration of the statement. The same happened when Secretary Rice canceled a meeting with Egyptian officials over the arrest of a liberal politician.[113] But as Jordanian columnist Fahid al-Fanik wrote, "The fault is not in the principles that America calls for but rather in the American practices that contradict them." Indeed, for more than 30 years, Egyptians witnessed the United States stand by a tyrannical regime and tacitly endorse its agenda of repression.[114]

A Troubled Democratic Interlude and the Rise of the el-Sisi Dictatorship

Washington's reaction to Mohamed Morsi's election and performance as president did not indicate any fundamental change in U.S. attitudes. That point became all too apparent in early July 2013 when the disgruntled Egyptian military ousted Morsi, the country's first democratically elected president, after barely one year in office. The Obama administration's response was ambivalent, at best. The coup was a crucial test of whether Washington's professed commitment to the Arab Spring and democracy was genuine. Developments on that score were not encouraging. Indeed, they seemed to validate many of the cynical accusations long made by anti-American groups throughout the Middle East.

Morsi's supporters, both in Egypt and other Arab countries, were convinced that U.S. officials knew about the impending coup. Many even seemed to believe that those officials actually encouraged the military to take action.[115] There is little credible evidence to support even the former allegation, much less the latter one, but Washington's extensive ties with the Egyptian military since the early 1980s understandably fed suspicions that the United States was something more than an innocent spectator.

It was clear that U.S. policymakers were not pleased with Morsi's election, much less with the Islamist agenda that his government seemed intent on pursuing. To leaders in Washington, Morsi was the spearhead of a Muslim Brotherhood regime intent on imposing Sharia law and systematically undermining secular values and institutions. Key opinion groups in the United States also fretted that, sooner or later, Cairo would reignite tensions with Israel, perhaps even repudiate the Camp David Accords, despite Morsi's emphatic denials of such intent.[116] Washington may not have prodded the Egyptian generals to remove Morsi, but U.S. leaders shed few tears at his fall from power.

The Obama administration's statements and actions after the coup fostered further suspicions and cynicism. Indeed, the White House refused to call the coup a "coup."[117] But if a military assault removing an elected president from power is not a coup, then the term has no meaning. The administration's refusal to acknowledge an obvious reality came across as both cowardly and deceitful. President Obama and his advisers, though, had a strong (albeit cynical) reason for declining to label Morsi's ouster as a coup. Using that term would create an obligation under U.S. law to terminate all aid to a military that removed a duly elected leader. Washington did not want to take that step with respect to Egypt, fearing that it would further destabilize the most populous country in the Arab world. Perhaps equally pertinent, suspending aid would reduce whatever leverage the United States might have with the new military regime.

Nevertheless it would have been an honorable act for the United States to cut off aid to the Egyptian military. American taxpayers have been saddled far too long with subsidizing a notoriously corrupt, autocratic institution. But that aspect, while important, is not the main reason to terminate aid. Not only were the Egyptian people watching Washington's response, so were populations throughout the Middle East and beyond. The new crisis and the U.S. reaction to it begged the question: Does the United States truly want a democratic Middle East, or do American policymakers favor democracy only when voters in a country choose leaders that Washington likes?

Many of the values that Morsi and the Muslim Brotherhood represent are repugnant to most Americans—and to people elsewhere who embrace secularism and individual liberty. But he and his colleagues were chosen in free and fair elections. It would be easier for U.S. officials, of course, if Egyptian and other Middle Eastern voters favored secular, democratic, pro-Western candidates. In a few areas, most notably Iraqi Kurdistan, that appears to be the case. Unfortunately, in most of the Middle East, voters tend to endorse more conservative, religious parties. The question remains whether Washington will respect their decisions if they run counter to U.S. wishes—and, sometimes, U.S. interests. The Obama administration's behavior following the coup against Morsi and the rise of a new military dictator, General Abdel Fattah el-Sisi, strongly indicated that U.S. leaders were not willing to accord such respect.

As expected, when the Egyptian generals finally held a new presidential election (after months of a bloody crackdown on Morsi supporters), that election confirmed el-Sisi as the country's new leader. It was not exactly the model of a free and fair election, though. Not only had el-Sisi, as the leader of the coup that ousted Morsi, been Egypt's de facto ruler for months, but his military colleagues (and their weaponry) were firmly behind his presidential candidacy. Security forces had killed nearly a thousand Muslim Brotherhood members—Morsi's political base—and jailed thousands of others, including Morsi himself. Subservient Egyptian judicial tribunals imposed death sentences on hundreds of regime opponents, following trials that did not meet even the most meager standards of due process, in just the two months immediately before the election.[118]

Western observers, including Cato Institute senior fellow Doug Bandow, who traveled to Egypt, noted the pervasive censorship throughout the period leading up to the election. Government-run media outlets maintained a steady barrage of images vilifying Morsi and hailing el-Sisi as the savior of the nation. The images in the so-called private outlets (the ones that the junta had not shut down) provided images and editorial commentary nearly indistinguishable from the official government publications.[119]

Under such circumstances, the outcome was as predictable as the sham elections that Mubarak routinely "won" by large margins. It also was disturbingly similar to the Crimean "referendum" that ratified Russia's takeover of that territory a short time before the Egyptian balloting. El-Sisi won with more than 96 percent of the vote. The only flaw in that orchestrated farce was a low voter turnout, the one permissible way people had to protest Egypt's slide back into dictatorship. But while the Obama administration repeatedly and harshly criticized the electoral charade that had taken place just weeks earlier in Crimea, U.S. officials portrayed the Egyptian election as modest progress toward democracy.[120] There was a time when U.S. leaders routinely castigated bogus elections in communist countries that produced wildly lopsided majorities for the incumbent regime. No such criticism was forthcoming in this case, just as Washington didn't denounce the earlier balloting for the new Egyptian constitution, drafted by the military's handpicked "representatives," that produced a 98 percent favorable vote.

The Obama administration's hypocrisy is certain to deepen the already alarming cynicism throughout the Muslim world about U.S. policy. One need not show enthusiasm for Morsi and the Muslim Brotherhood, who embodied ugly theocratic values and practices. But basic decency, as well as prudence regarding the state of popular opinion in the Muslim world, should have dictated a policy of U.S. neutrality regarding Egypt's political convulsions. Instead, Washington moved quickly to embrace the new "friendly tyrant," just as a succession of administrations had embraced Hosni Mubarak for three decades. Washington even agreed to deliver 10 Apache attack helicopters to Cairo.[121] Repressive regimes have never been reluctant to use such high-tech aircraft to intimidate or slaughter anti-regime forces. It was inappropriate for the Obama administration to approve such a delivery to the Egyptian junta, and one can anticipate the anti-U.S. reaction of el-Sisi's opponents if they see those aircraft flying over Tahrir Square the next time there are anti-government demonstrations.

U.S. officials may engage in an abundance of wishful thinking or outright sophistry, but the evidence confirms that el-Sisi intends to be as much a dictator as Mubarak ever was.[122] Not only has he created a cult of personality typical of Third World tyrants, replete with giant photographs of the supreme leader posted throughout urban areas, but he shows a pettiness that may even exceed Mubarak's. As the *New York Times* reported, el-Sisi promised to remedy Egypt's fuel shortages by installing energy-efficient light bulbs in every home, even if he has to send a government employee to carry out each installation.[123] "I'm not leaving a chance for people to act on their own," el-Sisi stated in a television interview. "My program will be mandatory." Yet this is the ruler that Washington has embraced as a new strategic and political partner.[124]

Conclusion

For decades the United States defended cooperation with Egypt's dictators on strategic, ideological, and economic grounds. But the assistance supported by a generation of U.S. officials ultimately rested on problematic premises. The consequences of collaboration matter at least as much as the justifications, and they should have undergone proper scrutiny. There is little evidence that such scrutiny ever took place.

Beyond the effect on Israel, the U.S. relationship with Egypt has other important geostrategic aspects. Keeping open the Suez Canal is important to America and its allies, and Egypt is a crucial Arab power with influence throughout the region. Incorporating Egypt into America's global counterterrorism strategy helped eliminate hundreds of suspected terrorists. But as a long-standing prop to an authoritarian government, Washington also created a deep reservoir of antagonism from which al Qaeda–style terrorism emerged. Moreover, Washington forfeited its claim to moral authority through its complicity with the crimes of torturers. That many experts and officials in Washington were slow to recognize the revulsion such actions inspire around the world, and especially across the Middle East, merits serious reflection.

With respect to ideology, Washington and Cairo shared an affinity for restraining the ascendance of Egypt's deeply conservative Islamist forces at odds with their mutual interests. Unfortunately, Egypt's repression marginalized moderate, reform-minded critics and progressive, secular opponents of the regime. As a result, Islamists filled the political void that enabled their social—and ultimately, their political—agenda to flourish.

On the economic level, three decades of continued U.S. military aid shored up a "cold peace" between Egypt and Israel, with Egypt at times undermining the necessary dialogue and outreach for substantive normalized relations. Part of the problem was legitimacy. Sadat, Mubarak, and their military successors drew their authority from policy planners in Washington and not from their own people. Anger toward U.S.-sanctioned policies could not be ignored indefinitely, and constant domestic upheaval should have called into question the long-term viability of the most populous Arab country's geopolitical orientation. Finally, with respect to economic aid as a tool for reforming Egypt's decrepit economic and political institutions, the key challenge was not the lack of external assistance, but the absence of meaningful pressure on the regime to reform. Thirty years of unstinting cooperation diminished incentives for change while simultaneously aggrandizing the power of a harsh dictatorship.

Officials in Washington implicitly ignored the flagrant hypocrisy at the heart of U.S. policy regarding Egypt. They routinely proclaimed their commitment to human rights, but their conduct often contradicted those values. Although the United States had no writ to impose its liberal ethos on Egypt, it was definitely not duty-bound to support the tyrants who oppressed their own people. We made that error far too often during the Cold War, and it appears that some policymakers have learned nothing from that experience. The embrace of el-Sisi indicates a continuation of a thoroughly amoral, if not immoral, policy toward Egypt.

13. From "Golden Chain" to Arab Spring: The Sordid Tale of U.S.-Saudi Relations

One of the strongest beliefs about American foreign policy in the Middle East has been that policymakers base most political engagements and military interventions upon the geostrategic value of oil. Former Federal Reserve Chairman Alan Greenspan caught flack when he said of the 2003 U.S.-led invasion of Iraq, "I am saddened that it is politically inconvenient to acknowledge what everyone knows: the Iraq war is largely about oil."[1] James A. Baker, secretary of state in George H. W. Bush's administration, went further. He argued in the context of longtime U.S. ally, the Kingdom of Saudi Arabia: "I worked for four administrations under three presidents. And in every one of those, our policy was that we would go to war to protect the energy reserves in the Persian Gulf."[2] That "oil-for-security" thesis not only diverged from well-known facts about contemporary energy markets but also overlooked the unforeseen consequences from an alliance in need of reexamination.

"It's been a huge recruiting device for al Qaeda," former deputy secretary of defense Paul Wolfowitz said of the 12-year U.S. troop presence at Prince Sultan Air Base in Riyadh, Saudi Arabia. That base served as Washington's command-and-control center for aerial patrols of Iraqi airspace, the so-called "no-fly zone," following the Persian Gulf War (1990–1991). "In fact if you look at [Osama] bin Laden, one of his principal grievances was the presence of so-called crusader forces on the holy land, Mecca and Medina."[3]

As Wolfowitz explains above, Osama bin Laden, who had emerged from the dark recesses of Afghanistan's decade-long rebellion against its Soviet occupation (1979–1989), turned his focus westward, invoking the presence of U.S. troops on holy soil to rally war-hardened militants to attack U.S. allies and interests across the globe. But often unmentioned in discussions of U.S.-Saudi relations was his movement's web of support from private Saudi donors, financial facilitators, and Saudi-based charitable foundations. That funding system, collectively called the "Golden Chain," overlapped with the Saudi monarchy's multidecade campaign to spread its ultra-conservative brand of Sunni Islam, called Wahhabism in the West and Salafism by its followers. Once confined to the Arabian Peninsula, Salafism gained significant influence in all countries with large Muslim populations, where its unique interpretation of Islam promoted some of the most oppressive social restrictions and metamorphosed alongside other rigid Islamist doctrines to become the ideological source of Salafi extremism exemplified by al Qaeda ("the base") and the Islamic State of Iraq and Syria (ISIS).

Reams of documentation from U.S. government investigations, previously classified documents from George Washington University's National Security Archive, and first-hand accounts from former U.S. national security and intelligence officials show that the United States government suffered massive policy and intelligence failures in the years, months, and even days leading up to 9/11: egregious aviation security lapses, communication breakdowns between the Federal Bureau of Investigation (FBI) and the Central Intelligence Agency (CIA), and a reluctance among cabinet-level U.S. officials, collectively known as "the Principals," to pressure their counterparts in the kingdom about Saudi charitable assistance and terrorist financing. Revelations about 9/11's perpetrators jolted the U.S.-Saudi alliance: 15 of the 19 hijackers were Saudi nationals; their murderous conspiracy was assisted by an exile of one of the kingdom's most powerful and wealthiest families; and private Saudi support helped sustain much of the terrorist activity that led up to and followed the 9/11 attacks.

Following the 2003 Iraq War, the 2011 Arab Spring, and the 2013 consolidation of ISIS, when the Arab Sunni kingdom feared encirclement from Persian Shiite Iran and its allies, Saudi-inspired and funded Salafists blossomed across North Africa and the Middle East. They acquired Saudi weapons and support in Iraq, Lebanon, and Syria; formed factions and political parties in Bahrain, Kuwait, Algeria, Libya, and Yemen; and won pluralities in post-revolutionary elections held in Tunisia, Morocco, and Egypt. Washington's long-standing, oil-rich ally made Salafism and its reactionary worldviews far broader than either bin Laden or the violent religious nationalism he spawned.

Issues surrounding the U.S.-Saudi alliance and the unintended byproducts of that association warrant considerable attention, especially given the consequences to the United States. Those consequences include the blood and treasure expended to fight terrorism, the fractious domestic political debates that Washington's anti-terrorism policies have generated, the scope of U.S. government surveillance in the struggle against terrorism, and the troubling short-term distraction of the Middle East from longer-term great-power politics. The American people—a major target of international terrorism—deserve to know the truth about the U.S.-Saudi alliance. Indeed, misguided policies and costly intractable wars partly reflect a public too ill-equipped to refute the misinformation given to them by officials vested in continuing the Middle East status quo. Until the public fully understands the U.S.-Saudi partnership, it will fail to comprehend the unexpected dangers that come from that alliance, which has enjoyed decades of Washington's political validation and military protection.

The Golden Chain

As a 2006 U.S. State Department report to Congress concluded, "Saudi donors and unregulated charities have been a major source of financing to extremist and terrorist groups over the past 25 years."[4] How those donors and charities grew to become the leading source of terrorist financing relates directly to the oil-rich kingdom's centrality in the Islamic world.

As the "Custodian of the Two Holy Mosques" in Mecca and Medina, the holiest sites in Islam, the kingdom holds tremendous sway over the global community of Muslims (*umma*). For decades, its religious scholars and conservative citizens devoted themselves to exporting their country's puritanical Salafist movement within Sunni Islam. During the Cold War, Riyadh founded and partially funded transnational charities that spread its austere religiosity and promoted pan-Islamism against pan-Arab nationalists in Egypt, Iraq, and Syria, and later, revolutionary Islamists in Libya, Iran, and at home. As noted in chapter 5, Saudi-based charities, including the Muslim World League (1962), the World Assembly of Muslim Youth (1972), the International Islamic Relief Organization (1979), and many others, underwrote the building of mosques, religious schools, medical facilities, potable water systems, and other social projects and programs to educate poor orphans and feed hungry refugees.

From Angola to Nicaragua, and most notably, Afghanistan—a longtime target of Saudi-Salafist proselytizing and the country from which the 9/11 attacks were planned—Riyadh's charitable activities often overlapped U.S.-Saudi policies that backed anti-communist insurgencies. From 1979 to 1989, under Operation Cyclone, the CIA—alongside the external spy agencies of Saudi Arabia's General Intelligence Directorate (GID) and Pakistan's Inter-Services Intelligence Directorate (ISI)—armed, trained, and financed Afghanistan's most radical guerilla commanders to ensnare the large ground combat forces of the Soviet Union. The conflict's most infamous religious volunteers from the Arab world, the "Arab Afghans," included Palestinian militant and Muslim Brotherhood scholar Abdullah Azzam—who established the seemingly innocuous Mekhtab al Khidemat (the "Services Office") in 1984, the precursor to al Qaeda—and Saudi national and religious philanthropist Osama bin Laden—who between 1980 and 1983 distributed cash donations to anti-Soviet rebels.[5] Azzam reportedly exposed bin Laden to the concept of transnational jihad, which insisted that all Muslims had a religious obligation to expel unbelievers from Muslim lands.[6] Accordingly, bin Laden, who later formed a committee within the Services Office promoting media and education, used graphic depictions and video imagery in charity marketing to promote the Afghan rebels and deify innocent orphans.[7]

Director of the GID General Prince Turki al'Faisal and longtime Saudi ambassador to America Prince Bandar bin Sultan claimed their government had little direct contact with bin Laden during this period. However, compelling evidence suggests more routine interaction.[8] Ahmed Badeeb, bin Laden's former high school teacher and Turki's former chief of staff, claimed bin Laden "had a strong relation with the Saudi intelligence and with our embassy in Pakistan."[9] During the war's early years, according to bin Laden's former friend, Jamal Khashoggi, GID supported "the military part," while private religious philanthropists would "support the humanitarian and relief work."[10]

Among a hoard of al Qaeda documents discovered in Bosnia after 9/11, a 1988 memorandum identified wealthy and influential Saudi families, financial backers, and one former Saudi government minister as early supporters of bin Laden—the "Golden Chain," as his movement called it.[11] Private donations for the purchase of medicine and food blended with funds to buy Kalashnikovs and rocket-propelled grenades. The Saudi government collected charitable giving required of all observant Muslims (*zakat*)—one of Islam's five pillars—and used a portion of the donations for charities to build religious schools and mosques around the world. Some charities wittingly helped bin Laden. Sympathetic facilitators infiltrated other organizations covertly, using mosque and civic-center charity boxes to mask the transfer of funds.[12] Human couriers also moved cash within and across borders and relied on a system of paperless funds (*hawala*) similar to Western Union.[13] As Azzam said before his death in 1989, the year the Soviets withdrew in defeat from Afghanistan, "Saudi [Arabia] is the only country which stood by the Afghani jihad as a government and peope."[14] However, another war in the Muslim world soon turned the Arab Afghans and their Saudi benefactors into mortal enemies.

On August 2, 1990, Iraq invaded Kuwait. Saudi Arabia, on Iraq's southern border, lay militarily vulnerable despite having spent billions on sophisticated American weaponry and equipment.[15] Bin Laden offered to save the cradle of Islam, laying out his plan in a 60-page paper offering to recruit and lead his guerilla-trained jihadist veterans against Saddam Hussein.[16] Instead, based upon a religious edict (fatwa) from the Council of Senior Ulema, a select group of some 20 scholars of Islamic law appointed by the monarch, within a matter of days Saudi Arabia's King Fahd bin Abdulaziz Al Saud welcomed the offer of protection from U.S. President George H. W. Bush, who then dispatched 2,300 U.S. paratroopers to the Arabian Peninsula under Operation Desert Shield.[17]

The following month, Secretary of Defense Dick Cheney claimed before the Senate Armed Services Committee that Iraq would control about 20 percent of the world's known oil reserves by conquering Kuwait. That position would give Saddam Hussein "a position to be able to dictate the future of worldwide energy policy" and a "stranglehold on our economy and on that of most other nations of the world."[18]

Secretary Cheney furnished no evidence to support his claim about Iraq's prospective domination of "worldwide energy policy." Uncertainty over the erratic dictator's intentions did loom large, but the commitment to combat was divorced from the fundamental realities of international commodity markets. Indeed, the United States acquires energy resources from many places, including its own hemisphere, because market forces, rather than a specific supplier, determine the supply of oil.[19] Other oil producers could have replaced the lost oil capacity even if a major long-term disruption occurred—a nightmare scenario that was unlikely.[20] Another fear, as President Bush wrote in his diary on August 2 about his reason for scrambling U.S. fighter squadrons to the Gulf, was "that the Kuwaiti puppet government set up by Iraq would try to move billions of dollars out of Western banks and out of U.S. banks illegally."[21]

Saddam, a demonic figure renowned for his ruthlessness, presumably had few incentives to stifle the availability of oil, particularly if self-enrichment motivated his pillaging. His country's bloody eight-year war against Iran—despite varying degrees of support to him from Washington and Riyadh—ended in 1988 with a stalemate and left Iraq depleted.[22] Some critics later claimed that the Bush administration misrepresented the threat by vastly overestimating the number of Iraqi troops poised on Saudi Arabia's borders: not 547,000 troops, as originally claimed, but barely one-third of that, about 183,000.[23] President Bush had also equated Saddam to Adolf Hitler, casting him as the archvillain in a millenarian dichotomy between "good and evil."[24] In any event, international sanctions and diplomatic efforts failed to remove Iraqi forces from Kuwait, and in January 1991 the U.S. Senate authorized a more robust military deployment under Operation Desert Storm. That month, when President Bush announced in a televised address that the United States and a coalition of 34 countries, including Arab states, had begun air attacks against Iraqi forces, Bush castigated the dictator: "Saddam Hussein systematically raped, pillaged, and plundered a tiny nation."[25]

A week after the U.S.-led coalition completed its rout of Iraqi forces on February 28, President Bush asserted that America's motives were altruism and the mediation of international conflict.[26] Before a joint session of Congress, he declared that America's intervention in the conflict would usher "the very real prospect of a new world order . . . A world where the United Nations, freed from cold war stalemate, is poised to fulfill the historic vision of its founders."[27]

America's Founders had elaborated a different, and far more humble and pragmatic, philosophy—one that cautioned against foreign entanglements. Conversely, Bush asserted that the continued triumph of global economic and political freedom in the post-Soviet age depended on U.S. global leadership to enforce nonaggression and international law. Most important, in a line of thought that led many U.S. leaders to conflate America's strategic and moral interests, Bush clearly implied that stamping out a recalcitrant thug such as Saddam through United Nations (UN) multilateralism demonstrated the value of alliances and the benefits of U.S. dominance and credibility. To some in Saudi Arabia, however, Washington harbored malicious motives.

The arrival of more than 500,000 U.S. soldiers, sailors, and airmen on Saudi soil provoked tremendous discontent in the most closed of Arab societies. The liberation of Kuwait indicated how U.S.-led intervention in the Middle East could promote democracy, and the kingdom's liberal-leaning business elites, journalists, women, and university professors called for political reforms.[28] But in some circles, the U.S. troop presence on Muslim holy land also triggered religious fervor, political resistance, social panic, and rabid patriotism. To bin Laden and other Saudi Islamists, the calls for liberal reform confirmed their suspicions that the U.S.-Saudi alliance—and King Fahd's invitation to foreign, predominately Christian, troops to save the holiest sites in Islam—would lead to mass secularization and corrupt their society's Islamic principles.[29] Humiliated and outraged over Fahd's refusal to accept his rebellious legions, bin Laden left Saudi Arabia for Sudan in May 1991.

Many observers have come to identify the Persian Gulf War (1990–1991) as bin Laden's impetus to attack American interests. But it was the Afghan-Soviet War's preexisting financial and logistical network of private donors and charities that enabled bin Laden to launch his strikes against the Saudi regime, autocratic Arab rulers, and the West. "Financial jihad," as bin Laden later wrote, "likewise, is an obligation."[30]

In the years to come, bin Laden's name appeared on cassette tapes and jihadi promotional material in disparate locations: Eritrea, Kashmir, the Balkans, and the Philippines. Bin Laden paired his philanthropy with guerilla violence around the world by funding local Islamic insurgencies. Even before he left Afghanistan for Saudi Arabia in the late 1980s, he had trained and housed rebels fighting South Yemen's communist government.[31]

By May 1991, according to a report later recovered from its Illinois office, the Saudi relief organization Benevolence International

Foundation (BIF) had started services in Sudan. Around that same that time, bin Laden's movement also began training the Sudanese militia, Popular Defense Force, in guerilla war tactics against Sudanese Christians and animists.[32] The BIF's two closely linked, but separately incorporated, entities aided the Bosnian army and its irregular warfare unit, the Black Swans.[33] The U.S. Treasury Department would later designate BIF a racketeering enterprise supporting al Qaeda.[34] The movement's wealthy Saudi founder also extended moral support to independent acts of anti-American terror.

In February 1993 terrorists linked to bin Laden attacked the North Tower of the World Trade Center in New York City, killing six people and injuring more than a thousand. The following year, when the Saudi government revoked bin Laden's Saudi citizenship, bin Laden was financing rebels from a half-dozen countries at terrorist training camps in northern Sudan.[35] He praised Saudi pro-Hezbollah operatives who, in November 1995, detonated a car bomb that killed five Americans at the Saudi National Guard training center in Riyadh—the location from which more than one hundred U.S. Air Force fighter aircraft patrolled Iraq's southern no-fly zone under Operation Southern Watch. He also commended the June 1996 Khobar Towers bombing that killed 19 U.S. Air Force servicemen and injured more than three hundred others.[36]

Despite the terrorist financier's string of attacks and global reach, U.S. leaders only began paying serious attention to al Qaeda after January 1996. President Bill Clinton's National Security Advisor Tony Lake and National Coordinator for Security and Counterterrorism Richard Clarke pushed to create a special unit within the CIA's Counterterrorism Center to track bin Laden and his terrorist financing. Yet few policymakers or intelligence analysts truly understood radical Islam and the international scope of bin Laden's activities. Far fewer could exercise the necessary influence to pressure Riyadh to help bring bin Laden to justice.

Pre-9/11 Intelligence

Throughout the 1990s, the Principals, those cabinet-level U.S. officials charged with formulating high-level policies with the kingdom, were disinclined to ask too much from their Saudi counterparts about retarding extremism or terrorist financing. Meanwhile, bureaucratic turf wars within and among the Federal Bureau of Investigation, the Central Intelligence Agency, and other departments led the U.S. government's national security complex to miss preparations for the deadliest terror attacks on American soil.

Sudan, under heavy U.S. diplomatic pressure, expelled bin Laden in May 1996. The terrorist financier revitalized his Golden Chain funding stream after he, his militia, and their families fled to Afghanistan. That July, the U.S. Embassy in neighboring Pakistan reported the "existence of religious madrassas and other institutions, including youth training camps which could be spawning terrorism." It continued, "The most recent indications are that institutions of this nature are funded from Saudi Arabia."[37] U.S. intelligence had also uncovered links between the Saudi-based charity Al Haramain Islamic Foundation (HIF) and support for militant Islamist activity in Chechnya, Azerbaijan, the Balkans, and al Qaeda more generally.[38] As one of the most prominent al Qaeda–linked Saudi charities, which former U.S. officials described as the "United Way" of the kingdom, at one point it raised $40 to $50 million a year in contributions.[39]

As Saudi charities underwrote the building of thousands of mosques, missions, and branch offices in 50 countries across Africa, Asia, Europe, and North America, U.S. troops in the region remained forward deployed in Saudi Arabia, Kuwait, Bahrain, Diego Garcia, and Turkey, among other locations. In response, bin Laden's philosophy evolved. He began framing the stationing of U.S. troops in Saudi Arabia within the broader picture of U.S. military intervention and political interference across the Islamic world.[40] In his August 1996 fatwa, "Declaration of War against the Americans Occupying the Land of the Two Holy Places," he demanded the United States "desist from aggressive intervention against Muslims in the whole world" and exhorted the violent overthrow of Arab police states and corrupt Muslim tyrannies such as those in Morocco, Jordan, Egypt, Saudi Arabia, and other countries that were complicit in America's crimes.[41] Bin Laden deemed them un-Islamic, and hence, apostate.[42]

"A man with human feelings in his heart does not distinguish between a child killed in Palestine or Lebanon, in Iraq or in Bosnia," bin Laden told CNN in 1997. "So how can we believe your claims that you came to save our children in Somalia while you kill our children in all of those places?"[43] Bin Laden had taken to citing the more than "600,000 Iraqi children" killed, he claimed, by the U.S.-

led no-fly zone mission to control Iraqi airspace and the economic sanctions pushed by Washington.[44] While those measures certainly took a toll on innocent children, competing evidence also points to Saddam's diversion of $2 billion in humanitarian aid for the killing of Iraqi civilians. Regardless, bin Laden invoked the grievances perpetrated against innocent Muslims to exploit concepts of human rights and other basic values to delegitimize American policies. To bin Laden and his followers, the trail of civilian deaths that Washington's policies left in their wake vindicated the killing of American civilians. Even though the Quran explicitly forbids the taking of innocent lives and the murder of women and children, the American people, bin Laden claimed, "are not exonerated from responsibility" because they choose their government "despite their knowledge of its crimes."[45]

The punishments bin Laden wanted for America's crimes steadily expanded. By late February 1998, Ayman al-Zawahiri, the former head of Egyptian Islamic Jihad, the militant group that assassinated Anwar Al-Sadat, joined his militant forces with bin Laden's under the banner International Islamic Front for Jihad on the Jews and Crusaders.[46] The movement, as it subsequently became known—al Qaeda—exhorted all Muslims to attack U.S. military and civilian targets anywhere in the world. It also talked ominously about "bringing the war home to America."[47] That May, bin Laden boasted, "I am confident that Muslims will be able to end the legend of the so-called superpower that is America."[48] Having observed America's ignominious departure from Lebanon in 1983 after Hezbollah bombed the U.S. Embassy and Marine barracks and its departure again from Somalia in 1993 after militants thought to be trained by bin Laden killed 18 U.S. servicemen, bin Laden saw America, as he said in May 1998 to ABC News, as being casualty averse—"just a paper tiger."[49]

Bin Laden effectively stood U.S. grand strategy on its head, turning U.S. foreign policy into a threat to U.S. national security. As opposed to a conventional war fought for limited aims, bin Laden's Salafi-inspired religious nationalism remained ostensibly a defensive war fought for unlimited aims. That was a critical point, and one not appreciated nearly enough. His zealotry and reactionary worldview, cited plentifully in the militant Islamist literature, seemed unstable: it went from evicting U.S. troops from Saudi Arabia to expelling U.S. troops from the entire region and stopping U.S. interference against all Muslims to calling for America's collapse. Even if Washington complied with al Qaeda's demands, bin Laden likely would have found other justifications for violence.

Regional experts, retired diplomats, military and intelligence officials, and investigative reporters analyzed those and other perceived injustices before, and especially after, 9/11. Like Cold War–era Kremlinology, their findings examine enemy doctrine, including the enemy's grotesque justifications for violence. Beneath such aims and depredations lie motives for understanding what specific interests and assets an enemy seeks to target. They can reveal secretive processes and indirect clues and point to approaches required among diplomatic, economic, military, and intelligence tools. In this case, such research contributed to a richer understanding of the iconic figure who possessed an exceptional ability to recruit from all over the world and attract millions of sympathizers to his violent extremism.

That inspiration and the ideology's ever-expanding transformation occurred as American leaders diverged over how much priority the cooperation with Saudi Arabia on counterterrorism should have over other mutual interests.

The Principals

As early as 1996, FBI Counterterrorism Chief John O'Neill believed bin Laden and al Qaeda threatened America's security. He also believed that powerful figures in the Saudi kingdom had close ties to bin Laden. Yet, according to O'Neill, America's dependence on Saudi oil seemingly gave the kingdom more leverage on Washington than Washington had on Riyadh.[50] American lawmakers had expressed similar concerns over Riyadh's financial power as early as 1979 and again in 1985 when U.S. Treasury officials refused to publicly divulge how much the Saudis held in U.S. securities. Critics feared those investments would give Saudi Arabia undue influence over U.S. foreign policy and erode America's political and economic independence.[51] That erosion may have occurred, but in less conspicuous ways.

In Washington, the most senior-level cabinet officials—a committee of the secretaries of state and defense, the director of the CIA, the chairman of the joint chiefs (and, under President Bush, often the vice president)—formulated U.S. policy toward Saudi Arabia. Collectively called "the Principals," many of those leaders formed close personal friendships with high-ranking Saudi leaders and members of the royal family. For example, former president George W. Bush recounted in his memoirs a 2002 meeting with Crown Prince Abdullah bin Abdulaziz Al Saud in Crawford, Texas. "The next day," wrote Bush, "I got a call from Mom and Dad. The crown prince had stopped in Houston to visit them."[52] Such casual interactions carried over into intelligence and diplomacy. In the late 1990s, CIA Director George Tenet reportedly traveled once a month from the CIA headquarters in Virginia to the nearby McLean home of Prince Bandar, the longtime Saudi ambassador to America.[53]

On the one hand, such personal relations can protect and advance America's official diplomatic partnerships by helping officials curry favor with powerful, well-connected foreign leaders in times of crisis or on matters of extraordinary importance. On the other hand, such cliquish insularity has the potential to discourage officials and policymakers from acknowledging certain realities. According to investigations by the 2004 National Commission on Terrorist Attacks upon the United States (the 9/11 Commission), lower-level U.S. officials with knowledge of private Saudi terrorist financing had no interaction with the Saudis. Higher-level U.S. officials who did, however, acceded to the strong Saudi preference to bypass the U.S. bureaucracy and "did not push the issue of terrorist financing because their concerns were different."[54] By 1997, the CIA analytical unit charged with monitoring bin Laden and al Qaeda issued a memorandum to CIA Director Tenet identifying Saudi intelligence as a "hostile service": the CIA term used to describe such entities as Cuban and Iranian intelligence.[55]

Perhaps out of a seeming reluctance to impute guilt, officials with greater influence failed to press their Saudi counterparts for more cooperation on terrorist financing. That reluctance could not have occurred at a more critical time. In early 1998, CIA surveillance and National Security Agency (NSA) eavesdropping revealed that bin Laden spent much of his time at Tarnak Farms, a compound in Kandahar, southern Afghanistan. Some in the agency developed a plan to capture bin Laden, while others proposed an immediate cruise missile strike. Tenet and Clarke, among others, objected and deemed the plans too risky. After canceling the operation, and underscoring the leverage of personal ties, Director Tenet flew to Saudi Arabia that May to seek Riyadh's help to capture bin Laden.[56]

Unfortunately, on that occasion, personal familiarity apparently failed to bear fruit. That June, Prince Turki met in Kandahar with Taliban spiritual leader Mullah Muhammad Omar. Allegedly, they agreed to explore ways to formally hand over bin Laden, and as down payment for the arrangement, the kingdom sent the Taliban 400 pick-up trucks and material assistance.[57] But on August 7, 1998, three months after Director Tenet's trip to Saudi Arabia, al Qaeda–rigged truck bombs blew up the U.S. Embassies in Kenya and Tanzania within five minutes of each other. The attack, eight years to the day after U.S. troop deployments to Saudi Arabia, killed 224 people and wounded more than 4,600 others.[58]

By the late 1990s and early 2000s, U.S. officials seemed to react to the repeated al Qaeda threats and attacks in a similar fashion: unsurprised, given existing intelligence, yet seemingly hapless and confused over how and when to respond. After the U.S. embassy attacks, President Clinton slapped sanctions on bin Laden and his organization and approved an order to launch cruise missile strikes against targets in Afghanistan and Sudan. The strikes hit largely abandoned camps, making it look, as Clinton's successor later wrote, "impotent and ineffectual."[59] To his credit, Clinton later claimed he inquired about a commando raid on al Qaeda training operations in Afghanistan, but senior U.S. military leaders recommended against it "perhaps because of Somalia."[60] That policy paralysis happened again in October 2000 after al Qaeda's attack on the USS *Cole*, which killed 17 American sailors in Yemen. Between a Special Forces operation shelved by the Pentagon and a bombing campaign of Afghanistan called off at the last minute due to unreliable intelligence, the White House, in the end, did nothing.[61]

According to Ahmad Zaidan, the Pakistan bureau chief for Al Jazeera television who interviewed bin Laden twice before 9/11, bin Laden wanted the USS *Cole* bombing to drag the Americans into Afghanistan and have fellow Muslims fight them as they did in Somalia and against the Soviets.[62] It is believed that Zawahiri, bin Laden's deputy, encouraged bin Laden to divert al Qaeda's emphasis from the "near enemy"—apostate Muslim states and societies—to the "distant enemy"—the United States and its Western allies.[63] In a policy developed before 9/11 and expounded upon thereafter, al

Qaeda now viewed its terrorism as a calculated maneuver to elicit U.S. and Western reprisals in Arab and Muslim lands, ensnaring them in protracted ground campaigns to the point of financial insolvency. Bin Laden envisioned a protracted ground campaign in the Afghan mountains. Rather than repelling U.S. troops, bin Laden's strategy welcomed them.

Another astonishing aspect of pre-9/11 Washington was the intra-agency turf wars that hamstrung America's intelligence bureaucracy over suspected Saudi terrorist assistance and financing. By nearly all accounts, problems at the FBI were particularly disturbing. Counterterrorism czar Richard Clarke described the efforts of more than 50 FBI field offices before 9/11 as "extremely poor and not coordinated," and former National Security Council official Paul Kurtz described his dealings with the pre-9/11 FBI as "totally infuriating."[64]

In the mid-1990s, the FBI reportedly declined 14,000 pages of documents from defecting Saudi diplomat Mohammed al-Khilewi that allegedly showed the Saudi regime's official support for terrorism.[65] In 2000, two years after FBI field offices had learned that a large number of Arabs were attending American flight schools, an al Qaeda recruit in New York who got cold feet told the FBI he was recruited to hijack passenger planes. Although he passed two lie detector tests, the FBI returned him to England.[66] Most infamously, Mawaf al-Hazmi and Khalid al-Mihdhar, two future 9/11 hijackers, had close and repeated contact with an FBI counterterrorist informant but nothing came of it.[67]

Another problem, as with the Principals, was conflicting objectives. After 9/11, a U.S. Department of Justice (DOJ) investigation of the FBI discovered that, by early 2000, FBI headquarters made counterterrorism the bureau's top concern: however, the FBI field office in San Diego, California, where Saudi Arabian national Omar al-Bayoumi had spent a "significant amount of time" with the two hijackers mentioned above, continued to pursue drug trafficking as its top concern.[68]

One FBI source opined that Bayoumi, an active member of San Diego's Muslim community, "must be an agent of a foreign power or an agent of Saudi Arabia." Regardless of the accuracy of that suspicion, an FBI case agent told the DOJ's Inspector General that "Saudi Arabia was not listed as a threat country and the Saudis were considered allies of the United States."[69] Most significant, a squad supervisor also told the DOJ's Inspector General that "before September 11, the Saudi Arabian government was considered an ally of the United States and that a report of an individual being an agent of the Saudi government would not have been considered a priority."[70] By this time, the CIA's bin Laden unit had already deemed Saudi intelligence "hostile."[71]

That discrepancy between the FBI and the CIA represented yet another problem with the passing of critical information. In the months leading up to the October 2000 USS *Cole* bombing, the perpetrators met in Kuala Lumpur, Malaysia. Among them were the two 9/11 hijackers. Although the FBI, according to the DOJ investigation, had several opportunities to uncover information on the plotters, the CIA, which had worked with the Malaysian authorities, did not share that information with the FBI.[72] Among its many findings, the DOJ investigation found "systemic problems" within the FBI and between the FBI and the CIA with the "gathering or passing of information" about the two 9/11 hijackers mentioned above.[73] From Kuala Lumpur the two aspiring hijackers flew first to Los Angeles then to San Diego. As 9/11 Commission member Senator Bob Kerrey (D-NE) revealed later during the commission's hearings, one of the biggest mistakes made after 1998 was "allowing al Qaeda to come inside the United States. . . . We continued to allow them to come to the United States."[74] Indeed, before 9/11, al Qaeda operatives traveled to Florida, Georgia, California, Arizona, and Virginia. Ostensibly, the U.S. State Department could have put the bombers' names on a terrorist watch list to stop them from entering the United States, but it was kept in the dark until August 24, 2001—less than three weeks before the 9/11 attacks and after the hijackers had already entered America.[75]

The ineffective handling of pre-9/11 intelligence called into question the strength of America's byzantine intelligence system. Michael Scheuer, with the CIA from 1982 to 2004 and the head of the CIA's bin Laden unit from 1996 to 1999, argued that leaders executing policy had underestimated al Qaeda and missed multiple opportunities to strike at bin Laden. Some setbacks involved political choices unrelated to the intelligence analytical process. For instance, in 1996, Sudan reportedly offered to arrest bin Laden and hand him to the Saudis, but the Saudis balked. U.S. diplomats privy to the details of the arrangement believed that other priorities dominated the U.S.-

Saudi alliance, including Washington's reliance on Saudi territory to patrol Iraq, and thus, "the White House did not press the Saudis very hard."[76]

Moreover, some Principals lacked focus on al Qaeda, a point confirmed in counterterrorism czar Richard Clarke's January 2001 memorandum that pleaded to incoming National Security Advisor Condoleezza Rice: "We *urgently* need such a Principals level review on the *al Qida* network."[77] Other times, the Principals spurned intelligence or claimed it offered no immediate action, such as the infamous August 2001 President's Daily Brief, "Bin Laden Determined the Strike in US." That brief dismissed outright al Qaeda's intent to hijack U.S. aircraft, calling it "the more sensational threat reporting."[78]

Despite many attempts to pin the blame for the events that were to follow on craven politicians or inept bureaucrats, the fact remains that policy planners, law enforcement authorities, and intelligence officials at every level of the U.S. government failed the American people. A month before the infamous brief, Attorney General John Ashcroft snapped at FBI acting Director Thomas Pickard: "I don't want to hear about al Qaeda anymore."[79] That snap had followed repeated FBI attempts to get Ashcroft's attention on al Qaeda. But in a truly mystifying development, a month later the Justice Department told the media that Ashcroft would be flying exclusively by leased jet aircraft, not commercial, because of a "threat assessment" from the FBI.[80] Neither the FBI nor the Justice Department identified the threat, and left Americans—the primary targets of al Qaeda terrorism—in the dark.

The Post-9/11 Decade

The government often conceals information it thinks may harm U.S. national security. But more often than not, as in the case with 9/11, the government suppresses information it deems potentially embarrassing or incompatible with existing grand strategy. After 9/11, U.S. officials found it politically convenient to conceal disturbing details about private Saudi donors and semiofficial charities that funded bin Laden. America's closest Arab ally had failed to stop the propagation of Salafism and indirect funding of terrorists, much less kill or capture bin Laden before the largest enemy attack on American soil. Past Saudi behavior, and Washington's previous failures, were downplayed and suppressed.

Critics have extensively covered the joint meeting between President Bush and Prince Bandar at the White House on the evening of September 13, 2001,[81] and the permission by a senior U.S. official to allow more than 140 Saudis residing in the United States, including bin Laden family members, to fly on chartered jets and commercial planes immediately following the federal government's grounding of all private flights after 9/11.[82] Points made about those events are valid, but all have been aired before. Far less discussed were the findings of a December 2002 Joint Inquiry by the U.S. Senate and House Intelligence Committees.[83]

Most revealing about the 832-page Joint Inquiry into the U.S. intelligence community's activities before and after 9/11 was what it failed to disclose. The Bush administration redacted virtually an entire 28-page section detailing the role of foreign governments in aiding the 9/11 hijackers. According to one official who read the censored section, it described "very direct, very specific links" between Saudi officials and two of the 9/11 hijackers, links that "cannot be passed off as rogue, isolated or coincidental."[84] Citing a CIA memorandum, the Joint Inquiry referred to "incontrovertible evidence that there is support for these terrorists" from a foreign government; congressional sources said the reference was to Saudi Arabia.[85] Former Florida governor and retired U.S. senator Bob Graham cochaired the Joint Inquiry and claimed unambiguously that the redacted section specified Saudi government assistance to the 9/11 terrorists.[86] "By 'the Saudis,'" Graham later asserted, "I mean the Saudi government and individual Saudis who are for some purposes dependent on the government—which includes all of the elite in the country."[87]

Prince Bandar said before 9/11, "If U.S. security authorities had engaged their Saudi counterparts in a serious and credible manner, in my opinion, we would have avoided what happened."[88] Historical evidence indicates otherwise. "Before 9/11," claimed one CIA source, "the Saudis gave us almost nothing on al Qaeda."[89] Case in point: before 9/11, the CIA asked the Saudis for copies of bin Laden's passport, bank records, and birth certificate. The CIA had still not received the documents after 9/11.[90] Another case was the June 1998 meeting in Kandahar between Prince Turki and the Taliban's Mullah Omar after CIA Director Tenet's visit to the kingdom. Former

Taliban intelligence chief Mohammed Khaksar claimed that, instead of an arrangement to hand over bin Laden, bin Laden agreed not to attack Saudi targets in return for the Saudi government's willingness to provide funds and material assistance to the Taliban—not a demand for bin Laden's extradition or pressure for the closure of al Qaeda training camps.[91]

Yet another case in point: Jordanian intelligence officials who toured Saudi military and security facilities before 9/11 reportedly saw a number of Osama bin Laden screensavers on the office computers of Saudi officials.[92] Indeed, as one CIA source stated after seeing documents and computer files seized from bin Laden operatives, "al Qaeda had the run of Saudi Arabia."[93]

To some observers, Saudi laxity resembled complicity. Bin Laden may have denounced the royal family as an agent of the "Zionist-Crusader alliance" and invoked the liberation of Mecca and Medina from the corrupt hands of the Al Saud family, but decrying the family's self-indulgence as profoundly un-Islamic tells us little about how strongly the Saudis were committed to countering extremists or about the incentives that drove their objectives.

Presumably, private Saudi citizens who knowingly funded al Qaeda sympathized with its cause and remained ideologically committed to bin Laden's worldview. A more charitable explanation, though no less damning, was that Saudis aided al Qaeda in order to inoculate the kingdom from its terrorism. A senior Kuwaiti official would later confirm to America's ambassador in Riyadh about Saudi Defense Minister Prince Sultan bin Abdulaziz Al Saud and Interior Minister Prince Nayef bin Abdulaziz Al Saud, "both had accommodated extremists, in order to keep peace."[94] (Interestingly, in the 1970s the CIA gave Prince Nayef a new desk, which he later discovered contained a listening device.[95]) Similarly, in his 2002 book, *Does America Need a Foreign Policy?* Henry Kissinger said the kingdom "made a tacit bargain with terrorists, so long as terrorist actions were not directed against the host government."[96]

Personal accounts of those connected to bin Laden and his organization also cast doubt on Al Saud claims of financial and emotional distance from bin Laden after his exile from the kingdom. Carmen bin Laden, once married to Osama's half-brother Yeslam, wrote that during the period after bin Laden fled from Sudan to Afghanistan that "Osama, [Yeslam] said, was under the protection of conservative members of the Saudi royal family."[97] In another account, before pleading guilty in 2012 of disclosing classified information, John Kiriakou, the former CIA chief of counterterrorist operations in Pakistan who played a leading role in the 2002 capture of one of bin Laden's top lieutenants, claims he and his CIA colleagues had known for years that elements of Al Saud were funding al Qaeda.[98] Even chief Saudi spokesman and future Saudi Ambassador to Washington Adel Al-Jubeir said that, among the thousands of members of the royal family, a government investigation had uncovered "wrongdoing by some."[99]

The Saudis appeared to try to correct that wrongdoing by getting serious about fighting extremism, especially after al Qaeda's May 2003 attack in Riyadh that killed 36 people and wounded more than 160 others. The government fired 2,000 mosque leaders for voicing support for terrorism, killed hundreds of others, and arrested thousands more. The Ministry of Islamic Affairs issued circulars to clerics and imams encouraging them to reject bigotry in their sermons.[100] Saudi leaders had their work cut out for them. In the immediate aftermath of 9/11, nearly 80 percent of mosques in Saudi Arabia voiced support for bin Laden.[101] And in late 2001, the largest contingent of "enemy combatants" captured by U.S. forces in Afghanistan was Saudi.[102] Even the most well-intentioned government-led campaign to eradicate domestic extremism and redefine Salafism could seemingly be a multigenerational effort.

In Washington, a few observers, mainly neoconservative commentators, made their case against the kingdom in the court of public opinion. *Weekly Standard* editor William Kristol called for deposing the Saudi royal family. In a paper for the Pentagon's Office of Net Assessment, an independent consultant advocated an invasion to secure the kingdom's oil fields. And in a brief to the Defense Policy Board on U.S. policy toward Saudi Arabia, a Rand Corporation analyst proposed targeting the kingdom's oil resources, financial assets, and the holy places of Mecca and Medina.[103] U.S. officials had thought through such issues before during the 1973–1974 OPEC oil embargo, but nothing came of those grandiose plans.[104] In the end, Kristol and other like-minded pundits moved on to mobilize public opinion for war against Iraq's secular dictator, whom the U.S. had fought to keep Iraqi troops off the kingdom's doorstep in the early 1990s.

As the old adage goes, the cover-up can be worse than the crime. After three main justifications for invading Iraq later proved categorically false—Iraq had weapons of mass destruction, Iraq was behind 9/11, and Iraq would welcome foreigners as liberators—White House efforts to focus on Iraq and overlook the kingdom became the subject of widespread speculation.[105] Twenty-one year CIA veteran Robert Baer argued in his 2004 book, *Sleeping with the Devil: How Washington Sold Our Soul for Saudi Crude,* that Washington's cozy ties with Riyadh created a "consent of silence" over the Saudi funding chain for al Qaeda and other violent extremists.[106]

"Consent" indeed. U.S. officials had stated repeatedly that Americans and the world must never forget the terrorist attacks on 9/11. Yet, senior American leaders primarily responsible for shaping U.S. policy toward the kingdom routinely gave their Saudi counterparts the benefit of the doubt—either explaining away the ties between its stateless renegades and the kingdom as coincidental or claiming the Saudis lacked the capability to staunch the flow of terrorist financing.[107] More likely, U.S. policymakers became vested in continuing relations with Riyadh despite other relevant factors.

Other commentary also called the long-standing alliance into question. American journalist Craig Unger detailed the personal and financial connections between the Bush family and the Al Saud monarchy in his *New York Times* bestseller, *House of Bush, House of Saud.* Political commentator and social activist Michael Moore generated significant controversy with his 2004 documentary, *Fahrenheit 9/11,* which argued that the administration's relentless attempt to depict Iraq as America's supreme threat distracted the public from 9/11's real culprits: the Saudis. President Bush was assailed from all sides when critics harped on Unger's and Moore's charges of past and ongoing business and personal relations between the Bush family and the royal family at the helm of an Islamic theocracy. But rather than an explicit cover-up driven by personal allegiances, it was strategic decisions and shared financial, energy, and diplomatic interests that primarily drove Washington's deference to Riyadh; personal connections merely reinforced existing policies.

The Council on Foreign Relations' Middle East Studies Director Rachel Bronson, author of *Thicker Than Oil: America's Uneasy Partnership with Saudi Arabia,* later explained "there is little evidence to suggest that such support has led the Bush family to make decisions at odds with U.S. interests. All previous presidents have sought close relations with the kingdom."[108] Contrary to prevailing assumptions, the fact that previous presidents preserved the U.S.-Saudi alliance, or any alliance for that matter, does not preclude incompetence in Washington. Past presidents' pursuit of close relations with the kingdom does not mean that continuing such support would not harm U.S. interests.

To that point, Pulitzer Prize–winning investigative reporter James Risen—who so accurately detailed CIA activities that the Barack Obama administration served him a subpoena—wrote in a remarkable and revealing passage about Saudi Arabia and the continuing status quo:

> So many people in Washington's power circles— lawyers, and lobbyists, defense contractors, former members of Congress and former White House aides, diplomats and intelligence officers, and even some journalists—rely so heavily on Saudi money or Saudi access that ugly truths about Saudi links to Islamic extremists have been routinely ignored or suppressed.[109]

The revelation of "ugly truths" continued. In June 2004, the U.S. Treasury Department called Al Haramain Islamic Foundation, the largest Saudi-based charity with links to the royal family, "one of the principal Islamic NGOs providing support for the al Qaida network and promoting militant Islamic doctrine worldwide."[110] That September, the U.S. Treasury disclosed that HIF branches in Afghanistan, Albania, Bangladesh, Bosnia, Ethiopia, Indonesia, Kenya, the Netherlands, Pakistan, Somalia, and Tanzania were all providing financial, material, and other operational support to al Qaeda and its affiliates.[111]

Unfortunately, coverage of the war in Iraq excluded these revelations almost entirely from the dominant U.S. media narrative. More exposure to such controversial details may have upset Saudi leaders and sharply reduced Washington's ability to shape policies. But diverting the public's attention to another enemy also perpetuated the public's ignorance about one of the most significant financial sponsors of militant Islamic extremists activities and the alleged necessity of oil security that spurred Washington's unwavering protection of Riyadh.

Despite those developments, the Bush administration's "freedom agenda" reinforced Washington's political engagement in the region. Bush preached the virtues of human liberty and explained how by addressing the "root causes of terrorism" through increased aid for education, democracy promotion, economic cooperation, and development, the United States could plant the seeds of reform. Of course, democratic elections neither diminished the threat of terrorism nor eliminated the underlying grievances that inspired it, as terrorist groups have thrived in free societies, including the Baader-Meinhof Group in West Germany, the Irish Republican Army in Northern Ireland, and the Weather Underground in the United States. Finally, U.S. intelligence agencies monitoring, identifying, and countering Islamic extremism, as detailed in a 2005 Government Accountability Office investigation of U.S. efforts to counter extremism, came to a different conclusion than the White House:

> The Defense Intelligence Agency and other experts agree that the rise in Islamic extremism stems from various factors, including economic stagnation; a disproportionate concentration of population in the 15-to-29-year-old range ("youth bulges"), especially in most Middle Eastern countries; repressive and corrupt governments; and anti-Western sentiments, particularly due to negative perceptions of the United States' foreign policy.[112]

Additionally, an unclassified report by the Pentagon's Defense Science Board commented on the subject of unconditional U.S. support for the Middle East's repressive regimes: "The United States finds itself in the strategically awkward—and potentially dangerous—situation of being the longstanding prop and alliance partner of these authoritarian regimes."[113]

Outside experts agreed. By bolstering tyranny in the Muslim world, a Council on Foreign Relations Independent Task Force argued, U.S. foreign policy strengthened the pull of extremist ideologies that fueled violence against America.[114] Moreover, a Pew Research Center survey stated that support for terrorism was positively correlated with negative views of America.[115] The message was clear: U.S. policies that required the compliance of regimes that oppressed their people were perceived as trying to weaken Islam, not only re-inforcing militant Islamist propaganda, but incentivizing attacks on America.

But like previous American presidents, Bush tolerated despotism in Saudi Arabia. In the deeply conservative kingdom, the Al Saud family monarchy *is* the political system. It owned most print and broadcast media; censored most domestic television and radio out-lets; restricted freedoms of speech, assembly, association, and move-ment; and forbade political parties or similar associations. Bush's oft-repeated warning that "America must confront threats before they fully materialize" overlooked the kingdom's Salafi extremism that threatened freedom. In March 2002, in a horrifying example of how the kingdom's rigid concepts of Islam and social relations could carry life-and-death consequences, its morality police prevented fire-fighters from entering a burning building to rescue female students trapped inside because they were not wearing their head coverings. Fifteen young girls became casualties of strict gender segregation. The head of the Presidency of Girls' Education called the fire "God's will."[116]

Despite the lack of access to accurate information about the threat of Salafi-inspired terrorism, the U.S. policies to counter it were pro-voking further resentment. The declassified judgments of the April 2006 National Intelligence Estimate, which includes input from the country's 16 intelligence agencies, concluded that "the global jihadist movement" was "spreading and adapting," and that activists iden-tifying themselves as jihadists were "increasing in both number and geographic dispersion."[117] That December, the Iraq Study Group, the congressionally mandated assessment of the Iraq war, found that "funding for the Sunni insurgency comes from private individuals within Saudi Arabia and the Gulf States, even as those governments help facilitate U.S. military operations in Iraq by providing basing and overflight rights and by cooperating on intelligence issues."[118]

The perpetual issue of terrorist financing offers an excellent case study of inconsistency in the conduct of foreign policy. To stem the flow of private Saudi funds to terrorists, the Riyadh government issued numerous decrees and created new institutions to increase government supervision over charitable donations. It removed col-lection boxes in shopping malls, prohibited cash contributions at mosques, and adopted new restrictions on the banking activities of Saudi-based charities.[119] "The Saudis are now arguably our most important counterterrorism intelligence partner," wrote David Rundell, the U.S. deputy chief of mission in Riyadh, in April 2009.[120] But U.S.-Saudi intelligence sharing and cooperation also depended upon senior-level American leaders communicating the U.S. government's counterterrorism priorities and fostering among their Saudi counterparts the necessary political will to address the problem of terrorist financing. On that score, the results were indisputably negative.

"Still, donors in Saudi Arabia constitute the most significant source of funding to Sunni terrorist groups worldwide,"[121] wrote Secretary of State Hillary Clinton in a December 2009 diplomatic cable to U.S. Embassies in Riyadh, Kuwait, Abu Dhabi, Doha, and Islamabad. "Saudi Arabia," Clinton continued, "remains a critical financial support base for al-Qa'ida, the Taliban, LeT, and other terrorist groups, including Hamas."[122] Despite important progress in combating terrorism, particularly in investigating and detaining financial facilitators, Saudi seriousness about combating extremists inside the kingdom was seemingly limited when it came to preventing extremists' permeation abroad.[123] That same year, U.S. State and Treasury Department officials found that, despite Saudi restrictions regarding funds, multilateral charitable organizations still operate "largely outside of the strict Saudi restrictions covering domestic charities."[124]

In these circumstances, two widely circulated images encapsulated criticism of America's subservience to the monarchy: one in 2005 of President Bush holding hands with and giving a ceremonial kiss to then Crown Prince Abdullah at the Crawford ranch, which struck many observers as symbolically inappropriate; and one in 2009 of President Barack Obama bowing to King Abdullah at the G20 summit in London, which ignited a media uproar. But despite the mutual admiration, old problems have resurfaced in the U.S.-Saudi alliance.

Arab Sunni Ally, Persian Shiite Enemy

"Thank God for bringing Obama to the presidency," Saudi Arabia's King Abdullah gushed to U.S. officials in 2009.[125] Such high hopes faded fast. In 2010, the pro-democracy research institute Freedom House reported a net decline in liberty across the world for the fifth consecutive year.[126] President Bush's Freedom Agenda and

President Obama's attempts to revive it coincided with the longest continual decline of political and civil rights in the institute's four decades of recordkeeping. Meanwhile, America's image around the world had plummeted to record lows, along with perceptions of its moral leadership, following revelations of torture and violations of human rights, targeted killings, indefinite detention, and preventive invasion. The world perceived the United States as unconstrained by the rules and values it imposed upon others; soon, it appeared to retreat from its oft-stated claim to oppose policies that subvert human freedom.

In January 2011, American leaders faced a serious moral challenge when authoritarian allies across North Africa and the Middle East violently suppressed public demonstrations known as the Arab Spring. The uprisings sent Tunisia's President Zine El Abidine Ben Ali into exile in Saudi Arabia and Egypt's Hosni Mubarak to a presidential palace in the Red Sea resort of Sharm el-Sheikh. Critics contended that the Saudis saw the Obama administration as a threat to their domestic security, as the Saudis had wanted aggressive U.S. measures to retain the regional status quo. Obama's failure to do so showed either that he discarded America's long-standing policy or that he lacked the capability to protect those allies from their own people.[127] Some alleged that regional upheavals had put the allies "on a collision course."[128]

In actuality, the Obama administration, much like its predecessors, projected the image that it attempted to balance American interests with ideals. Yet, it continued to back execrable Arab regimes. Only when such support proved intolerable to continue did the administration present itself as a consummate protector of human freedom, then proceeding to support new rulers that abandoned revolution in order to reinstate the principal features of its previous regime.

Moreover, far from peaceful protests, the Saudis saw behind the Arab Spring an Iranian-backed strategy to subvert Arab Sunni states. A year before the Arab Spring, U.S. diplomats reported that senior Saudi leaders "have been openly critical of U.S. policies they describe as having shifted the regional balance of power in favor of arch-rival Iran."[129] Those "U.S. policies" included the invasion and occupation of Iraq, which knocked off Saddam Hussein; Iraq was, until then, Persian Shia Iran's primary foe. Thereafter, Washington and Riyadh explicitly strove to contain Iranian influence and thwart its nuclear capabilities (explained in detail below). To senior Saudi leaders, the nuclear issue also symbolized Iran's drive for regional supremacy, and Riyadh encouraged Gulf countries to consider stationing nuclear weapons as a deterrent.[130]

With political values at cross purposes and decades of U.S.–Middle East doctrine unraveling, Washington scored an indisputable foreign policy achievement. On May 1, 2011, President Obama announced that U.S. Special Forces had entered northern Pakistan and killed Osama bin Laden. That essential U.S. objective deprived extremists of an iconic figure. But the greatest tragedy of the post-9/11 experience was that the war on terror could never be truly "won." Threats continued. That December, the Philippine and Indonesian offices of Saudi-based charity International Islamic Relief Organization came under international scrutiny for actively providing assistance to al Qaeda.[131]

Beyond organizations and established charities, the more insidious threat came from terrorism's inherent fragmentation. The uncontrollable spread of Salafist ideology continued to turn disenchanted young Muslims into hardened militants. Documents recovered from bin Laden's compound found that he appeared to lack an organized system to direct worldwide operations. In fact, bin Laden and other senior leaders of al Qaeda central wanted stunning attacks against America and its allies and disdained al Qaeda affiliates that promoted independent, lone-wolf attacks. One such affiliate was al Qaeda in the Arabian Peninsula (AQAP) and its local propagandist, Anwar al-Awlaki. The American-born and raised Al-Awlaki used reasoned arguments similar to bin Laden's, but he used social media and AQAP's English-language Web-based publication *Inspire* to promote violence, strict adherence to religious devotion, and belief in a worldwide Islamic caliphate.[132]

On April 15, 2013, Tamerlan and Dzhokhar Tsarnaev, two ethnic Chechen brothers, set off pressure-cooker bombs at the finish line of the Boston Marathon, killing 3 people, maiming 200 others, and severing the limbs of over a half-dozen blast victims. Preliminary investigations showed no connection to international terrorism but suggested the brothers were influenced by the Saudi-inspired Salafist concept of an international Islamic caliphate. The social media account of the younger Tsarnaev linked to Salafist videos and referenced Islamist insurgents in Russia's rebellious North Caucasus, including the Muslim republics of Dagestan and Chechnya.[133] Friends of the elder Tsarnaev, who attended a mosque attended by Salafists while in Dagestan, say he grew to oppose Western sensibilities and customs and regularly read militant Islamist propaganda, including AQAP's *Inspire*.[134] Interestingly, after the Cold War, Saudi Arabia had sent millions of Qurans to post-Soviet Central Asian republics for their large Muslim populations.[135] And, in the 1990s, many young Muslims from Dagestan traveled to the kingdom to study.

The legacy of the unintended consequences of Saudi Salafism arose once again in shaping the Middle East's political transformation. In elections held in the post–Arab Spring Middle East, ultra-conservative Salafists formed political parties and factions in Algeria, Bahrain, Kuwait, Libya, and Yemen and won pluralities in Tunisia, Egypt, and Morocco.[136] Salafists rejected minority and women's rights, restricted personal and political liberties, and opposed the secular interests and values of Western societies. In its competition for religious and regional dominance with Iran, the Sunni Arab kingdom continued aggressive policies directly and by proxy across the region.

Amid fears of Iranian encirclement, the Arab kingdom backed Salafists who challenged what Jordan's King Abdullah called the "Shiite Crescent," the arc of Shiite brethren and influence spanning Iran, Iraq, Bahrain, Lebanon, Syria, Saudi Arabia's Eastern Province, and elsewhere. In Bahrain, for instance, home to a major U.S. naval base for the U.S. Fifth Fleet, the Saudis had sent troops in March 2011 to support the Al-Khalifa ruling family of Bahrain and its privileged Arab Sunni minority and to crush peaceful protests among the country's disadvantaged Shiite majority. The United States colluded with a Saudi police state that not only denied its own subjects political and personal freedoms, but also obstructed regional progress.

"At its core," said commentator Hazem Amin, who in October 2013 believed Syrian Salafists were increasingly embracing radical views close to al Qaeda, "the new Syrian Salafism is jihadist in nature. It is moving towards extremism."[137] Washington refused to abide by the policies of its oil-rich ally, particularly in Syria, where U.S.-Saudi interests genuinely diverged. Saudi Arabia, along with Qatar, furnished weapons and other supplies to well-organized rebel Sunni and Salafi militant groups to fight against Syrian dictator Bashar Al-Assad and his minority Alawites, a small Shiite sect, that were allied with Shiite Iran and Lebanon's Shiite political-terrorist group, Hezbollah.[138] Saudi and Qatari funding to their "Salafi Crescent" turned Syria's civil war into a terror attraction and a reflection of the region's intra-Islamic turmoil. Militants attracted young, middle-class Australians, Canadians, Americans, Germans, French, and other aspiring jihadists—a virtual cornucopia of terrorism. Militants flocked to join the rebel cause and seek martyrdom, including those formerly fighting U.S. and coalition forces in Iraq.

Although the United States later sold $640 million worth of U.S.-made cluster bombs to Saudi Arabia, despite their ban by 83 countries and the U.S. State Department's admission of "international concern," the partners began to vent their differences publicly and pursue policies without consultation.[139] In August 2013, after Syrian opposition groups claimed Assad used chemical weapons, President Obama appeared to back away from his earlier "red line" vow to take military action against Assad if the Syrian dictator used chemical weapons against his own people. With some noticeable reluctance, Obama turned to Congress for approval of missile strikes, thereby putting his own policy prescription at risk. In response, Ahmed al-Ibrahahim, an adviser to some of the kingdom's royals and officials, claimed Obama had "lost credibility after Syria."[140] He continued: "The bond of trust between America and Saudi Arabia has been broken in the Obama years. . . . We feel we have been stabbed in the back by Obama." Prince Turki followed by calling the president's approach to Syria "lamentable."

In reality, America's longtime Arab ally was finally forced to pay the price for the violence, repression, and bloodshed its policies had inflicted at home and spread overseas. Far from constituting a vital component of U.S. national security, the Saudi government was supporting militant Islamist extremists and funding the propagation of worldviews that threatened U.S. political interests and the secular values of Western societies. Indeed, years before on Capitol Hill, on the subject of Afghanistan and Pakistan that applies equally to events in Syria, Secretary Clinton was remarkably frank about past U.S. government policies:

> I mean, let's remember here, the people we are fighting today, we funded 20 years ago. And we did it because we were locked in this struggle with the Soviet Union. . . . And it was President Reagan, in partnership

with the Congress, led by Democrats, who said you know what, it sounds like a pretty good idea. Let's deal with the ISI and the Pakistani military and let's go recruit these Mujahedeen and that's great. Let's get some to come from Saudi Arabia and other places, importing their Wahabi [*sic*] brand of Islam so that we can go beat the Soviet Union. And guess what? They retreated. They lost billions of dollars and it led to the collapse of the Soviet Union. So there's . . . a very strong argument, which is it wasn't a bad investment to end the Soviet Union, *but let's be careful what we sow, because we will harvest.*[141]

Alliance commitments have the tendency to push American leaders to adopt policies they might not otherwise take. This time, when Saudi and American proponents of overthrowing Assad called for deeper U.S. involvement, they faced fierce resistance from Congress and the public. After more than a decade, with more than 8,000 Americans dead; 40,000 wounded and traumatized; $4 trillion spent, with the meter still running; sectarian chaos; and al Qaeda, ISIS, and other militant cells active in Iraq, Libya, Pakistan, Yemen, Somalia, and Syria, it appears that the war on terror's tumultuous aftermath hardened the public's cynicism about becoming entrapped yet again in a region where anti-Western hatreds run deep. Ironically, Riyadh's incessant proselytizing bred much of the hatred that prompted Washington's reluctance to become more involved.

Conclusion

Although Saudi Arabia has played a major role on many issues of critical importance to the United States, and the kingdom's wealth and influence accords it considerable clout in Washington, it is impossible to have an informed debate about that pivotal alliance when key factual questions surrounding it remain unanswered. Before and after 9/11, American leaders whitewashed the conduct of private Saudi-based donors and charities that funded bin Laden's movement and the affiliates who fought under its flag. In the course of forgiving irredeemable behavior, U.S. leaders engaged in their own: downplaying their responsibility for doing too little to stop those offenses, misleading the public with clumsy attempts to cast suspicion upon Iraq, and supporting an ally that continued to sponsor Salafist insurgencies and spread sectarianism through intra-Islamic civil wars. Even after Washington stood by Riyadh, the Saudi regime raised objections to Washington for expanding Shiite Iranian influence by overthrowing Iraq's Sunni Arab dictator and for refusing to crush revolutions during the Arab Spring. Decades of collaboration had bred a false sense of entitlement.

Shortly after the 2011 revolutionary upheavals swept the region, many aspects of the alliance also began to transform. Former U.S. Ambassador to Saudi Arabia Chas Freeman recounted a comment made by King Abdullah, then crown prince, on the kingdom and theme of Salafism that "a friend who does not help you is no better than an enemy who does you no harm." Freeman explained that the "automaticity of friendship, a willingness to go out of your way to do things notwithstanding the absence of any interest of your own is gone."[142] Moreover, on the subject of oil, Saudi Arabia's inability to bring new supply for a sustained period of time, combined with its domestic energy consumption used to quell internal political unrest, and impressive new developments in the U.S. energy sector, means that the relevance of Saudi oil to America became greatly diminished.[143]

Given these and other changing dynamics, the United States must govern its future policies toward the kingdom based upon legitimate disagreements and genuine constraints, not slavish attempts to promote a flawed alliance through pervasive misinformation. With Saudi Arabia, as with Pakistan, American leaders must ensure that its allies make concerted efforts against militants at home *and* abroad. If allies fail to move against militants or their funding sources quickly enough, U.S. leaders should not hesitate to take action themselves. Moreover, after tragedies like 9/11, U.S. officials must be willing to censure the Saudis and redefine the parameters of America's security commitment.

Finally, a richer public dialogue about terrorism, its sources, and its consequences could have helped the American public make better decisions about U.S. involvement in the Middle East and allowed for a wider range of policy choices. Without that knowledge, the public cannot know what policies to avoid repeating. To the extent that U.S. officials keep the public in the dark, the public will continue to be critically endangered for it.

14. Janus-Faced Partners: America and Pakistan after 9/11

Despite America's intense focus on South and Central Asia in the years after 9/11, the duplicity between the United States and the Islamic Republic of Pakistan remained staggering. Early on, U.S. officials praised Islamabad's military dictator, General Pervez Musharraf, and his corrupt civilian successor, President Asif Ali Zardari, who perpetuated their country's political and economic dysfunction. Pakistan sat at the turbulent crosscurrents of key U.S. policy concerns that ranged from nuclear weapons safety and stability, to Afghanistan, to forging a concord with the world's Muslims and neutralizing violent jihad. As a major non–North Atlantic Treaty Organization (NATO) ally and for a time the second leading recipient of U.S. foreign aid, Pakistan helped kill and capture over 700 al Qaeda suspects, provided the CIA with bases to carry out targeted killings with drones, and offered the U.S.-led coalition overland support for transporting supplies into landlocked Afghanistan.

But in spite of that assistance, Pakistani leaders lacked broad public support for the battle against terrorism and cooperated only when their interests aligned with those of Washington. On regional issues, the bulk of Pakistan's armed forces remained on the Indian frontier, and on counterterrorism cooperation, leaders engaged in political maneuvering by accommodating religious extremists and forming political alliances with pro-Taliban political parties.

Elements of Pakistan's armed forces and its military-dominated external spy agency, the Directorate for Inter-Services Intelligence (ISI), actively facilitated anti-U.S. insurgents and militant infiltration into Afghanistan to undermine the viability of any Afghan government aligned with New Delhi. Indeed, in the seven-year period leading up to 9/11, Islamabad funded, armed, and advised the Taliban regime that harbored al Qaeda.

For the United States and Pakistan, differences over the concept of sovereignty became a crucial, yet overlooked, feature of their al-

427

liance, and one that merits deeper consideration. The most widely recognized definition of sovereignty is a population with a defined territory and a government that has relations with other states.[1] But international relations scholar Stephen Krasner, in his 1999 book *Sovereignty: Organized Hypocrisy*, elaborates four types of state sovereignty in the international system that countries often fail to meet.[2] Post-9/11 Pakistan repeatedly—and sometimes deliberately—failed to meet the most basic standards of sovereignty: It failed to exercise control within the state (domestic sovereignty); it lacked the capacity to control cross-border movement (interdependence sovereignty); and it competed for domestic authority with political organizations, religious associations, and external agents (Westphalian sovereignty). Yet, despite those serious deficiencies in controlling its territory, borders, and people, Pakistan successfully maintained full legal recognition by other sovereign states (international legal sovereignty).

Sovereignty, in the context of the U.S.-Pakistan post-9/11 alliance, came to imply a false sense of equality as Islamabad complained bitterly about Western interference inside its territory while also resigning itself to radical forces that devoured its sovereignty from within.[3] For a sovereign right that the UN declares inviolable, Pakistan's situation epitomized hypocrisy. Nevertheless, Washington recognized Islamabad as a fully autonomous and independent nation-state eligible for arms and aid, even as Islamabad (by choice or by circumstance) failed to enforce the rule of law within its territory. In ways seldom understood, the outcome forced Washington to accommodate Islamabad's corrupt and repressive government at the cost of America's values and regional priorities, allowing a duplicitous yet "indispensable" ally to play both sides of the global war on terror.

Past as Prologue

Two days after hijacked airliners slammed into the World Trade Center, the Pentagon, and a field in Pennsylvania, U.S. Deputy Secretary of State Richard Armitage met in Washington with Pakistan's ambassador to the United States, Maleeha Lodhi, and ISI Director Lt. General Mahmud Ahmed, a vociferous Taliban supporter and self-professed, born-again Islamic fundamentalist.[4] Armitage said the United States had seven nonnegotiable demands for Pakistan's support in the war on terror. First, stop al Qaeda operatives at its border and end all logistical support for Osama bin Laden. Second, give the United States blanket overflight and landing rights for all necessary military and intelligence operations. Third, provide territorial access to U.S. and allied military intelligence and other personnel to conduct operations against al Qaeda. Fourth, provide the United States with intelligence information; and fifth, continue to publicly condemn terrorist acts. Sixth, halt all shipments of fuel to the Taliban and stop recruits from going to Afghanistan; and seventh, if evidence was found that implicated Osama bin Laden and al Qaeda—and the Taliban continued to harbor them—Pakistan was to break relations with the Taliban government.[5]

That afternoon, Pakistan's President and Army Chief of Staff General Pervez Musharraf and his top military commanders agreed to all seven demands. Musharraf promised his country's "unstinted cooperation in the fight against terrorism."[6] Such promises provided a flimsy basis for a war on terror alliance dedicated to eliminating terrorists and punishing states providing them sanctuary.

No sovereign nation "worth its salt" could have acceded to all of the Bush administration's demands, wrote Shuja Nawaz, director of the South Asia Center of the Atlantic Council.[7] As that perspective implies, Pakistan's military regime found itself on the horns of a dilemma. It could stand with its regional proxies and incur unimaginable levels of U.S. military and economic retaliation or join the U.S.-led anti-terror coalition and provoke the fury of state-sanctioned militants. Musharraf, as the sovereign head of state, confronted unpalatable options to save face.

American policymakers expected their Pakistani counterparts to have control over what is internationally accepted to be Pakistani territory. But its legislature, under Articles 247 and 248 of Pakistan's 1973 constitution, does not extend the jurisdiction of Pakistan's Supreme Court to the country's treacherous tribal region along its border with Afghanistan, known as the Federally Administered Tribal Areas (FATA). That lack of jurisdiction created a void that posed a critical problem to NATO's war in Afghanistan and is explored more in detail below. As the Bush administration rallied Afghan and international allies and prepared to invade Afghanistan, some observers grew concerned.

"Are you really sure you are not going to be creating more Osama bin Ladens by what you will do?" Senate Foreign Relations Committee Chairman Joseph Biden asked Secretary of State Colin Powell in October 2001.[8] The region had served as a multidecade transit hub for chaotic bloodletting: holy warriors waged jihad against the Soviets in the 1980s, Kashmiri extremists fought Indian troops in the 1990s, and guerilla insurgents would attack coalition forces in Afghanistan in the 2000s.

Some of the most important groups were the Haqqani network, a Pakistani tribal-based network run by Jalaluddin Haqqani, a former U.S. ally in the 1980s, and later by his son, Sirajuddin Haqqani, which held sway over large parts of Paktika, Paktia, and Khost provinces in post-9/11, U.S.-occupied Afghanistan; the Hizb-e-Islami Group (HiG), led by Gulbuddin Hekmatyar, the anti-Soviet jihad's most radical militant outfit and an ISI favorite, which became a leading insurgent group in post-9/11 Afghanistan; Jaish-e-Mohammad (JeM), a radical, al Qaeda–connected group with separate militant and missionary structures that strives to unite Kashmir with Pakistan; Lashkar-e-Taiba (LeT), an extremist assortment that aimed to join Kashmir with Pakistan, enjoyed a following among lower ranks of Pakistan's armed forces and launched high-profile attacks against India; Harkut-ul-Mujahideen (HuM), a Pakistan-based, Kashmiri jihadi group, with close ties to ISI, that threw acid in women's faces, demanded bans on televisions and maintained recruiting offices throughout Pakistan in the mid-1990s, along with LeT; and Jamiat-Ulema-e-Islam (JUI), a politically powerful, pro-Taliban religious party that operated a network of Islamic religious schools in Baluchistan, Punjab, and Khyber Pakhtunkhwa (formerly the British colonial-sounding North-West Frontier Province, NWFP, until 2010).[9]

Incredibly, it seemed that wherever Pakistan lacked a strong and definable border, its military and civilian leaders made common cause with tribal auxiliaries and religious zealots who then turned their areas into hotbeds of violence. Accordingly, U.S. ambitions ran into trouble whenever the region's tribal populations got restless.

In modern times, Afghanistan has refused to recognize the Durand Line, the international border separating its dominion from Pakistan. The contested boundary divides indigenous Pashtun tribes—most of whom live as minorities in densely populated Pakistan. Although fewer of them live in rural Afghanistan, they represent Afghanistan's ethnic majority. That imbalance was a major part of U.S.-Pakistan post-9/11 duplicity. When Pakistan was founded as a homeland for India's Muslims (see chapter 4), tribal loyalties within the country transcended identity to a particular state; those loyalties fragmented further when tribes were eventually displaced. Indeed, as a newly formed nation-state, Pakistan failed by succeeding: given its ethnic composition, Pakistan had created a Muslim homeland that its government could not control.

For Islamabad, Pashtun separatism remained a reality. Its tribes had long called for an independent homeland uniting Afghanistan with parts of Pakistan beyond Islamabad's writ, including in Baluchistan, FATA, and Khyber Pakhtunkhwa. Compounding that fierce tribal agitation was nuclear-armed India, to which Pakistan had lost four wars (1947, 1965, 1971, and 1999). India and Pakistan's entry into the nuclear weapons club during the Cold War made the subcontinent the most politically sensitive region in the world. Moreover, in 1971, India helped Pakistan's geographically isolated and ethnically distinct eastern wing gain independence and form Bangladesh—which for many in Pakistan remains a vivid memory of ethnic division, communal unrest, political instability, and ultimately, issues of separatism and sovereignty.

Against irredentist Afghan governments and conventional and nuclear Indian threats, Pakistan has long sought to secure its regional backyard through "strategic depth" west of the Indus, the geographic barrier dividing the country's Pashtun minority in the west and its Punjabi majority in the east. By the 1990s, after a decade of acting as a covert pipeline for American arms and Saudi aid to holy warriors in Afghanistan, Pakistan's ISI repurposed the anti-Soviet jihad's most radical militias and the domestic political parties supporting them.

Radical religious schools also played a significant role in rising religious extremism. Wealthy private donors and Arab sheikhdoms in the Persian Gulf, particularly Saudi Arabia, provided major financial backing for Pakistan's network of Islamic religious schools (madrasahs). Although propagating militancy was not the original intent upon their establishment in 11th-century Baghdad, madrasahs in late 20th-century Pakistan indoctrinated students with anti-Western worldviews and a blend of the Arabian Peninsula's puritanical strain of Salafi Islam with South Asia's fundamentalist strand of Deobandism. Although 60 percent of Pakistani Sunnis adhere to South Asia's moderate, and more prevalent, Barelvi Islam, by the early 1990s Deobandi religious schools were churning out tens of thousands of students, transforming the anti-Soviet era's young war refugees into foot soldiers for the Taliban.

Moreover, the Taliban's "Islamic Emirate" consolidated its conquests with help from Pakistan's senior military and civilian leaders. By late 1993 the ISI had filled training camps throughout Afghanistan's Khost and Jalalabad regions with thousands of militants from across the Islamic world. Benazir Bhutto, a Sindhi politician and chair of the center-left Pakistan People's Party (PPP), during her second term as democratically elected prime minister, appointed ethnic Pashtun Naseerullah Babar as interior minister. Together, they worked with JUI and financed Afghanistan's Taliban movement through the civilian budget. They aimed to weaken ISI influence in foreign policy decisions as well as undermine Bhutto's Punjab-based political rival, former Prime Minister Nawaz Sharif.[10] Pakistani army advisers led the Taliban's Sunni-Pashtun movement to weapons depots on the Afghan border and aided its tactical sophistication on the battlefield once again in 1995 with ammunition for its push into Herat. Only Pakistan, Saudi Arabia, and the United Arab Emirates extended diplomatic recognition to the Taliban when it finally seized Kabul in September 1996.

Taliban-controlled territory gave Pakistan lucrative access to Central Asian trade routes and oil and natural gas pipelines; but, most critically, it sheltered militants and provided strategic depth. At Darunta, west of Jalalabad, the capital of eastern Afghanistan's Nangarhar province bordering Pakistan, ISI instructors assisted militants and used 16 separate camps, known collectively as the al-Badr complex, to train them.[11] Meanwhile, the Taliban government outlawed singing and dancing, amputated limbs for thievery, and publicly executed apostates. Pakistan continued its political, moral, and economic assistance, despite Afghanistan's totalitarian behavior and medieval reputation.

In ways American Cold War leaders could never have imagined, Afghanistan and Pakistan became the epicenter of global terrorism. That impression sharpened in 1996, when al Qaeda leader Osama bin Laden, his jihadi followers, and their family members departed Sudan and gained refuge in Afghanistan. Despite strong disagreement among the Taliban's senior ranks about whether to host bin Laden, Taliban spiritual leader Mullah Mohammad Omar permitted bin Laden and his associates to use the Afghan territory under Taliban control, notwithstanding their plots for international terrorist activity. After al Qaeda bombed the U.S. embassies in Kenya and Tanzania in August 1998, U.S. efforts to capture, extradite, and kill bin Laden failed, as did toothless United Nations (UN) resolutions for the Taliban to cease providing training and sanctuary to international terrorists.

Pakistan, in part because of its support to Afghanistan's repressive regime, also became an international pariah. Its reputation plummeted for its sponsorship of radical militancy in Kashmir, its nuclear weapons test in May 1998, and its military coup against its sitting civilian government in August 1999. During this time, Afghanistan's extremism fed from and back into Pakistan. In December 1998, Deobandis in Quetta, Baluchistan's capital across the border from Afghanistan's Kandahar province—the Taliban's political headquarters and spiritual heartland—sought to expunge the city of video rental shops, video records, and televisions. In late 2000 madrasah teachers and mullahs ordered Deobandi students in present-day Khyber Pakhtunkhwa to burn televisions, video players, and satellite dishes—essentially the new-age equivalent of book burning.[12]

"Afghanistan's majority ethnic Pashtuns have to be on our side," declared General Pervez Musharraf at a May 2000 press conference in Islamabad. "This is our national interest. . . . The Taliban cannot be alienated by Pakistan."[13] His government insisted bin Laden was not a Pakistani national. It told Washington to talk with the Taliban directly and called Afghanistan a sovereign state—a right Pakistan demanded for itself but rarely respected for its neighbors. In fact, insofar as Pakistan's policies were aiding the Taliban, Islamabad was facilitating al Qaeda's presence in Afghanistan. Yet, even after 9/11, no amount of U.S. pressure or persuasion would convince Pakistan's Islamic Republic to abandon Afghanistan's Islamic emirate.

Also in May 2000, before a select group of journalists, U.S. Under Secretary of State Thomas Pickering said he found it difficult to believe that "Pakistan's continued support for the Taliban [was] irrelevant to the questions of the possibility of Pakistan playing a very constructive role in bringing Osama bin Laden to justice."[14] Other top officials reached the same conclusion. Within a month of taking office, President George W. Bush sent a strong private message to President General Musharraf encouraging him to convince the

Taliban to turn over bin Laden. In June 2001 U.S. National Security Advisor Condoleezza Rice delivered a similarly resolute message to Pakistan's foreign minister, which according to her was "met with a rote, expressionless response."[15]

Geography as Destiny

After the September 11, 2001, terrorist attacks, NATO, for the first time in its history, invoked Article 5: the pledge that an attack on one member is considered an attack on all. In early October, allied military campaigns, Operation Enduring Freedom and Operation Crescent Wind, pounded Taliban air-defense systems, command- and-control bunkers, airfields and warplanes, and terrorist training camps. U.S. Secretary of Defense Donald Rumsfeld, who described the tempo of air and sea strikes as "more or less around the clock," emphasized the targeting of the Taliban, "not the people of Afghanistan." And yet, despite reasonable efforts to select targets with the least "unintended damage" (collateral civilian fatalities), hundreds of civilians, including children, lay dead in homes and hamlets thought to be Taliban command centers.[16]

As coalition explosions lit up Afghanistan's nighttime sky, feelings of shared Islamic identity dominated Pakistan's national mood. The day after the start of hostilities, Musharraf publicly urged Bush to terminate the war in "one or two days."[17] The war was stirring intense animosities among many in Pakistan who viewed it as a hostile action thrust upon the region. "Now the image is no longer the Taliban against everyone, but America mindlessly bombing a poor country," opined prominent journalist and former parliamentarian Ayaz Amir.[18] In Quetta, anti-American rioters riled up by fundamentalist religious parties set fire to movie theaters, looted shops, and forced foreigners to barricade themselves inside the city's main hotel. In Karachi, Sindh's capital and Pakistan's commercial trading hub, tens of thousands of anti-American demonstrators attacked cars, fast-food outlets, and the offices of international relief agencies.[19]

"A vast majority of Pakistan is with us," Musharraf assured the Bush administration.[20] Such reassurances provided comfort—but only up to a point. In Pakistan, the war revived Cold War memories of past U.S. abandonment and betrayal. That experience chastened many citizens, explains Quaid-i-Azam University Professor Rifaat Hussain:

> There is an emerging current of anti-Americanism that is turning people by default into Taliban sympathizers. People do not want Pakistan to act as a proxy for the Americans, and they are not sure if there is an exit strategy for our entanglement in the Afghan crisis. They fear the Americans will leave and we will end up holding the bag.[21]

Of course, Pakistani leaders helped pull their country into that mess by aiding and abetting the Taliban. Nevertheless, from English-speaking liberals to illiterate masses, the public opposed transforming their fragile country into a frontline state for another disastrous war. The unstated premise underlying that concern was that America's war on terror constituted an existential crisis to their country.

Islamic solidarity, which entailed more than a dollop of sympathy for Afghanistan's Taliban regime, overrode Musharraf's public support for the anti-terror campaign. He encountered stiff resistance from the military and spy establishments regarding his attempts to transform them from institutions aiding Islamist jihadists into organizations combating those same militants. The duplicity was subtle and deniable. For instance, by providing overland routes and flyover rights, Pakistan did little to hinder the coalition's entrance into Afghanistan. But Islamabad strived to gain the upper hand once coalition forces arrived. Few officials in Washington seriously reckoned with that difficulty. Those underlying issues surfaced early on, as Bush prepared for war in Afghanistan. Inter-Services Intelligence Director Ahmed met twice with Mullah Omar, purportedly to convince him to hand over bin Laden. But senior Taliban leaders allege that Ahmed urged Omar to resist American pressure. Musharraf later forced Ahmed and other top generals into early retirement for opposing his pro-American policies. Regardless, among the ISI's roughly 2,500 officers, at least several hundred continued to reject Pakistan's alliance with the United States.[22]

Some ISI officers allowed and assisted thousands of militants, including JeM fighters, to resist the U.S. invasion alongside the Taliban. At the Afghan border, the Pakistani army captured between 600 and 700 foreigners, while ISI commanders ensured that other useful proxies were freed. By mid-November, the Taliban high command, Osama bin Laden, and his top aides slipped across Afghanistan's porous border into Pakistan. While some escaped by various means—by foot, mule, motorbike, SUVs, buses, and trucks—Pakistan's secret service airlifted some, a move approved by senior Bush administration officials reportedly unaware of who was being lifted where.[23]

That befuddlement conflicted with the confidence among active and former senior U.S. officials that America would punish not just al Qaeda but the states that provided it sanctuary. Bush officials rejected Clinton-era policies that targeted terrorist commanders one cruise missile at a time. President Bush, in his words, "was tired of swatting flies."[24] Pentagon Defense Policy Board Chairman Richard N. Perle explained that "we have to make the cost to the governments that support terrorism so high that they stop supporting them." But, as later discovered, the government Perle served was unwilling to conduct a scorched-earth policy. Former Secretary of State George P. Shultz argued for the need to be "relentless" against "states that harbor terrorists."[25] The Bush administration implicitly agreed with that approach. Unaddressed, however, was how the United States would, or could, handle states such as Pakistan, which quietly supported terrorist forces. Musharraf alleges that Armitage threatened that Pakistan "should be prepared to be bombed back to the Stone Age" if it chose the terrorists over Washington.[26]

Whether or not Armitage laced Washington's nonnegotiable demands with such an explicit military threat, America's gloves were not coming off to that extent. Indeed, in a widely reported background briefing, Pentagon officials found "reasonable certainty" that in mid-December 2001 bin Laden was in the caves of Tora Bora in eastern Afghanistan's White Mountains. Opposite Tora Bora, in rugged FATA, the Pakistan army launched one of its first operations in Kurram Agency—the first point of refuge for al Qaeda and the Taliban after the U.S. and allied invasion of Afghanistan. Although administration policy statements seemingly affirmed Washington's readiness to attack state sponsors of terrorism aggressively, the White House rejected the idea of using U.S. troops to block southern escape routes, telling U.S. officers on the ground that Pakistani troops would cut off Osama bin Laden.[27] They did not.

Despite the outpouring of global sympathy and support, even a military superpower such as the United States did not launch a unilateral incursion to chase down foreign aggressors in Pakistan as a matter of self-defense, and at a time when such an incursion would have been most justified and permissible. Advocates of a strong military response to the 9/11 attacks were blocked by the implicit limits a nuclear-armed state could impose. Notwithstanding the harsh rhetoric that Perle and Armitage employed, sending U.S. troops into Pakistan was deemed a clear red line that Washington dare not cross. Secretary Rumsfeld firmly rejected the suggestion that U.S. forces might pursue al Qaeda fighters into Pakistan. And, years later, U.S. officials looking for a silver bullet to solve the Pakistan problem immediately dismissed the idea of invading a country that possessed nuclear weapons, calling such an option "beyond madness."[28]

As the window of opportunity was closing to capture 9/11's perpetrators, Bush deferred to Musharraf. Whether the administration displayed willful blindness or gross incompetence is unclear. But, for numerous reasons, Washington faced a unique problem with Pakistan. Musharraf, despite his country's track record, apparently convinced Bush that he was an enthusiastic ally in the war on terror. Strong rhetoric and arm-twisting fell short of squeezing Pakistan to bend to Washington's will.

With limited means to overcome its geographical and historical complexities, the region's stubborn militancy persisted and almost set off a nuclear confrontation. On December 13, 2001, five terrorists armed with grenades, plastic explosives, and AK-47s killed 12 people and injured 18 others in an attack on India's parliament. Officials in New Delhi accused LeT, the Pakistan army–trained and al Qaeda–affiliated militant outfit, and JeM, a group with a following among the lower ranks of Pakistan's armed forces, of carrying out the attacks. On January 12, 2002, Musharraf banned LeT, JeM, and other groups. He also closed Hizb-ul-Mujahedeen's Muzaffrabad office, condemned religious extremism, and announced reforms to Islamic schools.[29]

The general's sweeping measures made little difference. It was one of the earliest indications of a central problem with Pakistan: its inability to behave like a typical sovereign state, despite its claims to the contrary. LeT merely regrouped under another name. New militant offshoots also defied Musharraf's crackdown and continued to support attacks in Afghanistan and Kashmir. Other sectarian and Islamist radical groups were so large and so well financed they could operate independent of the state. Additionally, Musharraf's government neither regulated radical madrasahs nor prosecuted the militants who fed their ideology.[30] Of greater significance, Pakistan and India amassed troops along their international border for nearly a year. No large-scale hostilities ensued, but the tension kept the bulk of Pakistani troops away from the Afghan border where they might have impeded, or at least monitored, the movements of Taliban and al Qaeda operatives.

Pakistan's official support in the anti-terror coalition still earned it $3 billion in assistance, debt relief, and rescheduled debt payments over the next several years. But the military's loyalties in favor of the militants lingered. In a matter of months, U.S. Special Operations Forces and Central Intelligenge Agency (CIA) paramilitary operatives, alongside Afghanistan's Northern Alliance, a loose confederation of warlords, achieved victory over the Taliban. But the triumph of largely white, Christian soldiers apparently struck a deep chord of anger among conservative elements of Pakistan's military. "To accept a U.S. occupation of a Muslim state that they had helped set up was too much for some of the officers," wrote journalist Tariq Ali. "For some soldiers too it was a shameful defeat."[31] That spring, in memoranda to Musharraf, senior officials attached to the ISI speculated that the United States would leave Afghanistan in 5 to 15 years. They recommended that Pakistan's proxies be well placed to fill the vacuum and help install an Afghan government friendly to Islamabad's interests.[32]

"A Genie of Frightening Proportions"

In January 2002 the Bush administration made a stunning shift in its foreign policy, turning U.S. attention from Afghanistan to Iraq and labeling the latter a part of the "axis of evil." The message Washington conveyed to Islamabad was disinterest in the future of Afghanistan, an assumption that prompted the regeneration of the Taliban and Pakistan's other religious extremist proxies in Afghanistan. For senior U.S. officials, Pakistan's supposedly firm commitment against al Qaeda terrorism mattered most. President General Musharraf and his country's military and civilian leaders were beardless, Westernoriented, whiskey-swilling, secularized Muslims; they largely embodied the antithesis of reactionary and regressive Islamists. But in an alliance, a duplicitous partner can be hostile in subtle ways. Although Pakistan's military dictator pledged support for strategic realignment, he secured U.S. military and political support against terrorism while promoting the military's interests within the state, including bolstering radical elements that Washington sought to eliminate.

Musharraf promoted military interests in many ways. In October 1999, as army chief of staff, he overthrew democratically elected Prime Minister Nawaz Sharif in a bloodless coup and promised to lay the foundations of "true democracy." Many in Pakistan initially welcomed the jarring transition. Like many patriotic Americans, Pakistanis respected their military and believed it had their country's best interests at heart. Moreover, Pakistan's military had governed the country for half of its postcolonial existence, as many citizens held the belief that their country's civilian leaders looked out primarily for themselves, distrusting them because of their corruption, venality, and incompetence.

Musharraf leveraged his people's discontent by blurring the line between military and civilian authority so fundamental to democracy. In June 2001, to legitimize his reign, he declared himself president despite never standing for election. In April 2002, ahead of parliamentary elections in October—the first since his extraconstitutional seizure of power dissolved the National Assembly—voters gave the army general five more years in office as president, allowing him to serve as both army chief and president simultaneously. Under Pakistan's 1973 constitution, parliament and the provincial assemblies elect the president, not the people by direct vote.[33] But under Musharraf, an awkward military-led democracy prevailed. The April referendum gave the president the power to dismiss parliament and block parliament's constitutional right to remove the president from office.[34]

"This is the beginning of a process that will lead to democratic elections," the U.S. embassy spokesperson in Islamabad said of the referendum.[35] Belief that a military dictator's bogus rewriting of a constitution would usher in democratic elections indulged dangerously wishful thinking. Ironically, that thinking came just as a vocal minority of political opponents in parliament and civil society began openly opposing Musharraf; however, lacking the wherewithal to directly challenge a dictator's monopoly on power, they derided Musharraf's American backers.

"Democracy is not the principle that first drives U.S. policy," PPP spokesperson Farhatullah Babar remarked scornfully. "If the U.S.

thinks its own national interests are being served, the U.S. normally closes its eyes, [and] tolerates the dictator."[36]

That view, however strident, contained a grain of truth. When President Bill Clinton visited Islamabad in March 2000, according to retired State Department South Asia specialist Dennis Kux, Clinton's message to the new dictator expressed America's concerns about Pakistan's direction, but "he neither lectured nor scolded Musharraf."[37] After all, Washington had grown accustomed to the Pakistani military's derailment of the democratic process, with its overhauled constitutions (1956, 1962, 1973), protracted periods of martial law (1958–1962, 1969–1972, 1977–1985), and the frequent deposing of civilian governments (1958, 1970, 1977, 1999).

Bush administration officials declined to openly criticize a war on terror ally even as he tightened his authoritarian grip, since control implied stability. But control in this context also strengthened the military's interests within the state to promote Islamist sentiments. A 2002 law required that parliamentary candidates have a bachelor's degree, a qualification that would bar 90 percent of the population from office, but aided religious parties by allowing madrasah certificates to substitute for university degrees.[38] In August the president general incorporated into the constitution a sweeping package of amendments known as the Legal Framework Order. The president now had the authority to dismiss legislative assemblies; issue orders that were immune from challenges in court; amend the constitution unilaterally; appoint military service chiefs, judges, and provincial governors; and institutionalize the military's decision-making role through a permanent National Security Council.[39]

Those powers expanded progressively after October 2002. In parliamentary elections, Muttahida Majlis-e-Amal (MMA), a coalition of six hard-line Islamist political parties, became the third largest bloc in Pakistan's National Assembly and formed a coalition government with Musharraf's political party, Pakistan Muslim League-Quaid-i-Azam (PML-Q).[40] The Muttahida Majlis-e-Amal's religious parties, though varied, all backed the strict application of Sharia law and openly glorified militant jihad, vigilantism, and intolerance.[41] Influential alliance party Jamaat-e-Islami (JI) had close ties to the Saudis, and another, Jamiat Ulema-e-Islam (JUI), operated the largest network of Deobandi mosques and madrasahs in Pakistan's Pashtun-dominated tribal region.[42] JUI comprised two factions. One led by

Maulana Fazlur Rehman, chair of the National Assembly's standing committee for foreign affairs under Benazir Bhutto, had, after 9/11, directed the large anti-U.S., anti-Musharraf, and pro-Taliban rallies in major Pakistani cities.[43] The other JUI faction was led by Maulana Sami ul-Haq, the so-called "Father of the Taliban," who directed Darul Uloom Haqqania madrasah, the infamous "University of Jihad."

In line with ISI speculations about the endgame in Afghanistan, the MMA pledged to prioritize and restore Pakistani support for the Taliban and end the U.S. presence in Afghanistan, according to MMA spokesman Mansoor Jafar.[44] Benazir Bhutto, under self-imposed exile in Dubai since 1999, described the MMA as "a genie of frightening proportions." She added that "the military wants to say 'Look, West, you need a military dictatorship, because if there's not, then pro-Taliban parties are going to come to power.'"[45] The West got the worst of both worlds under that "mullah-military alliance," as some citizens began to call it. Religious parties dissatisfied with the war on terror advanced the military's interest by providing a hospitable environment for militant proxies in tribal regions bordering Afghanistan. In essence, the military pushed the interests of religious parties and rigged elections against civilian political rivals who opposed the military's role in governance.[46]

The mullah-military alliance gained a decisive say over events in Afghanistan. The MMA victory "placed a crucial border province entirely at the disposal of Islamist extremists directly linked to the Afghani Taliban," wrote *South Asia Intelligence Review* editor Ajai Sahni.[47] In actuality, the MMA victory did far more. The MMA won an absolute majority in Khyber Pakhtunkhwa's provincial legislature and emerged as the second-largest party in Baluchistan, two border provinces that the MMA's hard-line Islamist parties could re-Talibanize with harsh fundamentalist laws. In June 2003, with the Hisba Bill, which Pakistan's Supreme Court later struck down, Khyber Pakhtunkhwa's legislative assembly voted unanimously to impose fundamentalist Sharia law and entrench it throughout the education, finance, and judiciary systems.

The MMA ordered shops, offices, and schools to close in adherence to Islam's five daily prayers, and a Saudi-inspired Department of Vice and Virtue patrolled the streets. The critical part is that the military looked the other way. Pakistan did not function as a typical state, nor as U.S. interests would dictate. The military government allowed a separate state within Pakistan to operate virtually unmolested, by choice or otherwise, despite Musharraf's initial outlawing of jihadist groups. In Baluchistan, in and around Quetta, MMA ministers regularly attended the funerals of slain Taliban fighters; and, on the orders of MMA representatives, local jails released dozens of militants. Senior cleric, JUI senator, and Khyber Pakhtunkhwa junior minister Mualana Rahat Hussain boasted of being a former classmate of senior Taliban insurgents at Binoria madrasah in Karachi.[48]

State Department spokesperson Richard Boucher said about the success of Pakistani fundamentalists linked to the Taliban, "Let's not assume that everything that happens in the world is a failure of the United States."[49] That was a valid observation. Regardless of whether the existence of the MMA represented a U.S. failure, though, certain policies Washington pursued had some connection to the MMA victory and its appalling consequences. Less than a year after Operation Enduring Freedom, the White House instructed U.S. Central Command Chief General Tommy R. Franks to pull most of America's Special Operations Forces and CIA paramilitary operatives off the hunt for bin Laden for redeployment to Iraq. That decision dealt a severe blow to NATO's unity of effort.

Many European allies "have a problem with our involvement in Iraq and project that to Afghanistan," said U.S. Defense Secretary Robert Gates. Those forthright remarks were echoed by William Maley and Daoud Yaqub, a professor and research scholar at Australian National University, respectively. "To many observers in Europe," they wrote, "Iraq is a war of choice, and as a result Europe has no particular duty to shoulder a heavier burden in Afghanistan. The Afghan government and people are victims of this tension."[50]

Iraq not only diverted scarce resources, public attention, and congressional oversight from Afghanistan and Pakistan but also relieved pressure on remaining Taliban and al Qaeda forces. In 2003 U.S. military commanders were already complaining of al Qaeda and Taliban attacks on troops in Afghanistan, with the militants escaping across the Pakistani frontier.

Inflaming the region's Islamic fanaticism, the March 2003 U.S.-led invasion and occupation of Iraq provoked a wave of resistance to the United States and its policies, both in the region generally and in Pakistan specifically. The Iraq War inspired and mobilized Muslims worldwide. Viewing the conflict as an assault on Islam, revenge was deemed defensive and justified—exactly what bin Laden and his ilk had hoped for. Before 9/11, he had framed Western policies as aggressive attacks on Islam and argued that defensive jihad was binding on all Muslims. Accordingly, MMA leader Maulana Shah Ahmed Noorani described Iraq as part of a broader U.S. crusade against Muslims and demanded that jihad become an obligation for all followers of Islam.[51] JUI leader Maulana Fazlur Rehman, in support of Iraq's secular dictator, said, "I want to give this message to Saddam Hussein that the people are with him. . . . America is a terrorist."[52]

Inside Pakistan, the deeply unpopular war in Iraq emboldened domestic opposition to Musharraf's alignment with Bush. The war on terror alliance became a major liability, as Musharraf was seen as complicit in the diabolical Western plot to weaken Islam. On December 14, 2003, and again on Christmas Day, in the tightly guarded city of Rawalpindi, home to the Pakistan Army headquarters, Musharraf narrowly escaped two assassination attempts.

"I have been saying that the greatest danger to our nation is not external," said an undeterred Musharraf, "it is internal and it comes from religious and sectarian extremists."[53] A military court convicted two soldiers for their involvement and, in total, tried four junior army officers and six air force personnel for their role in the plots. The revelation reflected years of the Pakistani military's close relations with Islamic militant groups and showed that an increasingly radical younger rank-and-file recruited from lower- and middle-class urban families was receptive to radical Islam.[54]

In condemning the assassination attack, Deputy Secretary Armitage praised Musharraf, calling him "absolutely terrific" and "one of our closest allies in the global war on terror . . . Had we not had Pervez Musharraf at the helm in Pakistan, then we could have quite a different equation in South Asia."[55] Despite the sincerity of U.S. support, the "different equation in South Asia" that Armitage referenced may have looked the same even without Musharraf. Indeed, with Musharraf in charge and elections rigged in his favor, his government ceded institutional power in two of Pakistan's four provinces to radical parties—the very regions where just a year and a half earlier, U.S. forces had swept the Taliban from power. Moreover, the mullah-military alliance, despite its outward appearance of strength, was gradually fracturing, creating conditions for even greater chaos.

Along his country's political spectrum, Musharraf occupied the moderate left, and pro-Taliban religious parties occupied the extreme right. Musharraf allied with the right, marginalized the left, and, eventually, alienated both. He called for a more "tolerant, progressive and civilized" Pakistan, not a "backward and intolerant Islam,"[56] and later pleaded in the editorial pages of the *Washington Post* for Muslims to shun militancy and extremism for "enlightened moderation."[57] Yet, in another political compromise with fundamentalist parties, the MMA voted in December 2003 to pass a 17th amendment to the Pakistani constitution that validated Musharraf's coup on his pledge to resign his military commission by the end of 2004. Alliance members did not adhere to the military's line on every issue. Some rejected the army's political role and Musharraf's demand to serve as president and army chief. Others praised Musharraf and the army's commitment to Islam. That discord, combined with squabbling among opposition parties in parliament, rendered legislative sessions in the National Assembly completely chaotic and left whole chunks of the country teetering on the edge of violent extremist anarchy.

Into the Fray

Washington continued to compromise its democratic principles for the sake of security and got neither. In 2003, for the 11th consecutive year, the nonpartisan Freedom House labeled Pakistan "not free" regarding political rights and civil liberties. A report from Human Rights Watch concluded that four years of military power had "led to serious human rights abuses." And the U.S. State Department, in its *Pakistan Country Report on Human Rights Practices, 2003*, found that Islamabad's record on human rights "remained poor" and listed "acute" corruption, extrajudicial killings, lack of judicial independence, political violence, terrorism, and "extremely poor" prison conditions—including police abuse and rape of citizens with apparent impunity—among the areas in which "serious problems remained."[58] Despite those offenses, Washington had long embraced and funded Pakistan's rulers, a record that was widely understood by the country's population. Little wonder that in January 2004 testimony before the Senate Foreign Relations Committee, one senior expert had to admit that "Pakistan is probably the most anti-American country in the world right now, ranging from the radical Islamists on one side to the liberals and Westernized elites on the other side."[59]

In the face of that pervasive antipathy, and perhaps to some extent because of it, Washington elevated the importance of intelligence sharing and tightened nuclear security measures over the importance of pushing democratic ideals. U.S. officials emphasized that the Pakistani government had captured more terrorists and committed more troops than almost any other nation in the war on terror. After all, the United States depended on Pakistan's air bases and intelligence sharing to capture senior al Qaeda fugitives, including 9/11 mastermind Khalid Sheikh Mohammad and bin Laden senior lieutenant Abu Zubaydah.[60]

After deploying 70,000 troops to capture foreign terrorist suspects in Operation Kalusha in South Waziristan in early March 2004, Musharraf claimed, "We do not want such elements to misuse our soil for activities against any other country, including Afghanistan." He demurred, though, when asked if he believed bin Laden, or his second-in-command, Ayman al-Zawahiri, were hiding there.[61] In reality, killing and capturing militants proved problematic in FATA's seven tribal agencies (Bajaur, Mohmand, Khyber, Orakzai, Kurram, North Waziristan, and South Waziristan). FATA fell within Pakistani territory but lay outside of its constitution. The Frontier Crimes Regulation, a British imperial relic imposed in 1901, gave councils of tribal elders (*jirgas*) absolute power to hold their populations accountable.[62] Beyond that administrative ambiguity, FATA's mountainous topography made monitoring insurgent activity and military infiltration of the region difficult. Much of that area can support only foot traffic or pack animals. Sealing the border would have been a daunting task for even the most capable military force.

Nevertheless, as a reward for Pakistan's bold steps against militancy, that June the Bush administration hosted Musharraf at the presidential retreat in Camp David, Maryland. Bush promised to work with Congress to establish a five-year, $3 billion aid package, split evenly between military and economic aid. Over a decade later, the nearly $20 billion total included Coalition Support Funds for reimbursing Pakistan's operational and logistical security support in U.S.-led counterterrorism operations and for F-16 combat aircraft and related U.S. military equipment for long-term modernization. Senior policy planners and lawmakers pushed for assistance packages that would make Pakistan the second leading recipient of U.S. foreign aid after Afghanistan—an amount even greater than that given to Israel.

The United States also designated Pakistan a major non-NATO ally, an exclusive club that included close U.S. allies Israel and South Korea. Moreover, Pakistan became eligible for foreign-aid benefits and military items under the Arms Export Control Act. The gestures proved badly timed. In February, Abdul Qadir Khan, Pakistan's infamous nuclear scientist and national hero, confirmed the existence of a global proliferation network that had illicitly transferred Pakistan's sensitive nuclear weapons technology to Iran, Libya, North Korea, and other countries. After Khan's pardon, and placement under a genteel house arrest, many citizens and security officials claimed he was a scapegoat whose black-market smuggling network could not have operated without official government-to-government assistance and military contacts.

More grave doubts about the mutual interests underpinning the U.S.-Pakistan alliance arose that July. In Washington, the congressionally authorized investigation into the 9/11 attacks accused Pakistan of helping the Taliban shelter bin Laden before 9/11. Pakistan's stance against terrorism proved shaky. But reflecting Washington's embrace of Islamabad's "enlightened moderation," the 9/11 Commission identified Musharraf as Pakistan's best hope for stability. The Commission's report recommended that the United States make a long-term commitment to the rapidly radicalizing, nuclear-armed Islamic Republic, specifically, with comprehensive aid and support for democratization, economic modernization, and education reform.

"His army has been incredibly active and very brave in southern Waziristan," proclaimed President Bush in December 2004 at the White House alongside President General Musharraf. "[The army is] flushing out an enemy that had thought they had found safe haven."[63] But even as Bush commended Musharraf for asserting his country's authority in Waziristan, his military faced hurdles of motivation and capability. On the ground, Western officials discovered that senior Taliban and Haqqani figures somehow learned of impending raids at the last minute and reported constant communication between Taliban figures and active and retired Pakistani military officials.[64] In 2005 a CIA attempt to capture militant leader Sirajuddin Haqqani was thwarted by the ISI. "Our guys couldn't believe it," a former

CIA officer told journalist Matthew Cole. "CIA had worked on this thing for some time, and the son of a bitch tipped Haqqani off."[65]

Compounding problems of divided loyalty, Pakistan's military offensives were disastrous and uncoordinated. In addition to FATA's colonial-era administration and inhospitable geography, its human terrain proved formidable. The Punjabi-dominated army and its repeated intrusions into quasi-autonomous Pashtun areas inflamed tribal sentiment. The army's conventional force structure—geared to fight India's standing armies—was ill-equipped and poorly trained to fight elusive and adaptive guerrillas. Desertions and mutinies mounted as the army suffered severe losses in confrontations with insurgents. Some officers admitted morale had plummeted to a level unseen since the 1971 civil war that halved the country's territory and shattered its political structure. "This is one country where soldiers are slaughtered," one soldier told the BBC. "Their bodies may be found, but not their heads."[66]

Out of desperation, Pakistan negotiated peace arrangements with militants. The government pledged to stop air and ground attacks, lift restrictions on travel, and resolve security issues in accordance with local customs. Militants later scrapped many of those deals either because of army offensives in other tribal agencies or U.S. missile strikes in FATA (discussed below).[67] Although efforts other than armed conflict were theoretically worth exploring, such "Sharia for peace" deals were dead on arrival. Instead of preserving the country's territorial integrity, Islamabad tried to save the integrity of its military by withdrawing the writ of the state. Its actions stemmed not just from impotence, but an unwillingness to suppress tribal insurrection. The notion of any state permitting its citizens to violently resist government control is a concept fundamentally alien to Western policymakers. The peace deals demanded little from militants to the government yet helped further radicalize Pakistan's Islamic identity. Worse, they gave militants virtual free rein so long as they focused their fire on U.S. and NATO military personnel in Afghanistan.

"When the president looks me in the eye and says, 'The tribal deal is intended to reject the Talibanization of the people,' and that there won't be a Taliban and won't be Al Qaeda, I believe him," President Bush said at a September 2006 press conference with Musharraf, praising the military leader's most recent peace accord.[68] Hindsight proved otherwise, as Bush wrote years later in his memoirs:

> Over time, it became clear that Musharraf either would not or could not fulfill all his promises. . . . Part of the problem was Pakistan's obsession with India. . . . A related problem was that Pakistani forces pursued the Taliban much less aggressively than they pursued al Qaeda.[69]

At the time, however, Musharraf made himself appear as the only leader capable of remedying his fractious country's myriad problems. For years, top officials in Washington backed Musharraf as the lesser of two evils when compared to the threat of extremism. Yet, extremism kept rising. In 2006, the U.S. State Department's Country Report on Terrorism called Pakistan "a major source of Islamic extremism and a safe haven for top terrorist leaders."[70] That homegrown Islamist militancy converged with a countrywide democratic struggle to remove Musharraf from office.

The Unraveling of "Bush and Mush"

Predating the 2011 Arab Spring, the Islamic world's earliest post-9/11 pro-democracy protests erupted in Pakistan in 2007. Evidence mounted that America's ally was illegally detaining its citizens and engaging in other abuses. In late 2006 the Human Rights Commission of Pakistan issued a 340-page report describing a "highly disturbing trend" of forced disappearances of Pakistani citizens stretching back to 2001. Domestic intelligence agencies picked up many of the missing persons and either detained them in secret locations or handed them over to the United States as accused terrorists. That year alone, the Asian Human Rights Commission on Pakistan estimated that some 600 persons had disappeared.[71] Interior Ministry spokesperson Brigadier Javed Iqbal Cheema claimed that the missing people had joined militant organizations. Senator Talha Mehmood scorned that explanation and retorted that accused terrorists should have been presented before a court of law. Mehmood blasted the disappearances as a "gross violation of human rights."[72] Human rights groups and families of victims appealed to Pakistan's Supreme Court to undertake the missing persons' cases. When the high court finally did, it commenced the highest profile proceedings in Pakistan's judicial history.

Ironically, the private satellite providers, Urdu and English newspapers, local and international radio and television stations, and Internet-based media that Musharraf helped liberalize played a major role in mobilizing the spontaneous demonstrations that hastened his downfall. On March 9, 2007, in an awkward showdown broadcast live on Pakistani television, Musharraf ordered Supreme Court Chief Justice Iftikhar Muhammad Chaudhry to either resign from office or face charges over abuse of his authority. Almost no one believed the charges. But in a scene vividly symbolizing the military's arrogance, police dragged Chaudhry by his hair into a waiting vehicle to be placed under house arrest. Soon after, riot police attacked Geo News, a private television station, after it broadcast images of baton-wielding police beating barristers. What began as an incipient lawyers' movement against Musharraf's authority expanded into countrywide upheaval for a return to civilian democracy.[73]

As police tear-gassed tens of thousands of lawyers, students, and political opponents, U.S. Vice President Dick Cheney addressed the turmoil in Pakistan directly. "We've got Musharraf in Pakistan and Karzai in Afghanistan who put their lives on the line every day, in effect, supporting our efforts to deal with the extremists and the terrorists in that part of world." He continued, "If they see us bail out in Iraq, they clearly would lose confidence in our capacity to carry through and get the job done." Cheney emphasized Iraq's importance to Afghanistan and Pakistan in "supporting our efforts to deal with extremists."[74] Yet at a time when Washington was supposedly seeking stability and democracy in Iraq, it overlooked their outright suppression in Pakistan. Cheney refused to acknowledge that the administration had gotten into bed with an odious strongman in a desperate, stop-gap measure to curb religious militants.

In his second inaugural address, President Bush promised to "support the growth of democratic movements and institutions in every nation and culture, with the ultimate goal of ending tyranny in our world." Pakistan was a prominent test of that proposition. But Musharraf, like a typical dictator, perceived a threat to his power from an increasingly assertive supreme court, whose activities he derisively labeled "judicial activism."[75] Previously, the court had stopped his government from selling a majority stake in a state-owned steel mill to acting Prime Minister Shaukat Aziz, allegedly at below market value. Fears that the court would challenge Musharraf's presidential powers on security issues intensified his anger. When the court demanded that ISI representatives account for missing persons, the hotheaded president general took it personally.[76]

In addition to that discrepancy in democracy promotion, the Bush administration also differentiated between Iraq and Pakistan militarily. The urgency of invading Iraq stemmed from a professed desire to avert a surprise attack through preventive war, yet the administration resisted that strategy with respect to Pakistan. That double standard is particularly curious in light of Washington's post-9/11 "weapons of mass destruction" obsession. The world knew that Pakistan possessed nuclear weapons and supported religious zealots, the very thing Bush accused Iraq of doing, yet one situation led to preventive war while another rendered it a remote possibility. In spite of the Bush administration's press blitz the following month, "Setting the Record Straight: Iraq Is the Central Front of al Qaeda's Global Campaign," developments far worse would rock nuclear-armed Pakistan—the real al Qaeda central front.[77]

In Islamabad, radical Islamist brothers Abdul Rashid Ghazi and Maulana Abdul Aziz headed the Red Mosque (Lal Masjid), a state-run madrasah of nearly 10,000 religious students. The clerics publicly supported the Taliban and urged their students to fight infidel troops in Afghanistan. They backed those pronouncements with vows to unleash a wave of suicide attacks if Musharraf's government failed to impose Sharia law in the federal capital.[78]

The threat was credible. The religious students were prepared to establish a parallel judicial system to compete with state courts, a Red Mosque leader told reporters.[79] Aziz ordered local video-store owners to either close their businesses or face punishment, and religious students burned thousands of Pakistani, Indian, and English CDs and DVDs. As in the hinterland, government officials appeased the capital's militants. Prime Minister and Pakistan Muslim League-Quaid-i-Azam leader Chaudhry Shujaat Hussain expressed a willingness to enforce Sharia in the heart of Pakistan. Religious students soon began hoarding caches of weapons and barricading themselves inside the mosque. After negotiations between the government and the Red Mosque administration failed to resolve the standoff, on July 3 hundreds of troops and army commandos stormed the shrine in a gory week-long raid. Public support for the crackdown quickly evaporated after it learned the level of the casualties. Local television stations reported fatality figures nearly double the government's official count of 76 militants and 11 soldiers.[80]

"I like him and I appreciate him," President Bush said of Musharraf the following day in Cleveland, Ohio, calling the dictator a "strong ally in the war against these extremists."[81] Assistant Secretary of State for South and Central Asia Richard Boucher acknowledged the militant buildup had been decades in the making but called the Red Mosque raid "a decisive move against extremism."[82] Ghazi and Aziz had been detained in 2004, only to be released by Religious Affairs Minister Ijazul Haq, who sympathized with their cause. Further ignoring the Red Mosque's provocations, the Musharraf government allowed the fundamentalists to foment trouble and remain unmolested for years. Hassan Abbas, who served under Musharraf from 1999 to 2000, criticized the regime's response:

> Delay in effectively tackling the defiant stance of Lal Masjid not only complicated the crisis, but gave ample opportunity to Ghazi to entrench his forces militarily, start an effective media campaign and draw sympathy from segments of society by claiming that he and his comrades were merely asking for the enforcement of religious laws in the country.[83]

Islamist political parties and their Talibanization of the volatile tribal belt were altering the state's Islamic character as the country's security spiraled downward.

"We have a firm belief in God that our blood will lead to a revolution," Ghazi wrote in a statement three days before his death in the grisly shootout. "God willing, Islamic revolution will be the destiny of this nation," he wrote.[84] In Bajaur Agency, days after the siege, renowned mujahid Maulana Faqir Mohammed stood before 20,000 armed tribesmen, some shouldering rocket-propelled grenades, and declared defiantly, "We beg Allah to destroy Musharraf, and we will seek revenge for the atrocities perpetrated on the Lal Masjid."[85]

Musharraf's Downward Spiral

To quote the King James Bible, Hosea 8:7, "For they have sown the wind, and they shall reap the whirlwind." In the months and years that followed the standoff in Islamabad, militants launched a wave of highly coordinated suicide bombings and explosions against military installations and civilian officials. Insurgents who turned against the state in the restive tribal areas now emerged in large and densely populated cities. Urban centers under Pakistani military control were now the targets of frequent and intense militant revenge attacks. It seemed the Islamic Republic was reaping the extensive destructive potential of the Islamic fanaticism it recklessly and foolhardily sowed. The state then confronted another setback, this time more explicitly of Musharraf's making.

On November 3, 2007—after the Pakistani Supreme Court filed six petitions challenging Musharraf serving as president and army chief simultaneously and challenging his eligibility the previous month to run for president as army chief—systematic government repression began. Musharraf again ordered Justice Chaudhry's arrest; abrogated the constitution; banned public demonstrations; blacked out privately owned television news stations; imposed a fusion of martial law and state of emergency; forbid courts from issuing orders against the president and the prime minister; and criminalized defamation of Musharraf, the army, and the government. Hundreds of army rangers manned checkpoints on Islamabad's streets. Squads of police raided the homes of opposition figures and arrested Musharraf's critics. More than 60 judges refused to take their oath of office sanctioning Musharraf's extraconstitutional act under a suspended constitution. They were summarily placed under house arrest.[86]

The next day in a nationally televised, 50-minute speech, Musharraf declared that necessity dictated his decision to preserve the country over the constitution. He even quoted America's 16th president, Abraham Lincoln, claiming that he, too, broke laws, violated the constitution, and trampled individual liberties to keep the union together. For Pakistan, Musharraf insisted, such powers were "the simplest way to save Pakistan" and "put it back on the right track."[87] His speech echoed the self-assurance of previous army chiefs who ruled the broken country:

- "This is a drastic and extreme step taken with great reluctance but with the deepest conviction

that there was no alternative to it except the disintegration and complete ruination of the country."
—Ayub Khan, October 8, 1958;

- "The armed forces could not remain idle spectators of this state of near anarchy. They have to do their duty and save the country from utter disaster." —Yayha Khan, March 26, 1969; and,

- "I was obliged to step in to fill the vacuum created by the political leaders." —Zia ul-Haq, July 5, 1977.[88]

Senior U.S. officials greeted Musharraf's actions with a mixture of opprobrium and approbation. Gordon Johndroe, the National Security Council spokesperson, stated bluntly, "They need to release the people that they've arrested, they need to stop beating people in the streets, they need to restore press freedom and they need to get back on the path to democracy soon—now."[89] Deputy Secretary of State John D. Negroponte was less emphatic, but still critical of Musharraf's behavior: "The United States believes that the best way for any country to counter violent extremism is to develop and nurture a moderate political center."[90]

National Security Advisor Stephen J. Hadley, however, struck a discordant note, saying "President Musharraf has been responsive to calls from his own people for clarity on these subjects." Raising the stakes, Negroponte backed away from his previous implied criticism, now calling Musharraf an "indispensable ally."[91] President Bush, after a meeting with German Chancellor Angela Merkel in Crawford, Texas, expressed fondness for Musharraf and his stand with America after 9/11: "He was given an option," Bush said. "Are you with us, or are you not with us? And he made a clear decision to be with us, and he's acted on that advice."[92]

Bush's unwavering loyalty reflected genuine convictions and rested on a set of widely held assumptions. Policymakers often downplay the significance of their public displays of admiration for a dictator and how it identifies the United States as a pillar of support for that tyrant's repression. According to U.S. intelligence agencies, total Pakistani casualties in 2007, including injured security forces and civilians, exceeded the cumulative total for all years between 2001 and 2006. A significant segment of Pakistan's society saw Musharraf's so-called "U.S. dictated" military policies as the central cause of the spate of suicide bombings that plagued the country from 2007 to early 2008.[93] After 9/11, a Gallup poll found that Muslims worldwide associated Western democracy and liberty most strongly with the United States, but saw America promoting those principles nearly everywhere except in the Muslim world. Furthermore, they perceived the disconnect between America's principles and how America treats them as a sign the United States does not view Muslims as equals.[94]

"Pressure mounted on me to cut ties with Musharraf," Bush recalls in his memoirs. "I worried that throwing him overboard would add to the chaos."[95] U.S. officials assumed that autocrats such as Musharraf could control their populations and keep a lid on events. The Bush administration grudgingly tolerated Musharraf's disdain for democratic reform by invoking the justification of "stability." But propping up a dictator made true stability elusive when his clumsy agenda continually intensified popular resentments against him. Martial law, the dismissal of independent judges, media blackouts, and arrests of political opponents made an already dangerous situation lethal. Between the Talibanization of the tribal regions and religious radicalization sweeping major cities, Pakistan's president, military, and government agencies had created an explosive combination.

U.S. policymakers also tend to emphasize personal ties to foreign leaders, a debilitating strategy when policies do not go according to plan. Although State Department officials denied "somehow stage-managing" Islamabad's internal affairs, reports suggest that U.S. policymakers turned to former Prime Minister Benazir Bhutto to arrest Pakistan's slide into chaos.[96] In Dubai and London, Bhutto talked with Musharraf senior aides, meetings that U.S. and British officials encouraged allegedly to forge a deal allowing Musharraf to remain president and army chief and allowing Bhutto to return from exile if her corruption cases could be dropped.[97]

On October 18, 2007, Bhutto returned to Pakistan's political scene after eight years of self-imposed exile in Dubai. The PPP chairwoman had fled Pakistan to escape trial for cases alleging that she and her husband, Asif Ali Zardari—infamously known for his corruption as

"Mr. 10 Percent"—had used questionable schemes to steal nearly $2 billion from their poor country's coffers. Her return came under the auspices of the National Reconciliation Ordinance (NRO), a statute that cleared current and former senior officials from all pending corruption cases. For many citizens, the NRO was yet another example of their government's rampant criminality and America's support for its policies.[98]

Whatever the NRO's backroom mechanics and string-pulling to keep Musharraf in power, they failed to stem Pakistan's deepening crisis. A month after Musharraf lifted emergency rule, restored the constitution, and resigned as army chief—traditionally the country's most powerful office—a crisis struck. On December 27, Benazir Bhutto was assassinated as she was leaving a campaign rally in Rawalpindi. Baitullah Mehsud, the head of the Waziristan-based Tehrik-e-Taliban Pakistan (TTP), was the primary suspect, although Bhutto's death remained shrouded in mystery. Mass looting and lawlessness soon followed her murder. Under headlines declaring, "The World's Most Dangerous Place," images of angry bearded men burning American flags and political effigies dominated international news coverage of the state.

In exchange for not rebuking Musharraf's ravaging of the democratic process, Washington got, at best, a schizophrenic ally. Even as the Islamic Republic cooperated with U.S. efforts to capture and kill al Qaeda, its Pashtun and Balochi areas operated as de facto safe havens for the Taliban, the Haqqani network, the Hizb-e-Islami Group, and other insurgent factions deliberately underming America's war on terror. In January 2008, the Director of National Intelligence, J. Michael McConnell, told the White House, "the Pakistani government regularly gives weapons and support to insurgents to go into Afghanistan and attack Afghan and coalition forces." Those safe havens, McConnell stated, permitted al Qaeda to regain strength and allowed the Taliban to "train, recruit, rest and recuperate and then come back into Afghanistan to engage."[99] In February, in testimony before the House Permanent Select Committee on Intelligence, U.S. officials assessed that Pakistan-based Lashkar-e-Taiba and other Kashmir-focused militant groups would continue attacks in India and support attacks in Afghanistan. One section of the ISI, known as Directorate S, was a known financier and nurturer of the Taliban and other terrorist groups.[100]

After years of Afghanistan being the forgotten war, events came as a rude awakening when news coverage finally caught up with reality. In March, CIA Director General Michael Hayden said he agreed with other top U.S. officials that another terrorist attack on the U.S. homeland would likely originate from the region. And in late May 2008 an intelligence intercept revealed that Pakistan's Army Chief of Staff, General Ashfaq Kayani, had referred to Jalaluddin Haqqani as a "strategic asset."[101] Outgoing commander of NATO forces in Afghanistan U.S. General Dan McNeill said he was "troubled" by Pakistan's negotiations with insurgents, observing that violence in eastern Afghanistan increased significantly when Pakistan arranged peace deals on its side of the Durand Line. A discussion paper later published by the London School of Economics and Political Science accused the ISI of funding the Taliban insurgency and maintaining representation on the movement's leadership council.[102]

Those troubling developments exposed a core weakness of U.S. policy: it remained hostage to an ally that was both key to regional stability and a major contributor to its violence. In this case, doing nothing was still doing something. Refusing to attack insurgents or control tribal regions for one reason or another amounted to obstruction of the war in Afghanistan. By August, Musharraf resigned ignominiously as president, and by October, Bush was winding down his second term. The two unpopular presidents left their successors a war gone horribly wrong. Not only had the conflict undergone a dramatic shift, from mixed levels of relative stability to a guerilla insurgency expanding political and economic influence, but also three-quarters of NATO provisions bound for Afghanistan traveled through Pakistan, a saboteur of the security environment in Afghanistan. Black-market trucking mafias and criminal gangs sanctioned by Islamabad launched coordinated attacks on supply convoys to steal commodities, flak jackets, and M-4 rifles. Police refused to interfere and often provided cover for the operations. One study found that nearly 95 percent of all NATO containers were broken into before reaching their destination.[103]

No less alarming was that President Bush, for all his "dead or alive" rhetoric, displayed great reticence for years over appalling disclosures of Pakistani duplicity. As early as September 2006, the NATO Supreme Allied Military Commander overseeing U.S. and NATO operations in Afghanistan told a U.S. Senate Foreign Relations Committee that it was "generally accepted" that the Afghan Taliban's headquarters was in the vicinity of Quetta—a Pakistani provincial capital, not a tribal region.[104] Until 2008 the Bush administration had decided against disturbing relations with a regime whose major spy agency colluded with militants launching cross-border attacks that killed U.S. military and coalition forces. The administration's distractions and passivity pointlessly sacrificed American and foreign lives. Bush's successor, Barack Obama, attempted to rectify the situation with ambitious goals of restoring order and enforcing peace, underestimating the difficulty of subduing a region resistant to foreign-imposed lethal force.

Afghanistan: America's Longest War

Afghanistan went from being called "the good war" and "the forgotten war" to "Obama's war" when, in 2009, President Barack Obama more than doubled the number of U.S. troops in that country, boosting Washington's commitment to over 100,000 personnel. The president had deepened the U.S. entanglement even as an increasing number of Americans believed the conflict was not worth fighting. Attempting to reconcile the two trends, Obama set a timeline for beginning the withdrawal of the newly deployed troops while declining to set an end date for a full withdrawal.

That same year, President Obama appointed veteran diplomat Richard C. Holbrooke to explore political and diplomatic solutions to end the war as America's special representative for Afghanistan and Pakistan. He also selected former CIA official and harsh critic of President Bush's "halfhearted effort" in Afghanistan, Bruce Riedel, to chair the White House's high-level, intra-agency strategic review of the newly coined "Af-Pak" region.[105]

"So the theme of this process is to be flexible, adaptable and comprehensive, and self-regulating with periodic reviews," Riedel said in March 2009.[106] Despite claims of a "flexible" process, few of Obama's senior diplomatic, military, and intelligence advisers taking part in the no-holds-barred debate pressed forcefully for limiting America's commitment in Afghanistan. While the review recommended an increased focus on Pakistan, it also suggested a broad counterinsurgency campaign in Afghanistan and massive investments in governance and economic development.

"I don't think you win this war. I think you keep fighting," Army General David H. Petraeus said in a widely quoted statement. "This is the kind of fight we're in for the rest of our lives and probably our kids' lives."[107] After the White House asked the Pentagon for a range of troop options to exit Afghanistan, Petraeus publicly endorsed an open-ended increase of 40,000 troops before the president made his final decision.

Stephen Biddle, a civilian adviser to General Stanley McChrystal, the commander of U.S. troops on the Afghan front, argued that "this is the single greatest U.S. interest in Afghanistan: to prevent it from aggravating Pakistan's internal problems and magnifying the danger of an al-Qaida nuclear-armed sanctuary there."[108] Of course, Pakistan has been harmful to regional stability and remains Afghanistan's key destabilizer, not the other way around. Indeed, Pakistan's reliance on tribal auxiliaries since 1947 should have informed the review. The Islamic Republic exploited the loose authority it wielded over its territories and impudently demanded recognition of its sovereignty. That Pakistan had a longer track record than Afghanistan of harboring al Qaeda should have constituted a standard against which U.S. policies were assessed.

Vice President Joe Biden advised President Obama, "If you don't get Pakistan right, you can't win."[109] He believed that sending more troops to Afghanistan would be counterproductive for that larger objective. There was no strong evidence that Taliban leaders would host al Qaeda again in Afghanistan, and Washington's goal of denying terrorists sanctuary in Afghanistan need not require pacification of the entire country.

But in September 2009, an op-ed in the *Wall Street Journal* by the most outspoken advocates of greater U.S. military involvement around the world, Senators Lindsey Graham, Joseph Lieberman, and John McCain, echoed Petraeus. "More troops will not guarantee success in Afghanistan," they argued, "but a failure to send them is a guarantee of failure."[110] A pessimistic Holbrooke, however, concluded that Obama's 30,000-trooop-decision "can't work."[111] He interpreted his duty as priming the Taliban for talks, if the movement disowned al Qaeda and peacefully entered the Afghan political system. According to Holbrooke's senior adviser, Vali Nasr, the Taliban was ready for talks as early as April 2009, but the White House, "did not want to try anything as audacious as diplomacy."[112]

As the U.S. military commitment to Afghanistan expanded, Congress also authorized a tripling of nonmilitary assistance to Pakistan, contending that the long-term interests of stability in South Asia rested on stable, democratic, and prosperous states. The Enhanced Partnership Act of 2009, which provided $1.5 billion in annual nonmilitary aid until fiscal year 2014, was also intended to strengthen the bonds of cooperation between the American and the Pakistani peoples and support democratic institutions and the rule of law.

Whether aid was the best vehicle to bring about or reward such transformations remained debatable. On February 18, 2008, in what Musharraf called the "mother of all elections," Pakistanis voted for Asif Ali Zardari, Bhutto's widower, and Nawaz Sharif, who had served twice before as prime minister. Both civilian leaders, who then formed a unity government, had toilet-paper-thin reputations for integrity, and neither embraced an ethos of democratic accountability or displayed bureaucratic competence. President Zardari appointed as defense minister his former cellmate and PPP veteran Ahmad Mukhtar, who had no background in military affairs, but who did own more than 400 shoe stores.

The Islamist political party, JUI, supported Zardari's election. In return the government reopened Lal Masjid's all-male seminary (Jamia Faridia) and appointed ultra-orthodox senator Mualana Sherani to chair the council of Islamic ideology. Sharif held even greater sway among religious conservatives, although he was remembered as a dull politician of mediocre talent. During his second term as prime minister, he was so disconnected that he learned Islamabad had extended diplomatic recognition to the Taliban only when he heard the news on Pakistani television.[113]

Incompetent Pakistani leaders faced daunting challenges, yet few in Washington considered whether U.S. aid actually served the stated interest of providing sustainable economic development. For example, endemic tax evasion in Pakistan irritated Washington. Secretary of State Hillary Clinton epitomized that annoyance. Speaking to an audience at the U.S. Global Leadership Coalition conference, she stated: "Pakistan cannot have a tax rate of 9 percent of GDP when land owners and all of the other elites do not pay anything or pay so little it's laughable, and then when there's a problem everybody expects the United States and others to come in and help."[114] Her listeners greeted that comment with enthusiastic applause, but despite such uncompromising rhetoric, neither Clinton nor other U.S. policymakers did anything of substance to pressure Pakistani officials to improve their abysmal performance.

Pakistani leaders often diverted aid to themselves rather than the country's economic and social development. In turn, many Pakistanis connected U.S. aid with their country's deteriorating condition, as such aid allowed leaders to avoid confronting their country's rampant corruption and budgetary problems with the necessary urgency. Developments in Pakistan also showed that whatever public diplomacy and goodwill benefits U.S. aid intended, it failed to offset the widespread anti-American sentiment that resulted from aid abuses and other U.S. policies. The Enhanced Partnership's conditions attached to nonmilitary aid were widely viewed as infringements on Pakistan's sovereignty. Moreover, years of ample U.S. military and economic assistance had failed to turn Pakistan into a reliable ally. Most of the world's jihadi terror plots had some connection to Pakistan-based elements, including those responsible for the November 2008 attacks in Mumbai.

After years of neglect, leaders in Washington pledged to get serious about pursuing al Qaeda in Pakistan. The Obama administration relied heavily on the U.S. military's clandestine Joint Special Operations Command and the CIA's covert program of unmanned aerial vehicles, or drones, as instruments of targeted killing. President Bush had dramatically ramped up drone strikes in the waning months of his presidency, but whereas drone strikes averaged once every 40 days under Bush, they increased to once every 4 days under Obama. This shadowy, secret war, according to U.S. officials, shook al Qaeda's ability to plan, prepare, and train. Drones killed al Qaeda spokesperson Abu Laith al-Libi in January 2008, al Qaeda chemical weapons expert Abu Khabab al-Masri in July 2008, and other senior al Qaeda terrorists. But despite the campaign's touted success, the CIA never officially confirmed the existence of the covert drone program, apparently in deference to the wishes of the Pakistani government. Moreover, Islamabad continued to forbid entry into FATA unless granted special permission.

Although the New America Foundation and the Bureau of Investigative Journalism compiled civilian casualty data, each organization disputed the others' analysis.[115] With few researchers able to independently verify the drone program's effectiveness and evaluate its second- and third-order consequences to make an adequate cost/benefit tradeoff, rumors, speculation, and conspiracy theories became rampant. Only 53 percent of the Pakistani public favored using its military to fight extremist groups in FATA and neighboring Khyber Pukhtunkhwa.[116] To minimize the political uproar, Pakistani officials condemned drones publicly while consenting to them privately. Retired Pakistani military officers, right-wing politicians, conservative clerics, and civil society figures spread the perception that Pakistan was fighting America's war and that drones violated their country's sovereignty and slaughtered innocent civilians. Unidentified government sources from the ISI's propaganda arm and army mouthpiece, the Inter-Services Public Relations Directorate, sought to conceal the ISI's cooperation with the CIA. Yet, drones took off from Shamsi airfield in Baluchistan and Shahbaz military base (Jacobabad) in Sindh while the Pakistan Army provided protection to the drone launch bases and human intelligence support.[117]

Pakistani citizens were not the only ones misled. Pakistani leaders leveraged public outrage over civilian casualties and violations of sovereignty to pressure U.S. officials to gain a greater say over drone-strike policy to target domestic enemies.[118]

"We have certain evidence that there is a close connection, links and that there are similarities between Al-Qaeda and TTP," Interior Minister Rehman Malik told reporters in Islamabad. "If Al-Qaeda is to move in a tribal area, they have to look to the TTP to get a refuge. . . . The TTP is a host to Al-Qaeda and is their mouthpiece."[119] Pakistani militants constantly fractured, regrouped, and changed sides, making it difficult to draw conclusions. The TTP, for instance, pledged fealty to Mullah Omar, but compared with the Afghan Taliban it lacked a unified leadership and had more limited, localized political objectives.[120] Of the many unintended consequences generated by the war's deceitful façade, targeting Pakistan's enemies turned them into America's enemies. Some U.S. officials understood that point, but they seemed willing to tolerate that outcome as a necessary cost of the war on terror.

"Anti-US sentiment has already been increasing in Pakistan . . . especially in regard to cross-border and reported drone strikes, which Pakistanis perceive to cause unacceptable civilian casualties," General Petraeus wrote in a May 2009 declassified statement. That same year, Washington's ambassador to Pakistan, Anne Patterson, warned her superiors that "unilateral targeting of al-Qaeda operatives and assets," while important to countering terrorism, "risks destabilizing the Pakistani state, alienating both the civilian government and the military leadership, and provoking a broader government crisis without finally achieving the goal."[121]

In August 2009, a CIA drone killed TTP leader Baitullah Mehsud. Although he was not a top al Qaeda operative, U.S. officials believed his death would strike a blow to his movement. The strike predictably opened a leadership vacuum, and a power struggle among rival factions ensued. But whereas Baitullah was content with waging attacks against Pakistani soldiers and police, Baitullah's cousin Hakimullah Mehsud, who succeeded him, constituted a more serious threat. In addition to the fact that Hakimullah was as virulently anti-American as his predecessor, U.S. intelligence agencies observed that more TTP fighters began to align with al Qaeda and carry out raids and attacks against U.S. troops in Afghanistan.[122]

That December, blowback hit Khost Province in southeastern Afghanistan. A suicide bomber killed seven CIA officers at Forward Operating Base Chapman in the deadliest day for the intelligence agency in a quarter century. The attack was believed to be a strategic hit by Pakistan-based radicals who intended to degrade U.S. capabilities at Chapman, the center of the CIA's drone program.[123]

Spy Games

Manifesting the U.S.-Pakistan alliance's unstable, seesawing dynamic was an unprecedented phase of successful but low-profile CIA-ISI cooperation to arrest and capture terrorists. CIA-operated drones raining hellfire missiles from the sky coincided with major Pakistani military offensives on its border with Afghanistan. Cooperation reached a high point in February 2010, when the allies arrested more militants than in the previous eight-and-a-half years combined.[124] Despite new tactics and cooperative action, blowback persisted thanks to a resurgence of the very threat the U.S. sought to neutralize: Pakistan-based groups plotting anti-Western attacks. In June, TTP-trained Pakistani-naturalized citizen Faisal Shahzad attempted to detonate an explosive-laden SUV in downtown Manhattan. His motive was anger over Muslim deaths by U.S. drones. To U.S. intelligence officials, attempts like Shahzad's undoubtedly grew out of CIA drone strikes. They made the TTP, according to one official, "increasingly determined to seek revenge by finding any way possible to strike at the United States."[125]

The Obama administration's drone warfare campaign dramatically limited his domestic political costs of war by not putting U.S. military personnel directly at risk. Of course, as the administration later tacitly admitted with its repeated justifications to critics, drone bombing also weakened accepted standards of domestic and international law, such as waging conflicts in countries upon which Congress had not formally declared war and violating international principles of sovereignty it once declared to be unbreakable. The drone campaign may have provoked terrorism (by Shahzad among others), but American leaders seemed to embrace the spirit of Thomas Hobbes, "Every independent commonwealth has a right to do what it pleases to other commonwealths."[126]

Moreover, as regional experts and senior officials began to grasp, drone strikes did little to change the region's bigger picture: Pakistan's strategic interest in supporting militants. ISI officers continued to recruit madrasah students as suicide bombers inside Afghanistan, sometimes even with the help of Afghan police. U.S. intelligence reported conversations between attackers and ISI officers on logistics for strikes against Afghan-based Indian targets.[127] The Pakistani military succeeded in rooting out militants in the Bajaur, Mohmand, and Orakzai tribal agencies, but continued its foot-dragging against the North Waziristan–based Haqqani network, which posed one of the greatest threats in large parts of Afghanistan's Paktika, Paktia and Khost provinces. Senate Armed Services Committee Chairman Carl Levin (D-MI) explained the situation in a September 2010 report: "The Pakistan military continued to avoid military engagements that would put it in direct conflict with Afghan Taliban or al-Qa'ida forces in North Waziristan. This is as much a political choice as it is a reflection of an under-resourced military prioritizing its targets."[128]

The partners cooperated on narrow transactional issues, such as drone bases and intelligence sharing, but they worked at cross-purposes when larger interests slipped out of sync. In Afghanistan especially, Pakistan sought equilibrium. Pakistani diplomats and officials argued repeatedly that their country's military and intelligence institutions wanted to enable a Taliban victory; Pakistan's military and intelligence institutions provided just enough support to forestall a Taliban defeat and pressure sufficient to eventually represent Pakistani interests in Afghanistan.[129] Raza Rumi, a director who studies the conflict for the Jinnah Institute in Islamabad, suggested that the military considered the Haqqanis as a means to shape the future of Afghanistan once the Americans left. "They do not act against the militants in North Waziristan because they are in a tactical relationship with them for the last eleven years to ensure a stake in the Afghanistan end game," he said.[130]

As Pakistanis soon discovered, espionage machinations were a two-way street. In January 2011 an incident exposed a web of unilateral U.S. intelligence collection in a country already rife with self-denial, anti-Americanism, and fears of malevolent foreign influence. U.S. Embassy employee (and undercover CIA contractor) Raymond Davis shot and killed two Pakistani robbers later discovered to be ISI agents. Scores of demonstrators across Pakistan called for Davis's execution. After weeks of misinformation, Davis was freed after victims' families allegedly received around $2.3 million in hush money.[131]

Another crisis in the bilateral alliance erupted on May 1. Seventy-nine members of the U.S. Navy's Sea, Air, Land Team entered northwest Pakistan by helicopter in a stealth assassination mission against Osama bin Laden. President Obama justified the raid as an appropriate and necessary act of vengeance for 9/11, and Americans rejoiced. But in a *New York Times* op-ed headline, al Qaeda specialist Gilles Kepel aptly captured the waning power and influence of the al Qaeda leader: "Bin Laden Was Dead Already." Indeed, documents obtained during the mission, Operation Neptune Spear, suggest that he no longer exercised control over the actions and statements of al Qaeda in the Arabian Peninsula or of many jihadi "affiliates" or "fellow travelers," such as the TTP. After combing through the trove of documents, the Department of Social Sciences at the U.S. Military Academy at West Point concluded that bin Laden was no "puppet master pulling the strings that set in motion jihadi groups around the world."[132] In fact, al Qaeda central had no formalized or unified command over regional jihadi groups that acted in its name. Washington's achievement with bin Laden's death was, therefore, more symbolic than substantive.

What was more significant was the location of bin Laden's exile haven. He lived in austere comfort at a safe house in Abbottabad, a sleepy garrison town just 35 miles north of Islamabad and home to retired army officers and Pakistan's main military academy. The presence of al Qaeda's leader on Pakistani soil, and so near a large military personnel center, raised grave questions, ranging from Pakistani government complicity in hiding bin Laden to institutional incompetence in not knowing the whereabouts of a major international terrorist. Rather than offer credible justifications either way, retired senior Pakistani army officers and political commentators spread conspiracy theories about bin Laden's death and charged that America had transgressed Pakistan's sovereignty.

The unilateral U.S. intrusion ignited a quick and ferocious backlash in Pakistan. On May 14, its Senate and National Assembly passed a resolution condemning the U.S. raid as a violation of Pakistan's sovereignty and the drone strikes as an assault on the UN Charter, international law, and humanitarian norms. The resolution called for a foreign policy for Pakistan independent of America, echoing Article 40 of Pakistan's 1973 constitution.[133] Prime Minister Yousaf Raza Gilani warned that, should another violation of Pakistan's sovereignty occur, Pakistan reserved the right to retaliate with full force.

Amid pious denunciations and unabashed recalcitrance, Pakistan experienced the adverse consequences of its own policies. On May 22, a team of 10 to 15 heavily armed TTP militants, in retaliation for the death of Osama bin Laden, stormed Mehran naval base in Karachi. They triggered a 16-hour gun battle with security forces in the most significant attack against a Pakistani military facility.[134] Sparking long-standing concerns over Pakistan's nuclear security, the dramatic assault occurred just 15 miles from a depot believed to house nuclear weapons.

A day later, Brigadier General Ali Khan and three other military officers were arrested for alleged links to Hezb-ut-Tahrir, an international pan-Islamic organization that aimed to unify Muslim countries into a single nation-state. The group had a large following among retired Pakistani army officers and former soldiers who desired Islamist reforms within Pakistan. Khan wrote letters to army generals with suggestions on how to become "self-reliant" and "purge the army of the American influence." The terror attack was an insurgent hydra—a monstrosity that even involved members of Pakistan's navy and the army's elite Special Services Group that trained TTP in North Waziristan.[135]

At long last, Islamabad's duplicity was fraying Washington's patience. In September, Chairman of the Joint Chiefs of Staff Admiral Michael Mullen publicly charged that Pakistan was "exporting" violence. America's top military officer told Congress, "The Haqqani network, for one, acts as a veritable arm of Pakistan's intelligence." That open secret, the disclosure of which was long considered taboo among Western politicians, diplomats, and journalists, made front-page news. Yet Pakistan's Foreign Minister Hina Rabbani Khar addressed Mullen's accusations succinctly in an interview with Geo television in New York: "You cannot afford to alienate Pakistan. You cannot afford to alienate the Pakistani people."[136] Mullen more or less agreed. In his congressional testimony, Mullen stated his belief that despite Pakistan's duplicity, flawed relations were better than none. Giving up on Pakistan, in his view, was not an acceptable option.

Conclusion

For American leaders, Pakistan was indispensable. It was too disloyal to keep as an ally, yet too dangerous to make into an enemy. Pakistan cooperated on hundreds of operations to kill and capture senior al Qaeda operatives and terrorists—more than any other American partner. But, put crudely, Afghanistan birthed the Taliban and Pakistan birthed al Qaeda; conceivably, Pakistan's ability to counter its terrorists reflected its inextricable links to them.

The key point underlying much of the alliance's duplicity was the question of sovereignty. A nation-state, which Pakistan claims to be, exercises, by definition, a monopoly on violence for the purpose of retaining control of its people and territory. The inability or unwillingness of Pakistan to fully cooperate with anti-terrorism measures reflected Western misperceptions about how a state should act. Pakistan exploited its sovereignty, as it has since its birth. But the notion that any state, for whatever reason, could not or would not control violent and treasonous elements within its borders was perplexing to U.S. officials and contributed greatly to the frustrating outcome in Afghanistan.

Three successive U.S. administrations knew what they wanted from their Pakistan counterparts: cooperation against al Qaeda. But efforts were impeded by Pakistan's intransigence and Washington's own misperceptions of what Islamabad could or would do. The country's possession of nuclear weapons made more dramatic U.S. efforts, such as an invasion, impossible, or at least politically unfeasible and not worth the consequences. But the main issue, the disconnect between how Pakistan should behave as a sovereign state and how Pakistan actually behaved, prompts a simple question: Where is the sovereignty Pakistan claims to possess?

The search for an answer begins next door. The Afghan war amplified existing problems; it did not create them. Indeed, events after 9/11 appeared to vindicate the prescriptions contained in the 1979 book, *The Quranic Concept of War*. With a forward by former dictator General Zia ul-Haq, the book, written by Pakistani Brigadier General S. K. Malik, lays out the case for Islamic warfare in which all means are just and righteous "for the cause of Allah."[137] The umma expanded beyond the traditional territorial boundaries of a state. Malik's view proved to be a prescient look into the post-9/11 world and asymmetric warfare. Radicals viewed existing government bodies as constructs of imperialism that impeded the umma's advancement.

The collective duty of Islam compelled Muslims to agitate against injustice, constituting a supranational force that transcended Islam's separate communities. After 9/11, even though seemingly inconceivable, Islamabad officially allied with Washington, while its supranational radical proxies made it Washington's de facto enemy.

15. Tangled Trails of the Silk Road: Washington and Central Asia's Tyrants

The Soviet Union's sudden disintegration at the end of 1991 created 15 newly independent states in what had been the territory of the USSR. Washington had two top priorities during the early phase of this new era. One was to integrate, as rapidly as possible, the successor countries in the European portion of the former Soviet empire into Western institutions. Thus began the lobbying effort to secure membership in the European Union—and ultimately the North Atlantic Treaty Organization (NATO)—for not only the formerly captive nations in Central and Eastern Europe, but for at least some Soviet republics, especially the Baltic states (Estonia, Latvia, and Lithuania.) Some ambitious U.S. foreign policy activists even embraced the long-term goal of incorporating Ukraine and Georgia in those Western institutions.

A second crucial objective was to get Ukraine, Belarus, and Kazakhstan to relinquish the nuclear weapons stationed in their territory, which they now inherited as independent countries. Kazakhstan's intentions were especially a matter of concern, since many Soviet missile launch sites had been located there, and there were apparently some 1,400 nuclear warheads on Kazakh soil. Uncertainty about the country's future stability and political orientation added to U.S. and Western worries.

Washington adopted a concerted carrot-and-stick strategy to persuade the newly minted states to turn over their nukes to Russia. The main carrots were rather vague U.S. guarantees of their security against any future depredations by Moscow and far more specific promises of lucrative aid packages to those governments now struggling with an assortment of major economic woes.[1] Both the security pledges and the financial inducements, though, were predicated on their willingness to fully cooperate in Washington's effort to roll back the proliferation that had occurred with the USSR's disintegration. The stick was an unsubtle warning that if the successor states insisted on keeping their newly acquired nuclear capabilities, the United States would treat them as it would any other "rogue" proliferators and lead an international effort to isolate them diplomatically and economically.

The strategy worked. A handful of nationalists in both Ukraine and Kazakhstan, suspicious of the Kremlin's long-term intentions, believed that an independent nuclear deterrent was the best way to guarantee that there would be no Russian effort to reconstitute the Soviet empire. A few international relations experts in the United States made similar arguments and derided the anti-nuclear campaign as shortsighted. University of Chicago professor John Mearsheimer, widely considered the dean of hard-core foreign policy realists in the academic community, was especially outspoken on that point. Writing in the pages of *Foreign Affairs*, Mearsheimer argued that the possession of a nuclear deterrent by Russia's neighbors, especially Ukraine, was the most reliable—perhaps the only reliable—way to prevent a future leader in the Kremlin from seeking to reassemble the Russian empire.[2] But Mearsheimer and other academic dissidents had little influence and were unable even to slow, much less halt, the drive to denuclearize all successor states, except for Russia.

Although that aspect of U.S. policy may have played into Moscow's hands, Washington was not about to concede that Russia rightfully had a sphere of influence beyond its borders, much less that it could enjoy a dominant position in Central Asia or any other portion of the former USSR.[3] To the contrary, the administrations of George H. W. Bush and Bill Clinton moved to maximize Western, especially U.S., influence in the newly independent countries.[4] Nowhere was that more evident than in Central Asia. Washington's objectives there were threefold. One was to blunt any effort by Russia to establish a de facto hegemony in the remnants of the former empire. Another goal was to create a buffer against China's increasingly evident attempt to maximize its influence among Central Asian states. The third objective was to thwart Iran from appealing to religious solidarity to expand its influence among Central Asia's Muslim societies. James A. Baker, George H. W. Bush's secretary of state, was quite candid about that last motive for U.S. policy in the region. "We, of course, were concerned about Iran, and supportive of Turkey's efforts to bring Central Asia into its sphere of influence."[5]

Even during the decade-long interlude between the end of the Cold War and the onset of the war on terror, the United States had powerful strategic and economic motives for trying to enhance its ties with the Central Asian republics. U.S. policymakers remained suspicious of both Moscow and Beijing and did not want to see the diplomatic or strategic reach of either country increase.[6] Aside from the normal competitive dynamics of relations between great powers, prospects for meaningful, lasting democracy in Russia were uncertain, at best, under Boris Yeltsin, strengthening Washington's wariness about Moscow's future international as well as domestic behavior. Likewise, U.S. policymakers viewed China as a worrisome authoritarian state with possible expansionist ambitions. That perception grew after the Tiananmen Square massacre in 1989 dashed hopes that China might evolve into a democratic state anytime soon. Beijing's growing economic power and diplomatic assertiveness, including a variety of territorial claims along China's perimeter during the 1990s and the initial years of the new century, also dampened any expectations that China would be content to support the U.S.-led status quo in Asia. U.S.-Chinese trade and other economic ties continued to grow, but officials in Washington increasingly viewed China as an emerging "strategic competitor"—a term that presidential candidate George W. Bush and his foreign policy advisers used until, once in office, they concluded that it was too toxic in terms of bilateral diplomacy. Although the rivalry between the United States and China became most evident in East Asia, it existed in Central Asia as well.

U.S. leaders also worried about the growth of Iranian political and diplomatic influence in the region and the possible mischief that Tehran could create. Tehran worked to cultivate political and commercial ties with various Central Asian states, especially Turkmenistan, Tajikistan, and Afghanistan. A key goal of that strategy was to maximize Iranian influence throughout the Caspian Basin and its environs, thereby protecting Iran's eastern flank. Analyst Stephen J. Blank aptly described Tehran's diplomatic offensive as one of "smiles and energy."[7] Of the two elements, the energy links—pipeline plans and other oil and gas relationships—were the more important.

If relations between Tehran and Washington had been reasonably normal, U.S. leaders might have viewed the Iranian initiatives as nothing particularly menacing. But given the extremely hostile

471

relations between the United States and Iran, U.S. administrations worried at least as much about Tehran's machinations as they did about the maneuvers of Moscow and Beijing. Thwarting the expansion of Iranian influence became yet another reason why the United States wanted to establish close working relationships with the new Central Asian states.

That goal became a major feature of Washington's policy in Central Asia even during the administration of the elder Bush. James Baker admitted that U.S. officials were especially worried about the potential for the development of close ties between Iran and Tajikistan. Unlike the populations of the other Central Asian countries, Baker noted, "the Tajiks are Persian, most of them speak a language similar to Farsi, and thus they have more ties and contacts with Tehran." Given those factors, "Iran was a primary topic of our discussion" with Tajikistan's leader, Rakhman Nabiyev, during Baker's 1992 trip through Central Asia. "Nabiyev ominously noted that the Iranians 'are showing a lot of interest' in Tajikistan."[8] Baker cautioned the Tajik leader that Iran sought to export its revolution and cautioned Nabiyev to be careful in his dealings with Tehran.

There was, however, one inconvenient aspect to Washington's strategy of courting Central Asian regimes. Even as U.S. political figures and policymakers touted America's robust commitment to democracy, free markets, and human rights in the post–Cold War era, there was little evidence of any of those practices in the Central Asian republics. In fact, corrupt autocratic systems were the norm.

U.S. leaders devoted much of their initial courtship efforts in the security arena to two countries: Kazakhstan and Uzbekistan. The relationship with the former noticeably deepened with the approval of a security-assistance program to that country in 1994. In May of the same year, Kazakhstan joined NATO's Partnership for Peace Program, widely viewed in the West as a halfway house for countries that might aspire to join the alliance at a later time. The Partnership for Peace Program's association with Kazakhstan was rather ironic, given that one of the program's stated objectives was to establish and strengthen civilian democratic control of the armed forces. Since Kazakhstan's government under strongman Nursultan Nazarbayev was not democratic even under the most flexible definition of that term, it was unclear how such control of the military would be achieved. Nevertheless, bilateral U.S. ties with Astana also deepened after 1994. At one point, U.S. defense attachés in Kazakhstan even decided what types of military equipment should be ordered for the country's armed forces.[9]

The Bush and Clinton administrations also worked hard to strengthen ties with Uzbekistan during the 1990s. The Uzbeks had historically exercised an outsized degree of influence in Central Asia. One reason for that was that they made up some 40 percent of the region's population, not only being the majority in Uzbekistan itself but constituting sizable minorities in Afghanistan and other countries. Uzbekistan's authoritarian president, Islam Karimov, clearly wanted the new great-power player in Central Asia, the United States, to recognize that preeminence and help perpetuate it. During Baker's visit, he gently chided the secretary of state for concentrating too much on Kazakhstan, as evidenced by the decision to make that country his first stop on his itinerary.

Despite Karimov's lobbying for close ties with the United States, Baker viewed the Uzbek leader with some caution, describing him as "more authoritarian than democratic."[10] Among other manifestations of authoritarianism, Karimov's government refused to register opposition parties or let them participate in the political process under anything even faintly resembling fair and equal conditions. Despite Baker's wariness, Washington's security ties continued to grow over the next 13 years, and during that period Uzbekistan was second only to Kazakhstan among Central Asian countries in terms of the breadth and depth of its military relationship with the United States.

The economic motives for an activist U.S. policy in Central Asia seemed equally compelling as the security rationales to U.S. policymakers. Early on, there were strong indications of major oil and gas deposits in the region—as well as deposits of valuable strategic minerals. Washington wanted American companies to control that new reservoir of wealth—or at a minimum, prevent potential rivals from doing so. Evidence has continued to mount that the speculation in the 1990s about oil and gas reserves was not misplaced or even premature. In September 2013, for example, Turkmenistan began pumping natural gas from a vast field near the Afghan border. An independent British auditing firm estimated that the new South Yolotan field might hold up to 750 trillion cubic feet of natural gas. If true, the South Yolotan field would be the world's second-largest

473

deposit of natural gas, surpassed only by the South Pars field stretching across Iran and Qatar.[11]

There was no doubt that Moscow and Beijing were deeply interested in those riches. China, with its voracious appetite for energy to run its rapidly growing economy, was especially determined to forge close ties with the newly independent Central Asian states.[12] And over the next two decades that strategy paid off handsomely. By 2006 Kazakhstan began exporting oil to China, and those exports were set to expand dramatically with the completion of a new pipeline in 2014. Turkmenistan began exporting natural gas to China in 2009, using a pipeline that took that gas through Uzbekistan and Kyrgyzstan on the way to its final destination.[13] It was not coincidental that Chinese President Xi Jinping was at the side of Turkmenistan's president at the ceremony inaugurating gas production from the South Yolotan field. Turkmenistan was committed to boost gas exports to China by some 250 percent—reaching the impressive figure of 65 billion cubic meters by 2020.[14] Since China was already the largest purchaser of Turkmen gas, the existing substantial economic relationship was certain to grow.

But Turkmenistan was just one component of the Chinese strategy along the new Silk Road. Xi's appearance in that country was part of his week-long trip through Central Asia. In Kazakhstan, the Chinese president further consolidated Beijing's role in that country's oil industry, signing economic deals worth nearly $30 billion. In Uzbekistan, he concluded agreements regarding gas, oil, and gold worth $15 billion. And in Kyrgyzstan, he finalized a $3 billion pipeline deal.[15] As Washington predicted in the 1990s, Beijing is striving to be a major player in all the Central Asian republics, primarily because of their importance as energy suppliers.

But Beijing's desire to establish a new "hydrocarbon highway" to Central Asia is not motivated solely by economic considerations.[16] Rosemary A. Kelanic, associate director of the Institute for Security and Conflict Studies at George Washington University's Elliott School of International Affairs, contends that "a major advantage of obtaining oil from Siberia and Central Asia is that it could travel to China overland—and thus beyond the reach of U.S. naval power."[17] Beijing's interest in Central Asia, at least as much as Washington's, is a combination of economic and security concerns.

New Allies in the War on Terror

The 9/11 attacks significantly increased the incentive for Washington to build close strategic ties with Central Asian regimes. As the war against al Qaeda and its allies began, the United States needed logistical support for the campaign in landlocked Afghanistan. George W. Bush's administration obtained the right to develop bases in Uzbekistan and Kyrgyzstan to meet that need. George Mason University professor Eric McGlinchey just slightly overstates the nature and rapidity of the change in U.S. policy toward Kyrgyzstan. That country, "once of minimal importance to U.S. geopolitics, suddenly became a strategic partner in the post-9/11 'War on Terror,'" he concludes. An especially important development took place in December 2001, when Askar Akaev's government agreed to President George W. Bush's request for an air base at the Manas airport outside the capital, Bishkek. The new relationship increased the resources available to Akaev's regime and helped consolidate his dictatorial rule. McGlinchey notes that "economic rents—both literal rents for the air base and rents from logistics and supply contracts for the base—began accruing directly to Akaev and his family."[18]

U.S. policy was governed by an overriding concern about preventing instability in the region, which administration officials believed was a goal that an ongoing U.S. military presence would help advance. In the years immediately after 9/11, Washington's concerns about stability in Central Asia verged on an obsession—especially as the U.S. military mission in Afghanistan persisted and eventually escalated. As early as 2004 Deputy Secretary of State Richard Armitage told an audience in Kazakhstan that "stability in the region is of paramount importance" to the United States and had become a "vital national interest."[19]

U.S. intelligence agencies were even more adamant about the danger of instability, fretting that the Central Asian republics could degenerate into the kind of chaos that afflicted Afghanistan in the 1990s and eventually produced the Taliban regime that gave safe haven to al Qaeda. Director of National Intelligence John Negroponte made that point explicitly in congressional testimony in December 2006. In a worst-case scenario, he warned, "central authority in one or more of these states could evaporate as rival clans or regions vie for power—opening the door to an expansion of terrorist and criminal activity on the model of failed states like Somalia and, when it was under Taliban rule, Afghanistan."[20]

Negroponte's successor, J. Michael McConnell, was equally worried when he testified before the Senate Armed Services Committee a year later. McConnell emphasized that there "is no guarantee that elite and societal turmoil across Central Asia will stay within the confines of existing autocratic systems."[21] Like Negroponte, he raised the specter of possible failed states and their potentially deadly consequences for America's security.

In retrospect, those fears were excessive, but not entirely unfounded. The region is a cauldron of ethnic animosities as well as corrupt authoritarianism. Turmoil began early in the post-Soviet period, when Tajikistan erupted into a full-blown civil war in 1992. (Ironically, while U.S. officials such as James Baker feared Iranian machinations in that country, the catalysts appeared to be bitter ethnic divisions aided and abetted by guerrilla factions in neighboring Afghanistan.)[22]

Ethnic and cross-border tensions have been persistent problems elsewhere in the region. For example, Turkmenistan has had a history of tense relations with Uzbekistan, especially since the Uzbek government conspired with insurgents who launched an unsuccessful coup against Turkmen dictator Sapirmurat Niyazov in 2002.[23]

Tensions between the majority Kyrgyz population and minority Uzbeks exploded again in the southern portion of Kyrgyzstan in 2010, resulting in hundreds of fatalities (primarily Uzbeks) and creating thousands of Uzbek refugees, most of whom fled across the border into Uzbekistan. According to a Human Rights Watch report, more than 2,600 homes were destroyed, and the number of refugees fleeing the country reached nearly 100,000. Yet, "Kyrgyz authorities failed to contain or stop the killings and large-scale destruction."[24]

A much worse episode of violence, though, occurred in the Uzbek city of Andijan in May 2005, and that incident caused more than a little embarrassment and consternation for U.S. foreign policy officials. The Bush administration had cultivated close ties with Uzbek President Islam Karimov, despite the latter's decidedly authoritarian rule and pervasive corruption.[25] The centerpiece of security ties between Uzbekistan and the United States was the U.S. air base at Karshi-Khanabad. That facility was especially important for troop rotation and logistical supplies for the war in Afghanistan.

But domestic discontent with Karimov's rule had been building for years, especially among the Kygryz ethnic minority, and on the night and early morning of May 12–13, 2005, that discontent exploded in violence in the eastern city of Andijan. Gunmen attacked several government buildings on May 12 and broke into the local prison to free 23 businessmen who were on trial for alleged religious extremism. Later on the morning of May 13, activists organized a march on the city's Bobur Square, with several thousand people eventually filling the area. During the day, security forces shot into the crowd from armored personnel carriers on several occasions, and, just before evening, those forces cordoned off the square and then conducted a systematic slaughter of unarmed civilians. Human Rights Watch later estimated that hundreds died during those attacks and reported that "after the peak of the carnage, government forces swept through the area and executed some of the wounded where they lay."[26]

Washington's initial reaction to the Andijan massacre could best be described as tepid. When reporters asked State Department spokesman Richard Boucher about the episode, his response was a classic example of fence straddling. He stated that the United States had been "consistently critical of the human rights situation in Uzbekistan," which was a considerable overstatement of the actual U.S. position. Furthermore, he proceeded to place much of the blame for the Andijan massacre on the demonstrators. The U.S. government, he said, was concerned about the deaths of innocent civilians, but he added that "it's becoming increasingly clear that the episode began with an armed attack on the prison and other government facilities." Furthermore, the State Department was worried about the "escape of prisoners, including possible members of the Islamic Movement of Uzbekistan, an organization we consider a terrorist organization."[27] Those arguments tracked closely with the increasingly discredited version of events that the Karimov government was putting out.

Washington's anemic response drew rebukes from a variety of sources. A bipartisan group of senators criticized the State Department's comments and called for a United Nations (UN) investigation of the killings in Andijan.[28] The British ambassador to Uzbekistan, Craig Murray, reportedly blasted U.S. conduct as a "sickening response," and even some officials within the State Department advocated severing ties with Karimov's government. Defense Department officials vehemently objected to any move along those lines, since they considered bilateral security cooperation vital to the mission in Afghanistan and the overall war on terror.[29]

Gradually, public and congressional pressure caused the administration to distance itself from its Uzbek client. But that change, in turn, produced a hostile reaction from Karimov and his associates. When the United States belatedly joined the call for an international investigation, the Karimov government ordered the closing of the U.S. air base at Karshi-Khanabad.[30] Relations deteriorated further over the next few years, and Washington tempered its hope of making Uzbekistan another linchpin (along with Kazakhstan) of the U.S. military presence in Central Asia.

Political and ethnic tensions continue to be a major concern in Uzbekistan, Turkmenistan, and elsewhere in the region. Domestic resistance is even growing to the rule of president-for-life Nazarbayev in Kazakhstan. His government instituted a crackdown in late 2012 on opposition groups and semi-independent media outlets that dared to criticize his authoritarian practices.[31] None of the Central Asian rulers seem to have a secure grip on power, and mechanisms for the orderly, peaceful transfer of power are largely absent.

The withering of close ties with the Uzbek government following the Andijan incident, and the failure of the Tulip Revolution in Kyrgyzstan that same year, led to the first stage of a hesitant, sporadic transition to a more restrained and realistic U.S. policy in Central Asia. Political conditions in that region made such a policy shift at least somewhat palatable to U.S. officials. Although several Central Asian republics have experienced their share of political turbulence in the years after 2005–2006, there has not been the cascade of imploding states as U.S. officials feared in the initial period following the 9/11 attacks. And that receding danger should have made it easier for both the Bush and Barack Obama administrations to avoid the pitfall of excessively close ties with the autocratic Central Asian regimes. U.S. policy, though, has just partially reflected that reality. American officials have not entirely given up their goal of maintaining strong security ties to friendly Central Asian governments.

Following the 9/11 attacks, Nursultan Nazarbayev seemed, along with Karimov, to be the most receptive of Central Asia's rulers to Washington's security overtures, further intensifying his defense relations with the United States and its Western allies. In February 2008 Kazakhstan signed a new five-year military cooperation plan with the United States, building on previous agreements and expanding into more ambitious areas, especially with respect to counterterrorism measures. Nazarbayev's government has actively combated al Qaeda and other terrorist operatives inside the country, even while insisting that Kazakhstan does not have a major domestic terrorist problem. Beyond the actions taken inside the country, the regime in Astana has aided Western anti-terrorism efforts in a variety of ways, including providing some logistical assistance to Afghanistan's government.[32]

But Nazarbayev also hedged his bets from the outset regarding external security ties. Writing in 2009, Jamestown Foundation senior fellow Roger N. McDermott noted that since 9/11 "Kazakhstan's defense posture has favored closer links with the United States and the North Atlantic Treaty Organization (NATO), while it has also pursued inconsistent efforts to extract better defense cooperation from Moscow."[33] Such an approach is "inconsistent," though, only if one assumes that Nazarbayev ever intended to be a reliable ally of the West. His actions suggest that he is, and has always been, an opportunistic nationalist, willing to cut a deal with any country offering appealing terms. Library of Congress scholar Jim Nichol cites the importance of Nazarbayev's comment that the "geographic location of Kazakhstan and its ethnic makeup dictate its 'multi-vector orientation toward both West and East.'" Consequently, he pursued "close ties with Turkey, trade links with Iran, and better relations with China," as well as a productive security relationship with the United States and other Western powers.[34]

In fact, shortly after renewing the U.S.-Kazakhstan five-year plan for defense cooperation in February 2008, Nazarbayev's government also deepened the country's defense relationship with Russia.[35] The ties with Moscow have both historical and institutional bases with which the United States cannot hope to compete. Despite some inroads by Washington, most of the Kazakh military still uses Russian hardware, and the military doctrine of the armed forces is heavily Russian influenced. Moreover, as McDermott emphasizes, "Kazakhstan protects Russia from challenges and substate threats from Central Asia and at the same time serves as a link with Asian countries from Russia."[36]

Despite Nazarbayev's caution about alienating Moscow, the Bush administration's willingness to overlook his regime's suppression of political dissent and its unsavory overall human rights record did seem to pay some initial geopolitical dividends. The Kazakh government allowed NATO to use its airspace for Operation Enduring Freedom in Afghanistan, principally for emergency landings at airfields in Kazakhstan. Elements of the country's new peace support battalion were sent to Iraq in 2003 to support the U.S.-led occupation following the overthrow of Saddam Hussein.[37] Following the Andijan clashes in 2005 that highlighted the political (and to some extent, ethnic-based) instability in Uzbekistan and the faltering of the Tulip Revolution in Kyrgyzstan, the United States and its allies increasingly regarded Kazakhstan under Nazarbayev as the region's security leader and a comparative bastion of stability.[38] McDermott notes that "NATO officials referred to Kazakhstan as NATO's 'anchor' in Central Asia." But that designation, he argues, was "way beyond Kazakhstan's capabilities," and by 2009 Western officials had "mostly dropped these claims from official discourse."[39]

Nevertheless, Nazarbayev's regime went to great lengths to foster the image of Kazakhstan as a modernizing society with a military that was useful to the United States and its allies in the war on terror. For the country's political elite, McDermott argues, "it was more important to showcase an image of Kazakhstan's armed forces that would promote a more positive image of the country internationally."[40] Taking steps such as sending the peace support battalion to Iraq advanced that public-relations strategy.

The gap between Washington's professed goal of supporting enlightened rule, if not full-fledged democracy, and the depressing political reality in Central Asia is all too apparent. Stephen Blank succinctly describes the nature of the Central Asian regimes, "all of which are despotic and often dominated by families and clans."[41] Writing in the *National Interest Online*, Ilan Greenberg, a visiting scholar at the Woodrow Wilson Center, adopts a slightly more charitable view, arguing that heads of state in Central Asia "range from outright dictators (Kazakhstan, Turkmenistan) to façade democrats (Kyrgyzstan)."[42] That is still hardly a compelling case for a close U.S. embrace of Central Asian regimes. None of them qualify as even reasonably enlightened economic, political, and military partners.

Even Washington has had to make the grudging admission that some of its Central Asian partners have major human rights issues. A 2012 State Department report on Kazakhstan cited a litany of authoritarian practices. "The most significant human rights problems were severe limits on citizens' rights to change their government; restrictions on freedoms of press, assembly, religion, and association; and lack of an independent judiciary and due process, especially in dealing with pervasive corruption and law enforcement and judicial abuse." If that weren't enough, there was also evidence of "arbitrary or unlawful killings," discrimination against ethnic minorities, "detainee and prisoner torture," and "arbitrary arrest and detention," among other abuses.[43] The action of Kazakhstan's largely rubber-stamp legislature in proclaiming Nazarbayev "Leader of the Nation" with lifetime ruling responsibilities and privileges in 2010 is markedly inconsistent with the Obama administration's stated strategic aim of helping the country develop into "a stable, secure, and democratic country that embraces free market competition and the rule of law."[44]

The unrealistic nature of U.S. and Western hopes for truly democratic systems certainly has been evident in Turkmenistan, both under the initial post–Cold War leader, Sapirmurat Niyazov, and his successor, Kurbanguly Berdymukhamedov. "Sapirmurat Niyazov ruled Turkmenistan," analyst Stephen Blank concludes, "like a sultan or latter-day Stalin." He "fully incarnated the idea of *l'etat, c'est moi*. In fact, he systematically disempowered the state's formal institutions." Niyazov "relentlessly promoted the idea of his being the father of the entire country, not least to reduce the influence of clans and other tribes in government." His ruling style was hardly unique, though. "In this respect," Blank argues, "he only represented an extreme form of the policies pursued by his colleagues as presidents of the other Central Asian regimes."[45] The behavior of Berdymukhamedov lends credence to that observation, since he has been just marginally less egocentric, despite the dubious legality of his rise to the presidency.[46]

There certainly is no semblance of democracy in Turkmenistan. Berdymukhamedov exercises virtually unlimited power, as did his predecessor, Niyazov, before his death in 2006. Indeed, Berdymukhamedov's preferred title "Arkadag" has the creepy, Orwellian translation of "the Patron." The cult of personality that has grown up around Berdymukhamedov has managed nearly to match that of the egocentric Niyazov—which is no small feat. Niyazov even re-named months of the year after his family members and mandated that all school children study his "spiritual guide." At one point, he claimed that reading the spiritual guide three times would guaran-tee the reader a place in heaven. Such bizarre manifestations of a cult of personality were reminiscent of the absurdities that could be found in North Korea throughout the decades or in China during the rule of Mao Zedong.

The ruling style of Niyazov's successor has not been quite as weird, but the stifling authoritarianism is just as evident. And it extends be-yond policy and politics to matters that should be mundane or even trivial. For example, the 55-year-old Berdymukhamedov partici-pated as rider in a horse race in late April 2013. Two developments in that race were quite revealing about how Turkmenistan is run. As the horses neared the finish line, it appeared that Berdymukham-edov, although near the front of the pack, was not going to win. The chief challenger, though, rather obviously throttled back his mount in the home stretch, allowing the president to win. That triumph proved to be short lived, for Berdymukhamedov's horse stumbled just after crossing the finishing line, throwing his rider face-first onto the track. Although the president was not hurt seriously, the fall was embarrassing at best and humiliating at worst. However, no one in Turkmenistan saw the incident, since all television video deleted it, and newspaper photos apparently disappeared.[47] Given that at-titude, it is unsurprising that outright criticism of the nation's infal-lible leader is not tolerated.

Yet Washington remains determined not to lose out on economic, diplomatic, and strategic opportunities in Turkmenistan merely be-cause of the country's repellent political system and egomaniacal leader. Not only is Turkmenistan's location important, given the U.S.-Russian-Chinese-Iranian rivalry in the region, but the former Soviet republic holds the world's fourth-largest known reserves of natural gas. And Washington was pleased that Berdymukhamedov seemed serious about continuing to pursue policies that eased con-trols on small-scale businesses and encouraged more entrepreneur-ial activity. Among other consequences, those reforms opened up the country to possible investment by American businesses.

Washington's willingness to overlook the repulsive policies of Central Asian regimes and instead establish close diplomatic ties has been most evident with regard to Kazakhstan and Turkmenistan (and until 2005, Uzbekistan). To some extent, that attitude has also affected relations with Kyrgyzstan. U.S. policy toward other countries in the region has been more tentative, ambivalent, and sometimes inconsistent. Indeed, policy has sometimes oscillated between very different approaches.

At times, Washington appeared inclined to encourage supposedly democratic "color" revolutions akin to the earlier upheavals such as the Orange Revolution in Ukraine and the Rose Revolution in Georgia. There was, for example, a considerable amount of initial support within the American foreign policy community for the so-called Tulip Revolution in Kyrgyzstan in 2005. But disillusionment about that uprising faded even faster than it did for the Orange and Rose predecessors. Indeed, evidence soon emerged that the allegedly democratic motives for the Tulip Revolution were interspersed with parochial, if not unsavory, objectives by various clans and leading families. One analyst speculates that a significant factor in the rebellion was not a thirst for democracy, but an effort by key clans "to stop President Askar Akayev's family from gaining even more wealth and power through their official connection."[48]

Perhaps because of a growing realization that social and political conditions in Central Asia were not conducive to the development of Western-style democracy, U.S. policymakers at other times seemed to adopt the more cautious strategy of realpolitik. Officials worked with existing authoritarian rulers and sought to maximize U.S. influence while trying to wean those regimes away from excessive economic and military dependence on either Moscow or Beijing. But as Washington discovered in its courtship of Turkmenistan's Niyazov, just because a Central Asian leader might be uneasy about an over-reliance on Russia or China, that did not necessarily translate into a wish for close ties with the United States. Niyazov, in particular, was ostentatious in pursuing a nonaligned course, much to Washington's mounting frustration.[49]

The competing impulses between democracy promotion and realpolitik sometimes gave U.S. policy in Central Asia an ambivalent, if not muddled, quality. Washington often seemed to be groping for a coherent overall strategy but found itself reacting on an ad hoc basis to a variety of crises and unpleasant trends. The pertinent lesson should have been that the United States was simply not in a position to implement a comprehensive regional strategy, whether based on the promotion of democracy or an amoral realpolitik. Historical, geographic, and economic factors combine to render such an ambitious approach impractical.

Stephen Blank overstates matters just slightly when he argues that the United States has been fatally handicapped in its contest for regional influence against Russia, China, and Iran. "Most of all, it is disadvantaged," Blank contends, "because, unlike Russia, it has previously been unwilling to spend large amounts of political and economic resources to subsidize Central Asian states, bribe rulers, or ensure that energy and other rents flow securely to them first, guarantee these rulers' physical security against insurgency, potentially guarantee their chosen successor, support them against demands for greater liberalization and democracy or completely overlook their misrule."[50]

Although those observations are generally accurate, Washington has been willing to go to some lengths on occasion to overlook misrule by Central Asian regimes considered friendly to the United States. That is especially true in cases where a regime, such as Nursultan Nazarbayev's dictatorship in Kazakhstan, has backed U.S. strategic goals in Afghanistan and more generally in the war on terror. Likewise, even though a State Department report conceded that "Uzbekistan is an authoritarian state with limited human rights," that conclusion did not entirely derail the U.S. effort to forge cooperative bilateral security ties. That point is also true to some extent when access to major resource riches is at stake, as in Turkmenistan. Washington's commitment to democracy and human rights tends to fade on those occasions, but alliances with autocratic regimes also have remained somewhat tentative, uncertain, and perhaps a bit self-conscious.

There even have been instances in which U.S. policymakers abandoned an autocratic client in Central Asia. Eventually, the Bush administration distanced itself from Islam Karimov's regime in Uzbekistan, although it did so with some reluctance. Perhaps more surprising, Washington supported a color revolution that toppled its erstwhile ally in Kyrgyzstan, Askar Akaev. But U.S. leaders have more typically downplayed criticism or even looked the other way—

as they did for years regarding Karimov—with respect to repressive policies that Central Asian regimes pursue.

The potentially embarrassing and morally compromising factors that U.S. policy in the region has had to confront were illustrated during an April 2013 special session of the United Nations Human Rights Council that examined the performance of Turkmenistan's government. U.S. delegates admitted that officials in Turkmenistan "are not held accountable for torture or other human rights violations," and that journalists and other critics of the regime, as well as religious and ethnic minorities, were systematically detained and otherwise abused.[51]

The Human Rights Council report may actually understate the degree of repression. Freedom of expression is so severely curtailed as to be barely noticeable. All domestic radio and television broadcasting is state run, and efforts are made to discourage residents from attempting to access the BBC and other foreign outlets. All newspapers are either state run or are under such heavy government "supervision" that there is no meaningful difference. Media outlets, whether state-owned or not, provide a consistent content: effusive praise for the government and no hint of criticism.

The perceived need for logistical and other military assistance from compliant Central Asian regimes has diminished just modestly, despite the passage of time since the 9/11 attacks and the gradual drawdown of the U.S. war in Afghanistan. The Obama administration waged a determined effort to gain an extension on the lease to Manas air base in Kyrgyzstan, which was set to expire in July 2013. Secretary of Defense Leon Panetta stopped in the Kyrgyz capital, Bishkek, in March 2012 for talks on extending the lease. Nearly a year later, Assistant Secretary of State Robert O. Blake Jr. conceded during an interview with the Voice of America that "Manas is a very important logistics operation" for the United States, being a transshipment point for fuel, ammunition and other supplies, and it was also "the center through which almost all of our troops pass to go into Afghanistan."[52] It was an accurate description. In 2011 alone, some 580,000 U.S. military personnel traveled through Manas going into and out of Afghanistan.

Washington regarded the facility to be important enough to pay an annual rent of $60 million. That was a considerable sum in a place like Kyrgyzstan, but the country's president, Almazbek Atambaev, appeared determined to extract even more money, vowing to terminate the lease at the end of its current run. The United States had been down that road before. Washington nearly lost access to Manas in 2009 when Kyrgyzstan threatened to evict the U.S. and close the base in August of that year. Kyrgyz authorities relented, though, when the Obama administration agreed to triple the rental fee.

In addition to the periodic financial haggling, the Manas facility was not located in a stable strategic environment. Political turmoil in Kyrgyzstan has long been a problem. In April 2010, for example, military flights had to be suspended for nearly a month when violent demonstrations against the Kyrgyz government reached a crescendo. A substantial portion of the public not only exhibited anger about the regime's systematic corruption but also objected to their country's territory being used for operations against fellow Muslims in Afghanistan.

Despite the concerted efforts during the Bush and Obama administrations to retain Manas, the policy ultimately failed. On June 3, 2014, the United States officially relinquished control of the base to the Kyrgyz government.[53] Washington had little choice in the matter. A year earlier, the parliament in Kyrgyzstan had voted to require the United States to vacate the facility by July 11, 2014. American officials were unhappy about having to leave Manas, even though President Obama had already announced that the U.S. troop presence in Afghanistan would decline to 9,800 at the end of 2014, with a complete withdrawal planned for the end of 2016. Such changes would greatly reduce the importance of the Manas facility as a logistical transport hub, but the expulsion was still humiliating. U.S. officials and regional experts believed that Russian pressure was a key factor in Kyrgyzstan's decision.[54] Given the rising tensions between the United States and Russia following the onset of the Ukraine crisis, and Moscow's long-standing wish to limit U.S. influence in Central Asia, that interpretation was likely correct.

Washington's association with Kyrgyzstan was less morally compromising than many of the associations with other autocratic regimes. As Ilan Greenberg mentions, Kyrgyzstan is the only country in the region that maintains a functioning parliament—even if its independence is akin to Russia's parliament under Vladimir Putin's suffocating presidency. The degree of autocratic rule is even worse in neighboring Central Asian countries, and the extent of ethnic tensions is typically at least as bad. Tajikistan may be the most fragile of the lot. Greenberg argues that "Tajikistan is less a coherent nation-state than a confederation of tribal regions," much like Afghanistan.[55] The country also has tense relations with several neighboring states, most notably Uzbekistan.

Such factors should impel U.S. policymakers to assess carefully whether the strategic and economic stakes in Central Asia are sufficient to justify attempts to maintain an ongoing U.S. presence. Geographic and historical factors alone put the United States at a considerable disadvantage in the competition for influence with China, Iran, and especially Russia.

Moscow remains determined to retain its status as the dominant power in the region, despite inroads from the United States, China, and Iran. While not happy about Beijing's growing influence, Russian leaders seem even more wary about Washington's intentions.[56] Although a Russian-Chinese rivalry is likely to emerge over the long term, in the meantime there are ample reasons for both governments to contain those inclinations. Julia Nanay, a Central Asian specialist at PFC Energy, notes that all governments in the region maintain strong ties to Moscow.

Even Beijing's role, while growing, remains secondary.[57] Moreover, both Moscow and Beijing have some important reasons to cooperate regarding Central Asian policy. Not only do they have common interests in thwarting terrorism, Islamic extremism, and secessionist impulses, but they have the mutual goal of curbing Washington's ambitions. Those overlapping interests are expressed both bilaterally and multilaterally—the latter chiefly through the Shanghai Cooperation Organization.

Russia certainly is keeping a wary eye on Washington's role. In September 2012 President Putin announced a preliminary agreement with the Kyrgyz government to keep a military base in that country after the current lease expires in 2017. A new treaty would extend the tenure of the Russian military through 2032.[58] In the meantime, Kyrgyzstan had the status of being the only country in the world to have both a U.S. and a Russian military base on its soil.[59] Russia's military influence in the region could grow even more significant as U.S. troop levels in Afghanistan shrink. That trend was already apparent during the 1990s and the early years of the 21st century. Uzbekistan granted Russia access to the Navoi airfield (supposedly in cases of emergency), which facilitated Moscow's ability to deploy forces in the region to combat terrorism or, perhaps, to help suppress an uprising against a client regime. In 2005 the Russian government successfully pressured Turkmenistan into agreeing not to accept foreign (i.e., U.S.) military bases without first notifying Russia. That agreement reflected a long-standing effort by Moscow to establish a de facto veto over Washington's goal of securing access to such bases—ostensibly to support the war in Afghanistan.

Russia's economic and political influence does not necessarily enjoy the same prospects as its military influence, however. Putin's ambitious proposal for a vast Eurasian Union, starting with a customs union stretching from Belarus and Ukraine in the west to the Chinese border in the east, appears to be stillborn.[60] Not only have ultranationalist Russians reacted badly (including engaging in some riots) to the prospect of workers emigrating to Russia from Central Asia, but some of the Central Asian countries are so poor they would be a major drain on Moscow in any close economic relationship. For example, Kyrgyzstan's per capita gross domestic product is $1,070 and Tajikistan's a mere $837, compared to Russia's $14,037.[61] A growing number of Russians seem unenthused about linking their country to such economic weaklings and potential dependents.

Those factors diminish the credibility of arguments advocates of U.S. activism make that the United States must play a larger role in Central Asia lest Moscow rebuild the Soviet empire and again pose a global challenge to America. On the other hand, the obstacles to the Kremlin's geopolitical clout in the region may tempt U.S. officials, who perceive a potential power vacuum that a notorious adversary like Iran or nonstate terrorists might exploit. There is also a more ambitious, assertive version of that thesis—one that argues that an optimistic, offensive U.S. strategy could turn a regional power vacuum to Washington's advantage.

Fears about Central Asian countries becoming possible sanctuaries for terrorist groups have some validity, but the past decade has shown that such groups can set up shop in numerous areas of the world, not just in Afghanistan and its neighbors. Concerns about political instability in Central Asia and the potential that terrorists might be able to exploit such a situation are not sufficient reasons for the United States to assign the region a high strategic priority. Equally important, those worries are not sufficiently compelling to justify compromising American values by maintaining close ties with authoritarian Central Asian regimes and invoking the justification of strategic necessity.

All of this suggests that a relatively low-profile strategy with limited objectives is the most advisable approach. Promoting stability and blocking, or at least trying to limit, the influence of Russia, China, and Iran might arguably be a worthwhile U.S. foreign policy objective, but those goals fall far short of transforming Central Asia into an arena involving vital U.S. interests. Nothing in that region warrants an expensive, high-priority policy for Washington.

Conclusion: A Muddled but Only Modestly Unsavory Policy

U.S. policy toward the Central Asian autocrats has been neither a great success nor an odious failure that unduly besmirches American values. During the 1990s—and especially in the years immediately following the 9/11 attacks—U.S. officials did engage in some questionable actions. The courtship of Nazarbayev certainly was reminiscent of some of the worst aspects of U.S. policy toward authoritarian allies during the Cold War. And both the Clinton and G. W. Bush administrations were willing to overlook the human rights abuses of Central Asian regimes that were willing to cooperate with Washington. The half-hearted attempt to excuse the abuses that Islam Karimov's government in Uzbekistan committed was especially embarrassing.

Furthermore, the hopes of establishing a substantial U.S. security and economic presence in Central Asia and being able to compete on equal terms with Russia and China were always unrealistic. Beijing—and especially Moscow—have geographic, cultural, historical, and institutional advantages that the United States cannot duplicate. It is likely that Washington will always be a secondary player in Central Asia. Indeed, the United States is more akin to a peer competitor with Iran than it is with Russia and China in that region.

To the credit of Obama administration officials, the United States seems to be gradually scaling back its Central Asian ambitions to more realistic and attainable levels. The drawdown of U.S. forces in Afghanistan, although too tardy and far too gradual, is symbolic of the overall shift of U.S. policy in the region. And, despite the early flirtations with the likes of Nazarbayev, Karimov, and Nizayov, Washington has managed to avoid the worst excesses of its Cold War relationships in terms of compromising American principles. Almost no one in an official capacity, for example, speaks any longer of Kazakhstan being NATO's anchor in Central Asia. There is an implicit recognition that Nazarbayev and other strongmen may occasionally serve as temporary tactical allies, but they are not suited to be close long-term partners of the democratic West.

Washington has gained some limited cooperation from the various regimes in the campaign against radical Islamic forces, and it has created the conditions for some modest economic opportunities for American-based businesses. But the risk that Central Asian tyrants might become the Mobutus or Marcoses of the 21st century for U.S. foreign policy has receded.

16. Closing the Values Gap: Protecting Security, Preserving Values

Americans want to believe that their country is a bastion of moral principles and that their government does not violate those values in the course of implementing the nation's foreign policy. Lamenting the bitter divisions over foreign policy that had marked the years of his administration, Ronald Reagan harkened back to a golden age of bipartisanship that supposedly existed before the 1970s. And according to Reagan, that bipartisan consensus "was based on the support of peace, democracy, individual liberty, and the rule of law."[1]

That may have been the ideal, but the record throughout the Cold War era pointed to a different, less savory conclusion. U.S. foreign policy certainly did not hew to those principles on a consistent basis. All too often, Washington's actions not only were inconsistent with professed ideals, but they also directly undermined such ideals. It is difficult to square the notion of allegiance to the values of peace, democracy, individual liberty, and the rule of law with the overthrow of democratically elected governments, the provision of financial aid and political support for corrupt autocrats, and in some cases, aid to install and sustain in power murderous sociopaths. Yet at times the U.S. government did all of those things.

Such moral agnosticism did not entirely abate even when the Cold War ended. There was some improvement between 1990 and 2001, and Washington's commitment to democracy and human rights seemed more genuine than during the Cold War. That did not always produce wise policies, however. Bill Clinton's administration intervened in Haiti to restore the elected president, Jean Bertrand Aristide, to office and reverse the military coup that had ousted him. But Aristide and many of his followers were hardly models of democratic leadership and, in some ways, were as repulsive as the generals who had conducted the coup. Moreover, even in the midst of a more serious U.S. commitment to democracy and human rights, U.S. officials still engaged in some morally questionable initiatives.

The fawning support of Kuwait's corrupt, autocratic ruling family during the Persian Gulf War and the de facto partnership with the sleazy governments in Bosnia and Kosovo are not episodes that should generate pride.

Once the United States embarked on a new crusade, targeting radical Islamic movements and regimes following the 9/11 terrorist attacks, there was a tendency to revert to old habits and cut ethical corners without sufficient reflection. Evidence that U.S. officials have learned only weak and incomplete lessons about the perils of getting too close to friendly tyrants in light of the bruising experiences of the Cold War period can be gauged from two incidents during the first term of Barack Obama's administration.

As demonstrators surged into the streets of Cairo in late January 2011, demanding that President Hosni Mubarak step down, U.S. Vice President Joe Biden opined that Mubarak was not a dictator and should not be asked to relinquish his office. Such an astonishing statement surely baffled or angered people in Egypt and was greeted with derision by knowledgeable people in the United States and around the world. If the leader of a regime that routinely jailed political opponents, banned or harassed critics who sought to form opposition parties, imposed comprehensive censorship on the news media, and blatantly rigged elections to stay in power for three decades is not a dictator, then the term has no meaning. That Biden made such a clueless statement at any time was bad enough, but to have voiced it during the early stages of a popular uprising against a notoriously corrupt and repressive ruler confirmed that he was diplomatically and politically tone deaf. It also may have confirmed to the people of Egypt and other nations ruled by pro-U.S. autocrats that Washington's long-standing policy of backing friendly tyrants regardless of what they did to their own people remained entrenched. The Obama administration's refusal in 2013 to term the Egyptian military's overthrow of elected President Mohammed Morsi a "coup" and the grudging, belated, and only partial cutting of U.S. aid to Egypt under the new junta likely reinforced that impression.

The second, less prominent, incident involved a U.S. embassy cable revealed by Wikileaks in February 2011. In that May 2009 cable, Anton K. Smith, the ranking U.S. diplomat in the small West African nation of Equatorial Guinea, told his superiors in Washington: "There are good guys and bad guys here. We need to strengthen the good guys—for all his faults, President Obiang among them—and undercut the bad guys." Obiang, Smith stated, exercised a "mellowing, benign leadership."[2] That "good guy," Teodoro Obiang, was actually a stereotypical dictatorial ruler. There is strong evidence that he had used his office to enrich himself and his extended family. In addition to such corruption, the U.S. State Department's annual human rights report documented multiple abuses in Equatorial Guinea, including onerous restrictions on freedom of expression, the arbitrary jailing of critics and others who ran afoul of the regime, and torture of prisoners. Smith's comments made a farce of Washington's professed support for democracy and the rule of law around the world.

It is, however, mildly encouraging that U.S. policymakers in the post-9/11 period have exhibited somewhat greater caution than their Cold War predecessors about crawling into bed with supposedly friendly authoritarian allies. That caution is evident in several places, but most notably in Central Asia. Despite Washington's considerable strategic and economic ambitions in that region, misrepresentations about the nature of prospective client regimes and the exaggeration of the stakes involved, which were far too common features of U.S. policy throughout the Third World during the Cold War, are not as prominent in post–Cold War Central Asia. There was an early temptation to flirt with Kazakhstan's dictator, Nursultan Nazarbayev, and a few other Central Asian tyrants in the immediate post-9/11 years, but that tendency has diminished. It has been replaced by more practical, limited relationships with such regimes. That is a mildly encouraging sign that U.S. foreign policy may have regained a healthy measure of realism.

A key factor in resolving the dilemma of securing important American foreign policy objectives while not betraying American values is to establish reasonably explicit standards or guidelines. There were times during the Cold War when Washington needed to cooperate with unsavory regimes to contain the security threat that the Soviet Union posed. The Nixon administration's initial rapprochement with China in 1971–1972 and the era of de facto security cooperation that ensued over the next two decades was one such instance. That move significantly altered the diplomatic and military balance in both East and Central Asia and thereby complicated Moscow's global strategic calculations. It did not alter the reality, though, that liberal, democratic America was collaborating with a regime that brutally repressed its own people. U.S. officials could plead that the moral compromise in that case was necessary, but it was a moral compromise nonetheless.

Most of Washington's other collaborative efforts with unsavory regimes during the Cold War did not have the same justification of necessity. In some cases, they did not even have a plausible plea of necessity. The arguments for supporting the likes of Ferdinand Marcos, Mobutu Sese Seko, Anastasio Somoza, and a parade of murderous Guatemalan generals ranged from weak to pathetic. Those associations were a betrayal of fundamental American values for meager benefits.

Whether a compelling case of necessity can be made is the crucial test regarding the establishment of ties with an authoritarian foreign partner. Perhaps the best illustration of that test comes from the realm of fiction, an episode during the third season of the Emmy-winning television drama *The West Wing*. In that episode, "The Women of Qumar," the administration has just concluded a $1.5 billion arms sale to the fictional country of Qumar in the Persian Gulf in exchange for an extended lease on a base for the U.S. Air Force. C. J. Gregg, the president's press secretary, is furious about the deal because of the horrific way the Qumari government treated the country's women. (The parallel with the conduct of the governments of Saudi Arabia and Bahrain was not terribly subtle.) As a woman, Gregg considers a close relationship between the United States and such an odious regime utterly unacceptable. In the climactic scene she confronts the president's national security adviser, also a woman, about the deal. The national security adviser justifies the arrangement as strengthening the U.S. military's position in that part of the world. Gregg will have no part of such an excuse, and she wrings an admission out of her colleague that the military base was not essential; it was merely "convenient."

That level of justification should never be acceptable in the real world. Yet, the evidence is overwhelming that U.S. administrations tacitly adopt that standard almost routinely. The willingness of Anton Smith to urge Washington to embrace Teodoro Obiang is a classic example. Except for some modest oil resources, there is nothing in Equatorial Guinea to warrant Washington's backing a corrupt, repressive government. In fact, given its limited economic relevance to the United States, and its even more limited strategic relevance, Equatorial Guinea barely even rises to the level of "convenient."

The convenience standard for backing corrupt, thuggish rulers is especially worrisome given Washington's excessively interventionist foreign policy. Indeed, there are many initiatives that are considered necessities in that policy that would come nowhere close to clearing the bar if the United States had a more restrained and cautious policy largely confined to the defense of vital American security interests. Convenience would not be a sufficient standard even to execute that more rigorous policy, but it is an abomination to cite convenience as an adequate justification for an initiative within a promiscuously interventionist security strategy. America risks the loss of its most cherished values if it continues down that path.

Because there may be times when, for legitimate security reasons, it may be necessary to make ethical compromises, it is imperative to establish some standards to determine when a situation warrants making that sacrifice and when it does not. Three crucial factors must be considered. First, what level of U.S. interest is at stake? Is it a vital interest; a substantial, but less than vital, interest; or something more marginal? Second, assuming that it is a substantial interest, how seriously is that interest threatened? Finally, just how odious is Washington's prospective partner? The first consideration is the most important one, but the second and third are far from minor.

In determining what kind of interest—security, economic, or political—is involved and how important it is to the well-being of the American people, it is essential to define the pertinent terms. Unfortunately, that is something U.S. officials often fail to do at all, or at best do in a perfunctory, slipshod fashion. But not all interests are created equal; some are vastly more important than others, and threats to less important ones mandate greater restraint about making ethical compromises.

Determining the nature and level of national interests is a complex exercise, and the following is merely a rough guide to that task. In general, though, interests can (and should) be divided into four broad categories: vital, secondary or conditional, peripheral, and barely relevant.[3] Each category warrants a different level of response from the United States and a different degree of association with potential authoritarian partners.

Unfortunately, in both the Cold War and the so-called war on terror, U.S. leaders have had a tendency to lump almost everything into the "vital interest" category. That is unfortunate on several levels, not the least because such thinking provides a justification for unnecessarily embracing repulsive regimes. The reality is that for any nation, but especially for the United States, truly vital interests are few in number. National survival is obviously the most important interest, but the preservation of political independence, domestic liberty, and economic well-being from external threats all are part of the mix as well. How secure those vital interests are depends heavily on both the threat environment and the capabilities of the adversary in question.

America's position is extraordinarily enviable using both criteria. Small, weak nations must constantly worry about the capabilities and intentions of powerful neighbors. Even most major powers typically operate in a strategic environment where they face potential challenges from peer rivals. In some cases, the security task of nations large and small is complicated by borders that are difficult to defend. The United States, however, may be the most secure great power in history. Not only does it benefit from having two vast oceans on its eastern and western flanks, which renders a large-scale conventional attack on the American homeland virtually impossible, but it has the luxury of dealing with an assortment of weak, and for the most part, friendly, neighbors throughout the hemisphere. There is no country that even approaches being a serious military peer competitor in America's neighborhood. And for all the talk of Brazil's rise as an economic power, even that country has an enormous distance to go before it could achieve the status of economic peer competitor. In the Western Hemisphere, the United States is, and is likely to remain for the foreseeable future, the utterly dominant strategic and economic player.

Even viewing the security environment on a global basis, it is difficult to identify many credible threats to America's vital interests. Although there are a handful of rising powers (most notably China and India), the United States still has a sizable economic edge and an enormous military advantage. Moreover, both of those rising powers have a considerable stake in maintaining decent relations with the United States. Indeed, India's strategic interests substantially overlap those of the United States. The situation with China is more complex and ambivalent, and there are some issues that could lead to significant bilateral tensions, most notably China's claim of sovereignty over Taiwan and Beijing's expansive territorial claims in the energy-rich South China Sea, a body of water through which key sea lanes pass. Even so, there are important factors, especially the mutually lucrative trade relationship, that serve to mute those tensions.

Moreover, even if China, another major power, or an alliance of major powers did seek to challenge the United States, it is difficult to see how they could menace America's survival, political independence, domestic liberty, or economic health. A direct threat to any of those interests seems far-fetched. Even a campaign to so substantially alter the global distribution of power that the shift could pose an indirect threat to America's vital interests is an extremely remote danger. That scenario would require a hostile power or an alliance of hostile powers being poised to dominate multiple regions that have crucial security and economic assets. Specifically, in today's world, such an adversary would have to be capable of gaining control of Europe *and* East Asia *and* the South Asia/Persian Gulf region.

U.S. policymakers feared precisely that kind of outcome during World War II with the alliance between Nazi Germany and Imperial Japan, and Washington fretted about a similar danger during the late 1940s and early 1950s when Soviet power was ascendant. Whatever the legitimacy of those worries in earlier decades—and the danger was substantially overblown—the notion of an adversary or adversaries dominating all three regions today or in the foreseeable future is the stuff of paranoid fantasy.

The mere emergence of a global peer competitor—much less an outright global adversary on the scale of Nazi Germany or the Soviet Union—is improbable for the next several decades. Moreover, in the unlikely event that such an adversary did emerge, the United States is more than capable of dealing with the challenge. Despite its recent economic malaise—and the self-inflicted wounds caused by the federal government's fiscal mismanagement—the United States still has the largest and most impressive economy in the world, accounting for more than one-fifth of global output. Washington's military advantages are even more daunting. There was a flurry of agitation in the U.S. media in August 2011 when China deployed its first aircraft carrier—a refurbished Russian vessel. But sober individuals pointed out that the United States already had 11 carriers, any one of which was vastly superior to the modest Chinese version. That point underscored overall U.S. conventional military superiority. No nation can come close to fielding the type or extent of America's conventional forces and weapons systems.

497

Washington's advantage in nuclear weaponry is equally apparent. The only country that has an arsenal comparable to that of the United States is Russia. And Russia's economic, political, and demographic (a shrinking population with a declining life expectancy) problems make that country a one-dimensional, anemic peer competitor. China deploys a meager arsenal of a few hundred nuclear weapons, most of which are configured to be useful only in a second-strike (i.e., a response to a nuclear attack) scenario. It would take at least a decade, and probably much longer, for China to mount a nuclear capability that comes close to matching America's.

A direct military challenge by a would-be peer competitor is far-fetched and would require a suicidal mentality by that country's political leadership. America's other adversaries are strictly second-tier or even third-tier powers, such as Iran and North Korea. Such countries are totally outclassed by Washington's conventional military power, and although Pyongyang and Tehran seem intent on barging into the global nuclear weapons club, any arsenals that they might develop would be miniscule compared to the vast U.S. arsenal. Indeed, their purpose in developing a small nuclear weapons capability appears to be primarily to deter the United States from making them the target of the kind of coercion that Washington employed against such nonnuclear adversaries as Serbia, Iraq, and Libya.

What about the possible threat that terrorism (either state-sponsored or nonstate) poses to America's vital interests? Experts who highlight that threat note that the logic of deterrence that applies to states may not be relevant to nonstate actors. America's vast military superiority, including its strategic nuclear deterrent, they argue, would mean little, since there would often be no return address for a retaliatory strike. Furthermore, terrorists are much more likely than leaders of nation states to be suicidal, since they benefit little or nothing from the status quo and, therefore, have far less to lose by engaging in rash actions.

Some pundits and policy experts contend that the leadership of certain countries, especially Iran, might be similarly indifferent to the consequences to themselves or their populations of launching an attack on the United States or U.S. allies, such as Israel. But there is little evidence to support that thesis and considerable evidence to refute it, especially in the case of Iran. Even Meir Dagan, the former chief of Mossad, Israel's intelligence agency, concluded that the

Iranian government, while ruthless, behaves in a rational fashion.[4] Tehran's conduct over the past three-and-a-half decades supports that conclusion. Despite vowing never to make peace with Saddam Hussein's government after Iraqi forces attacked Iran at the beginning of the 1980s, the Ayatollah Khomeini agreed to a peace accord at the end of that decade. Iran did so when Khomeini and other officials concluded that the costs of continuing the war would exceed any probable benefits and that a favorable outcome, even after more years of warfare, was anything but certain. That behavior reflected sober calculation, not suicidal impulses. Attacking the United States, which has thousands of nuclear weapons, or even Israel, which experts estimate possesses between 150 and 300 nuclear weapons, would constitute the height of suicidal irrationality.

It is also indicative of rational Iranian conduct that there is no evidence Tehran has given chemical weapons to Hezbollah, Hamas, or other extremist, nonstate allies. That restraint is all the more impressive because Iran has had those weapons in its arsenal since the days of the Shah. Again, the behavior of the mullahs regarding chemical weapons indicates that they understand the dire consequences of provoking the United States or its allies by distributing such nonconventional weapons to third parties, and they apparently have decided that the costs and risks overshadow any plausible benefits. That is a characteristic of rational and calculating, rather than suicidal, reasoning.

The attacks of 9/11, of course, demonstrated that expectations of similar cautious logic apparently do not apply to al Qaeda and other terrorist groups. Those attacks also created the impression of this country's extreme vulnerability to terrorism in the minds of many Americans. But it is important to put that terrible day—and the more general threat that terrorism poses—into perspective. Terrorism is, and always has been, a tactic used by weak parties, not strong ones. That is especially true of nonstate actors.

Al Qaeda got lucky on 9/11; not only did U.S. intelligence and law enforcement agencies failed to detect blatant signs of a terrorist plot using aircraft in the months leading up to the attack, but the execution (especially the complete collapse of both World Trade Center towers) was extraordinary. It would be extremely difficult for al Qaeda or any other terrorist organization to carry off another assault on the scale of 9/11—much less anything larger. Indeed, all of the other

499

attacks conducted since 9/11 have been much smaller in nature. The nightmare scenario of a terrorist group gaining control of a nuclear weapon—the one development that could produce an attack on a massive scale—cannot be ignored, but it is also a scenario that is exceedingly improbable.[5]

Terrorism is more accurately viewed as a chronic security annoyance that must be managed rather than as an existential threat to America. Despite the horrible anguish that 9/11 caused, it is pertinent to remember that 10 times as many Americans die in automobile accidents each year than perished on that awful day. The terrorist problem, while worrisome, can never pose a threat to America's survival as a nation. It cannot—unless our policymakers overreact—even pose a serious menace to our economic health or domestic liberty. Most of the adverse consequences on those fronts since 9/11 were not the result of that attack but of policies (the so-called Patriot Act, the wars in Iraq and Afghanistan, and the pervasive domestic spying perpetrated by the National Security Agency) that overzealous U.S. leaders adopted.

The bottom line is that vital interests are rare, and serious threats to those interests are equally rare. And in most cases the United States would be able by itself, or in cooperation with democratic allies, to neutralize such a threat. If and when a sufficiently lethal threat exists, there is a legitimate case for working with almost any security partner, however odious. British statesman Winston Churchill, a staunch anti-communist, undoubtedly had to hold his nose when his country forged an alliance with Josef Stalin's Soviet Union. But the threat that Nazi Germany posed to Britain's security, perhaps even to its existence as an independent nation, made such a moral concession necessary. The only bona fide criticism that could be made of the British (and U.S.) willingness to work with Stalin was the tendency of some policymakers to pretend (or delude themselves into believing) that their security partner was anything other than a genocidal monster.

When national survival or another vital interest is truly in jeopardy, close relationships with even the most repulsive leaders and regimes are justified. But that ought to be the great exception, not the rule, when it comes to the conduct of America's foreign policy. Even an effort to protect the next highest category of interests, secondary or conditional interests, requires a different, more rigorous, cost-benefit calculation.

Secondary interests are assets that are pertinent but not indispensable to the preservation of America's physical integrity, independence, domestic liberty, and economic health. For example, if one of the regions listed above came under the domination of an adversary, it would not automatically threaten the vital interests of the United States. America could still do reasonably well, for instance, even if China became the hegemon of East Asia, as long as Europe and the South Asia/Persian Gulf region remained outside Beijing's orbit. Chinese dominion over East Asia, however, would make for a significantly more uncomfortable existence, and U.S. leaders would quite understandably want to prevent such an outcome. There are limits, though, to how far policymakers should go adopting amoral, much less immoral, measures to contain China's power.

Unlike the defense of vital interests, the defense of (or promotion of) secondary interests justifies only modest exertions. Washington might deem it beneficial to encourage and lend political and diplomatic support to the efforts of friendly countries to resist the growing power of an emerging, adversarial regional hegemon. In some cases, the transfer of militarily relevant technology, and even direct arms sales, to such countries might be warranted. But whereas the United States must be willing even to risk war to defend vital interests, that stance is usually not warranted in the case of secondary interests.

Such a distinction also applies to the willingness to cooperate with unsavory foreign security partners. When secondary rather than vital interests are at stake, the bar should be higher for taking on such allies. It might be too much to insist that such a partner be a full-fledged democracy or have a squeaky clean record on the issue of corruption, but at the same time there needs to be limits to Washington's tolerance. Partnering with a Stalin (or a Chiang Kai-shek) was arguably necessary to counter the security threat to the United States that Nazi Germany and Imperial Japan posed after Pearl Harbor, but one could not make the same argument for embracing such individuals merely for the defense of secondary interests. To use a contemporary example, it would not be acceptable to establish a close relationship with the murderous Burmese junta or North Korea's totalitarian regime (in the unlikely event such an association was possible) merely to blunt China's growing power in East Asia—even though preventing Chinese hegemony in that region is a secondary interest of the United States.

The cost-benefit calculation shifts further in the direction of caution when the matter involved is one of peripheral interests. That category consists of assets that marginally enhance America's security, liberty, and economic well-being, but the loss of which would be more of an annoyance than a significant blow. The existence of a hostile regime in a midsize country in Latin America (Venezuela comes to mind) is an example of a threat to a peripheral interest. Another example would be the onset of extensive political turbulence in the Middle East or Persian Gulf, given the probable impact on oil prices. It is asking too much for Washington to be indifferent to such matters, but there is nothing at stake that normally requires more than diplomatic exertions. Joint naval maneuvers between Venezuelan and Russian forces, which occurred in 2008, or a spike in oil prices, which occurred in 2011 during the so-called Arab Awakening political upheavals, were unsettling developments, but they hardly warranted any kind of U.S. military response or even a covert Central Intelligence Agency operation.

Restraint about creating relationships with autocratic security partners is even more essential in the case of peripheral interests than it is with secondary interests. To establish alliances with brutal and corrupt regimes in such cases is simply unwarranted. Unfortunately, most of the close relationships that Washington developed with such allies and clients during the Cold War involved little more than the protection or promotion of peripheral interests. That was certainly true of the ties with such tyrants as Marcos, Somoza, and Mobutu. One would have been hard pressed to make a credible case that those associations advanced even legitimate secondary American interests, much less vital ones.

Many situations in the world do not rise even to the level of peripheral interests. They instead fall into the category of barely relevant matters. Whether Bosnia remains intact or divides into a Muslim-dominated ministate and a Serb republic or whether East Timor is well governed, can and should be a matter of indifference to the United States. It is highly improbable that such developments would have a measurable impact on America's security, liberty, or economic health. Washington ought to confine any role to one of routine diplomatic involvement on the margins—and sometimes not even that. In settings where not even peripheral U.S. interests are at stake, there is no justification at all for compromising American values to create security partnerships with unsavory allies or clients.

While the nature and extent of U.S. interests should be the principal screening mechanism for determining whether an alliance with an authoritarian regime is justified, an important secondary screening mechanism should be a determination of just how bad is the prospective partner. It is one thing if a candidate to be an ally or client is engaged in garden variety corruption or harassment of political opponents. It is quite another if the corruption is pervasive, or even worse, if Washington's new "friend" perpetrates systematic torture and murder.

The hardest call regarding a moral balancing act occurs when secondary interests are at stake. U.S. leaders can and should take a firm position against acquiring dubious partners when only peripheral interests are involved—much less when the issue is one of a barely relevant matter. Conversely, as noted earlier, the defense of vital interests requires making sometimes painful moral compromises. The defense of secondary interests constitutes a grey area, and it is in that situation that judgment calls about the severity of the moral deficiency of a potential ally take on special importance. There are instances in which the balance may tilt in favor of establishing or maintaining a cooperative relationship with a morally defective ally.

At some point, though, the repulsive quality of a security partner is so bad that nothing except thwarting a serious threat to vital American interests justifies a close working relationship. Only repelling such a threat could possibly warrant backing the likes of Mobutu, the Guatemalan military dictators, or even Egypt's Hosni Mubarak. That Washington supported such partners—often enthusiastically—even though far milder interests were at stake, is an especially damning indictment of U.S. policy during the Cold War and its aftermath.

U.S. leaders sometimes seem inclined to make similar casual compromises of fundamental American values in the campaign against radical Islamic terrorism. That is unfortunate for two reasons. On a practical level, crawling into bed with the likes of the Saudi royal family or the Pakistani military leadership risks incurring serious blowback from angry populations. Indeed, Washington's willingness to back such corrupt and brutal elites provides fodder for the very terrorist movements we seek to neutralize.

But beyond the practical foreign policy and security considerations, those kinds of relationships create a moral rot within America's own polity. It is not merely hypocritical, it is destructive to America's values and sense of self-worth to betray fundamental principles for anything less than compelling reasons. We made that mistake far too often during the Cold War, and we ought to be doubly on guard to make sure that it does not happen again.

The most practical way to minimize the temptation to back unsavory clients needlessly, and incur the likely unpleasant consequences, is to adopt a policy of ethical pragmatism. That approach recognizes that world affairs are not akin to a fairy tale with easy moral lessons and preordained happy endings. Instead, world conditions require that the United States be flexible and practical in its conduct of foreign policy. But there is a great deal of territory between adopting cynical, Machiavellian practices and adhering to starry-eyed idealism that cannot work in the real world. The self-proclaimed realism of a Henry Kissinger leans too far toward the first pole, while the policy preferences of pacifist organizations tilt too far toward the second.

Ethical pragmatism endeavors to strike a balance between the extremes of those two approaches. It accepts the need for some dilution of moral standards in the conduct of foreign policy—but only if the American interests at stake are sufficiently important, the threat to those interests is serious, and the compromise of values is not excessive, given the circumstances. Admittedly, all of that is dependent on the subjective judgment of policymakers, with all their human frailties. But ethical pragmatism at least provides some guidance for officials as they make their decisions. It guards against an "anything goes" mentality that needlessly sacrifices important principles. Applying such a standard might well have prevented the United States from engaging in some embarrassing, and at times truly shameful, actions during the Cold War and its aftermath. Developing and applying that standard minimizes the danger of repeating such behavior in the future.

Notes

Chapter 1

1. The best account of U.S. policy toward Cuba during this period remains David F. Healy, *The United States in Cuba, 1898–1902: Generals, Politicians, and the Search for Policy* (Madison, WI: University of Wisconsin Press, 1963).

2. Senator Henry Cabot Lodge, an especially avid proponent of U.S. imperialism, even worried about foreign corporations, not just foreign governments, establishing an excessive foothold. In 1912, he proposed his own addition to the Monroe Doctrine, prohibiting any non-U.S. "corporation or association" from taking possession of "any harbor or other place in the American continents." Quoted in Richard H. Immerman, *Empire for Liberty: A History of American Imperialism from Benjamin Franklin to Paul Wolfowitz* (Princeton: Princeton University Press, 2010), p. 156.

3. Robert Kagan, *A Twilight Struggle: American Power and Nicaragua, 1977–1990* (New York: Free Press, 1996), p. 3.

4. For a discussion of the role of United Fruit's extensive role in the politics of Central American states, see Stephen Schlesinger and Stephen Kinzer, *Bitter Fruit: The Story of the American Coup in Guatemala*, 2005 rev. ed. (Cambridge, MA: Harvard University Press, 2005), pp. 65–77.

5. Ted Galen Carpenter, "Threat to the Monroe Doctrine: Axis Penetration of South America, 1936–1941" (master's thesis, University of Wisconsin–Milwaukee, 1971).

6. Grace Livingstone, *America's Backyard: The United States and Latin America from the Monroe Doctrine to the War on Terror* (London: Zed Books, 2009), pp. 19–20.

7. Livingstone, *America's Backyard*, p. 20.

8. Lyndon Baines Johnson, *The Vantage Point: Perspectives of the Presidency, 1963–1969* (New York: Holt, Rinehart, and Winston, 1971), p. 191.

9. Accounts of the intervention, its motives, and the results include Russell Crandall, *Gunboat Democracy: U.S. Interventions in the Dominican Republic, Grenada, and Panama* (New York: Rowman & Littlefield, 2006), pp. 35–94; Abraham F. Lowenthal, *The Dominican Intervention* (Baltimore: Johns Hopkins University Press, 1994); and Lawrence A. Yates, *Power Pack: U.S. Intervention in the Dominican Republic, 1965–1966*, Leavenworth Papers Series, no. 15 (Leavenworth, KS: Combat Studies Institute, 1988).

10. Crandall, *Gunboat Democracy*, pp. 48–49; 90–93.

11. Ronald Reagan, *An American Life: The Autobiography* (New York: Simon & Schuster, 1990), p. 450. Emphasis in original.

12. Reagan, *An American Life*, pp. 457–58.

13. Mark Falcoff, "Argentina under the Junta, 1976–1982," in *Friendly Tyrants: An American Dilemma*, ed. Daniel Pipes and Adam Garfinkle (New York: St. Martin's Press, 1991), p. 158. For a more detailed treatment of the junta's behavior and U.S. policy toward Argentina, see Mark Falcoff, *A Tale of Two Policies: U.S. Relations with the Argentine Junta, 1976–83* (Philadelphia: Foreign Policy Research Institute, 1989).

14. Memorandum of conversation, Santiago, Chile, June 6, 1976, National Security Archive. Quoted in Livingstone, *America's Backyard*, p. 68.

15. Memorandum of conversation, October 7, 1976, "Secretary's Meeting with the Argentine Foreign Minister Guzzetti," Department of State, National Security Archive. Quoted in Livingstone, *America's Backyard*, p. 69.

16. Embassy Buenos Aires, to Secretary of State, Washington, October 19, 1976, "Foreign Minister Guzzetti Euphoric Over Visit to the United States ," Department of State. Quoted in Livingstone, *America's Backyard*, p. 69.

17. For a thoroughly sanitized view of the U.S. role—which essentially argues that Washington bore no responsibility whatever for the coup—see Henry Kissinger, *Years of Upheaval* (Boston: Little, Brown and Company, 1982), pp. 374–406. The extent of Washington's involvement in the 1973 coup remains murky, but there is strong evidence that Nixon ordered the CIA to foment an earlier coup against Allende. Indeed, Nixon instructed Director Richard Helms in September 1970 to organize such a covert operation shortly after it became apparent that Allende had won the three-way contest for Chile's presidency. Such an attempt occurred the following month but failed. See Jack Devine, "What Really Happened in Chile," *Foreign Affairs* 93, no. 4 (July / August 2014): 26–35.

18. Mark Falcoff, "Uncomfortable Allies: U.S. Relations with Pinochet's Chile," in *Friendly Tyrants*, pp. 276–77.

19. Ibid., p. 266.

20. Dwight D. Eisenhower, *The White House Years: Mandate for Change, 1953–1956* (Garden City, NY: Doubleday & Company, 1963), p. 3.

21. Ibid., p. 421.

22. Ibid., p. 422.

23. Quoted in ibid.

24. Quoted in ibid., p. 423, n. 10.

25. For a reasonably balanced discussion of the nature of Árbenz and his government, see Stephen M. Streeter, *Managing Counterrevolution: The United States and Guatemala, 1954–1961* (Athens, OH: Ohio University Center for International Studies, 2000), pp. 16–23.

26. Walter LaFeber, *Inevitable Revolutions: The United States in Central America*, rev. ed. (New York: W.W. Norton, 1984), p. 119.

27. John P. Powelson and Richard Stock, *The Peasant Betrayed: Agriculture and Land Reform in the Third World*, rev. ed. (Washington: Cato Institute, 1990).

28. Jonathan Kwitny, *Endless Enemies: The Making of an Unfriendly World* (New York: Congdon and Weed, 1984), p. 222. Emphasis in original.

29. For example, the brother of Assistant Secretary of State John Moors Cabot was a recent president of United Fruit, and the Cabot family still owned large blocs of stock. And Undersecretary of State Walter Bedell Smith reportedly had expressed the wish in an early 1954 conversation to become president of that company once he retired from government service. Kwitny, *Endless Enemies*, pp. 223, 225.

30. Tim Weiner, *Legacy of Ashes: The History of the CIA* (New York: Doubleday, 2007), pp. 97–98.

31. Kwitny, *Endless Enemies*, p. 225.

32. For accounts of the extent of the U.S. involvement in both the preparation and execution of the coup, see Kwitny, *Endless Enemies*, pp. 225–227; Richard H. Immerman, *The CIA in Guatemala: The Foreign Policy of Intervention* (Austin: University of Texas Press, 1982), pp. 133–186; Schlesinger and Kinzer, *Bitter Fruit*, pp. 99–198;

John Prados, *Presidents' Secret Wars: CIA and Pentagon Covert Operations since World War II* (New York: Morrow, 1986), pp. 98–107; Livingstone, *America's Backyard*, pp. 26–29; and Streeter, *Managing Counterrevolution*, pp. 23–28.

33. Weiner, *Legacy of Ashes*, pp. 93–104.

34. Prados, *Presidents' Secret Wars*, p. 107.

35. Eisenhower, *Mandate for Change*, p. 425.

36. Eisenhower, *Mandate for Change*, p. 426. Critics present a very different view. See, for example, Streeter, *Managing Counterrevolution*, pp. 33–58.

37. Allen Dulles, *The Craft of Intelligence* (New York: New American Library, 1965), pp. 207–8.

38. Quoted in Immerman, *The CIA in Guatemala*, p. 141.

39. John Foster Dulles, radio and television address, June 30, 1954. U.S. Department of State, *American Foreign Policy, 1950–1955, Basic Documents*, vol. 1 (Washington: Government Printing Office, 1957), pp. 1311–15.

40. Streeter, *Managing Counterrevolution*, p. 39.

41. Quoted in ibid.

42. LaFeber, *Inevitable Revolutions*, p. 257.

43. Quoted in ibid., p. 260.

44. Tom Brown and Sarah Grainger, "Guatemalan Tied to Massacre Pleads Guilty in U.S.," Reuters, July 7, 2010.

45. Weiner, *Legacy of Ashes*, p. 458.

46. LaFeber, *Inevitable Revolutions*, pp. 260–61.

47. Kagan, *A Twilight Struggle*, p. 23.

48. Jeane J. Kirkpatrick, *Dictatorships and Double Standards: Rationalism and Reason in Politics* (New York: Simon & Schuster, 1982), p. 24. Emphasis added.

49. Ibid., p. 25.

50. Ibid., pp. 71, 74.

51. Ibid., p. 71.

52. Ibid., p. 70.

53. For examples of such excuses, see ibid., pp. 71, 73.

54. Kagan, *A Twilight Struggle*, p. 28.

55. Bernard Diederich, *Somoza and the Legacy of U.S. Involvement in Central America* (New York: Markus Wiener Publishers, 1981), p. 141.

56. Alan Riding, "Nicaraguan Bishops Accuse Government of Resorting to Widespread Torture," *New York Times*, March 2, 1977.

57. Diederich, *Somoza and the Legacy of U.S. Involvement in Central America*, pp. 120–24.

58. For an overview of U.S. policy regarding both Somoza and the Sandinistas, see Morris H. Morley, *Washington, Somoza, and the Sandinistas: State and Regime in U.S. Policy toward Nicaragua, 1969–1981* (Cambridge: Cambridge University Press, 2010).

59. James Theberge, "The Collapse of the Somoza Regime," in *Friendly Tyrants*, p. 118.

60. Kagan, *A Twilight Struggle*, p. 29.

61. Examples of columns in that series included "Nicaragua Ruler Is World's Greediest," *Washington Post*, August 18, 1975; "Somoza Family's Power Is Pervasive," *Washington Post*, August 19, 1975; "U.S. Subsidizes Nicaragua's Dictator," *Washington Post*, August 26, 1976; "Latin Counterpart to Uganda's Amin," *Washington Post*, September 28, 1977; "Somoza: Caricature of a Dictator," *Washington Post*, September 29, 1977; and "Nicaragua Run for Somoza's Benefit," *Washington Post*, September 30, 1977.

62. For a discussion of the earthquake and the subsequent orgy of corruption, see Diederich, *Somoza and the Legacy of U.S. Involvement in Central America*, pp. 93–106.

507

63. LaFeber, *Inevitable Revolutions*, pp. 227–28.

64. Carter adds the observation in his memoirs that "because of the heavy emphasis that was placed on the Soviet-American competition, a dominant factor in our dealings with foreign countries became whether they espoused an anti-communist line. There were times when right-wing monarchs and military dictators were automatically immune from any criticism of their oppressive actions." Jimmy Carter, *Keeping Faith: Memoirs of a President* (New York: Bantam Books, 1982), p. 142.

65. Kirkpatrick, *Dictatorships and Double Standards*, p. 74.

66. William P. Bundy, "Who Lost Patagonia? Foreign Policy in the 1980 Campaign," *Foreign Affairs* 58, no. 1 (Fall 1979): 8–9.

67. Alexander M. Haig Jr., *Caveat: Realism, Reagan, and Foreign Policy* (New York: Macmillan, 1984), pp. 88–89.

68. Crandall, *Gunboat Democracy*, pp. 150–62.

69. See, for example, Douglas Schoen and Michael Rowan, *The Threat Closer to Home: Hugo Chavez and the War against America* (New York: Free Press, 2009); and Sean Goforth, *Axis of Unity: Venezuela, Iran and the Threat to America* (Dulles, VA: Potomac Books, 2011).

Chapter 2

1. Throughout this chapter, the name Taiwan will be used, except in quoted passages from the period before the 1970s when Formosa was the more common term for the island in Western countries. Likewise, modern terms will generally be used for the names of Chinese individuals and cities, for example, Mao Zedong, not Mao Tse-tung; Beijing, not Peking or Peiping.

2. Barbara W. Tuchman, *Sand against the Wind: Stilwell and the American Experience in China, 1911–1945* (New York: Macmillan, 1971), pp. 187–88.

3. Tuchman, *Sand against the Wind*, p. 188.

4. Useful accounts of the China Lobby and its activities include Joseph Charles Keeley, *The China Lobby Man: The Story of Alfred Kohlberg* (New Rochelle, NY: Arlington House, 1969); and Ross Y. Koen, *The China Lobby in American Politics* (New York: Octagon Books, 1974).

5. Jay Taylor, *The Generalissimo: Chiang Kai-shek and the Struggle for Modern China* (Cambridge, MA: Belknap Press, 2011), pp. 333–34.

6. Tuchman, *Sand against the Wind*, p. 252.

7. Jonathon Fenby, *Chiang Kai-shek: China's Generalissimo and the Nation He Lost* (New York: Carroll and Graf, 2004), p. 412.

8. Ibid., p. 321.

9. Tuchman, *Sand against the Wind*, p. 251.

10. Quoted in ibid., p. 371.

11. Quoted in Fenby, *Chiang Kai-shek*, p. 411. According to Stilwell, though, FDR had little confidence in Chiang and even indicated to the general that it might be advisable to take measures to remove Chiang and get better leadership. Fenby, pp. 412, 426–28.

12. Douglas MacArthur, *Reminiscences* (New York: McGraw Hill, 1964), p. 339.

13. Martin L. Lasater, "Taiwan under the Kuomintang: America and the China Puzzle," in *Friendly Tyrants: An American Dilemma*, ed. Daniel Pipes and Adam Garfinkle (New York: St. Martin's Press, 1991), pp. 353–54.

14. Lasater, "Taiwan under the Kuomintang," p. 354.

15. For a discussion of the extent of the corruption in the Kuomintang (KMT), see Taylor, *The Generalissimo*, pp. 221–22, 357–58, 370–74.

16. Taylor, *The Generalissimo*, p. 373.

17. Ibid., p. 374.

18. Ibid.

19. Ibid., p. 375.

20. For President Truman's perspective on the Marshall Mission and its eventual failure, see Harry S. Truman, *Years of Trial and Hope, 1946–1952* (Garden City, NY: Doubleday and Company, 1956), pp. 71–92.

21. Quoted in Fenby, *Chiang Kai-shek*, p. 469.

22. Taylor, *The Generalissimo*, p. 376.

23. Dean Acheson, *Present at the Creation: My Years in the State Department* (New York: W.W. Norton, 1969), p. 206.

24. Letter reprinted in Truman, *Years of Trial and Hope*, pp. 82–83.

25. Acheson, *Present at the Creation*, p. 369.

26. Truman, *Years of Trial and Hope*, p. 90.

27. Taylor, *The Generalissimo*, pp. 425–26.

28. Dean Rusk, as told to Richard Rusk, *As I Saw It* (New York: Penguin Books, 1990), p. 157.

29. Rusk, *As I Saw It*, p. 158.

30. 81 Cong. Rec., 2nd sess. (January 11, 1950), p. 298.

31. Quoted in James T. Patterson, *Mr. Republican: A Biography of Robert A. Taft* (Boston: Houghton Mifflin, 1972), p. 489.

32. Quoted in Richard P. Stebbins, *The United States in World Affairs, 1950* (New York: Harper and Brothers, 1951), p. 57. For Acheson's reaction to such charges, see Acheson, *Present at the Creation*, p. 364.

33. Acheson, *Present at the Creation*, pp. 365–66.

34. That decision represented a significant change in U.S. policy. Just a few months earlier, both Acheson and Truman had emphasized that the U.S. government considered Taiwan to be Chinese territory and that the United States "would not get involved militarily in any way" regarding the island's future status. Acheson, *Present at the Creation*, p. 351.

35. MacArthur, *Reminiscences*, p. 359.

36. Michael Schaller, *The United States and China in the Twentieth Century* (New York: Oxford University Press, 1979), p. 133.

37. John W. Garver, *The Sino-American Alliance: Nationalist China and the American Cold War Strategy in Asia* (Armonk, NY: M. E. Sharpe, 1997), p. 36.

38. Ibid., pp. 35–36.

39. Ibid., p. 36.

40. MacArthur, *Reminiscences*, p. 341.

41. Excerpt of Harriman memo to President Truman in Truman, *Years of Trial and Hope*, p. 353.

42. Patterson, *Mr. Republican*, p. 485.

43. The bitterness expressed by one of the prominent targets of the purge still comes through decades later. See John Paton Davies Jr., *China Hand: An Autobiography* (Philadelphia: University of Pennsylvania Press, 2012). The book was published 13 years after Davies's death in 1999.

44. John Newhouse, "Diplomacy, Inc.: The Influence of Lobbies on U.S. Foreign Policy," *Foreign Affairs* 88, no. 3 (May–June 2009): 90.

45. Daniel H. Johnson, "The Committee of One Million against the Admission of Communist China to the United Nations," February 21, 2014, Brown University, Hall-

Hoag Collection of Dissenting and Extremist Printed Propaganda, Part II, https://blogs.brown.edu/hallhoag/2014/02/21/the-committee-of-one-million-against-the-admission-of-communist-china-to-the-united-nations/.

46. Dwight D. Eisenhower, *The White House Years: Mandate for Change, 1953–1956* (Garden City, NY: Doubleday and Company, 1963), p. 462.

47. See Dwight D. Eisenhower, *White House Years: Waging Peace, 1956–1961* (Garden City, NY: Doubleday and Company, 1965), p. 564.

48. For discussions of the extent of repression during Chiang Kai-shek's rule on Taiwan, see Amber Parcher, "Remembering the White Terror," *Foreignpolicy.com* (blog), October 12, 2012, http://www.foreignpolicy.com/articles/2012/10/12/remembering_the_white_terror; and Julie Wu, "Remembering Taiwan's White Terrror," *The Diplomat* (Tokyo) (blog), March 8, 2014, http://thediplomat.com/2014/03/remembering-taiwans-white-terror/.

49. Winston Hsiao, "The Development of Human Rights in the Republic of China on Taiwan: Ramifications of Recent Democratic Reforms and Problems of Enforcement," *Pacific Rim Law and Policy Journal* 5, no. 1 (1995): 161–204.

50. Garver, *The Sino-American Alliance*, p. 231.

51. "Document No. 295: National Intelligence Estimate," in *Foreign Relations of the United States, 1952–1954*, vol. XIV, part 1 (China and Japan), para. 23 (September 14, 1954), pp. 632–33.

52. Eisenhower, *Waging Peace*, p. 464.

53. Quoted in Eisenhower, *Mandate for Change*, p. 462.

54. Eisenhower, *Waging Peace*, p. 56.

55. Eisenhower's perspective on the two Taiwan Strait crises can be found in Eisenhower, *Mandate for Change*, pp. 459–83; and Eisenhower, *Waging Peace*, pp. 292–304. Also see Taylor, *The Generalissimo*, pp. 472–79, 493–502; and Garver, *The Sino-American Alliance*, pp. 123–43.

56. Eisenhower, *Waging Peace*, p. 293. Garver describes that maneuver as Chiang's attempt to "entrap" the United States into a more vigorous defense commitment to Taiwan, including an explicit commitment to defend the offshore islands. Garver, *The Sino-American Alliance*, pp. 133–39.

57. Dwight D. Eisenhower, *The Eisenhower Diaries*, ed. Robert H. Ferrell (New York: W.W. Norton, 1981), p. 296.

58. Lasater, "Taiwan under the Kuomintang," p. 355.

59. Taylor, *The Generalissimo*, p. 475.

60. Eisenhower, *Waging Peace*, p. 296.

61. Eisenhower, *Mandate for Change*, p. 459.

62. Ibid., pp. 465–66.

63. Quoted in Garver, *The Sino-American Alliance*, p. 139.

64. Garver, *The Sino-American Alliance*, p. 139.

65. Rusk, *As I Saw It*, pp. 282–83.

66. George W. Ball, *The Past Has Another Pattern: Memoirs* (New York: W. W. Norton, 1982), p. 166.

67. Rusk, *As I Saw It*, p. 288.

68. Ibid.

69. Richard M. Nixon, *RN: The Memoirs of Richard Nixon* (New York: Grosset and Dunlap, 1978), p. 556.

70. Henry Kissinger's version of the various maneuvers during the 1969–1971 period regarding the issue of Taiwan's UN membership is in Henry Kissinger, *White House Years* (Boston: Little, Brown and Company, 1979), pp. 733, 770–74, 784–86.

71. Ibid., p. 785.

72. James Mann, *About Face: A History of America's Curious Relationship with China, from Nixon to Clinton* (New York: Vintage, 2000), p. 71.

73. Jimmy Carter, *Keeping Faith: Memoirs of a President* (New York: Bantam Books, 1982), p. 187.

74. Ibid., p. 200.

75. Ibid., pp. 187–88.

76. Harry Harding, *A Fragile Relationship: The United States and China since 1972* (Washington: Brookings Institution, 1992), pp. 84–85.

77. Carter, *Keeping Faith*, p. 200.

78. Portions of the speech were reprinted a short time later in Ronald Reagan, "Decency for Taiwan," *New York Times*, January 28, 1979.

79. See David Tawei Lee, *The Making of the Taiwan Relations Act: Twenty Years in Retrospect* (New York: Oxford University Press, 2000).

80. Harding, *A Fragile Relationship*, pp. 86–87.

81. Ronald Reagan, *An American Life* (New York: Simon & Schuster, 1990), p. 361.

82. Garver, *The Sino-American Alliance*, p. 232.

83. MacArthur, *Reminiscences*, pp. 343–44.

84. Lasater, "Taiwan under the Kuomintang," pp. 354–55.

85. The conviction and imprisonment of former president Chen Shui-bian on corruption charges is testimony to the persistence of the problem.

86. For a comparison of the gross domestic product of Brazil, Canada, China, the Russian Federation, Taiwan, and the United States between 1950 and 2000, see DataMarket.com, "Real GDP Per Capita," https://datamarket.com/data/set/1crb/real-gdp-per-capita#!ds=1crb!wra=3p.z.x.4n.1e.4m&display=line.

87. Garver, *The Sino-American Alliance*.

88. Fenby, *Chiang Kai-Shek*, p. 500.

Chapter 3

1. That has long been a bipartisan assumption. Even as he excoriated many aspects of the Truman administration's policy in East Asia in the aftermath of the communist revolution in China and the onset of the Korean War, Republican Senator Robert A. Taft concluded gloomily: "If we are forced out of Korea, it will be very difficult to defend Japan." Quoted in James T. Patterson, *Mr. Republican: A Biography of Robert A. Taft* (Boston: Houghton Mifflin, 1972), p. 485.

2. James Irving Matray, *The Reluctant Crusade: American Foreign Policy in Korea, 1941–1950* (Honolulu: University of Hawaii Press, 1985), pp. 52–124.

3. Callum A. MacDonald, *Korea: The War before Vietnam* (New York: Free Press, 1986), pp. 13–14.

4. Gregg Brazinsky, *Nation Building in South Korea: Koreans, Americans, and the Making of a Democracy* (Chapel Hill, NC: University of North Carolina Press, 2007), p. 13.

5. Douglas MacArthur, *Reminiscences* (New York: McGraw Hill, 1964), p. 319.

6. Chalmers Johnson, *Blowback: The Costs and Consequences of American Empire* (New York: Metropolitan Books, 2000), pp. 98–100.

7. Clay Blair, *The Forgotten War: America in Korea, 1950–1953* (New York: Times Books, 1987), p. 973.

8. Jean Edward Smith, *Eisenhower in War and Peace* (New York: Random House, 2012), p. 576.

9. Dwight D. Eisenhower, *The White House Years: Mandate for Change, 1953–1956* (Garden City, NY: Doubleday and Co., 1963), pp. 181–82.

10. Ibid., p. 182.

11. The recurring tensions between Washington and Seoul regarding the armistice negotiations are discussed in Ohn Chang-il, "South Korea, the United States, and the Korean Armistice Negotiations," in *Korea and the Cold War: Division, Destruction, and Disarmament*, ed. Kim Chull Baum and James Matray (Claremont, CA: Regina Books, 1993), pp. 209–29; and William Stueck, *The Korean War: An International History* (Princeton: Princeton University Press, 1995), pp. 210–15, 320–25, 330–39.

12. Eisenhower, *The White House Years: Mandate for Change*, p. 188.

13. Ibid., pp. 185–86.

14. Smith, *Eisenhower in War and Peace*, p. 577.

15. Eisenhower, *The White House Years: Mandate for Change*, p. 186.

16. Dwight D. Eisenhower, *The Eisenhower Diaries*, ed. Robert H. Ferrell (New York: W. W. Norton, 1981), p. 248.

17. Eisenhower, *The White House Years: Mandate for Change*, p. 187.

18. Hakjoon Kim, "The U.S.-Korean Alliance: Past, Present, and Future," *International Journal of Korean Studies* 7, no. 1 (Spring/Summer 2003): 2.

19. Eisenhower, *The White House Years: Mandate for Change*, p. 183.

20. Brazinsky, *Nation Building in South Korea*, p. 13.

21. See Melvin P. Leffler, *A Preponderance of Power: National Security, the Truman Administration, and the Cold War* (Stanford, CA: Stanford University Press, 1992), pp. 376–77, 395–96.

22. Brazinsky, *Nation Building in South Korea*, pp. 19–20.

23. Yong-Sup Han, "The May Sixteenth Military Coup," in *The Park Chung Hee Era: The Transformation of South Korea*, ed. Byung –Kook Kim and Ezra F. Vogel (Cambridge, MA: Harvard University Press, 2011), pp. 35–57. Both quotes are on p. 41.

24. Taehyun Kim and Chang Jae Baik, "Taming and Tamed by the United States," in *The Park Chung Hee Era: The Transformation of South Korea*, ed. Byung –Kook Kim and Ezra F. Vogel (Cambridge, MA: Harvard University Press, 2011), pp. 58–84. Quote is on p. 81.

25. Edward Olsen notes that the initial opposition in Washington to Park's coup gradually gave way to a more supportive attitude. Edward A. Olsen, "South Korea under Military Rule: Friendly Tyrant?" in *Friendly Tyrants: An American Dilemma*, ed. Daniel Pipes and Adam Garfinkle (New York: St. Martin's Press, 1991), pp. 336–37.

26. Kim and Baik, "Taming and Tamed by the United States," p. 58.

27. Ibid., p. 59.

28. Dae-Sook Suh, "The Centennial: A History," in *Korea and the United States: A Century of Cooperation*, ed. Youngnok Koo and Dae-Sook Suh (Honolulu: University of Hawaii Press, 1984), pp. 15–16.

29. Johnson, *Blowback*, p. 107.

30. Balanced discussions of Park's rule and the economic reforms that he implemented are found in Kim and Vogel, *The Park Chung Hee Era*. Especially useful chapters are Chung-in Moon, "Modernization Strategy: Ideas and Influences," pp. 115–39; Byung-Kook Kim, "The Leviathan: Economic Bureaucracy under Park," pp.

200–32; Eun Mee Kim and Gil-Sung Park, "The *Chaebol*," pp. 265–94; and Ezra F. Vogel, "Nation Rebuilders: Mustafa Kemal Atatürk, Lee Kuan Yew, Deng Xiaoping, and Park Chung Hee," pp. 513–41. Also see Brazinsky, *Nation Building in South Korea*, pp. 128–62.

31. President Ford, memorandum of conversation, November 22, 1974, http://www.fordlibrarymuseum.gov/library/document/0314/1552860.pdf.

32. Quoted in "President Park of South Korea Greeted Here as Firm U.S. Ally," *New York Times*, May 20, 1965.

33. Quoted in John F. Barton, "U.S. Aid at Stake—Korean Regime Stirs Criticism," *Youngstown Vindicator* (OH), August 7, 1974.

34. Yong-Jick Kim, "The Security, Political, and Human Rights Conundrum, 1974–1979," in *The Park Chung Hee Era*, pp. 457–82. Quote is on p. 458.

35. Zbigniew Brzezinski, *Power and Principle: Memoirs of the National Security Adviser, 1977–1981*, rev. ed. (New York: Farrar Straus Giroux, 1985), p. 127.

36. Olsen, "South Korea under Military Rule," p. 338.

37. Brzezinski, *Power and Principle*, p. 128.

38. Ibid. Emphasis added.

39. Ibid.

40. Cyrus R. Vance, *Hard Choices: Critical Years in America's Foreign Policy* (New York: Simon & Schuster, 1983), pp. 127–28.

41. Quoted in Kim Jin-wung, "Recent Anti-Americanism in South Korea: The Causes," *Asian Survey* 29, no. 8 (August 1989): 755. On Wickham's views and comments, also see Selig Harrison, "Dateline South Korea: A Divided Seoul," *Foreign Policy* no. 67 (Summer 1987): 157.

42. For a discussion of the December 1979 coup and Washington's apparent conduct, see Don Oberdorfer, *The Two Koreas: A Contemporary History*, 2nd ed. (New York: Basic Books, 2001), pp. 116–19, 121–24.

43. Linda Lewis, "'The Kwangju Incident' Observed," in *The Kwangju Uprising: Shadows Over the Regime in South Korea*, ed. Donald Clark (Boulder: Westview Press, 1988), p. 23.

44. Oberdorfer, *The Two Koreas*, p. 125.

45. Quoted in ibid., p. 128.

46. Johnson, *Blowback*, p. 110.

47. Alexander M. Haig Jr., *Caveat: Realism, Reagan, and Foreign Policy* (New York: Macmillan, 1984), p. 57.

48. Haig, *Caveat*, p. 90.

49. Quoted in "Banner Battle Rouses Crowd at Seoul Rally," *Washington Post*, July 19, 1987.

50. Walt W. Rostow, *The Diffusion of Power, 1957–1972* (New York: Macmillan, 1972), p. 206.

51. Gerald R. Ford, *A Time to Heal: The Autobiography of Gerald R. Ford*, 2nd ed. (New York: Berkley Books, 1980), pp. 207–8.

52. Ibid.

53. For a discussion of Washington's gradually increasing support for democracy in South Korea as that country became economically stronger and more mature, see Gregg Brazinsky, *Nation Building in South Korea*, especially pp. 245–60.

54. George P. Shultz, *Turmoil and Triumph: My Years as Secretary of State* (New York: Charles Scribner's Sons, 1993), p. 978.

55. Ibid., pp. 978–79.

56. Ibid., p. 980.

57. Quoted in Dorothy Collin, "Democrats in Congress Warn Seoul to Reform," *Chicago Tribune*, June 19, 1987.

58. Olsen, "South Korea under Military Rule," p. 340.

59. Richard M. Nixon, *RN: The Memoirs of Richard Nixon* (New York: Grosset and Dunlap, 1978), p. 395.

60. Quoted in Ralph N. Clough, *Deterrence and Defense in Korea: The Role of U.S. Forces* (Washington: Brookings Institution, 1976), p. 3.

61. See, for example, Holbrooke's 1975 article in the *New York Times Magazine*. Richard Holbrooke, "Escaping the Domino Trap," *New York Times Magazine*, September 7, 1975.

62. Richard Bernstein, "Restoring America's Role in Asia," in *The Unquiet American: Richard Holbrooke in the World*, ed. Derek Chollet and Samantha Power (New York: Public Affairs, 2011), p. 124.

63. Ibid. Also see Yong-Jick Kim, "The Security, Political, and Human Rights Conundrum, 1974–1979," in *The Park Chung Hee Era*, pp. 479–81.

64. "Weinberger Assures South Koreans 40,000 U.S. Troops Will Not Pull Out," *Washington Times*, April 3, 1986.

65. Oberdorfer, *The Two Koreas*, p. 106.

66. Claude A. Buss, *The United States and the Republic of Korea: Background for Policy* (Stanford, CA: Hoover Institution, 1982), p. 142.

67. Quoted in ibid., p. 144.

68. See Doug Bandow, *Tripwire: Korea and U.S. Foreign Policy in a Changed World* (Washington: Cato Institute, 1996), pp. 71–73.

69. For a discussion of the strong anti-American sentiment among South Koreans during the early 21st century, see Ted Galen Carpenter and Doug Bandow, *The Korean Conundrum: America's Troubled Relations with North and South Korea* (New York: Palgrave Macmillan, 2004), pp. 14–18, 32–33, 123–24.

70. Quoted in Oberdorfer, *The Two Koreas*, p. 124. Emphasis added.

Chapter 4

1. For insightful examinations of the Kashmir issue see Sumantra Bose, *Kashmir: Roots of Conflict, Paths to Peace* (Cambridge, MA: Harvard University Press, 2003); and Howard B. Schaffer, *The Limits of Influence: America's Role in Kashmir* (Washington: Brookings Institution Press, 2009).

2. Early planners considered South Asia important, but considerably less so compared to Western Europe and East Asia in terms of industrial might, skilled labor, and economic and material abundance. See, for example "Appraisal of U.S. National Interests in South Asia," Report by the SANACC (State-Army-Navy-Air Force Coordinating Committee) for the Near and Middle East, SANACC 360/14, April 19, 1949, Foreign Relations of the United States (hereafter cited as *FRUS*) 1949, vol. VI, doc. 6, pp. 8–28, http://images.library.wisc.edu/FRUS/EFacs/1949v06/reference/frus.frus1949v06.i0006.pdf; and "Memorandum of Conversation, by the Acting Secretary of State (Lovett)," April 2, 1948, *FRUS* 1948, vol. V, doc. 5, p. 506, http://images.library.wisc.edu/FRUS/EFacs/1948v05p1/reference/frus.frus1948v05p1.i0016.pdf.

3. Anita Inder Singh, *The Limits of British Influence: South Asia and the Anglo-American Relationship, 1947–56* (London: Pinter Publishers, 1993), pp. xi–xii.

4. American officials also took umbrage with Nehru's condemnation of America as imperialist and driven in its foreign policy by economic imperatives. Nehru also demanded the withdrawal of U.S. personnel from the UN peacekeeping mission in Kashmir and refused America to airlift supplies to French forces in Indochina using Indian airspace or territory. See Kenton J. Clymer, "Jawaharlal Nehru and the United States: The Preindependence Years," *Diplomatic History* 13 (Spring 1990): 143–61.

5. George McGhee, President Harry Truman's Assistant Secretary of State, believed "Nehru was the stumbling block . . . If he had cooperated, the Kashmir problem could have easily been solved." Dennis Kux, *Disenchanted Allies: The United States and Pakistan, 1947–2000* (Washington: Woodrow Wilson Center Press, 2001), p. 31; Dean Acheson, *Present at the Creation: My Years in the State Department* (New York: W.W. Norton, 1969), p. 336; and "Minutes of NSC Meeting," June 1, 1953, *FRUS 1952–1954*, vol. IX, pt. 1 (Washington: Government Printing Office, 1986), p. 147.

6. Quoted in Kux, *Disenchanted Allies*, p. 20.

7. On the generally secular nature of the early Pakistani state, see Lawrence Ziring, *Pakistan in the Twentieth Century: A Political History* (Karachi, Pakistan: Oxford University Press, 1997), p. 182; and Stephen Cohen, "India, Pakistan and Kashmir," paper presented at the University of Texas at Austin, December 2001, http://www.brookings.edu/~/media/research/files/articles/2002/12/india-cohen/cohens20011201. On Jinnah's willingness to offer forces to the Western Cold War cause, see George Crews McGhee, *Envoy to the Middle World: Adventures in Diplomacy* (New York: Harper & Row, 1983), pp. 92–93, 96–97; and M. S. Venkataramani, *The American Role in Pakistan, 1947–1958* (New Delhi: Radiant Publishers, 1982), pp. 103–6.

8. Keith B. Callard, *Pakistan, a Political Study* (London: Allen and Unwin Ltd, 1957), p. 325.

9. Lloyd I. Rudolph and Susanne Hoeber Rudolph, "The Making of US Foreign Policy for South Asia: Offshore Balancing in Historical Perspective," *Economic and Political Weekly* 41, no. 8 (February 25 to March 3, 2006): 703–09.

10. "Appraisal of U.S. National Interests in South Asia," SANACC.

11. As Eisenhower's National Security Council advised on July 23, 1954, the concept of the "northern tier" would include Turkey, Pakistan, Iran, and Iraq. See "U.S. Objectives and Policies with Respect to the Near East," Statement of Policy by the National Security Council, NSC 5428, July 23, 1954, *FRUS 1952–1954*, vol. IX, pt.1, p. 525 et seq., http://digicoll.library.wisc.edu/cgi-bin/FRUS/FRUS-idx?type=article&did=FRUS.FRUS195254v09p1.i0008&id=FRUS.FRUS195254v09p1&isize=M.

12. Ayub went to Washington on his own volition and ahead of a visit by Pakistan's civilian head of state. Shirin TahirKheli, *The United States and Pakistan: The Evolution of an Influence Relationship* (New York: Praeger, 1982), p. 3.

13. John P. Callahan, "US-Pakistan Talks on Arms Awaited," *New York Times*, November 2, 1953; and Dana Adams Schmidt, "Pakistan to Get Arms," *New York Times*, February 14, 1954.

14. As the governor of West Pakistan stated frankly, "When Pakistanis speak of 'defense' they speak of defense against India." See "Telegram from the Embassy in Pakistan to the Department of State," *FRUS 1955–1957*, South Asia, vol. VIII, doc. 219, http://history.state.gov/historicaldocuments/frus1955-57v08/d219 Secretary Dulles began to doubt the "northern tier" concept, blaming the scourge of "Arab politics." See "Letter from the Secretary of State to the Secretary of Defense (Wilson)," *FRUS 1955–1957*, vol. XII, doc. 126, April 23, 1956, http://history.state.gov/historicaldocuments/frus1955-57v12/d126.

15. See Fulbright's remarks in *Congressional Record—Senate*, March 2, 1954, 83rd Cong., 2nd sess, pp. 2481–82; and see Chester A. Bowles, *Promises to Keep: My Years in Public Life, 1941–1969* (New York: Harper & Row, 1971), pp. 477–78.

16. Dennis Kux, *India and the United States: Estranged Democracies* (Honolulu, HI: University of the Pacific, 2002), p. 127.

17. Department of State, Central Files, 110.11–DU/3–1156 (Secret), *FRUS* 1955–1957, vol. VIII, doc. 157, http://history.state.gov/historicaldocuments/frus1955-57v08 /d157; "Telegram from the Department of State to the Embassy in Iraq," November 20, 1956, *FRUS* 1955–1957, vol. XII, doc. 146, p. 338, http://digicoll.library.wisc .edu/cgi-bin/FRUS/FRUS-idx?type=turn&id=FRUS.FRUS195557v12&entity=FRUS . FRUS195557v12.p0367&q1=november%2016,%201956.

18. After a coup in Baghdad in 1958, the Baghdad Pact was renamed CENTO and continued to comprise Turkey, Iran, and Pakistan.

19. Mohammed Ayub Khan, "The Pakistan-American Alliance," *Foreign Affairs* 42, no. 2 (January 1964): 195.

20. Sexton was head of the U.S. mission set up to advise and guide the modernization of Pakistan's armed forces (U.S. Military Assistance Advisory Group). He reported that to raise existing force levels "would involve additional expenditures." See, "The Ambassador in Pakistan (Hildreth) to the DOS, Karachi," August 9, 1954, *FRUS* 1952–1954, vol. XI, pt. 2, p. 1860, http://images.library.wisc .edu/FRUS/EFacs2/1952-54v11p2/reference/frus.frus195254v11p2.i0007.pdf; see also "Editorial note" number 194 after "Telegram from the Department of State to the Embassy in Pakistan," April 15, 1955, *FRUS* 1955–1957, vol. VIII, doc. 193, p. 428, http://images.library.wisc.edu/FRUS/EFacs2/1955-57v08/reference/frus .frus195557v08.i0011.pdf. Sexton had met with General Ayub Khan in Rawalpindi, the headquarters of the Pakistani armed forces, and discussed the offer of a first year, $30 million aid package designated exclusively for military equipment and training. Ayub, however, anticipated receiving upwards of $300 million for unrestricted use. U.S. officials unveiled a more expansive aid package on October 12—$171 million in military assistance for three-and-a-half years to arm and equip five-and-a-half Pakistani divisions and $50 million in economic assistance for consumer goods and raw materials. "The Acting Secretary of State to the Embassy in Pakistan," October 22, 1954, *FRUS 1952–1954*, vol. XI, pt. 2, pp. 1869–71, http://images.library.wisc.edu /FRUS/EFacs2/1952-54v11p2/reference/frus.frus195254v11p2.i0007.pdf.

21. U.S. objectives for Pakistan included its increased identification with the free world community, its ability to help defend the free world, and a sound, developed economy. "National Security Council Report, Statement of Policy on U.S. Policy toward South Asia," January 10, 1957, NSC 5701, *FRUS* 1955–1957, vol. VIII, doc. 5, p. 29, http://history.state.gov/historicaldocuments/frus1955-57v08/d5.

22. "The Chargé in Pakistan (Emmerson) to the DOS," Karachi, 689.90D/10-2354: Telegram, October 23, 1954, *FRUS* 1952–1954, vol. XI, pt. 2, pp. 1871–74, http://images .library.wisc.edu/FRUS/EFacs2/1952-54v11p2/reference/frus.frus195254v11p2 .i0003.pdf; and "Memorandum by Assistant Secretary of Defense H. Struve Hensel," February 17, 1955, *FRUS* 1955–1957, vol. VIII, 418–20, http://images.library.wisc .edu/FRUS/EFacs2/1955-57v08/reference/frus.frus195557v08.i0011.pdf.

23. "Report by the Joint Strategic Plans Committee to Joint Chiefs of Staff," March 24, 1955; Joint Chiefs of Staff 2099/569, February 14, 1956, sec. 24, JCS Records; on "limited initial resistance" see "Memorandum of Discussion at the 308th Meeting

of the National Security Council, Washington, January 3, 1957," *FRUS* 1955–1957, vol. XIX, doc. 103, p. 397.

24. "Telegram from the Department of State to the Embassy in Pakistan," May 28, 1955, *FRUS* 1955–1957, vol. XII, Near East Region; Iran; Iraq, doc. 39, http://history .state.gov/historicaldocuments/frus1955-57v12/d39.

25. By 1957, Pakistan military expenses absorbed approximately 65 percent of government tax revenues. "Letter from the Ambassador in Pakistan (Langley) to the Assistant Secretary of State for Near Eastern, South Asian, and African Affairs (Rountree)," December 27, 1957, *FRUS* 1955–1957, vol. VIII, doc. 224, p. 487, http:// images.library.wisc.edu/FRUS/EFacs2/1955-57v08/reference/frus.frus195557v08 .i0011.pdf. See also John P. Callahan, "US-Pakistan Talks on Arms Awaited," *New York Times*, November 2, 1953; and ICA Report, "Evaluation of Pakistan Program," February 1, 1957, 790D.5-MSP/4-1557. On Pakistan's defense burden see JCS 1887/347, March 20, 1957, CCS 381 EMMA (11-19-47), sec. 56, JCS Records. Also see "National Security Council Report, Statement of Policy on U.S. Policy toward South Asia," January 10, 1957, NSC 5701, *FRUS* 1955–1957, vol. VIII, doc. 5, p. 29, http://images.library.wisc .edu/FRUS/EFacs2/1955-57v08/reference/frus.frus195557v08.i0008.pdf.

26. "National Intelligence Estimate: Probable Developments in Pakistan," March 15, 1955, NIE 52–55, *FRUS* 1955–1957, vol. VIII, doc. 190, p. 423, http://images .library.wisc.edu/FRUS/EFacs2/1955-57v08/reference/frus.frus195557v08.i0011 .pdf; "Memorandum from the Operations Coordinator (Bishop) to the Assistant Secretary of State for Near Eastern, South Asian, and African Affairs (Allen)," July 28, 1955, *FRUS* 1955–1957, vol. VIII, doc. 196, p. 433, http://images.library.wisc .edu/FRUS/EFacs2/1955-57v08/reference/frus.frus195557v08.i0011.pdf; "Telegram from the Embassy in Pakistan to the Department of State," October 1, 1955, *FRUS* 1955–1957, vol. VIII, doc. 201, p. 442, http://images.library.wisc.edu/FRUS /EFacs2/1955-57v08/reference/frus.frus195557v08.i0011.pdf; "Memorandum from the Deputy Under Secretary of State for Economic Affairs (Prochnow) to the Secretary of State," July 27, 1956, *FRUS* 1955–1957, vol. X, doc. 22, p. 85, http://images.library .wisc.edu/FRUS/EFacs2/1955-57v10/reference/frus.frus195557v10.i0008.pdf; and "Memorandum of Discussion at the 308th Meeting of the National Security Council, Washington, January 3, 1957," *FRUS* 1955–1957, vol. VIII, doc.103, p. 397, http:// images.library.wisc.edu/FRUS/EFacs2/1955-57v08/reference/frus.frus195557v08 .i0008.pdf. Military programs originally set to reach their goals in three-and-a-half years were refined to reach objectives in approximately 15 years. "Telegram from the Embassy in Pakistan to the Department of State," January 19, 1956, *FRUS* 1955–1957, vol. VIII, doc. 208, p. 454, http://images.library.wisc.edu/FRUS/EFacs2/1955 -57v08/reference/frus.frus195557v08.i0011.pdf. An interdepartmental committee report estimated that during the 1958–1960 fiscal years, if the United States accepted the costs of maintaining Pakistan's new equipment, assistance to Pakistan would cost between $765 million and $1.1 billion; the average cost per year after 1960 would be between $130 million and $235 million.

27. In terms of direct and indirect economic burden, inflationary pressures, competition for resources, and financing. See "Memorandum from the Deputy Under Secretary of State for Economic Affairs (Prochnow) to the Secretary of State," July 27, 1956, *FRUS* 1955–1957, vol. X, doc. 22, p. 85, http://images.library.wisc.edu/FRUS /EFacs2/1955-57v10/reference/frus.frus195557v10.i0008.pdf; and "Telegram from the Embassy in Pakistan to the Department of State," October 1, 1955, *FRUS* 1955–1957, vol. VIII, doc. 201, p. 442, http://images.library.wisc.edu/FRUS/EFacs2/1955-57v08

/reference/frus.frus195557v08.i0011.pdf. For influential Pakistani perspectives on the issue, see Ayesha Siddiqa, *Military Inc.: Inside Pakistan's Military Economy* (London: Pluto Press, 2007); and Hassan Abbas, *Pakistan's Drift into Extremism: Allah, the Army, and America's War on Terror* (Armonk, NY: M. E. Sharpe, 2005).

28. "National Intelligence Estimate 52–56: Probable Developments in Pakistan," November 13, 1956, *FRUS* 1955–1957, vol. VIII, doc. 216, p. 473, http://images.library .wisc.edu/FRUS/EFacs2/1955-57v08/reference/frus.frus195557v08.i0011.pdf. Also see Robert J. McMahon, *Cold War on the Periphery: The United States, India, and Pakistan* (New York: Columbia University Press, 1994).

29. Department of State, INR–NIE Files (Secret), *FRUS* 1955–1957, vol. VIII, doc. 216, http://history.state.gov/historicaldocuments/frus1955-57v08/d216; and "Progress Report by the Operations Coordinating Board, Progress Report on U.S. Policy Towards South Asia (NSC 5409)," March 30, 1956, *FRUS* 1955–1957, vol. VIII, p. 1, http://images.library.wisc.edu/FRUS/EFacs2/1955-57v08/reference/frus .frus195557v08.i0008.pdf.

30. Ayesha Jalal, *The State of Martial Rule: The Origins of Pakistan's Political Economy of Defence* (New York: Cambridge University Press, 1990), pp. 255–56.

31. "Memorandum of Discussion at the 308th Meeting of the National Security Council, Washington, January 3, 1957," Eisenhower Library, Whitman File, NSC Records (Top Secret). Drafted by S. Everett Gleason on January 4. *FRUS* 1955–1957, South Asia, vol. 8, doc. 4, http://history.state.gov/historicaldocuments/frus1955-57v08/d4.

32. The only reason why Pakistan was "able to keep going is U.S. aid," Langley warned, insisting that the partnership not become "a mutual 'suicide pact.'" "Letter from the Ambassador in Pakistan (Langley) to the Assistant Secretary of State for Near Eastern, South Asian, and African Affairs (Rountree)," December 27, 1957, *FRUS* 1955–1957, vol. VIII, doc. 224, p. 487, http://images.library.wisc.edu/FRUS /EFacs2/1955-57v08/reference/frus.frus195557v08.i0011.pdf.

33. "Memorandum of discussion by Gleason," October 31, 1958, Eisenhower Library, Whitman File, NSC Records; and "Memorandum of discussion by Gleason," October 17, 1958, Eisenhower Library, Whitman File, NSC Records, *FRUS* 1958–1960, vol. XV, doc. 291, http://images.library.wisc.edu/FRUS/EFacs/1958-60v15 /reference/frus.frus195860v15.i0013.pdf; and Department of State, Central Files, 790D.00/10–958 (Secret), *FRUS* 1958–1960, vol. XV, doc. 326, http://www.history .state.gov/historicaldocuments/frus1958-60v15/d326.

34. John F. Kennedy: "Joint Statement Following Discussions with the President of Pakistan," July 13, 1961, The American Presidency Project, http://www.presidency .ucsb.edu/ws/?pid=8237; http://www.millat.com/democracy/Foreign%20Policy /Briefing_Paper_english_11.pdf.

35. South Asia expert Stephen Cohen calls the generation of officers joining the Pakistan military from 1950 through 1965, and entering the middle ranks in 1971, the "American generation." Stephen P. Cohen, *The Pakistan Army* (Berkeley: University of California Press, 1984), p. 70.

36. Michael R. Beschloss, *Mayday: Eisenhower, Khrushchev, and the U-2 Affair* (New York: Harper & Row, 1986), pp. 267–68.

37. A May 1959 State Department Planning Board report spelled out U.S. policy in South Asia for the coming decade: "The problem of how great an effort the Western Powers should make to build up a position of greater Free World strength in South Asia is given new prominence by the rapid growth in Chinese Communist power. The likelihood that this growth will intensify the threat posed to Free World

interests in Asia over the next decade underlines the desirability of developing in India a successful alternative to Communism in an Asiatic context." Department of State, S/S–NSC Files: Lot 63 D 351, NSC 5701 Series (Secret). A slightly different version of this paper was first transmitted to the NSC on May 22. See Department of State, S/S–NSC Files: Lot 63 D 351, NSC 5701 Series, *FRUS* 1958–1960, vol. XV, doc. 1, http://history.state.gov/historicaldocuments/frus1958-60v15/d1.

38. Kennedy quoted in Arthur M. Schlesinger Jr., *A Thousand Days, John F. Kennedy in the White House* (Boston: Houghton Mifflin Company, 1965), p. 522.

39. John F. Kennedy: "Annual Message to the Congress on the State of the Union," January 30, 1961, The American Presidency Project, http://www.presidency.ucsb .edu/ws/?pid=8045. Rusk worked on Kashmir under Truman, Bowles was former ambassador to India, Talbot was a scholar-journalist-India specialist, and Galbraith was a visiting professor there in the mid-1950s.

40. *New York Times* Chronology, July 1, 1961, http://www.jfklibrary.org/Research /Ready-Reference/New-York-Times-Chronology/Browse-by-Date/New-York-Times -Chronology-July-1961.aspx; http://history.state.gov/departmenthistory/visits /pakistan; http://artandhistory.house.gov/house_history/Joint_Meetings/80to99 .aspx. For Ayub quote, see http://www.dawn.com/2011/07/13/know-your-friends -ayub-tells-us.html. For a slight variation of quote see Tariq Ali, *The Duel: Pakistan on the Flight Path of American Power* (New York: Scribner, 2008), p. 201.

41. Kennedy Library, National Security Files, Countries Series, India, General, 4/16/61-4/30/61 (Confidential). "Approved per RDungan to FAMau 4/22/61," Department of State, Central Files, 891.00-Five Year/4-1961, *FRUS* 1961–1963, vol. XIX, doc. 14, http://history.state.gov/historicaldocuments/frus1961-63v19/d14; Department of State, Central Files, 791.5-MSP/4-2361 (Confidential; Priority), *FRUS* 1961–1963, vol. XIX, doc. 16, http://history.state.gov/historicaldocuments/frus1961 -63v19/d16; and "Summary: *FRUS* 1961–1963, vol. 19, South Asia," Office of the Historian, Bureau of Public Affairs, U.S. Department of State, http://dosfan.lib.uic .edu/ERC/frus/summaries/960820_FRUS_XIX_1961-63.html.

42. Kennedy Library, National Security Files, Countries Series, India, General, 10/26/62-10/27/62 (Secret), *FRUS* 1961–1963, vol. XIX, doc.181, http://history.state .gov/historicaldocuments/frus1961-63v19/d181.

43. Kennedy highlighted the weapons' "limited" purpose. Kennedy Library, National Security Files, Countries Series, India, General, 10/26/62-10/27/62 (Secret), *FRUS* 1961–1963, vol. XV, doc. 181, http://history.state.gov/historicaldocuments /frus1961-63v19/d181; Department of State, Central Files, 691.93/10-2762 (Secret; Niact), received in the Department of State at 3:09 p.m.; repeated to New Delhi, *FRUS* 1961–1963, vol. XIX, doc. 183, http://history.state.gov/historicaldocuments /frus1961-63v19/d183. General Moin Haider, Pakistan's former Interior Minister, who had served in the army, recalled the growing bitterness that occurred. Malou Innocent interview with General Moin Haider, Karachi, August 5, 2008.

44. Timothy W. Crawford, "Kennedy and Kashmir, 1962–63: The Perils of Pivotal Peacemaking in South Asia," *India Review* 1 (July 2002): 6; Statement by Foreign Minister Mohammad Ali Bogra to the National Assembly of Pakistan, November 22, 1962, in "Pakistan, 1947–1965," Rajendra K. Jain, ed., *U.S.-South Asian Relations, 1947– 1982*, vol. 2 (Atlantic Highlands, N.J.: Humanities Press, 1983), p. 213.

45. Kennedy Library, President's Office Files, Staff Memoranda Series, R. Komer (Security Secret), *FRUS* 1961–1936, vol. XIX, doc. 257, http://history.state.gov /historicaldocuments/frus1961-63v19/d257; and Department of State, Central Files,

690D.91/1-1563 (Secret; Priority), *FRUS* 1961–1963, vol. XIX, doc. 239, http://history.state.gov/historicaldocuments/frus1961-63v19/d239.

46. "Telegram from the Department of State to the Embassy in India," January 4, 1963, *FRUS* 1961–1963, vol. 19, South Asia, doc. 235, http://history.state.gov/historicaldocuments/frus1961-63v19/d235.

47. Central Intelligence Agency, Job 80 B 01285A, Box 6, McCone Files, DCI Meetings with the President, January 1– March 31, 1963 (Top Secret), *FRUS* 1961–1963, vol. XIX, doc. 244, http://history.state.gov/historicaldocuments/frus1961-63v19/d244.

48. George L. Singleton, "Prelude to the 1965 India-Pakistan War," in Smithsonian Institute, *Cold War Magazine*, February 2011; Syed Hussain Shaheed Soherwordi, "US Foreign Policy Shift towards Pakistan between 1965 and 1971 Pak-India Wars," *South Asian Studies* 25, no. 1 (January 2010): 21–37; and *The Civil and Military Gazette* (CMG), June 18, 1963, http://pu.edu.pk/images/journal/csas/PDF/Shaheed%20Soherwordi%202.pdf.

49. W. M. Dobell, "Ramifications of the China-Pakistan Border Treaty," *Pacific Affairs* 37, no. 3 (Autumn 1964): 293.

50. Department of State, Central Files, POL 7 US/BALL (Secret; Repeated to Karachi eyes only Ambassador), relayed to the White House, *FRUS* 1961–1963, vol. XIX, doc. 330, http://history.state.gov/historicaldocuments/frus1961-63v19/d330.

51. Department of State, Central Files, POL 32-1 INDIA-PAK (Secret; Priority), repeated to New Delhi and London, *FRUS* 1961–1963, vol. XIX, doc. 308, http://history.state.gov/historicaldocuments/frus1961-63v19/d308.

52. See Dobell, "Ramifications of the China-Pakistan Border Treaty," p. 293.

53. "Report of June 3, 1963, meeting between Presidents Kennedy and Radhakrishnan," Kennedy Library, National Security Files, Countries Series, India, Subjects, Radhakrishnan Visit (Secret, approved by the White House on June 20). The meeting was held in the Cabinet Room of the White House. See *FRUS* 1961–1963, vol. XIX, doc. 304, http://history.state.gov/historicaldocuments/frus1961-63v19/d304.

54. McMahon, *Cold War on the Periphery*, p. 315.

55. Johnson Library, National Security File, Country File, India, vol. 2, Cables, 4/64–6/64 (Secret), *FRUS* 1964–1968, vol. XXV, doc. 53, http://history.state.gov/historicaldocuments/frus1964-68v25/d53; and Johnson Library, National Security File, Country File, India, vol. 2, Cables, 4/64–6/64 (Secret), *FRUS* 1964–1968, vol. XXV, doc. 44, http://history.state.gov/historicaldocuments/frus1964-68v25/d44.

56. Ayub's comments quoted in Zulfikar Ali Bhutto, *Myth of Independence* (London: Oxford University Press, 1969) p. 105; and Zulfikar Ali Bhutto, *Foreign Policy of Pakistan: A Compendium of Speeches Made in the National Assembly of Pakistan: 1962–64*, http://www.scribd.com/doc/4908434/FOREIGN-POLICY-OF-PAKISTAN, p. 109.

57. CIA report, "0900 Report: Pakistan and the Free World Alliance," July 10, 1964, p. 7; William J. Barnds, *India, Pakistan, and the Great Powers*, pp. 190–92; and McMahon, *Cold War on the Periphery*, p. 337.

58. "Memorandum from Robert Komer of the National Security Council Staff to President Johnson," *FRUS* 1964–1968, vol. 25, South Asia, doc. 142, http://history.state.gov/historicaldocuments/frus1964-68v25/d142; see also Robert J. McMahon, "Disillusionment and Disengagement in South Asia," in *Lyndon Johnson Confronts the World: American Foreign Policy, 1963–1968*, eds. Warren I. Cohen and Nancy Bernkopf Tucker (New York: Cambridge University Press, 1994), pp. 150–51. Scheduled to convene on July 27, Johnson postponed the session for two months. For the NSC statement, see Johnson Library, National Security File, Country File, India, vol. V,

Cables, 6/65–9/65 (Secret), *FRUS* 1964–1968, vol. XXV, doc. 140, http://history
.state.gov/historicaldocuments/frus1964-68v25/d140;http://dosfan.lib.uic.edu/ERC
/frus/summaries/960820_FRUS_XIX_1961-63.html.

59. Johnson Library, National Security File, "Memos to the President," McGeorge
Bundy, vol. 12, July 1965 (Secret), *FRUS* 1964–1968, vol. XXV, doc. 142, http://history
.state.gov/historicaldocuments/frus1964-68v25/d142;NationalArchivesandRecords
Administration, RG 59, Central Files 1964–66, AID9 PAK (Secret; Priority; Limdis),
FRUS 1964–1968, vol. XXV, doc. 141, http://history.state.gov/historicaldocuments
/frus1964-68v25/d141; and S. M. Burke and Lawrence Ziring, *Pakistan's Foreign Policy:
An Historical Analysis*, 2nd ed. (Karachi, Pakistan: Oxford University Press, 1991), pp.
315–17. For a fuller discussion of Pakistan's approach to India see Stephen P. Cohen,
The Pakistan Army, 2nd ed. (Karachi: Oxford University Press, 1998).

60. Timothy D. Hoyt, "Pakistani Nuclear Doctrine and the Dangers of Strategic
Myopia," *Asian Survey* 41, no. 6 (November–December 2001): 974; Shuja Nawaz,
Crossed Swords: Pakistan, Its Army, and the Wars Within (New York: Oxford University
Press, 2008), p. 207; and Ziring, *Pakistan in the Twentieth Century*, p. 288. On August
24 the Indians crossed the ceasefire line into southwestern Kashmir and advanced
rapidly.

61. 89 Cong. Rec., 1st sess., September 8, 1965, 23059-60, 23168, 23186-89; ibid.,
September 7, 1965, 23021; and McMahon, *The Cold War on the Periphery*, p. 329.

62. "Telegram from the Office in Pakistan to the Department of State," September
6, 1965, *FRUS* 1964–68, vol. 25, South Asia: 182, National Archives and Records
Administration, RG 59, Central Files 1964–66, POL 32–1 INDIA–PAK (Secret; Flash);
repeated to Karachi, London, New Delhi, DOD, CINCMEAFSA, and USUN),
FRUS 1964–1968, vol. XXV, doc. 187, http://history.state.gov/historicaldocuments
/frus1964-68v25/d187. McConaughy advised Bhutto that the administration was
relying on the UN to reach an immediate ceasefire, to which Bhutto replied indignantly
that if the only means to meet aggression was the UN "there would be no need for
bilateral alliances." National Archives and Records Administration, RG 59, Central
Files 1964–66, POL27 INDIA–PAK (Secret; Immediate); received at 8:41 p.m., and
passed to the White House, DOD, and CIA at 9 p.m. Repeated to London, New Delhi,
and CINCMEAFSA for POLAD, *FRUS* 1964–1968, vol. XXV, doc. 198, http://history
.state.gov/historicaldocuments/frus1964-68v25/d198.

63. National Archives and Records Administration, RG 59, Central Files
1964–66, POL27 INDIA–PAK (Secret; Immediate); repeated to Karachi, London,
New Delhi, USUN, andCINCMEAFSA for POLAD, and passed to the White
House, USIA, DOD, and CIA, *FRUS* 1964–1968, vol. XXV, doc. 200, http://history
.state.gov/historicaldocuments/frus1964-68v25/d200.

64. McMahon, *Cold War on the Periphery*, p. 348; and Memorandum from the
President's Deputy Special Assistant for National Security Affairs (Komer) to
President Johnson, Washington, October 1, 1965, 6 p.m., Johnson Library, National
Security File, Name File, Komer Memos, vol. 2 (Secret), http://webdoc.sub.gwdg
.de/ebook/p/2005/dep_of_state/www.state.gov/www/about_state/history/vol
_xxv/t.html.

65. Mujib declared publicly that his goal remained "emancipation," stopping short
of demanding a total break. The Awami League favored confederation rather than
succession and would leave defense and foreign policy to the central government
in West Pakistan. National Archives, RG 59, Central Files 1970–73, POLPAK–US
(Confidential; Priority; Limdis), repeated to Islamabad, Karachi, and Lahore, *FRUS*

1969–1976, vol. E-7, Documents on South Asia, 1969–1972, doc. 121, http://history .state.gov/historicaldocuments/frus1969-76ve07/d121.

66. Roedad Khan, *Pakistan: A Dream Gone Sour* (Karachi: Oxford University Press, 1998), p. 51.

67. National Archives, RG 59, Central Files 1970–73, POL 23–9 PAK (Confidential; Immediate; Exdis); also sent to Islamabad; repeated priority to London, Bangkok, New Delhi, Karachi, Lahore, Calcutta, CINCSTRIKE, CINCPAC, and MAC, *FRUS* 1969–1976, vol. E-7, Documents on South Asia, 1969–1972, doc. 125, http://history .state.gov/historicaldocuments/frus1969-76ve07/d125. Telegram 959 from the Consulate General in Dacca to the Department of State, March 28, 1971. *FRUS* 1969–1976, vol. E-7.

68. Sarmila Bose, "Anatomy of Violence: Analysis of Civil War in East Pakistan in 1971," in *Economic and Political Weekly* (October 8, 2000). See National Archives, RG 59, Central Files 1970–73, POL 23–9 PAK (Confidential; Priority); also sent to Islamabad; repeated priority to Bangkok, London, New Delhi, Calcutta, Karachi, Lahore, CINCPAC, CINCSTRIKE, and MAC, *FRUS* 1969–1976, vol. E-7, Documents on South Asia, 1969–1972, doc. 127, http://history.state.gov /historicaldocuments/frus1969-76ve07/d127. Also see Christopher Hitchens, *The Trial of Henry Kissinger* (New York: Verso Publishers, 2002), p. 46; "Tanks Crush Revolt in Pakistan," *Daily Telegraph* (London), March 30, 1971. A database of press reports at the time can be found at http://www.genocidebangladesh.org/?page _id=12. Also see "Memorandum from Samuel Hoskinson of the National Security Council Staff to the President's Assistant for National Security Affairs (Kissinger)," *FRUS* 1969–1976, vol. XI, South Asia Crisis, 1971, doc. 13, http://history.state.gov /historicaldocuments/frus1969-76v11/d13; and "Telegram 978 from the Consulate General in Dacca to the Department of State, March 29, 1971, 1130Z," *FRUS* 1969–1976, vol. E-7, Documents on South Asia, 1969–1976, doc. 126, http://history.state .gov/historicaldocuments/frus1969-76ve07/d126.

69. Quoted in Henry Kissinger, *White House Years* (Boston: Little, Brown, and Company, 1979), p. 853.

70. National Archives, RG 59, Central Files 1970–73, POL 23–9 PAK (Confidential; Immediate; Exdis); also sent to Islamabad; repeated priority to London, Bangkok, New Delhi, Karachi, Lahore, Calcutta, CINCSTRIKE, CINCPAC, and MAC, *FRUS* 1969–1976, vol. E-7, doc. 125, http://history.state.gov/historicaldocuments/frus1969 -76ve07/d125 and http://www.gwu.edu/~nsarchiv/NSAEBB/NSAEBB79/BEBB8.pdf.

71. "Excerpts from a World Bank Group's Report on East Pakistan," *New York Times,* July 13, 1971.

72. "Pakistan: Dacca, City of the Dead," *Time,* May 3, 1971, http://www.time.com /time/magazine/article/0,9171,876963,00.html; and Christopher Van Hollen, "The Tilt Policy Revisited: Nixon-Kissinger Geopolitics and South Asia," *Asian Survey* 20, no. 4 (April 1980): 342.

73. Anthony Mascarenhas, *Bangladesh: A Legacy of Blood* (London: Hodder and Stoughton, 1986); W. Norman Brown, *The United States and India, Pakistan, and Bangladesh* (Cambridge, MA: Harvard University Press, 1972), p. 217; Sumit Ganguly, *Conflict Unending: India-Pakistan Tensions since 1947* (New York: Columbia University Press, 2001), pp. 51–72; Ishaan Tharoor, "Bangladesh: Bringing a Forgotten Genocide to Justice," *Time,* August 3, 2010, http://www.time.com/time/world /article/0,8599,2008085,00.html; and Amnesty International, "UN Provides Welcome Support to Bangladesh War Crimes Investigations," April 7, 2009, http://www

.amnesty.org/en/news-and-updates/good-news/un-provides-welcome-support
-bangladesh-war-crimes-investigations-20090407.

74. Kissinger, *White House Years*, p. 913.

75. Nixon contended that pressing Pakistan publicly "would be totally counterproductive." Richard Nixon: "The President's News Conference," August 4, 1971. Posted online by Gerhard Peters and John T. Woolley, The American Presidency Project, http://www.presidency.ucsb.edu/ws/?pid=3100.

76. On West Pakistan's repression starting to concentrate on East Bengal's minority Hindu population, see "Memcon Kenneth Keating, Henry Kissinger, and Harold Saunders, June 3, 1971 (4:00 P.M.)." Attached to cover sheet dated June 21, 1971 (Secret /NODIS), 6 pp. Source: Nixon Presidential Materials Project (NPMP), National Security Council Files Country Files: Middle East, Box 596, http://www .gwu.edu/~nsarchiv/NSAEBB/NSAEBB79/BEBB13.pdf. Kissinger reported to the president on April 1—after the Indian Parliament threw its full support behind the Bengali insurrection—that India seemed to want to increase the already "high level of tension in the subcontinent and run the risk of touching off a broader and more serious international crisis." The warning proved prophetic. After Bengali representatives established a government in exile in Calcutta on April 14, the White House learned India was infiltrating thousands of trained guerillas into East Pakistan. See Kissinger, *White House Years*, p. 855.

77. White House, Telephone Conversations (Telcon), December 4 and December 16, 1971, 11 pp., NPMP, NSC Files, Country Files: Middle East, Box 643, http://www .gwu.edu/~nsarchiv/NSAEBB/NSAEBB79/BEBB28.pdf; National Archives, RG 59, Central Files 1970–73, POL 23–9 PAK (Confidential; Priority); repeated to Calcutta, Colombo, Dacca, Kabul, Karachi, Lahore, London, and New Delhi, *FRUS 1969–1976*, vol. E-7, doc. 128, http://history.state.gov/historicaldocuments/frus1969-76ve07/d128.

78. On May 28, after Gandhi publicly warned that India was "fully prepared to fight" in order to deal with West Pakistan's repression and the more than 2.8 million refugees, President Nixon sent her a personal letter informing her of his quiet diplomacy with Yahya, his interest in managing the humanitarian crisis, and a warning against her intervening militarily against Pakistan. For more on Gandhi's motives, see Richard Sisson and Leo E. Rose, *War and Secession: Pakistan, India, and the Creation of Bangladesh* (Berkeley: University of California Press, 1990), p. 214.

79. National Archives, Nixon Presidential Materials, White House Tapes, "Recording of Conversation between Nixon and Kissinger, Oval Office, Conversation No. 630–20." No classification marking. The editor transcribed the portions of the conversation published here specifically for this volume. See *FRUS 1969–1976*, vol. E-7, doc. 162, http://history.state.gov/historicaldocuments /frus1969-76ve07/d162. National Archives, Nixon Presidential Materials, White House Tapes, "Recording of Conversation among Nixon, Kissinger, and Haldeman, Oval Office, Conversation 615–4," *FRUS 1969–1976*, vol. E-7, doc. 150, http:// history.state.gov/historicaldocuments/frus1969-76ve07/d150; Van Hollen, "The Tilt Policy Revisited," p. 341; "Conversation between President Nixon and his Assistant for National Security Affairs (Kissinger), Washington, May 26 1971, 10:30–10:44 a.m.," *FRUS 1969–1976*, vol. E-7, Documents on South Asia, 1969–1972, doc. 135, http://history.state.gov/historicaldocuments/frus1969-76ve07/d135; and "Memcon Kenneth Keating, Henry Kissinger, and Harold Saunders June 3, 1971 (4:00 P.M.)." Attached to cover sheet dated June 21, 1971 (Secret /NODIS), 6 pp. Source: Nixon Presidential Materials Project (NPMP), National Security Council

Files Country Files: Middle East, Box 596, http://www.gwu.edu/~nsarchiv /NSAEBB/NSAEBB79/BEBB13.pdf.

80. Sisson and Rose, *War and Secession*, pp. 227–30.

81. "Texts of Secret Documents on Top-Level U.S. Discussions of Indian-Pakistani War," *New York Times*, January 6, 1972. Library of Congress, Manuscript Division, Kissinger Papers, Box 397, Telephone Conversations, Home File, December 1971, *FRUS* 1969–1976, vol. E-7, doc. 159, http://history.state.gov /historicaldocuments/frus1969-76ve07/d159.

82. Henry Tanner, "Russian Vote in U.N. Kills Troop-Pullback Proposal," *New York Times*, December 6, 1971. Kissinger said the president wanted "to take a line to condemn the Indians." Library of Congress, Manuscript Division, Kissinger Papers, Box 370, Telephone Conversations, Chronological File, 1–5 December 1971, *FRUS* 1969–1976, vol. E-7, doc. 158, http://history.state.gov/historicaldocuments/frus1969 -76ve07/d158.

83. In transcripts of telephone conversations from December 4 and 16, 1971, Kissinger and Nixon discuss providing fighter planes to Pakistan from China, the Middle East, and the United States through third-party transfers (see the database here: http://www.gwu.edu/~nsarchiv/NSAEBB/NSAEBB79/). White House, "Telephone Conversations (Telcon)," December 4 and December 16, 1971, 11 pp. Includes cover sheet dated January 19, 1972. Source: NPMP, NSC Files, Country Files: Middle East, Box 643, http://www.gwu.edu/~nsarchiv/NSAEBB/NSAEBB79 /BEBB28.pdf; on support for Chinese and Middle East supplies, see http://www .gwu.edu/~nsarchiv/NSAEBB/NSAEBB79/BEBB23.pdf and http://www.gwu .edu/~nsarchiv/NSAEBB/NSAEBB79/BEBB29.pdf. F-5 fighter aircraft, originally slated for Libya, were flown to Pakistan via Iran, United States Embassy (Tehran), Cable, "F-5 Aircraft to Pakistan" (Secret), December 29, 1971, 3 pp. Includes DOD cable. Source: NPMP, NSC Files, Indo-Pak War, Box 575, http://www.gwu.edu/~nsarchiv /NSAEBB/NSAEBB79/BEBB44.pdf

84. Kissinger, *White House Years*, p. 854.

85. In late June, the *New York Times* reported that two ships carrying military items were preparing to set sail from New York City to Pakistan. Viewing the episode in the context of the Pentagon Papers, the press condemned as deceitful the White House's explanation that the shipment of equipment had been purchased under licenses issued before the ban. Library of Congress, Manuscript Division, Kissinger Papers, Box 370, Telephone Conversations, Chronological File, 1–5 December 1971, *FRUS* 1969–1976, vol. E-7, doc. 158, http://history.state.gov/historicaldocuments/frus1969-76ve07/d158.

86. Kissinger, *White House Years* p. 886; and "Transcript of Telephone Conversation between the President's Assistant for National Security Affairs (Kissinger) and the Pakistani Ambassador (Raza), Washington, December 8, 1971, 2:47 p.m.," *FRUS* 1969–1976, vol. E-7, Documents on South Asia, 1969–1972, doc. 164, http://history.state .gov/historicaldocuments/frus1969-76ve07/d164#fn6.

87. Choudhury, "Reflections on Sino-Pakistan Relations," p. 266.

88. Richard Nixon, "Fourth Annual Report to the Congress on United States Foreign Policy. May 3, 1973," *Public Papers of the Presidents of the United States, Richard Nixon, 1973* (Washington: Government Printing Office, 1975), p. 455.

89. The Constitution of Pakistan, Article 40, http://www.pakistani.org/pakistan /constitution/part2.ch2.html.

90. Secretary Rusk once lamented that Ayub apparently "followed the anti-American line of Bhutto and other extremists." "Foreign Relations of the United

States, 1964–1968, vol. 25, South Asia, document 158," *FRUS* 1964–1968, vol. XXV, doc. 158, http://history.state.gov/historicaldocuments/frus1964-68v25/d158. Telegram from the Department of State to the Embassy in Pakistan, July 23, 1965, *FRUS 1964–68*, vol. 25, South Asia: 154.

91. For an insightful read on this subject see Pervez Hoodbhoy, "Myth-Building: The 'Islamic' Bomb," http://www.hraicjk.org/the_islamic_bomb.html.

92. There are different versions of this quote: Joel Sandhu, "The Nuclear Crescent: Pakistan and the Bomb," *Scholar Warrior* (Spring 2011), pp. 44–48, http://www.claws.in /images/journals_doc/Spring%202011-%20Final%20Issue.57-61.pdf; Masood Haider, "War Clouds Hovering over South Asia: Report," *Dawn.com*, May 19, 2002, http:// www.dawn.com/news/35501/war-clouds-hovering-over-south-asia-report; Carey Sublette, "Pakistan's Nuclear Weapons Program: The Beginning," January 2, 2002, http://nuclearweaponarchive.org/Pakistan/PakOrigin.html.

93. Major General Mahmud Ali (Ret.), "Pakistan's Strategic Thinking and the Role of Nuclear Weapons," paper 37 (Albuquerque: Cooperative Monitoring Center, Sandia National Labratories, July 2004), p. 18. Also see George Perkovich, "Could Anything Be Done to Stop Them? Lessons from Pakistan's Proliferating Past," *Pakistan's Nuclear Future: Worries beyond War*, ed. Henry D. Sokolski (Carlisle Barracks, PA: Strategic Studies Institute, 2008), p. 63. See also "Interagency Intelligence Memorandum 240" and "Interagency Intelligence Memorandum 76-047, Washington, December 30, 1976." Ford Library, NSC Institutional Files (H-Files), Box H-131, NSDM 273-290 (Top Secret; Noforn; Nocontract; Orcon). The report was one produced semiannually in response to NSDM 289 and incorporates intelligence from the Central Intelligence Agency, the Defense Intelligence Agency, and the Bureau of Intelligence and Research, Department of State. See "Interagency Intelligence Memorandum 76-047, Washington, December 30, 1976," *FRUS* 1969–1976, Documents on South Asia, 1973–1976, vol. E-8, doc. 240, http://history.state.gov/historicaldocuments/frus1969-76ve08/d240.

94. Adopted 1976. Sec. 101 of the Arms Export Control Act, formerly Sec. 669 of the Foreign Assistance Act of 1961 as amended. For more on efforts to roll back Pakistan's nuclear activities, see George Washington University, the National Security Archive, "The United States and Pakistan's Quest for the Bomb," http://www.gwu .edu/~nsarchiv/nukevault/ebb333/index.htm.

95. Adopted 1977. Sec. 102(b) of the Arms Export Control Act, formerly Sec. 670 of the Foreign Assistance Act of 1961 as amended; Robert M. Hathaway, "Confrontation and Retreat: The U.S. Congress and the South Asian Nuclear Tests —Key Legislation," *Arms Control Association* (blog), http://www.armscontrol.org/act/2000_01-02 /rhchart.

96. Adrian Levy and Catherine Scott-Clark, *Deception: Pakistan, the United States, and the Secret Trade in Nuclear Weapons* (New York: Walker and Company, 2007), pp. 48, 67.

97. Zulfikar Ali Bhutto, *If I Am Assassinated* (Lahore, Pakistan: Classic Books, 1994), cited in Levy and Scott-Clark, *Deception*, p. 60. See also Hoodbhoy, "Myth-Building: The 'Islamic' Bomb."

98. Steve LaMontagne, "India-Pakistan Sanctions Legislation Fact Sheet," The Center for Arms Control and Non-Proliferation, http://armscontrolcenter.org /policy/nonproliferation/articles/india_pakistan_sanctions/.

99. See Robert M. Gates, *From the Shadows: The Ultimate Insider's Story of Five Presidents and How They Won the Cold War* (New York: Simon & Schuster, 1997), pp. 144–45.

100. Levy and Scott-Clarke, *Deception*, p. 70.

101. Jimmy Carter, "Soviet Invasion of Afghanistan Address to the Nation," January 4, 1980, http://www.presidency.ucsb.edu/ws/?pid=32911. See also Terrence Smith, "Carter Embargoes Technology for Soviets and Curtails Fishing and Grain," *New York Times*, January 5, 1980.

102. Zbigniew Brzezinski, *Power and Principle: Memoirs of the National Security Adviser, 1977–1981* (New York: Farrar, Straus, and Giroux, 1983), p. 448.

103. William Borders, "Pakistani Dismisses $400 Million in Aid Offered by U.S. as 'Peanuts,'" *New York Times*, January 18, 1980.

104. Ronald Neumann, "Borderline Insanity: Thinking Big about Afghanistan," *The American Interest* 3, no. 2 (November/December 2007): 52–58. For more on the generals' strategic motivations, see Hassan Abbas, *Pakistan's Drift into Extremism: Allah, the Army, and America's War on Terror* (Armonk, NY: M. E. Sharpe, 2004), p. 121.

105. Brzezinski, *Power and Principle*, p. 448.

106. Peter R. Lavoy, "Islamabad's Nuclear Posture: Its Premises and Implementation," in *Pakistan's Nuclear Future: Worries Beyond War*, ed. Henry D. Sokolski (Washington: Strategic Studies Institute, 2008), p. 124, http://www.strategicstudiesinstitute.army.mil/pdffiles/pub832.pdf; and Levy and Scott-Clark, *Deception*, p. 85.

107. For more on the dispersal of weapons and money see Steve Coll, *Ghost Wars: The Secret History of the CIA, Afghanistan, and bin Laden, from the Soviet Invasion to September 10, 2001* (New York: Penguin, 2004), pp. 129–32.

108. Kux, *Disenchanted Allies*, p. 266; Testimony of Senator John Glenn before the Senate Committee on Foreign Relations, "U.S.-Pakistan Nuclear Issues," July 30, 1992, http://www.fas.org/news/pakistan/1992/920731.htm; and Robert Dreyfuss, *Devil's Game: How the United States Helped Unleash Fundamentalist Islam* (New York: Macmillan, 2013), pp. 277, 291. From 1982 through 1990, the United States gave more than $4 billion in assistance to Pakistan.

109. George Washington University, the National Security Archive, "The Pakistani Nuclear Program," June 23, 1983, http://www.gwu.edu/~nsarchiv/NSAEBB/NSAEBB6/ipn22_1.htm.

110. Levy and Scott-Clarke, *Deception*, pp. 116–17; and William E. Burrows and Robert Windrem, *Critical Mass: The Dangerous Race for Superweapons in a Fragmented World* (New York: Simon & Schuster, 1994). According to Richard Barlow, former Pakistan specialist analyst in the CIA's Office of Scientific and Weapons Research, the CIA tracked leads that the White House declined to pursue, enabling Islamabad to obtain components for its nuclear program. Barlow had code-word clearance that gave him access to a wide range of classified material, and his analysis was regularly included in the President's Daily Brief. Adrian Levy and Cathy Scott-Clark, "The Man Who Knew Too Much," *The Guardian* (London), October 13, 2007.

111. In an interview with the Urdu-language Awaz International newspaper, published in London, General Mirza Aslam Beg, the army chief of staff from 1988 to 1991, was quoted as saying, "Pakistan carried out the test in cold laboratory conditions." "Pakistani Quoted as Citing Nuclear Test in 1987," *New York Times*, July 25, 1993, http://query.nytimes.com/gst/fullpage.html?res=9F0CE3D8173EF936A15754C0A965958260. Also see Levy and Scott-Clark, *Deception*, p. 111.

112. Levy and Scott-Clark, *Deception*, pp. 118, 148.

113. Ibid., p 125.

114. The Bank of Credit and Commerce's dirty dealings were exposed in the cover story "The World's Sleaziest Bank: How BCCI and Its 'Black Network' Became a

Financial Supermarket for Crooks and Spies—and How the U.S. is Trying to Cover Up Its Role," *Time,* July 29, 1991.

115. Bruno Tertrais, "Kahn's Nuclear Exports: Was There a State Strategy?" http://www.strategicstudiesinstitute.army.mil/pdffiles/pub832.pdf, p. 27. See also "A Blind Eye to the Islamic Bomb," *Dateline,* Special Broadcasting Service, June 23, 2004; and "The BCCI Affair: A Report to the Committee on Foreign Relations United States Senate," by Sen. John Kerry and Sen. Hank Brown, December 1992, 102d Cong. 2d sess., Senate Print 102-140, pp. 66, 109.

116. Zahid Hussain, *Frontline Pakistan: The Struggle with Militant Islam* (New York: Columbia University Press, 2007), p. 19; and Joshua Hammer, "After Musharraf," *Atlantic Monthly,* October 2007, pp. 100–14.

117. Whereas an estimated 900 registered madrasahs existed in all of Pakistan 1971, by 1988 that number had swelled to 8,000, with another 25,000 unregistered. Ahmed Rashid, *Taliban: Militant Islam, Oil, and Fundamentalism in Central Asia* (New Haven, CT: Yale University Press, 2000), p. 89; and Husain Haqqani, "The Ideologies of South Asian Jihadi Groups," in *Current Trends in Islamist Ideology,* ed. Hillel Fradkin, Husain Haqqani, and Eric Brown (Washington: Hudson Institute, 2005), p. 21.

118. Levy and Scott-Clarke, *Deception,* p. 181.

119. Bob Woodward, "Pakistan Reported near Atom-Arms Production," *Washington Post,* November 4, 1986.

120. "Pakistan Has the A. Bomb," *The Observer,* March 1, 1987; and Levy and Scott-Clarke, *Deception,* pp. 156–58, 161.

121. Levy and Scott-Clarke, *Deception,* pp. 167–69.

122. Dennis Kux interview with Brent Scowcroft, quoted in Kux, *Disenchanted Allies,* p. 308.

123. Kux, *Disenchanted Allies,* p. 311. John Glenn, "Nuclear Arms Race in South Asia," 101st Cong., 1st sess. S. Rep. America Federation of Scientists, http://www.fas.org/news/pakistan/1989/891117.htm; "Pakistani Quoted as Citing Nuclear Test in 1987," *New York Times,* July 25, 1993.

124. Husain Haqqani, *Pakistan: Between Mosque and Military* (Washington: Carnegie Endowment for International Peace, 2005), p. 283; Perkovich, "Could Anything Be Done to Stop Them?" pp. 70–71; and David B. Ottoway, "U.S. Relieves Pakistan of Pledge Against Enriching Uranium," *Washington Post,* June 15, 1989.

125. Hassan Abbas, *Pakistan's Drift into Extremism,* p. 63.

126. Pyotr Romanov, "New Medal for American Uniform," Sputnik International, May 19, 2006, http://sputniknews.com/analysis/20060519/48366913.html.

127. Analysts dismissed the likelihood of cooperation between radical Shiite Iran and Sunni Islamic Pakistan, but Khan himself claimed that Pakistan's Army Chief of Staff from August 1988 to August 1991, General Mirza Aslam Beg, had explicitly authorized the transfers to Iran. Bruno Tertrais, "Kahn's Nuclear Exports: Was There a State Strategy?" in *Pakistan's Nuclear Future: Worries beyond War,* ed. Henry D. Sokolski (Washington: Strategic Studies Institute, 2008), http://www.strategicstudiesinstitute.army.mil/pdffiles/pub832.pdf, p. 19. The deal, he said, was "government-to-government." Naturally, high-level political and military leaders were also involved in nuclear exports, which became more decentralized in the late 1990s. Prime Minister Benazir Bhutto says she was involved in the inner circle of nuclear decisionmaking as early as 1989. She may have been dismissed because she knew too much.

128. Interview conducted by Malou Innocent in Karachi, August 5, 2008.

129. "Zia's recruits" (Zia Bharti) began reaching the pinnacle of their careers, taking over senior leadership positions. Nawaz, *Crossed Swords*, p. 572; and Coll, *Ghost Wars*, p. 475.

Chapter 5

1. For a history of the Arabian Peninsula and Saudi Wahhabism, see Alexei Vassiliev, *The History of Saudi Arabia* (New York: New York University Press, 2000).

2. Cairo's al-Azhar and Sunni scholars at other centers of Islamic learning dismissed Abd al-Wahhab's teachings, criticizing them as uncompromising and dismissing their permissibility of warfare against fellow Muslims. Hamid Algar, *Wahhabism: A Critical Essay* (Oneota, NY: Islamic Publications International, 2002); and Vassiliev, *The History of Saudi Arabia*, pp. 64–82.

3 King Abd al-Aziz bin Abd al-Rahman al-Saud.

4. John A. DeNovo, *American Interests and Policies in the Middle East, 1900–1939* (Minneapolis: University of Minnesota Press, 1963), pp. 167–209; Daniel Yergin, *The Prize: The Epic Quest for Oil, Money, & Power* (New York: Simon & Schuster, 1991), pp. 298–300.

5. Anthony Cave Brown, *Oil, God, and Gold: The Story of Aramco and the Saudi Kings* (New York: Houghton Mifflin, 1999), p. 52.

6. Chas W. Freeman Jr., *America's Misadventures in the Middle East* (Charlottesville, VA: Just World Books, 2010), p. 201n.

7. Joshua Teitelbaum, "Holier Than Thou: Saudi Arabia's Islamic Opposition," Washington Institute for Near East Policy, Policy Paper No. 52, November 1, 2000; Tim Niblock, ed., *State, Society, and Economy in Saudi Arabia* (New York: St. Martin's Press, 1981); and Anthony H. Cordesman and Nawaf Obaid, *National Security in Saudi Arabia: Threats, Responses, and Challenges* (Westport, CT: Praeger, 2005), p. 391.

8. Despite signing a treaty with King Ibn Saud on May 20, 1927, the British sided later with the Hashemites for their loyalty and compliance with British interests. See Timothy J. Paris, *Britain, the Hashemites, and Arab Rule, 1920–1925: The Sherifian Solution* (London: Routledge, 2003); and Nadav Safran, *Saudi Arabia: The Ceaseless Quest for Security* (Ithaca, NY: Cornell University Press, 1988), pp. 64–67.

9. Parker T. Hart, *Saudi Arabia and the United States: Birth of a Security Partnership* (Bloomington, IN: Indiana University Press, 1998), p. 38.

10. In April 1941, Moffett explained that the king could not hold on to his dominion with only the fees from the annual pilgrimage to Mecca (*hajj*). He encouraged Roosevelt to advance the king $6 million annually for five years against the value of oil to be purchased by Washington. See "Mr. James A. Moffett to President Roosevelt," April 16, 1941, in *Foreign Relations of the United States* 1941 (hereafter, *FRUS*), vol. III, pp. 624–25; see also Hart, *Saudi Arabia and the United States*, p. 29. Rodgers's push came in February 1943. See "Multinational Oil Corporations and U.S. Foreign Policy," Report by U.S. Senate Committee on Foreign Relations, Subcommittee on Multinational Corporations, 93rd Cong., 1st sess., http://www.mtholyoke.edu/acad/intrel/oil1.htm.

11. Michael A. Bernstein, *The Great Depression: Delayed Recovery and Economic Change in America, 1929–1939* (Cambridge: Cambridge University Press, 1987), pp. 201–2.

12. "President Roosevelt to the Lend-Lease Administrator (Stettinius)," February 18, 1943, *FRUS* 1943, vol. IV, The Near East and Africa (Washington: Government

Printing Office, 1943), p. 859, http://digicoll.library.wisc.edu/cgi-bin/FRUS/FRUS -idx?type=header&id=FRUS.FRUS1943v04; and Yergin, *The Prize*, p. 397.

13. For an analysis of why U.S.-Saudi relations were not always about oil, see Rachel Bronson, *Thicker than Oil: America's Uneasy Partnership with Saudi Arabia* (New York: Oxford University Press, 2006). According to William A. Eddy, the future U.S. Consul General in Dhahran, an account of the meeting contained no specific reference to agreements or commitments by the United States or by Saudi Arabia. See William A. Eddy, *F.D.R. Meets Ibn Saud*, repr. (Vista, CA: Selwa Press, 2005), http://www .susris.com/documents/2010/100222-fdr-abdulaziz-eddy.pdf.

14. "Draft Memorandum to President Truman," [n.d.], U.S. Political and Economic Policies [Annex], Prepared by the Chief of the Division of Near Eastern Affairs (Merriam) and to the Director of the Office of Near Eastern and African Affairs (Henderson) in early August 1945, *FRUS* 1945, vol. VIII, The Near East and Africa, p. 45, http://images.library.wisc.edu/FRUS/EFacs/1945v08/reference/frus .frus1945v08.i0013.pdf.

15. Central Intelligence Agency, "The Current Situation in the Mediterranean and the Near East," October 17, 1947. Truman Papers, PSF, Box 254. The CIA was primarily concerned with Iran, Turkey, Egypt, French North Africa, Libya, and Spain.

16. Robert Vitalis, *America's Kingdom: Mythmaking on the Saudi Oil Frontier* (Palo Alto, CA: Stanford University Press, 2009), p. 81. Memorandum from Under Secretary of the Navy to Acting Secretary of State, [n.d.], with attached Memorandum for the President, June 26, 1945, RG 59, F.245/6-2645.

17. "The Secretary of Defense (Forrestal) to Secretary of State," November 8, 1948, *FRUS* 1948, vol. V, p. 252. See also C. L. Sulzberger, "Saudi Arabia Base Key U.S. Airfield," *New York Times*, November 24, 1946.

18. For more on how the State Department under President Truman helped U.S. oil policy secure increased markets and additional sources of supply, see Michael James Lacey, ed., *The Truman Presidency* (New York: Cambridge University Press, 1989). A number of influential thinkers believed private corporations were complements to government. A perceptive law-review essay published in 1960 explored the legal and foreign policy ramifications of calling the corporation a "government" and the dominance this thinking had in the pre- and postwar years regarding oil. See Arthur S. Miller, "The Corporation as a Private Government in the World Community," *Virginia Law Review* 46, no. 8 (December 1960): 1551.

19. James R. Ralph Jr., "*U.S. Middle East Oil: The Petroleum Reserves Corporation* (Carlisle Barracks, PA: U.S. Army War College, 1972); Aaron David Miller, *Search for Security: Saudi Arabian Oil and American Foreign Policy, 1939–1949* (Chapel Hill: University of North Carolina Press, 1991), pp. 68–71, 92–97; and Michael B. Stoff, *Oil, War, and American Security: The Search for a National Policy on Foreign Oil, 1941– 1947* (New Haven, CT: Yale University Press, 1980), pp. 41–46, 58–61. King Ibn Saud was reportedly "astonished and annoyed" by the ultimatums. See Douglas Little, "Pipeline Politics: America, TAPLINE, and the Arabs," *Business History Review* 64 (Summer 1990): 270.

20. Miles Copeland, *The Game of Nations: The Amorality of Power Politics* (New York: Simon & Schuster, 1969), pp. 44–45.

21. That account and those from others are verified by other evidence. See Andrew Rathmell, "Copeland and Za'im: Re-evaluating the Evidence," *Intelligence and National Security* 11, no. 1 (January 1996): 89–105; Andrew Rathmell, *Secret War in the Middle East: The Covert Struggle for Syria, 1949–1961* (New York: I.B. Tauris Academic Studies,

1995); Douglas Little, "Cold War and Covert Action: The United States and Syria, 1945–1958," *Middle East Journal* 44 (Winter 1990): 55–57; and Douglas Little, "Pipeline Politics: America, TAPLINE, and the Arabs," *Business History Review* 64 (Summer 1990): 277–81. For Copeland quote, see *The Game of Nations,* p. 50.

22. The State Department also said that "other matters involving security were tied up in this relationship." Quoted in Miller, "The Corporation as a Private Government in the World Community," pp. 1546–47.

23. "President Truman to King Abdul Aziz Ibn Saud of Saudi Arabia," *FRUS* 1950, vol. V, October 31, 1950, pp. 1190–91, http://images.library.wisc.edu/FRUS /EFacs/1950v05/reference/frus.frus1950v05.i0014.pdf; "Memorandum by the Central Intelligence Agency," September 24, 1951, *FRUS* 1951, vol. I, National Security Affairs: Foreign Economic Policy, pp. 205–6.

24. Copeland, *The Game of Nations,* p. 58.

25. "Letter from William A. Eddy to Dorothy Thompson" [Christian-Muslim Anticommunist Propaganda Theme], June 7, 1951. National Archives. Record Group 59. Records of the Department of State. Lot Files. 57 D 298, http://www.gwu .edu/~nsarchiv/NSAEBB/NSAEBB78/propaganda%20026.pdf.

26. Ian Johnson, *A Mosque in Munich: Nazis, the CIA, and the Rise of the Muslim Brotherhood in the West* (New York: Houghton Mifflin Harcourt, 2010), pp. 41, 69.

27. After 1959, the U.S. Military and Advisory Group (MAAG) was known as the U.S. Military Training Mission (USMTM). For more on formal U.S.-Saudi security relations, and MAAG and USMTM, see David E. Long, *The United States and Saudi Arabia: Ambivalent Allies* (Boulder, CO: Westview Press, 1985), p. 35; and Brown, *Oil, God, and Gold,* p. 261.

28. U.S. intelligence had penetrated the Brotherhood during WWII, learning its leadership and activities. On Rida, see Dore Gold, *Hatred's Kingdom: How Saudi Arabia Supports the New Global Terrorism* (Washington: Regnery Publishing, 2003), pp. 54–55.

29. Kai Bird, *Crossing Mandelbaum Gate: Coming of Age between the Arabs and Israelis, 1956–1978* (New York: Scribner, 2010), p. 195.

30. For details of the visit, see Johnson, *A Mosque in Munich,* pp. 116–19.

31. Jefferson Caffery, U.S. Department of State, "Colloquium on Islamic Culture and Saeed Ramadan," Foreign Service Dispatch, National Security Archive, July 27, 1953, http://www.gwu.edu/~nsarchiv/NSAEBB/NSAEBB78/propaganda%20103.pdf. The CIA front organization was the Institute for the Study of the USSR in Munich. See Johnson, *A Mosque in Munich,* pp. 133–34.

32. Department of State, memorandum from Wilson S. Compton to David K. E. Bruce, "Colloquium on Islamic Culture to Be Held in September, 1953, under the Joint Sponsorship of the Library of Congress and Princeton University" [Attached to cover note dated January 16, 1953; includes enclosure], January 13, 1953, National Archives. Record Group 59. Records of the Department of State. Decimal Files, 1950–1954, http://www.gwu.edu/~nsarchiv/NSAEBB/NSAEBB78/propaganda%20089.pdf; http://www.archives.gov/research/guide-fed-records/groups/306.html#306.1.

33. Johnson, *A Mosque in Munich,* p. 117.

34. U.S. Assistant Secretary of State for Near Eastern Affairs William Rountree emphasized that poor nations provided fertile fields for anti-U.S. propaganda. "441. Memorandum of a Conversation, Department of State, Washington, November 26, 1956," Department of State, Central Files, 611.87/11–2656. Secret. Drafted by Newsom, http://history.state.gov/historicaldocuments/frus1955-57v12/d441. For NATO findings, see "Report by the Council Deputies to the North Atlantic Council:

Soviet Foreign Policy," Conference files, lot 59 D 95, CF 104, Top Secret. February 6, 1952, *FRUS, 1952–1954*, vol. V, pp. 280–85.

35. Saud bin Abdul Aziz.

36. For more on propaganda operations, see "Memorandum on the Substance of Discussions at the Department of State-Joint Chiefs of Staff Meeting, Pentagon, Washington, May 23, 1956, 11:30 a.m.," Department of State, State-JCS Meetings: Lot 61 D 417(Top Secret), http://images.library.wisc.edu/FRUS/EFacs2/1955-57v12/reference/frus.frus195557v12.i0008.pdf. The CIA eventually severed the cozy ties between Nasser and Saud, convincing the latter that Saudi money for Egyptian propaganda was assisting communists. See Copeland, *The Game of Nations*, pp. 245–46. Beforehand, though, after proclaiming the need for closer Arab and Islamic ties and opposition to the Baghdad Pact, King Saud concluded a defense pact with Egypt in October 1955 and a similar pact with Syria in March. See Vassiliev, *The History of Saudi Arabia*, pp. 338–53.

37. On the rich history of Zionism in America, see Peter Grose, *Israel in the Mind of America* (New York: Schocken-Random House, 1984). On American sympathy for the Jewish people and its impact on politics, see Aaron Berman, *Nazism, the Jews, and American Zionism, 1933–1948* (Detroit: Wayne State University Press, 1990); and David H. Shapiro, *From Philanthropy to Activism: The Political Transformation of American Zionism in the Holocaust Years, 1933–1945* (New York: Pergamon Press, 1994). Also see Michelle Mart, *Eye on Israel: How America Came to View Israel as an Ally* (Albany: State University of New York Press, 2006), pp. 73, 76; Peter L. Hahn, *Crisis and Crossfire: The United States and the Middle East Since 1945* (Washington: Potomac Books Inc., 2005); Paul Boyer, *When Time Shall Be No More: Prophecy Belief in Modern American Culture* (Cambridge, MA: Harvard University Press, 1992); and Yaakov Ariel, *On Behalf of Israel: American Fundamentalist Attitudes toward Jews, Judaism, and Zionism, 1865–1945* (Brooklyn: Carlson, 1991).

38. For excellent accounts of U.S. national security issues in the Middle East in the decade after World War II, see John C. Campbell, *Defense of the Middle East: Problems of American Policy* (New York: HarperCollins, 1958); and Melvin P. Leffler, *A Preponderance of Power: National Security, the Truman Administration, and the Cold War* (Palo Alto: Stanford University Press, 1992).

39. "Joseph Grew to Harry S. Truman," May 1, 1945, President's Secretary's Files, Truman Papers, Harry S. Truman Library and Museum, http://www.trumanlibrary.org/whistlestop/study_collections/israel/large/documents/newPDF/2-6.pdf; "Edward Stettinius to Harry S. Truman," April 18, 1945, President's Secretary's Files, Truman Papers, Harry S. Truman Library and Museum, http://www.trumanlibrary.org/whistlestop/study_collections/israel/large/documents/newPDF/2-5.pdf; "Joint Chiefs of Staff to State-War-Navy Coordinating Committee," June 21, 1946, President's Secretary's Files, Truman Papers, Harry S. Truman Library and Museum, http://www.trumanlibrary.org/whistlestop/study_collections/israel/large/documents/newPDF/2-14.pdf; "Correspondence between William L. Clayton and Harry S. Truman," September 12, 1946, President's Secretary's Files, Truman Papers, Harry S. Truman Library and Museum, http://www.trumanlibrary.org/whistlestop/study_collections/israel/large/documents/newPDF/72.pdf.

40. PPS 19, "Report by the Policy Planning Staff on Position of the United States with Respect to Palestine," January 19, 1948, *FRUS* 1948, vol. V, part 2, p. 552, http://digital.library.wisc.edu/1711.dl/FRUS.FRUS1948v05p2.

41. Dwight D. Eisenhower, *The White House Years: Waging Peace, 1956–1961* (New York: Doubleday, 1965), p. 114.

42. "Excerpts from Dulles Testimony to Senators on Arms Shipments to Middle East," *New York Times*, February 26, 1956.

43. See Henry J. Epstein, *American Jewish Congress v. Elmer A. Carter et al.*, 19 Misc. 2d 205 (July 15, 1959), http://ny.findacase.com/research/wfrmDocViewer .aspx/xq/fac.19590715_0044738.NY.htm/qx.

44. Eisenhower resorted to flashing lights and military police for the monarch. Wilbur Crane Eveland, *Ropes of Sand: America's Failure in the Middle East* (New York: W.W. Norton, 1980), p. 242.

45. Eisenhower, *Waging Peace*, p. 190.

46. Lawrence Wright, *The Looming Tower: Al-Qaeda and the Road to 9/11* (New York: Knopf, 2006), p. 147; and Carmen bin Laden, *Inside the Kingdom: My Life in Saudi Arabia* (New York: Grand Central Publishing, 2005).

47. Copeland, *The Game of Nations*, pp. 246–47.

48. "226. Diary Entry by the President," March 28, 1956, Eisenhower Library, Whitman File, Eisenhower Diaries. Top Secret. *FRUS* 1955–1957, vol. XV, Arab-Israeli Dispute, January 1–July 1956, doc. 226, http://history.state.gov/historicaldocuments /frus1955-57v15/d226; "Memorandum of Discussion at the 260th Meeting of NSC, October 6, 1955," *FRUS* 1955–1957, vol. XIII, Eisenhower Library, Whitman File, NSC Records (Top Secret; Eyes Only), Drafted by Gleason on October 7. http://images .library.wisc.edu/FRUS/EFacs2/195557v12/reference/frus.frus195557v12.i0008.pdf.

49. "Telegram from the Embassy in the United Kingdom to the Department of State," (in editorial note 106), March 28, 1956, *FRUS* 1955–1957, vol. XV, pp. 421 ff; Dulles to Eisenhower, DDE Library. For Department of State, Central Files, 674.84A/3-2656, Top Secret, Eyes Only, http://images.library.wisc.edu/FRUS/EFacs2/195557v12 /reference/frus.frus195557v12.i0008.pdf. For a detailed account of U.S. maneuvers in the Middle East during this period, see the memoir of defense intelligence officer, CIA adviser, and military attaché Wilbur Crane Eveland, *Ropes of Sand*, p. 247. See also John Ranelagh, *The Agency: The Rise and Decline of the CIA, from Wild Bill Donovan to William Casey* (New York: Simon & Schuster, 1986), p. 298.

50. Malcolm H. Kerr, *The Arab Cold War: Gamal Abd Al-Nasir and His Rivals, 1958– 1970* (London: Oxford University Press, 1967); and Malcolm H. Kerr, *The Arab Cold War, 1958–1964: A Study of Ideology in Politics* (London: Oxford University Press, 1965).

51. Stephen E. Ambrose, *Eisenhower: Soldier and President* (New York: Simon Schuster, 1990), p. 360; and Rashid Khalidi, *Resurrecting Empire: Western Footprints and America's Perilous Path in the Middle East* (Boston: Beacon Press, 2004), p. 125.

52. Pan-Arabism is understood as the feeling of belonging to one Arab nation. Arab nationalism is understood as the particular nationalist movements that emerged in various Arab states. See Hans E. Tütsch, *Facets of Arab Nationalism* (Detroit: Wayne State University Press, 1965); Tawfik E. Farah, ed., *Pan-Arabism and Arab Nationalism: The Continuing Debate* (Boulder: Westview Press, 1987); and Bassam Tibi, *Arab Nationalism: A Critical Inquiry*, trans. Marion Farouk-Sluglett and Peter Sluglett (London: Macmillan Press, 1981). On the rise of pro-Nasserite parties, see Ellis Goldberg, "Gamal Abdel Nasser" in *Political Leaders of the Contemporary Middle East and North Africa: A Biographical Dictionary*, ed. Bernard Reich (New York: Greenwood Press, 1990), p. 384.

53. Saïd K. Aburish, *Nasser: The Last Arab* (New York: St. Martin's Press, 2004), p. 114; Helen Chapin Metz, ed., *Saudi Arabia: A Country Study* (Washington: Government Printing Office, 1992), http://countrystudies.us/saudi-arabia/, p. 249; Eveland, *Ropes of Sand*, p. 243; Yergin, *The Prize*, pp. 491–92; and Vassiliev, *The History of Saudi Arabia*, p. 351.

54. Dwight D. Eisenhower, "Special Message to the Congress on the Situation in the Middle East," January 5, 1957. Text of the document the President signed and transmitted to the Senate and the House of Representatives (H. Doc. 46, 85th Cong., 1st sess.), and the Address as reported from the floor appears in the *Congressional Record* (vol. 103, p. 181). For the text of this speech online, see Gerhard Peters and John T. Woolley, The American Presidency Project, Santa Barbara, CA, http://www.presidency.ucsb.edu/ws/?pid=11007.

55. By February, Jordan supported Saudi Arabia's alliance with Washington. Vassiliev, *The History of Saudi Arabia*, pp. 352–53.

56. Dwight D. Eisenhower, "Address at the Annual Luncheon of the Associated Press, New York City," April 25, 1955, Gerhard Peters and John T. Woolley, The American Presidency Project, http://www.presidency.ucsb.edu/ws/?pid=10459.

57. For an array of in-depth interviews with former American diplomats and senior American officials, see Robert Dreyfuss, *Devil's Game: How the United States Helped Unleash Fundamentalist Islam* (New York: Metropolitan Books, 2005), especially p. 125.

58. Johnson, *A Mosque in Munich*, pp. 41, 127–28.

59. Eveland, *Ropes of Sand*, pp. 244–45; for Eveland interview with author Kai Bird on July 25, 1982, see Bird, *Crossing Mandelbaum Gate*, pp. 195, 394.

60. Eveland, *Ropes of Sand*, p. 131.

61. Steven L. Spiegel, *The Other Arab-Israeli Conflict: Making America's Middle East Policy, from Truman to Reagan* (Chicago: University of Chicago Press, 1985), p. 88. Regarding anti-communist posters for Iraq, see United States Embassy, Iraq Cable from Edward S. Crocker II to the Department of State, "Anti-communist Poster Material Prepared by USIS Baghdad," March 10, 1951, National Archives. Record Group 59. Records of the Department of State. Decimal Files, 1950-1954, http://www.gwu.edu/~nsarchiv/NSAEBB/NSAEBB78/propaganda%20021.pdf. Regarding the offering of "leadership grants" to even "mildly pinkish" Iraqis, see United States Embassy, Iraq Cable from Edward S. Crocker II to the Department of State. "Foreign Leader Grants for Iraqis," March 26, 1951, National Archives. Record Group 59. Records of the Department of State. Decimal Files, 1950-1954, http://www.gwu.edu/~nsarchiv/NSAEBB/NSAEBB78/propaganda%20022.pdf; Dwight D. Eisenhower, "Statement by the President following the Landing of United States Marines at Beirut," July 15, 1958, Gerhard Peters and John T. Woolley, The American Presidency Project, http://www.presidency.ucsb.edu/ws/?pid=11133.

62. "Briefing notes by Director of Central Intelligence Dulles," July 14, 1958, *FRUS* 1958–1960, vol. XII, doc. 110, https://history.state.gov/historicaldocuments/frus1958-60v12/d110.

63. "Briefing Notes by Director of Central Intelligence Dulles," July 14, 1958, *FRUS* 1958–1960, vol. XII, Near East Region, doc. 110; "226. Memorandum of Discussion at the 373d Meeting of the National Security Council, Washington, July 24, 1958," Eisenhower Library, Whitman File, NSC Records. Top Secret; Eyes Only. Drafted by Boggs on July 25. The full text of the discussion of item 2 is scheduled for publication in volume XII, http://history.state.gov/historicaldocuments/frus1958-60v11/d226.

64. David Tal, "Seizing Opportunities: Israel and the 1958 Crisis in the Middle East," *Middle Eastern Studies* 37, no. 1 (January 2001): 143–58; David Allan Mayers, *George Kennan and the Dilemmas of U.S. Foreign Policy* (New York: Oxford University Press, 1988), p. 261. See also, "White House Memorandum of Conversation with the President," July 23, 1958, 3:00 p.m., pp. 1–3 (the Senate in the Sudan had unanimously condemned U.S.-UK action in the Near East); "226. Memorandum of Discussion at the 373d Meeting of the National Security Council, Washington, July 24, 1958," Eisenhower Library, Whitman File, NSC Records. Top Secret; Eyes Only. Drafted by Boggs on July 25. The full text of the discussion of item 2 is scheduled for publication in volume XII, http://history.state.gov/historicaldocuments/frus1958-60v11/d226. As Eisenhower acknowledged, there was still no answer to America's overall problem in the Middle East, that being Arab sympathies toward Nasser. See "26. Memorandum of Conference with President Eisenhower," Washington, July 20, 1958, 3:45 p.m. Eisenhower Library, Whitman File, Staff Memos, July 1958. Top Secret. Drafted by Goodpaster on July 21, http://www.history.state.gov/historicaldocuments/frus1958-60v12/d26#fn-source.

65. From an unpublished portion of Eisenhower's memoirs. Quoted in Ambrose, *Eisenhower*, p. 360.

66. "226. Memorandum of Discussion at the 373d Meeting of the National Security Council, Washington, July 24, 1958," Eisenhower Library, Whitman File, NSC Records. Top Secret; Eyes Only. Drafted by Boggs on July 25. The full text of the discussion of item 2 is scheduled for publication in volume XII, http://history.state.gov/historicaldocuments/frus1958-60v11/d226.

67. Kennedy to National Security staffer and Robert Komer in May 1961, as quoted in Michael O'Brien, *John F. Kennedy: A Biography* (New York: St. Martin's Press, 2005), p. 878.

68. "Special Message to the Congress on Urgent National Needs," May 25, 1961, Gerhard Peters and John T. Woolley, The American Presidency Project, http://www.presidency.ucsb.edu/ws/?pid=8151.

69. Safran, *Saudi Arabia*, p. 92; and Hart, *Saudi Arabia and the United States*, pp. 82–87.

70. For a definitive work on the Yemen crisis, see Warren Bass, *Support Any Friend: Kennedy's Middle East and the Making of the U.S.-Israel Alliance* (New York: Oxford University Press, 2003). Britain, Jordan, and Iran later backed the royalists, too. See "Yemen: Pax Americana?" *Time*, December 28, 1962; and "Yemen: Trouble for the Sons of Saud," *Time*, November 23, 1962.

71. Bass, *Support Any Friend*, p. 99.

72. Department of State, Central Files, 786H.11/9-2162. Secret. Cleared by Harold W. Glidden of INR, http://history.state.gov/historicaldocuments/frus1961-63v18/d51.

73. Department of State, Central Files, 611.86H/11–1262. Confidential. Drafted by Seelye. Kennedy Library, National Security Files, Countries Series, Yemen, 11/1/62–11/15/62, http://history.state.gov/historicaldocuments/frus1961-63v18/d96.

74. Dana Adams Schmidt, *Yemen: The Unknown War* (New York: Holt, Rinehart, and Winston, 1968), p. 189; Fawaz A. Gerges, "The Kennedy Administration and the Egyptian-Saudi Conflict in Yemen: Co-Opting Arab Nationalism," *Middle East Journal* 49, no. 2 (Spring 1995): 296; and Spiegel, *The Other Arab-Israeli Conflict*, p. 103.

75. Despite a UN-brokered disengagement agreement reached in the spring of 1963 and an Egyptian-Saudi ceasefire brokered in August 1965, both sides resumed hostilities. On Nasser's reassurances, see March 9, 1963, *New York Times* Chronology, John F. Kennedy Presidential Library and Museum, http://www.jfklibrary.org

/Research/Research-Aids/Ready-Reference/New-York-Times-Chronology/Browse-by-Date/New-York-Times-Chronology-March-1963.aspx.

76. Talal bin Abdul Aziz Al Saud.

77. Faisal Bin Abd Al-Aziz Al Saud.

78. Safran, *Saudi Arabia*, p. 94; Simon Henderson, "After King Abdullah: Succession in Saudi Arabia," The Washington Institute for Near East Peace, Policy Focus no. 96 (August 2009); and Rayed Krimly, "Faisal Bin Abd Al-Aziz Al Saud," *Political Leaders of the Contemporary Middle East and North Africa: A Biographical Dictionary*, ed. Bernard Reich (New York: Greenwood Press, 1990), p. 182.

79. Robert Baer, *Sleeping with the Devil: How Washington Sold Our Soul for Saudi Crude* (New York: Crown Publishers, 2003), p. 99; and Bird, *Crossing Mandelbaum Gate*, p. 196.

80. Bird, *Crossing Mandelbaum Gate*, pp. 195–96; and Johnson, *A Mosque in Munich*, p. 238.

81. Gilles Kepel, *Jihad: The Trail of Political Islam* (Cambridge, MA: Harvard University Press, 2002), p. 52.

82. Dreyfuss, *Devil's Game*, p. 133; and Kepel, *Jihad*, p. 52.

83. Tellingly, the administration voiced regret that the issue was publicized, but never denied the story's validity. Bass, *Support Any Friend*, p. 130. The White House was considering another show of force in defense of the kingdom's southern border with Yemen after King Faisal fretted that Washington's fall 1962 fly-over covered only major Saudi cities, implying that border attacks were fair game.

84. "Saudi Arabia Lets Jews in US Units Serve on Her Soil," *New York Times*, June 10, 1963.

85. Bass, *Support Any Friend*, p. 131.

86. Hart, *Saudi Arabia and the United States*, pp. 210–33; and Safran, *Saudi Arabia*, pp. 96–97.

87. The deployment lasted until January 1964. "Editorial Note," *FRUS* 1961–1963, vol. XVIII, p. 581; Bass, *Support Any Friend*, pp. 129–30; Also see Spencer C. Tucker, ed., *The Encyclopedia of Middle East Wars: The United States in the Persian Gulf, Afghanistan, and Iraq Conflicts*, 5 vols. (Santa Barbara: ABC-CLIO, 2010), p. 523.

88. Douglas Little, *American Orientalism: The United States and the Middle East Since 1945* (Chapel Hill, NC: University of North Carolina Press, 2008), pp. 237, 239. Previous U.S. shows of force lacked a credible ability to defend the kingdom. See Tucker, *The Encyclopedia of Middle East Wars*, p. 523.

89. "Remarks at the Dinner of the Protestant Council of the City of New York," November 8, 1963, Gerhard Peters and John T. Woolley, The American Presidency Project, http://www.presidency.ucsb.edu/ws/?pid=9515.

90. "My Vietnam," quoted in Bird, *Crossing Mandelbaum Gate*, p. 193.

91. Former U.S. diplomat to Jeddah and Cairo Hermann Eilts said that Hassan al-Banna, the Brotherhood's founder, made frequent visits to Saudi Arabia "because Saudi Arabia was his principal source of financing." See Dreyfuss, *Devil's Game*, pp. 65, 126. See also Madawi Al-Rasheed, *A History of Saudi Arabia* (New York: Cambridge University Press, 2002), pp. 116, 144; Olivier Roy, *The Failure of Political Islam* (Cambridge, MA: Harvard University Press, 1998), p. 117; and Richard P. Mitchell, *The Society of the Muslim Brothers* (New York: Oxford University Press, 1993).

92. Some kings and princes were more pious than others, producing a struggle for supremacy between the royal family and the clerics. Dr. Ondrej Beranek, "The

Sword and the Book: Implications of the Intertwining of the Saudi Ruling Family and the Religious Establishment," Crown Center for Middle East Studies, no. 28 (April 2008), http://www.brandeis.edu/crown/publications/meb/MEB28.pdf. Herman Eilts also describes the "constant tug of war" between the royal and religious families. See also Dreyfuss, *Devil's Game*, pp. 129–30. Salafism, like Wahhabism, is an umbrella term. The doctrine combines Sunni religious and cultural traditions from Egypt and other regions, and its revivalist movement, which seeks a return to Islam as practiced by Muhammad, began with this intermingling. For a comprehensive account of this history, see Abdullah M. Sindhi, "King Faisal and Pan-Islamism," in Willard L. Beling, ed., *King Faisal and the Modernisation of Saudi Arabia* (Boulder: Westview Press, 1980); al-Rasheed, *A History of Saudi Arabia*, pp. 122–23, 144; Trevor Stanley, "Understanding the Origins of Wahhabism and Salafism," *Terrorism Monitor* 3, no. 14 (July 15, 2005), http://www.jamestown.org/programs/tm/single/?tx_ttnews%5Btt_news%5D=528&tx_ttnews%5BbackPid%5D=180&no_cache=1#.VPYYZbPF-1I.; John L. Esposito, *Unholy War: Terror in the Name of Islam* (New York: Oxford University Press, 2003); David E. Long, *The Kingdom of Saudi Arabia* (Gainesville, FL: University of Florida Press, 1997); Eleanor Abdella Doumato, "Manning the Barricades: Islam according to Saudi Arabia's School Texts," *The Middle East Journal* 57, no. 2 (2003): 230–48; and Michaela Prokop, "Saudi Arabia: The Politics of Education," *International Affairs* 79, no. 1 (January 2003): 77–89.

93. Kepel, *Jihad*, p. 78; and Gold, *Hatred's Kingdom*, p. 92.

94. British journalist David Holden died mysteriously in Cairo while writing his book, *The House of Saud*. Richard Johns, *Financial Times* Middle East specialist, completed Holden's book. For more on Sheikh bin Baz, see David Holden and Richard Johns, *The House of Saud: The Rise and Rule of the Most Powerful Dynasty in the Arab World* (New York: Holt, Rinehart, and Winston, 1981), p. 262; and Gold, *Hatred's Kingdom*, p. 110.

95. Kepel, *Jihad*, p. 51.

96. Vassiliev, *The History of Saudi Arabia*, p. 435.

97. James Akins, U.S. Ambassador to Saudi Arabia, believed that Saudi universities should train "fewer mullahs." Saudis told Akins he was speaking beyond his competence. Akins thought it was rank stupidity. Other U.S. officials, though, raised few questions. Dreyfuss, *Devil's Game*, p. 129. On Adham's network of Islamist agents and the CIA encouraging Adham, see Bird, *Crossing Mandelbaum Gate*, pp. 139, 196.

98. Quoted in Bird, *Crossing Mandelbaum Gate*, p. 195.

99. Quoted in Dreyfuss, *Devil's Game*, p. 134.

100. Quoted in Gold, *Hatred's Kingdom*, p. 93.

101. "Remarks of Welcome to King Faisal of Saudi Arabia on the South Lawn at the White House," June 21, 1966, Gerhard Peters and John T. Woolley, The American Presidency Project, http://www.presidency.ucsb.edu/ws/?pid=27664.

102. Bass, *Support Any Friend*, p. 141. "Memorandum of Conversation," June 21, 1966, *FRUS* 1964–1968, vol. XXI, doc. 275. Johnson Library, National Security File, Country File, Saudi Arabia, Memos, vol. I, 12/63-4/67. Secret; Exdis. Drafted by Sabbagh on June 22, *FRUS* 1964–1968, vol. XXI, doc. 275, http://history.state.gov/historicaldocuments/frus1964-68v21/d275. The time of the meeting is from the President's Daily Diary. The memorandum is Part I of II; Part II is Document 276.

103. "Message by Ford, Rockefeller Flying to Convey Sympathy of American People," *New York Times*, March 26, 1975.

104. William B. Quandt, *Peace Process: American Diplomacy and the Arab-Israeli Conflict Since 1967* (Washington: Brookings Institution; Berkeley: University of California Press, 1993), p. 109.

105. Henry Kissinger, *White House Years* (Boston: Little, Brown, and Company, 1979), pp. 661, 656–66; Richard Valeriani, *Travels with Henry* (Boston: Houghton, Mifflin, 1979), p 310; Edward R. F. Sheehan, *The Israelis, the Arabs, and Kissinger* (New York: Reader's Digest Press, 1976), pp. 71, 234; Holden and Johns, *The House of Saud*, p. 271; and Richard Nixon, *RN: The Memoirs of Richard Nixon* (New York: Doubleday and Company, 1978), p. 1012.

106. Paul Lewis, "U.N. Repeals Its '75 Resolution Equating Zionism with Racism," *New York Times*, December 17, 1991; and Krimly, "Faisal Bin Abd Al-Aziz Al Saud."

107. Some factions threatened Jordan's ruling dynasty while others sought the destruction of Israel. National Archives and Records Administration, RG 59, Central Files 1964-66, POL7UAR. Limited Official Use. Drafted by Slator C. Blackiston Jr. (NEA/NE), *FRUS* 1964–1968, vol. XXI, doc. 1, http://history.state.gov /historicaldocuments/frus1964-68v21/d1; P. J. Vatikiotis, *The History of Modern Egypt: From Muhammad Ali to Mubarak*, 3rd ed. (Baltimore: The Johns Hopkins University Press, 1985), pp. 405–06; Howard M. Sachar, *A History of Israel: From the Rise of Zionism to Our Time* (New York: Alfred A. Knopf, 1979), p. 616; and Robert McNamara, "Britain, Nasser, and the Outbreak of the Six Day War," *Journal of Contemporary History* 35, no. 4 (2000): 622.

108. Lyndon Johnson, *The Vantage Point: Perspectives of the Presidency 1963–1969* (New York: Holt, Rinehart, and Winston, 1971), p. 293.

109. Spiegel, *The Other Arab-Israeli Conflict*, pp. 119–20; "229. Memorandum for the Record," May 24, 1967. National Archives and Records Administration, RG 59, Records of the Department of State, Central Files, 1967-69, PET 6 SAUD. Secret; Exdis, *FRUS 1964–1968*, vol. XXXIV, doc. 229, http://history.state.gov/historicaldocuments /frus1964-68v34/d229. A note attached to the source text on White House letterhead reads, "May 24, 1967 To: S/S, Mr. Ben Read From: Bromley Smith FYI." A note on the source text by Harold Saunders reads, "President From—."

110. Michael B. Oren, *Six Days of War: June 1967 and the Making of the Modern Middle East* (New York: Oxford University Press, 2002), p. 84. Oren writes that Nasser's allegation concerned Israeli air cover. Joshua Pollack writes that Nasser's allegation was that U.S. and British carrier-based aircraft had attacked Egyptian airfields. Josh Pollack, "Saudi Arabia and the United States, 1931–2002," *Middle East Review of International Affairs* 6, no. 3 (September 2002): 81. In a letter to King Faisal, President Johnson wrote that the charges were "totally false." "Telegram from the Department of State to the Embassy in Saudi Arabia," June 8, 1967, *FRUS* 1964–1968, vol. XXI, Near East Region, Arabian Peninsula, doc. 290, http://history.state.gov/historicaldocuments /frus1964-68v21/d290. "Telegraph from the Department of State to the Embassy in Saudi Arabia, #290," June 8, 1967, *FRUS* 1964–1968, vol. XXI, doc. 290, National Archives and Records Administration, RG 59, Central Files 1967-69, POLSAUD-US. Secret; Immediate; Exdis. Drafted by Brewer on June 5, cleared by Battle and Bromley Smith, and approved by Secretary Rusk, http://history.state.gov /historicaldocuments/frus1964-68v21/d290#fn2.

111. Quoted in Thomas F. Brady, "Saudis Question Embargo on Oil," *New York Times*, July 1, 1967. Also see Yergin, *The Prize*, p. 555; and Brown, *Oil, God, and Gold*, pp. 268–80.

112. William B. Quandt, *Saudi Arabia in the 1980s: Foreign Policy, Security, and Oil* (Washington: The Brookings Institution, 1981), pp. 61–62.

113. The "three 'no's" has long been couched not as a preference of war over peace but as a firm rejection of coexistence with Israel. See Vatikiotis, *The History of Modern Egypt*, p. 408.

114. Kennedy was the first president to define U.S.-Israel relations as "special," but the defeat of the Soviet clients enhanced Israel's importance to Washington. Johnson noted the Russians "had lost their shirts" in the war. Robert Dallek, *Lyndon B. Johnson: Portrait of a President* (New York: Oxford University Press, 2005), p. 285. On U.S.-Israel relations, see Yitzhak Rabin, *The Rabin Memoirs* (Boston: Little, Brown, 1979), pp. 64–65; and Yaacov Bar-Siman-Tov, "The United States and Israel Since 1948: A 'Special Relationship'?" *Diplomatic History* 22, no. 2 (Spring 1998): 237–38. On states cutting diplomatic ties with the U.S., see Spiegel, *The Other Arab-Israeli Conflict*, p. 105, and George Lenczowski, *American Presidents and the Middle East* (Durham, NC: Duke University Press, 1990), pp. 112–13, 248. An April 1964 National Intelligence Estimate had warned presciently, "If US-Arab relations should deteriorate sharply, there would probably be a noticeable strengthening of Soviet influence." Similarly, the 1968 National Intelligence Estimate concluded, "The war and its aftermath have greatly reduced US influence in the Arab world and increased that of the USSR." Central Intelligence Agency, Job 79-R01012A, ODDI Registry of NIE and SNIE Files. Secret; Controlled Dissem., *FRUS* 1964–1968, vol. XXI, doc. 4, http://history.state.gov/historicaldocuments/frus1964-68v21/d4; and Central Intelligence Agency, Job 79-R01012A, ODDI Registry of NIE and SNIE Files. Secret; Controlled Dissem., *FRUS* 1964–1968, vol. XXI, doc. 32, http://history.state.gov/historicaldocuments/frus1964-68v21/d32.

115. See "297. Telegram From the Embassy in Saudi Arabia to the Department of State/1/Jidda, June 23, 1967, 1528Z. Source: National Archives and Records Administration, RG 59, Central Files 1967-69, POL 27 ARAB-ISR. Secret; Priority; Limdis. Repeated to USUN, http://www.state.gov/www/about_state/history/vol_xxi/zb.html.

116. See Moshe Dayan, *Breakthrough: A Personal Account of the Egypt-Israel Peace Negotiations* (New York: Random House, 1981), p. 87; Eitan Habar, Zeev Schiff, and Ehud Yaari, *The Year of the Dove* (New York: Bantam, 1979), pp. 13–14; and John Norton Moore, ed., *The Arab-Israeli Conflict: Readings and Documents*, vol. 4 (Princeton: Princeton University Press, 1974), pp. 1106–25.

117. On Saudi concerns, see Yergin, *The Prize*, p. 595.

118. James E. Akins, "The Oil Crisis: This Time the Wolf Is Here," *Foreign Affairs* 51, no. 3 (April 1973): 462–90.

119. Jim Hoagland, "Faisal Warns US on Israel," *Washington Post*, July 6, 1973; Jim Hoagland, "Saudis Ponder Whether to Produce the Oil US Needs," *Washington Post*, July 11, 1973; and Yergin, *The Prize*, pp. 596–97.

120. Yergin, *The Prize*, p. 597. Also see Chaim Herzog, *The Arab Israeli Wars: War and Peace in the Middle East, from the War of Independence through Lebanon* (New York: Vintage Books, 1983), p. 302; and Safran, *Saudi Arabia*, pp. 152–55.

121. James Schlesinger, *The House of Saud*, directed by Jihan El-Tahri (Paris: Alegria Productions, 2004), DVD.

122. Henry Kissinger, *Diplomacy* (New York: Simon & Schuster, 1995), p. 739; Yergin, *The Prize*, pp. 602–03; Spiegel, *The Other Arab-Israeli Conflict*, p. 247; and Nixon, *RN: The Memoirs of Richard Nixon*, p. 924.

123. Spiegel, *The Other Arab-Israeli Conflict*, p. 243; and Yergin, *The Prize*, p. 604.

124. Bird, *Crossing Mandelbaum Gate*, p. 222.

125. For Kissinger's perspective, see Henry Kissinger, *Years of Upheaval* (Boston: Little, Brown, 1982), pp. 468–515. Nixon's take can be found in Nixon, *RN: The Memoirs of Richard Nixon*, p. 787.

126. William B. Quandt, *Decade of Decisions: American Policy toward the Arab-Israeli Conflict, 1967–1976* (Berkeley: University of California Press, 1977), p. 184; Moshe Dayan, *Moshe Dayan: Story of My Life* (New York: Da Capo Press, 1992), pp. 421–22; and Nixon, *RN: The Memoirs of Richard Nixon*, pp. 927–28. The airlift proceeded on the condition that Israeli cargo plane would have the El Al markings painted out, as not to endanger U.S. interests by assisting an ally "too visibly." The planes, however, were detected. Memcon between Dinitz and Kissinger, 9 October 1973, 6:10–6:35 p.m. Source: RG 59, SN 70-73, Pol Isr-US, http://www.gwu.edu/~nsarchiv/NSAEBB /NSAEBB98/octwar-21b.pdf; William Quandt to Kissinger, "Middle Eastern Issues," October 9, 1973, Source: NPMP, NSCF, box 664, Middle East War Memos & Misc. Oct. 6–Oct. 17, 1973, http://www.gwu.edu/~nsarchiv/NSAEBB/NSAEBB98/octwar-22. pdf. Also see Yergin, *The Prize*, pp. 598–617; and Safran, *Saudi Arabia*, pp. 556–60.

127. Aramco president Frank Jungers claimed that the Saudis insisted on specific instructions to ensure embargo, setting up a system to determine "where the oil actually ended up, every barrel," under threat of complete nationalization. Aramco also got Saudi Arabia's tacit permission to supply oil to America's Sixth and Seventh Fleets. But it's alleged that Aramco ignored this. Brown, *Oil, God, and Gold*, pp. 294–96.

128. Kamal Adham was the conduit for President Sadat and Secretary Kissinger in the early 1970s. Sadat's wife also had business ventures with Kamal Adham. Holden and Johns, *The House of Saud*, pp. 289–93; Kissinger, *White House Years*, p. 1293.

129. The U.S. bill on foreign oil climbed from $3.9 billion to $24 billion between 1972 and 1973, and inflation doubled in many Western European nations. Still, in 1973, only 10 percent of U.S. total oil consumption came from the Persian Gulf and North Africa. See Yergin, *The Prize*, pp. 590–94; and "King Faisal: Man of the Year," *Time*, January 6, 1975.

130. "Excerpts from the Kissinger News Conference," *New York Times*, November 22, 1973. Kissinger implied the embargo was an "actual strangulation of the industrialized world." "Kissinger on Oil, Food, and Trade," *Business Week*, January 13, 1975, p. 69. President Ford also referred to the embargo as "economic strangulation." See "Gerald Ford: They Will See Something Is Being Done," *Time*, January 20, 1975, p. 21. Defense Secretary Schlesinger indicated "conceivably military measures in response" in the event of another oil embargo. "Now a Tougher U.S.: Interview with James R. Schlesinger, Secretary of Defense," *U.S. News & World Report*, May 26, 1975, pp. 26–27. Articles and essays on this confrontational approach include Robert Tucker, "Oil: The Issue of American Intervention," *Commentary*, January 1975; Tucker (writing under a pseudonym), "Seizing Arab Oil," *Harper's*, March 1975; Glen Frankel, "U.S. Mulled Seizing Oil Fields in 1973," *Washington Post*, January 1, 2004; and Owen Bowcott, "UK Feared Americans Would Invade Gulf During 1973 Oil Crisis," *The Guardian* (London), January 1, 2004.

131. Stephen Hayes, "Joint Economic Commissions as Instruments of US Foreign Policy in the Middle East," *Middle East Journal* 31, no. 1 (Winter 1977): 16–30. Edward R. F. Sheehan, *The Arabs, Israelis, and Kissinger: A Secret History of American Diplomacy in the Middle East* (New York: Reader's Digest Press, 1976), p. 116; Quandt, *Decade of Decisions*, p. 232; Kissinger, *Years of Upheaval*, p. 975; Henry Kissinger, *Years of Renewal* (New York: Simon & Schuster, 1999), p. 677.

132. "Remarks at the Conclusion of Discussions with King Faisal of Saudi Arabia," June 15, 1974, Gerhard Peters and John T. Woolley, The American Presidency Project, http://www.presidency.ucsb.edu/ws/?pid=4254.

133. Thomas W. Lippman, *Saudi Arabia on the Edge: The Uncertain Future of an American Ally* (Washington: Potomac Books, 2012); Anthony Sampson, *The Arms Bazaar: From Lebanon to Lockheed* (New York: Viking Press, 1977), pp. 331–37; and Martin Tolchin, "Foreigners' Political Roles in US Grow by Investing," *New York Times*, December 30, 1985. By 1979, American companies signed nearly $6 billion in nonmilitary contracts in Saudi Arabia. Tom McHale, "Flow of Funds," in *Saudi Arabia: A MEED Special Report* (Dubai: MEED, 1980), pp. 94–95.

134. Saudi Arabia, Kuwait, and the United Arab Emirates set up a special fund through which Syria and Egypt each received $570 million, Jordan $300 million, and the PLO $28 million. Esposito, *Unholy War*, pp. 107–8. These Western financial institutions acquired ownership, maintained complete Islamic subsidiaries, and opened branches as the Saudis invested their capital. In the late 1990s, Citibank's largest individual shareholder was the Saudi prince Al Walid Bin Talal. See Ibrahim Warde, *Islamic Finance in the Global Economy* (Edinburgh: Edinburgh University Press, 2000). Also see Clement M. Henry, "Islamic Financial Movements: Midwives of Political Change in the Middle East?" paper prepared for the 2001 Annual Meetings of the American Political Science Association, San Francisco (August 30–September 6, 2001), http://www.ifisa.co.za/Articles/Islamic%20Banking/Islamic%20Movements%20in%20finance_Banking.pdf; and Josh Martin, "Citibank Goes Islamic," *The Middle East* (London), July 1, 1996.

135. Khlaid bin Abdul-Aziz Al Saud.

136. Fahd bin Abd al-Aziz.

137. Vassiliev, *The History of Saudi Arabia*, p. 395.

138. Bernard Gwertzman, "US Jets Will Visit Saudi Arabia as Show of Support in Tense Area," *New York Times*, January 11, 1979. Saudi ambassador to the United States Prince Bandar said that the consequences were devastating and lived on. "We don't want you to put out a hand and then pull it back," the ambassador said. Quoted in Bob Woodward, *The Commanders* (New York: Simon & Schuster, 1991), p. 240.

139. Quoted in Peter A. Iseman, "Iran's War of Words against Saudi Arabia," *The Nation*, April 19, 1980. Also see James Buchan, "Secular and Religious Opposition in Saudi Arabia," in *State, Society, and Economy in Saudi Arabia*, pp. 117–20.

140. Quoted in Buchan, "Secular and Religious Opposition in Saudi Arabia," p. 122; Also see Yaroslav Trofimov, *The Siege of Mecca: The Forgotten Uprising in Islam's Holiest Shrine* (New York: Doubleday, 2007); and Steve Coll, *Ghost Wars: The Secret History of the CIA, Afghanistan, and bin Laden, from the Soviet Invasion to September 10, 2001* (New York: Penguin Books, 2004), pp. 27–29.

141. Robin Wright, *Sacred Rage: The Wrath of Militant Islam* (New York: Touchstone Press, 1985), p. 148; and Daniel Benjamin and Steven Simon, *The Age of Sacred Terror* (New York: Random House, 2002), p. 90.

142. Quoted in Bird, *Crossing Mandelbaum Gate,* p. 154.

143. Wright, *The Looming Tower,* p. 147; and Carmen Bin Laden, *Inside the Kingdom.*

144. Dreyfuss, *Devil's Game,* p. 258.

145. U.S. Embassy in Kabul to Department of State, Airgram A-77, "Afghanistan Clerical Unrest: A Tentative Assessment," June 24, 1970, Confidential, 7 pp. Source: National Archives, Record Group 59, Subject-Numeric Files, 1970 (hereinafter SN 70 -73), Pol 23-8 AFG, http://www.gwu.edu/~nsarchiv/NSAEBB/NSAEBB59/zahir02.pdf.

146. An October State Department cable reported: "The Saudis interpret Moscow's take over in Afghanistan last year as part of a Soviet-directed campaign to encircle the Persian Gulf and the Arabian Peninsula with radical regimes in preparation for the subversion of the conservative oil-rich monarchies." Marin J. Strmecki, "Power Assessment: Measuring Soviet Power in Afghanistan" (PhD diss., Georgetown University, 1994); and Bronson, *Thicker than Oil,* pp. 154–60n.

147. Zbigniew Brzezinski, *Power and Principle: Memoirs of the National Security Advisor, 1977–1981* (New York: Farrar Straus and Giroux, 1983), p. 449.

148. "The State of the Union Address Delivered before a Joint Session of the Congress," January 23, 1980, Gerhard Peters and John T. Woolley, The American Presidency Project, http://www.presidency.ucsb.edu/ws/?pid=33079.

149. "The President's News Conference," October 1, 1981, Gerhard Peters and John T. Woolley, The American Presidency Project, http://www.presidency.ucsb.edu/ws/?pid=44327.

150. David E. Long, "Fahd Bin Abd Al-Aziz Al-Saud," in *Political Leaders of the Contemporary Middle East and North Africa,* p. 178.

151. Esposito, *Unholy War,* p. 86; and Reinhard Schulze, *A Modern History of the Islamic World,* trans. Azizeh Azodi (New York: New York University Press, 2002), p. 201.

152. The Saudis also created the Riyadh-based GCC with conservative, Sunni-ruled regimes in the United Arab Emerates, Bahrain, Oman, Qatar, and Kuwait to regulate finance, trade, customs, and tourism; foster scientific and technical progress; and establish a unified military presence. See Safran, *Saudi Arabia,* pp. 172–76.

153. "Transcript of President's News Conference on Foreign and Domestic Politics," *New York Times,* October 2, 1981; Esposito, *Unholy War,* p. 86. On Reagan's anger at Israeli influence, see Alexander M. Haig Jr., *Caveat: Realism, Reagan, and Foreign Policy* (New York: Macmillan, 1984), pp. 189–90.

154. Majid Khadduri, *The Gulf War: The Origins and Implications of the Iran-Iraq Conflict* (New York: Oxford University Press, 1988), p. 124. Reagan threatened to punish one senator by closing a base in his district. See Melinda Beck, "AWACS: The Final Days," *Newsweek,* November 2, 1981. Also see Robin Allen, "Saudi Arabia Builds Defence of the Realm," *Financial Times* (London), November 23, 1988; Jim Mann, "Threat to Mideast Military Balance; U.S. Caught Napping by Sino-Saudi Missile Deal," *Los Angeles Times,* May 4, 1988; and John M. Goshko and Don Oberdorfer, "Chinese Sell Saudis Missiles Capable of Covering Mideast," *Washington Post,* March 18, 1988.

155. Turki bin Faisal al-Saud.

156. Saudi General Khaled bin Sultan relates that King Fahd sensed it would be unwise "to tie ourselves to an alliance which was likely to arouse the hostility of the Arab and Muslim world." HRH General Khaled bin Sultan with Patrick Seale, *Desert Warrior: A Personal View of the Gulf War by the Joint Forces Commander* (New York:

HarperCollins, 1995), p. 25; Hart, *Saudi Arabia and the United States*, p. 85–89; and Trofimov, *The Siege of Mecca*, p. 172.

157. In the mid 1980s, the president secretly shipped 400 Stinger missiles to Saudi Arabia for short-range air defense. Michael H. Armacost, "US Response to Saudi Request for Military Assistance-Transcript," US Department of State Bulletin, July 1984; Bernard Gwertzman, "Senators Assail Arms Sale to Saudis," *New York Times*, June 6, 1984; Robert M. Gates, *From the Shadows: The Ultimate Insider's Story of Five Presidents and How They Won the Cold War* (New York: Simon & Schuster, 1997), p. 311; Jeff Gerth, "The White House Crisis; Evidence Points to Big Saudi Role in Iranian and Contra Arms Deals," *New York Times*, November 30, 1986; David B. Ottaway, "Saudi Envoy Has Credibility Woes," *Washington Post*, February 28, 1987; and Lawrence E. Walsh, *Firewall: The Iran-Contra Conspiracy and Cover-Up* (New York: W.W. Norton, 1998), pp. 389–92.

158. Coll, *Ghost Wars*, p. 81; and Steven V. Roberts, "Prop for U.S. Policy: Secret Saudi Funds," *New York Times*, June 21, 1987. For more on aid policies, see Thomas W. Lippman, "Saudis Pledge $1 Billion Aid to Africa; Saudis Pledge $1 Billion Aid at Afro-Arab Talks in Cairo," *Washington Post*, March 8, 1977. Also see Bronson, *Thicker than Oil*, p. 135; and Kenneth Labich, "Saudi Power," *Newsweek* (International Edition), March 6, 1978.

159. Passed the House by a bipartisan vote of 411–0. See Gates, *From the Shadows*, p. 298.

160. For the $32 million figure, and the entire argument more generally, see Jonathan Marshall, "Saudi Arabia and the Reagan Doctrine," *Middle East Report* 18 (November/ December 1988), http://www.merip.org/mer/mer155/saudi-arabia-reagan-doctrine. (Marshall also cites *San Francisco Examiner*, March 12, 1987; and *Insight*, July 6, 1987.) See House of Representatives, Select Committee to Investigate Covert Arms Transactions with Iran, and Senate Select Committee on Secret Military Assistance to Iran and the Nicaraguan Opposition, report, "Iran-Contra Affair" (Washington: GPO, 1987), pp. 5, 45, 119–20, 128, https://archive.org/details/reportofcongress87unit. Related to the above citation (US Gov), Saudi Arabia is "Country 2": see "The Iran-Contra Report," The American Presidency Project, http://www.presidency.ucsb .edu/PS157/assignment%20files%20public/congressional%20report%20key%20 sections.htm. Bob Woodward, *Veil: The Secret Wars of the CIA, 1981–1987* (New York: Simon & Schuster, 1987), p. 401.

161. Sen. John Glenn (D-OH), testimony before the Senate Committee on Foreign Relations, U.S.—Pakistan Nuclear Issues, July 30, 1992, http:// www.fas.org/news /pakistan/1992/920731.htm. On dollar for dollar, see Gates, *From the Shadows*, p. 148. Also see Michael Scheuer, *Through Our Enemies Eyes: Osama bin Laden, Radical Islam and the Future of America* (Herndon, VA: Potomac Books, 2003), p. 41; Peter Dale Scott, *The Road to 9/11: Wealth, Empire, and the Future of America* (Berkeley, CA: University of California Press, 2007), pp. 62–63; and Jonathan Beaty and S. C. Gwynne, *The Outlaw Bank: A Wild Rise Into the Secret Heart of BCCI* (New York: Random House, 1993).

162. Coll, *Ghost Wars*, pp. 128–35; Adam Curtis, *The Power of Nightmares: The Rise of the Politics of Fear* (London: British Broadcasting Corporation, 2004), TV miniseries; James Bryce, "Arab Veterans of the Afghan War," *Jane's Intelligence Review* 7, no. 4 (1995); and Peter L. Bergen, *Holy War, Inc.: Inside the Secret World of Osama Bin Laden* (New York: Free Press, 2001), p. 70.

163. Chris Hedges, "Muslim Militants Have Afghan Links," *New York Times*, March 28, 1993, http://www.nytimes.com/1993/03/28/world/muslim-militants-share -afghan-link.html?pagewanted=all&src=pm; Esposito, *Unholy War,* pp. 87–88; Gold, *Hatred's Kingdom,* p. 94; and Kepel, *Jihad,* p. 147.

164. Coll, *Ghost Wars*, pp. 83, 154.

165. Gold, *Hatred's Kingdom*, p. 121.

166. Coll, *Ghost Wars*, pp. 278–79, 512.

167. Joe Stephens and David B. Ottoway, "From U.S., the ABC's of Jihad: Violent Soviet-Era Textbooks Complicate Afghan Education Efforts," *Washington Post*, March 2, 2002.

168. Thomas L. Friedman, "Foreign Affairs: In Pakistan, It's Jihad 101," *New York Times*, November 3, 2001.

Chapter 6

1. Dwight D. Eisenhower, *The White House Years: Mandate for Change, 1953–1956* (Garden City, NY: Doubleday and Company, 1963), p. 83.

2. For an account of the British anger at Mossadegh over the oil issue and London's subsequent attempts to draw the United States into efforts to overthrow the prime minister during the final months of Harry Truman's administration, see Tim Weiner, *Legacy of Ashes: The History of the CIA* (New York: Doubleday, 2007), pp. 81–83.

3. Saced Kamali Dehghan and Richard Norton-Taylor, "CIA Admits Role in 1953 Iranian Coup," *The Guardian* (London), August 19, 2013, http://www.theguardian .com/world/2013/aug/19/cia-admits-role-1953-iranian-coup.

4. Quoted in Stephen Kinzer, *All the Shah's Men: An American Coup and the Roots of Middle East Terror* (New York: John Wiley and Sons, 2003), p. 4.

5. Eisenhower, *Mandate for Change*, pp. 162–63.

6. Maziar Behrooz, "The 1953 Coup in Iran and the Legacy of the Tudeh," in *Mohammed Mosaddeq and the 1953 Coup in Iran*, ed. Mark J. Gasiorowski and Malcolm Byrne (New York: Syracuse University Press, 2003), pp. 100–11.

7. Kinzer, *All the Shah's Men*, p. 53.

8. Those documents were published on the website of the U.S. National Security Archive at George Washington University. See George Washington University, "CIA Confirms Role in 1953 Iran Coup," The National Security Archive, http://www2 .gwu.edu/~nsarchiv/NSAEBB/NSAEBB435/#_ftn1 (hereafter cited as National Security Archives documents summary), p. 6. Tim Weiner broke the story of the destroyed documents in 1997. Tim Weiner, "CIA Destroyed Files on 1953 Iran Coup," *New York Times*, May 29, 1997. Some U.S. documents remained classified, however, and the British government still steadfastly refuses to release the relevant information. Dehghen, "CIA Admits Role in 1953 Iranian Coup."

9. Kermit Roosevelt, *Countercoup: The Struggle for the Control of Iran* (New York: McGraw-Hill, 1979).

10. Abbas Milani, *The Shah* (New York: Palgrave Macmillan, 2011), pp. 172–73.

11. See, for example, Ray Takeyh, "What Really Happened in Iran: The CIA, the Ouster of Mossaddeq, and the Restoration of the Shah," *Foreign Affairs* 93, no. 4 (July/ August 2014): 2–12.

12. George Washington University, "CIA Confirms Role in 1953 Iran Coup," Documents 3 a & b: CIA History, *The Battle for Iran*, author's name excised, undated

(c. mid 1970s), in National Security Archives documents summary, http://www2 .gwu.edu/~nsarchiv/NSAEBB/NSAEBB435/, pp. 10–11.

13. Love's report reprinted in Jonathan Kwitny, *Endless Enemies: The Making of an Unfriendly World* (New York: Congdon and Weed, 1984), pp. 160–76.

14. Quoted in Dehghan, "CIA Admits Role in 1953 Iranian Coup."

15. Ibid.

16. Ibid.

17. Milani, *The Shah*, p. 174.

18. Kinzer, *All the Shah's Men*, p. 223.

19. Zbigniew Brzezinski, *Power and Principle: Memoirs of the National Security Adviser, 1977–1981*, rev. ed. (New York: Farrar, Straus, Giroux, 1985), pp. 356–57.

20. "Ministry of Security, SAVAK" Intelligence Resources Program, Federation of American Scientists: http://www.fas.org/irp/world/iran/savak/index.html; and "Nobody Influences Me!" *Time*, December 10, 1979, http://www.time.com/time /magazine/0,9263,7601791210,00.html, p. 6.

21. Amnesty International, Annual Report 1968–1969, http://www.amnesty.org /en/library/asset/POL10/001/1969/en/36325d2a-0429-4840-96ff-1f11b1f3762c /pol100011969eng.pdf, p. 11.

22. Amnesty International, Annual Report 1970–1971, http://www.amnesty.org /en/library/asset/POL10/001/1971/en/c21872f5-04d5-465d-aca2-aa97b36c25e3 /pol100011971eng.pdf, p. 36.

23. Amnesty International, Annual Report, 1971–1972, http://www.amnesty.org /en/library/asset/POL10/001/1972/en/76be8361-865c-40c1-a378-809d54c263ed /pol100011972eng.pdf , p. 26.

24. Ibid.

25. Ibid.

26. Amnesty International, Annual Report, 1972–1973, http://www.amnesty.org /en/library/asset/POL10/001/1973/en/13706937-b5fa-43a6-be13-e865f0424318 /pol100011973eng.pdf, p. 39.

27. Amnesty International, Annual Report, 1973–1974, http://www.amnesty.org /en/library/asset/POL10/001/1974/en/082dd4a9-28fe-4e8a-ac39-b076ba1dbd9e /pol100011974eng.pdf, p. 38.

28. Amnesty International Report, 1977, http://www.amnesty.org/en/library /asset/POL10/006/1977/en/561cfa94-80ee-45aa-add8-adc02121df2b /pol100061977eng.pdf, p. 150.

29. Ibid., p. 151.

30. Jack Anderson with Les Whitten, "Torture Is Used in Shah's Iran," *The Nevada Daily Mail*, May 30, 1976, http://news.google.com/newspapers?nid=1908&dat=1976 0530&id=V5ofAAAAIBAJ&sjid=Z9QEAAAAIBAJ&pg=3835,3334606.

31. *Public Papers of the Presidents of the United States, Jimmy Carter, 1977, Book 2: June 25– December 31, 1977* (Washington: Government Printing Office, 1978), pp. 2221–22.

32. Jesse Leaf, "Iran: A Blind Spot in U.S. Intelligence," *Washington Post*, January 18, 1979; Barry Rubin, *Paved with Good Intentions: The American Experience and Iran* (New York: Oxford University Press, 1980), p. 201.

33. Cyrus Vance, *Hard Choices: Critical Years in America's Foreign Policy* (New York: Simon & Schuster, 1983), p. 316.

34. Brzezinski, *Power and Principle*, p. 357.

35. Vance, *Hard Choices*, p. 316.

36. Ibid., p. 319.

37. Jimmy Carter, *Keeping Faith: Memoirs of a President* (New York: Bantam Books, 1982), p. 436.

38. Ibid., pp. 436–37.

39. Brzezinski, *Power and Principle*, p. 385. A few officials, such as Ambassador William Sullivan, thought that an Islamic republic would gradually drift toward democracy rather than communism. Yet it is telling that neither of the two major schools of thought in Washington seriously considered the possibility that the religious factions would be able to sustain their power over the long term. The dominance of such competing fallacies underscores just how badly U.S. officials misread Iran's political situation.

40. Brzezinski, *Power and Principle*. The term "without any reservation" crops up repeatedly regarding policy toward the Shah during the 1978 crisis in Brzezinski's memoirs. See pp. 363–65.

41. Ibid. See especially his comments on pp. 356, 363–64, 371.

42. Ibid., p. 371.

43. Quoted in Milani, *The Shah*, p. 387.

44. Brzezinski, *Power and Principle*, p. 378.

45. Carter, *Keeping Faith*, p. 446.

46. Ibid., p. 438.

47. Ibid., pp. 438–39.

48. Brzezinski, *Power and Principle*, p. 394

49. Henry Kissinger, *White House Years* (Boston: Little, Brown, and Company, 1979), p. 1261.

50. Ibid., p. 1262.

51. Ibid.

52. Ibid., pp. 1263–64.

53. Ibid., p. 1264.

54. See Eugene Gholz and Daryl G. Press, "Energy Alarmism: The Myths That Make Americans Worry about Oil," Cato Institute Policy Analysis no. 589, April 5, 2007, http://www.cato.org/publications/policy-analysis/energy-alarmism-myths -make-americans-worry-about-oil, especially pp. 11–16. Also see David R. Henderson, "Do We Need to Go to War for Oil?" Cato Institute Foreign Policy Briefing no. 4, October 24, 1990, http://object.cato.org/sites/cato.org/files/pubs/pdf/fpb004.pdf; M. A. Adelman, "The Real Oil Problem," *Regulation* (Spring 2004): 16–21; Jerry Taylor and Peter Van Doren, "An Oil Embargo Won't Work," *Wall Street Journal*, October 10, 2002; and Jerry Taylor and Peter Van Doren, "Driving Bin Laden?" *National Review*, March 6, 2006.

55. Kissinger, *White House Years*, pp. 1258, 1262.

56. Milani, *The Shah*, p. 374.

57. Kissinger, *White House Years*, p. 1261.

58. Richard Nixon, *RN: The Memoirs of Richard Nixon* (New York: Grosset and Dunlap, 1978), p. 133. Eisenhower's account of the "restoration" of the Shah to his throne is no more accurate or honest. See Eisenhower, *Mandate for Change*, pp. 162–64.

59. Kissinger, *White House Years*, p. 1261.

60. Dwight D. Eisenhower, *The White House Years: Waging Peace, 1956–1961* (Garden City, NY: Doubleday, 1965), p. 505.

61. Gerald R. Ford, *A Time to Heal*, rev. ed. (New York: Berkley Books, 1980), p. xvii.

62. Carter, *Keeping Faith*, p. 435.

63. Ibid., p. 440.

64. Vance, *Hard Choices*, p. 317.

65. Ibid.

66. Brzezinski, *Power and Principle*, p. 356.

67. Alexander M. Haig Jr., *Caveat: Realism, Reagan, and Foreign Policy* (New York: Macmillan, 1984), p. 96.

68. Ronald Reagan, *An American Life* (Simon & Schuster, 1990), p. 218.

69. Sean Hannity, *Deliver Us from Evil: Defeating Terrorism, Despotism, and Liberalism* (New York: William Morrow, 2004), pp. 89–90.

70. Max Boot, "The End of Appeasement," *Weekly Standard* 8, no. 21 (February 10, 2003).

71. Steven F. Hayward, *The Real Jimmy Carter: How Our Worst Ex-President Undermines American Foreign Policy, Coddles Dictators, and Created the Party of Clinton and Kerry* (Washington: Regnery Publishing, 2004), pp. 121, 122.

72. Ibid., p. 126.

73. Michael Ledeen, "The Willful Blindness of Those Who Will Not See," *National Review*, February 18, 2003.

74. Brzezinski, *Power and Principle*, p. 378.

75. The Shah received meager domestic political credit for those reforms, while opponents of his initiatives, especially the land reforms, directed intense criticism at his efforts. The land reforms attracted intense opposition from both social conservatives and free-market capitalists. Milani, *The Shah*, pp. 262–63, 292.

76. Brzezinski, *Power and Principle*, p. 360.

77. Milani, *The Shah*, pp. 371–73.

78. Kinzer, *All the Shah's Men*, preface to the 2008 edition, p. x.

Chapter 7

1. U.S. Department of State, *Department of State Bulletin* 22, no. 554 (February 13, 1950): 244, https://archive.org/details/departmentofstat2250unit.

2. John Foster Dulles, "Memorandum of Conversation with Eisenhower, March 24, 1953," *FRUS, 1952–1954*. Quoted in David L. Anderson, *Trapped by Success: The Eisenhower Administration and Vietnam, 1953–61* (New York: Columbia University Press, 1991), p. 17.

3. Quoted in Stephen E. Ambrose, *Eisenhower: The President* (New York: Simon & Schuster, 1984), p. 180. See also, Robert A. Divine, *Eisenhower and the Cold War* (New York: Oxford University Press, 1981), p. 41. Eisenhower seemed almost obsessed with the domino theory regarding East Asia. By the end of the 1950s, he argued that the fall of Laos could trigger a domino effect that would engulf Vietnam and then the rest of East Asia. On another occasion, he feared that Nationalist China's possible loss of Quemoy and Matsu to Communist China, two tiny islands barely a mile off the mainland coast, could cause the collapse of Chiang Kai-shek's regime on Taiwan and begin to engulf the entire region in a communist tide. See Dwight D. Eisenhower, *The White House Years: Waging Peace, 1956–1961* (Garden City, NY: Doubleday, 1965), pp. 294, 607.

4. *Public Papers of the Presidents of the United States: Dwight D. Eisenhower, 1953* (Washington: Government Printing Office, 1953).

5. George C. Herring and Richard H. Immerman, "Eisenhower, Dulles and Dienbienphu: 'The Day We Didn't Go to War' Revisited," *Journal of American History* 71, no. 2 (September 1984): 343–63.

6. Richard Nixon, *RN: The Memoirs of Richard Nixon* (New York: Grosset and Dunlap, 1978), p. 112.

7. Dwight D. Eisenhower, *The White House Years: Mandate for Change, 1953–1956* (Garden City, NY: Doubleday), p. 372.

8. Speech before the American Friends of Vietnam. Quoted in Guenter Lewy, *America in Vietnam* (New York: Oxford University Press, 1978), p. 12.

9. Eisenhower, *Mandate for Change*, p. 337.

10. Quoted in Jean Edward Smith, *Eisenhower in War and Peace* (New York: Random House, 2012), pp. 615–16.

11. Department of Defense, report for the House Committee on Armed Services, 92nd Cong., 1st sess., *United States-Vietnam Relations*, book 9, part V.B3, (Washington: Government Printing Office, 1971), p. 217.

12. Memorandum for the National Security Council, June 13, 1955, *United States-Vietnam Relations*, book 10, part V.B3, (Washington: Government Printing Office, 1971), p. 841.

13. Quoted in Fred Greenstein and Richard Immerman, "What Did Eisenhower Tell Kennedy about Indochina? The Politics of Misperception," *Journal of American History* 79, no. 2 (September 1992): 572.

14. Henry Luce, "Revolution in Vietnam," editorial, *Life*, May 16, 1955, p. 3.

15. See Seth Jacobs, *America's Miracle Man in Vietnam: Ngo Dinh Diem, Religion, Race, and U.S. Intervention in Southeast Asia* (London: Duke University Press, 2005), p. 208.

16. Ernest K. Lindley, "An Ally Worth Having," *Newsweek*, June 29, 1959, p. 31.

17. John F. Kennedy, *The Strategy of Peace* (New York: Harper & Row, 1960), p. 61.

18. "Reply to the Ambassador in France," *FRUS* 1955–1957, vol. I, May 11, 1955, pp. 393–99. Quote is on pp. 394–95.

19. John Foster Dulles, letter to Secretary of Defense Charles Wilson, August 18, 1954, *United States-Vietnam Relations*, book 10, part V.B, (Washington: Government Printing Office, 1971), pp. 768–69.

20. Quoted in Jacobs, *America's Miracle Man in Vietnam*, p. 211.

21. Quoted in General William C. Westmoreland, *A Soldier Reports* (New York: Doubleday, 1976), pp. 409–10.

22. Speech before the American Friends of Vietnam. Quoted in Lewy, *America in Vietnam*, pp. 12–13.

23. Mike Gravel, Noam Chomsky, and Howard Zinn, *The Pentagon Papers: The Defense Department History of United States Decisionmaking on Vietnam*, Senator Gravel ed., vol. 2 (Boston: Beacon Press, 1971), p. 72.

24. George W. Ball, *The Past Has Another Pattern: Memoirs* (New York; W. W. Norton, 1982), p. 365.

25. Ibid., p. 370.

26. Ibid., p. 372.

27. Robert S. McNamara, with Brian VanDeMark, *In Retrospect: The Tragedy and Lessons of Vietnam* (New York: Times Books, 1995), p. 43

28. Quoted in Tim Weiner, *Legacy of Ashes: The History of the CIA* (New York: Doubleday, 2007), p. 215.

29. McNamara, *In Retrospect*, pp. 41–42.

30. Tad Szulc, "Washington, with a Deep Commitment in the Area, Is Facing Major Decisions on Diem Regime," *New York Times*, September 1, 1963.

31. McNamara, *In Retrospect*, p. 42.

32. Ball, *The Past Has Another Pattern*, p. 370.

33. Quoted in Ball, *The Past Has Another Pattern*, p. 370.

34. Ibid.

35. Quoted in Anderson, *Trapped by Success*, p. 181.

36. Lyndon Baines Johnson, *The Vantage Point: Perspectives of the Presidency, 1963–1969* (New York: Holt, Rinehart, and Winston, 1971), pp. 60–61.

37. Ibid., p. 61.

38. Memorandum of conversation, Vietnam, August 29, 1963, 12:00 Noon. John F. Kennedy Presidential Library, Roger Hilsman Papers, Country Series, Box 4, folder: Vietnam: White House Meetings 8/26/63–8/29/63, State Department.

39. *The Pentagon Papers, New York Times* ed. (New York: Bantam Books, 1971), p. 197.

40. Department of State, Check-List of Possible U.S. Actions in Case of Coup, October 25, 1963, John F. Kennedy Presidential Library, Roger Hilsman Papers, Country File, Box 4, folder: Vietnam, 10/6/63–10/31/63.

41. Ball, *The Past Has Another Pattern*, p. 371.

42. For a discussion of the CIA's role in Diem's overthrow but the Agency's apparent chagrin at his murder, see Weiner, *Legacy of Ashes*, pp. 214–21.

43. Memorandum of Conference with the President, November 2, 1963, 9:15 a.m. John F. Kennedy Presidential Library, John F. Kennedy Papers, National Security File, Meetings & Memoranda Series, Box 317, folder: Meetings on Vietnam, 11/1/63–11/2/63.

44. United States Congress, Senate, Interim Report, Alleged Assassination Plots Involving Foreign Leaders, S. Rept. 465, 94th Cong., 1st sess., 1975 (Washington: Government Printing Office, 1975), p. 22.

45. "Embtel 917, Lodge to Rusk, November 4, 1963," *FRUS* 1961–1963, vol. IV, (Washington: Government Printing Office, 1978), pp. 560–62.

46. Quoted in Brian VanDeMark, *Into the Quagmire: Lyndon Johnson and the Escalation of the Vietnam War* (New York: Oxford University Press, 1991), p. 15.

47. Johnson, *The Vantage Point*, p. 64.

48. Ibid.

49. Leon T. Hadar, "Getting the Vietnam Analogy Right in Afghanistan," *Huffington Post*, October 21, 2009.

50. Quoted in McNamara, *In Retrospect*, p. 195. Such thinking epitomizes what Jonathan Schell aptly describes as the development of a "psychological domino theory." Increasingly, those who defended the Vietnam mission relied less on the argument that geostrategic forces unleashed by a defeat in Vietnam would cause other nations in East Asia to go communist and instead emphasized an amorphous loss of U.S. credibility that would produce disastrous outcomes on a global scale. Jonathan Schell, *The Time of Illusion* (New York: Vintage Books, 1976), pp. 9–10.

51. McNamara, *In Retrospect*, p. 195.

52. *The Pentagon Papers, New York Times* ed., p. 129.

53. Hadar, "Getting the Vietnam Analogy Right in Afghanistan."

54. Ball, *The Past Has Another Pattern*, p. 375.

55. Ibid., p. 383.

56. Ibid., p. 389.

57. Walt W. Rostow, *The Diffusion of Power, 1957–1972* (New York: Macmillan, 1972), p. 446.

58. Ibid., p. 447.

59. Interview with Nguyen Cao Ky, *Sunday Mirror* (London), July 4, 1965.

60. Quoted in McNamara, *In Retrospect*, p. 186.

61. Ball, *The Past Has Another Pattern*, p. 400.

62. Rostow, *The Diffusion of Power*, p. 455.

63. Lyndon B. Johnson, "Joint Statement Following Discussions in Canberra with President Thieu of Vietnam," John T. Woolley and Gerhard Peters, The American Presidency Project, http://www.presidency.ucsb.edu/ws/index.php?pid=28632&st=Thieu&st1.

64. Henry Kissinger, *White House Years* (Boston: Little, Brown, and Company, 1979), p. 236.

65. Max Frankel, "Nixon Visits India; He Again Praises Regime in Saigon," *New York Times*, August 1, 1969.

66. Kissinger, *White House Years*, p. 1035.

67. Rostow, *The Diffusion of Power*, p. 555.

68. Kissinger, *White House Years*, p. 1035.

69. Ibid., p. 1031–32.

70. Nixon, *RN: The Memoirs of Richard Nixon*, p. 348.

71. Ibid., p. 696.

72. See John Burnett, "Brown and Root: A Company with a History," *History News Network* (blog), December 24, 2003, http://hnn.us/article/2851; and Don Luce, "We've Been Here Before: The Tiger Cages of Vietnam," *History News Network* (blog), April 4, 2005, http://hnn.us/article/11001.

73. Robert Shaplen, *A Turning Wheel: Three Decades of the Asian Revolution as Witnessed by a Correspondent for the* New York Times (New York: Random House, 1979), p. 13.

74. One telling indicator is the surprising infrequency that Thieu is even mentioned (much less discussed in reasonable detail) in both Lyndon Johnson's and Richard Nixon's memoirs.

75. Nixon, *RN: The Memoirs of Richard Nixon*, p. 706. See also the January 16, 1973, ultimatum from Nixon that Kissinger personally delivered to Thieu.

76. Ibid., p. 392.

77. Regarding the growing gap between the policy preferences of Saigon and Washington, see Nixon, *RN: The Memoirs of Richard Nixon*, pp. 696–707.

78. Ibid., p. 706

79. Ball, *The Past Has Another Pattern*, p. 415.

80. Nixon, *RN: The Memoirs of Richard Nixon*, pp. 749–50.

81. Quoted in Johnson, *The Vantage Point*, p. 58.

82. "Robert Kennedy Assures Vietnam: Says U.S. Troops Will Stay until Reds Are Defeated—Calls Diem Brave," *New York Times*, February 18, 1962.

83. U.S. Department of State, *Department of State Bulletin* 31, no. 788 (August 2, 1954): p. 164, https://archive.org/details/departmentofstat311954unit.

84. Quoted in Johnson, *The Vantage Point*, p. 61.

85. McNamara, *In Retrospect*, p. 107.

86. Dean Rusk, as told to Richard Rusk, *As I Saw It* (New York: Penguin Books, 1990), pp. 294–95.

87. Quoted in Thad Szulc, *The Illusion of Peace: Foreign Policy in the Nixon Years* (New York: Viking Press, 1978), p. 158.

88. Daryl G. Press, *Calculating Credibility: How Leaders Assess Military Threats* (Ithaca, NY: Cornell University Press, 2005).

89. Nixon, *RN: The Memoirs of Richard Nixon*, p. 348.

90. Hadar, "Getting the Vietnam Analogy Right in Afghanistan."

91. Shaplen, *A Turning Wheel*, p. 12.

92. Quoted in Johnson, *The Vantage Point*, p. 417.

93. Ibid.

94. John J. Mearsheimer, "Hollow Victory," *ForeignPolicy.com*, November 2, 2009.

95. Lewis Sorley, *A Better War: The Unexamined Victories and Final Tragedy of America's Last Years in Vietnam* (Boston: Harcourt, Brace and Company, 2007). Sorley reprises a few of those arguments in his latest book, *Westmoreland: The General Who Lost Vietnam* (Boston: Houghton Mifflin Harcourt, 2011).

96. Richard Bergholz, "Reagan Shares Ford View of Congress in Viet Crisis," *Los Angeles Times*, April 2, 1975.

97. Richard Nixon, "Congress to Blame for Viet Defeat," *Chicago Tribune*, May 3, 1978.

98. Rusk, *As I Saw It*, p. 493.

99. Author's interview with Walt W. Rostow, April 1997.

100. Mearsheimer, "Hollow Victory."

101. Ball, *The Past Has Another Pattern*, p. 422.

102. Michael Lind, *Vietnam: The Necessary War: A Reinterpretation of America's Most Disastrous Military Conflict* (New York: Free Press, 2002).

Chapter 8

1. Dwight D. Eisenhower, *The White House Years: Waging Peace, 1956–1961* (Garden City, NY: Doubleday, 1965), pp. 571–76.

2. "Discussion at the 410th Meeting of the National Security Council," June 18, 1959, Box 2, NSC Summaries of Discussion, Dwight D. Eisenhower Library, p. 4.

3. Eisenhower, *Waging Peace*, pp. 573, 575.

4. Ibid., p. 575.

5. Quoted in Jonathan Kwitny, *Endless Enemies: The Making of an Unfriendly World* (New York: Congdon and Weed, 1984), p. 57.

6. Tim Weiner, *Legacy of Ashes: The History of the CIA* (New York: Doubleday, 2007), pp. 162–63.

7. Ibid., p. 163.

8. United States Cong., Senate. Church Committee. "Interim Report: Alleged Assassination Attempts Involving Foreign Leaders." 94 Cong., 1st sess., S. Rept. 94-465. (Washington: Government Printing Office, 1975,) pp. 1–25.

9. Michael G. Schatzberg, *Mobutu or Chaos? The United States and Zaire, 1960–1990* (Lanham, MD: University Press of America, 1991), p. 21. Also see Stephen R. Weissman, "What Really Happened in the Congo: The CIA, the Murder of Lumumba, and the Rise of Mobutu," *Foreign Affairs* 93, no. 4 (July/August 2014): 14–24.

10. Kwitny, *Endless Enemies*, p. 50.

11. For a succinct, insider account of the maneuvering regarding policy toward the Congo during the Kennedy administration, see the oral history interview with

Ambassador Sheldon Vance, who served in the State Department's Office of Central African Affairs and would later become U.S. ambassador to Zaire. Oral History Interview, Ambassador Sheldon Vance, July 26, 1989, Sheldon and Jean Vance Papers, Minnesota Historical Society Library, Locator 147 H3 2F., pp. 7–17.

12. See John Prados, *Presidents' Secret Wars: CIA and Pentagon Covert Operations Since World War II* (New York: W. Morrow, 1986), pp. 235–37.

13. Dean Rusk, as told to Richard Rusk, *As I Saw It* (New York: Penguin Books, 1990), p. 277.

14. "Memorandum of Conversation between President John F. Kennedy and General Joseph Mobutu, Commander-in-Chief of the Congolese Army," May 31, 1963, National Security Files (NSF), John F. Kennedy Library (JFKL). Cited in Sean Kelly, *America's Tyrant: The CIA and Mobutu of Zaire* (Lanham, MD: American University Press, 1993), p. 2.

15. Reuters, "Mobutu Leaves Congo Thursday for U.S. Visit," *Washington Post*, May 15, 1963; and J. Anthony Lukas, "U.S. to Help Congo Retrain Military," *New York Times*, May 15, 1963.

16. George Weeks, "U.S. Training Congolese Troops in Preparation for UN Pullout," *Washington Post*, July 3, 1963.

17. "U.S. Helping to Build Congo Policy Force," *New York Times*, February 19, 1964.

18. "Final U.S. Arms Aid Due in Congo in June," *New York Times*, April 30, 1964.

19. Kelly, *America's Tyrant*, p. 96.

20. George Shepherd, "Congo Intervention Again," *Africa Today* 14, no. 4 (August 1967): 3.

21. "Intelligence Cable Regarding Assassination Activities of Paracommandos in the Congolese Town of Leopoldville." Cable to Central Intelligence Agency, August 22, 1964. Reproduced in *Declassified Documents Reference System* (Farmington Hills, MI: Gale, 2015).

22. Sheldon Vance oral history interview, p. 17.

23. Rusk, *As I Saw It*, p. 280.

24. Sheldon Vance oral history interview, pp. 19–20.

25. Weiner, *Legacy of Ashes*, p. 281.

26. "Dictator Mobutu" *Chicago Defender*, July 9, 1966; "U.S. Makes Plea for Clemency," *New York Times*, June 3, 1966; and "Mobutu Cites Past to Defend Hangings," *New York Times*, June 5, 1966.

27. Directorate of Intelligence, Central Intelligence Agency (CIA), "Memorandum of Intelligence: The Congo's Joseph Mobutu," (June 1966), p. 3, http://www.foia.cia.gov/docs/DOC_0000333466/DOC_0000333466.pdf.

28. Ibid.

29. John Latz, "Mobutu Turns Congo into a Police State," *Chicago Tribune*, October 2, 1966.

30. George Godley cables Secretary of State Dean Rusk requesting he be removed from his post as U.S. ambassador to the Congo following accusations by Congolese President Joseph-Désiré Mobutu that Godley is supporting former Prime Minister Moise Tshombe in a bid to take over the government. Godley thinks it is in the best interests of the U.S. for him to leave the Congo. Cable to Department of State, October 10, 1966. Reproduced in *Declassified Documents Reference System* (Farmington Hills, MI: Gale, 2015).

31. Weeks, "U.S. Training Congolese Troops in Preparation for UN Pullout."

32. Russell Freeburg, "U.S. Backs Congo Rule by Mobutu," *Chicago Tribune*, July 7, 1967; and Russell Freeburg, "U.S. Sends 3 Air Carriers to Aid Congo," *Chicago Tribune*, July 10, 1967.

33. "Pres. Mobutu has requested US assistance, and Foreign Min. Bomboko has asked that the US send a battalion of paratroopers to quash the revolt before it becomes established. Bomboko feels even 'so-called progressive' African states would favor US intervention against mercenaries and Tshombists. Am Emb views that US failure to respond appropriately to Mobutu could eventually swing Congo towards UAR, Algeria, or Soviet Union." Telegram from the American Embassy in Kinshasa to the Department of State, July 6, 1967. Johnson Library, NSF, "Countries, Congo," vol. 13. Reproduced in *Declassified Documents Reference System* (Farmington Hills, MI: Gale, 2015).

34. Freeburg, "U.S. Sends 3 Aircraft Carriers to Aid Congo."

35. J. Y. Smith, "Hill Leaders Decry Air Aid for the Congo," *Washington Post*, July 11, 1967.

36. Benjamin Welles, "U.S. Terminating Airlift of Troops in Congo Revolt," *New York Times*, August 5, 1967.

37. "Leak in Washington of Amb. McBride's demarche to Foreign Min. re Tshombe against mercenaries. US Amb. McBride objected on grounds that too many people would try to board planes, making for a dangerous situation. Mobutu then claimed that US denial of mission was based on Congo's expulsion of three AP staffers. Matters worsened later when Foreign Min. Bomboko suggested that C-130's might as well leave now. An official request for their withdrawal may follow." Telegram no. 2049 from the American Embassy in Kinshasa to the Department of State, Aug. 5, 1967. Johnson Library, NSF, "Countries, Congo," vol. 13. Reproduced in *Declassified Documents Reference System* (Farmington Hills, MI: Gale, 2015).

38. Cable regarding Secretary of State Dean Rusk's recommendation that the U.S. discourage a U.S. visit by Congolese President Joseph-Désiré Mobutu." Cable to Department of State, September 29, 1967. Reproduced in *Declassified Documents Reference System* (Farmington Hills, MI: Gale, 2015).

39. Richard Nixon, "Remarks of Welcome to President Joseph Desire Mobutu of the Democratic Republic of the Congo," The American Presidency Project, August 4, 1970, http://www.presidency.ucsb.edu/ws/?pid=2610#axzz1oM9XnRD5.

40. Richard Nixon, "Toasts of the President and President Mobutu of the Democratic Republic of the Congo," The American Presidency Project, August 4, 1970, http://www.presidency.ucsb.edu/ws/?pid=2611#axzz1oM9XnRD5.

41. Schatzberg, *Mobutu or Chaos?*, p. 64.

42. National Archives, Nixon Presidential Materials, NSC Files, Box 1027, Presidential/HAK Memcons, April–November 1973. Secret. The meeting took place in the Oval Office of the White House. Kissinger had met with Mobutu on October 3, in New York, during the UN General Assembly, and previewed the issues discussed here. "Document 258: Memorandum of Conversation," in *FRUS 1969–1976*, Volume E-6, Documents on Africa, 1973–1976 (October 10, 1973), Washington, D.C., October 10, 1973, http://history.state.gov/historicaldocuments/frus1969-76ve06/d258.

43. Elise Forbes Pachter, "Our Man in Kinshasa: U.S. Relations with Mobutu, 1970–83; Patron Client Relations in the International Sphere," (PhD diss., School of Advanced International Studies, Johns Hopkins University, 1987), p. 243.

44. Gerald Ford, "Message from President Ford to Mobutu," telegram to the Department of State, November 1, 1974, from the American Embassy in Kinshasa, Zaire.

45. Walter Cutler, "Secretary's Trip to Zaire; Biographic Data on Mobutu Sese Seko; President of Zaire," telegram to the Department of State, April 21, 1976, from the American Embassy in Kinshasa, Zaire.

46. "Telegram 13019 from Secretary of State Kissinger in Oslo to the Embassy in Zaire, May 20, 1976, 1335Z," FRUS 1969–1976, Documents on Africa, 1973–1976, vol. E-6, doc. 296, http://history.state.gov/historicaldocuments/frus1969-76ve06/d296.

47. Sheldon B. Vance, on the subject of M-16s for Zaire, in "Telegram 1948 from the Embassy in Zaire to the Department of State, March 4, 1974, 1508Z," FRUS 1969–1976, Documents on Africa, 1973–1976, vol. E-6, doc. 261, http://history.state.gov/historicaldocuments/frus1969-76ve06/d261. Portugal was dealing with the issue of decolonization in Angola at this time, and Portuguese authorities were concerned about neighboring Zaire's intentions and policies. A close security relationship between Kinshasa and Beijing would have been viewed as extremely troubling.

48. Deane Hinton, "Arms Sales to Zaire," telegram to the Department of State, October 7, 1974, from the American Embassy in Kinshasa, Zaire.

49. Deane Hinton, "Press Attack on Ambassador Hinton," telegram to the Department of State, February 7, 1975, from the American Embassy in Kinshasa, Zaire.

50. Deane Hinton, "An American in Kinshasa," telegram to the Department of State, February 8, 1975, from the American Embassy in Kinshasa, Zaire.

51. Thomas A. Johnson, "An Anti-US Plan by Zaire Is Seen," New York Times, June 23, 1975.

52. Thomas A. Johnson, "Mobutu Reports a Coup Attempt," New York Times, June 18, 1975.

53. "Special U.S. Envoy Seeks Reconciliation," Washington Post, June 23, 1975; and Murrey Marder, "Top Aide to Quit at State Dept.," Washington Post, September 1, 1975.

54. "Vance-Mobutu: Angola: 2nd Meeting, July 20," telegram to the Department of State, July 20, 1975, from the American Embassy in Kinshasa, Zaire.

55. Tad Szulc, "Our Man Mobutu," The New Republic, February 21, 1976, p. 6. See also Kelly, America's Tyrant, p. 216.

56. James Brooke, "C.I.A. Said to Send Weapons Via Zaire to Angola Rebels," New York Times, February 1, 1987.

57. Prados, Presidents' Secret Wars, p. 347.

58. Henry Kissinger, Years of Renewal (New York: Simon & Schuster, 1999), p. 803.

59. Michael Newlin, "FAA Section 32—Political Prisoners," telegram to the Department of State, April 16, 1974, from the American Embassy in Kinshasa, Zaire.

60. "Mobutu Criticizes 'Certain Foreign Journalists' for 'Lies,'" telegram to the Department of State, September 24, 1974, from the American Embassy in Kinshasa, Zaire.

61. Walter Cutler, "Political Stability of Mobutu's Regime," telegram to the Department of State, July 10, 1976, from the American Embassy in Kinshasa, Zaire.

62. Henry Kissinger, "Congressional Request for Human Rights Information," telegram to the American Embassy in Kinshasa, Zaire, September 29, 1976, from Washington.

63. Walter Cutler, "Human Rights Report to Congress," telegram to Department of State, October 1, 1976, from the American Embassy in Kinshasa, Zaire.

64. Schatzberg, *Mobutu or Chaos?* p. 66.

65. Cyrus Vance, *Hard Choices: Critical Years in America's Foreign Policy* (New York: Simon & Schuster, 1983), p. 70.

66. Ibid., p. 70.

67. According to National Security Advisor Zbigniew Brzezinski, there were broader strategic motives for assisting the paratroop operation in Zaire. "This was not only an important step showing our determination," he said, but "will convey a message" to a high-level visiting Chinese delegation. Zbigniew Brzezinski, *Power and Principle: Memoirs of the National Security Adviser, 1977–1981*, 2nd ed. (New York: Farrar, Straus, Giroux, 1985), p. 209. His comment suggests that while Cyrus Vance may not have viewed the disorder in Zaire primarily through the lens of a global geopolitical contest, Brzezinski did not appear to share that opinion.

68. Vance, *Hard Choices*, p. 70.

69. Kelly, *America's Tyrant*, p. 238.

70. "Young Hails Carter's Africa Policy," *Chicago Tribune*, May 11, 1977.

71. David Lamb, "Since Shaba Invasion, Mobutu of Zaire Seems to Count U.S. among His Friends," *Los Angeles Times*, July 22, 1977.

72. Vance, *Hard Choices*, pp. 90–92.

73. President Jimmy Carter, "The President's News Conference," The American Presidency Project, March 24, 1977, http://www.presidency.ucsb.edu/ws/index.php?pid=7229&st=&st1=#axzz1oM9XnRD5.

74. Jimmy Carter, "Statement regarding President Meeting with Mobutu Sese Seko of Zaire," The American Presidency Project, September 11, 1979, http://www.presidency.ucsb.edu/ws/?pid=31320#axzz1oM9XnRD5.

75. Jack Foisie, "Zaire's Gen. Mobutu Is the Sort of Ally the U.S. Would Like to Do Without," *Los Angeles Times*, June 4, 1978.

76. Congressional Research Service, Library of Congress, "Human Rights Conditions in Selected Countries and the U.S. Response" (Washington: Government Printing Office, July 25, 1978), pp. 338–46.

77. U.S. House of Representatives, Committee on Foreign Affairs, Hearing before the Subcommittee on Africa, *Political and Economic Situation in Zaire—Fall 1981* (Washington: Government Printing Office, July 1982).

78. Dusko Doder, "Diplomat Charges Cables Were Ignored," *Washington Post*, December 30, 1979.

79. James M. Scott, *Deciding to Intervene: The Reagan Doctrine and American Foreign Policy* (Durham, NC: Duke University Press, 1996), pp. 137–38.

80. "White House Statement on a Meeting between President Reagan and President Mobutu Sese Seko of Zaire," December 1, 1981, The American Presidency Project, http://www.presidency.ucsb.edu/ws/?pid=43303#axzz1oM9XnRD5.

81. "Two versions of a letter to Zairian President Mobutu Sese Seko from President Ronald Reagan regarding: Soviet aggression in Angola; relations between Libya and Zaire; U.S. economic assistance to Zaire; U.S.-Zairian relations." Letter from the White House to President Mobutu Sese Seko, February 18, 1986. Reproduced in *Declassified Documents Reference System* (Farmington Hills, MI: Gale, 2015).

82. "House Panel Cuts Aid to 3 Nations in Africa," *New York Times*, May 12, 1982.

83. Don Oberdorfer, "Zaire, Stung by Criticism, to Renounce U.S. Aid," *Washington Post*, May 14, 1982.

84. U.S. House of Representatives, Committee on Foreign Affairs, Hearing before the Subcommittee on Human Rights and International Organizations and the Subcommittee on Africa, *The Human Rights Situation in South Africa, Zaire, the Horn of Africa, and Uganda* (Washington: Government Printing Office, 1985).

85. "Text of Zairian President Mobutu Sese Seko's (former Joseph-Désiré Mobutu) comments during U.S. Ambassador William Harrop's credential presentation ceremony in Kinshasa. Points include: Zairian support of U.S. policy in Angola; request for U.S. military assistance; cancellation of Mobutu's planned U.S. visit." Cable to the Department of State, January 29, 1988. Reproduced in *Declassified Documents Reference System* (Farmington Hills, MI: Gale, 2015).

86. Schatzberg, *Mobutu or Chaos?* p.70.

87. George Bush, "Remarks Following Discussions with President Mobutu Sese Seko of Zaire," The American Presidency Project, June 29, 1989, http://www .presidency.ucsb.edu/ws/index.php?pid=17223#axzz1oM9XnRD5.

88. Makau wa Mutua, "Zaire Doesn't Deserve That Aid," *Washington Post*, September 18, 1990.

89. Clifford Kraus, "U.S. Cuts Aid to Zaire, Setting Off Policy Debate," *New York Times*, November 4, 1990.

90. "SECTION NOTES: Administration's Warning to Zaire's Ruler," *CQ Weekly Online* (November 9, 1991): 3300, http://library.cqpress.com/cqweekly /WR102405284.

91. Quoted in Kelly, *America's Tyrant*, p. 254.

92. For a discussion of the final stages of Mobutu's dictatorship, see Jeanne M. Haskin, *The Tragic State of the Congo: From Decolonization to Dictatorship* (New York: Algora, 2005), pp. 73–82.

93. Ibid., pp. 87–129.

94. Kwitny, *Endless Enemies,* p. 48.

95. Ibid., p. 41.

96. Ibid., p. 42.

97. Interview with Sheldon Vance by Mike Wallace of *60 Minutes*, Tuesday, January 24, 1984,. Transcript, p. 13. Sheldon and Jean Vance Papers, Minnesota Historical Society, Locator 147, H3, 2F.

98. Ibid., p. 23.

99. Sheldon Vance oral history interview, p. 20.

100. Quoted in Stephen R. Weissman, *American Foreign Policy in the Congo, 1960– 1964* (Ithaca, NY: Cornell University Press, 1974), p. 280.

101. Kissinger, *Years of Renewal*, p. 803.

102. Ibid., pp. 800–01,804–05, 943–44.

103. A similar lack of attention emerges in the memoirs of various secretaries of state. With the exceptions of Henry Kissinger and Cyrus Vance, most of them scarcely mention the U.S. relationship with Zaire. The country is treated as little more than an afterthought.

Chapter 9

1. Ronald Reagan, *An American Life* (New York: Simon and Schuster, 1990), p. 362.

2. "Philippine 'No. 1': Ferdinand Edralin Marcos," *New York Times*, November 13, 1965.

3. Lyndon Baines Johnson, *The Vantage Point: Perspectives of the Presidency, 1963–1969* (Holt, Rinehart, and Winston, 1971), p. 363.

4. Ibid., p. 359.

5. Quoted in Raymond Bonner, *Waltzing with a Dictator: The Marcoses and the Making of American Policy* (New York: Times Books, 1987), p. 53.

6. Sterling Seagrave, *The Marcos Dynasty* (New York: Harper and Row, 1988), p. 205.

7. Ibid., p. 205.

8. Mark R. Thompson, *The Anti-Marcos Struggle: Personalistic Rule and Democratic Transition in the Philippines* (New Haven, CT: Yale University Press, 1995), pp. 34–45.

9. Bonner, *Waltzing with a Dictator*, p. 5.

10. Ibid., p. 6.

11. Ibid., p. 96.

12. Ibid., pp. 107–10.

13. Ibid., p. 63.

14. Thompson, *The Anti-Marcos Struggle*, p. 54.

15. Quoted in Bonner, *Waltzing with a Dictator*, p. 168.

16. Testimony of Patricia Derian, U.S. Congress, House, Committee on Foreign Affairs, "Reconciling Human Rights and U.S. Security Interests in Asia," Hearings before the Subcommittee on Asian and Pacific Affairs and on Human Rights and International Organizations, 97th Cong., 2nd sess., 1982, p. 4.

17. Quoted in George Russell, "A Test for Democracy," *Time*, February 3, 1986, http://content.time.com/time/magazine/article/0,9171,960545,00.html.

18. For a discussion of how Marcos and his wife built and then consolidated their family's political and economic power, see Seagrave, *The Marcos Dynasty*.

19. Thompson, *The Anti-Marcos Struggle*, pp. 114–17.

20. Seagrave, *The Marcos Dynasty*, pp. 385–86.

21. Jonathan Kwitny, *Endless Enemies: The Making of an Unfriendly World* (New York: Congdon and Weed, 1985), p. 302.

22. Ibid., p. 304.

23. Bonner, *Waltzing with a Dictator*, p. 326.

24. Theodore Friend, "Timely Daring: The United States and Ferdinand Marcos," in *Friendly Tyrants: An American Dilemma*, ed. Daniel Pipes and Adam Garfinkle (New York: St. Martin's Press, 1991), pp. 206–7.

25. Ibid., p. 207.

26. Ross H. Munro, "The New Khmer Rouge," *Commentary* 80, no. 6 (December 1985): 19–38.

27. Ibid., p. 19.

28. Ibid., p. 38.

29. A. James Gregor, "The Key Role of U.S. Bases in the Philippines," Heritage Foundation, Asian Backgrounder no. 7, January 10, 1984, p. 10.

30. Ibid., p. 8.

31. Ibid., p. 11.

32. Ibid., p. 9.

33. William F. Buckley Jr., "What to Do about the Philippines," *Pittsburgh Post-Gazette*, October 31, 1985.

34. Jeane Kirkpatrick, "The Philippines in Global Chess Game," *Bangor Daily News*, December 14–15, 1985.

35. Anthony Lewis, "Abroad at Home: Reagan Faces Life," *New York Times*, February 10, 1986.

36. Munro, "The New Khmer Rouge," p. 19.

37. George P. Shultz, *Turmoil and Triumph: My Years as Secretary of State* (New York: Charles Scribner's, 1993), pp. 608–9.

38. Ibid., p. 610.

39. Ibid.

40. Vanderbilt University has the actual clip available on loan: see "CBS Evening News for Tuesday, May 15, 1984," Vanderbilt Television News Archive, http://tvnews.vanderbilt.edu/program.pl?ID=296964. The quote first appeared in print in Associated Press, May 15, 1984, Domestic News, PM Cycle, Dateline New York.

41. Shultz, *Turmoil and Triumph*, p. 611.

42. Ibid., p. 613.

43. On Armacost's role in helping to shift U.S. policy, see Thompson, *The Anti-Marcos Struggle*, pp. 107, 121.

44. Shultz, *Turmoil and Triumph*, p. 613.

45. For a discussion of the gradual build up of the domestic opposition to Marcos, culminating in the 1986 demonstrations, see Thompson, *The Anti-Marcos Struggle*, pp. 146–61.

46. Shultz, *Turmoil and Triumph*, p. 618.

47. Ibid., p. 625.

48. Thompson, *The Anti-Marcos Struggle*, pp. 149–61.

49. Quoted in Shultz, *Turmoil and Triumph*, pp. 630–31. Emphasis in original.

50. Reagan, *An American Life*, p. 364.

51. Ibid., p. 366.

52. Commission on Presidential Debates, "The Second Reagan-Mondale Presidential Debate," October 21, 1984, http://www.debates.org/index.php?page=october-21-1984-debate-transcript.

53. Friend, "Timely Daring," p. 201.

54. Bonner, *Waltzing with a Dictator*, p. 7.

55. Ibid., p. 7.

56. Ibid., p. 50.

57. Shultz, *Turmoil and Triumph*, p. 614.

58. Quoted in Alex R. Seith, "George Says It," *Blue Island Sun Standard* (Blue Island, IL), June 19, 1977, p. 13, http://www.newspapers.com/newspage/18243555/.

59. Gregor, "The Key Role of U.S. Bases in the Philippines," p. 10.

60. Carl Rowan, "Repeating Bad History," *Newsday*, September 2, 1983.

61. Quoted in "U.S. Warns It Would Act to Hold Bases in Philippines," *Deseret News* (Salt Lake City), December 12, 1985.

62. Ronald Reagan, "The President's News Conference," February 11, 1986, The American Presidency Project, http://www.presidency.ucsb.edu/ws/index.php?pid=36870#axzz1r5TdfKpn.

63. See John D. Lawlor, "No Need for Review; U.S. Must Have Bases," *USA Today*, February 2, 1990.

64. Both quotes in Al Kamen, "East Asia Alignments Altered with Ending of the Cold War," *Washington Post*, November 26, 1990.

65. "U.S. Bases Pullout from Philippines to Weaken Military," *Japan Economic Newswire* (Tokyo), August 21, 1991.

66. For a contemporary discussion of the modest—at most—strategic relevance of the Philippine bases, see Ted Galen Carpenter, "The U.S. Military Presence in the Philippines: Expensive and Unnecessary," Cato Institute Foreign Policy Briefing no. 12, July 29, 1991.

67. A good profile of Aquino and her views is found in Robert H. Reid and Ellen Guerrero, *Corazon Aquino and the Brushfire Revolution* (Baton Rouge, LA: Louisiana State University Press, 1995).

Chapter 10

1. John Lewis Gaddis, *The Long Peace: Inquiries into the History of the Cold War* (New York: Oxford University Press, 1989).

2. "The Ambassador in Yugoslavia ([Richard C.] Patterson) to the Secretary of State [Stettinius]," April 9, 1945, FRUS 1945, vol. V, p. 1218, http://digital.library.wisc .edu/1711.dl/FRUS.FRUS1945v05.

3. "Memorandum of Meeting with the President at Twelve O'Clock, August 31, 1945 at the White House," Papers of Richard C. Patterson Jr., Truman Presidential Library.

4. Lorraine M. Lees, *Keeping Tito Afloat: The United States, Yugoslavia, and the Cold War* (University Park, PA: Pennsylvania State University Press, 1997), p. 6.

5. "Telegram from Clark M. Clifford to President Truman, September 15, 1947." Papers of Robert L. Dennison, Truman Presidential Library.

6. See, for example, "Yugoslavia: Biting the Hand," editorial, *Newsweek*, August 26, 1946.

7. U.S. Department of State, "Policy and Information Statement on Yugoslavia, July 30, 1946." Papers of James F. Byrnes, Truman Presidential Library.

8. See Peter Stavrakis, *Moscow and Greek Communism, 1944–1949* (Ithaca, NY: Cornell University Press, 1989); and Vladislav Zubok and Constantine Pleshakov, *Inside the Kremlin's Cold War: From Stalin to Khrushchev* (Cambridge, MA: Harvard University Press, 1996), pp. 56–57.

9. Jeronim Perović, "The Tito-Stalin Split: A Reassessment in Light of New Evidence," *Journal of Cold War Studies* 9, no. 2 (Spring 2007): 32–63; and Leonid Gibianskii, "The Origins of the Soviet-Yugoslav Split," in *The Establishment of Communist Regimes in Eastern Europe, 1944–1949*, ed. Norman Naimark and Leonid Gibianskii (Boulder, CO: Westview Press, 1997), pp. 291–312. Documents released from the Soviet archives since the disintegration of the USSR in 1991 indicate that the depth and bitterness of the split between Stalin and Tito was even deeper than previously thought.

10. Robert A. Garson, "American Foreign Policy and the Limits of Power: Eastern Europe 1946–50," *Journal of Contemporary History* 21, no. 3 (July 1986): 347–66.

11. Lees, *Keeping Tito Afloat*, p. 53.

12. Policy Planning Staff 35, "The Attitude of This Government toward Events in Yugoslavia," June 30, 1948, Papers of Harry S. Truman, President's Secretary's Files, Truman Presidential Library, p. 3.

13. Ibid., pp. 4–5.

14. Lees, *Keeping Tito Afloat*, p. 111.

15. In a speech before the Veterans of Foreign Wars shortly before Congress approved MDAP, Truman stressed that the aid program was needed because "our European partners in the North Atlantic Treaty are not strong enough today to

defend themselves effectively." He added: "We can strengthen them, and ourselves, by transferring some military means to them, and joining with them in a common defense plan." Harry S. Truman, *Years of Trial and Hope, 1946–1952* (Garden City, NY: Doubleday and Company, 1956), p. 251.

16. For a historical assessment that echoes some of the contemporary conservative criticism, see Nora Beloff, *Tito's Flawed Legacy: Yugoslavia and the West Since 1939* (Boulder, CO: Westview Press, 1986).

17. Stephen E. Ambrose, *Eisenhower: The President* (New York: Simon & Schuster, 1984), p. 380.

18. Lees, *Keeping Tito Afloat*, pp. 156–58, 215–16, 226.

19. Dwight D. Eisenhower, *The White House Years: Mandate for Change, 1953–1956* (Garden City, NY: Doubleday and Company, 1963), p. 412.

20. Ibid., p. 414.

21. Josip Močnik, "United States-Yugoslav Relations, 1961–1980: The Twilight of Tito's Era and the Role of Ambassadorial Diplomacy in the Making of America's Yugoslav Policy" (PhD diss., Bowling Green State University, 2008), pp. 10–11.

22. Ibid., p. 11.

23. Ibid., pp. 16–17.

24. "Memorandum of Conversation between the President and George F. Kennan, American Ambassador to Yugoslavia, March 22, 1961," Yugoslavia General Folder, National Security Files, Box 209A, JFK Library. Cited in Močnik, p. 17.

25. John R. Lampe, Russell O. Prickett, and Ljubiša S. Adamović, *Yugoslav-American Economic Relations since World War II* (Durham, NC: Duke University Press, 1990), p. 47.

26. John Lewis Gaddis, *Strategies of Containment: A Critical Appraisal of American National Security Policy during the Cold War*, revised edition (New York: Oxford University Press, 2005), pp. 266–67.

27. George Christian, press release, White House Press Corps, October 14, 1968.

28. John C. Campbell, *Tito's Separate Road: America and Yugoslavia in World Politics* (New York: Harper & Row, 1967), p. 22. Other analysts of this period reach a similar conclusion. See, for example, Nick S. Ceh, "United States-Yugoslav Relations during the Early Cold War, 1945–1957" (PhD diss., University of Illinois–Chicago, 1998).

29. Useful accounts of both Tito's ideology and conduct in power include Neil Barnett, *Tito* (London: Haus Publishing, Ltd., 2006); and Geoffrey Swain, *Tito: A Biography* (London: I. B. Taurus, 2010).

30. Močnik, "United States-Yugoslav Relations, 1961–1980," p. 74.

31. Quoted in ibid., p. 78.

32. "Comments of a Yugoslav Official Concerning Vietnam," Intelligence Information Cable, March 11, 1965, Country File: Yugoslavia, vol. 1. Cables 1/64–4/66, NSF, Box 232, Lyndon B. Johnson Presidential Library.

33. Henry Kissinger, *White House Years* (Boston: Little, Brown, and Company, 1979), p. 928.

34. Ibid., p. 928.

35. Ibid., pp. 928–29.

36. "Incoming Telegram from Belgrade to Secretary of State," No. 587, February 7, 1961, Yugoslavia General Folder, National Security Files, Box 209A, John F. Kennedy Presidential Library. Cited in Močnik, "United States-Yugoslav Relations, 1961–1980," p. 15.

37. William Zimmerman, *Open Borders, Nonalignment, and the Political Evolution of Yugoslavia* (Princeton: Princeton University Press, 1987), p. 29.

38. Kissinger, *White House Years*, p. 929.

39. "The Maverick Who Defied Moscow," *Time*, May 12, 1980.

40. Welles Hangen,"Peaceful Shifts in Rumania Seen," *New York Times*, October 26, 1956.

41. David Binder, "Ceausescu of Rumania: Man Battering at the Kremlin Wall," *New York Times*, May 29, 1966.

42. John M. Lee, "Ceausescu Takes Steps to Protect Rumanian Independence from Soviet Attack," *New York Times*, August 23, 1968.

43. "Rumania: Winner Take All," *Time*, December 15, 1967.

44. Lyndon Baines Johnson, *The Vantage Point: Perspectives of the Presidency, 1963–1969* (New York: Holt, Rinehart, and Winston, 1971), p. 268.

45. Richard M. Nixon, *RN: The Memoirs of Richard Nixon* (New York: Grosset and Dunlap, 1978), pp. 395–96.

46. Kissinger, *White House Years*, p. 930.

47. Henry Kissinger, *Years of Renewal* (New York: Simon and Schuster, 1999), p. 661.

48. Jimmy Carter, *Keeping Faith: Memoirs of a President* (New York: Bantam Books, 1982), p. 472.

49. Alexander M. Haig Jr., *Caveat: Realism, Reagan, and Foreign Policy* (New York: Macmillan, 1984), p. 258.

50. Ibid.

51. Kissinger, *Years of Renewal*, pp. 660–61.

52. See Kissinger, *Years of Renewal*, pp. 657–63; and Gerald R. Ford, *A Time to Heal: The Autobiography of Gerald R. Ford*, rev. ed. (New York: Berkley Books, 1980), pp. 408–9. Indeed, President Ford's enthusiasm about the beneficial effects of the independent behavior that Yugoslavia and Romania (and to lesser extent, Poland) exhibited at Helsinki was a major cause of his overstatement about Eastern Europe's supposed lack of domination by the USSR in the presidential campaign debate with Jimmy Carter.

53. "The Attitude of This Government toward Events in Yugoslavia," p. 2.

Chapter 11

*The modern Chinese names for cities and other locales (e.g., Beijing, not Peking; Taiwan, not Formosa) will be used throughout this chapter (except in quoted passages), even though those names were often not the norm until well into the 1970s or 1980s.

1. Dean Rusk, as told to Richard Rusk, *As I Saw It* (New York: Penguin Books, 1991), p. 284.

2. For Acheson's intense opposition to either a Communist Chinese seat in the United Nations or U.S. diplomatic recognition of the Beijing regime, see Dean Acheson, *Present at the Creation: My Years in the State Department* (New York: W.W. Norton, 1969), pp. 357–58, 378, 394, 401, 418–20.

3. Harry S. Truman, *Years of Trial and Hope* (Garden City, NY: Doubleday and Company, 1956), p. 404.

4. Dwight D. Eisenhower, *The White House Years: Mandate for Change, 1953–1956* (Garden City, NY: Doubleday and Company, 1963), pp. 248–49.

5. Ibid., p. 473.

6. There were actually hints a decade earlier that the Soviets were suspicious of their Chinese colleagues and reluctant supporters of their revolution. Truman recalled that, at Potsdam, Stalin stated that the Chinese communists were "not really proper" communists. The president later dismissed that statement as merely Stalin's attempt to deceive the West about the extent of his significant support for Mao and his followers. See Truman, *Years of Trial and Hope*, p. 91. That may well have been true, but the possibility also exists that simmering tensions between the two Leninist movements may already have been present during the late 1940s.

7. Author Ted Galen Carpenter's conversation with former Kennedy administration and Johnson administration foreign policy official Walt W. Rostow, April 1997.

8. Henry Kissinger, *White House Years* (Boston: Little, Brown, 1979), p. 168.

9. Ibid., p. 183.

10. Ibid., p. 178.

11. For a discussion of the State Department bureaucracy's relentless hostility toward any notion of a balanced, triangular policy toward the Soviet Union and China—much less a triangular policy with a tilt toward China—see Kissinger, *White House Years*, pp. 178, 182, 189–90.

12. White House Staff Member and Office Files, President's Personal Files, Box 67, "Thursday, July 15, 1971" Folder, Richard Nixon Presidential Library.

13. For a good discussion of the complex domestic and international background to Nixon's opening to China, see Patrick Tyler, *A Great Wall: Six Presidents and China, an Investigative History* (New York: Public Affairs, 1999), pp. 45–103.

14. Richard M. Nixon, "Asia after Vietnam," *Foreign Affairs* 46, no. 1 (Fall 1967): 121–22.

15. Ibid., p. 123.

16. Richard M. Nixon, *RN: The Memoirs of Richard Nixon* (New York: Grosset and Dunlap, 1978), p. 545.

17. Kissinger, *White House Years*, p. 191.

18. Nixon, *RN: The Memoirs of Richard Nixon*, p. 546.

19. Ibid., p. 556. Emphasis added.

20. Quoted in ibid., p. 552

21. Ibid., pp. 553–54.

22. Ibid., p. 563.

23. Kissinger, *White House Years*, p. 165.

24. Ibid., pp. 171–72.

25. Ibid., pp. 172–73.

26. Ibid., p. 177.

27. Ibid., p. 178.

28. Nixon, *RN: The Memoirs of Richard Nixon*, p. 577.

29. Ibid., p. 571.

30. John W. Garver, *The Sino-American Alliance: Nationalist China and American Cold War Strategy in Asia* (Armonk, NY: M. E. Sharpe, 1997), p. 3.

31. Ibid., p. 4.

32. The Chinese leadership became even more candid about their fears of and hostility toward Moscow during the post-Nixon period. On his visit to China in 1975,

President Gerald Ford was struck by how blunt the Chinese leaders were on that issue. See Gerald Ford, *A Time to Heal* (New York: Berkley, 1980), p. 325.

33. Henry Kissinger, *Years of Renewal* (New York: Simon & Schuster, 1999), p. 872.

34. James Mann, *About Face: A History of America's Curious Relationship with China, from Nixon to Clinton* (New York: Vintage, 2000), p. 65.

35. Kissinger, *White House Years*, p. 191.

36. Mann, *About Face*, p. 71.

37. William F. Buckley Jr., "Nixon Diplomacy Won't Work," *Washington Star*, February 23, 1972.

38. Mann, *About Face*, p. 71.

39. Both quotes in ibid., pp. 78–79.

40. Vance insisted in his memoirs that "from the very outset, normalizing relations with the People's Republic of China was my goal and that of President Carter." Cyrus Vance, *Hard Choices: Critical Years in America's Foreign Policy* (New York: Simon & Schuster, 1983), p. 75. For Vance's concerns about trying to preserve Taiwan's independence and security within the context of establishing diplomatic relations with China, see pp. 76–79.

41. See David Tawei Lee, *The Making of the Taiwan Relations Act: Twenty Years in Retrospect* (New York: Oxford University Press, 2000).

42. For candidate Reagan's murky, often inconsistent, statements regarding China policy, see Hong N. Kim and Jack L. Hammersmith, "U.S.-China Relations in the Post-Normalization, 1979–1982," *Pacific Affairs* 59, no. 1 (Spring 1986): 69–91.

43. Alexander M. Haig Jr., *Caveat: Realism, Reagan, and Foreign Policy* (New York: Macmillan, 1984), p. 50.

44. Ibid., p. 195.

45. Ronald Reagan, *An American Life* (New York: Simon & Schuster, 1990), p. 361.

46. Tyler, *A Great Wall*, pp. 298–301, 306–10.

47. The full text of the third communiqué can be found in "Joint Communiqué of the United States of America and the People's Republic of China," August 17, 1982, http://www.taiwandocuments.org/communique03.htm.

48. George P. Shultz, *Turmoil and Triumph: My Years as Secretary of State* (New York: Charles Scribner's Sons, 1993), p. 385.

49. Ezra F. Vogel, *Deng Xiaoping and the Transformation of China* (Cambridge, MS: Harvard University Press, 2011).

50. Harry Harding, *A Fragile Relationship* (Washington: Brookings Institution, 1992), p. 169.

51. Quoted in Tyler, *A Great Wall*, p. 359.

52. For a good, concise discussion of the public and congressional reaction to the Tiananmen Square crackdown—and the congressional pressure on the administration to take a stronger stance against the Chinese government—see Harding, *A Fragile Relationship*, pp. 230–34.

53. James A. Baker III, with Thomas M. DeFrank, *The Politics of Diplomacy: Revolution, War, and Peace, 1989–1992* (New York: G. P. Putnam's Sons, 1995), p. 104.

54. Ibid., p. 105.

55. Letter to His Excellency Deng Xiaoping, June 20, 1989, reprinted in George Bush, *All the Best: My Life in Letters and Other Writings* (New York: Scribner, 1999), pp. 428–31.

56. Ibid., p. 431.

57. Letter to His Excellency Deng Xiaoping, July 21, 1989, reprinted in Bush, *All the Best*, pp. 435–37.

58. Ibid., p. 437.

59. For a discussion of Deng Xiaoping's cautious, only slightly compromising, response to the Bush administration's post-Tiananmen Square policy toward China, see Vogel, *Deng Xiaoping and the Transformation of China*, pp. 648–54; and Harding, *A Fragile Relationship*, pp. 235–39.

60. Tyler, *A Great Wall*, pp. 386–87.

61. Ibid., pp. 394–416.

62. Aaron L. Friedberg, *A Contest for Supremacy: China, America, and the Struggle for Mastery in Asia* (New York: W. W. Norton, 2011), p. 188.

63. Pew Research Center for the People and the Press, "U.S. Seen as Less Important, China as More Powerful," December 3, 2009, http://www.people-press.org/2009/12/03/us-seen-as-less-important-china-as-more-powerful/.

64. Andrew Dugan, "Americans View China Mostly Unfavorably," *Gallup Politics*, February 20, 2014, http://www.gallup.com/poll/167498/americans-view-china-mostly-unfavorably.aspx.

65. Ted Galen Carpenter, "Obama's Dangerous South China Sea Strategy," *National Interest Online*, October 21, 2013, http://www.cato.org/publications/commentary/obamas-dangerous-south-china-sea-strategy.

66. Ted Galen Carpenter, "Island Wars," *National Interest Online*, October 1, 2012, http://www.cato.org/publications/commentary/island-wars.

67. For sophisticated cases critical of the bipartisan, "soft" policy toward China, see Friedberg, *A Contest for Supremacy*; and James Mann, *The China Fantasy: How Our Leaders Explain Away Chinese Repression* (New York: Viking, 2007). For examples of shrill China-bashing, see Jed Babbin and Edward Timperlake, *Showdown: Why China Wants War with the United States* (Washington: Regnery Publishing, 2006); and Constantine C. Menges, *China: The Gathering Threat* (Nashville, TN: Nelson Current, 2005).

68. Friedberg, *A Contest for Supremacy*.

69. Mann, *About Face*, p. 8.

70. Ibid., p. 60.

Chapter 12

1. John L. Esposito, *Unholy War: Terror in the Name of Islam* (New York: Oxford University Press, 2003), p. 86.

2. Reinhard Schulze, *A Modern History of the Islamic World*, trans. Azizeh Azodi (New York: New York University Press, 2002), p. 201.

3. In a toast to the Egyptian leader, President Gerald Ford commended Sadat for "his courage, his wisdom, his broad view, and his dedication to what was needed and necessary in the Middle East." Gerald R. Ford, "Toasts at a Dinner in Jacksonville Honoring the President and President Sadat of Egypt," November 2, 1975, The American Presidency Project, http://www.presidency.ucsb.edu/ws/?pid=5354.

4. William B. Quandt, a member of President Carter's National Security Council, writes that Sadat was fed up with Carter's inability to pressure Israel. See William B. Quandt, *Peace Process: American Diplomacy and the Arab-Israeli Conflict Since 1967* (Berkeley: University of California Press, 2005), p. 268.

5. P. J. Vatikiotis, *The History of Modern Egypt: From Muhammad Ali to Mubarak* (Baltimore: Johns Hopkins University Press, 1991), p. 412; and Tewfik E. Farah, *Pan-Arabism and Arab Nationalism: The Continuing Debate* (Boulder, CO: Westview, 1987), p. 144.

6. Sadat's address to the Knesset, November 20, 1977, in William B. Quandt, "Camp David and Peacemaking in the Middle East," *Political Science Quarterly* 101, no. 3 (1986): 351–53.

7. Jimmy Carter, "The President's News Conference," November 30, 1977, The American Presidency Project, http://www.presidency.ucsb.edu/ws/?pid=6962; and Quandt, *Peace Process*, p. 257.

8. Elias Shoufani, "The Reaction in Israel to the Sadat Initiative," *Journal of Palestine Studies* vol. 7, no. 2 (Winter 1978): 3–25.

9. Boutros Boutros-Ghali, *Egypt's Road to Jerusalem: A Diplomat's Story of the Struggle for Peace in the Middle East* (New York: Random House, 1997), p. 22.

10. Before becoming president, Carter endorsed a controversial December 1975 Brookings Institution report on an Arab-Israeli settlement. It called for: (1) Arabs to accept Israel's right to exist behind secure borders; (2) Israel to withdraw from the occupied territories; and (3) a "provision for Palestinian self-determination." Many of the report's suggestions were incorporated into policy. Brookings Middle East Study Group, *Toward Peace in the Middle East* (Washington: Brookings Institution, 1975). For more on Carter's conception of a "comprehensive" settlement and what it would entail, see Jimmy Carter, *White House Diary* (New York: Farrar, Straus, and Giroux, 2010), p. 71. See also Quandt, *Peace Process*, pp. 260–63. On Carter's endorsement of the Brookings study, see Zbigniew Brzezinski, *Power and Principle: Memoirs of the National Security Adviser, 1977–1981* (New York: Farrar Straus and Giroux, 1983), pp. 84–85, 256.

11. Palestinians were a "quasi-independent force with veto over policy in Jordan, and perhaps even in Lebanon." Henry Kissinger, *White House Years* (Boston: Little, Brown, 1979) p. 573. Also see Steven L. Spiegel, *The Other Arab-Israeli Conflict: Making America's Middle East Policy, from Truman to Reagan* (Chicago: University of Chicago Press, 1985), pp. 285, 288.

12. See Jimmy Carter, "Aliquippa, Pennsylvania, Remarks and a Question-and-Answer Session at a Town Meeting," in *Public Papers of the Presidents of the United States, September 23, 1978* (Washington: Government Printing Office, 1979) p. 1612 (the quote is on 1612); see also Jimmy Carter: "Aliquippa, Pennsylvania, Remarks and a Question-and-Answer Session at a Town Meeting," September 23, 1978, The American Presidency Project, http://www.presidency.ucsb.edu/ws/?pid=29846.

13. Cyrus Vance, *Hard Choices: Critical Years in America's Foreign Policy* (New York: Simon & Schuster, 1983), pp. 162–63.

14. Wilbur Crane Eveland, *Ropes of Sand: America's Failure in the Middle East* (New York: W.W. Norton, 1980), p. 245.

15. Boutros-Ghali, *Egypt's Road to Jerusalem*, pp. 53, 166.

16. Mohamed Ibrahim Kamel, *The Camp David Accords: A Testimony by Sadat's Foreign Minister* (London: KPI Limited, 1986), p. 313; Quandt, "Camp David and Peacemaking," p. 365; Boutros-Ghali, *Egypt's Road to Jerusalem*, p. 165; and Brzezinski, *Power and Principle*, pp. 260, 262.

17. Boutros-Ghali, *Egypt's Road to Jerusalem*, pp. 21, 46, 133, 166.

18. Others who resigned include Minister of Foreign Affairs Ismail Fahmy and Minister of State for Foreign Affairs Mohamed Riad. See Kamel, *The Camp David Accords*, p. 292. For Kamel on Israeli policies, see p. 366. Also see Boutros-Ghali, *Egypt's Road to Jerusalem*, p. 146.

19. Brzezinski, *Power and Principle*, p. 258.

20. George Lenczowski, *American Presidents and the Middle East* (Durham, NC: Duke University Press, 1990), pp. 175–77.

21. Quandt, *Peace Process*, p. 268; see also William B. Quandt, "Camp David and Peacemaking," pp. 125–31; and Martin Gilbert, *The Routledge Atlas of the Arab-Israeli Conflict* (London: Routledge, 1993), pp. 45–89.

22. Brzezinski, *Power and Principle*, pp. 279–80.

23. Boutros-Ghali, *Egypt's Road to Jerusalem*, pp. 144, 159.

24. Marvine Howe, "P.L.O. Condemns Speech by Sadat, Calls for 'Sanctions' against Him," *New York Times*, November 21, 1977; Baghdad Summit: "The Palestinian Question is the Essence of the Conflict," *Middle East Research and Information Project Reports*, no. 73 (December 1978): 22–23; and "Radical Arabs Win Fight to Punish Egypt, but Can They?" *New York Times*, April 9, 1979.

25. Nations with which Cairo cut ties included Algeria, Syria, Libya, and South Yemen. "Radical Arabs Win Fight to Punish Egypt, but Can They?" See also Brzezinski, *Power and Principle*, p. 283; Quandt, *Peace Process*, p. 271; and Quandt, "Camp David and Peacemaking," p. 152.

26. The figures declined somewhat in the mid-1990s, but they remained considerable. The United States gave Israel nearly $3.2 billion in aid between 1949 and 1973 and nearly $75 billion between 1974 and 1997. "The Final, Extra Mile," *Time*, March 19, 1979. Aid was granted to the countries as part of the Pentagon's Foreign Military Financing as grant transfers and USAID's Economic Support Fund (ESF). According to the State Department, ESF's purpose is to support "strategically significant friends" and provide "economic assistance to allies and countries." See "Special International Security Assistance Act of 1979," S. 1007, 96th Cong., http://thomas.loc.gov/cgi -bin/bdquery/z?d096:SN01007:@@@L&summ2=m& | TOM:/bss/d096query.html. Under special circumstances, additional assistance was offered, such as in 1990 when Congress wrote off nearly $7 billion of Egypt's military debt from previous years. See Quandt, *Peace Process*, p. 416; and "The Final, Extra Mile."

27. Robert Satloff and Patrick Clawson, "U.S. Economic Aid to Egypt: Designing a New, Pro-Growth Package," Policy Watch no. 324, Washington Institute for Near East Policy, July 7, 1998. By 2000, the Egyptian government employed one-third of Egypt's labor force. The U.S. government spent about $200 million to develop Egypt's domestic cement industry, even though cement could be imported more cheaply. Ibrahim Elbadawi and Norman Loayza, "Informality, Employment and Economic Development in the Arab World," *Journal of Development and Economic Policies* 10, no. 2 (July 2008): 25–75.

28. Anwar al-Sadat, "Message to the Middle East Development Conference," June 7, 1976, http://sadat.umd.edu/archives/Written_Works/AAHP%20MidEast%20 Develop%206.7.76.pdf.PDF. Many of these policies were implemented under pressure from the International Monetary Fund.

29. Robert Dreyfuss, *Devil's Game: How the United States Helped Unleash Fundamentalist Islam* (New York: Metropolitan Books, 2006), p. 163; Brzezinski, *Power and Principle*, p. 280; and Henry F. Jackson, "Sadat's Perils," *Foreign Policy* 42 (Spring 1981): 58–73.

30. Anwar al-Sadat, "The Glorious Days of October: From the October Working Paper by President Mohamed Anwar El Sadat," April 1974, http://sadat.umd.edu /archives/Written_Works/AAFB%20Glorious%20Days%20of%20Oct5.71.pdf.PDF.

31. Although Sadat blamed the attack on Libya, Salih Sirriya, a member of the Islamic Liberation Party (Hizb-ut Tahrir), an Islamist movement dedicated to restoring the caliphate, was the ringleader. Sirriya was from Ijzim, a small town near Haifa, Israel. See Gilles Kepel, *Muslim Extremism in Egypt: The Prophet and Pharaoh* (Berkeley: University of California Press, 1986), p. 93.

32. "Cracking Down," *Time*, September 14, 1981; and Anwar El Sadat, *In Search of Identity: An Autobiography*, (New York: Harper and Row, 1978), p. 224.

33. Egyptian Islamist group Al-Gama'a al-Islamiyya may have also been involved in the conspiracy, as Omar Abdel-Rahman (the "blind sheikh"), the group's spiritual leader, was charged, but not convicted, of issuing a fatwa resulting in the assassination. Some believe that to assassinate Sadat, Islamists had to have infiltrated the military. Lawrence Wright, *The Looming Tower: Al-Qaeda and the Road to 9/11* (New York: Vintage, 2007), p. 49; Marie-Christine Aulas, "Sadat's Egypt: A Balance Sheet," *MERIP Reports* 107 (July–August 1982): 6–18, 30–31; Henry F. Jackson, "Sadat's Perils," *Foreign Policy* 42 (Spring 1981): 58–73.

34. Ronald Reagan, *An American Life* (New York: Simon & Schuster, 2009), p. 420. Also, during the anti-Soviet jihad in Afghanistan, Egypt encouraged religious fighters to go to that country to combat the Soviets. John K. Cooley, *Unholy Wars: Afghanistan, America, and International Terrorism* (London: Pluto Press, 2002), pp. 31–32. By 2011, it was estimated the U.S. aid accounted for as much as 80 percent of the Egyptian Defense Ministry's weapons procurement costs. Egypt also routinely allocated just the minimum amount of FMF funds necessary for adequate support for weapon system sustainment. See Government Accountability Office, *Security Assistance: State and DOD Need to Assess How the Foreign Military Financing Program for Egypt Achieves U.S. Foreign Policy and Security Goals* (Washington: GAO, 2006); and Jeremy M. Sharp, *Egypt: Background and U.S. Relations* (Washington: Congressional Research Service, 2011), p. 22, http://fpc.state.gov/documents/organization/155979.pdf.

35. Marie-Christine Aulas, "Sadat's Egypt." See *Aviation Week and Space Technology*, December 14, 1981; January 4, 1982; February 1, 1982; and March 22, 1982, issues.

36. Quandt, "Camp David and Peacemaking," p. 358; Boutros-Ghali, *Egypt's Road to Jerusalem*, p. 195; and Brzezinski, *Power and Principle*, p. 273.

37. Ezer Weizman, *Battle for Peace* (New York: Bantam, 1981), pp. 190–91; and Kamel, *The Camp David Accords*, p. 87.

38. After Camp David, with the freedom to fortify and settle occupied territories, Israel formally annexed East Jerusalem, extended Israeli law into the Golan Heights, and increased its presence in the West Bank and Gaza. As Avner Yaniv writes, "The Egyptian defection was bound to have a critical effect. Israel would be freed of the need to attend to an Egyptian front. Syria would become the mainstay of any future Arab campaign. Syria could not be expected to rally the same broad coalition that Egypt had so far led. The P. L. O. itself would lose much of its hard-won freedom of action and become as uncomfortably dependent on Syria's good will as it had been in the 1960s. Israel would be free to sustain military operations against the P. L. O. in

Lebanon as well as settlement activity on the West Bank." See Avner Yaniv, *Dilemmas of Security: Politics, Strategy, and the Israeli Experience in Lebanon* (New York: Oxford University Press, 1987), p. 70; and Quandt, "Camp David and Peacemaking," pp. 364, 370.

39. Hisham Sharabi, *Arab Intellectuals and the West: The Formative Years, 1875–1914* (Baltimore: Johns Hopkins University Press, 1970), pp. 133–36. Barry Rubin, "Pan-Arab Nationalism: The Ideological Dream as Compelling Force," *Journal of Contemporary History* 26, no. 3–4 (1991): 535–51.

40. Rubin, "Pan-Arab Nationalism"; Jehuda Reinharz and George L. Mosse, eds., *The Impact of Western Nationalisms: Essays Dedicated to Walter Z. Laqueur on the Occasion of His 70th Birthday* (London: Sage Publications, 1992), p. 542.

41. Marvine Howe, "Radical Arabs Win Fight to Punish Egypt, but Can They?" *New York Times*, April 9, 1979.

42. Aside from intelligence sharing, the United States also had both an extradition and a mutual legal assistance treaty with Egypt for law enforcement and counterterrorism issues. See U.S. Embassy, Cairo, Cable 10 Cairo 179, "Scenesetter for FBI Director Mueller," February 10, 2010, https://www.wikileaks.ch/cable/2010/02/10CAIRO179.html. For more on President George W. Bush's covert action programs, see also Bob Woodward, *Bush at War* (New York: Simon & Schuster, 2001), pp. 76–77.

43. See "Extraordinary Rendition in U.S. Counter Terrorism Policy: The Impact on Transatlantic Relations," House Committee on Foreign Affairs, Subcommittee on International Organizations, Human Rights, and Oversight, Subcommittee on Europe, 110th Cong., 1st sess., April 17, 2007, http://foreignaffairs.house.gov/110/34712.pdf.

44. Robert Baer, as quoted in American Civil Liberties Union, "Fact Sheet: Extraordinary Rendition," December 6, 2005, https://www.aclu.org/national-security/fact-sheet-extraordinary-rendition.

45. For more information, see Amnesty International, "Egypt: Systematic Abuses in the Name of Security," April 11, 2007, http://www.amnesty.org/en/library/info/MDE12/001/2007 and "Extraordinary Rendition in U.S. Counter Terrorism Policy," House Committee on Foreign Affairs, April 17, 2007.

46. U.N. Doc, Egypt, A/51/44, para. 220. (Inquiry under Article 20), May 3, 1996, http://www.redress.org/downloads/country-reports/Egypt.pdf. Ron Suskind quoted in Matthew Cole, "Mubarak to Grant VP Omar Suleiman More Power," ABC News, February 10, 2011. Kate Allen's comments in "Egypt Torture Centre, Report Says," *BBC News*, April 11, 2007.

47. U.S. Embassy, Cairo, Cable 06 Cairo 2933, "Scenesetter for Deputy Secretary Zoellick's Visit," May 16, 2006, https://wikileaks.ch/cable/2006/05/06CAIRO2933.html.

48. Michael John Garcia, *Renditions: Constraints Imposed by Laws on Torture* (Washington: Congressional Research Service, 2009), p. 12; ACLU, "Fact Sheet: Extraordinary Rendition." See comments from Federal Bureau of Investigation (FBI) Director Robert Mueller in Ron Suskind, *The One Percent Doctrine: Deep Inside America's Pursuit of Its Enemies Since 9/11* (New York: Simon & Schuster, 2006), p. 114.

49. See Part I of "Military Studies in the Jihad against the Tyrants" at www.usdoj.gov/ag/manualpart1_1.pdf.

50. Chris Zambelis, "Is There a Nexus between Torture and Radicalization?" *Terrorism Monitor* 6, no. 13 (June 26, 2008), http://www.jamestown.org/programs/tm/single/?tx_ttnews%5Btt_news%5D=5015&tx_ttnews%5BbackPid%5D=167&no

_cache=1#.VQ8eUWTF-1I; Thomas Heghammer, "Terrorist Recruitment and Radicalization in Saudi Arabia," *Middle East Policy* 13, no. 4 (December 2006): 39–60; and Lawrence Wright, *The Looming Tower*, p. 52.

51. Montassir al-Zayyat, *The Road to Al-Qaeda: The Story of Bin Laden's Right-Hand Man*, ed. Sara Nimis, trans. Ahmed Fekry (London: Pluto Press, 2004), pp. 31–32. See also Suskind, *The One Percent Doctrine*, p. 129.

52. In October 2001, when the FBI released its list of the 22 most-wanted terrorists, seven of them were Egyptian, making Egypt the largest country represented. See "Most Wanted 'Terrorists' List Released," *CNN*, October 10, 2001. Also see "U.S. Foreign Policy and the Terrorist Threat," *Conversations with History: Michael Scheuer*, U.S. Berkeley Events, March 20, 2008, https://www.youtube.com/watch?v=gxdb5nnRMrU.

53. Scott Horton, "Kill or Capture: Six Questions for Matthew Alexander," *Harpers*, February 18, 2011, http://harpers.org/blog/2011/02/kill-or-capture-six-questions -for-matthew-alexander/.

54. "Report of the Defense Science Board Task Force on Strategic Communication," Office of the Under Secretary of Defense, Department of Defense, September 2004, http://www.dod.mil/pubs/foi/dsb/05-F-0422.pdf. Emphasis added.

55. Eric Neumayer and Thomas Plümper develop a rational theory of international terrorism over the period 1978 to 2005: "Applied to the U.S. case, our theory predicts that more anti-American terrorism emanates from countries that receive more U.S. military aid and arms transfers and in which more American military personnel are stationed, all relative to the country's own military capacity." See Eric Neumayer and Thomas Plümper, "Foreign Terror on Americans," *Journal of Peace Research* 48, no. 1 (2011): 3–17. For more on al Qaeda's twisted vindication of indiscriminate killing, see Thomas H. Kean and Lee H. Hamilton, *The 9/11 Commission Report: The Authorized Report* (New York: W.W. Norton and Company, 2004), pp. 47–53.

56. Committee on Government Reform, House of Representatives, "The 9/11 Commission Recommendations on Public Diplomacy: Defending Ideals and Defining the Message," August 23, 2004. Emphasis added.

57. For analysis on the Brotherhood, see Robert S. Leiken and Steven Brooke, "The Moderate Muslim Brotherhood," *Foreign Affairs* 22 (March/April 2007): 107–21.

58. "Egypt—Systematic Abuses in the Name of Security," Amnesty International, May 4, 2007, http://www.amnesty.org/en/library/asset/MDE12/001/2007/en /27dc4dc8-d3c5- 11dd-8743-d305bea2b2c7/mde120012007en.pdf.

59. "Egypt Sentences Newspaper Editors," *Al Jazeera* (Riyadh), September 13, 2007; "Egyptian Blogger Jailed for Insulting Islam," *The Guardian* (London), February 22, 2007; "Egyptian Blogger Jailed for 'Insult,'" *BBC News*, February 22, 2007; "Human Rights Watch World Report 2001—Egypt," Human Rights Watch, December 1, 2000; and Jailan Halawi, "Prison Limelight," *Al-Ahram Weekly Online*, no. 519 (February 1–7, 2001).

60. U.S. Embassy, Cairo, "Scenesetter for Deputy Secretary Zoellick's Visit."

61. Maye Kassem, *Egyptian Politics: The Dynamics of Authoritarian Rule* (London: Lynne Rienner, 2004), p. 66.

62. Ibid., pp. 69–73; and Jihad Ouda, Negad El-Borai, and Hafez Abu Se'ada, *A Door onto the Desert: Egyptian Legislative Elections of 2000, Course, Dilemmas, and Recommendations for the Future* (Cairo: United Group, 2000), p. 64, http://www.ug -law.com/downloads/door-onto-the-desert-en.pdf.

63. David Remnick, "Going Nowhere," *New Yorker*, July 12, 2004, pp. 74–83.

64. In an especially clever move, Mubarak permitted the Brotherhood to participate as "independents." They won 88 seats, some 20 percent of the assembly. See U.S. Embassy, Cairo, Cable 07 Cairo 2871, September 23, 2009, "Egypt in Transition: Sadat and Mubarak," https://www.wikileaks.ch/cable/2007/09/07CAIRO2871.html. Also see David Ottaway, "The Arab Tomorrow," *Wilson Quarterly* (Winter 2010): 48–64.

65. Jackson Diehl, "Mubarak Outdoes Himself," *Washington Post,* December 5, 2005.

66. U.S. Embassy, Cairo, "Scenesetter for Deputy Secretary Zoellick's Visit."

67. Over the years, members of the Brotherhood influenced by a fundamentalist interpretation of Islam, Wahhabism, have been dubbed the "Saudi clan." They have come to dominate the movement's thinking on matters of social politics. See David B. Ottaway, "Egypt at the Tipping Point?" Woodrow Wilson International Center for Scholars, Middle East Program Occaisonal Paper Series (Summer 2010). For more on the 2005 elections and their impact on the Brotherhood, see Marina Ottaway and Amr Hamzawy, *Getting to Pluralism: Political Actors in the Arab World* (Washington: Carnegie Endowment for International Peace, 2009), p. 86.

68. Esposito, *Unholy War: Terror in the Name of Islam,* p. 94; and David B. Ottaway, "Egypt at the Tipping Point?"

69. Scott Atran, "Calling the Muslim Brotherhood," *The National Interest Online,* February 2, 2011.

70. U.S. Embassy, Cairo, "Egypt in Transition: Sadat and Mubarak."

71. Ottaway and Hamzawy describe in detail "the plethora of legal and political restrictions imposed by the government to limit the role of liberal and leftist opposition parties." See Ottaway and Hamzawy, *Getting to Pluralism,* p. 49.

72. Over the decades, the proportion of nonmilitary to military aid has fallen almost continuously, with U.S. military aid to Egypt becoming five times as large as all other aid. See *State and DoD Need to Assess How the Foreign Military Financing Program for Egypt Achieves U.S. Foreign Policy and Security Goals;* and Jeremy M. Sharp, *Egypt in Transition* (Washington: Congressional Research Service, 2011). For USAID total, see "Egypt Health and Population Legacy Review," USAID, March 2011, http://www.newsecuritybeat.org/2011/05/usaid-egypts-health-and-population-legacy-review/. See also Ashley Barnes, "Creating Democrats? Testing the Arab Spring," *Middle East Policy* 20, no. 2 (Summer 2013): 55–72, http://www.mepc.org/journal/middle-east-policy-archives/creating-democrats-testing-arab-spring?print; and "Egypt: USAID Struggles to Find Common Ground," *Business Today Egypt* (Cairo), April 12, 2012, http://www.egypt-business.com/Web/details/1215-xg-USAID-Struggles-to-Find-Common-Ground/4776. For yearly funding, see U.S. Embassy, Cairo, Cable, 2-10-010, https://www.wikileaks.ch/cable/2010/02/10CAIRO181.html.

73. U.S. Embassy, Cairo, "Egypt in Transition: Sadat and Mubarak."

74. For military exercises, see Julie Stahl, "Egyptian War Games Cause for Concern in Israel, Lawmaker Says," *CNS News,* October 29, 2008; and Harun ur Rashid, "Israel's Peace Opportunity with Palestinians," *The Daily Star* (Dhaka, Bangladesh), March 2, 2011; U.S. Embassy, Cairo, Cable 08 Cairo 2543, "Scenesetter for General Petraeus' Visit to Egypt," December 21, 2008, https://www.wikileaks.ch/cable/2008/12/08CAIRO2543.html.

75. State-run newspaper *Al-Ahram* also had a ban on reporters interviewing Israelis. See David B. Ottaway, "Egypt at the Tipping Point?" Mustapha quoted in Peter Kenyon, "Israel's 'Cold' Peace with Egypt, Jordan Grows Chillier," NPR.org, October 26, 2009, http://www.npr.org/templates/story/story.php?storyId=114170104.

76. As early as March 1980, Egypt's Foreign Ministry had instructed officials to keep cooperation with Israel to a minimum. See Yediot Aharonot, cited in Kenneth W. Stein, "Egyptian-Israeli Relations," *Middle East Review of International Affairs* 1, no. 3 (September 1997), http://www.gloria-center.org/1997/09/stein-1997-09-05/. Stein cites an Israeli Foreign Ministry report analyzing the normalization process, which says there was "an Egyptian tendency, particularly at the subpresidential level, [to] deliberately slow down progress and the rate of normalization." Little has changed. U.S. officials relayed in a cable back to Washington in 2009 that "broader elements of peace with Israel, e.g. economic and cultural exchange, remain essentially underdeveloped." For U.S. perceptions of this "cold peace," see U.S. Embassy, Cairo, "Scenesetter for President Mubarak's Visit to Washington."

77. U.S. Embassy, Tel Aviv, Cable 07 TelAviv 3258, "DAS Danin and DASD Kimmit Discuss Gaza Smuggling," November 9, 2007, https://www.wikileaks.ch/cable/2007/11/07TELAVIV3258.html; and U.S. Embassy, Cairo, "Scenesetter for General Petraeus' Visit to Egypt."

78. "Egyptian FM complains of 'Israel lobby,'" *Jerusalem Post*, December 26, 2007; and "Egypt Warns Israel Not to Undermine Ties to U.S.," Reuters, December 31, 2007.

79. Cairo viewed Iran as a threat because of its nuclear ambitions and support for terrorist proxies. "President Mubarak sees Iran as Egypt's—and the region's—primary strategic threat." Quoted in U.S. Embassy, Cairo, "Scenesetter for FBI Director Mueller." Also see U.S. Embassy, Tel Aviv, Cable 09 TelAviv 2757, December 22, 2009, "U/S Tauscher's December 1-2 Visit to Israel," https://www.wikileaks.ch/cable/2009/12/09TELAVIV2757.html.

80. As scholar Robert L. Tignor writes, the Egyptian-Israeli relationship "has suffered whenever the Israelis repressed Palestinian dissidents in Gaza and the West Bank." See Robert L. Tignor, *Egypt: A Short History* (Princeton: Princeton University Press, 2010), p. 287.

81. Amira Howeidy, "Solidarity in Search of a Vision," *Al-Ahram Weekly* (Cairo), April 11–17, 2002.

82. In an effort not to alienate a major Arab ally whose support he needed for the 2003 invasion of Iraq, President Bush demanded that Israel halt incursions into Palestinian-controlled areas, and later that year, White House Press Secretary Ari Fleischer told reporters that Israel's actions were "very unhelpful" and "contrary to peace," adding, "Notice I didn't say anything about Israelis defending themselves." See "U.S. Proposes Resolution Urging Israel to End Ramallah Siege," *CNN.com*, September 24, 2002. For more on the protests and boycott, see Samer Shehata, "Egypt After 9/11: Perceptions of the United States," *Contemporary Conflicts*, March 26, 2004, http://conconflicts.ssrc.org/archives/mideast/shehata/; and Amira Howeidy, "Solidarity in Search of a Vision."

83. Egypt withdrew its ambassador until 2005. See "Egypt Scales Down Israel Contacts," BBC *News*, April 3, 2002.

84. "Cablegate: Tfle01: Egypt: July 26 Demonstrations," *Scoop Independent News* (Wellington, NZ), July 27, 2006, http://www.scoop.co.nz/stories/WL0607/S00368/cablegate-tfle01-egypt-july-26-demonstrations.htm; U.S. Embassy, Cairo, "Scenesetter for President Mubarak's Visit to Washington"; U.S Embassy, Cairo, Cable 10 Cairo 181, February 9, 2010, "Scenesetter for Admiral Mullen," https://wikileaks.ch/cable/2010/02/10CAIRO181.html; "Global Protests Condemn Gaza War," *Al Jazeera* (Riyadh), January 10, 2009; and "Israel/Gaza-Operation 'Cast Lead': 22 Days of

Death and Destruction," Amnesty International, 2009, https://www.amnesty.org/en/documents/MDE15/015/2009/en/.

85. U.S. Embassy, Doha, Cable 10 Doha 71, February 24, 2010, "Senator Kerry's Meeting with Qatar's Prime Minister," https://wikileaks.ch/cable/2010/02/10DOHA71.html.

86. Hillary Rodham Clinton, Testimony before the House Appropriations Subcommittee on State, Foreign Operations, and Relations Programs, March 10, 2011.

87. "Text: Obama's Speech in Cairo," *New York Times,* June 4, 2009.

88. Grants are made through Foreign Military Financing. See *State and DoD Need to Assess How the Foreign Military Financing Program for Egypt Achieves U.S. Foreign Policy and Security Goals*; Sharp, "Egypt in Transition," http://www.gao.gov/assets/220/218386.pdf.

89. Ahmad Al-Sayed El-Naggar, "U.S. Aid to Egypt: The Current Situation and Future Prospects," Carnegie Endowment for International Peace, June 17, 2009, http://carnegieendowment.org/2009/06/17/u.s.-aid-to-egypt-current-situation-and-future-prospects.

90. Sharp, *Egypt: Background and U.S. Relations.* Quote by Council on Foreign Relations scholar Steven Cook, in Amir Rosen, "The U.S. and Egypt Sure Look Like Allies, at Least on Military Matters," *The Atlantic,* September 14, 2012, http://www.theatlantic.com/international/archive/2012/09/the-us-and-egypt-sure-look-like-allies-at-least-on-military-matters/262411/.

91. U.S. Department of Defense, "Contracts: Air Force, No: 160-10," Press Operations, DoD, March 2, 2010, http://www.defense.gov/contracts/contract.aspx?contractid=4228; U.S. Department of Defense, "Contracts: Air Force, No: 294-10," Press Operations, DoD, April 14, 2010, http://www.defense.gov/contracts/contract.aspx?contractid=4259; U.S. Department of Defense, "Contracts: Navy, No: 428-09," Press Operations, DoD, June 17, 2009, http://www.defense.gov/contracts/contract.aspx?contractid=4050; U.S. Department of Defense, "Contracts: Army, No: 367-10," Press Operations, DoD, May 7, 2010, http://www.defense.gov/contracts/contract.aspx?contractid=4276; U.S. Department of Defense, "Contracts: Army, No. 157-10," Press Operations, DoD, March 1, 2010, http://www.defense.gov/Contracts/Contract.aspx?ContractID=4227; Sue Sturgis, "U.S. Defense Contractors with the Most at Stake in Egypt," The Institute for Southern Studies, February 1, 2011, http://www.southernstudies.org/2011/02/us-defense-contractors-with-the-most-at-stake-in-egypt.html.

92. For more on community policing training program, see "Interior Ministry Eager to Continue Police Training," *The Telegraph* (London), February 15, 2011; "Wikileaks: Police Brutality in Egypt," *CrethiPlethi,* January 30, 2011, http://www.crethiplethi.com/wikileaks-police-brutality-in-egypt/usa/2011/. For more on U.S.-sponsored anti-terrorism classes, see U.S. Embassy, Cairo, "Scenesetter for General Petraeus' Visit to Egypt"; "FBI Deputy Director Meets with Head of State Security," *The Telegraph* (London), February 9, 2011; U.S. Embassy, Cairo, "Scenesetter for FBI Director Mueller"; and "Scenesetter for Deputy Secretary Zoellick's Visit," Cable 06CAIRO2933, https://wikileaks.ch.cable/2006/05/06CAIRO2933.html.

93. U.S. Embassy, Cairo, "Scenesetter for FBI Director Mueller"; and "Human Rights in the Arab Republic of Egypt," Amnesty International, 2010, http://www.refworld.org/topic,50ffbce582,50ffbce59a,4c03a82fc,0,,,EGY.html.

94. U.S. State Department, "2009 Human Rights Report: Egypt," March 11, 2010; and U.S. Embassy, Cairo, Cable 09 Cairo 79, January 15, 2009, "GOE Struggling to Address Police Brutality," https://wikileaks.ch/cable/2009/01/09CAIRO79.html.

95. Quoted in U.S. Embassy, Cairo, "Scenesetter for FBI Director Mueller."

96. U.S. Embassy, Cairo, "Scenesetter for General Petraeus' Visit to Egypt."

97. Paul Amar, "Why Mubarak Is Out," *Jadaliyya*, February 1, 2011, http://www.jadaliyya.com/pages/index/516/why-mubarak-is-out-; and U.S. Embassy, Cairo, Cable 08 2091, September 8, 2009, "Academics See the Military in Decline, but Retaining Strong Influence," https://www.wikileaks.ch/cable/2008/09/08CAIRO2091.html.

98. Peter T. Bauer, *Equality, the Third World and Economic Delusion* (Cambridge, MA: Harvard University Press, 1981), pp. 103–4.

99. Ken Stier, "Egypt's Military-Industrial Complex," *Time*, February 9, 2011; and U.S. Embassy, Cairo, "Academics See the Military in Decline, but Retaining Strong Influence."

100. $28.6 billion total. Department of State, *Summary and Highlights: International Affairs Function 150* (Washington: DoS, 2010), http://www.state.gov/documents/organization/122513.pdf. See also USAID, *Audit of USAID/Egypt's Democracy and Governance Activities* (Washington: USAID, 2009), http://oig.usaid.gov/sites/default/files/audit-reports/6-263-10-001-p.pdf.

101. An example is Ismail Sabry Abdallah, the former Egyptian minister of development and planning, now an independent economist. Charles Levinson, "$50 Billion Later, Taking Stock of US Aid to Egypt," *Christian Science Monitor*, April 12, 2004.

102. USAID, *Audit of USAID/Egypt's Democracy and Governance Activities*.

103. "Scenesetter for Deputy Secretary Zoellick's Visit," https://www.wikileaks.ch.cable/2006/05/06CAIRO2933.html. For Mubarak comments in September 2006, see U.S. Embassy, Cairo, Cable 06CAIRO6171, October 2, 2006, "Jeddah for the Secretary's Traveling Party," https://wikileaks.org/cable/2006/10/06CAIRO6171.html. Also see "US Funded Egypt Pro-Democracy Movement," *Herald Sun*, January 29, 2011.

104. U.S. Embassy, Cairo, "Scenesetter for President Mubarak's Visit to Washington."

105. U.S. Embassy, Cairo, "Scenesetter for General Petraeus' Visit to Egypt."

106. Hillary Rodham Clinton, secretary of state, "Interview with Randa Aboul Azem of Al-Arabiya," March 2, 2009, http://www.state.gov/secretary/rm/2009a/03/120115.htm.

107. "Ayman Nour Requests the Secretary Push GOE for AN," Cable 06CAIRO6171, https://wikileaks.ch.cable/2006/10/06CAIRO6171.html.

108. David Welch, U.S. ambassador to Egypt, public lecture on U.S. foreign policy in the Middle East, American University in Cairo, January 28, 2002. Quoted in Issandr Elamrani, "The Cost of Friendship," *Cairo Times*, January 31–February 6, 2002.

109. "U.S. Urges Restraint in Egypt, Says Government Stable," Reuters, January 25, 2011.

110. "VP Biden Calls Egyptian President Mubarak an 'Ally'—and Would Not Call Him a Dictator," ABC *News*, January 27, 2011.

111. In contrast, Germany and France froze arms exports to Egypt. See Mina Kimes, "Egypt Uprisings, American Weapons. Now What?" *CNN Money*, February 14, 2011; and "Egypt Protests: Hilary Clinton Urges 'Orderly Transition,'" BBC *News*, January 30, 2011.

112. "Egyptians Embrace Revolt Leaders, Religious Parties and Military, as Well," Pew Research Center, April 25, 2011, http://www.pewglobal.org/2011/04/25/egyptians-embrace-revolt-leaders-religious-parties-and-military-as-well/.

113. Marc Lynch, "Anti-Americanisms in the Arab World," in *Anti-Americanism in World Politics*, ed. Peter J. Katzenstein and Robert O. Keohane (Ithaca, NY: Cornell University Press, 2007), p. 203.

114. A U.S. diplomat wrote that an Egyptian political activist agitating for democratic reform charged the United States with "being responsible" for Mubarak's crimes. See U.S. Embassy, Cairo, Cable 08 Cairo 2572, December 30, 2008, "April 6 Activist on His U.S. Visit and Regime Change in Egypt," https://wikileaks.ch/cable/2008/12/08CAIRO2572.html.

115. For examples of such allegations, see Emad Mekay, "Exclusive: U.S. Bankrolled Anti-Morsi Groups," *Al Jazeera* (Riyadh), July 10, 2013; Michel Chossudovksy, "Was Washington Behind Egypt's Coup d'Etat?" Global Research, July 4, 2014; and "West Backs Military Coup against Morsi, Muslim Brotherhood Says," *PressTV*, July 7, 2013.

116. Dan Ephron, "Morsi's Win in Egypt Sparks Fear in Israel," *Daily Beast*, June 19, 2012, http://www.thedailybeast.com/articles/2012/06/19/morsi-s-win-in-egypt-sparks-fear-in-israel.html.

117. Julian Pecquet, "Obama Administration Won't Label Toppling of Egypt's Morsi a Coup," *The Hill*, July 26, 2013.

118. Asma Alsharif, "Egyptian Court Sentences 529 Brotherhood Members to Death," Reuters, March 24, 2014; and "U.S. 'Shocked' by Egypt Death Sentences," Agence France Presse, March 24, 2014.

119. Ted Galen Carpenter interview with Doug Bandow, May 28, 2014.

120. "Egypt Declares El-Sisi Winner of Presidential Election," *CNN.com*, June 4, 2014.

121. Phil Stewart and Arshad Mohammed, "U.S. to Deliver Apache Helicopters to Egypt, Relaxing Hold on Aid," Reuters, April 23, 2014; and Sandra Maier, "U.S. to Deliver 10 Apache Helicopters to Egypt—Pentagon," Reuters, September 20, 2014. For an incisive criticism of the resumption of generous U.S. aid to Egypt, see Andrew Bacevich, "If We Have to Let Generals Run Egypt, Must We Pay for Them Too?" *The Spectator* (London), May 31, 2014.

122. Lin Nouelhed, "From Jubilation in Tahrir, Egypt Returns to Mubarak-Era Politics," Reuters, September 26, 2014.

123. David D. Kirkpatrick, "Egypt's New Strongman, Sisi Knows Best," *New York Times*, May 24, 2014.

124. "U.S. Backing of El-Sissi Reminiscent of Mubarak Era," *Deutsche Welle,* August 6, 2014.

Chapter 13

1. Alan Greenspan, *The Age of Turbulence: Adventures in a New World* (New York: Penguin, 2007), p. 463.

2. PBS *Frontline*, "Saudi Time Bomb? Interview James Baker," October 1, 2001.

3. "Deputy Secretary Wolfowitz Interview with Sam Tannenhaus, *Vanity Fair*," Defense.gov, May 9, 2003, http://www.defense.gov/transcripts/transcript.aspx?transcriptid=2594. According to CNN's Peter Bergen, who recounts his meeting with bin Laden, what most enraged the Saudi terrorist was the American military presence in Saudi Arabia. Incensed that the Saudis invited U.S. troops to their defense after the Iraqi invasion of Kuwait, bin Laden—like many Muslims—considered the continued

presence of these armed infidels in Saudi Arabia the greatest possible desecration of the holy land and contended that they must be driven out.

4. Bureau for International Narcotics and Law Enforcement Affairs, *International Narcotics Control Strategy Report—Volume II: Money Laundering and Financial Crimes* (Washington: Department of State, 2006), http://2001-2009.state.gov/p/nea/ci/sa/80179.htm.

5. Azzam studied and taught Islamic politics in Egypt and Jordan, but when his views became too subversive he found refuge in the kingdom, where he won appointment to the faculty of King Abdulaziz University. By 1981 he was sent to Islamic University in Islamabad, Pakistan, with $35 million in Saudi funds. See Steve Coll, *The Bin Ladens: An Arabian Family in the American Century* (New York: Penguin Press, 2008), p. 253.

6. The Afghan war was meant to strengthen the *umma* to liberate Palestine. The larger war with Israel, the West, and other unbelievers was part of some millenarian conflict leading to Judgment Day, as forecast in the Quran. See Coll, *The Bin Ladens*, pp. 256–57.

7. Bin Laden leveraged his experience with advertisers and promotional products from his earlier years at his family's Bin Laden Company. See Coll, *The Bin Ladens*, p. 259.

8. Pakistan officially restricted U.S. and Saudi access to rebels. But for narrative accounts of bin Laden's connections to GID, see James Risen, *State of War: The Secret History of the CIA and the Bush Administration* (New York: Simon and Schuster, 2006), p. 180; Lawrence Wright, *The Looming Tower: Al-Qaeda and the Road to 9/11* (New York: Knopf, 2006), p. 103–20; and Steve Coll, *Ghost Wars: The Secret History of the CIA, Afghanistan, and bin Laden, from the Soviet Invasion to September 10, 2001* (New York: Penguin Press, 2004), pp. 87–88.

9. After Turki Al-Faisal, as chief of foreign intelligence, named Ahmed Badeeb his chief of staff. For Badeeb quote about bin Laden, see Coll, *The Bin Ladens*, p. 295.

10. Coll, *The Bin Ladens*, p. 251.

11. According to Pulitzer Prize-winning journalist and author Steve Coll—who wrote that as early as 1988, wealthy Saudi merchants may have been among the most generous contributors to bin Laden's fundraising network and militia—American investigators and prosecutors confirmed that the documents uncovered were authentic and credible. See Coll, *The Bin Ladens*, p. 341–42. For more on bin Laden and Saudi charities, see "Government's Evidentiary Proffer Supporting the Admissibility of Co-Conspirator Statements," *United States v. Enaam Arnaout*, No. 02-CR-892 (N.D. Ill, filed January 6, 2003). For more on the trove of al Qaeda documents, see Glenn R. Simpson, "List of Early al Qaeda Donors Points to Saudi Elite, Charities," *Wall Street Journal*, March 18, 2003.

12. National Commission on Terrorist Attacks upon the United States, *The 9/11 Commission Report: Final Report of the National Commission on Terrorist Attacks upon the United States* (hereafter *The 9/11 Report*), (Washington: National Commission on Terrorist Attacks upon the United States, 2004), pp. 372.

13. Robert M. Guido, "U.S. Efforts to Combat Terrorism Financing: Progress Made and Future Challenges," *Small Wars Journal*, August 19, 2010.

14. Coll, *The Bin Ladens*, p. 341. *Al-Jihad*, a magazine supported by the Services Office, praised Saudi support of seven charities in its December 1986 issue. One was the Mecca-based Muslim World League. See Alex Strick van Linschoten and Felix Kuehn,

An Enemy We Created: The Myth of the Taliban–Al Qaeda Merger (New York: Oxford University Press, 2012), pp. 359–60, n140.

15. The militarily defenseless Kuwaitis, despite their purchase of sophisticated American weaponry, used their commanding economic positions to pay 55 percent of what would become Operation Desert Storm. Saudi Arabia and Kuwait paid approximately $33 billion toward the total cost of Desert Storm and Desert Shield, which was $60 billion. The U.S. share was only $6 billion (10 percent), according to a Defense Department press release (125-M) issued on May 5, 1992. Oil revenues are 70–80 percent of Saudi government revenues. See the citation in Jerry Taylor and Peter VanDoren, "The Soft Case for Soft Energy," *Journal of International Affairs* 53, no. 1 (1999): 225.

16. Bin Laden claimed he worked for the true interest of the royal family. At the time, Saudi Bin Laden Group, when Osama bin Laden was still a shareholder, signed contracts with the U.S. Army to build facilities supporting U.S. troop presence. Bin Laden likely profited from those construction projects. Coll, *The Bin Ladens*, pp. 375–76.

17. *Ulema* (sometimes spelled *ulama*) were trained in the interpretation of Islamic (*Sharia*) law, Islamic jurisprudence, and Islamic sciences and doctrines.

18. Statement of Secretary of Defense Dick Cheney, "Crisis in the Persian Gulf Region: U.S. Policy Options and Implications: Hearings before the U.S. Senate Armed Services Committee," 101st Congress, 2nd Session (1990).

19. The oil myth is based on the false assumption of a "fair and reasonable price" for oil. The reality is that oil is a commodity openly traded on the worldwide market, and the price of oil is determined by supply and demand, not by some perception of what it should cost. As Massachusetts Institute of Technology economist Morris Adelman points out, "The world oil market, like the world ocean, is one great pool. The price is the same at every border. Who exports the oil Americans consume is irrelevant." For more on the myth of oil security, see Morris Adelman, *Genie out of the Bottle: World Oil since 1970* (Cambridge, MA: MIT Press, 2008); and Jerry Taylor and Peter Van Doren, "The Energy Security Question," *Georgetown Journal of Law and Public Policy* 6, no. 2 (Summer 2008): 475–85.

20. The only real issue was immediate price spikes: the 1970s oil shocks. Only after coalition forces entered the conflict did Saddam's forces set fire to hundreds of Kuwaiti oil wells. Even then, that action failed to generate a major imbalance in the world's oil market.

21. George Bush, *All the Best, George Bush: My Life in Letters and Other Writings* (New York: Scribner, 1990), p. 476. The majority of foreign securities are U.S. treasury bills, of which Saudi Arabia has considerable holdings, and private Saudi business families hold large portfolio investments in the U.S. See U.S. Department of the Treasury, "Major Foreign Holders of Treasury Securities," http://www.treasury.gov/resource-center/data-chart-center/tic/Documents/mfh.txt.

22. For more on U.S. aid to Saddam during the Iran-Iraq War (1980–1988), see Shane Harris and Matthew M. Aid, "Exclusive: CIA Files Prove America Helped Saddam as He Gassed Iran," *ForeignPolicy.com*, August 26, 2013.

23. The *New York Times* reported that General H. Norman Schwarzkopf, the commander of U.S. military forces during the Persian Gulf War, reduced Iraq's "combat effectiveness" by 50 to 100 percent. See Eric Schmitt, "Study Lists Lower Tally of Iraqi Troops in Gulf War," *New York Times*, April 24, 1992. On discrepancies over the threat posed by Saddam, see Scott Peterson, "In War, Some Facts Less Factual," *Christian Sci-*

ence Monitor, September 6, 2002; and Dave Kehr, "The Hidden Wars of Desert Storm: Questioning U.S. Motives in the Persian Gulf War," *New York Times,* April 20, 2001.

24. Ann Reilly Dowd and Suneel Ratan, "How Bush Decided," *Fortune,* February 11, 1991.

25. Kuwait, Iraq's "small and helpless neighbor," was not attacked, but "crushed," and the Kuwaiti people "brutalized." For more, see George Bush, "Address to the Nation Announcing Allied Military Action in the Persian Gulf," January 16, 1991," Gerhard Peters and John T. Woolley, The American Presidency Project, http://www .presidency.ucsb.edu/ws/?pid=19222.

26. Implying such control was political, not purely economic. Secretary Baker later said about U.S. involvement in the Middle East, "We're their security because we have a self-interest in making sure that those energy reserves in the Persian Gulf *don't fall under the control of a country that is adverse to the United States.*" [Emphasis added.] PBS *Frontline,* "Saudi Time Bomb?"

27. George Bush, "Address before a Joint Session of the Congress on the Cessation of the Persian Gulf Conflict," March 6, 1991," Gerhard Peters and John T. Woolley, The American Presidency Project, http://www.presidency.ucsb.edu/ws/?pid=19364.

28. In November, 47 women shocked Saudi society by driving through Riyadh in violation of the kingdom's ban on female drivers. In early 1991, 43 liberal-leaning businessmen, journalists, and university professors signed a petition to Fahd asking for broader political participation. Coll, *The Bin Ladens,* p. 378.

29. Khashoggi, bin Laden, and others feared more than individual irreligious or sinful behavior, such as "a mass movement of secularization, mixed schools, top-down changes." See Coll, *The Bin Ladens,* pp. 260, 378–79.

30. Osama bin Laden, *Messages to the World: The Statements of Osama bin Laden,* ed. Bruce Lawrence (London, UK: Verso, 2005), p. 203.

31. In Yemen, before his retreat from Afghanistan, bin Laden was sponsoring militants attempting to overthrow South Yemen's communist government. Later that decade, bin Laden's militants received advice and training from Shiite Muslim terrorists, although their intra-Islamic enmity could take collaboration only so far. For more, see *The 9/11 Commission Report,* p. 240.

32. About private charitable funds intended for poor refugees rather than terrorists, a Benevolence International Foundation official stated, "That is our mission—Lying to people." Also, BIF began services in Sudan "after the agreement of *the base* in Sudan with the Sudanese Government." [Emphasis in original.] For more on the training of Sudanese forces, see *United States v. Enaam Arnaout,* p. 22. For more on BIF activities, see pp. 48, 58. The Benevolence International Foundation, according to its own report, supported jihad, mujahideen, and, in the service of Islamic proselytizing (*dawah*), "to make Islam supreme on this Earth." The Benevolence International Foundation was formerly known as Lajnatt Al-Birr Al-Islamiah. See *United States v. Enaam Arnaout,* pp. 51, 57.

33. An article from the era reported that the Black Swans spent around $700,000 per month in cash on weapons, equipment, and supplies. The article, citing Brigadier Tiric, states, "He said that some of the funds come through the army's general command but that most come from 'private sources.'" See Chuck Sudetic, "Bosnia's Elite Force: Fed, Fit, Muslim," *New York Times,* June 16, 1995. See also *United States v. Enaam Arnaout,* pp. 25, 66, 68. In addition, Pulitzer Prize–winning reporter Karen Elliot House, who spent the past 30 years writing about Saudi Arabia as a diplomatic

correspondent, foreign editor, and publisher of the *Wall Street Journal,* writes that the Saudi government "gave billions of dollars to aid jihadists fighting in Afghanistan, Chechnya, and Bosnia." See Karen Elliot House, *On Saudi Arabia: Its People, Past, Religion, Fault Lines—and Future* (New York: Knopf, 2012), p. 29.

34. Office of Public Affairs, "Treasury Designates Benevolence International Foundation and Related Entities as Financiers of Terrorism," November 19, 2002, http:// www.investigativeproject.org/documents/misc/27.pdf.

35. For more on bin Laden's desire to extend his operations outside of Afghanistan before the end of the Afghan-Soviet War, see Michael Scheuer, *Osama bin Laden* (New York: Oxford University Press, 2012), p. 104. On training camps in Sudan, see PBS *Frontline,* "Osama bin Laden: A Chronology of His Political Life," http://www .pbs.org/wgbh/pages/frontline/shows/binladen/etc/cron.html; and Jeff Gerth and Judith Miller, "Funds for Terrorists Traced to Persian Gulf Businessmen," *New York Times,* August 14, 1996.

36. For more on the training facility in Riyadh, see "U.S. Vows Terrorist Bomb 'Won't Affect Saudi Relationship,'" *CNN,* November 13, 1995.

37. Thomas W. Simons Jr., "Pakistan, Islamic Terror and Hua (96ISLAM-ABAD5972)," American Embassy Islamabad, July 14, 1996.

38. And by 1997, Al Haramain Islamic Foundation (HIF) employees in Kenya were arrested for planning a terrorist attack against the U.S., with some planning conducted inside the HIF office. See *The 9/11 Commission Report,* chap. 7, "Al Haramain Case Study." A U.S. State Department memorandum later uncovered that top-level HIF officials condoned funding militants, and that charity field offices and representatives around the world, including HIF headquarters in Riyadh, appeared to provide financial and logistical support to al Qaeda. Colin Powell, "Terrorist Financing–Updated Nonpaper on Al Haramain (03STATE23994)," Washington, D.C., January 28, 2003.

39. Douglas Jehl, "Saudis Are Shutting Down a Charity Tied to Terrorists," *New York Times,* June 3, 2004; *The 9/11 Commission Report,* chap. 7, "Al Haramain Case Study."

40. "U.S. Strength in the Persian Gulf," *Washington Post,* February 24, 1998, http:// www.washingtonpost.com/wp-srv/inatl/longterm/iraq/military/usstrength.htm.

41. His fatwa appeared in an edition of the London-based, Arabic-language newspaper *Al-Quds Al-Arabi.* See "Bin Laden's Fatwa," PBS *NewsHour,* August 23, 1996, http://www.pbs.org/newshour/updates/military/july-dec96/fatwa_1996.html. According to bin Laden biographer Yossef Bodansky, radical clerics offered Quranic backing to bin Laden's bloodshed, insisting that all methods of war, including terrorism, are justified in the battle against the infidels. See Yossef Bodansky, *Bin Laden: The Man Who Declared War on America* (New York: Random House, 2001).

42. Michael Scheuer, "Extraordinary Rendition in U.S. Counterterrorism Policy: The Impact on Transatlantic Relations," Joint Hearing before the Subcommittee on International Organizations, Human Rights, and Oversight, and the Subcommittee on Europe, April 17, 2007, p. 32.

43. "CNN March 1997 Interview with Osama bin Laden," news.findlaw.com/cnn /docs/binladen/binladenintvw-cnn.pdf.

44. "Bin Laden's Fatwa," PBS *NewsHour.*

45. See the Quran, Surahs 5:32 and 5:33, for another opinion. "CNN March 1997 Interview with Osama bin Laden" For more on the deaths of Iraqi children, see UNICEF, "Iraq Surveys Show 'Humanitarian Emergency,'" Unicef.org, August 12, 1999, http://www.unicef.org/newsline/99pr29.htm.

46. The front, including three other militant groups, said in its founding manifesto: "We—with God's help—call on every Muslim . . . to comply with God's order to kill Americans." Andrew Higgins and Alan Cullison, "Saga of Dr. Zawahiri Sheds Light on the Roots of al Qaeda Terror," *Wall Street Journal,* July 2, 2002.

47. Bill Clinton, *My Life* (New York: Knopf, 2004), p. 797.

48. "Bin Ladin Creates New Front against US, Israel, Islamabad," *The News in English* (Islamabad), May 28, 1998, p. 12; Foreign Broadcast Information Service Report, "Compilation of Usama Bin Ladin Statements, 1994–January 2004," pp. 68–69. For "the so-called superpower that is America," see "Time magazine interview, January 11, 1999"; "Compilation of Usama Bin Ladin Statements, " p. 98; and PBS, "Osama bin Laden v. The U.S.: Edicts and Statements," April 1999, http://www.pbs.org/wgbh/pages/frontline/shows/binladen/who/edicts.html; and Scheuer, *Osama bin Laden,* p. 129.

49. PBS *Frontline,* "Interview: Osama bin Laden," (May 1998)," http://www.pbs.org/wgbh/pages/frontline/shows/binladen/who/interview.html.

50. In August 2001, O'Neill quit the FBI to head security at the World Trade Center, where his remains were recovered after 9/11. For snippets of O'Neill's conversations with Jean-Charles Brisard, author of a study of terrorist financing for a French intelligence agency, see Anthony Summers and Robbyn Swan, *The Eleventh Day: The Full Story of 9/11* (New York: Ballantine Books, 2011), p. 396.

51. The officials said the Saudis would rather sell their securities than acquiesce. Martin Tolchin, "Foreigners' Political Roles in U.S. Grow by Investing," *New York Times,* December 30, 1985.

52. Bush also described Saudi Prince Bandar, longtime Saudi ambassador to America, as "a friend of mine since Dad's presidency." George W. Bush, *Decision Points* (New York: Crown Publishers, 2010), pp. 403, 247.

53. In a 2003 profile of Bandar in *The New Yorker,* Elsa Walsh wrote that Tenet showed up at Bandar's home during the interview. For more on the friendship, see James Risen, *State of War,* p. 188.

54. That quote from the 9/11 Commission came from a former National Security Council official. See *The 9/11 Commission Report,* chap. 7, "Al Haramain Case Study," p. 116.

55. Risen, *State of War,* p. 181. According to Michael Scheuer, head the CIA's bin Laden unit, the Saudis refused to help perhaps because they wanted to protect themselves from U.S. investigations into their private collaboration with bin Laden in the past. See Coll, *The Bin Ladens,* pp. 436–37.

56. On Tenet and Clarke's objections, see Lawrence Wright, *The Looming Tower,* p. 291. On Tenet's trip to the kingdom, see p. 266.

57. Ibid., p. 267.

58. Risen, *State of War,* pp. 183–84.

59. Bush, *Decision Points,* p. 191.

60. Clinton also admits, however, that Americans had to absorb the news of the strike and his grand jury testimony into his "personal behavior." See Bill Clinton, *My Life* (New York: Knopf, 2004), p. 797. For the quote on Somalia, see p. 804.

61. Ibid., p. 797. The Aldrich Ames case had also done "severe damage" to the CIA, according to Clinton's recollection of Tenet's concern. See p. 818.

62. PBS *Frontline,* "In Search of Al Qaeda," interview with Ahmad Zaidan, http://www.pbs.org/wgbh/pages/frontline/shows/search/interviews/zaidan.html. Re-

porter Peter Bergen also recounts Zaidan's meeting with al Qaeda member Moham-med Atef after the attack on the USS *Cole*, who said how the group wanted America to react: "We did [the USS] *Cole* [attack] and we wanted the United States to react. And if they reacted, they are going to invade Afghanistan and that's what we want. . . . We want them to come to our country. . . . And then we will start holy war against the Americans, exactly like the Soviets." Peter L. Bergen, *The Osama bin Laden I Know: An Oral History of al Qaeda's Leader* (New York: Free Press, 2006), p. 255.

63. Wright, *The Looming Tower*, p. 46.

64. For Kurtz, see Summers, *The Eleventh Day*, p. 286. For Clarke, see Bob Graham, *Intelligence Matters: The CIA, the FBI, Saudi Arabia, and the Failure of America's War on Terror* (New York: Random House, 2004), pp. 136–37.

65. Seymour M. Hersh, "King's Ransom: How Vulnerable Are the Saudi Roy-als?" *The New Yorker*, October 22, 2001; "Kidnap Team Stalks Ex-U.N. Envoy: Saudi Diplomat is Terror Target," *New York Post*, August 1, 1994; U.S. Department of State, "Saudi Arabia and Human Rights Practices, 1994," February 1995, http://dosfan.lib .uic.edu/ERC/democracy/1994_hrp_report/94hrp_report_nea/SaudiArabia.html; Summers, *The Eleventh Day*, p. 392. At the time, FBI Director Louie Freeh did not use email, an aversion to computers that may have explained his reluctance to update the FBI's computer system or develop a central counterterrorism database. Prince Bandar hired Freeh to be his legal representative after he retired from the bureau. See the full program: PBS *Frontline*, "Black Money," April 7, 2009, http://www.pbs.org/wgbh /pages/frontline/blackmoney/view/.

66. Lisa Myers, "The Missed Opportunities of 9/11: Could the Attacks on America Have Been Disrupted or Delayed?" *NBS News*, July 26, 2004, http://www.nbcnews .com/id/5469870/#.Ur7N2fRDs50; Anthony Barnet, Lee Hanno, and Martin Bright, "UK Spymasters Shrugged off al-Qaeda 'Recruit's Warning,'" *The Guardian* (London), June 6, 2006, http://www.theguardian.com/world/2004/jun/06/september11.ter rorism; Summers, *The Eleventh Day*, pp. 294, 302–03.

67. One future hijacker lived for four months with an informant. For more, see Of-fice of the Inspector General, *A Review of the FBI's handling of Intelligence Information Related to the September 11 Attacks* (Washington: Department of Justice, 2004), http:// www.justice.gov/oig/special/s0606/final.pdf, p. 335; and Graham, *Intelligence Mat-ters*, pp. 160–61, 164–65, 168–69, 204.

68. Omar al-Bayoumi was employed by the Saudi Presidency of Civil Aviation from 1975 until 1995 and later paid by a Saudi company that contracted with the Saudi government. See *A Review of the FBI's Handling of Intelligence Information Related to the September 11 Attacks*, p. 331.

69. Ibid., p. 332.

70. Ibid., p. 334.

71. Risen, *State of War*, p. 181.

72. *A Review of the FBI's Handling of Intelligence Information Related to the September 11 Attacks*, pp. 361, 247–48. FBI sources who spoke to Lawrence Wright offered a range of explanations for why the CIA had intelligence but neglected to provide it: the CIA feared that FBI prosecutions might compromise relations with foreign services; the FBI was too clumsy to be trusted with sensitive intelligence; and—more cynically— the CIA, desperate for a source inside al Qaeda to recruit, was running a joint venture with Saudi intelligence. See Wright, *The Looming Tower*, pp. 310–13.

73. *A Review of the FBI's Handling of Intelligence Information Related to the September 11 Attacks*, pp. 315, 361.

74. The full quote by Bob Kerrey (D-NE) was that, of the "three big failures, mistakes" made in the Clinton and Bush administrations after 1998, one was with "allowing al Qaeda to come inside the United States. . . . We continued to allow them to come to the United States; we didn't put a full-scale effort on with consular offices and INS and FBI and all sorts of other people in the United States to try to prevent them from coming into the United States." See "National Commission on Terrorist Attacks upon the United States, Tenth Public Hearing," April 13, 2004, http://www.9-11commission.gov/archive/hearing10/9-11Commission_Hearing_2004-04-13.htm.

75. Mihdhar had already returned to the United States in early July 2001. See *A Review of the FBI's Handling of Intelligence Information Related to the September 11 Attacks*, p. 302; Wright, *The Looming Tower*, pp. 310–13; and Summers, *The Eleventh Day*, p. 384.

76. Barton Gellman, "U.S. Was Foiled Multiple Times in Effort to Capture Bin Laden or Have Him Killed," *Washington Post*, October 3, 2001, http://www.washingtonpost.com/wp-dyn/content/article/2006/06/09/AR2006060900911_pf.html.

77. Richard A. Clarke, "Memorandum for Condoleezza Rice," National Security Council January 25, 2001, http://www2.gwu.edu/~nsarchiv/NSAEBB/NSAEBB343/osama_bin_laden_file09.pdf. Emphasis in the original.

78. Reference to President's Daily Brief, "Bin Laden Determined to Strike in US," Central Intelligence Agency (CIA), August 6, 2001, (declassified and publicly released on April 10, 2004), http://nsarchive.gwu.edu/NSAEBB/NSAEBB343/osama_bin _laden_file02.pdf. President Bush later claimed the CIA "could not confirm any concrete plans." See Bush, *Decision Points*, p. 135.

79. Philip Shenon, *The Commission: The Uncensored History of the 9/11 Investigation* (New York: Hachette Book Group, 2008), p. 247. See also Lisa Myers, "Did Ashcroft Brush off Terror Warnings?" *NBS News*, June 22, 2004.

80. "Ashcroft Flying High," *CBSNews.com*, July 26, 2001; "Bin Laden Determined to Strike in US."

81. In Bandar's company, Bush cut off one reporter who began to raise the subject of 9/11. See Summers, *The Eleventh Day*, p. 406.

82. The FBI had interviewed some, but not all, of the departing Saudis. No doubt many were likely innocent of any crime, but U.S. government documents reveal that the FBI was uncertain as to whether those who left had information pertinent to the 9/11 investigation. Summers, *The Eleventh Day*, p. 406.

83. "Joint Inquiry into Intelligence Community Activities before and after the Terrorist Attacks of September 11, 2001," House Permanent Select Committee on Intelligence and Senate Select Committee on Intelligence, 107th Cong., 2nd sess., S. Rep. 107-351 and H. Rep. 107-792, http://www.gpoaccess.gov/serialset/creports/pdf/fullreport_errata.pdf.

84. Josh Meyer, "Report Links Saudi Government to 9/11 Hijackers, Sources Say," *Los Angeles Times*, August 2, 2003; James Risen and David Johnson, "Report on September 11 Suggests a Role by Saudi Spies," *New York Times*, August 2, 2003; Mike Allex, "Bush Won't Release Classified September 11 Report," *Washington Post*, July 30, 2003; David Johnson and Douglas Jehl, "Bush Refuses to Declassify Saudi Section of Report," *New York Times*, July 30, 2003.

85. Dana Priest, "White House, CIA Kept Key Portions of Report Classified," *Washington Post*, July 25, 2003; Helen Kennedy, "New Rage Over 9/11 & Saudis Pols Get Censored Report," *New York Daily News*, July 25, 2003.

86. Graham, *Intelligence Matters*, p. 215.

87. Summers, *The Eleventh Day*, p. 416.

88. "Ex-Saudi Ambassador: Kingdom Could Have Helped U.S. Prevent 9/11," *CNN.com*, November 2, 2007, http://www.cnn.com/2007/WORLD/meast/11/01/saudiarabia.terrorism/index.html.

89. Risen, *State of War*, p. 181.

90. Ibid. Steve Coll cites the head of the CIA's bin Laden unit, Michael Scheuer, as the one who submitted the request to the Kingdom of Saudi Arabia for basic information about Osama bin Laden. The agency received no reply. See Coll, *The Bin Ladens*, pp. 416–17.

91. Alex Strick van Linschoten and Felix Kuehn, *An Enemy We Created: The Myth of the Taliban-/Al Qaeda Merger in Afghanistan, 1970–2010* (New York: Oxford University Press, 2012), p. 165; Summers and Swan, *The Eleventh Day*, pp. 393–94.

92. Risen, *State of War*, p. 182.

93. Some in the CIA had also begun to suspect that the highly classified intelligence and communications intercepts it was sharing with GID were being passed to al Qaeda. See Risen, *State of War*, p. 182.

94. Richard H. Jones, "GOK Sees Strong Saudi Commitment against Terrorism (03KUWAIT4680)," American Embassy in Kuwait, October 14, 2003.

95. Coll, *The Bin Ladens*, p. 437.

96. Henry Kissinger, *Does America Need a Foreign Policy? Toward a Diplomacy for the 21st Century* (New York: Simon and Schuster, 2001), p. 293.

97. Carmen bin Ladin, *Inside the Kingdom: My Life in Saudi Arabia* (New York: Grand Central Publishing, 2004), p. 4.

98. See Summers, *The Eleventh Day*, p. 419.

99. Josh Meyer, "Report Links Saudi Government to 9/11 Hijackers, Sources Say," *Los Angeles Times*, August 2, 2003.

100. State Department, Bureau of Democracy, Human Rights and Labor, "Country Report on Human Rights Practices for 2012: Saudi Arabia," http://www.state.gov/j/drl/rls/hrrpt/humanrightsreport/index.htm?year=2012&dlid=204381 #wrapper.

101. James B. Smith, "Saudi Arabia: General Jones' Jan. 12, 2010 Meeting with Prince Mohammed Bin Naif, Assistant Minister of Interior (10RIYADH90)," American Embassy in Riyadh, January 19, 2010; Lawrence Wright, "The Kingdom of Silence," *The New Yorker*, January 5, 2004.

102. David Ottoway, "The King and Us," *Foreign Affairs* 88, no. 3 (May/June 2009): 121–31, https://www.foreignaffairs.com/articles/middle-east/2009-05-01/king-and-us.

103. Thomas E. Ricks, "Briefing Depicted Saudis as Enemies," *Washington Post*, August 6, 2002; Jack Shafer, "The PowerPoint that Rocked the Pentagon?" *Slate*, August 7, 2002.

104. Kissinger called the embargo an "actual strangulation of the industrialized world" and implied the West had plans to seize Persian Gulf oil militarily. "Kissinger on Oil, Food, and Trade," *Business Week*, January 13, 1975, p. 69; and "Excerpts from the Kissinger News Conference," *New York Times*, November 22, 1973. President Gerald Ford also referred to the embargo as "economic strangulation." See "Gerald

Ford: They Will See Something Is Being Done," *Time*, January 20, 1975, p. 21. Defense Secretary James Schlesinger indicated "conceivably military measures in response" in the event of another oil embargo. See "Now a Tougher U.S.: Interview with James R. Schlesinger, Secretary of Defense," *U.S. News and World Report*, May 26, 1975, pp. 26–27. For more articles and essays on this confrontational approach, see Miles Ignotus, "Oil: The Issue of American Intervention," *Commentary*, January 1975; "Seizing Arab Oil," *Harper's*, March 1975; Glen Frankel, "U.S. Mulled Seizing Oil Fields in 1973," *Washington Post*, January 1, 2004; and Owen Bowcott, "UK Feared Americans Would Invade Gulf During 1973 Oil Crisis," *Guardian* (London), January 1, 2004.

105. The Senate Intelligence Committee, in July 2004, concluded there was no Iraq–al Qaeda link, and stated that claims made in the October 2002 National Intelligence Estimate about Iraq's alleged WMD were "either *overstated, or were not supported by, the underlying intelligence reporting.*" [Emphasis added]. The committee later expanded their investigation. See "Report of the Select Committee on Intelligence on the U.S. Intelligence Community's Prewar Intelligence Assessments on Iraq," http://www.intelligence.senate .gov/108301.pdf; "Senate Report on Intelligence Activities Relating to Iraq Conducted by the Policy Counterterrorism Evaluation Group and the Office of Special Plans within the Office of the Under Secretary of Defense for Policy," June 2008, 110th Cong., 2nd sess., http://www.intelligence.senate.gov/080605/phase2b.pdf. The 9/11 Commission also found "no evidence" that Iraq and al Qaeda "ever developed into a collaborative operational relationship." See *The 9/11 Commission Report*. And a declassified 2007 Pentagon investigation concluded that civilians under Secretary of Defense Donald Rumsfeld and Under Secretary of Defense for Policy Douglas Feith "developed, produced, and then disseminated alterative intelligence assessments." Inspector General, United States Department of Defense, "Review of the Pre-Iraqi War Activities of the Office of Under Secretary of Defense for Policy," Report No. 07-Intell-04, February 9, 2007 http://www.fas.org/irp/agency/dod/ig020907-decl. pdf.

106. Robert Baer, *Sleeping with the Devil: How Washington Sold Its Soul for Saudi Crude* (New York: Crown, 2003).

107. *The 9/11 Commission Report*, chap. 7, Al Haramain Case Study.

108. Rachel Bronson, "5 Myths about U.S.-Saudi Relations," *Washington Post*, May 21, 2006, http://www.washingtonpost.com/wp-dyn/content/article/2006/05/19 /AR2006051901758_pf.html.

109. Risen, *State of War*, p. 177.

110. U.S. Department of the Treasury, "Additional Al-Haramain Branches, Former Leader Designated by Treasury as Al Qaida Supporters Treasury Marks Latest Action in Joint Designation with Saudia Arabia," press release, June 2, 2004, http://www .treasury.gov/press-center/press-releases/Pages/js1703.aspx.

111. U.S. Department of the Treasury, "U.S.-Based Branch of Al Haramain Foundation Linked to Terror Treasury Designates U.S. Branch, Director," press release, September 9, 2004, http://www.treasury.gov/press-center/press-releases/Pages/js1895 .aspx.

112. The quote and core finding is from a 2005 Government Accountability Office report. See "*International Affairs: Information on U.S. Agencies' Efforts to Address Islamic Extremism*" (Washington: GAO, 2005), http://www.gao.gov/assets/250/247784 .html.

113. Office of the Under Secretary of Defense, *"Report of the Defense Science Board Task Force on Strategic Communication,"* (Washington: DOD, 2004), http://www.dod.mil/pubs/foi/Science_and_Technology/DSB/05-F-0422.pdf.

114. Council on Foreign Relations, "In Support of Arab Democracy: Why and How," Independent Task Force Report No. 54, June 2005.

115. Richard Wike and Nilanthi Samaranayake, "Where Terrorism Finds Support in the Muslim World," Pew Research Center, May 23, 2006.

116. "Saudi Police 'Stopped' Fire Rescue," March 15, 2002, *BBC.com;* Lawrence Wright, "Kingdom of Silence," *New Yorker,* January 5, 2004.

117. Office of the Director of National Intelligence (ODNI), "Declassified Key Judgments of the National Intelligence Estimate 'Trends in Global Terrorism: Implications for the United States," (Washington, D.C.: Office of the Director of National Intelligence, April 2006), http://www.governmentattic.org/5docs/NIE-2006-02R.pdf.

118. James A. Baker III and Lee H. Hamilton, cochairs, et al., "Iraq Study Group Report," United States Institute of Peace, December 6, 2006), p. 25, http://media.usip.org/reports/iraq_study_group_report.pdf.

119. Christopher M. Blanchard and Alfred B. Prados, "Saudi Arabia: Terrorist Financing Issues," CRS Report for Congress, September 14, 2007; and *The 9/11 Commission Report,* chap. 7, "Al Haramain Case Study." For more on joint U.S.-Saudi efforts against terrorist financing, see testimony of Deputy Assistant Secretary of the Treasury Juan Zarate and Deputy Assistant Director of the FBI Counterterrorism Operational Support Branch Thomas Harrington, U.S. Congress, House of Representatives, Hearing of the Subcommittee on the Middle East and Central Asia of the House Committee on International Relations on "Saudi Arabia and the Fight Against Terrorism Financing." March 24, 2004.

120. U.S. Embassy, Riyadh, Cable 09 Riyadh 496, "Scenesetter for Senator Bond's April 6–8 Visit to Saudi Arabia," March 31, 2009, http://wikileaks.org/cable/2009/03/09RIYADH496.html.

121. "Terrorist Finance: Action Request for Senior Level Engagement on Terrorism Finance," *The Guardian* (London), December 30, 2009, http://www.theguardian.com/world/us-embassy-cables-documents/242073.

122. Ibid. For more on Saudi private and charitable giving inadvertently going to militant groups, see the analysis of former FBI counterterrorism intelligence analyst Matthew Levitt, "Stemming the Flow of Terrorist Financing: Practical and Conceptual Challenges," *The Fletcher Forum of World Affairs* 27, no. 1 (Winter/Spring 2003): 59–70, http://ui04e.moit.tufts.edu/forum/archives/pdfs/27-1pdfs/Levitt3.pdf. See also, "Charitable and Humanitarian Organizations in the Network of International Terrorist Financing," testimony of Matthew A. Levitt before the Subcommittee on International Trade and Finance, Committee on Banking, Housing, and Urban Affairs, United States Senate (August 1, 2002), http://www.washingtoninstitute.org/media/levitt/levitt080102.htm; and Matthew A. Levitt, "Tackling the Financing of Terrorism in Saudi Arabia," The Washington Institute for Near East Policy, Policy Watch #609, March 11, 2002, http://www.washingtoninstitute.org/watch/index.htm.

123. Government Accountability Office, "Combating Terrorism: U.S. Agencies Report Progress Countering Terrorism and Its Financing in Saudi Arabia, but Continued Focus on Counter Terrorism Financing Efforts Needed," September 24, 2009, http://www.gao.gov/assets/300/295873.pdf.

124. United States Department of State, Bureau for International Narcotics and Law Enforcement Affairs, "International Narcotics Control Strategy Report: Volume II Money Laundering and Financial Crimes," March 2009, p. 435, http://www.state.gov/documents/organization/120055.pdf.

125. Quote from U.S. Embassy Riyadh, in a cable dated March 22, 2009, "Counterterrorism Adviser Brennan's Meeting with Saudi King Abdullah," https://wikileaks.org/plusd/cables/09RIYADH447_a.html.

126. Freedom House, "Freedom in the World 2010: Global Erosion of Freedom," January 12, 2010, http://www.freedomhouse.org/article/freedom-world-2010-global-erosion-freedom.

127. A former high-ranking official on Middle East policy in the Clinton administration contended that the Saudis saw the Obama administration as a threat to their domestic security. Martin Indyk, "Amid the Arab Spring, Obama's Dilemma over Saudi Arabia," *Washington Post,* April 8, 2011.

128. The *Los Angeles Times* spoke of the "longtime allies" being "put on a collision course" by regional upheavals. Paul Richter and Neela Banerjee, "U.S.-Saudi Rivalry Intensifies," *Los Angeles Times,* June 19, 2011.

129. U.S. Embassy, Riyadh, "Scenesetter for Secretary Clinton's Feb. 15–16 Visit to Saudi Arabia (10RIYADH178)," February 11, 2010, http://wikileaks.org/cable/2010/02/10RIYADH178.html.

130. Prince Turki and other Saudi leaders feared an Iranian SCUD missile could hit Saudi oil facilities and warned U.S. diplomats that Gulf countries might be compelled to station nuclear weapons as a deterrent. On nuclear weapons, see Scott Mcgehee, "Saudi Exchange with Russian Ambassador on Iran's Nuclear Plans," American Embassy in Riyadh, January 28, 2009, http://www.theguardian.com/world/us-embassy-cables-documents/189229]. On fears of SCUD missile strikes, see U.S. Embassy, Riyadh, "APHSCT Townsend's November 16 Meeting with Saudi NSA Bandar Bin Sultan on Iranian Threats (06RIYADH9095)," December 16, 2006, https://wikileaks.org/plusd/cables/06RIYADH9095_a.html; and U.S. Embassy, Riyadh, "APHSCT Townsend February 6 Meeting with Foreign Minister Prince Saud Al-Faisal (07RIYADH367)," February 24, 2007, https://www.wikileaks.org/plusd/cables/07RIYADH367_a.html.

131. "Security Council Al-Qaida Sanctions Committee: Amends 111 Entries on its Sanctions List," December 13, 2011, http://www.un.org/News/Press/docs//2011/sc10483.doc.htm.

132. Sally Jacobs, David Filipov, and Patricia Wen, "The Fall of the House of Tsarnaev," *Boston Globe,* December 15, 2013, http://www.bostonglobe.com/Page/Boston/2011-2020/WebGraphics/Metro/BostonGlobe.com/2013/12/15tsarnaev/tsarnaev.html.

133. Tim Lister and Paul Cruickshank, "Older Brother in Boston Bombings Grew Increasingly Religious, Analysis Shows," *CNN.com,* April 20, 2013.

134. Ksenia Svetlova, "The Saudi Connection Linking the Boston Marathon to September 11," *Ha'aretz* (Tel Aviv), April 20, 2013; "Boston Bombing Suspect Tamerlan Tsarnaev's Wife Katherine Russell 'Had No Idea of Plot,'" *Courier-Mail* (Brisbane), April 25, 2013.

135. Alexei Vassiliev, *The History of Saudi Arabia* (New York: New York University Press, 2000), p. 473.

136. Experts also report Salafism's spread to Mali, a former democratic U.S. ally overthrown by domestic insurgency, military coup, and fighters with weapons from Libya following the 2011 NATO invasion. Antoine Basbous, head of the Paris-based Observatory of Arab Countries, said "the Salafism we hear about in Mali and North Africa is in fact the export version of Wahhabism." See Antoine Basbous, quoted in Marc Daou, "How Saudi Petrodollars Fuel Rise of Salafism," *France 24* (Paris), September 30, 2012, http://www.france24.com/en/20120929-how -saudi-arabia-petrodollars-finance-salafist-winter-islamism-wahhabism-egypt/; Robin Wright, "Don't Fear Islamists, Fear Salafis," *New York Times,* August 19, 2012.

137. "Ibid.

138. Khaled Yacoub Oweis, "Insight: Saudi Arabia boosts Salafist rivals to al Qaeda in Syria," Reuters, October 1, 2013.

139. U.S. Department of Defense, "Contracts: Press Operations, No: 593-13," August 20, 2013, http://www.defense.gov/contracts/contract.aspx?contractid=5116; U.S. Department of State, "Cluster Munitions," http://www.state.gov/t/pm/wra /c25930.htm.

140. Richard Miniter, "Saudis Lament, 'We Have Been Stabbed in the Back by Obama,'" *FoxNews.com,* December 27, 2013.

141. "The Situation Room," April 23, 2009, http://transcripts.cnn.com/TRAN SCRIPTS/0904/23/sitroom.02.html; Robin Wright, "Don't Fear Islamists, Fear Salafis," *New York Times,* August 19, 2012. Emphasis in original.

142. Ambassador Chas Freeman attributes that problem to 2001 peace talks. See *Ten Years After 9/11: Managing U.S.-Saudi Relations* (Washington: Carnegie Endowment for International Peace, 2011), http://carnegieendowment.org/files/91211_transcript _SaudiPanelTwo.pdf.

143. Summer Said and Benoit Faucon, "Shale Threatens Saudi Economy, Warns Prince Alwaleed," *Wall Street Journal,* July 29, 2013.

Chapter 14

1. See Malcolm N. Shaw, *International Law* (New York: Cambridge University Press, 2003), p. 178.

2. Stephen Krasner, *Sovereignty: Organized Hypocrisy* (Princeton: Princeton University Press, 1999).

3. George Kennan explores this concept briefly in his memoirs. See George F. Kennan, *Around the Cragged Hill: A Personal and Political Philosophy* (New York: W.W. Norton, 1993), pp. 87–88.

4. For more on ISI Director Mahmood Ahmed, see Ahmed Rashid, *Descent into Chaos: The United States and the Failure of Nation Building in Pakistan, Afghanistan, and Central Asia* (New York: Penguin, 2008), p. 24.

5. National Commission on Terrorist Attacks upon the United States, *The 9/11 Commission Report: Final Report of the National Commission on Terrorist Attacks upon the United States* (hereafter *The 9/11 Report*), (Washington: National Commission on Terrorist Attacks upon the United States, 2004), pp. 331–32.

6. For more on Washington's demands, confirmed by the U.S. embassy in Islamabad, see *The 9/11 Report*, p. 331; and Tom Carter, "U.S. Pressures Pakistan to Help Fight Terrorism," *Washington Times*, September 13, 2001.

7. Shuja Nawaz, *Crossed Swords: Pakistan, Its Army, and the Wars Within* (New York: Oxford University Press, 2008), p. 541.

8. Jane Perlez, "A Nation Challenged: Congress; Powell Tries to Allay Worry of Senators on Muslim Rage," *New York Times*, October 4, 2001.

9. Owen Bennett Jones, *Pakistan: Eye of the Storm* (New Haven, CT: Yale University Press, 2002), p. 9.

10. Jason Burke, *Al Qaeda: The True Story of Radical Islam* (New York: I.B. Tauris, 2006), p. 89, 125–26; and Jones, *Pakistan: Eye of the Storm*, p. 240.

11. "Pakistan: 'The Taliban's Godfather?'" National Security Archive Electronic Briefing Book No. 227, ed. Barbara Elias, George Washington University National Security Archive, http://nsarchive.gwu.edu/NSAEBB/NSAEBB227/; Burke, *Al Qaeda*, p. 188; and Jones, *Pakistan: Eye of the Storm*, p. 27.

12. Jones, *Pakistan: Eye of the Storm*, p. 9.

13. Rashid, *Descent into Chaos*, p. 50.

14. See "US Diplomat Asks Pakistan, India to Reduce Violence in Kashmir," Agence France Presse, May 27, 2000. See also Ahmed Rashid, "Pakistan's Explicit Pro-Pashtun Policy and Pro-Taliban Support," June 21, 2000.

15. Condoleezza Rice, "Opening Remarks" (speech, Commission on Terrorist Attacks, Washington, April 8, 2004).

16. Donald H. Rumsfeld, "DoD News Briefing—Secretary Rumsfeld and General Myers," (Washington, October 9, 2001), http://www.defense.gov/transcripts/transcript.aspx?transcriptid=2034; Carl Conetta, "Strange Victory: A Critical Appraisal of Operation Enduring Freedom and the Afghanistan War," *Project on Defense Alternatives Research Monograph* no. 6 (January 30, 2002): 1–87, http://www.comw.org/pda/0201strangevic.pdf; and Craig Nelson, "Concern Grows over US Strategy, Tactics in Afghanistan," *Cox News Service*, October 29, 2001.

17. John F. Burns, "Pakistan Is Already Calling on U.S. to End Airstrikes Quickly," *New York Times*, October 9, 2001.

18. Pamela Constable, "Anti-U.S. Sentiment Spreading in Pakistan; Growing Street Protests Precede Visit by Powell," *Washington Post*, October 15, 2001.

19. Ibid.

20. Burns, "Pakistan Is Already Calling on U.S. End to Airstrikes Quickly."

21. Constable, "Anti-U.S. Sentiment Spreading in Pakistan."

22. Alex Strick van Linschoten and Felix Kuehn, *An Enemy We Created: The Myth of the Taliban–Al Qaeda Merger in Afghanistan* (New York: Oxford University Press, 2012), p. 223; Jones, *Pakistan: Eye of the Storm*, p. 26; Kathy Gannon, *I Is for Infidel. From Holy War to Holy Terror: 18 Years inside Afghanistan* (New York: Public Affairs, 2006), pp. 93–94; Ahmed Rashid, "Pakistan and the Taliban," in *Fundamentalism Reborn? Afghanistan and the Taliban*, ed. William Maley (London: C. Hurst and Company, 1998), p. 30; Muhammad Amir Rana and Rohan Gunaratna, *Al Qaeda Fights Back inside Pakistani Tribal Areas* (Lahore, Pakistan: Pak Institute for Peace Studies, 2007), p. 52; Gilles Dorronsoro, *Revolution Unending: Afghanistan, 1979 to the Present* (London: C. Hurst and Co., 2005), p. 321; John F. Burns, "Pakistanis Fail in Last-Ditch Bid to Persuade Taliban to Turn over bin Laden," *New York Times*, September 28, 2001; Michael Zielenziger and Juan O. Tamayo, "U.S. Finds Itself Relying on Information from Former Taliban

Allies," Knight Ridder, November 2, 2001. Also see Rory McCarthy, "Dangerous Game of State-Sponsored Terror that Threatens Nuclear Conflict: Pakistani Leader's Attempt to Rein in Militants Is Met with Defiance," *The Guardian* (London), May 24, 2002, http://www.guardian.co.uk/world/2002/may/25/pakistan.india.

23. Jason Burke, *The 9/11 Wars* (New York: Allen Lane, 2011), p. 366. For more on foreigners captured, see pp. 63–64. For more on proxies let go, see p. 69. Also see Seymour Hersh, "The Getaway"; Douglas Frantz, "Pakistan Ended Aid to Taliban Only Hesitantly," *New York Times*, December 8, 2001; and Rashid, *Descent into Chaos*, pp. 90–93.

24. Rice, "Opening Remarks," p. 3; Bob Woodward, *Bush at War* (New York: Simon and Schuster, 2002), p. 98; and Steven Mufson, "U.S. Urged to Target Nations that Aid Terrorism; N.Y., Pentagon Attacks Are Called Acts of War," *Washington Post*, September 12, 2001.

25. Both quotes in Mufson, "U.S. Urged to Target Nations that Aid Terrorism."

26. Pervez Musharraf, *In the Line of Fire: A Memoir* (New York: Free Press, 2006), p. 201.

27. Tariq Mahmood, "The Durand Line: South Asia's Next Trouble Spot" (master's thesis, Naval Postgraduate School, June 2005), http://www.dtic.mil/cgi-bin/GetTRDoc?AD=ADA435574; Burke, *The 9/11 Wars*, p. 65.

28. Bob Woodward, *Obama's Wars* (New York: Simon and Schuster, 2010), p. 100.

29. Celia W. Dugger, "India Says Arrests Link Militants in Pakistan to Attack," *New York Times*, December 17, 2001; Bruce Riedel, "Al Qaeda Five Years after the Fall of Kandahar," Brookings Institution, January 18, 2007; and Steve Coll, "The Stand-Off," *The New Yorker*, February 13, 2006, pp. 126–39.

30. John Lancaster and Kamran Khan, "Extremist Groups Renew Activity in Pakistan; Support of Kashmir Militants Is at Odds with the War on Terrorism," *Washington Post*, February 8, 2003; Owen-Bennett Jones, "U.S. Policy Options toward Pakistan: A Principled and Realistic Approach," in *Stanley Foundation Policy Analysis Brief* (Muscatine, IA: The Stanley Foundation, 2008), http://www.stanleyfoundation.org/publications/pab/JonesPAB208.pdf; Husain Haqqani, "The Ideologies of South Asian Jihadi Groups," in *Current Trends in Islamist Ideology*, eds. Hillel Fradkin, Husain Haqqani, and Eric Brown (Washington: Hudson Institute, 2005), p. 21; Sharon Otterman, "Pakistan: Threats to Musharraf's Rule," *Council on Foreign Relations*, January 16, 2004, http://www.cfr.org/pakistan/pakistan-threats-musharrafs-rule/p7743; and John Lancaster, "Pakistan's Heartland Under Threat," *National Geographic*, July 2010, pp. 82–107.

31. Tariq Ali, *The Duel: Pakistan on the Flight Path of American Power* (New York: Scribner, 2008), p. 148.

32. Quoted in Burke, *9/11 Wars*, p. 368. Also see Rashid, *Descent into Chaos*, p. 241.

33. Additionally, foreign journalists, the Human Rights Commission of Pakistan, and even Musharraf himself conceded that irregularities blighted the election. "Musharraf Wins Huge Backing," *BBC News*, May 1, 2002; and Ihtasham ul Haque, "Polls to Be Held from Oct 7-11: We Won't Initiate War: Musharraf," *Dawn* (Karachi, Pakistan), May 28, 2002.

34. The vice chair of the Pakistan Muslim League-Nawaz (PML-N) Tehmina Daultana condemned the referendum as "totally illegal and unconstitutional." See Seth Mydans, "A Nation Challenged: Pakistan; Musharraf Plans a Referendum to Let Him Stay in Power," *New York Times*, April 6, 2002.

35. Karl Vick, "U.S. Offers Musharraf Leeway on Democracy; Warnings of the Past Absent as Opposition Decries Referendum," *Washington Post*, April 13, 2002.

36. Quoted in ibid.

37. Dennis Kux, *Disenchanted Allies: The United States and Pakistan: 1947–2000* (Washington: Woodrow Wilson Press, 2001), p. 357.

38. International Crisis Group, "Pakistan: Madrasas, Extremism, and the Military," *ICG Asia Report No. 36* (Islamabad: ICG, 2002), http://merln.ndu.edu/archive/icg/pakistanmadrasasextremismandthemilitary.pdf.

39. Bushra Asif and Teresita C. Schaffer, "Pakistan: Parliamentary Elections and After," *South Asia Monitor* 66 (January 1, 2004), http://csis.org/files/media/csis/pubs/sam66.pdf.

40. John Lancaster, "Musharraf Struggling for Ruling Coalition; Pakistan's Religious Parties Emerge from October Elections as Power Brokers," *Washington Post*, November 11, 2002; and International Crisis Group, "Islamic Parties in Pakistan," *Asia Report No. 216* (Islamabad: ICG, 2011), http://www.crisisgroup.org/en/regions/asia/south-asia/pakistan/216-islamic-parties-in-pakistan.aspx.

41. Civil society groups, opposition parties, and European Union observers widely criticized the October 2002 elections as "deeply flawed." See K. Alan Kronstadt, "Pakistan's Domestic Political Developments: Issues for Congress," *CRS Report*, March 27, 2003.

42. Samina Ahmed, South Asia Project Director for the International Crisis Group, "Extremist Madrasas, Ghost Schools, and U.S. Aid to Pakistan: Are We Making the Grade of 9/11 Commission Report Card?" testimony before the United States House of Representatives Subcommittee on National Security and Foreign Affairs, Committee on Oversight and Government Reform Hearing, May 9, 2007.

43. On Rahman's protests see Haroon Rashid, "Profile: Maulana Fazlur Rahman," *BBC News*, November, 6, 2002; Syed Saleem Shahzad, "Taliban's Call for Jihad Answered in Pakistan," Asia Times (Hong Kong), January 16, 2006; and Imtiaz Ali, "The Father of the Taliban: An Interview with Maulana Sami ul-Haq," *Spotlight on Terror* 4, no. 2 (May 23, 2007), http://www.jamestown.org/programs/tm/single/?tx_ttnews%5Btt_news%5D=4180#.VR7sVJTF-1I.

44. Liz Sly, "Fundamentalists Gain in Pakistan; Coalition Linked to Taliban Wins Big in Border Area," *Chicago Tribune*, October 12, 2002.

45. Mazhar Abbas, "Islamists Send Message to Pakistan's Government with Huge Anti-War Rally," Agence France Presse, March 2, 2003.

46. Ahmed Rashid, "America's War on Terror Goes Awry in Pakistan," *YaleGlobal* (New Haven, CT), June 4, 2003; Magnus Norell, "The Taliban and the Muttahida Majlis-e-Amal (MMA)," *China and Eurasia Forum Quarterly* 5, no. 3 (2007): 61–82; International Crisis Group, "The State of Sectarianism in Pakistan," *Asia Report* 95, no. 18 (April 18, 2005); and Lionel Beehner, "Musharraf's Taliban Problem," *Council on Foreign Relations*, September 11, 2006, http://www.cfr.org/pakistan/musharrafs-taliban-problem/p11401.

47. Ajai Sahni, "The Taliban Revisited in Pakistan," *Asia Times* (Hong Kong), June 11, 2003.

48. Jann Einfeld, *Pakistan*, History of Nations (Farmington Hills, MI: Greenhaven Press, 2004), p. 245; and Burke, *The 9/11 Wars*, p. 369.

49. Quoted in David Rohde, "Muslim Parties' Election Strength Weakens Musharraf," *New York Times*, October 12, 2002.

50. Quotes are from the Bucharest Conference Papers, "NATO in Afghanistan: Saving the State-Building Enterprise," Daoud Yaqub and William Maley (Washington: The German Marshal Fund of the United States, 2008), pp. 5–17. Also see K. Alan Kronstadt, "Addressing the U.S.-Pakistan Strategic Relationship," testimony before the U.S. Senate Committee on Homeland Security and Governmental Affairs Subcommittee on Federal Financial Management, Government Information, Federal Services, and International Security, June 12, 2008, http://www.hsgac.senate.gov//imo/media/doc/KronstadtTestimony.pdf.

51. C. Christine Fair, Clay Ramsay, and Steve Kull, "Pakistani Public Opinion on Democracy, Islamist Militancy, and Relations with the U.S.," United States Institute of Peace Working Paper, February 2008; and Saleem Shahid, "MMA Urges Unity against U.S.," *Dawn* (Karachi, Pakistan), April 3, 2003.

52. Abbas, "Islamists Send Message to Pakistan's Government."

53. "Musharraf Undeterred, Reiterates Stance on Extremism," Associated Press of Pakistan, December 14, 2003.

54. "Two Soldiers Convicted in Musharraf Assassination Attempts," Voice of America, October 29, 2009.

55. "US Condemns Musharraf Assassination Bid," Agence France Presse, December 17, 2003.

56. Gohar Ali, "Musharraf Wades into Islamist Heartland with Anti-Talibanisation Campaign," Agence France Presse, June 12, 2003.

57. Pervez Musharraf, "A Plea for Enlightened Moderation," *Washington Post*, June 1, 2004.

58. U.S. Department of State, "2003 Country Reports on Human Rights Practices," February 25, 2004, http://www.state.gov/j/drl/rls/hrrpt/2003/.

59. The Pew Global Attitudes Project, *Views of a Changing World, June 2003* (Washington: Pew Research Center, 2003), http://www.people-press.org/files/legacy-pdf/185.pdf; Pew Research Center, "A Year after Iraq War," March 16, 2004; John Lancaster, "Pakistan Struggles to Put Army on Moderate Course," *Washington Post*, April 4, 2004; "Statement of Stephen P. Cohen before the Senate Foreign Relations Committee," January 28, 2004; and Zaffar Abbas, "Musharraf and the Mullahs," *BBC News*, December 30, 2003.

60. C. Christine Fair, "Pakistan: An Uncertain Partner in the Fight against Terrorism," in *The Counterterror Coalitions: Cooperation with Pakistan and India* (Santa Monica: Rand, 2004), p. 27. For more on KSM, see "Kashmiri Militant Killed in Pak Drone Strike," *Hindustan Times* (New Delhi, India), August 25, 2012. For more on Zubaydah, see Stephen Tankel, "Lashkar-e-Taiba: Past Operations and Future Prospects," New America Foundation, April 27, 2011, http://newamerica.net/publications/policy/lashkar_e_taiba.

61. For more on Operation Kalusha, see Hassan Abbas, *Militancy in Pakistan's Borderlands: Implications for the Nation and for Afghan Policy* (New York: Century Foundation, 2010). For more on Musharraf's views, see Salman Masood, "Link to Qaeda Cited in Effort to Assassinate Pakistan Chief," *New York Times*, March 16, 2004; and "Pakistani Sources: Al-Zawahiri Surrounded," *CNN.com*, March 18, 2004, http://www.cnn.com/2004/WORLD/asiapcf/03/18/pakistan.alqaeda/.

62. Pashtun tribes who controlled FATA adhered to a pre-Islamic tribal code (*pashtunwali*) that by custom extends assistance to strangers who request protection.

63. Quoted in Robin Wright and Peter Baker, "Musharraf: Bin Laden's Location Is Unknown; Pakistani Presses U.S. on Rebuilding Afghan Army," *Washington Post*, December 5, 2004.

64. Burke, *The 9/11 Wars*, p. 370.

65. Quoted in Matthew Cole, "Killing Ourselves in Afghanistan," *Salon.com,* March 10, 2008, http://www.salon.com/2008/03/10/taliban/.

66. Quoted in M. Ilyas Khan, "Pakistan Army's Tribal Quagmire," *BBC News*, October 9, 2007.

67. "Pakistani Militants Abandon Deal," *BBC News*, June 30, 2009.

68. Quoted in Eli Lake, "U.S. Allies in Asia Argue Over Bin Laden Whereabouts," *New York Sun*, September 26, 2006.

69. George W. Bush, *Decision Points* (New York: Crown, 2010), p. 213.

70. United States Department of State, *Country Reports on Terrorism 2006* (Washington: United States Department of State, 2007), p. 120, http://www.state.gov/documents/organization/83383.pdf.

71. Jamal Shahid, "Disappearances New Form of Abuse: HRCP," *Dawn* (Karachi, Pakistan), February 9, 2007; Asian *Human Rights Commission, Pakistan: The Human Rights Situation in 2006* (Hong Kong: Asian Human Rights Commission, 2006); and Amnesty International, *Denying the Undeniable: Enforced Disappearances in Pakistan* (London: Amnesty International, 2008).

72. "Govt Urged to Efforts for Release of Missing Persons," *Daily Times* (Lahore, Pakistan), May 8, 2010, http://www.dailytimes.com.pk/default.asp?page=2010%5C05%5C08%5Cstory_8-5-2010_pg11_6; and "Culprits in Missing Person Case Will Be Punished: SC," *Daily Times* (Lahore, Pakistan), June 7, 2007, http://www.dailytimes.com.pk/default.asp?page=2007%5C06%5C07%5Cstory_7-6-2007_pp. 7_20.

73. Somini Sengupta, "Musharraf Finds Himself Weakened after the Firing of a Judge Stirs Anger in Pakistan," *New York Times*, March 25, 2007; and Ardeshir Cowasjee, "Mismanaged and Dysfunctional," *Dawn* (Karachi, Pakistan), March 18, 2007.

74. Richard B. Cheney, interview by Rush Limbaugh, *The Rush Limbaugh Show*, April 5, 2007. Gerhard Peters and John T. Woolley, The American Presidency Project, http://www.presidency.ucsb.edu/ws/?pid=83551.

75. Quoted in Ihtasham ul Haque, "Emergency to End Judicial Activism," *Dawn* (Karachi, Pakistan), November 4, 2007.

76. Ahmed Hassan, "Opposition Says Govt. 'Thoroughly Corrupt': Calls for PM's Resignation Rejected," *Dawn* (Karachi, Pakistan), August 11, 2006; and Carlotta Gall and Salman Masood, "Pressures Increase on Pakistan's Government," *New York Times*, August 30, 2006.

77. George W. Bush, "Setting the Record Straight: Iraq Is the Central Front of Al Qaeda's Global Campaign," May 3, 2007. Gerhard Peters and John T. Woolley, The American Presidency Project, http://www.presidency.ucsb.edu/ws/?pid=83469.

78. Ahmed, "Extremist Madrasas, Ghost Schools, and U.S. Aid to Pakistan."

79. Syed Irfan Raza, "Lal Masjid Threatens Suicide Attacks," *Dawn* (Karachi, Pakistan), April 7, 2007.

80. Istasham ul Huque, "Seminaries Use as Terror Havens Won't Be Allowed; Musharraf Says Operation Was Inevitable," *Dawn* (Karachi, Pakistan), July 13, 2007, http://www.dawn.com/2007/07/13/top1.htm. Hassan Abbas, "The Road to Lal Masjid and its Aftermath," *Terrorism Monitor* 5, no. 14 (July 19, 2007), http://www.jamestown.org/single/?no_cache=1&tx_ttnews%5Btt_news%5D=4322#.VR7xmJTF

-1I; and William Dalrymple, "Days of Rage: Challenges for the Nation's Future," *The New Yorker,* July 23, 2007, pp. 26–35.

81. Quoted in Anwar Iqbol, "Musharraf Gets a Pat from Bush," *Dawn* (Karachi, Pakistan), July 12, 2007, http://www.dawn.com/2007/07/12/top8.htm.

82. Richard Boucher, "Briefing on Pakistan," U.S. Department of State, July 17, 2007, http://2001-2009.state.gov/p/sca/rls/rm/2007/88582.htm.

83. Hassan Abbas, "The Road to Lal Masjid and Its Aftermath"; Syed Shoaib Hasan, "Profile: Islamabad's Red Mosque," *BBC News,* July 27, 2007; and "Musharraf Wins Presidential Vote," *BBC News,* October 6, 2007.

84. Quoted in Dalrymple, "Days of Rage."

85. Quoted in Nicholas Schmidle, "My Buddy, the Jihadi," *Washington Post,* July 15, 2007.

86. "Pakistan: Constitutionality of the Proclamation of Emergency," Library of Congress, September 16, 2014; and *"Proclamation of Emergency," Dawn* (Karachi, Pakistan), November 4, 2007. "It is one man against the nation," exclaimed Chaudhry's attorney only hours before being arrested. Political analyst Hasan Askari Rizvi said of Musharraf, "He's pretty much carrying out a second coup." Quoted in Griff Witte, "Musharraf Declares Emergency Rule in Pakistan; Constitution Suspended; Chief Judge Fired," *Washington Post*, November 4, 2007.

87. Witte, "Musharraf Declares Emergency Rule in Pakistan"; and Ihtasham ul Haque, "Emergency to End Judicial Activism," *Dawn* (Karachi, Pakistan), November 4, 2007.

88. Bennett Jones, *Pakistan: Eye of the Storm,* p. 269.

89. Anwar Iqbal, "US Patience Not Never-Ending," *Dawn News* (Karachi, Pakistan), November 8, 2007, http://www.dawn.com/2007/11/08/top7.htm.

90. John D. Negroponte, "Remarks to the Press in Islambad, Pakistan," Department of State, November 18, 2007, http://2001-2009.state.gov/s/d/2007/95337.htm.

91. Corey Flintoff, "U.S. Could Lose 'Indispensable Ally' in Pakistan," *NPR.org,* February 17, 2008, http://www.npr.org/templates/story/story.php?storyId=19095161.

92. Quoted in Michael Abramowitz, "Bush, Rice Defend Musharraf as an Ally," *Washington Post,* November 11, 2007.

93. J. Michael McConnell, "Annual Threat Assessment of the Intelligence Community for the House Permanent Select Committee on Intelligence," statement before the House Permanent Select Committee on Intelligence, February 7, 2008, http://www.dni.gov/files/documents/Newsroom/Testimonies/20080207_testimony.pdf; and K. Alan Kronstadt, "Addressing the U.S.-Pakistan Strategic Relationship," text of statement given before the U.S. Senate Committee on Homeland Security and Governmental Affairs, June 12, 2008.

94. *Inside Islam: What a Billion Muslims Really Think,* directed by Robert Gardner, (Potomac Falls, VA: Unity Productions Foundation, 2009), DVD.

95. Bush, *Decision Points,* p. 216.

96. Anwer Iqbal, "US Avoids Taking Sides," *Dawn News* (Karachi, Pakistan), October 6, 2007, http://www.dawn.com/2007/10/06/top12.htm; and Paul Wiseman, "Official: U.S. Forced Pakistan to Allow Bhutto Back; Pakistani Government Spokesman Cites Her Willingness to Cooperate," *USA Today,* October 29, 2007.

97. Musharraf signed the National Reconciliation Ordinance on October 5, which allowed him to stand for—and win—reelection as president the following day. Much of parliament boycotted the vote in opposition to the NRO's unconstitutionality.

Members of Bhutto's PPP, however, merely abstained, a move perceived as quid pro quo in a power-sharing arrangement between Musharraf and Bhutto brokered by Washington. For more, see "Bhutto Faces Corruption Setback," *BBC News,* October 12, 2007; and Isambard Wilkinson, "Bhutto Enters Coalition Talks with Musharraf," *London Telegraph,* April 21, 2007.

98. "She says what America wants to hear," Deputy Information Minister Tariq Azim Khan told *USA Today.* On U.S. officials forcing Bhutto's return from exile, Khan complained bitterly, "You twisted our arm." Wiseman, "Official: U.S. Forced Pakistan to Allow Bhutto Back; Pakistani Government Spokesman Cites Her Willingness to Cooperate."

99. Pam Benson, "Intelligence Chief: Taliban Making Gains in Afghanistan," *CNN.org,* February 28, 2008.

100. McConnell, "Annual Threat Assessment of the Intelligence Community," February 7, 2008, http://www.dni.gov/files/documents/Newsroom/Testimonies /20080207_testimony.pdf. Also see Woodward, *Obama's Wars,* p. 4.

101. "CIA: Pakistan Border 'Clear and Present Danger,'" Associated Press, March 30, 2008; and David E. Sanger, *The Inheritance: The World Obama Confronts and the Challenges to American Power* (New York: Broadway Publishers, 2009), p. 248.

102. "ISAF Commander 'Troubled' by Pakistan Negotiations," *Jane's Defense Weekly* (London), May 21, 2008; and "Nato 'Concerned' Over Pakistan," *BBC News,* May 27, 2008. Also see Matt Waldman, "The Sun in the Sky: the Relationship between Pakistan's ISI and Afghan Insurgents," Discussion Paper 18 (June 2010), Crisis States Research Centre, London School of Economics and Political Science, http://www.lse.ac.uk /internationalDevelopment/research/crisisStates/download/dp/DP%2018.pdf.

103. Aamir Latif, "Pakistan's Black Marketers Cheer Reopening of NATO Supply Lines," *Christian Science Monitor* (Boston), August 21, 2012.

104. Comments reported by Barnett Rubin, "Saving Afghanistan," *Foreign Affairs* (January/February 2007): 57–78. Also see Seth Jones, "Terrorism's New Central Front," Center for Conflict and Peace Studies-Afghanistan, September 26, 2006.

105. Julian E. Barnes, "Obama Team Works on Overhaul of Afghanistan, Pakistan Policy," *Los Angeles Times,* February 11, 2009, http://articles.latimes.com/2009 /feb/11/world/fg-us-afghan11.

106. Bruce Riedel and Michelle Flourney, White House Press Briefing, March 27, 2009, http://www.whitehouse.gov/the_press_office/Press-Briefing-by-Bruce-Riedel -Ambassador-Richard-Holbrooke-and-Michelle-Flournoy-on-the-New-Strategy-for -Afghanistan-and-Pakistan.

107. Woodward, *Obama's Wars,* p. 332.

108. Stephen Biddle, "Is It Worth It?" *The American Interest* (July/August 2009), pp. 4–11.

109. Woodward, *Obama's Wars,* p. 167.

110. Lindsey Graham, Joseph I. Lieberman, and John McCain, "Only Decisive Force Can Prevail in Afghanistan," *Wall Street Journal,* September 13, 2009.

111. Quoted in ibid., pp. 171, 333.

112. Vali Nasr, "The Inside Story of How the White House Let Diplomacy Fail in Afghanistan," *Foreign Policy* (March 4, 2013), http://foreignpolicy.com/2013/03/04 /the-inside-story-of-how-the-white-house-let-diplomacy-fail-in-afghanistan/.

113. During his second term as prime minister, in October 1998, he pushed an amendment to make Sharia supreme law, but was overthrown by Musharraf be-

fore he secured a two-thirds majority in the Pakistan Senate. Steve Coll, *Ghost Wars: The Secret History of the CIA, Afghanistan, and Bin Laden, from the Soviet Invasion to September 10, 2001* (New York: Penguin Press, 2004), p. 349.

114. Quoted in Josh Rogin, "Clinton Presses Pakistan to Raise Taxes on Wealthy," *ForeignPolicy.com,* http://thecable.foreignpolicy.com/posts/2010/09/28/clinton_presses_pakistan_to_raise_taxes_on_wealthy.

115. See, for example, Joshua Foust, *Understanding the Strategic and Tactical Considerations of Drone Strikes* (Washington: American Security Project, 2013), http://www.scribd.com/doc/121483783/Understanding-the-Strategic-and-Tactical-Considerations-of-Drone-Strikes. For up-to-date tracking of CIA drone strikes and other U.S. covert actions, see the Bureau of Investigative Journalism, "Covert Drone War," http://www.thebureauinvestigates.com/category/projects/drones/; and the New America Foundation's similar and ongoing project, "Drone Wars Pakistan: Analysis," http://securitydata.newamerica.net/drones/pakistan/analysis.html; Chris Woods, "Analysis: CNN Expert's Civilian Drone Death Numbers Don't Add Up," the Bureau of Investigative Journalism, July 17, 2012, http://www.thebureauinvestigates.com/2012/07/17/analysis-cnn-experts-civilian-drone-death-numbers-dont-add-up/; and Meg Braun, "Counting Civilian Casualties in CIA's Drone War," *Foreign Policy's AfPak Channel,* November 2, 2012, http://afpak.foreignpolicy.com/posts/2012/11/02/counting_civilian_casualties_in_cia_s_drone_war.

116. "Pakistani Public Opinion Ever More Critical of U.S.," Pew Research, June 27, 2012, http://www.pewglobal.org/2012/06/27/pakistani-public-opinion-ever-more-critical-of-u-s/.

117. Chris Woods, "CIA Drones Quit One Pakistan Site—But US Keeps Access to Other Airbases," the Bureau of Investigative Journalism (London), December 15, 2011.

118. Jonathan Landay, "Pakistan-U.S. Feud Boils over CIA Drone Strikes," *McClatchy Newspapers* (Washington), April 22, 2011.

119. "Pakistani Taliban 'An Extension of Al-Qaeda': Official," Agence France Presse, September 1, 2008; and "TTP Is an Extension of Al Qaeda: Rehman," *Daily Times* (Lahore), September 2, 2008.

120. Rahimullah Yusufzai, "The Emergence of the Pakistani Taliban," in *Jane's Terrorism and Insurgency Centre* (London: December 11, 2007).

121. Karen DeYoung, "Al-Qaeda Seen as Shaken in Pakistan," *Washington Post,* June 1, 2009.

122. Joby Warrick, *The Triple Agent: The al-Qaeda Mole Who Infiltrated the CIA* (New York: Vintage, 2011), p. 90.

123. Alissa J. Rubin and Mark Mazzetti, "Suicide Bomber Killed C.I.A. Operatives," *New York Times,* December 30, 2009.

124. Mark Mazzetti and Dexter Filkins, "Secret Joint Raid Captures Taliban's Top Commander," *New York Times,* February 15, 2010.

125. Quoted in Mark Mazzetti and Scott Shane, "Evidence Mounts for Taliban Role in Bomb Plot," *New York Times,* May 5, 2010. Also see Andrea Elliot, "Militant's Path from Pakistan to Times Square," *New York Times,* June 22, 2010.

126. Chas. W. Freeman Jr., *The Diplomat's Dictionary,* rev. ed. (Washington: United States Institute of Peace, 2006), p. 270.

127. Mark Mazzetti, Jane Perlez, Eric Schmitt, and Andrew W. Lehren, "Pakistan Aids Insurgency in Afghanistan, Reports Assert," *New York Times*, July 25, 2010; and Burke, *The 9/11 Wars*, p. 327.

128. U.S. Senator Carl Levin, "Report on Afghanistan and Pakistan, September 2010," September 30, 2010, http://www.fas.org/man/eprint/wh-afpak.pdf.

129. Mazzetti, "Secret Joint Raid Captures Taliban's Top Commander."

130. Taha Siddiqui, "Fattening Breed in Fata," *PIQUE* (Islamabad), September 2012, p. 38.

131. Josh Rogin, "Who Paid the 'Blood Money' to Set Raymond Davis Free?" *Foreign Policy Online*, March 16, 2011, http://thecable.foreignpolicy.com/posts/2011/03/16/who_paid_the_blood_money_to_set_raymond_davis_free.

132. Additionally, bin Laden had become burdened by what he saw as the incompetence of al Qaeda affiliates. He held neither al-Qaeda in the Arabian Peninsula (AQAP) leader Anwar Al-Awlaki in great esteem, nor AQAP's *Inspire* English-language magazine. For more, see Don Rassler, Gabriel Koehler-Derrick, Liam Collins, Muhammad al-Obaidi, and Nelly Lahoud, "Letters from Abbottabad: Bin Laden Sidelined?" The Combating Terrorism Center, Department of Social Sciences, United States Military Academy at West Point, May 3, 2012, p. 52.

133. Article 40 of the Constitution of the Islamic Republic of Pakistan: http://pakistanconstitution-law.org/article-40-strengthening-bonds-with-muslim-world-and-promoting-international-peace/.

134. Salman Masood and David E. Sanger, "Militants Attack Pakistani Naval Base in Karachi," *New York Times*, May 22, 2011, http://www.nytimes.com/2011/05/23/world/asia/23pakistan.html.

135. Imtiaz Gul, *Pakistan: Before and After Osama* (New Delhi: Roli/Lotus Books Private Limited, 2012), p. 128.

136. Quoted in Qasim Nauman and Missy Ryan, "Pakistan Warns U.S.: 'You Will Lose an Ally,'" Reuters, September 23, 2011.

137. Brigadier S. K. Malik, *The Quranic Concept of War* (Lahore: Associated Printers, 1979).

Chapter 15

1. "U.S. Envoy Explains Security Guarantees," *Foreign Broadcast Information Service Daily Report: Central Eurasia*, SOV-94-014, January 21, 1994, p. 39. The secret security protocols to the agreements relinquishing those countries' nuclear arsenals still have not been made public more than two decades after their signing.

2. John J. Mearsheimer, "The Case for a Ukrainian Nuclear Deterrent," *Foreign Affairs* 72, no. 3 (Summer 1993): 50–66.

3. Washington's opposition to a sphere of influence for Russia (or virtually any country other than the United States) is even stronger now than it was in the early 1990s. See Ted Galen Carpenter, "Accepting Spheres of Influence in the 21st Century," *Aspenia Online*, May 7, 2014, https://www.aspeninstitute.it/aspenia-online/article/accepting-spheres-influence-21st-century.

4. Western advocacy of that strategy was already well underway by the first year of the Clinton administration. See, for example, Stephen Page, "The Great Game Revisited? The Quest for Influence in Independent Central Asia," in *NATO's Eastern Dilemmas*, ed. David G. Haglund, S. Neil MacFarlane, and Joel J. Sokolsky (Boulder: Westview Press, 1994), pp. 67–90.

5. James A. Baker III, with Thomas M. DeFrank, *The Politics of Diplomacy: Revolution, War and Peace, 1989–1992* (New York: G. P. Putnam's Sons, 1995), p. 629.

6. E. Wayne Merry, *Russia and China in Asia: Changing Great Power Roles* (Washington: American Foreign Policy Council, 2002). See especially chapter 8, "Central Asia: Making Way for a New Player in the 'Great Game,'" pp. 41–46.

7. Stephen J. Blank, *Turkmenistan and Central Asia after Niyazov* (Carlisle, PA: Strategic Studies Institute, 2007), pp. 53–61.

8. Baker, *The Politics of Diplomacy*, p. 631.

9. Roger N. McDermott, *Kazakhstan's Defense Policy: An Assessment of the Trends* (Carlisle, PA: Strategic Studies Institute, 2009), p. 4.

10. Baker, *The Politics of Diplomacy*, p. 632.

11. "Turkmenistan Starts Pumping Gas from Vast Field," Associated Press, September 4, 2013, http://www.khou.com/news/world/222376701.html.

12. Blank, *Turkmenistan and Central Asia after Niyazov*, pp. 34–35. Also see Philip Andrews-Speed, Xuanli Liao, and Roland Dannreuther, *The Strategic Implications of China's Energy Needs* (New York: Oxford University Press, 2002), pp. 58–61.

13. "Turkmenistan Starts Pumping Gas from Vast Field."

14. Ibid.

15. Barry Wood, "China Stakes out Investments along New Silk Road," *Market Watch*, September 27, 2013, http://www.marketwatch.com/story/china-stakes-out -investments-along-new-silk-road-2013-09-27?siteid=yhoof2.

16. See Rosemary Kelanic, "China's Changing Oil Calculus," *National Interest Online*, November 12, 2013, http://nationalinterest.org/commentary/chinas-changing -oil-calculus-9385.

17. Ibid.

18. Eric McGinchley, *Chaos, Violence, Dynasty: Politics and Islam in Central Asia* (Pittsburgh: University of Pittsburgh Press, 2011), p. 87.

19. Quoted in Jim Nichol, *Central Asia: Regional Developments and Implications for U.S. Interests* (Washington: Congressional Research Service, 2004), p. 3.

20. John D. Negroponte, "Annual Threat Assessment of the Director of National Intelligence for the Senate Select Committee on Intelligence," December 10, 2004.

21. J. Michael McConnell, "Annual Threat Assessment of the Director of National Intelligence for the Senate Armed Services Committee," February 27, 2007.

22. Baker, *The Politics of Diplomacy*, p. 631.

23. Blank, *Turkmenistan and Central Asia after Niyazov*, pp. 3–4.

24. Human Rights Watch, Kyrgyzstan, *Where Is the Justice? Interethnic Violence in Southern Kyrgyzstan and Its Aftermath*, August 16, 2010, http://www.hrw.org/en/re ports/2010/08/16/where-justice-0. Also see Human Rights Watch, *Distorted Justice: Kyrgyzstan's Flawed Investigation and Trials on the 2010 Violence*, June 8, 2011, http:// www.hrw.org/reports/2011/06/08/distorted-justice.

25. McGlinchey, *Chaos, Violence, Dynasty*, pp. 114–17.

26. Human Rights Watch, "The Andijan Massacre: One Year Later, Still No Justice," http://www.hrw.org/legacy/backgrounder/eca/uzbekistan0606/1.htm, p. 1.

27. Quoted in Robert Rand, *Tamerlane's Children: Dispatches from Contemporary Uzbekistan* (Oxford: Oneworld, 2006), p. 189.

28. "U.S. Senators Ask for UN Action in Uzbekistan," *Financial Times* (London), June 9, 2005.

29. R. Jeffrey Smith and Glenn Kessler, "U.S. Opposed Calls at NATO for Probe of Uzbek Killings," *Washington Post*, June 14, 2005.

30. Robin Wright and Ann Scott Tyson, "U.S. Evicted from Air Base in Uzbekistan," *Washington Post*, July 30, 2005.

31. Human Rights Watch, "Kazakhstan: Growing Crackdown on Free Speech," December 13, 2012, http://www.hrw.org/news/2012/12/13/kazakhstan-growing -crackdown-free-speech.

32. Jim Nichol, "Kazakhstan: Recent Developments and U.S. Interests," in *Kazakhstan: Conditions, Issues and U.S. Relations*, ed. Randell M. Hoyt and Morris B. Weston (New York: Nova Science Publishers, 2013), pp. 9–12.

33. McDermott, *Kazakhstan's Defense Policy*, p. v.

34. Nichol, "Kazakhstan: Recent Developments and U.S. Interests," p. 23.

35. McDermott, *Kazakhstan's Defense Policy*, pp. 41–45.

36. Ibid., p. 45.

37. Ibid., p. 21.

38. Nichol, "Kazakhstan: Recent Developments and U.S. Interests," p. 27.

39. McDermott, *Kazakhstan's Defense Policy*, p. vi.

40. Ibid., p. 13.

41. Blank, *Turkmenistan and Central Asia after Niyazov*, p. v. For detailed accounts of authoritarian, often clan-based, politics in the Central Asian countries and how that social reality makes dim prospects for modern democratic states anywhere in the region, see McGlinchey, *Chaos, Violence, Dynasty*; John Glenn, *The Soviet Legacy in Central Asia* (New York: St. Martin's Press, 1999); Edward Schatz, *Modern Clan Politics: The Power of "Blood" in Kazakhstan and Beyond* (Seattle: University of Washington Press, 2004); and E. Wayne Merry, "The Politics of Central Asia: National in Form, Soviet in Content," in *In the Tracks of Tamerlane: Central Asia's Path to the 21st Century*, ed. Dan Burghart and Theresa Sabonis-Helf (Washington: National Defense University, 2004), pp. 36–42.

42. Ilan Greenberg, "Rough Year Ahead for Central Asia," *National Interest Online*, December 28, 2012, http://nationalinterest.org/commentary/rough-year-ahead-cen tral-asia-7912.

43. U.S. Department of State: Bureau of Democracy, Human Rights and Labor, "Kazakhstan 2012 Human Rights Report," pp. 37–38, http://www.state.gov/docu ments/organization/204612.pdf.

44. Quoted in Nichol, "Kazakhstan: Recent Developments and U.S. Interests," pp. 1–2.

45. Blank, *Turkmenistan and Central Asia after Niyazov*, pp. v, 12.

46. For a discussion of the murky succession struggle upon Niyazov's death, see ibid., pp. 4–6.

47. Jim Hentz, "Turkmen Leader's Horse Fall Hidden from Nation," Associated Press, May 1, 2013.

48. Blank, *Turkmenistan and Central Asia after Niyazov*, p. 7.

49. Ibid., pp. 29, 65.

50. Ibid., p. 28.

51. Robert Evans, "West Ramps up Accusations of Systemic Repression in Turkmenistan," Reuters, April 22, 2013.

52. Quoted in John Vandiver, "U.S. Seeking Extension of Manas Air Base Lease," *Stars and Stripes* (Washington), January 16, 2013.

53. Olga Dzyubenko, "U.S. Vacates Base in Central Asia as Russia's Clout Rises," Reuters, June 3, 2014, http://www.reuters.com/article/2014/06/03/us-kyrgyzstan-usa-manas-idUSKBN0EE1LH20140603.

54. Ibid.

55. Greenberg, "Rough Year Ahead for Central Asia."

56. For a discussion of the complex, often ambivalent, economic and security relationship between Russia and China, both bilaterally and through the Shanghai Cooperation Organization, see Elizabeth Wishnick, *Russia, China, and the United States in Central Asia: Prospects for Great Power Competition and Cooperation in the Shadow of the Georgian Crisis* (Carlisle, PA: Strategic Studies Institute, February 2009), pp. 27–36.

57. Wood, "China Stakes out Investments along New Silk Road."

58. "Russia to Keep Kyrgyzstan Military Base," Agence France Presse, September 20, 2012.

59. Moscow moved adeptly to undercut Washington's military influence with President Kurmanbek Bakiev, who took power after Askar Akaev was ousted from power in 2005, and that effort paid dividends, including obtaining a base in Kyrgyzstan.

60. Anton Barbashan and Hannah Thoburn, "The Kremlin's Collapsing Eurasian Sandcastle," *National Interest Online*, September 11, 2013, http://nationalinterest.org/commentary/the-kremlins-collapsing-eurasian-sandcastle-9042.

61. Ibid.

Chapter 16

1. Ronald Reagan, *An American Life* (New York: Simon & Schuster, 1990), p. 483.

2. Quoted in Michelle Faul, "U.S. Diplomat Calls African Dictator a Good Guy," *Washington Post*, February 11, 2011.

3. For an earlier, more detailed discussion of the first three categories, see Ted Galen Carpenter, *A Search for Enemies: America's Alliances after the Cold War* (Washington: Cato Institute, 1992), pp. 174–79.

4. Meir Dagan, interview, *60 Minutes*, CBS.com, March 11, 2012.

5. See John Mueller, *Overblown: How Politicians and the Terrorism Industry Inflate National Security Threats, and Why We Believe Them* (New York: Free Press, 2009); and John Mueller and Mark G. Stewart, *Terror, Security and Money: Balancing the Risks, Benefits, and Costs of Homeland Security* (New York: Oxford University Press, 2011).

Index

About the Authors

Ted Galen Carpenter is senior fellow for defense and foreign policy studies at the Cato Institute. He is the author of 10 books and the contributing editor of 10 on international affairs, including *The Fire Next Door: Mexico's Drug Violence and the Danger to America*, *Smart Power: Toward a Prudent Foreign Policy for America*, and *The Captive Press: Foreign Policy Crises and the First Amendment*.

Malou Innocent is an adjunct scholar at the Cato Institute. She was a foreign policy analyst at Cato from 2007 to 2013. She is a member of the International Institute for Strategic Studies, and her primary research interests include Middle East and Persian Gulf security issues and U.S. foreign policy toward Pakistan, Afghanistan, and China.

Cato Institute

Founded in 1977, the Cato Institute is a public policy research foundation dedicated to broadening the parameters of policy debate to allow consideration of more options that are consistent with the principles of limited government, individual liberty, and peace. To that end, the Institute strives to achieve greater involvement of the intelligent, concerned lay public in questions of policy and the proper role of government.

The Institute is named for "Cato's Letters," libertarian pamphlets that were widely read in the American Colonies in the early 18th century and played a major role in laying the philosophical foundation for the American Revolution.

Despite the achievement of the nation's Founders, today virtually no aspect of life is free from government encroachment. A pervasive intolerance for individual rights is shown by government's arbitrary intrusions into private economic transactions and its disregard for civil liberties. And while freedom around the globe has notably increased in the past several decades, many countries have moved in the opposite direction, and most governments still do not respect or safeguard the wide range of civil and economic liberties.

To address those issues, the Cato Institute undertakes an extensive publications program on the complete spectrum of policy issues. Books, monographs, and shorter studies are commissioned to examine the federal budget, Social Security, regulation, military spending, international trade, and myriad other issues. Major policy conferences are held throughout the year, from which papers are published thrice yearly in the *Cato Journal*. The Institute also publishes the quarterly magazine *Regulation*.

In order to maintain its independence, the Cato Institute accepts no government funding. Contributions are received from foundations, corporations, and individuals, and other revenue is generated from the sale of publications. The Institute is a nonprofit, tax-exempt, educational foundation under Section 501(c)3 of the Internal Revenue Code.

CATO INSTITUTE
1000 Massachusetts Ave., N.W.
Washington, D.C. 20001
www.cato.org